# THE EARTH IS ALL
# THAT LASTS

## ALSO BY MARK LEE GARDNER

*To Hell on a Fast Horse: The Untold Story of
Billy the Kid and Pat Garrett*

*Shot All to Hell: Jesse James, the Northfield Raid, and
the Wild West's Greatest Escape*

*Rough Riders: Theodore Roosevelt, His Cowboy
Regiment, and the Immortal Charge Up San Juan Hill*

*George Armstrong Custer: A Biography*

*Geronimo: A Biography*

*Wagons for the Santa Fe Trade: Wheeled Vehicles and
Their Makers, 1822–1880*

*The Mexican War Correspondence of
Richard Smith Elliott* (with Marc Simmons)

*Brothers on the Santa Fe and Chihuahua Trails:
Edward James Glasgow and William Henry Glasgow,
1846–1848*

# THE EARTH IS ALL THAT LASTS

*Crazy Horse, Sitting Bull, and the*
*Last Stand of the Great Sioux Nation*

## MARK LEE GARDNER

MARINER BOOKS

*Boston    New York*

HarperCollins books may be purchased for educational, business, or sales promotional use. For information, please email the Special Markets Department at SPsales@harpercollins.com.

FIRST EDITION

*Designed by Lucy Albanese*
*Map designed by Jeffrey L. Ward*

Library of Congress Cataloging-in-Publication Data has been applied for.

ISBN 978-0-06-266989-6

22 23 24 25 26   LSC   10 9 8 7 6 5 4 3 2 1

TO MY UNCLE

**Curly Gardner,**

A TRUE MISSOURIAN

*Notice how many noble things there are in men*
*in spite of the meanness that you see.*

JOHN G. NEIHARDT

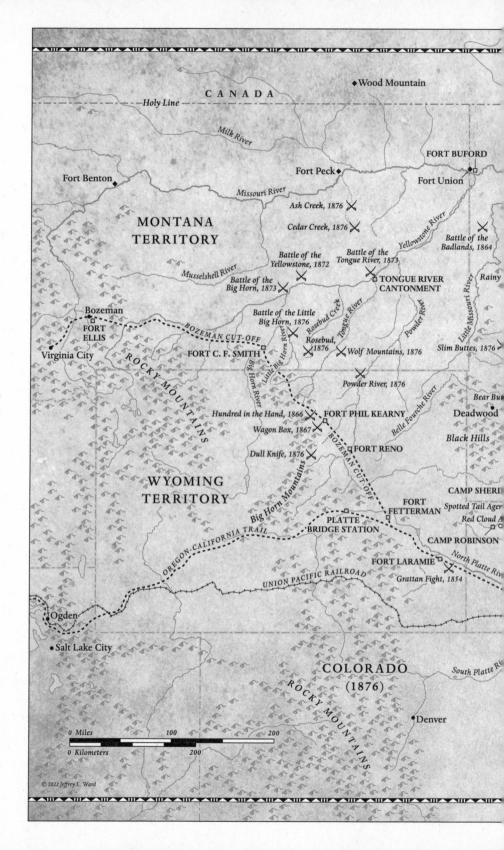

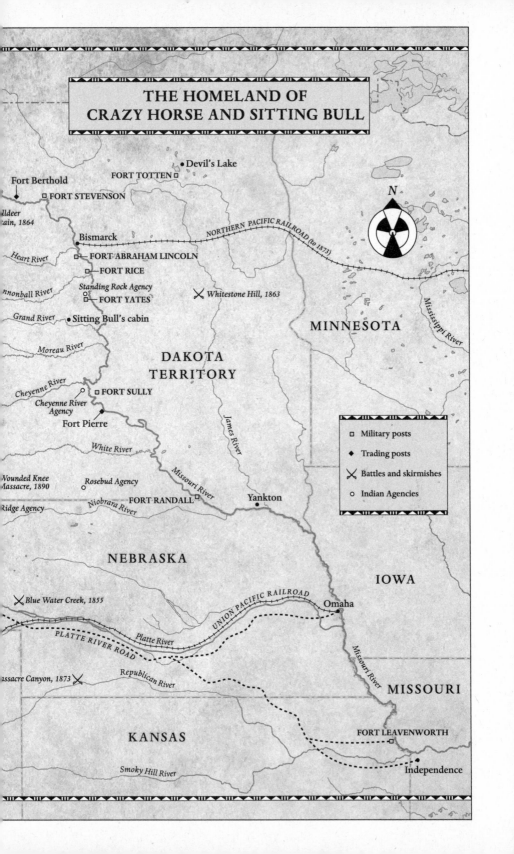

# THE HOMELAND OF
# CRAZY HORSE AND SITTING BULL

Devil's Lake
FORT TOTTEN □

Fort Berthold
□ FORT STEVENSON

*lldeer
ain, 1864*

N

Bismarck
NORTHERN PACIFIC RAILROAD (to 1873)

*Heart River*

□—FORT ABRAHAM LINCOLN

□—FORT RICE

*nnonball River*

*Standing Rock Agency*
□—FORT YATES

✕ Whitestone Hill, 1863

MINNESOTA

*Grand River* ● Sitting Bull's cabin

*Mississippi River*

*Moreau River*

## DAKOTA
## TERRITORY

*Cheyenne River*
○ □ FORT SULLY

*Cheyenne River
Agency*
Fort Pierre

*White River*

*James River*

*Missouri River*

*Wounded Knee
Massacre, 1890*

○ *Rosebud Agency*

*Niobrara River* FORT RANDALL □

Yankton

*Ridge Agency*

□ Military posts

♦ Trading posts

✕ Battles and skirmishes

○ Indian Agencies

## NEBRASKA

IOWA

✕ *Blue Water Creek, 1855*

UNION PACIFIC RAILROAD

Omaha

*Platte River*

PLATTE RIVER ROAD

*Missouri River*

*assacre Canyon, 1873* ✕

*Republican River*

MISSOURI

## KANSAS

FORT LEAVENWORTH □

*Smoky Hill River*

● Independence

# CONTENTS

# THE EARTH IS ALL THAT LASTS

# Hóka Hé!

*A charger, he is coming
I made him come.
When he came, I wiped him out.
He did not like my ways; that is why.*

KILL SONG OF STEPHEN STANDING BEAR, MINICONJOU

Sitting Bull carefully dressed and painted himself. Then he cut a few small pieces of tobacco from a tobacco twist and wrapped them in supple buckskin, making several little packets. He tied each one to a thin stick of cherrywood. All this he did with great care as well, for these were offerings intended for *Wakan Tanka*, the Great Spirit. Sitting Bull slid the sticks into a leather bag, picked up his pipe and a buffalo robe, and stepped out of his tipi to a clear night sky glistening with stars.

The Lakota holy man, now in his forty-third year, stood about five feet, ten inches tall, was stoutly built, and carried himself with an erect, stately bearing. He parted his long, black hair in the middle, and in the part he painted his skin crimson. Sitting Bull walked with a slight limp, the result of an old wound given him by a Crow chief twenty years earlier. That Crow died with a bullet in his gut from Sitting Bull's gun, and his spirit left this world without its scalp—Sitting Bull made sure of that.

Wading the Greasy Grass River to its east side, Sitting Bull climbed a long ridge lush with prairie grasses and scattered clumps of sagebrush, finally stopping at a high prominence overlooking the valley. Below him, a thousand buffalo hide tipis, their earflaps blackened from the smoke of many fires, stretched for one and a half miles along the river's west bank.

The village counted more than five thousand souls, most of whom were members of seven Lakota (Western Sioux) tribes: Oglala, Húnkpapa, Miniconjou, Sihásapa, Two Kettle, Sans Arc, and Brulé. Some Yanktonais and Santees, Middle and Eastern Sioux, had joined their Lakota relatives that summer. And there was also a camp circle of Northern and Southern Cheyennes, age-old friends and allies of the Lakotas. No one among the thousands camped on the Greasy Grass could remember ever having seen such a big village. It was, in fact, one of the largest gatherings of free-roaming Plains Indians in history.

But trouble lay ahead for these people. Sitting Bull, who was well known for his ability to see into the future, could sense it. In addition to being a Húnkpapa holy man, he was also the recognized leader of all the Lakotas making up this great village; he would do whatever he could to protect them. So Sitting Bull removed the offering sticks with their packets of tobacco from his bag and pushed each one into the ground, forming a circle. Then, standing, he began to sing a Thunder song. His voice was deep, and it reached far out into the still darkness:

> Great Spirit, pity me. In the name of the tribe I offer you
> this sacred pipe. Wherever the sun, the moon, the earth,
> the four points of the wind, there you are always. Father
> save the tribe, I beg you. Pity me, we wish to live. Guard
> us against all misfortunes or calamities. Pity me.

The following day, as the sun climbed high in the June sky, men, women, and children sought relief from the heat in the cool waters of the Greasy Grass, its banks lined with tall cottonwoods. Many slept late, for there had been several social dances the night before, some lasting until dawn. It was a joyous time, the hunting had been good, and the Lakotas and Cheyennes were still reveling in the great victory they had won over the "Long Knives" (white soldiers) just eight days earlier.

That fight had occurred on Rosebud Creek some thirty miles to the southeast. About eight hundred warriors, dressed in their best colorful finery, surprised a column of more than one thousand United States cavalry, infantry, and Shoshone and Crow scouts. The Long Knives had come a great distance to find and attack these very same Indians.

Fierce charges and countercharges stretched over miles of rolling hills, and the feats of bravery were too many to count. When a Southern Cheyenne chief, Comes in Sight, had his horse shot out from under him, his sister, Buffalo Calf Road Woman, kicked the flanks of her pony and galloped into a storm of flying lead to her brother. The chief jumped up behind her and they raced away to safety. The Cheyennes would always refer to the Rosebud fight as "where the girl saved her brother."

The battle lasted for hours, from early morning to midafternoon. Crazy Horse, the mysterious Oglala war chief, led several bold attacks that day, and whenever his men seemed to tire or hesitate, Crazy Horse urged them on, shouting and shaking his lever-action Winchester above his head. The white soldiers and their commanders were stunned by the aggressiveness and determination of these warriors, and when the Indians finally broke off the battle and started back on the trail to their village, the Long Knives did not follow them.

And that is exactly what Sitting Bull and Crazy Horse wanted: to be left alone. These two remarkable Lakotas were unwavering in their resolve to live separate from the white men steadily encroaching upon their lands. They recognized no treaties and no reservations. They did recognize the arrogance in the white man telling the Lakotas what they could and could not do, where they could live and where they could hunt. And if the white man would not let them follow the buffalo and live free as Lakotas, then they would fight.

In the Greasy Grass village the morning after Sitting Bull's offering to *Wakan Tanka,* very few feared the coming of more Long Knives. An aged and nearly blind Cheyenne holy man in the camp named Box Elder had the gift of prophecy much like Sitting Bull, and Box Elder had been disturbed by a dream in which he saw soldiers bearing down on their village. He sent a crier to warn everyone and to tell them to keep their horses tied close to their tipis, but the people didn't believe him.

"We had driven away the soldiers, on the upper Rosebud," recalled Wooden Leg, a Northern Cheyenne who was eighteen that summer. "It seemed likely it would be a long time before they would trouble us again."

Wooden Leg had danced with the Lakota girls all night long, and after taking a midday swim with his brother, Yellow Hair, they both lay down in the shade of the rustling cottonwoods and fell sound asleep. Elsewhere along the river, away from the splashing and playing, boys were sitting on the banks fishing. A number of women were out digging turnips—this time of year was known as the Moon of the Wild Turnip. Others were tending to thin strips of buffalo meat hanging and drying in the air, food to be stored up for winter. And here and there through the camps, a few lodges were being taken down, for the village would be moving soon. Such a large gathering could not remain in one place for long. The enormous herd of horses—far outnumbering the

Indians—quickly exhausted the available forage, dead wood for campfires was soon used up, and killing enough game to keep the hundreds of families fed took more and more effort.

Iron Hail, a fourteen-year-old Miniconjou, had also gone swimming and was returning to his family's tipi for food when he was approached by an uncle.

"When you finish eating," the uncle said, "go to our horses. Something might happen today. I feel it in the air."

All Lakotas knew that the wind carried messages, but not all could hear them. Iron Hail did not question his uncle, and he quickly finished his meal and rode off to join his younger brother, who was already herding together the family's ponies. Just as Iron Hail reached the herd, shouts and yells began coming from the village.

Wooden Leg, still napping under the cottonwoods, dreamed there were lots of people making a terrible racket. Startled, he bolted awake, as did his brother. The commotion was real. The brothers jumped up and ran from the cottonwoods. Women and children dodged past them screaming. In the distance, they distinctly heard gunfire—*pop-pop-pop-pop-pop-pop.*

All the things Wooden Leg had sensed before drifting asleep— the pleasant smell of woodsmoke, the buzz of summer insects, the meadowlark's singing, the intense heat of the midday sun— instantly vanished. The cries of the tribal elders cut through the cacophony in the camp: "Soldiers are here! Young men, go out and fight them!"

The shooting came from the southern end of the village, and the pandemonium moved as a wave down the valley and among the lodges. Horses hurriedly driven into the camps kicked up thick dust. Some of the ponies, frightened by the gunfire and yelling, snorted and reared as women and children struggled to catch and hold them for the warriors. The village dogs barked incessantly.

Men too old to fight did what they could to assist the young men: faces must be painted, old clothes exchanged for fancy dress saved for just such an occasion. Nothing but the best when riding into battle.

The Húnkpapa camp, Sitting Bull's people, was where the Long Knives struck first. Mixed with the screams of the fleeing Lakotas was the peculiar buzzing sound of the soldiers' conical lead bullets. When a round ripped through a hide lodge, it sounded like a bug flicking into the tipi's side. Those that struck the tipi poles created a rattling noise. A sickening *slap* meant a bullet had found flesh and bone.

One Bull, a twenty-three-year-old nephew of Sitting Bull, ran into the lodge he shared with his uncle and grabbed his trade gun, an old muzzleloader. But Sitting Bull rushed in right after him and took the gun away, handing him in its place a stone-headed war club. In close-quarter fighting, a warrior had no time to reload a single-shot muzzleloader, but a stout club could crack skulls again and again.

Sitting Bull also gave One Bull his personal buffalo hide shield. The stiff shield held tremendous significance and power. It had been made by Sitting Bull's father, who had painted on the shield's face a bird of prey with large talons over a bluish-green sky. A thick border encircling the bird, colored red on one side and black on the other, represented a rainbow. Four eagle feathers hung from the shield's edge honoring the four cardinal directions, thus giving the warrior who carried it luck wherever he might travel.

"Go right ahead," Sitting Bull told his nephew as he positioned the shield. "Don't be afraid. Go right on." One Bull jumped onto the back of his pony and started off through the village, heading for the sound of the gunfire.

Once outside the tipi, Sitting Bull mounted a black horse and left to find his aged mother and help lead the women and children to safety—as an "old man chief," the holy man was not expected to fight the Long Knives. Quickly disappearing into the throng of Indians hurrying to and fro, Sitting Bull could be heard shouting to the warriors: "Brave up, boys. It will be a hard time. Brave up."

As One Bull rode through the camps, he held his uncle's shield high so all could see. By displaying Sitting Bull's shield, he was instantly recognized as carrying the authority of the leader of the Lakotas, and many warriors flocked to him. One Bull sang to the shield, a sacred song Sitting Bull's father had received in his vision. This song was important to realize the full protection the shield offered. Then One Bull prayed to *Wakan Tanka* to have mercy on him.

In the Cheyenne camp, Chief Two Moons called out to his people: "I am Two Moons, your chief. Don't run away. Stay here and fight. You must stay and fight the white soldiers. I shall stay even if I am to be killed."

Wooden Leg, now astride his favorite pony, raced in the direction of the Húnkpapa camp circle. The air was so full of dust he could barely see. All he could do was keep his horse headed in the same direction as the crowd around him.

In the Oglala camp, situated near the Northern Cheyennes, impatient warriors rode their ponies back and forth outside Crazy Horse's lodge as they waited for their leader to finish readying himself for battle. But as Lakotas, these warriors knew that entering a fight without first carefully preparing one's "medicine" risked defeat and even death. A warrior might still be hurt, but a warrior was also meant to suffer at one time or another, and there were few greater honors than a battle wound. Nevertheless, when it came to medicine, Crazy Horse was more meticulous than most.

The Oglala leader's battle preparations came mostly from Horn Chips, a legendary holy man and a cousin of Crazy Horse.

A "Stone Dreamer," Horn Chips's war medicine always involved, in some way, small stones imbued with special power. He'd given Crazy Horse a black stone the size of a marble with a hole in it, encased in buckskin, and told him to wear it under his left arm, held in place by a leather thong over the shoulder.

Horn Chips also presented Crazy Horse with the two center tail feathers of a spotted eagle and told him to attach one to the stone. The other he was to fix in his hair. Crazy Horse was never to wear a warbonnet, only this feather and a few straws of grass. Additionally, the war chief was to take into battle an eagle wing-bone whistle, suspended from his neck.

These talismans could be gathered and arranged fairly quickly, but that was not all. Paint had to be applied in a very special way as well. With one finger dabbed in a paint made from red earth, Crazy Horse drew a zigzag line down one side of his face from his forehead to his chin. This represented the lightning of the Thunder Beings, whom Crazy Horse had dreamed would give him power and protection. Over his body, Crazy Horse lightly rubbed the spotted eagle's dried heart.

Also requiring protection from the enemy was a warrior's horse, for a Lakota lived and breathed as one with his mount. The war medicine for Crazy Horse's pony came from the dry dirt of a gopher hill, which Crazy Horse dusted over the animal, front and back, and rubbed in streaks in the pony's hair. The war chief would then dab a little of the same dirt into his own hair. If all these things were done, and done correctly, Horn Chips had told Crazy Horse, no bullet could touch him.

No one can say for sure how much time passed during this ritual, only that Crazy Horse would not be hurried. When he finally jumped up on his white-faced pony, he wore only a breechclout and moccasins. Yet there was something magnificent and even magical about this unassuming, quiet man. Just under six feet tall, lean and strong, Crazy Horse was always at the front in a fight, constantly exposing himself to enemy bullets and arrows—it was said he had had eight horses shot out from under him. The thirty-five-year-old Oglala was a warrior's warrior, and his men would follow anywhere he led. Now they galloped to help the Húnkpapas, Crazy Horse in the lead, his long hair streaming behind him.

The battle had commenced with three companies of cavalry and a few Arikara scouts, about 150 men total, charging the village. The Arikaras, bitter enemies of the Lakotas, rode in advance of the troopers and shot down ten women and children hurrying back to their lodges. But the soldiers curiously halted in an open flat just a few hundred yards from the Húnkpapa tipis. There they dismounted and formed a skirmish line while their horses were led to the protection of the cottonwoods along the river on their right. The raking fire from the soldiers' Springfield carbines terrorized the village, but the halt gave the warriors critical time to concentrate at the point of attack. Within minutes, the Long Knives found themselves on the defensive as hundreds of warriors massed on their front and quickly began to outflank the soldiers' thin line.

Without warning, the troopers suddenly retreated to the timber. "Hay-ay! Hay-ay!" cried the warriors, emboldened now to advance closer. The sky rained arrows, and puffs of gray-white smoke belched from guns on both sides. Tree leaves and small twigs, clipped by flying lead, sprinkled down upon the soldiers. The warriors dashed in and out of the dust and smoke like phantoms, glints of sunlight reflecting off gun barrels and dangling metal adornments such as hair plates and gorgets.

Then, from the direction of the village, eagle-bone whistles pierced the air, followed by thundering hooves and shouts: "Crazy

Horse is coming!" Women and children who'd fled to the low hills west of the Húnkpapa camp thrilled at the sight of Crazy Horse's arrival, crying *"Hóka hé!"* (Come on!). Several women voiced the distinctive, high-pitched tremolo.

The surging, always moving swarm of mounted warriors, now numbering perhaps a thousand, began to wrap around the wooded loop the cavalrymen had retreated to; others on foot stealthily slipped into the timber on each side. Crazy Horse, recognizing the troopers' desperate situation, turned to his men and anyone else within hearing and said, "Here are the soldiers after us again. Do your best, and let us kill them all off today that they may not trouble us anymore. All ready! Charge!"

At that same moment, a flood of soldiers poured out from the trees and raced headlong back up the valley in the direction from which they had come, keeping close to the winding stream. Most were mounted on their horses, but some were on foot. The mad dash of the cavalrymen across the open prairie resembled buffalo fleeing, remembered Two Moons.

The warriors quickly closed on the Long Knives, and, just as in a buffalo chase, the slaughter began. The terrified soldiers soon veered into the Greasy Grass and splashed into the fast current to cross to the other side. It was not a good place to ford, and men and horses floundered in the river as they attempted to climb the opposite bank, which was steep and well above their horses' heads—it was now every man for himself.

The warriors paid little heed to the few white men who turned to shoot at their pursuers. They rode pell-mell into the midst of the soldiers, swinging war clubs and rifle butts, and shooting at point-blank range. A young Oglala named Red Hawk watched Crazy Horse charge a soldier riding a sorrel horse. The soldier shot at the war chief with his revolver but missed. As the scared trooper spun his cavalry mount around to flee, a bullet from

Crazy Horse's Winchester struck the soldier's horse but failed to drop the animal. Red Hawk dashed up and barely missed the soldier's back with his lance. The desperate cavalryman fired twice at Red Hawk, the gunpowder burning the warrior's face. Red Hawk let go of his lance and grabbed the Spencer carbine hanging from his shoulder. As the two horses bumped together, Red Hawk slammed the butt of his Spencer into the white man's head, sending him tumbling to the ground.

With a cousin, Kicking Bear, riding at his side, Crazy Horse plunged his horse into the river. The two rode into the sweaty mob of men and horses and began pulling troopers off their floundering mounts. "We killed many on the river bank and in the water," recalled One Bull. "I rode up behind one soldier and knocked him over with my war club. Then I slid off my pony and held the soldier's head under water until he was dead. I killed two more soldiers in the water."

Long Knives clawed up a narrow buffalo path on their hands and knees, some leading their horses, others mercilessly spurring their exhausted mounts upward. Those lucky soldiers who escaped to the opposite bank still had a challenging climb to the top of the high bluffs to the east, two hundred feet above the river. And although not as many Indians followed them, those who did kept it hot for the fleeing troopers and continued to inflict casualties until the surviving soldiers found limited protection in a natural basin at the bluff's summit.

Down below, in the trees and brush next to the river, the grass was set on fire in an attempt to force out any soldiers who might be hiding. "Lots of Indians were hunting around for dead soldiers or for wounded ones to kill," Wooden Leg remembered. "I got some tobacco from the pockets of one dead man. I got also a belt having in it a few cartridges. All of the weapons and clothing and all other possessions were being taken from the bodies."

The military ammunition was important because the warriors' battle trophies now included several Springfield breechloading carbines in .45-55 caliber, and very few, if any, of the Indian guns were chambered for that round. When Wooden Leg discovered two pasteboard boxes in a leather saddlebag, he was elated to find they contained the proper cartridges for the carbine he'd captured.

Black Elk, a thirteen-year-old Oglala and a second cousin of Crazy Horse, had ridden up from the camps with two other boys just in time to see the warriors stripping the bodies of the soldiers. As they watched the intense plundering, Black Elk spotted a trooper on the ground kicking his legs. A warrior motioned to the kicking man and shouted to Black Elk: "Boy, get off and scalp him." Black Elk got off his pony and approached the dying soldier.

The boy was dismayed to find that the soldier had short hair, but he did his best, cutting a circle in the scalp and yanking it free. The excruciating pain caused the wounded trooper to grind his teeth, but he did not speak. "After I did this," Black Elk recalled, "I took my pistol out and shot him in the forehead."

When Black Elk returned to a hilltop where his mother and other women were observing the battle's progress, his mother saw the bloody enemy scalp and gave a shrill tremolo to honor her son. Then Black Elk heard a young woman singing, exhorting the warriors to take courage. Her song ended with a reminder of the consequences of defeat: "Would you see me taken captive?"

Blood spatters, dead men, and dead horses marked the route of the soldiers' flight from near the village to the river crossing. Following this death trail was a Húnkpapa woman on horseback named Her Eagle Robe. She'd just learned that her ten-year-old brother had been killed and in her rage set out to seek vengeance upon the Long Knives. Her Eagle Robe came upon a wounded Black man pinned under his bullet-riddled horse. This man was well known to many Lakotas, for he was married to a Santee woman and spoke their language fluently. He was with the Long Knives as an interpreter. The Lakotas knew him by the name Teat.

Teat had propped himself up, blood oozing from his chest. Between painful gasps, he told Her Eagle Robe that it was likely her husband or son had also been shot in the fight, which only served to anger the woman more.

"Do not kill me," Teat pleaded, "because I will be dead in a short while, anyway."

"If you did not want to be killed," Her Eagle Robe said, "why did you not stay home where you belong and not come to attack us?"

Her Eagle Robe carried a Colt revolver. She raised the gun and pointed it at Teat and squeezed the trigger. The revolver misfired. She worked the action of the weapon and again took deliberate aim at the black man. This time a bullet smashed into Teat's skull.

Other women came up to Teat's limp corpse and began to strike it repeatedly with stone clubs and slash it with knives. Young warriors riding by counted coup on the dead man by shooting arrows into the body until it bristled with feathered shafts. And to ensure that Teat would enter the hereafter at a supreme disadvantage, a picket pin was driven through his testicles and his penis cut off and stuffed into his mouth. Although Teat was considered a Sioux relative through his Santee wife, he and the white men he rode with were there to kill them.

With an apparent lull in the fighting, many women ran back to their lodges to retrieve possessions and food. But on the high ridgetops east of the river, an ominous dust cloud could be seen rolling northwest, parallel to the village. Soon, a shouted warning spread from camp to camp: "Other soldiers are coming!" Scattered gunshots erupted from near the river, about a mile downstream from the Húnkpapa camp, and the faint sound of a bugle floated across the air from the same direction.

Two companies of cavalry had galloped down a large, dry gulch to the Greasy Grass in an apparent attempt to find a crossing and strike the camps. These troopers were not the same ones who had been routed earlier up the valley. The goal of the Long Knives, it seemed, was to encircle the village, to hit it from both ends. And because many women and children had fled downstream, away from the first attack, they were now in danger from these other soldiers.

Only a handful of warriors were in this part of the village to meet the new threat, but they opened fire from their side of the river anyway, quickly knocking as many as three troopers out of their saddles. The Long Knives returned fire, but they didn't press their attack. Bullets screamed back and forth across the Greasy Grass for a time, and then the Long Knives slowly withdrew up to the ridgetops, where more soldiers waited. Great numbers of Lakotas and Cheyennes, some with magnificent feather headdresses running down their backs, began arriving and plunging their horses into the river. "It appeared there would be no end to the rushing procession of warriors" across the Greasy Grass, remembered Antelope Woman, a Southern Cheyenne. "They kept going, going, going." They followed the Long Knives to the high ground.

Wooden Leg, riding with other warriors to this second fight, stopped at his family's lodge to get a fresh horse. He showed his father his plunder from the dead white men, being especially proud of his new gun and cartridges.

"You have been brave," his father told him. "You have done enough for one day. Now you should rest."

"No, I want to fight the other soldiers," Wooden Leg said forcefully. "I can fight better now, with this gun."

His father relented, but reminded his young son that his

brother was also fighting the Long Knives. "I think there will be plenty of warriors to beat the soldiers, so it is not needful that I send both of my sons. You have not your shield nor your eagle wing-bone flute. Stay back as far as you can and shoot from a long distance. Let your brother go ahead of you."

Wooden Leg's father watched as his son jumped up on a fresh mount and galloped away with two other warriors, the new gun grasped firmly in his hand.

Leading a group of Oglalas and Cheyennes, Crazy Horse galloped through the camps to the sound of the gunfire. At his side was another cousin and friend, Flying Hawk. Like Crazy Horse, Flying Hawk was driven to kill every last one of these white men who had attacked their homes. "No good soldiers would shoot into the Indian's tipi where there were women and children," Flying Hawk would say later. "These soldiers did, and we fought for our women and children."

Crazy Horse's party rode past the point on the river where other warriors had been crossing and continued downstream for another mile, just beyond the northern edge of the village. They forded the Greasy Grass there and headed up a deep ravine that led to the high ridge, three-quarters of a mile away. Crazy Horse and his men kept to the bottom of the ravine as it made a wide turn to the right, getting ever closer to the increasing gunfire above them. Finally coming to a place within shooting range of the soldiers, Crazy Horse slid off his horse and handed the reins to Flying Hawk.

The Long Knives—five companies, numbering slightly more than two hundred men—were spread out in bunches along the ridge, with some companies separated from the others by a distance of several hundred yards. The shooting from the troopers now approached a roar. "The bullets flew past our ears like angry bees," recalled one warrior.

Crazy Horse crawled to a good vantage point. He had a known preference to shoot from the ground instead of on horseback—no chance of his pony spoiling a shot. But in this fight, many warriors had abandoned their horses so as to stay low, partially hidden in the grasses and clumps of sagebrush.

The Oglala war chief rose up from the ground on his knees and shot several rounds at the troopers closest to him, rapidly working the lever action of his Winchester until it was empty. He quickly dropped prone again and reloaded. Then he backed down to Flying Hawk, retrieved his pony, and led his cousin and several warriors through the haze of gunsmoke to the top of the hogback and over to the east side. Here, too, warriors cautiously inched toward the besieged white men.

The troopers were dismounted, their horses gathered together and held by other soldiers, a minimum of four horses to each holder. Arcing arrows gashed the sides of some horses, and more than a few stuck in their rumps, causing the terrified animals to rear and plunge. Crazy Horse directed his men to aim for the horse holders, and when a holder was killed or wounded, the warriors waved blankets and yelled to scare the loose horses west toward the village. Women and old men who had crossed the river caught the mounts, most of which carried precious packs of ammunition for the white man guns.

Shrill notes from eagle wing-bone whistles cut the air. Warriors sang their "brave songs" to bolster their nerve. Shouts of "Hóka hé! This life will not last forever," and, "Take courage, the earth is all that lasts," floated in and out of the deafening gunfire.

To the amazement of all those near him, Crazy Horse remained on his pony. "It is a good day to fight, a good day to die," he shouted. "Strong hearts, brave hearts, to the front. Weak hearts and cowards to the rear!"

Crazy Horse "was the bravest man I ever saw," recalled one old Arapaho fighter. "He rode closest to the soldiers, yelling to his warriors. All the soldiers were shooting at him, but he was never hit."

Crazy Horse saw a dip or depression in the ridge above him. If he were to ride through this, he could possibly split the troopers into two groups, and if he could get most of them to fire all at once, his warriors might have an opportunity to charge in while the troopers were reloading, a favorite Indian tactic when fighting the Long Knives. This dangerous feat was known to the Lakotas as a "bravery run," and Crazy Horse was its undisputed master.

Crazy Horse believed his medicine to be strong, but if *Wakan Tanka* willed his death, then he would die brave and free. The Oglala war leader leaned forward on his saddle, spoke to his pony, then slapped his heels against its sides. The animal lurched ahead and broke into a gallop, its hooves kicking up dirt and small rocks. Crazy Horse slid down onto the animal's side and clung there, his Winchester leveled across the pony's mane.

Lakotas and Cheyennes cheered as they watched him guide his pony toward the ridgetop. Streaks of flame and gunsmoke erupted from carbine and revolver muzzles as Crazy Horse neared the gap, the gunfire stopping for only a second or two as he passed between both groups of soldiers. Then, as suddenly as his ride had begun, Crazy Horse was through the gauntlet, disappearing from view on the other side of the ridge.

Now came a rush of warriors. The soldiers, all semblance of discipline lost, began to run—again, like buffalo, scared and sensing death.

# Becoming Warriors

*Son, I never want to see you live to be an old man. Die
young on the battlefield. That is the way a Lakota dies.*

**LAKOTA FATHER TO HIS SON**

In the early 1880s, as a prisoner of war at Fort Randall, Dakota
Territory, Sitting Bull told his life story through a series of colorful drawings, at least fifty of them. In these paper tableaus, flat
figures on flat horses act out various war deeds or coups of the
Húnkpapa holy man and chief. Like all warriors, Sitting Bull saw
his life as a series of individual heroics in battle.

With a palette of graphite, colored pencils, crayon, and watercolors, Sitting Bull drew himself delivering the coup de grâce to
one enemy warrior after another: Crow, Flathead, Assiniboine,
and Chippewa. The victims' feet are in the air, the figures falling
backward from a gunshot or the thrust of a feathered lance. In
some drawings, Sitting Bull's victims have open mouths showing
pain, a panicked gasp for air, or the enemy's surprise upon receiving a death blow.

Glaringly absent from Sitting Bull's pictographic résumé, however, are any depictions of white victims. Long before he was a

prisoner, Sitting Bull did create drawings showing his killings of white soldiers and settlers, but he wisely thought better of chronicling such episodes while at the mercy of his white hosts. Consequently, to view his Fort Randall oeuvre is like trying to read an autobiography that's missing several key chapters. For in all his years, Sitting Bull and his people had never known a world without the white man. Even these drawings of Sitting Bull's early life as a Lakota warrior were made on white man's paper using white man's pencils. And like the lines and colors permanently fixed on that paper, Sitting Bull's story is inseparable from that of the white interloper.

No one can say with absolute certainty the exact date of Sitting Bull's birth—even Sitting Bull wasn't sure. But most biographers, including Sitting Bull's own great-grandson, have settled on 1831, possibly in March. The place? "I don't know where I was born and cannot remember," Sitting Bull told a needling newspaper reporter in 1881. "I know I was born, though, or I would not be here. I was born of a woman. I know this is a fact, because I exist."

Sitting Bull's uncle, Four Horns, was present at the interview and informed his nephew that he was born at a camp on Willow Creek, below where the Cheyenne River empties into the Missouri (in present-day South Dakota).

The calendar year for the Lakotas and other Plains tribes began with the first snow of winter and continued until the next winter's first snow. An Indian record that keeps track of these years, be it on buffalo hide, cloth, or paper, is known as a "winter count," with each year having its own pictograph illustrating a single unusual or remarkable event. For the year of Sitting Bull's birth, a pictograph showing two wagons in front of a tipi is found on the winter count kept by American Horse, a prominent Oglala chief. A white man is in one of the wagons. The remarkable event depicted was, "They saw wagons for the first time." The white man was a trader, his wagons packed with "Indian goods."

Not only did many Lakotas see their first wagons in 1831, but they also saw their first "fireboat." That spring, the American Fur Company's new side-wheeler *Yellow Stone* chugged up the Missouri as far as the trading post of Fort Tecumseh, in the heart of Sioux country and but a few miles from Sitting Bull's birthplace. The steamboat belched black smoke and sparks from two smokestacks as it pushed against the Missouri's swift current, its hold crammed full of standard trade items such as wool point blankets, glass beads, sewing awls, skinning knives, brass kettles, sugar, tobacco, Northwest trade guns, gun flints, and several tons of gunpowder and lead.

As much as a thousand gallons of whiskey was also stowed away beneath the *Yellow Stone's* decks. Although "ardent spirits" were forbidden by law as a trade item in Indian country, some tribes wouldn't bargain without it. Fortunately for the fur companies, an exception was granted allowing liquor for boatmen employed along the river and at various posts. Consequently, all a company had to do was claim the alcohol brought upstream was intended for its employees. Problem solved.

When the *Yellow Stone* returned to St. Louis in mid-July, it offloaded hundreds of heavy packs of buffalo robes and assorted peltries and ten thousand pounds of salted buffalo tongues, the latter a delicacy craved by both Indians and whites. Each and every one of the thousands of robes had been fully tanned with the hair on, a tedious job that fell to Indian women—it easily took ten days for a woman to process just one robe. The results of their labors generally ended up as lap robes for use in the white man's carriages and sleighs during winter months in the United States and Europe. Numerous robes were also purchased by clothing manufacturers, who fashioned them into heavy but warm coats, mittens, and hats.

By the time Sitting Bull was born, then, the Lakotas and other tribes were already firmly tied to a global market economy. And having become wedded long ago to the traders' manufactured goods—and their revolutionizing effect on the Lakotas' material culture and way of life—they had found there was no going back. At least the fur traders didn't want their land, only what the land provided. But by their harvesting buffalo far in excess of the Indians' own needs, the days of vast herds darkening the prairies from horizon to horizon could not last forever.

In a particularly shocking instance of wasteful slaughter in 1832, a large herd of buffalo appeared one day across the Missouri from the Fort Pierre trading post (successor to Fort Tecumseh). A band of several hundred Indians—their tribal affiliation is not recorded—forded the river and began to very efficiently bring down one woolly beast after another. The Indians returned to the fort a few hours later with fourteen hundred fresh buffalo tongues. As prairie wolves feasted on the meat left behind to rot, the Indians enjoyed several gallons of whiskey they'd accepted in trade for the tongues.

The white man did his share of wanton killing, too, but that was more in his nature. For the Lakotas, the buffalo were their sacred providers and central to many of their spiritual beliefs. When a man killed a buffalo, the soul of that animal joined with its hunter. A gift to the Lakotas from the Spirit of the Earth, the buffalo was their primary source of food, clothing, and shelter—everything the people needed to live free. To waste such a sacred gift was to travel the "black road." One who travels this metaphoric road, as related by the Oglala holy man Black Elk, "is ruled by his senses, and who lives for himself rather than for his people."

While the steamboat *Yellow Stone* brought tidings of dramatic changes to come for Sioux country, it also brought white intellectuals—ethnologists and artists who often marveled at the splendor of the native peoples they encountered. "There is no tribe on the Continent, perhaps, of finer looking men than the Sioux," wrote the artist George Catlin, who visited Fort Pierre in 1832, "and few tribes who are better and more comfortably clad, and supplied with the necessaries of life."

To the artist's eyes, the Sioux appeared "very fine and prepossessing, their persons tall and straight, and their movements elastic and graceful." In their pursuit of buffalo and wild horses, no tribe was "more bold in destroying one for food, and appropriating the other to their use." However, even though a good many men had obtained guns from the traders, Catlin wrote, they preferred hunting with the bow and lance, "killing their game from their horses' backs while at full speed." The bow and arrow was easier and faster to manage at close range during a headlong buffalo chase than the muzzleloading firearms available at the time. And guns required lead and powder, which had to be traded for. Arrows shot into a buffalo, their metal points also obtained from the traders, could be retrieved and used again.

German explorer-naturalist Prince Maximilian of Wied traveled up the Missouri a year after Catlin, reaching Fort Pierre on May 31, 1833. In his copious journal, the fifty-year-old prince noted that it wasn't uncommon to see eight or nine hundred tipis of Middle and Western Sioux camped on the plains along the river. "Life and activity everywhere," he wrote, "in one place they are dancing and playing; in another they are working and tanning hides; others come to pack or load their animals, etc. A most interesting sight."

While at and around Fort Pierre, the prince had numerous friendly interactions with the Sioux and other tribes, interviewing chiefs and warriors, feasting in their lodges, bartering for garments and weapons for later study, and observing daily camp routines. About the latter, Maximilian noted that most of the burden fell upon Sioux women: "They have to do all the work, the women in general, and the men lead a very easy and comfortable life once they have provided food. [The men] sit about all day, smoke their pipes, or walk about leisurely."

"Wealthy" Sioux men might own thirty to forty horses, Maximilian wrote. They could also have as many as nine wives. Multiple horses and wives correlated directly with the enticements of the robe trade. Being able to choose from several fresh mounts was a definite advantage when the hunting was heavy, and the more wives one had, the more buffalo hides that could be processed during robe season.

Upon meeting a hunting party of Húnkpapas (Sitting Bull's tribe) and Yanktonais, Maximilian was similarly impressed as Catlin: "They were mostly strong, slender, good-looking men with long, wildly disheveled hair. [They were] mostly naked; some of them had buffalo-hide blankets, others [woolen] blankets [as well as] fine bags and hides embroidered with beads and porcupine quills. But most of them were dressed simply, because they were on a hunting expedition."

In their villages, however, the Indians' personal artistic expressions were in full view: faces painted with vermillion, blue and white glass beads and shells dangling from ears and around necks, feathers carefully placed just so on the head to signify some exploit, shirts fringed with human hair, and supple summer robes painted with intricate geometric designs of red and white. Elaborate bead- and quillwork adorned moccasins, leggings, shirts, knife sheaths, bow quivers, and cradleboards, to name just a few. It was unthinkable to the Lakotas, it seemed, to leave any blank space undecorated.

As this was still six years before the Frenchman Louis Daguerre would introduce daguerreotype photography to the world, Maximilian had brought along a superbly talented draftsman and engraver, Karl Bodmer, to visually document his expedition. With wonderful detail, Bodmer sketched in watercolor the Sioux and other Indians they met on their journey up the Missouri, as well as the breathtaking landscape and its equally beautiful flora and fauna.

But Bodmer's watercolors are much more than just scientific illustrations. In his intimate portraits of native men and women, the artist also captured the dignity and pride of a people. Together, Bodmer's sketches and Maximilian's journals reveal a vibrant culture—a buffalo culture—in its prime. This was the culture Sitting Bull was born into.

The baby boy who would one day become the renowned and feared leader of the Lakotas was the second child of Returns Again and Her Holy Door. By all accounts, Returns Again was a brave and wise man, and his name, which could also be translated as "Forsakes His Home," had everything to do with bravery and warfare. As explained by Sitting Bull's nephew One Bull, the name referred to a warrior who, after starting home from a war expedition, stopped and turned back in search of more Lakota enemies to battle.

Not only was Returns Again a noted warrior, but he was something of a holy man himself and was known to have powerful dreams or visions. In one dream, a humanlike being appeared in the form of a bird of prey and sang a sacred song to Returns Again. The being gave the Húnkpapa instructions on how to make and decorate a shield, which had to be done at once to receive the power of the great gift. Returns Again made and decorated not one, but four identical shields. The number four was sacred to the Lakotas—many things in the world came in fours: the four directions, the four seasons, and the four ages of human life. Returns Again kept one shield and gave the remaining three away as gifts.

Sitting Bull's father also had a reputation as someone with a knowledge of nature's medicines and healing. It was often Returns Again who would treat and bind a battle wound or injury. Despite his many fine qualities and skills, though, Returns Again was not a "big chief" of the Húnkpapas, a leadership position commonly inherited. He was, however, the ranking headman of his lodge group. A lodge group could number as many as one hundred people, mostly family and extended family that hunted and camped together. Several lodge groups formed a band, and Returns Again's people belonged to the Bad Bow band. At least nine bands made up the Húnkpapa tribe.

Her Holy Door, Sitting Bull's mother, was remembered as very social, a good talker who could make people laugh. In addition to her many daily tasks as a Lakota woman, she nurtured her babe so that he would grow straight and strong. Before sleep each night, she took care to cleanse the boy by rubbing buffalo tallow over his body and then tenderly massage his muscles and limbs. As one Lakota explained, manhood was planned in babyhood. The Lakotas' survival depended upon raising fit men to hunt, protect their people, and maintain their homeland.

The name Returns Again chose for his child was Jumping Badger—the adult name "Sitting Bull" would not come for several more years. Why Returns Again decided upon this name is unknown, but bestowing an animal name within a personal name allowed for a connection to that animal's traits or powers. The badger is an amazingly strong mammal for its size. With its long, sharp foreclaws, it burrows deep into the earth in search of its prey: gophers, prairie dogs, and even rattlesnakes. It is fierce, unrelenting, and fearful of no other creature, certainly very good qualities to possess for any boy aspiring to be a warrior.

But as Jumping Badger grew into a boy, he acquired an unusual nickname. Its English translation is "Slow" or "Slow-Moving." According to one Lakota account, he got this nickname because he was physically slow (his short legs did not lend themselves to speed), and he spoke slowly as well. In playful contests with other children, he consistently lost. In fact, Slow "was always last in everything." Other accounts, however, tell us that the nickname came from a certain deliberateness that was remarkable in a child, a tendency to carefully think things out at his own pace. In any event, the boy was rarely if ever called Jumping Badger. Family and friends called him by his nickname, Slow.

As with all Lakota children, Slow's education and training began soon after he could walk. He would learn to ride horseback, to shoot an arrow so that it flew straight and true, and to catch fish in the rivers and creeks. He would learn the ways of the "winged peoples" and the "four leggeds" and of the earth's many wonders that flood a child's mind and senses. "There was no such thing as emptiness in the world," one Lakota remembered from his childhood. "Even in the sky there were no vacant places. Everywhere there was life, visible and invisible, and every object possessed something that would be good for us to have also—even to the very stones."

The boy would also learn about the Lakotas' enemies—such tribes as the Crows, the Assiniboines, the Hidatsas, and the Flatheads. Many were the coups Returns Again counted on Crow warriors. The hatred for the Crows ran so deep, in fact, that even decades later, one old warrior described them as the "most cowardly tribe [that] ever lived on earth." Why did the Lakotas fight the Crows? Because Crow lands were rich with buffalo, and the Crows had lots of horses.

Of course, the Lakotas' enemies had nothing good to say about their opponents, either. A Pawnee Indian warned an English adventurer in 1835 that the Lakotas and their allies, the Cheyennes, were "bad men." In an obvious acknowledgment of the Lakotas' ferocity, the universal hand sign for the tribe was made by holding the index finger of the right hand near the left shoulder and moving it, in one swift motion, across the throat to the right shoulder, thus mimicking the very unpleasant act of slitting a throat.


Naturally, father and mother played an important role in Slow's upbringing, but so did the village elders, men and women of his parents' age and his grandparents' age, regardless of blood relationship. For Slow was not just the son of Returns Again and Her Holy Door, but a son of the lodge group as a whole, which had a vested interest in his development into a good and brave Lakota.

Slow's most significant mentor, perhaps even more influential than his father, was his uncle Four Horns, the younger brother of Returns Again. Tall and stoutly built, Four Horns was an important chief, the leading headman of the Bad Bow band, and he saw potential in this boy who seemed so methodical and deep-thinking.

Foremost in a Lakota boy's preparation for adulthood was instilling the importance of the four virtues of Lakota men: bravery, generosity, endurance, and wisdom. Bravery always ranked first. Four Horns and other elders counseled Slow again and again that "You must be brave" and "You must grow into a brave man." And from an early age, Lakota boys were expected to be like men. When a boy was caught misbehaving, nothing hurt so much as when his mother scolded him by saying a *man* wouldn't have done such a thing.

According to One Bull, a common practice to train a boy to have a "brave heart" was to roughly throw him into the cold waters of a river—more than once. The aim was "to teach him patience and to give him a chance to show that he could control his anger," explained One Bull. "He had to learn to endure this kind of thing and other hardships as well." One Bull spoke from experience—his father threw him into the river three times.

Another vital aspect of the boy's training was the horse, without which the nomadic Lakotas couldn't follow the buffalo, transport their lodges and gear, or seek out their enemies. It started when Slow was so young and small that he had to be tied to his pony's back to keep from sliding off while learning to ride. When he was older, Slow's morning chore was retrieving mounts from the camp herd for Four Horns and his father.

With other youths, Slow was enlisted to help train ponies for warfare. One exercise involved having a boy hide in the brush or tall grass near the animal being trained and firing a gun until the pony became used to the blast and would not recoil or flinch. Another was riding and mounting a pony double, the two riders getting on and off the animal multiple times. Thus, in a fight, if a warrior was knocked off his pony—or his pony was killed—he could climb up behind another rider without the pony shying.

Lakota children were also taught to be giving to those with less. "The greatest brave was he who could part with his most cherished belongings," recalled one Lakota, "and at the same time sing songs of joy and praise." Four Horns was well known for his kindness to the elderly, and his young nephew was no different. Slow took care to make sure the old and infirm of their camp had plenty to eat, and at his urging, Her Holy Door frequently prepared feasts for them.

Slow demonstrated his willingness to give with those his own age as well. A favorite story told by those who knew him relates how Slow, as a ten-year-old, participated in a contest with other boys to see who could harvest the most beautifully feathered bird. They used blunt arrows to stun or kill the birds without bloodying or otherwise damaging the feathers. When one boy's best arrow became stuck in the top of a tree, Slow agreed to try to dislodge it with a well-placed shot from his own bow. Several boys watched in awe as Slow's arrow struck the snagged arrow, sending it plummeting to the ground. But when they ran up to the arrow, it was found to be broken in two. The young owner of the arrow became angry and demanded that Slow replace it.

Instead of arguing with the boy, or becoming upset himself, Slow remained calm. He held out his own arrow, which he considered his best also, saying, "Here, take my blunt point arrow that caused you so much grief. Keep it and get your bird."

At the end of the day, when it was learned what Slow had done to avoid a fight, he was awarded the prize that was to be presented to the contest's winner: a bow and arrows made by one of the camp's best arrow makers.

Slow's people took inspiration and knowledge not only from elders and their teachings but also from the creatures they shared the world with. On occasion, the winged peoples and the four-leggeds spoke to them, delivering sacred messages of great power. When Slow was still a boy, his father returned from a buffalo hunt and related how a large bull buffalo had appeared near the campfire around which Returns Again and three men were roasting meat from a freshly killed buffalo. The bull grunted and bellowed, its great shaggy head swaying from side to side. Returns Again's companions were awestruck; the buffalo seemed to be communicating with them, but only Returns Again understood what the animal was saying. Returns Again heard the bull speak four names: Buffalo Bull Sits Down, Jumping Bull, Bull Stands with Cow, and One Bull. Then the buffalo disappeared into the darkness.

Returns Again believed these four names—again, the sacred number four—were a gift for him to bestow as he saw fit. He announced to his family and the village that he was no longer to be called Returns Again. He was now to be known as Sitting Bull.

At age thirteen, Slow had his first of several mystical encounters with animals. One day, as he was out searching for wild horses, he thought he heard a man singing. He followed the mournful sound to the top of a hill, where a large golden eagle was perched. To Slow's astonishment, the singing was coming from this great bird. The eagle sang, "My father gave me this nation to care for, and I am trying to fulfill my duty." For Slow, it was both a prophecy and a challenge. Slow determined to make the song and its sacred message his own.

By his middle teens, Slow was no longer "last in everything." Far from it. His hand-eye coordination was exceptional; few were as adept in the use of the bow and the lance. He excelled at the hoop game, for example, in which contestants attempted to hit marks on a rolling hoop with a spear, and his skill in this game brought him many prizes, from knives to buffalo robes to new arrows. And he was already an excellent hunter and superior horseman. "When I was ten years old, I was famous for a hunter," he recalled years later. "My specialty was buffalo calves. I gave the calves I killed to the poor that had no horses."

The teenager known as Slow even became a very good long-distance runner. If anyone had outgrown a nickname, he had. All that awaited Slow in his path to manhood was the counting of his first coup. That came when he was fourteen.

It happened while he was out with a small Húnkpapa raiding party looking for enemies, specifically Crows. Because Slow had not yet accomplished any warrior deeds, he was naked except for a breechclout and beads. No feathers adorned his head. His body, covered entirely in yellow paint, was the only thing that distinguished him.

When scouts patrolling in advance of the raiding party returned with the exciting news that a band of Crow warriors was just out of sight, traveling in their direction, the Húnkpapas quickly rode to the back of a nearby rise. There they dismounted and waited for the unwitting Crows to arrive. Once their enemy was too close to escape, the Húnkpapas would pounce.

Soon the hated Crows appeared, riding slowly in single file, getting closer and closer to the hill that hid Slow's party. The Húnkpapa warriors began to silently remove arrows from quivers and remount their ponies in preparation for the charge when suddenly a lone rider galloped out from their ranks. It was Slow, his body leaning forward, his horse at full speed. He was heading straight for the Crows, but he carried no weapon. In his right hand Slow grasped a long coupstick given him by his uncle, Four Horns.

The rest of the raiding party took off after Slow, yipping as they emerged from behind the rise. The Crows, surprised and terrified by the sight of the oncoming Húnkpapas, wheeled around and fled. But Slow's pony was a good one, and he steadily cut the distance to an enemy warrior falling behind the others. Without warning, the Crow jumped off his speeding mount, a bow and arrow in his hand. Spinning around, the Crow drew back his bowstring, a deadly arrow nocked and aimed at his pursuer. Slow didn't deviate from his course, and in an instant, he was on the warrior. Just as the Crow released the metal-tipped arrow, Slow sharply struck his arm with the coupstick, ruining the warrior's aim. Slow's horse crashed into the Crow, flipping him backward and onto the ground.

The Húnkpapas following Slow killed the stunned warrior and several of his companions. It was a great victory, with valuable booty in weapons, horses, and scalps, but it was of even greater importance for Slow. He had touched an enemy in battle. He had counted coup.

Shortly after the raiding party returned to the village, Slow's father led his son, mounted on a handsome bay horse, among the many tipis. The young man was completely naked, and in place of yellow body paint, Slow was now covered entirely in black. A single eagle tail feather stuck out from his hair, signifying his first coup. His father told those who gathered round that his son was very brave, and he had given him a new name befitting a warrior. In a gesture of both love and generosity, the name he gave his son was the one he had taken for himself. From this momentous day forward, the father announced, his son was to be known as Sitting Bull, and he himself would take the name Jumping Bull.

At the time young Sitting Bull counted his first coup, far to the southwest, in the Cheyenne River country just east of the sacred Black Hills, a five-year-old Lakota boy was beginning his own journey to manhood. The boy's grandfather was an Oglala holy man, and so too was his father. The father went by the name Crazy Horse, also translated as His Horse Foolish. The boy's mother, Rattle Blanket Woman, was of the Miniconjou tribe, and her young son was the couple's second child, the first being a daughter named Looks at Her. Their family belonged to the Hunkpatila band of the Oglalas.

The child had a very light complexion and light-colored or "yellow" hair. One Lakota said it was the color of hair you would find on a white man. The boy's appearance was indeed unusual, perhaps slightly suspicious. In a moment of anger, Crazy Horse is supposed to have insinuated to Rattle Blanket Woman that their son had been fathered by a white man.

Another curious thing about the boy's hair was its curls. Friends and family called the child by a nickname, Curly. He did have the black eyes of a Lakota, however, although he seldom looked anyone square in the face. But as a friend said years later, those eyes "didn't miss much that was going on all the same."

Unfortunately for Curly, those young eyes couldn't help but see upsetting things between his father and mother. According to family stories passed down through generations, Rattle Blanket Woman fell in love with her husband's younger brother, Male Crow. When Male Crow and thirty Oglalas were killed in a desperate fight with Shoshone and Crow warriors, Rattle Blanket Woman became sick with grief. The strained relationship with Crazy Horse weighing on her as well, she was last seen leaving the village clutching something close to her dress. Sometime later, her lifeless body was found dangling from a tree. The thing she'd been carrying was a rawhide rope. Rattle Blanket Woman's only son, Curly, was just four years old.

Soon Curly's father married two Miniconjou sisters, who tried to bring a sense of normalcy back to the lodge. Like Sitting Bull, young Curly was taught the virtues expected of a Lakota, and also like Sitting Bull, he took these virtues to heart. A story is told of a hard winter when buffalo were not to be found and many in Curly's village were suffering. His father hunted hard, pushing through the snowdrifts day after day in search of game. Finally, he got lucky, killing two pronghorn antelope. When Crazy Horse arrived back at the village with the pronghorns, Curly excitedly rushed through the camp inviting the elderly to come share in the meat.

Crazy Horse and his wives, who were not aware of Curly's generous invitation, were surprised when the old ones began to line up at their lodge. But to turn anyone away, no matter the small amount of meat available, was utterly unthinkable. When the last portion was handed out, all that remained for Curly's family was enough meat for two meals. The following day, when Curly asked one of his stepmothers for some fresh pronghorn, she told him it was gone—the old and weak, at his invitation, had taken the better part of it. But, she added, "they went home singing praises in your name, not my name or your father's. You must be brave. You must live up to your reputation."

At around age ten, Curly received a new name. It sprang from an astonishing event, the first of many that would eventually be connected to the enigmatic Oglala. Curly and an uncle were hunting wild horses and spied a good-size herd guarded by a handsome stallion. Normally, catching wild horses was an involved affair requiring numerous mounted hunters to surround a herd from a distance, blocking all escape routes. The horse hunters carried long willow poles with forked ends to which rawhide ropes with large loops were attached. As the hunters closed in from different directions, the wild herd would race back and forth until slowed by exhaustion, allowing the hunters to ride near enough to slip their loops over the horses' necks.

"Aren't those fine horses?" the uncle remarked to Curly.

"Yes, Uncle, especially that one."

Curly pointed to the stallion, and, at that moment, the stallion seemed to cast its gaze directly at the boy. Without another word, Curly dismounted, rope in hand, and began walking toward the stallion. The two continued to lock eyes, and the uncle watched in amazement as Curly approached the stallion and placed a loop over the animal's head. Curly then led the stallion back to his uncle, the rest of the herd following close behind. It was as if the song of the Lakota Horse Dance—danced as an offering for better and larger Indian herds—were coming to life before the uncle's very eyes:

> *Watch the horses are come dancing*
> *Watch the horses are come dancing*
> *Watch the horses are come dancing*
> *Watch closely a herd of black horses come dancing*

When Curly and his uncle returned to their camp with the horses, his uncle related the incredible story of how Curly had caught them, and he announced that his young nephew would now be called His Horse Stands Looking.

With boyhood friends He Dog, Pretty Weasel, Lone Bear, Short Bull, and Lone Man, His Horse Stands Looking honed the skills that made a warrior—they stalked game, held contests with bow and arrow, practiced mounting ponies running at full speed, and pretended to count coup on imaginary enemies. And like Sitting Bull, His Horse Stands Looking benefited from an important mentor, a Miniconjou relative by the name of High Backbone. Only about five years in age separated the two, but it was customary for older boys to take younger ones in charge, to be their helpmates and protectors. Such bonds lasted for life. High Backbone is said to have made his young protégé his first bow. The two became fast friends, and when they were seen together, people called them "the grizzly and his cub."

As it turned out, His Horse Stands Looking's first display of nerve, bravery, and quick thinking came one summer at the hands of a very real, jaw-snapping grizzly bear. The boy, then about twelve, and his younger half brother, Little Hawk, had gone to find their father's ponies, locating them near a tree-lined stream. Nearby were several sand cherry bushes loaded down with the dark purple fruit. Forgetting about the horses for the moment, the boys began to stuff their mouths with the tart cherries. Suddenly a distant growl startled them, and His Horse Stands Looking turned his head to see a large grizzly on its haunches, sniffing the air. Bears are just as fond of sand cherries as humans, and the boys had interrupted its meal.

His Horse Stands Looking quickly pushed his brother up a tree and then jumped onto the back of a pony as the large bruin began to lumber toward them. But the pony bolted when it glimpsed the charging grizzly and nearly ran out of sight before its rider gained control of the terrified animal. His Horse Stands Looking then yanked his pony around and galloped straight at the threatening beast, shouting and swinging his rawhide rope in the air. The bear hesitated and finally turned tail, disappearing into the bushes. As one old Lakota explained, His Horse Stands Looking, though not yet in his teens, already "had some power, so that even a grizzly did not care to tackle him."

When exactly His Horse Stands Looking began to seek that "power"—that is, seek a vision or dream through which spiritual power would come—is not known. Some visions came unexpectedly, others through specific ritual and fasting with the help of a holy man, who would both prepare the vision seeker and afterward interpret his dreams. But whether a vision seeker took pains to follow the instructions of a holy man or not, great visions came only to those who were worthy. His Horse Stands Looking would be blessed with many potent visions that guided him throughout his life. The white intruders scoffed at such notions, but as one Lakota explained, they "did not understand the Indian's touch with nature."

His Horse Stands Looking's first vision came in a dream in which the Thunder Beings appeared. Their power was incredibly strong, and His Horse Stands Looking understood it had the potential to protect not only himself but also his people. This dream visited him over and over again for years. The holy man Horn Chips, who had grown up with His Horse Stands Looking, provided crucial guidance on how to honor and channel this great gift—failing to carry out the wishes of the Thunder Beings risked being struck by their lightning.

Another time, His Horse Stands Looking sat alone on a hilltop—solitude was often his preferred companion. As a light breeze cooled his face, he felt something touch his head. His Horse Stands Looking reached up and pulled a bit of grass from his hair and studied it. What happened next he described to his friend Flying Hawk:

> There was a trail nearby and I followed it; it led to the water; I went into the water; there the trail ended and I sat down in the water; I was nearly out of breath; I started to rise out of the water, and when I came out I was born by my mother. When I was born I could know and see and understand for a time, but afterwards went back to it as a baby; then I grew up naturally. . . . That was the reason I always refused to wear any war-dress; only a bit of grass in the hair; that was why I always was successful in battles.

What His Horse Stands Looking experienced seems to have been a waking dream in which he'd been reborn by the Water Spirit and consequently received the water's great power. It had all started with the piece of grass, so His Horse Stands Looking wore straws of grass in his hair before a fight to call forth that power for protection.

Horn Chips also provided protections or charms created specifically for his cousin. But the holy man offered a warning as well. Horn Chips was one of a few holy men who had the ability to see far into the future. Death would come, he told his cousin, from a knife while his arm was held. The medicine Horn Chips prepared would protect His Horse Stands Looking from the knife only if his arm wasn't restrained. Despite this chilling prophecy, the young Oglala came to believe he had an important destiny. "If anything happens to myself," he once said, "I will return to the Thunder [Beings] and from there I will look after my people with the power of the Thunder [Beings]."

At the age of sixteen, His Horse Stands Looking finally had the chance to prove his courage in battle. In a measure of the esteem and confidence his mentor, High Backbone, had in the boy, he invited him to join a war expedition he was leading northward against the Hidatsas, age-old foes of the Lakotas. The Hidatsas lived in villages along the upper Missouri River and were primarily farmers, but they occasionally ventured onto the plains to harvest buffalo and other game.

The details of just where High Backbone's warriors encountered the Hidatsas and under what circumstances were lost long ago. But meet them they did, and both sides were prepared for combat. High Backbone and his warriors charged, His Horse Stands Looking close behind his mentor. As they galloped near the Hidatsas' line, puffs of black powder smoke spewed from the muzzleloading trade guns of the Hidatsas, and metal-tipped arrows streaked through the sky. High Backbone and his men flared to the side of the enemy's advance in an attempt to flank them when High Backbone's pony was hit by a musket ball and collapsed.

Thrown from his saddle, High Backbone somersaulted along the hard ground as his warriors raced on. Seeing the horseless Lakota stunned and all alone, several Hidatsas rushed forward to finish him off. But His Horse Stands Looking had seen his leader fall. With a shout, he pulled tight on the reins of his pony and turned back. Upon reaching High Backbone, the young Oglala jumped to the ground and jerked his friend upright. Hidatsa bullets buzzed uncomfortably close; ominous thuds came from arrows striking the ground near them. But High Backbone quickly recovered his senses and climbed into the saddle. He held out his arm so that His Horse Stands Looking could pull himself up behind. High Backbone then dug his heels into the pony and they galloped away, several Hidatsas giving chase. But the two Lakotas could not be caught, not this day.

His Horse Stands Looking had easily proved he had a brave heart. But the most important step in becoming a warrior was to count coup, a step that came not long after he rescued High Backbone, and it came in spectacular fashion. His friend He Dog remembered the story well. He said that Oglala warriors were in a fight with Arapahos, who had taken a strong position among large rocks on high ground overlooking a river. His Horse Stands Looking charged alone more than once into the giant rocks, disappearing for a moment each time before returning. Such dangerous bravado was perfectly in keeping with the Lakota way of fighting, which emphasized the individual over the group, a warrior's personal record of coups more important than achieving victory. In the words of Horn Chips, "All tried to get their names up the highest, and whoever did so was the principal man in the nation."

After his last charge into the rocks, His Horse Stands Looking emerged with blood running down his body from a slight wound. Even bloodier, however, were the two Arapaho scalps he held triumphantly in the air.

As per custom, His Horse Stands Looking's proud father held a feast to celebrate his son's exploit. "I throw away [my son's] old name," he announced to the crowd, "and give him a new one. I give him the name of his father and of many fathers before him. I give him a great name—I call him Crazy Horse!"

# Native Ground

*Most of our troubles were over boundary lines or hunting grounds.*

LUTHER STANDING BEAR

The Lakotas hadn't always roamed the Great Plains. Once they lived hundreds of miles east of the Missouri River, in the woods and scattered prairies of present-day Minnesota. They stalked buffalo, harvested berries and wild rice, and tended to small patches of corn. And it was there they received the name Sioux, a corruption by French traders of an Ojibwa word meaning "people of an alien tribe." The simple definition? "Enemy."

These Lakotas traveled between winter and summer camps on foot, transporting their possessions using dogs strapped to travois. And for the longest time they had no "medicine irons" (guns), while such enemies as the Crees and Assiniboines did. Through a combination of pressure from these enemies and a desire to find better buffalo hunting, the Lakotas gradually migrated south and west to lands new to them and rich in game.

In 1804, when the American explorers Lewis and Clark ascended the Missouri, the Lakotas were already living on the river's west side. And they'd become expert horsemen, having acquired the "holy dog" some three decades earlier. They were also well supplied with British firearms, which came from Canada through trade networks with their Eastern Sioux cousins. With these two things—horses and guns—the Lakotas whom Lewis and Clark encountered had, in a remarkably short time, transformed themselves from a people once fearful of their enemies to a people dreaded by all tribes who were not Lakota allies (and allies were few). In 1809, a member of a party of trappers ascending the Missouri observed that the Lakotas, whom he likened to the Bedouins of Arabia, "are the terror and in fact lordly masters of all their neighbors, claiming tribute (presents) from all other tribes."

Horseback Lakotas now traveled vast distances, primarily westward—hunting, exploring, and raiding. During the Lakota year 1775–76, an Oglala leader named Standing Bull ventured far across the plains with several fellow tribesmen—farther than any other Lakotas before them—and returned to the Missouri River country with, among other things, a small tree or sapling. He wished for others to see it, because it was a type of pine that was strange to him. Standing Bull and his Oglalas, it turns out, had discovered the Black Hills.

The Lakotas were by no means the first Indians to visit the Black Hills, nor the first to make use of their natural resources, but they would lay claim to them as a life-sustaining reserve and a spiritual touchstone. They saw in the dark, pine-forested hills the shape of a reclining woman. From her breasts emanated everything the Lakotas needed: game, spring-fed waters, and sturdy pines for their lodgepoles. In the curves and recesses of her body she would protect them from the winter winds. As explained by Luther Standing Bear, the Lakotas went to the Black Hills "as a child to its mother's arms."

At the time of Crazy Horse's birth, the various Lakota tribes were indeed the lords of the northern plains, imposing their will from the Yellowstone and Powder River country in the northwest to the North Platte River on the south, with the sacred Black Hills the beating heart at the center of their domain. And yet, a worrisome threat had already penetrated deep into their territory.

The Cheyennes had a name for the white man. They called him *vèho*. It was the same word they used for "spider." And like a spider, the white man spun an ever larger web onto the plains. A main strand of that web followed the Platte River. Fur traders and mountain men had beaten a hard path along it in going to the Rocky Mountains and back. But some white men traveled the road specifically to barter with the various Lakota tribes for buffalo robes and peltries, and they established trading posts far up the North Platte and elsewhere in Sioux country to be as close as possible to their hunting grounds.

Most Lakotas desired this trade. It gave them weapons and ammunition needed to kill game and enemies, as well as manufactured items and foodstuffs they had grown accustomed to. But at the same time, they were mindful of the effects of these non-Lakotas on the buffalo herds—white men killing and eating buffalo potentially took food out of the mouths of their families and also robbed them of robes they could use in trade. And even if the number of buffalo the traders killed was few, the simple act of buffalo hunting drove the shaggy beasts away, thus making the hunting harder for the Lakotas.

In November 1841, the supply of meat at Fort Laramie, near the junction of the Laramie and North Platte Rivers, was running low. The trading post's bourgeois (head trader) sent three employees out to kill some buffalo. His men soon located a herd and brought down a few animals, but on their return, they made the mistake of passing too near an Oglala village. The village was that of the Hunkpatila band, Crazy Horse's people, and its chief was called They Fear Even His Horses.

Warriors poured out of the village to confront the white men, and when they saw the mounds of fresh meat strapped to the men's saddle mounts and pack mule, the warriors became enraged. They pulled the men off their horses and began to beat and whip them and slash them with their knives. Next the warriors killed the horses and mule. The traders had been warned, the warriors shouted, not to hunt buffalo where the Oglalas hunted them. Several warriors wanted to kill the men on the spot, but there were others who were on friendly terms with the traders, so it was decided to take the white men as prisoners to the village and hold a council to decide their fate.

The trembling white men, their hair matted with blood and dirt and blood oozing from cuts to their faces and hands, were placed in the lodge of They Fear Even His Horses while the warriors and headmen met. Several Oglalas still wanted to kill the prisoners, but They Fear Even His Horses spoke strongly in favor of sparing the men's lives. All agreed later that if it had not been for the chief's pleading, the white men would have lost their scalps. They Fear Even His Horses went to his lodge and handed back the men's firearms and told them they were free to return to Fort Laramie. But he sent with them a stern message for the fort's bourgeois. Tell him, the chief said, if his men are caught "running" their buffalo again, the Oglalas will not hesitate to kill the men and their horses.

But the killing of buffalo and other game by whites would not stop, no matter how many threats the Lakotas made. And the white man's web grew. The white man even had a name for it: Manifest Destiny.

It began as a trickle. The year 1841 saw the first emigrant wagon train on what some would call the "Platte River Road." Less than a hundred men, women, and children made up the party bound for Oregon and California. The emigrants on the trail the following year didn't amount to more than two hundred. But in 1843, the number jumped to one thousand, and the next year, two thousand. In 1845, an estimated five thousand emigrants in hundreds of creaking, slow-moving prairie schooners raised dust along the Platte. These emigrants viewed the "desolate" Lakota lands as nothing more than something that must be crossed, and the Lakotas and other tribes as a potential hazard to avoid if at all possible. For the most part, though, encounters between the several Plains tribes and the emigrants during those years were peaceable.

In the summer of 1845, the U.S. government sent a military expedition—five companies of the First U.S. Dragoons (precursors to the U.S. Cavalry) with two pieces of artillery—up the trail with the main goal of overawing the tribes along the route. It was believed that if the Indians saw the might of the U.S. Army, they would think twice about any run-ins with the overland emigrants. As for impressing the tribes, the expedition did have the desired effect. Days before the military column reached Fort Laramie, several excited Lakotas reported its advance to the traders. The men and horses were so many, they said, that they "blackened the land." The Lakotas also said that up until they saw these soldiers with their long knives, they thought the only white people in the world were traders and emigrants.

The commander of the expedition, Colonel Stephen Watts Kearny, held a short council with the Lakotas at nearby Fort Platte, a competing post to Laramie. Some twelve hundred Oglala and Brulé men and women, dressed in their finest attire, gathered to hear what the colonel had to say. Through an interpreter, Kearny used the language a young United States, and other nations before it, had always used in asserting authority over a people it really had no authority over. That is, he spoke down to them:

Your great father has learned much of his red children, and he has sent me with a few braves to visit you. . . . I am opening a road for the white people, and your great father directs that his red children shall not attempt to close it up. There are many whites now coming on this road, moving to the other side of the mountains; they take with them their women, children, and cattle. They all go to bury their bones there, and never to return. You must not disturb them in their persons or molest their property. Should you do so, your great father would be angry with you, and cause you to be punished.

Kearny also warned the Lakotas not to trade for the whiskey offered by "bad white men" from Taos (known to the traders as "Taos Lightning") and to destroy it whenever found. After concluding his talk, he ordered the distribution of some of the trade goods he'd brought as gifts to the Lakotas. And as his soldiers began to hand out bolts of scarlet and blue cloth, blankets, tobacco, knives, beads, and other prized items, several old Lakota men broke out in chants, singing their approval. Following the distribution of the gifts, Kearny's artillerymen fired three rounds of spherical case shot from one of their two mountain howitzers. Each artillery blast shook the ground, followed five seconds later by another blast when the fused case shot exploded high in the air, leaving a puff of white smoke against the blue sky. The Lakotas had never witnessed such a thing, and it thrilled them. They named the mighty howitzer "the gun that shoots twice."

Kearny and his dragoons marched away confident that the Indians would remember what they'd seen and were told, that they now knew the Long Knives could travel anywhere in their country and that there was no place the Lakotas could hide that the Long Knives couldn't find them. At least that's what Kearny wrote

in his report. Nowhere in that report, however, did he write anything of the concerns of the Lakotas or how the "Great Father"
would make sure their lands, their buffalo, their water, wood, and
grass, were respected.

The Lakotas' own Indian agent, appointed by the U.S. government the following year, had no answer, either. That agent
was Thomas Fitzpatrick, a seasoned mountain man who'd immi-
grated to America from Ireland at the age of sixteen. For years
he led trapping parties all over the Rockies and later served as a
trusted guide for emigrants, army officers, and exploring expeditions, specifically those of John C. Fremont, "the pathfinder
of empire." He was well liked by many among the Plains tribes,
who knew him as The Broken Hand—one of his hands had been
mangled when his gun's barrel burst during firing. No white
man had more knowledge of the Indians of the northern and southern plains, and it was that close familiarity with their culture, and
the tribal leaders, that gave Fitzpatrick a sense of foreboding.

To Agent Fitzpatrick, it was not a matter of protecting a way
of life for the Plains peoples in his charge—as it arguably should
have been—but instead a simple matter of time until that way of
life would end. "I consider them a doomed race," he wrote the
superintendent of Indian affairs in St. Louis, "and [they] must fulfill their destiny." Fitzpatrick also warned his superior of troubles
to come. As the buffalo herds shrank and other game decreased
due to overhunting, there would be "a great struggle for the ascendancy" among the various tribes concentrated on and around
the northern hunting grounds. Actually, that struggle was already
occurring, with the powerful and more numerous Lakotas clearly
holding the upper hand.

Fitzpatrick repeated his warnings yearly. In May 1849, he wrote
that the Plains tribes were getting louder with their grievances.
And, he added, since U.S. government policy recognized these

tribes as owning the soil and everything on it, their complaints were justified. But at the time Fitzpatrick penned his letter, the full impact of that year's migration had not yet been felt. That season would see an unprecedented thirty thousand emigrants and gold seekers in thousands of ox-drawn wagons snake their way along the "Great Medicine Road of the Whites," as some Indians called it. And if the deep ruts left by the wagon wheels weren't enough of a road map, one could easily follow the route by what the trains left strewn in their wake: shoes with worn-out soles, torn pieces of clothing, crownless hats, crushed tinware, broken glass jars, scattered playing cards, an occasional cast-iron cookstove, carcasses of oxen, broke-down wagons—and fresh mounded graves.

Some of these emigrants unwittingly brought a killer to the High Plains—Asiatic cholera—and the disease spread like a prairie fire, proving especially deadly to the Lakotas. The wailing of those mourning for deceased relatives was heard in the villages night and day, and the stench of death from decomposing bodies wafted over the plains for miles. In the winter count of the Oglala American Horse, it was the year "Many died of the cramps." More than a few angry Lakotas suspected the whites of purposely introducing the disease to eradicate them.

The U.S. Army purchased Fort Laramie that summer of 1849 to use as a base for protecting emigrants, but a garrison of Long Knives wasn't going to relieve the mounting tensions between the tribes and white travelers. What was needed, said the superintendent of Indian affairs, was a treaty, and no ordinary treaty at that. In addition to setting out terms for safe passage through Indian lands and compensation for Indian losses, the treaty he proposed would carve up all of "Indian country," with the several tribes supposedly deciding among themselves who got what. The superintendent was convinced his was a brilliant plan, that once the tribes knew the fixed boundaries of their territories, their constant warring with one another would come to an end. The only thing more surprising than the superintendent's absurd belief that his plan would work—the Lakotas and their enemies were long practitioners of might makes right—is that Agent Fitzpatrick seemed to believe in it as well.

The "Great Indian Council" convened on Horse Creek, thirty miles below Fort Laramie, in early September 1851. More than ten thousand members of the Sioux, Cheyenne, Arapaho, Crow, Assiniboine, Gros Ventre, Shoshone, Mandan, Arikara, and Hidatsa tribes—men, women, and children—set up camps near the council grounds. Gathered on the same smoke-filled plain were tribes that had been bitter enemies for generations. Three tribes, the Comanches, Kiowas, and Apaches, refused outright to attend. The meeting place was too far away, they said, but more importantly, in no way would they risk having their horses and mules so close to such notorious horse thieves as the Sioux and the Crows.

Also in attendance was the famed Jesuit missionary Pierre-Jean De Smet. By 1851, the fifty-year-old priest had already spent more than ten years in the Rocky Mountain West and traveled thousands of miles establishing missions and converting natives. Known as a "Black Gown" to the Indians, the passionate and dignified De Smet captivated those in attendance at Horse Creek. De Smet had been personally invited by the superintendent of Indian affairs so as to use his considerable influence with the tribes to bring about a successful council and treaty.

Over ten days, the headmen of the various nations listened to the proposals of the commissioners and wrangled over each tribe's claimed hunting grounds. However, every word spoken was filtered through interpreters, most of them mixed-bloods (individuals of Indian and white parentage). Not one chief or headman among the several tribes was fluent in English. Fitzpatrick, a treaty commissioner, once characterized interpreters on the frontier as men "ignorant and weak minded . . . who had neither a proper knowledge of their own mother tongue, or of that of the Indian." And indeed, the language barrier was acknowledged by at least one Sioux chief during the council. "Father, this is the third time I have met the whites," he explained. "We don't understand their manners or their words. We know it is all very good, and for our good, but we don't understand it all. We suppose the half breeds understand it, and we leave it to them to speak for us."

One chief carefully studied the commissioners, traders, and De Smet clustered around a table, intently working on a map showing the western country and the new tribal boundaries. When it was explained to him what the white men were doing, the chief suggested that while the Great Father was in the process of remaking the Indians' land, he also put down a few more buffalo for his people, as the animals weren't as numerous as they used to be.

When it came time to "touch the pen," the chiefs were shown how to make their marks on the prepared treaty document, but not every Lakota headman signed. Some Lakota leaders had pushed to have each band's chief represented, but the commissioners demanded that the tribes name an overall chief for the entire Sioux nation, a demand that caused confusion and resentment. In the end, only six Sioux chiefs made their marks on the treaty. No chiefs from Crazy Horse's people, the Oglalas, or Sitting Bull's people, the Húnkpapas, signed that day. In fact, not one Húnkpapa is known to have made the trip south from the Upper Missouri country to attend the council.

The chiefs who obligated their tribes to abide by the treaty almost certainly didn't comprehend all its provisions. The treaty called for a "lasting peace" between the tribes assembled and restitution from any tribe that might commit wrongs against Americans. It gave the United States the right to make roads and establish military posts on Indian lands, and in exchange for this right, the government promised to protect the tribes from depredations by whites. Also by signing the treaty, the chiefs agreed to the boundaries of tribal lands set forth in it. Fortunately for the Sioux, their boundary lines encompassed their sacred Black Hills, which was not so fortunate for other tribes with legitimate claims to the same region (the Cheyennes, for example).

If the treaty provisions were upheld, the United States agreed to distribute $50,000 worth of goods annually for ten years, to be divided equally between all the tribes that signed. It was, in fact, a paltry sum when the total number of Indians that were a party to the treaty was estimated by one of the commissioners at fifty thousand.

At the conclusion of the council, several wagonloads of trade goods were distributed. First to be called up in front of the piles of merchandise were the chiefs. Each received a colorful military uniform complete with pantaloons and a "long knife," which they immediately donned. The superintendent of Indian affairs called the goods given out that day "presents," but they were no gift or gesture of goodwill. The goods were actually a payment for all past claims by the tribes for the destruction of buffalo, grass, and timber caused by white travelers on the Platte River Road. It doesn't appear that anyone explained to the chiefs strutting about as native Napoleons that their past claims were now considered settled by the U.S. government.

The different tribes departed the council grounds in high spirits. Much feasting, dancing and singing, smoking of pipes, horse racing, and bartering had occurred. Dog meat being a standard dish of several Plains tribes and much in evidence at the different feasts, De Smet wrote that "no epoch in Indian annals, probably, shows a greater massacre of the canine race." De Smet turned away none of the dog meat offered him, nor did he turn away any souls. By the end of the council, he'd baptized 1,194 Indian children, including sixty-one mixed-bloods.

De Smet, as well as the commissioners and other whites present, truly believed the council and its great treaty to have been a tremendous achievement. The treaty was the beginning of a new era, De Smet wrote, an era of peace. "In future, peaceable citizens may cross the desert unmolested, and the Indian will have little to dread from the bad white man, for justice will be rendered to him." The superintendent of Indian affairs was confident the tribes would uphold the treaty terms. The only thing that could possibly break it would be "some untoward misfortune."

In August 1854, many Lakotas along the Platte were hungry. Buffalo herds seldom appeared near the white man's road, where they'd been heavily hunted for years. Several Oglala and Brulé bands, with a few Miniconjous, were camped about eight miles downstream from Fort Laramie, awaiting the arrival of their agent and the distribution of their annuities, supplies that included such edibles as salt pork and flour. A small Mormon emigrant train bound for Salt Lake City passed near these Indian camps, and as it did so, a lame cow belonging to one of the Mormons slowly fell behind and wandered into the village of the Brulés, where it was promptly killed and butchered. Sometime after the Mormon train arrived at the fort, the bovine's owner learned his cow had been eaten, and he demanded that the post commander do something about it.

Two days later, as a strong, hot wind began to blow down the valley of the North Platte, twenty-nine soldiers and one mixed-blood interpreter headed out of Fort Laramie under the command of Brevet Second Lieutenant John Lawrence Grattan, a twenty-four-year-old West Point graduate. They were to locate and make a prisoner of the cow killer, believed to be a Miniconjou staying with the Brulés, and bring him back to the fort. The lieutenant, not unlike many of his fellow soldiers, had little respect for the Lakotas or their ways. He often boasted that "with thirty men he could whip the combined force of all the Indians of the prairie." Grattan had pleaded with the post commander to send him after the guilty party and seems to have hoped the Indians would be belligerent. With no war going on for an ambitious young lieutenant to win laurels and advancement in rank, a skirmish with the Sioux would give him a chance to distinguish himself. And he relished the idea of showing the Indians "the power of the white man's arms."

Grattan's detachment included a mule-drawn wagon, in which several of his infantrymen rode, and two twelve-pounder howitzers. Riding along with Grattan was the Oglala They Fear Even His Horses, long a friend of the whites. As was his nature, They Fear Even His Horses volunteered to go to the camps alone to try and convince the Miniconjou to come to the fort. The Oglala chief sensed this whole affair could go bad in a hurry, and for good reason—the Lakota villages contained some six hundred lodges, home to several thousand men, women, and children, more than fifteen hundred of them warriors. But the post commander refused his offer. He feared the Miniconjou would run away once he learned he was to be arrested. Let the soldiers go first, he told the chief.

When Grattan's force arrived at the village of the Brulés, his interpreter, Auguste Lucien, was drunk. Apparently Lucien shared the same worries as They Fear Even His Horses, saying more than once that he believed he was going to die. Grattan wasted no time in confronting the Brulé chief, Conquering Bear, a signer of the great treaty three years earlier. There was no smoking of tobacco, no exchange of gifts, no pleasant introductions. The young West

Pointer formed his men in a line on both sides of the howitzers, facing the village, and demanded that Conquering Bear hand over the Miniconjou. Making matters worse, Lucien, fully feeling the effects of his liquor, began to insult and threaten the Brulés, calling the Lakota warriors women.

Conquering Bear had no authority over a Miniconjou and tried to explain to Grattan that if he turned over the cow killer, he would be blamed by everyone in the village. Besides, he said, they had all eaten of the cow, so they were all guilty. The chief offered to pay for the cow, but Grattan would hear none of it. "You tell the Bear," he said angrily to a trader who was present, "that I have come down here for that man, and I'll have him or die."

The Brulé leader replied in a raised voice: "For all I tell you, you will not hear me; today you will meet something that will be very hard. I would strike you were I not a chief, but as I am a chief and am made so by the whites, [I] will not do it. But you will meet something very hard."

They Fear Even His Horses interrupted. "You are talking very bad," he said to Conquering Bear. "The Brulés have a great many soldiers; why do you not get them together and do something that will be good? Today you are acting the fool."

As the meeting became increasingly heated, hundreds of warriors began to gather. Behind their blankets, they held guns, bows, trade axes, and war clubs. Many of them remembered an incident from the previous year that left three Miniconjous dead—killed by Long Knives. The relatives of those Indian victims welcomed a fight this day just as much as Grattan did.

To the shock of everyone, a soldier's musket went off with a sharp crack. Whether the man fired intentionally or accidentally is unknown, but a Lakota fell to the ground. The warriors dropped their blankets, revealing their weapons. Lucien, scared sober, shouted at They Fear Even His Horses to tell the Lakotas to stop. "Yes," the Oglala replied, "but you have killed one of us."

Grattan barked at his men to prepare to fire. Conquering Bear began to walk away rapidly, looking over his shoulder as he retreated. Grattan gestured at the chief and shouted for a volley. Flame and smoke erupted from the muzzles of the leveled muskets, and three lead balls struck the Brulé chief, one delivering a mortal wound. The warriors swiftly returned the attack with their guns and bows. The soldiers touched off the two howitzers, but the barrels were elevated too high, and their rounds crashed into the tops of the lodges. Within seconds, Grattan and five of his men lay dead. The remaining soldiers panicked and fled, some attempting to get away in the wagon, but the warriors pursued them. Only one soldier escaped, although he would die later from his wounds.

Lucien jumped on Grattan's horse and galloped off. Because he had a Lakota wife, the interpreter was at first allowed to flee— until his Lakota brother-in-law decided otherwise. The warrior rapidly overtook Lucien, and when he came up alongside his terrified relative, he shot him in his ears, for the reason that the interpreter "would not listen to anything he was told."

The other man who would not listen, Lieutenant Grattan, was found draped across one of the howitzers with several ugly bullet wounds and two dozen arrows sticking out of his corpse like a pincushion. One arrow had been shot at point-blank range so that it punched entirely through the officer's head. Grattan's boots had been removed and stuffed into the muzzle of the fieldpiece— along with a good quantity of manure. Such was how the Lakotas showed their hatred for the rude West Pointer.

In the winter count of Moses Red Horse Owner, an Oglala, the year 1854 is identified as "They killed thirty white men." The era of peace, if it ever really began, had been short.

If Sitting Bull heard about the 1851 treaty council on Horse Creek, it meant nothing to him. A full-fledged Húnkpapa warrior at the peak of his fighting prowess, he thirsted for coups, to battle the Crows and other enemies, and to steal horses from anyone who had them. His Húnkpapas were the northernmost of the Lakota tribes, ranging from the Grand River north to the junction of the Yellowstone and Missouri. No emigrant road crossed their lands, and they had not been ravaged by white man diseases as had their Oglala and Brulé cousins. And yet the Húnkpapas were becoming increasingly hostile toward whites in their country, even traders. To Sitting Bull's people, the whites were just another tribe—albeit one rich with goods—that as yet had given the Húnkpapas no reason to see them as equals in anything. And the Húnkpapas had absolutely no use for a white agent who scolded and threatened them regarding a treaty they'd never agreed to and who spoke of a Great Father far to the east they'd never seen.

That agent met with several Húnkpapa and Sihásapa chiefs in 1854 at the Upper Missouri trading post of Fort Clark. The chiefs shocked and angered the agent by refusing the "presents" he brought them as required by the 1851 treaty. According to the agent's written report, the chiefs told him, quite forcefully, "that they preferred the liberty to take scalps, and commit whatever depredations they pleased, in preference to goods from their Great Father." These Lakotas, in the agent's opinion, were the most dreaded Indians on the Missouri.

The Húnkpapas, Sihásapas, and other Sioux made good on their word. They raided and murdered among the Missouri River villages of tribes friendly to the whites and made any kind of travel in the region perilous. White men caught outside the gates of their trading posts, if lucky enough not to be killed outright, were stripped of their clothing, beaten, and relieved of their weapons and horses. A typical case occurred in early May 1855, when a party of seven fur company employees traveling between posts had the misfortune of running into a very unhappy band of Húnkpapa and Sihásapa warriors. Although the Lakotas let the men live, they left them naked and without food, with their destination far up the Yellowstone, 150 miles away. By some miracle, all seven men reached the trading post, but the arduous journey took them more than two weeks and left them little more than living skeletons, their skin blistered and peeling from exposure to the sun.

The exasperated Indian agents for the Sioux called for troops. Talking wasn't working, "presents" weren't working, and the treaty definitely wasn't working. The agents reasoned that if a strong force were to show itself at the villages of the depredating tribes, the "murders, robberies, and horse stealing would no longer be heard of." It was wishful thinking at best, but the U.S. government was no longer interested in simply awing the tribes. That had been tried before. The Lakotas had killed thirty soldiers and a government interpreter on the white man's road. It didn't matter that an arrogant and insensitive lieutenant was to blame for what became known as the "Grattan massacre." Those killings required a harsh response.

It came on September 3, 1855, as the sun's rays spilled into the valley of Blue Water Creek, a tributary of the North Platte. Along the creek's banks, white slivers of smoke streamed high into the air from fifty-two Brulé and Oglala lodges. The Brulés were the same band that Grattan had provoked the year previous, now led by a chief named Little Thunder. Poised to attack those camps that morning was an army of approximately six hundred dragoons and infantry. But these Long Knives were different from others the Lakotas had encountered. The infantrymen no longer carried old, inaccurate smoothbore muskets. The long guns in their hands this day were rifled and fired conical minié balls that were more accurate and could punch through bone and muscle at much greater range.

As the infantry advanced up the grassy valley toward the village, their tromping feet and clanking of canteens disrupting the morning calm, Little Thunder rode out to meet the American commander, Brevet Brigadier General William S. Harney. Harney was an imposing white man. Fifty-five years old and sporting a thick, white beard, he stood an impressive six feet, two inches tall. And he was hell-bent to punish the Lakotas. When the Brulé chief told Harney he didn't want to fight, the general curtly replied that "he had not come out here for nothing." Little Thunder returned to his people, and the march continued, but now at a brisk pace. Then came the crash of the infantry's first volley, reverberating off the steep bluff overlooking the creek, followed by a steady popping as the soldiers fired at will at dodging and running Indians in the distance.

The Lakotas, numbering as many as four hundred men, women, and children, attempted to flee, but their escape was partially blocked by mounted Long Knives who had silently positioned themselves in the rear of the village in the early-morning darkness. These Long Knives, mostly dragoons, now charged in among the panicked Lakotas, shooting at any living thing that moved.

Many Lakotas climbed up to shallow caves and crevices in the bluff, from which warriors made desperate stands to protect their families. Those caves became death traps. Unable to direct fire into one of the caves from below, the Long Knives climbed onto an outcropping above the entrance, lay on their stomachs, and reached over to fire their Colt Dragoon revolvers nearly point-blank at those inside.

The result, as one officer wrote in his journal, was "heart

rending—wounded women & children crying and moaning, horribly mangled by the bullets." Another officer claimed that the killing of women and children was unavoidable; they were huddled with the warriors. And besides, he argued, they showed no signs of surrendering. That officer neglected to mention that most of the Lakotas were never given any "signs" that surrender was an option. In their eyes, they were clearly fighting for their lives.

By noon that day, eighty-six Lakotas lay dead and about seventy women and children taken prisoner. The rest, Little Thunder among them, were scattered over the prairie for miles, putting as much distance between themselves and the Long Knives as possible. Left behind were nearly all the Lakotas' belongings and food, including breakfasts still cooking over campfires. Also left behind in the village were several pieces of mail, souvenirs from a Lakota attack on a mail train near Fort Laramie the previous November in which three white men were murdered. This, along with the discovery of bayonets believed taken from Grattan's dead men, convinced Harney's command they'd been justified in spilling so much blood into Blue Water Creek. As one officer wrote, it showed "there were plenty of bad Indians in Camp."

It's said that a young Crazy Horse rode through the abandoned village shortly after the fight and saw firsthand the bloodied corpses and the lodges plundered by the Long Knives. (Most of those lodges would soon be burned by Harney's men, "some as pretty tepees as I ever saw," wrote one soldier.) Whether Crazy Horse visited Blue Water Creek or not, word of the violent blow delivered by the Long Knives to Little Thunder's camp spread quickly among the Lakotas and other tribes.

As far as the Indian agent for the Sioux on the Upper Missouri was concerned, the harsh punishment dealt at Blue Water Creek was nothing but a good start. The army now needed to exterminate the entire Yanktonai tribe and one-third each of the Húnkpapas and Sihásapas. Those Sioux allowed to live would, in the agent's opinion, be peaceful and happy—and the agent's job would be much easier minus all those troublemakers. Fortunately, his recommendation wasn't attempted. Instead, General Harney summoned several Sioux tribes to Fort Pierre on the Missouri River the following March for a treaty council. A special incentive for the Brulés and Oglalas to attend were the captive women and children from Blue Water Creek that Harney hadn't yet released. Other tribes and bands came because of a cautious respect for the white leader and his Long Knives—the Lakotas named Harney "Mad Bear" for the vicious way he'd handled Little Thunder's people. Still others traveled to Fort Pierre because they were hungry.

The Mad Bear conducted the council as if he'd conquered the entire Sioux nation, presenting a set of demands that sounded more like surrender terms, with no possibility of negotiation. The Sioux were to turn over all stolen property, surrender warriors guilty of committing murders of whites, stay off the emigrant road, and cease hostilities with other tribes. And once again, the Lakotas were forced to pick chiefs to be officially recognized and held responsible for any treaty violations. Each selected chief received a handwritten commission and a handshake from the Mad Bear, although they very likely would have preferred the usual gift of brightly colored uniforms known as "chief's coats."

One astute Yanktonai leader at the council by the name of Two Bears perfectly understood the white man's intentions when it came to the Sioux. "I am going to tell you something," he said to the Mad Bear. "I think that from this day you want to raise me, and make a new nation out of an old one." In a word, subjugation.

The following year, in September, a U.S. government exploring party of approximately twenty-two men entered the sacred Black Hills of the Lakotas. Led by Lieutenant Gouverneur K. Warren of the Topographical Engineers, their primary mission was to map the region, but when the expedition was discovered by the Lakotas, they didn't like it one bit. They strongly suspected the white men with all their strange equipment of making another road through their lands. A Sihásapa chief named Black Shield angrily told Warren to turn back. The Mad Bear had said no white men were to enter the Black Hills, he told the lieutenant. The Lakotas had given the Great Father enough roads, and even the Missouri River was now crowded with fireboats. This place, these Black Hills, he emphasized with a broad sweep of his hand, was all they had left. Without it, they would starve.

Warren assured Black Shield and, later, the Húnkpapa chief Bear's Rib, that he was not making a road. He was on a mission from the Great Father "only to see what was in their country." The Lakotas didn't care who sent him; he was scaring their buffalo. And, Bear's Rib warned, it was a rule to kill anyone who frightened away the buffalo. Warren would not be dissuaded, however, no matter how much the Lakotas protested and threatened to harm him and his men. He even climbed the sacred mountain known as Bear Butte (near present-day Sturgis, South Dakota).

To the lieutenant, Bear Butte was nothing more than an interesting geologic formation. To the Cheyennes, it was the place the Great Spirit had given a Cheyenne holy man the four Sacred Arrows that protected their people. For Crazy Horse's father, it was the place where *Wakan Tanka* had come to him in the form of a bear and given him great powers. And in 1840, in sight of that very same mountain, the Oglala warrior Crazy Horse had come into the world.

Warren completed his Black Hills explorations by the middle of October and returned to his post in Washington, D.C., his trunks brimming with notebooks and papers containing daily journal entries, weather and astronomical observations, maps, and sketches. His work had been thorough, as would be his final report, published in 1858. The Black Hills were rich with timber, he wrote in that report, covering some fifteen hundred square miles, and although the first attempts at harvesting it would likely start an Indian war, the scarcity and high price of lumber at the Missouri River settlements might just offset any such "difficulties." Furthermore, the fertile lands around Fort Laramie were being wasted. If the Lakota, Cheyenne, and Arapaho title to those lands could be extinguished, and if adequate protection could be provided for settlers, "there would soon spring up a settlement that would rival that of Great Salt Lake."

But sometime after Warren submitted his report, he began to feel deep remorse. He believed that war between the whites and Lakotas was inevitable, and now his detailed surveys would serve as a road map of sorts to invade their lands and defeat them. "I almost feel guilty of crime," Warren wrote in a letter, "in being a pioneer to the white men who will ere long drive the red man from his last niche of hunting ground." It was exactly what Black Shield and Bear's Rib had tried to warn him of. As the Lakotas would have put it, the lieutenant had no ears.

# Visions of the Future

*What we see is largely determined by what we are.*

ELAINE GOODALE EASTMAN

The U.S. government's "treaties," boundary lines, and numerous patronizing instructions to the Lakotas meant nothing far out on the High Plains, where it was a never-ending fight for survival with other tribes over shrinking buffalo herds. It was either defend your hunting grounds, take new hunting grounds, or starve. The Lakotas had wrested the Powder River country away from the Crows because it was rich in buffalo and other game. Granted, some Lakota bands became content to depend upon the white man's handouts—they earned the name "Sticks around the Fort" and "Loafers"—but not Sitting Bull's people.

And for the white man to demand that the Lakotas cease raiding on their enemies showed a complete lack of understanding of who these people were. Their culture and political system revolved around the individual deeds of its men—coups counted, horses stolen, captives taken. It was why warriors took great care to keep track of their coups, even to documenting each one with witnesses. It's why Sitting Bull could easily fill page after page with drawings picturing his numerous deeds—a warrior never forgot his coups. And the braver the man, the more coups recorded, opening a path to increasing leadership within one's band and tribe—if that's what he desired. That was especially important for someone like Sitting Bull, who did not have a "big chief" for a father and who held an ambition to lead.

Sitting Bull had plenty of witnesses to perhaps his most famous fight, when he killed a Crow chief in 1856. Even better, though, was the bullet hole in his shield and the permanent limp that resulted from the encounter. The fight had happened in the winter, in the broken country near the junction of the Powder and Yellowstone Rivers. In an early-morning raid on a Crow village, Sitting Bull and a number of his fellow Húnkpapas had made off with more than a hundred Crow horses. They were soon pursued by angry Crow warriors, but the Crows seemingly lost their appetite for fight when they caught up with the large party of Húnkpapas, who halted and turned to face them. After the usual taunting from both sides and a few harmless, long-range shots with their flintlock trade guns, the Crows turned back—all except one.

A Crow warrior in a red blanket coat, a man whom they would later determine was a chief, rode forward, alone. The rest of the Crows halted their retreat to see if any Húnkpapas would accept what was an obvious challenge for individual combat. Indeed one would.

Sitting Bull instantly dashed out from the line of Húnkpapas on a black horse, the morning sunlight dancing off his splendid regalia. On his head, Sitting Bull wore a distinctive buffalo horn bonnet with numerous white ermine tails dangling behind. This bonnet identified him as a member of the Strong Hearts, a prominent warrior society that also functioned as camp rule enforcers. Only the four bravest Strong Hearts were permitted to wear the bonnet. A long, narrow strip of red trade cloth festooned with several eagle feathers hung from his shoulders, nearly touching the ground behind him. Sitting Bull was one of two "sash-wearers" among the Strong Hearts. In battle, a sash-wearer staked one end of the cloth strip to the ground and fought all comers while tethered to the stake, never retreating. He could be freed only by a comrade. Otherwise, it was kill or be killed.

This fight with the Crow chief unfolded too quickly for Sitting Bull to make use of the sash. The two warriors galloped toward each other. When less than fifty yards apart, the Crow jumped to the ground, quickly took aim with his smoothbore trade gun, and jerked the trigger. Smoke and flame shot out from the muzzle. The Crow had loaded his gun with "buck and ball": one large ball and several buckshot. Hot lead ripped through the sole of Sitting Bull's left foot, and one of the buckshot pierced his shield and gashed his wrist or forearm. Deep red blood spewed from both wounds, but Sitting Bull had been lucky.

The Crow expected to see the charging Sitting Bull topple from his horse, but instead he saw the muzzle flash of Sitting Bull's gun, followed instantly by the sickening feeling of a punch to his gut. The Crow collapsed and doubled up on the ground, grabbing at his stomach. Sitting Bull circled back to the dying Crow, slid off his horse, and finished the warrior with a knife thrust to his heart. He then cut away the dead enemy's scalp and held it aloft for both sides to see. The Crows spurred their ponies and rode away back to their village.

Sitting Bull took stock of his wounds and then examined the hole in his shield, the one given him by his father. He did not doubt the shield's power. As with any war medicine, there was always a reason why the medicine failed, and it nearly always had to do with something, some taboo, that had been broken or some ritual the warrior didn't perform properly. In the case of a shield, no woman was allowed to touch it. It was also taboo for a man to eat out of a bowl another man had eaten out of or touched. And only a man's mother or wife could touch his food. Once, when Sitting Bull's nephew White Bull was away from his lodge, his brother made the mistake of drinking out of White Bull's cup. When White Bull found out, he severely scolded his wife for allowing such a thing to happen. A short time later, White Bull was wounded in a fight, and when he got back to his village, the first thing he did was throw the cup away.

Still, Sitting Bull's wounds were not life-threatening, not even close. And he had been victorious in a duel with a Crow chief, whose bloody scalp now hung from the bridle of Sitting Bull's horse. Perhaps Sitting Bull's war medicine hadn't failed at all. Instead, it had kept him alive. On this day, the Húnkpapa's medicine had been stronger than the Crow's.

Even with his limp, Sitting Bull could hold his own in a footrace, and the limp certainly didn't affect his fighting skills, for most fighting was done from the back of a horse. Sitting Bull's many drawings of his war deeds show him again and again as a mounted warrior. One of those pictographs portrays an event that occurred a year after the duel with the Crow chief—1857 by the white man's calendar. Sitting Bull is depicted wearing his Strong Heart bonnet and a white blanket coat. His leggings are colored green and his horse yellow, which suggests he was riding a buckskin. Sitting Bull appears to be in the act of throwing a lance at a short warrior on foot and striking him, but there is much more to the story.

A raiding party of Húnkpapas had ridden in the cold and snow to near where the Yellowstone flows into the Missouri (near present-day Buford, North Dakota). They found the Missouri frozen, a crust of snow covering the ice. Across the river, they could see a thin plume of smoke curling up from a small Indian camp. This was Assiniboine country, a tribe the Lakotas knew as Hohes.

In all likelihood, this was an Assiniboine camp. The Húnkpapas urged their ponies across the ice and charged the camp, which turned out to contain only one lodge, the home of a single Assiniboine family.

The Húnkpapas made quick work of the family—men, women, children, they were all enemies, and they were slaughtered in the same way Assiniboines would have slaughtered Lakotas if the circumstances were reversed. However, a boy of about ten stood his ground bravely, shooting his arrows at the Húnkpapas until he was down to one. As Sitting Bull rode toward him, the last arrow slipped from the boy's bow. Sitting Bull struck the boy with his lance, not a killing or even wounding blow but a blow to count coup. "Big brother, save me!" the boy cried—the Assiniboines speak a Siouan language easily understood by the Lakotas. Sitting Bull was awed by the boy's courage, and he was well known for his affection for children. The Húnkpapa leader reached down and pulled the boy up behind him.

Sitting Bull immediately let it be known that this boy was not to be touched, and because he'd always wanted a brother, he would adopt this Assiniboine lad. The boy was small for his age, and some began to call him Little Assiniboine. Sitting Bull indeed treated Little Assiniboine like a brother, and the strong bond that developed between the two would last to the end of their days. In fact, sometime after Sitting Bull made the boy his brother, relatives of Little Assiniboine reached out to the Húnkpapas to negotiate a return to his people, but Little Assiniboine chose to remain with Sitting Bull and the Húnkpapas. For this reason, the Húnkpapas gave the boy a new name: Stays Back.

In the Badlands near the headwaters of the Cannonball River, a butte eroded and sculpted by time rises to more than thirty-five hundred feet. It always seemed to rain when the Lakotas camped in sight of it, and for this reason they called it Rainy Butte. In 1858, during the Moon of Changing Leaves (September), various bands of the Húnkpapas, Miniconjous, Two Kettles, and Sans Arcs happened to be camping in the area. One morning, the Lakotas awoke to a heavy fog that choked off the sunlight and created an ethereal, colorless world around them. With no trace of even the slightest breeze, every voice, every sound in the camps seemed as close as the nearest tipi.

A Húnkpapa hunting party left their village early that morning, after which the women busied themselves taking down their tipis for a short move. By midmorning they were ready to start, with lodge skins, poles, and personal possessions secured to numerous travois and the spare horses herded together. But just as the assemblage started out, a raiding party of Crow warriors appeared out of the mist and swooped down upon the Húnkpapas. What followed was a cacophony of commotion, with women and children screaming, the camp dogs barking, and the Crows shouting war whoops. As their families looked on in horror, two boys walking in advance of the Húnkpapa column were struck first and one of the boys killed.

The Crows, as many as fifty, split into three groups, some going after the horse herd, others charging the few Húnkpapa warriors rallying to resist the attack, and the last chasing the fleeing women and children. To the Crow warriors, it appeared the village and its tremendous booty of horses, camp goods, and women was theirs for the taking. But they did not know of the other Lakota villages nearby, and within minutes a large party of Sans Arc warriors came galloping out of the heavy mist.

Now outnumbered and their force divided, the Crow warriors panicked and fled in different directions, each group followed by a healthy number of Lakotas eager to count coup. The pursuit would go on for miles, and so would the death toll for the Crows, as warriors with exhausted mounts gradually fell behind their comrades. Some Crow leaders sacrificed themselves by bravely reining in their mounts and confronting the oncoming Lakotas to allow the others time to escape.

By midday, the sun had burned off the fog, revealing a bright blue sky, as well as the several life-and-death clashes as they played out upon the prairie. One group of Crows briefly halted to rest their sweat-lathered horses, and the Húnkpapas chasing them did the same. In this interim, a particularly fierce Crow warrior named Big Otter rode out in front of the Crow line and began to taunt the Lakotas. Holding his trade gun up high and shaking it, he shouted, "You are like old women. Come fight me, if any among you are brave!"

Sitting Bull's father, now known as Jumping Bull, was in the group of Húnkpapas watching Big Otter's antics, and he told his companions that he would go and fight this braggart. The aged warrior was more than sixty years old and well past his prime as a fighting man, but he'd lost none of his fearlessness and pride. Jumping Bull dismounted, and as he withdrew two arrows from his quiver and checked his bow, he explained that he'd suffered from a toothache the night before. The pain had been so severe that he'd wished he was dead. If he died at the hands of this Crow, at least the tooth would no longer trouble him. "Leave him to me," Jumping Bull said finally, meaning that he did not want his companions to intervene.

When Big Otter saw his challenger come forward on foot, he dismounted as well. As the two closed the distance with each other, Jumping Bull shot an arrow at the Crow, which grazed the side of Big Otter's head, causing no serious harm. Jumping Bull quickly nocked his second arrow and let it fly at Big Otter, striking the man's shoulder, but the point failed to penetrate much beyond the skin. The Crow fired his trade gun at nearly the same moment that Jumping Bull loosed his second arrow, and the musket ball struck the Húnkpapa in the shoulder, but it did not slow the old warrior's momentum. Not wanting to give Big Otter time to reload, Jumping Bull now ran at Big Otter to fight hand to hand.

As the two men came together, Big Otter unsheathed a large knife. Jumping Bull grabbed for his own knife also, but it had slipped around to his back, and he couldn't reach it while trying to fend off the blows of Big Otter. Big Otter was the taller and stronger man by far, and as he clutched Jumping Bull, he brought his long knife down again and again, stabbing the old Húnkpapa around the collarbone and neck and slashing open his chest. Jumping Bull collapsed to his knees, his blood squirting from multiple wounds with each remaining heartbeat. Then Big Otter slammed the point of his knife into the top of Jumping Bull's head. The blow was so fierce that part of the blade broke off in the old man's skull, after which Big Otter roughly pushed the lifeless Húnkpapa to the ground.

Big Otter returned to his companions, and the bunch rode off, leaving the Lakotas agasp at what they'd witnessed. One of the Húnkpapas galloped away to find Sitting Bull, who was fighting other Crows not too far distant. In a short time, Sitting Bull was staring down at his father's bloody remains, but he didn't pause for long, for his only thought now was to avenge his father's death. Sitting Bull took charge of the Lakotas gathered around him, leading them in pursuit of Big Otter's retreating band. Urging his pony forward at full speed, Sitting Bull eventually caught sight of the Crows. Their horses were nearly played out, and Sitting Bull rapidly overtook a Crow warrior who had fallen behind the others. In an instant, Sitting Bull thrust his lance into the Crow's side, knocking him from his saddle. As the Crow screamed and writhed on the ground, Sitting Bull leveled his trade gun and shot him. Then Sitting Bull kicked his heels into his pony's flanks and started after the rest.

The Lakotas say that Sitting Bull killed five or six more Crows before his fellow Húnkpapas convinced him it was too danger-ous to continue on—they were already thirty miles from their village, and the sun was slipping low on the horizon. Sitting Bull, tears streaming down his face, acquiesced, but he stopped at the body of the first Crow he killed, dismounted, and spent a good amount of time cutting the corpse up into small pieces. When Sitting Bull was done, the Crow was disfigured beyond all rec-ognition. The dead Crow would now enter the spirit land in that same revolting condition, and if the Crow's relatives later found his corpse and became incensed, Sitting Bull's revenge would be even sweeter.

The fight would be remembered as "The Battle of the Long Chase." In all, eighteen Crows fell that day. The Lakotas lost ten warriors. And Big Otter, the slayer of Jumping Bull, had gotten away. When Sitting Bull and his men returned to their people, they learned that another party of Húnkpapas had captured three Crow women (one with a baby in a cradleboard), and a teenage boy from the Crow camp. Seeing Sitting Bull's grief, several Húnkpapas suggested killing the captives, but Sitting Bull would have none of it. "Take good care of [the] women and boy," he told them. "It may be you have captured them for my sake, but don't harm them. My father was a warrior and it is well that he died fighting." The virtue of generosity was cherished by the Lakotas, but it was an even greater virtue to be generous to one's enemies.

For four days Sitting Bull mourned the loss of his father. He cut his hair short, removed his leggings and moccasins, and covered his skin with mud. Others who'd lost family members mourned during this time as well. To ensure that his father's mem-ory and sacred name were not lost to the past, Sitting Bull, in time, would bestow the name Jumping Bull on his adopted younger brother, Stays Back. When the four days of mourning were con-cluded, Sitting Bull allowed that a victory dance was in order.

They'd sent many Crows on the mysterious trail to the land of ghosts, and it was good.

Because of Sitting Bull's great bravery, his many coups, his well-known generosity, and his kindness to women and children, he'd steadily advanced within the tribe's power structure. By 1860 on the white man's calendar, Sitting Bull had become "soldier chief" of the Strong Hearts, chief of a derivative but intertribal group called the Midnight Strong Hearts, and a full-fledged war chief of the Húnkpapas. Sitting Bull fully earned everything he accomplished, but it also didn't hurt that he'd gained the esteem of his uncle, Four Horns, now one of four governing chiefs of the Húnkpapas, called "Shirt Wearers."

And Sitting Bull had "given flesh" to *Wakan Tanka*. That is, he'd danced the Sun Dance—more than once. Both religious and social, the Sun Dance was at the heart of Lakota existence. Occurring each year in early summer, several tribes of the Lakota nation gathered at a preselected location to observe and participate in what Luther Standing Bear described as a tribute to the Great Spirit "for life and its blessings."

Lasting as many as six days, the gathering actually involved a number of ceremonial dances as well as singing and feasting, the culmination being the sacred Sun Dance itself. The male dancers (sometimes as few as one or two) were often fulfilling a vow they'd made to *Wakan Tanka*. They may have asked the Great Spirit to protect them and bring them home safely from a future horse-stealing expedition, promising to dance before the sun if their wish was granted. For leaders like Sitting Bull, they might dance to ask for something beneficial to their people. Long before anyone living, long before the time of their grandfathers' grandfathers, the Lakotas had been promised that if they danced the

Sun Dance and asked the sun for buffalo to eat, they would have plenty of buffalo meat.

A tall, painted "medicine pole" fixed solidly in the ground stood in the center of the open dance area, which was surrounded by a circular shade arbor covered by either buffalo robes or brush. As hundreds of Lakota men, women, and children watched in silence, a holy man pierced the skin of the dancers just above their nipples and inserted a small wooden skewer on each side of the breast. To these skewers he tied leather thongs that were then fastened to a rawhide rope, the other end of which was secured to the pole. Several Lakota musicians seated around a large drum now began to strike the drum and sing. The dancers commenced jerking back violently over and over in an attempt to rip the skewers out of their breasts, all the while staring just beneath the sun's fiery orb.

The most excruciating pain came with the first jerk against the taut rope. After that, the nerves soon became deadened. As the dancers pulled with all their might, their skin stretched several inches away from the body. It could take several hours for the dancers to break free, especially as they were already in a weakened state from fasting prior to the dance. Oftentimes, as the ritual progressed, female relatives of the dancers would have small pieces of flesh cut from their arms to share in the sacrifice of their loved ones and to ask *Wakan Tanka* for their speedy release.

Giving flesh for the Sun Dance took on a number of variations. One white observer in 1866 saw a tall, muscular Lakota with three heavy buffalo skulls dangling from skewers stuck in his skin just below his ribs. Sitting Bull had numerous Sun Dance scars on his breast and back, as well as scars on his arms from where pieces of his flesh had been cut out. The raised scars were an indisputable record of one's sacrifice and courage.

No such scars would ever be found on Crazy Horse. Within his

Hunkpatila band of Oglalas at least, a tenet existed that no man who'd killed another man could be a Sun Dancer, nor could he be a holy man. And this rule applied as well to the man's descendants for four generations. Crazy Horse's father was a Sun Dance chief, but after the death of his brother, Male Crow, at the hands of the Shoshones and Crows, he vowed revenge. In the winter count of the Oglala historian Cloud Shield, the Lakota year 1844–1845 is represented with a drawing of a Lakota man standing in profile holding a pipe vertically. The man is Crazy Horse's father, and he is said to be saying his prayers before going to war. He has thus relinquished his position as Sun Dance chief and holy man and become a warrior.

Other Lakota bands, including Sitting Bull's people, didn't have this rule, and for anyone who aspired to be a great holy man, which Sitting Bull did, the Sun Dance and the visions that sometimes came to the dancers were an integral part of that journey. Many a young Lakota strove to become a holy man by seeking a vision in hopes that *Wakan Tanka,* or one of several spirits, would speak to him. For the Lakotas, everything in the world has a spirit, from the four-leggeds and winged peoples, to the lakes and mountains, to inanimate objects such as a weapon or a drum. It was through a holy man that *Wakan Tanka* and any of these spirits made their wishes known. And by making offerings and prayers to these sacred beings, a holy man hoped to please them and gain their aid.

Very few Lakotas who sought to be holy men succeeded, and perhaps that was the will of *Wakan Tanka.* When exactly Sitting Bull became an acknowledged holy man is not known, but he would have first been mentored by other holy men. A holy man had to know all the Lakotas' ceremonies intimately, as well as their laws and customs. Learning these things took time, although a chief like Sitting Bull would have some of this same knowledge.

More important than anything else, though, was a holy man's supernatural powers, his ability to communicate with the Great Spirit and other beings. In this, Sitting Bull had been blessed more than most. As one Lakota explained it, "He was a man medicine seemed to surround someway."

Sitting Bull's followers witnessed his incredible powers on many occasions. His nephew One Bull distinctly remembered the time they had stolen several horses from the Assiniboines and were on their way home when Sitting Bull suddenly stopped beneath a tree in which a blue speckled bird was singing. Sitting Bull listened for a moment and then turned to his fellow Húnkpapas and told them the little bird had given him a disturbing message. The bird said that a false report had reached their village that Sitting Bull's party had all been killed. They must hurry home before their families begin mourning the loss of their loved ones. A short time later, when they arrived at the village, the people were ecstatic with joy, as they had indeed been told that Sitting Bull and his men were all wiped out.

Another time, after a strong winter storm, One Bull could not find one of his horses. He went to his uncle, and again a blue speckled bird began to chatter. Sitting Bull relayed to his anxious nephew what the bird had told him, which was that the horse was mired in a snowdrift and that another man would find the horse and bring him in. Within a little while, a Húnkpapa walked into their village leading One Bull's horse.

An exceptionally devout Lakota, Sitting Bull prayed more often than anyone else, and he conducted more sacred ceremonies than other holy men. That the Great Spirit always answered Sitting Bull's prayers there was no doubt. One Bull recalled another occasion when he was a young man of twenty and he saw his uncle alone on a hill, crying to *Wakan Tanka* for food for his people. The Húnkpapas had plenty of food that year.

And Sitting Bull never failed to give thanks for the gifts and favors received by him and his followers. The story is told that when
Sitting Bull came across the bones of buffalo on the prairie, their
horn-tipped skulls a chalky white, he would get off his mount and
carefully turn each skull to face the rising sun, and thus please the
Buffalo Spirit. "Friends, we must honor these bones," he would
announce to his companions. "These are the bones of those who
gave their flesh to keep us alive last winter." And sometimes after killing a buffalo, Sitting Bull would approach the magnificent
beast and pray over its large, warm body. Then he would order
that the animal not be touched, and they would leave it where it
fell, a gift for *Wakan Tanka*.

By far Sitting Bull's greatest power as a holy man, the one
for which he was most known and revered, was his ability to
see into the future. His premonitions came to him most often in
visions or dreams, but one time he saw a future battle and its outcome in the smoke from his pipe. Sitting Bull could not foresee
everything in his people's future, of course, only what *Wakan
Tanka* chose to tell him, but what he did see invariably came
true.

Late in his life, Sitting Bull was told the future by a meadowlark. The meadowlark was sometimes called the Sioux bird; it
thrived on the lush, green prairies where the Lakotas camped and
hunted. And Sitting Bull could often be heard imitating the songs
of the yellow-throated bird with his voice, and quite remarkably
at that. The message the meadowlark gave Sitting Bull that day
was simple and ominous: "Lakotas will kill you." The bird did
not say when or how, but that his own people would be the cause
of his death Sitting Bull did not doubt—the meadowlark had told
him so. When the Húnkpapa leader related to others the meadowlark's message, they believed as well.

Only humans lied.

The Lakotas knew the Shoshones as the "Grass House People," a reference to their traditional lodges made of long, thick grasses. In the time of Sitting Bull and Crazy Horse, the Eastern Shoshones lived in the region of the Wind and Green Rivers of present-day Wyoming—or tried to. These Shoshones were so fearful of the Lakotas that they retreated west through the mountains during the summer, returning only in the late fall to hunt buffalo on the western fringes of the Great Plains during the winter. How long the Shoshones and Lakotas had been enemies, no one knows for sure, but the Shoshones had horses, and that's all that really mattered to the Lakotas.

One of Crazy Horse's early exploits came against the Shoshones about 1860. Crazy Horse was a member of a raiding party that also included his younger half brother, Little Hawk. The two had always been close, and now Little Hawk was old enough to ride with the warriors. Many believed that Little Hawk would be an even greater fighter than Crazy Horse, but the boy could be a little too foolhardy.

The Oglalas found the Shoshones, or the Shoshones found the Oglalas—how the enemies met is no longer known. What's been passed down in the oral histories, however, is that there was a running fight, and the Oglalas were badly outnumbered. As the Oglalas fled before the Shoshones, Crazy Horse and Little Hawk hung back and fought a delaying action to cover their comrades' retreat. Soon Crazy Horse's mount gave out from exhaustion, and he had no choice but to turn it loose and fight on foot. A warrior on foot against mounted enemies does not have long to live, yet Little Hawk suddenly jumped off his pony and turned it loose as well. He would fight with his brother to the end.

Two Shoshone warriors bore down on the defiant Oglalas.

"Take care of yourself," Crazy Horse said to his brother. "I'll do the fancy stunt." In an instant, Crazy Horse drew back his bow and let an arrow fly, knocking the leading Shoshone warrior from his saddle. He was dead when he hit the ground. The other Shoshone, seeing the odds now reversed, spurred his horse and galloped away.

The rest of the Shoshones were nowhere to be seen, apparently having continued after the escaping Oglala warriors. Crazy Horse scalped the dead Shoshone, the bloody ritual giving him extra satisfaction, for Crazy Horse bore a scar in the calf of his left leg from a Shoshone bullet he'd received in a previous fight. Next Crazy Horse caught the Shoshone's horse, and the brothers both got on it and started in the direction of their companions, keeping a good watch for more Shoshones. The two eventually made it home safely, as did the rest of the raiding party. And long would the Oglalas talk about the day when Crazy Horse had saved his fellow warriors, killed and scalped an enemy in single combat, and captured that enemy's horse.

Some things about Crazy Horse were not talked about, at least openly, and one of those occurred when he was in his late teens, maybe even before he had first counted coup and received his father's name. In fact, it would be completely forgotten today except for a brief mention—the length of a single sentence—from Crazy Horse's old friend He Dog. According to He Dog, Crazy Horse had gone to live for a time with the Brulés—Crazy Horse was a nephew through his stepmothers of the famed Brulé warrior and chief Spotted Tail. After about a year, Crazy Horse returned to his Oglala band. He Dog wondered why Crazy Horse came back but, curiously, he did not ask Crazy Horse himself. Instead, He Dog sought the information from others. "I was told," He Dog recalled decades later, "he had to come back because he had killed a Winnebago woman."

He Dog said nothing more about this killing, but his phrasing, "he had to come back," strongly suggests that Crazy Horse committed a crime, or at the least the killing was deemed highly offensive. If so, Crazy Horse would have looked to his friend and holy man Horn Chips for spiritual guidance. Horn Chips possibly led Crazy Horse through a ceremony known as "Wiping of Blood from the Hands." But the circumstances surrounding the killing, whether it was intentional or an accident, and whether Crazy Horse even felt any remorse, will remain questions forever. If there's anything to take away from this tragic and enigmatic episode, it's that Crazy Horse, like all humans before and after, was not perfect.

A kingdom of gold. The folktales, rumors, and speculation titillated Europeans' minds for generations. Spanish conquistadors had traveled many hard miles from the south and suffered numerous privations to reach the Great Plains in search of it. They knew it as Cibola, the Seven Cities of Gold. But there were no cities, and they found no gold. However, gold hadn't been found in California until decades after Spaniards first settled there, discovered by Americans shortly after California was seized from Mexico during the U.S.-Mexican War. Some whites believed that if California's rich goldfields could be overlooked for so long, gold was likely still waiting to be discovered in the vast Rocky Mountain West. Actually, its presence there was a closely guarded secret.

William Bent, an Indian trader, had gotten hints of its existence from the Southern Cheyennes ever since he located a trading post on the upper Arkansas River in the early 1830s. After the California gold discoveries, he pressed his Indian trade partners for more details about where they might have seen the precious mineral, but the Cheyennes refused to divulge more. As an old Southern Cheyenne chief explained to Bent later, they believed that if the white man found gold in their country, he would take from them their "best and last home."

But time is hard on secrets. In the summer of 1858, as Sitting Bull and Crazy Horse and their fellow tribesmen battled Crows and Shoshones and hunted buffalo on the northern plains, a party of gold seekers found what they'd been looking for on a small creek just east of the Front Range of the Rocky Mountains. By that winter, the town of Denver City had been established, and the following spring saw hordes of eager prospectors cramming the trails that crossed the central plains. Other boomtowns quickly sprang up as well, and in 1861, the white man's government established Colorado Territory.

Quiet valleys where the Plains Indians had once located their villages and grazed their horse herds were now defiled with hastily constructed wood buildings and muddy streets. And the fact that the land itself belonged to the Cheyennes and Arapahos—officially designated as theirs at the Fort Laramie Treaty of 1851—meant little to those consumed by gold fever. Just what the Cheyennes had feared was coming to pass, and it was happening faster than anyone could've ever imagined.

What was occurring in Colorado wasn't far from the lands of the Lakotas, who had a secret of their own to guard. Sometime in the 1860s, or maybe even earlier, Father De Smet and a number of Lakotas were camped on Rapid Creek, where it spills out of the Black Hills. Eagle Woman That All Look At, a Two Kettle Lakota who often served as De Smet's interpreter, went off with several other women to cut lodgepoles. In the midst of this task, she came across a curious piece of metal and brought it back to show the father. When De Smet saw it, his usually jovial face turned serious.

"This is the white man's money," he said to Eagle Woman, "and you must never tell that you have found it here, for if you do he will come and drive your people away from the country and take it for his own."

Eagle Woman took De Smet's warning to heart, and she told no one of the yellow metal. But, again, time is hard on secrets.

# The Invasion of Good Horse Grass Country

*At present [the Indians] are only a nuisance on the
face of the earth; and if they will not be improved,
they must be exterminated. No milk-and-water
policy will do for the North American Indians.*

AMERICAN PHRENOLOGICAL JOURNAL, 1864

*Fort Pierre, Dakota Territory, June 1862*

Bear's Rib was dead. A leading chief of the Húnkpapas, he'd come
to believe that the only way the Lakotas could survive was to find
a way to coexist with the white man. The news of his death was
stunning in and of itself, but the manner in which he died was
shocking. Bear's Rib had been assassinated by Sans Arc Lakotas because the chief had been accepting the Great Father's annual annuities. Many Lakotas feared that by accepting the Great Father's
gifts, they were relinquishing all claims to their lands. A few weeks
after the chief's murder, the Indian agent on the Upper Missouri
received a letter crafted by an interpreter on behalf of nine Húnkpapa chiefs. "We beg of you for the last time not to bring us any
more presents," the letter stated, "as we will not receive them."

*We notified the Bear's Rib yearly not to receive your goods;
he had no ears, and we gave him ears by killing him. We now
say to you, bring us no more goods; if any of our people receive
any more from you we will give them ears as we did the Bear's
Rib. We acknowledge no agent, and we notify you for the last
time to bring us no more goods. We have told all the agents the
same thing, but they have paid no attention to what we have
said. If you have no ears we will give you ears, and then your
Father very likely will not send us any more goods or agent.*

*We also say to you that we wish you to stop the whites from
traveling through our country, and if you do not stop them, we
will. If your whites have no ears, we will give them ears.*

That the chiefs sent a letter and touched the pen to sign it reveals just how much they'd learned about the white man's ways, as does their severe threats if their demands weren't met. But just like the treaties they'd signed, they'd soon see that no document, no matter how many signatures it contained, would stand in the way of what the white man wanted. And there wasn't much, it seemed, that the white man didn't want.

That very same summer, prospectors found paying quantities of gold on a small creek just east of the Beaverhead Mountains in what would soon become Montana Territory. The town of Bannack City sprang up nearly overnight and in six months' time boasted four stores, several gambling establishments, dancing and boxing schools, and a population of six hundred, including several families. Reports of some of the luckier strikes quickly made their way east. A Bannack City prospector's letter published in an Iowa newspaper in the spring of 1863 told of new "diggings" that generated $611 from eighteen wheelbarrow-loads of dirt. Such reports guaranteed a full-blown rush.

Thousands of gold seekers traveled to southwestern Montana

via Missouri River steamboats to the trading post of Fort Benton and from there continued overland another 280 miles by wagon or horseback. But others quickly discovered another, more direct route to the goldfields, this one entirely by land. The same Bannack City prospector wrote that he'd met some men at Fort Benton who'd come there from Fort Laramie, "and they say it is a good route for a road along the base of the mountains. They came through with wagons." Whether or not those men knew they were trespassing on Indian land, the letter writer didn't say. If they did know, they certainly didn't care, nor would the many who were soon to follow. They also didn't care that this new wagon route, soon to be known as the Bozeman Cut-off, passed through a region rich in game—outside the Black Hills, one of the last unspoiled pockets on the northern plains—that several tribes held dear and considered crucial to their survival. No, none of these things mattered to the white gold seekers and freighters.

Not yet.


Probably few Lakotas in the early 1860s were aware that white men were fighting each other in a horrendous civil war. The various Lakota winter counts for that period mostly chronicle their conflicts with the hated Crows: "Young Rabbit, a Crow, was killed in a battle by Red Cloud" (1861–62), "Crows scalped an Oglala boy alive" (1862–63), and "Oglalas and Miniconjous took the warpath against the Crows and stole 300 horses" (1863–1864). But a very different and quite significant entry is found in the winter count of Long Soldier, a Húnkpapa chief. For the Lakota year 1864 to 1865, Long Soldier drew a white soldier and a Lakota shooting at each other. The event is titled "First fight with white men." The Lakota is identified as Sitting Bull, and he is fighting a soldier who is "taking lands."

The fight Long Soldier recorded was known by whites as the Battle of Killdeer Mountain. It took place on the eastern edge of the broken Badlands country of the Little Missouri River on July 28, 1864, and it very likely was indeed the first time Sitting Bull fought the Long Knives in a pitched battle. The story of how this battle came to be actually has its beginnings in Minnesota two years earlier. There, the Eastern Sioux tribes were suffering from starvation, disreputable agents, a flood of white settlers, and forced reduction of their lands. Pent-up anger and frustration exploded into violence in August 1862 when hundreds of Eastern Sioux warriors went on a killing spree, slaying dozens of white families in what a Minnesota newspaper described as "one awful holocaust of blood and fire." This Sioux uprising, labeled the Dakota War, lasted only a few weeks before many of the Sioux participants were forced to surrender. Yet some escaped west as far as the Missouri River, and many white settlers in Minnesota feared the Indians would reorganize and strike again. They demanded the Sioux be thoroughly punished—at the very least.

So in the summer of 1863, as two great armies converged on a Pennsylvania farming town called Gettysburg, two much smaller armies converged on various Sioux bands reported to be buffalo hunting just east of the Missouri River in present-day North Dakota. These bands included Lakotas who'd had nothing to do with the Minnesota uprising, as well as large factions of their Eastern Sioux cousins, particularly the Yanktonais, who'd not taken part in the uprising and wished to remain at peace with the whites. Yet those leading the military expeditions, as well as the common soldiers in the ranks, were not interested in such distinctions. Their primary objective was vengeance upon the Sioux, and any Sioux they encountered would suffice.

Bluecoats and Sioux clashed three times in July with few casualties on each side, but in early September, seven hundred Long

Knives attacked a village of approximately thirty-five hundred Yanktonais, Santees, Sihásapas, and Húnkpapas at Whitestone Hill. The commander of the Long Knives, Brigadier General Alfred Sully, had been transferred from the Civil War's Eastern theater less than four months earlier. Forty-two years old, tall and slim with a scraggly beard, the West Point graduate led troops in some of the Civil War's bloodiest engagements thus far: Antietam, Fredericksburg, and Chancellorsville. But Sully was by no means unfamiliar with the Sioux. He'd served with the army on the Upper Missouri in the late 1850s, where he fathered a child by a Yankton woman named Red Crane. Sully may not have known of the child, called Soldier Woman by her mother's people, but he doesn't seem to have made any inquiries for his Indian lover on his return to the West, at least none that we know of.

Sully's troops surprised the peaceful village at Whitestone Hill late in the day on September 5. When darkness finally forced a halt to the fighting—or, rather, slaughter—as many as three hundred Sioux lay dead, including many women and children, and more than 150 captured. The next day, the soldiers destroyed three hundred lodges left behind by the fleeing inhabitants and more than four hundred thousand pounds of precious dried buffalo meat. The surviving Sioux fled to the west side of the Missouri, where Sitting Bull undoubtedly soon learned of the calamity, for the Húnkpapa chief Black Moon, a cousin to Sitting Bull, had been in the ill-fated village with his followers.

The Long Knives believed they'd delivered a major blow to the Sioux, but their summer campaign served only to enrage the Sioux bands they'd harassed and make enemies of those who'd not been enemies before. In February 1864, worrying reports came from the Upper Missouri that the Sioux wintering in the Powder River country were plotting to "clear out all the whites," including the trading posts of Fort Union and Fort Berthold. In fact, Fort

Union, near the junction of the Yellowstone and Missouri Rivers, was already in a virtual state of siege. That same winter, the Sioux attacked a wagon train of Pierre Chouteau & Company along the Missouri in present-day eastern Montana, killing a white trader and making off with one hundred packs of buffalo robes and more than $4,000 in trade goods. "This whole section of country is in a terrible foment," wrote Chouteau's agent at Fort Union.

But the whites were already plotting, too. Hardly had the wisps of smoke disappeared from the charred lodgepoles at Whitestone Hill before plans for another military campaign the following summer began. But this one had far greater objectives than simple revenge. Steady news of richer and richer yields by the miners in Idaho and Montana resulted in more bonanza-crazed whites determined to go there. The 1864 military campaign aimed to secure the water and land routes to and from the goldfields by both defeating the "savage demons," as one Minnesota newspaper referred to the Sioux, and establishing a series of permanent military posts in Sioux country. The power of the Lakotas and Yanktonais, observed the general commanding the U.S. Army's Department of the Northwest, "must be broken to pieces."

On July 19, more than twenty-five hundred Long Knives set out from the newly established Fort Rice, on the west bank of the Missouri, just north of the mouth of the Cannonball River, on a seek-and-destroy mission. General Sully led the expedition, and if an army of white soldiers with several lumbering artillery pieces invading the buffalo plains wasn't enough of an affront to the Sioux, following close behind was a train of gold seekers bound for Montana: 123 wagons and 250 men, women, and children.

Despite the intimidating size of the invaders' column, the Sioux were more than willing to give battle to these Long Knives and either annihilate them or drive them away for good. But they would do it on the ground of their choosing. Near the end of July, at "the place where they kill deer"—Killdeer Mountain—some eight thousand Sioux congregated in an enormous village. Approximately sixteen hundred hide lodges stretched for four miles, homes to Húnkpapas, Sihásapas, Sans Arcs, Miniconjous, Yanktonais, and Santees. The campsite had been selected specifically with its defensive potential in mind. A series of steep hills with rocky outcroppings rose to several hundred feet behind the village, and a labyrinth of deep, timbered ravines notched the hillsides. Thus, the village could not be attacked from the rear or flanked. The only approach was from the rolling prairie to the front.

Among the approximately two thousand warriors in the Sioux camps were some of their most renowned fighting men. These included Sitting Bull, now thirty-three years old; his uncle, Four Horns, now an old man chief; and a rising Húnkpapa warrior named Phizí, who would become known to whites as Gall. Leading a small contingent of Santees was the fearsome Inkpaduta (translated as "Red End"), a forty-eight-year-old chief whose name had been notorious to white settlers in Iowa and Minnesota for years, ever since he'd led his followers in the slaying of nearly forty whites in Iowa in 1857, known as the Spirit Lake Massacre.

In August 1863, Inkpaduta and his men, along with a band of Húnkpapas, had attacked a party of returning Montana miners traveling down the Missouri by boat. Fearing trouble, the miners had equipped their craft with a small cannon, but the firing of the cannon shook the boat so violently that it sprang several leaks, and it sank in shallow water. The Sioux made quick work of the miners, killing the entire party: eighteen men, one woman, and three children. The miners carried nearly $20,000 in gold dust and money, some of which the Sioux left scattered on the riverbank, along with the mutilated bodies of their victims.

Confident in their numbers, the Lakotas and their Eastern Sioux cousins saw no reason to flee the Bluecoats. For several days, their scouts shadowed Sully's column and signaled its movements by shooting fire-tipped arrows high into the night sky. On July 27, those scouts warned the village leaders the Bluecoats would be there the next day. Shortly before noon on the twenty-eighth, Sitting Bull's nephew White Bull was out watering his horses when he heard a commotion coming from the village. He drove the horses back to camp, where he was told the Long Knives were close. White Bull found his uncle and Four Horns, and together they rode up onto the high ground behind the lodges to get a better view.

The coolness of the morning was long gone, and the temperature now stood at more than one hundred degrees. In fact, the temperature had hovered around the one-hundred-degree mark for the last few days, hard on people, horses, and a land that was in the midst of a two-year drought. Looking south through a thin mirage shimmering above the prairie, the three Lakotas saw a strange sight. Sully's Long Knives approached in the shape of a large, hollow square. The white man clearly liked squares; he lived in square houses and square trading posts. But these hard lines seemed as alien in the Lakotas' world as the white man himself. Neither belonged here.

Sully had left the emigrant wagon train at a camp more than sixty miles behind under the protection of a strong guard, thus reducing his strike force to a still-formidable twenty-two hundred men. He placed his artillery, batteries of six-pounder and twelve-pounder guns, in the center of the square, along with ambulances and supply wagons. And as he'd ordered a portion of his cavalry to fight dismounted, the riderless horses were also placed within the protection of the formation, which was more than a mile across.

The Sioux warriors had ample time to prepare their war medicine and don their best shirts and leggings, elaborately decorated with colorful bead- and porcupine work and human hair. Some men wore only breechclouts and moccasins, with an eagle feather or two in their hair. Sitting Bull retrieved his shield and sang its song. Warriors prayed to *Wakan Tanka*. Eagle-bone whistles cut the air. Women, children, and old men gathered in front of the village to see their warriors off, the women voicing the shrill tremolo as the warriors galloped away.

When the Long Knives advanced to within two miles of the village, the warriors suddenly appeared, hundreds and hundreds of them. They raced back and forth on their ponies, kicking up great dust clouds, and shouted taunts at the Bluecoats. But they didn't fire their weapons. A Húnkpapa warrior named Lone Dog suggested that he make a dash close to the soldiers. "If they shoot at me," he said, "we will then all shoot at the soldiers." Lone Dog was known to possess a powerful charm, and in a battle, a ghost or spirit rode with him. "It was hard to shoot him," recalled White Bull.

Lone Dog kicked his pony's sides and galloped toward the Long Knives, waving a war club high above his head. As he came within range of their guns, he swung his horse around so that for a few seconds he was racing parallel to their line. The soldiers opened up with their rifles, and bullets buzzed all around Lone Dog, several kicking up dust from the ground beneath his pony's hooves, but neither was hit. The Sioux warriors knew better than to make a direct frontal assault on Sully's formation, instead sweeping around to the sides, using the low hills and draws as cover. Lone Dog made a second ride in front of the Long Knives and this time White Bull, just fifteen years old, followed him. The soldiers "all took a shot at us," White Bull remembered, but his medicine was also strong that day, and the two Húnkpapa dare-devils returned to their fellow warriors unharmed.

The Sioux warriors quickly learned the range of the soldiers' rifles and charged in and out of it, trying to find a weak point or a few Bluecoats they could isolate from the rest. From the soldiers' perspective, the Sioux charges were equally awe-inspiring and ter-rifying, like "the imps of hell let loose." It soon became painfully obvious, however, that the bows and arrows and smoothbore trade guns of the Sioux were no match for the long-range rifles and carbines of the Long Knives. And none of the Sioux were pre-pared for the artillery.

As the cannons boomed, sending shrieking rounds of spheri-cal case shot through the air, warriors fired up into the sky to try to kill this invisible enemy. When a large body of warriors threat-ened the rear of Sully's formation, an exploding artillery shell in-stantly killed five Sioux and their mounts as well, the shot and shrapnel shredding three of the warriors beyond recognition. The Sioux women and children weren't safe from the cannons, either. The artillerymen specifically targeted a large group of noncom-batants watching the battle from a high butte a mile away. The first shell exploded short of the butte, but the second exploded directly over the women and children, causing them to run for their lives. The Sioux women now began to frantically take down their lodges, but with the shells continuing to rain deadly shrap-nel into the village, the task became too risky. Some threw their possessions and food bundles into nearby ravines, thinking they could retrieve them once the fighting stopped. Then they fled into the hills with their children.

The fighting became more desperate as the Long Knives neared the village, with the warriors trying to buy time for their families to escape. When a Sioux fell, another warrior daringly raced forward on horseback, looped a rawhide rope around the wounded or dead man, and drug him away. One Sioux, however, did not wish to be saved—he wished to die. As shells exploded overhead and bullets pinged and ricocheted off the rocks, a Sioux warrior appeared in the open, leading a horse with a travois and loudly singing as he walked in the direction of the Long Knives. The travois carried an unarmed forty-year-old man named Bear's Heart. In his song, the warrior told how Bear's Heart had been crippled all his life and that he was of no use. Bear's Heart wished to be killed in battle by a bullet. His song finished, the warrior whipped the rump of the horse with a quirt, and the horse lunged forward.

Several soldiers directed their fire at the easy target. They killed the horse first, which collapsed hard to the ground, along with the travois. Bear's Heart's arms instinctively reached out as the travois fell, then flopped about as several bullets struck his body. And then Bear's Heart moved no more.

The Húnkpapas, along with other Lakotas, were concentrated on the west end of the Sioux line. Mounted on a fast sorrel horse and armed with a trade gun and his bow and arrows, Sitting Bull seemed to be everywhere. He shouted at the warriors to be brave and to keep the Long Knives from reaching the camps. Close by rode Four Horns and White Bull. Suddenly Four Horns yelled, "I am shot!" A bullet had ripped into the back of the chief's ribs, and blood was now streaming from the wound. Although in great pain, Four Horns kept his saddle as Sitting Bull hurriedly led him back to the village and to his lodge, where he kept his medicines. White Bull followed and watched Sitting Bull treat and bandage the wound and give his uncle medicine to drink.

As Sitting Bull left the battlefield, the Yanktonais and Santee warriors under Inkpaduta, fighting on the east end of the line, made a last, desperate attempt to flank the Bluecoats and stop their advance on the village. It was at this moment that Sully un-leashed his cavalry. With sabers drawn, the troopers charged the Sioux warriors. Sweat-lathered cavalry horses and Indian ponies collided, the troopers slashing with their sabers and firing their carbines at point-blank range while the warriors swung their war clubs at the Bluecoats. Thirteen warriors died in this initial clash, the rest retreating to nearby cover, where they continued to fight, shooting their arrows as fast as they could draw their bowstrings.

Because of the broken terrain, the cavalry commander now ordered his men to dismount and fight on foot. They pushed for-ward, driving the warriors from one rocky outcropping to the next, one copse of trees and brush to the next, one ravine to the next. Finally, exhausted, outnumbered, and outgunned, the San-tee and Yanktonais warriors broke off the fight and fled, leaving a total of twenty-seven of their comrades dead on the ground. The Lakotas also retreated, and suddenly a strange stillness replaced the life-and-death chaos of battle. As long shadows from the sink-ing sun crept over the village, the only living things remaining were several colts and dogs the Indians had abandoned, still tied to their stakes.

When the Long Knives tallied up their casualties, they counted five killed and ten wounded. Of the Sioux, General Sully be-lieved his men had killed from 100 to 150. Because many of the dead and wounded warriors were carried away by their compan-ions, it was difficult to come up with an exact figure. What was clear, however, was that most of those killed were victims of the artillery shelling. Four Horns survived his ugly bullet wound, thanks in part to Sitting Bull's doctoring. The bullet remained in his body for the rest of his life and, for a short time, caused him some discomfort. But, according to Four Horns, the bullet eventually dropped into his stomach and troubled him no more.

Sully ordered the village and its contents destroyed, a formidable task, for in addition to the sixteen hundred lodges, the camps contained tons of dried buffalo meat packed in large parfleches, heaps of dried berries, countless decorated buffalo robes, tanned elk, deer, and antelope skins, brass and copper kettles, saddles, and travois poles. Thousands of personal items also littered the ground, the things one soldier explained as "worth little to a white man, but prized highly by the Indians."

Eighteen hundred Bluecoats worked for several hours the following day to destroy the immense village, piling the Indian possessions on the dismantled lodgepoles and setting them ablaze. The several bonfires sent up huge plumes of smoke visible for miles. A Bluecoat who found the task distasteful wrote that it "was wicked to destroy the work of a lifetime, and every particle of that work done by poor over-worked squaws."

A number of Sioux secretly watched from a large bluff overlooking the village, and to witness the Long Knives methodically go about eliminating all trace of their camps was nothing short of heart-wrenching. Overcome with emotion, these Sioux made themselves visible to the soldiers and waved a white flag. Maybe they could negotiate with the white men to spare some of their food and belongings or let them retrieve a loved one's body. But the officer in charge of the operation claimed he "could not interpret the meaning [of the flag] at this particular time." Some of his men chose to ignore the white flag as well and began shooting at the Indians, who ran for cover and were not seen again.

As evening approached, and with much of the village's contents still remaining, the Bluecoats set fire to the surrounding timber and undergrowth, already a tinderbox from the extreme drought conditions. The flames licked upward, racing over the entire encampment, burning not just hides and lodgepoles, but Indian corpses, too.

After hastily regrouping in the twisted and broken country behind Killdeer Mountain, the several Lakota bands traveled southwest, putting more than fifty miles between them and the battlefield in a few days' time. Hungry and tired, they laid out their camp circles in the Good Horse Grass Country (Badlands) west of the cottonwood-lined Little Missouri River. Safe from the Long Knives, they now began proper mourning for those slain at Killdeer. Sad, pitiful wailing echoed among the bare, eroded buttes. Women and men cut the flesh on their arms and legs. With faces painted black and their hair shorn, grieving relatives wandered among the lodges, tears streaming down their cheeks.

Buffalo were scarce, and hunters rode great distances looking for game. As one white soldier explained, the Indians "live very fat when they fall in with buffalo, but when they have to depend on small game they nearly starve." But the impoverished camps were soon joined by Brulés, more Miniconjous, their allies the Cheyennes, and others, who didn't hesitate to share all they had in the way of food and shelter. In return, the veterans of Killdeer shared numerous stories of bravery—Lone Dog's death-defying ride and the honorable death of the crippled Bear's Heart—and the terrible power of the Long Knives' cannons.

During this time, General Sully had countermarched to the camp where he'd left the emigrant wagon train and its guard detachment. Short on rations, he made the risky decision to cut across the Badlands, believed impassable for wagons, to get to the Yellowstone River. There, two small steamboats with much-needed provisions would be waiting for him. His route led him in the direction of the new Lakota and Cheyenne encampments, and as soon as Sioux scouts alerted their people of that fact, they were keen to exact their revenge.

Sully's long column, three to four miles in length, wended its way through a fairyland of petrified tree trunks, multicolored hoodoos, and deeply carved earthen mounds from a few feet to several hundred in height that reminded the white men of the ruins of some immense ancient city. With picks and shovels, Sully's men worked in the extreme heat to make a road where no road had previously existed. In places where it was too steep and high, they used ropes to lower the wagons. Occasionally, a wagon got loose and wrecked, but no men were hurt. All was going much better than expected. Once Sully crossed to the west side of the Little Missouri, however, the Sioux and Cheyennes pounced.

Over three days, at least a thousand warriors harassed the column and its road builders. In parties large and small, the Indians struck here and there, using the deep gorges and castlelike formations to shield their approach. But time and again, the warriors were driven back by the superior firearms of the watchful Bluecoats and especially the artillery, which had been placed strategically along the length of the slow-moving train. Tiring of the surprise attacks, Sully directed the artillery to fire at likely hiding places as they appeared up ahead. And just like at Killdeer Mountain, the exploding shells decimated the warrior ranks. In several places, the column encountered the bodies of warriors sprawled on the hard earth, bloodied and mangled, as it proceeded westward.

When nightfall brought an end to the Indian assaults on the second day, and knowing that the Sioux were still lurking just beyond the darkness, one of Sully's Indian scouts called out to them.

"We are about thirsty to death and want to know what Indians are you?"

"Húnkpapas, Sans Arcs, Yanktonais, and others," Sitting Bull shouted. "Who are you?"

"Some Indian with soldiers and one Indian badly shot through

[the] arm," the scout answered. "Most [of the] white boys are starved and thirsty to death, so just stay around and they will be dead."

Sitting Bull was indignant that this scout, likely a mixed-blood Sioux, was helping the Long Knives. "You have no business with the soldiers," he yelled. "The Indians here want no fights with [the] whites," the Húnkpapa leader continued. "Why is it the whites come to fight with [the] Indians?"

That last question—the question of all Lakotas—was met with silence.

Sitting Bull didn't believe the Long Knives were close to death. In fact, the only ones dying were Sioux warriors. And it was hard for Sitting Bull to imagine the Long Knives being hungrier than his own people. Consequently, by the next morning, he'd had enough and urged the Húnkpapa warriors to stay away from the Bluecoats. Ammunition was running low, he reminded them, and they desperately needed to direct their energies to hunting buffalo to feed their people. "Let them go," he said, "and we will go home."

But the young warriors, eager to add to their résumés of coups, couldn't resist making another attempt at inflicting damage upon the Long Knives. They should have listened to Sitting Bull, for the fighting was largely a repeat of what had gone before. However, the Long Knives this day borrowed a tactic from their adversaries. Fearful of the long-range rifles and artillery, the warriors generally kept at a safe distance. To lure them in, a small party of soldiers would charge the warriors, stop and fire their weapons, and then wheel their horses and race back to their lines. The warriors invariably gave chase, only to discover, too late, that more soldiers were waiting unseen behind various formations and mounds. In other words, an ambush. The volley that came from the Long Knives seldom failed to empty a few saddles.

The warriors finally gave up the fight about noon, and a large dust cloud rose in the southwest as the Sioux and Cheyenne bands scattered in advance of Sully's column. Reaching the western edge of the Badlands that day, Sully and his men came upon the Indian campsites, which stretched for three miles and were three-quarters of a mile wide. Some of the campfires were still burning, and the dead bodies of several warriors were found scattered about the camp. The Indians had obviously left in a hurry.

In his official report, Sully estimated that his men killed at least one hundred warriors in the Badlands fighting; some of his officers, however, believed it was double or triple that number. Sully's casualties amounted to only nine wounded and none killed. "I don't think the Indians will ever again attempt to unite and make a stand against the whites," the general wrote triumphantly on August 18. "They are fully convinced that they can do nothing; and the Unkpapas, who have been the great boasters that they alone could clean out any body of whites sent against them, were the poorest fighters in the whole crowd that opposed me."

Sully's claim was pure hyperbole, but the white man's mode of warfare was nothing short of a revelation to Sitting Bull. He'd heard accounts from other Sioux, but now he'd experienced it firsthand. The Long Knives had no interest in unnecessarily risking their lives for personal glory; they didn't count coup. They would just as soon kill Indians from a mile away with shrapnel and shot from their artillery if that would get the job done.

Sitting Bull, his people, the Húnkpapas, and the other Sioux tribes suffered terribly at Killdeer Mountain and in the Badlands, but they were by no means defeated. Nor had their resolve to defend their homeland from the whites been weakened, but they would have to fight smarter.


The next opportunity for Sitting Bull's Húnkpapas to "clean out" some whites came a few weeks later when they discovered a wagon train far out on the plains, about 160 miles west of Fort Rice. It was another group of gold seekers headed for the Montana diggings—nearly two hundred men, women, and children, with close to a hundred wagons and carts. The captain of the train had convinced the commander at Fort Rice to provide the emigrants with an escort of forty-seven cavalrymen. Additionally, the caravan had a single mountain howitzer.

On September 2, 1864, shortly after noon, the long train navigated a deep ravine situated below picturesque red-colored buttes. One by one, the lumbering ox-drawn wagons rolled down the steep bank. As the oxen strained against their loads on the opposite side, the teamsters shouted and cursed and cracked their long whips, making a sound like so many firecrackers going off. Suddenly, several men began yelling as a heavily loaded wagon began to tip, its wheels lifting off the ground on one side. The wagon's momentum couldn't be stopped, and it careened over, spilling much of its contents on the ground.

The wagon itself suffered no real damage, so it was only a matter of righting the vehicle and repacking its load, which would take a little time. Rather than halt the entire train, another team with two men remained behind to assist in the repacking, along with the train's rear guard of nine cavalrymen. Soon the main caravan disappeared in the hills to the west and the sounds of creaking wagons and cracking whips grew fainter and fainter until they disappeared as well. The teamsters, with the help of some of the guard, busied themselves organizing the jumbled load with not the slightest inkling they were being watched.

From behind those red buttes, Sitting Bull and one hundred Húnkpapa warriors prepared for battle. Carefully studying the terrain surrounding the two wagons, Sitting Bull determined that the best route for surprise was the deep ravine. The Húnkpapa war chief took the lead, racing down into the gulch on horseback with the warriors following. The roar of thundering hooves from up the ravine got the white men's attention, and when the yipping warriors burst into view seconds later, they ran for their weapons, but it was too late. The Húnkpapas swarmed the white men.

The wagon train had traveled a mile to the west when a messenger alerted the military escort of the attack. Together with some of the teamsters, they immediately started on the back trail and soon came upon the milling Húnkpapas and charged them. The fighting became hand to hand. A warrior named White Buffalo Chief grappled with a soldier who'd raced ahead of the others, thirty-one-year-old Corporal Jefferson Dilts, a scout for the wagon train. Yanking at each other, both men fell to the ground, where they continued to wrestle. When Dilts seemed to be getting the better of White Buffalo Chief, another warrior, Fool Buffalo, jumped off his pony to help. In his hand was a revolver he'd acquired just before the attack from an emigrant unlucky enough to be walking along the trail looking for a stray ox. The warriors had made sure the white man would never worry about lost oxen or anything else ever again.

Fool Buffalo wanted to shoot the corporal, but he was afraid of hitting his fellow Húnkpapa. Finally, as Dilts lay on top of White Buffalo Chief, his hands tightening around the warrior's neck, Fool Buffalo began to strike Dilts's back with the revolver. This caused Dilts to release his grasp and turn on Fool Buffalo. In an instant, he snatched the revolver from the surprised warrior and then used it to strike a gasping White Buffalo Chief, breaking the Húnkpapa's collarbone. Fool Buffalo ran as Dilts stood up and leveled the revolver. Another warrior dashed close, but returned to the warrior line when he saw that Dilts was armed.

Now Sitting Bull made a charge at the corporal, rapidly drawing his bow and firing an arrow as he bore down on the brave white man. The arrow sank deep into Dilts's body but the corporal stood his ground, firing his revolver as the war chief passed within touching distance. The ball from Dilts's weapon entered Sitting Bull's left hip and exited out the small of his back. A searing pain ripped through Sitting Bull's side, and he could feel the wetness as blood spurted from the wound. He maintained his grip on his pony, however, and turned the animal away from the fight.

Dilts, an arrow sticking out of his stomach and blood now streaming from his mouth, grabbed the reins of his horse, which was still standing nearby, quickly pulled himself up into the saddle, and galloped off. Several warriors shot arrows at the corporal as he hurried away, and two found their mark, but, incredibly, the soldier didn't fall.

The rescue party was able to save a few of the oxen and carry off a wounded guard, the only survivor of the initial attack, but the warriors were too many, and the soldiers were forced to abandon the two wagons. One contained several carbines and muskets and four thousand rounds of ammunition. The other was crammed with kegs of liquor, cigars, tobacco, tents, clothing, and foodstuffs. The wagonloads amounted to an absolute windfall for the Lakotas.

Sitting Bull had a painful ride back to the village, a distance of six miles. Jumping Bull, his adopted Assiniboine brother, rode close alongside, helping to keep Sitting Bull upright on his pony. White Bull rode near his uncle as well. Upon arriving at the camp, the wound was carefully cleaned and treated. It was by no means life-threatening, but the extreme soreness meant Sitting Bull would be forced to take some time to rest and heal and leave any fighting to others, at least for the next few days. Those days would see no rest, however, for his fellow Húnkpapas, for their harassment of the emigrants had just begun.

The warriors started from the village at first light the following morning and soon reached the train. Fully expecting to see the

Indians again, the emigrants had positioned their mountain how-itzer on a rise that overlooked the length of the moving caravan. Any gullies or ridges in front that could hide Indians received a round or two of spherical case shot, and when several warriors were observed bunched together, the gunner touched off a round that exploded near the group, causing them to scatter. When the last wagon passed the howitzer, it was rushed ahead to the next knoll and performed the same duty.

The Húnkpapas alternately charged the front and rear of the train as it moved along but were repulsed each time. Yet the warriors refused to give up, endlessly circling and making feints all day long. And they made good use of the long-range guns and am-munition they'd captured from the abandoned wagons, wounding several emigrants. After traveling eight miles, the train corralled for the evening. It had been a hellish day for the gold seekers, but more than a few admitted to being in awe of the Húnkpapas' bravery.

That night, some of the emigrants decided they'd deal with their antagonists like they would a pack of wolves or similar var-mints. Retrieving stacks of hardtack from one of the wagons, they used a syringe to lace the hard crackers with strychnine. The poi-soned hardtack was then placed in a half-burned box and left on top of a doused campfire so that the Indians would find it after the wagon train had departed. The next day, their depraved scheme played out exactly as they'd imagined, with the hardtack being taken to the village and quickly consumed. Between twenty-five and one hundred Lakotas of all ages died a slow, torturous death.

That same day saw the warriors again surrounding the wagon train, and their numbers appeared to the emigrants to have in-creased dramatically. After traveling only two miles, the train abruptly halted and corralled. In the distance, the emigrants could see the Badlands, and they had no desire to enter that broken coun-try where the warriors could spring from any number of hidden ravines or pick them off one by one from behind countless buttes. They simply couldn't proceed without strong reinforcements. The men thus set to work building a sod fortification around their corral, which they named Fort Dilts in honor of the courageous corporal, who had succumbed to his wounds and was buried within the perimeter. That evening, well after dark, a squad of soldiers started for Fort Rice to get help.

The next morning, the gold seekers observed two to three hundred warriors congregated on a hill about a mile away, the sunlight making their figures glow against the deep blue sky. Eventually, three warriors emerged carrying a white flag and a stick, which they planted in the ground midway to the fort and then stepped back a short distance. They waved for someone from the fort to come to them. One of the emigrants and two mixed-blood interpreters cautiously obliged and returned with the stick, which had a piece of paper attached. To the emigrants' surprise, the paper was a note written in English. It revealed that the writer was a white woman with the last name Kelly. Just eighteen years old, Fanny Kelly had been captured by Oglalas near Fort Laramie on July 12 and subsequently traded to a Húnkpapa named Brings Plenty.

Fanny's captors instructed her to tell the emigrants to proceed, that they would not attack the wagons. But this was certainly a ruse, she wrote, and she cautioned the emigrants not to move. Additionally, her captors demanded forty head of cattle. She also related that the Húnkpapas "had many killed by the goods they brought into camp"—the poisoned hardtack. Fanny closed her note with a plea to be rescued. "Buy me if you can, and you will be satisfied," she wrote. "They have killed many whites. Help me if you can."

This note set off a flurry of negotiations. In a second letter from Fanny, the Húnkpapas now demanded sugar, coffee, flour, gunpowder, knives, axes, barrel hoop metal for making arrow-heads, the forty head of cattle, and four wagons. "They say this is their ground," she wrote. "They say, 'Go home, and come back no more.' . . . They are very anxious for you to move now. Do not, I implore you, for your life's sake." The captain of the emigrant party answered that he would trade three of his own horses and some supplies for Fanny, but he did not offer the cattle or wagons. When at last it seemed a deal had been reached, the Húnkpapas showed up for the ransom but did not bring Fanny. Thus ended the negotiations.

The Lakotas left the vicinity the next day in search of better hunting grounds. Many families were hungry, which is why they coveted the emigrants' oxen. The few buffalo in the area had been driven off by the constant booming of the emigrants' howitzer and its exploding shells. On September 20, a relief force of 850 men from Fort Rice—cavalry, infantry, and artillery—arrived at the gold seekers' encampment. With this large military escort, the entire wagon train started back for the Missouri River. In something of a Pyrrhic victory, the fierceness of the Húnkpapas had prevented the emigrant train from penetrating farther into Lakota lands; they'd made them "go home." But, at the same time, the wailing of mourning relatives seemed to come from everywhere in the Húnkpapa camps.

In late November, a party of Sihásapas arrived at Fort Sully, a recently established military fort on the Missouri a few miles downstream from the Fort Pierre trading post. One of the Indians asked to see the "big chief," indicating that he had something for him. That something was a letter written by Fanny Kelly. The Sihásapa told the fort's commanding officer that the white woman was in a village on the Grand River distant about two days' travel. The officer immediately negotiated with the Sihásapas to take several horses to the village and trade them for Kelly and bring her to the fort. The leader of the group sent on this mission was a chief named Slohan but known to the whites as Crawler.

Crawler had been a friend of Sitting Bull since childhood, and it was to the Húnkpapa war chief's lodge that he first went after arriving at the village. Sitting Bull, ever considerate of captives, was well aware of Kelly's unhappiness. "I can see in her face she is homesick," he said. Sitting Bull instructed Crawler to go to Brings Plenty, give him the horses from the fort, and then bring Kelly back to his lodge. Like all the tipis in the village, a warm fire burned in the center of Brings Plenty's, for the weather was bitterly cold. When Crawler entered the tipi, he saw on the far side, behind the fire, the warrior Brings Plenty. On the Húnkpapa's left sat Fanny Kelly.

"My friend, I have come to secure the white woman," Crawler said. "I have brought horses to pay you for her."

"My friend," Brings Plenty replied, "I have no use for your horses. I will keep the captive."

Crawler left and returned to Sitting Bull's lodge and told him Brings Plenty refused to give the woman up. Sitting Bull sent Crawler back to again request Kelly, and Brings Plenty again refused to trade. "My friend," he said sternly to Crawler, "I have no desire to part with the captive."

Upon learning that Brings Plenty had turned Crawler away a second time, Sitting Bull got up from his fire and with Crawler made his way to the recalcitrant warrior's tipi. Brings Plenty was more than a little surprised to see the war chief.

"My friend," Sitting Bull said, "I sent for this woman to be brought to me at my tent and you wouldn't give her up."

Brings Plenty, cowed by a visibly angry Sitting Bull, said nothing, and Crawler motioned to Kelly to come to him. Frightened and confused, Kelly nevertheless scurried out of the lodge with Crawler and Sitting Bull. Two days later, Crawler and the other Sihásapas delivered her safely to Fort Sully. Her ordeal was over, in part thanks to Sitting Bull.

Fanny Kelly would eventually write a book of her experiences as a Sioux captive. Although with the Oglalas and then the Húnk-papas for only five months, she witnessed nearly everything that touched their daily lives. She even learned some of the Lakota language. In her narrative, Fanny had little good to say about her captors, other than the times she was treated by them with kindness. She had, after all, experienced a murderous attack on the wagon train of her family and friends. Very few of the Lakotas' customs she understood or cared for. She did come to understand, however, what drove them, beyond the basic need to survive:

> The youth are very fond of war. They have no other ambition, and pant for the glory of battle, longing for the notes of the war song, that they may rush in and win the feathers of a brave. They listen to the stories of the old men, as they recall the stirring scenes of their youth, or sing their war songs, which form only a boasting recapitulation of their daring and bravery. They yearn for the glory of war, which is the only path to distinction.

Sitting Bull and Crazy Horse would not disagree. And if they could win that distinction in stopping the white man from further encroachment of Lakota lands, so much the better.

# The Hundred in the Hand

*So, like wolves we travel all over the country to prey upon white men. So when they quarrel with us, I hunt them down.*

SITTING BULL

*Piney Creek, Just East of the Big Horn Mountains,*
*December 21, 1866*

Crazy Horse gazed at the white man's stockade fort less than five hundred yards in the distance. Largely hidden from the fort's view by thick cottonwoods and brush growing along the creek, more than thirty warriors fidgeted about on each side of him—they'd been waiting there since before dawn. Some of the men wore buffalo robes, woolly side in, draped over their shoulders. Others sported colorful wool blanket coats. The Indian ponies stomped their hooves on the hard ground and occasionally dropped their heads to nose around for a piece of cottonwood bark or a morsel of dry, brown grass. The sun, making its shortest appearance of the year, remained hidden behind dreary, overcast skies, but the weather was actually unseasonably mild, which is generally the case as a winter storm approaches. And a storm was definitely coming to the High Plains.

If the Long Knives in the fort did what they did every morning, soon a train of some twenty empty wagons with a strong guard would leave the main gate of the fort and head slowly west for about six miles to logging camps located near heavy timber. The post was not yet complete, and these wagons would be loaded with long sawlogs for the fort's two sawmills. And if the Indian warriors did what they did every morning, they would attack this outbound train once it was a couple of miles from the fort. And also like every morning, the train would immediately corral and wait for reinforcements from the post to scare off the attacking warriors.

But this morning was to be different—at least that was the hope of the leaders of the allied tribes who'd been carefully planning this day for some time. Warriors would still attack the wood train, but once the relief column started from the fort, those warriors would break off their attack and withdraw. At the same time, those with Crazy Horse—and a few others lurking on the treeless bluffs behind them—would do their best to lure the Long Knives away from the wagon road and up and over a long ridge to the north, which the white man called Lodge Trail Ridge. Just over that ridge waited approximately two thousand warriors itching to kill and scalp.

Crazy Horse watched the wood train leave the post as usual and clatter along toward the pinery. When it was about a mile and a half away, he heard the *pop-pop-pop-pop* of the attack. Now the warriors on the open slopes behind him began to make a commotion, shouting at the soldiers in the fort to come out and fight. The answer to their challenge came in the form of a loud boom and a shrieking projectile from a twelve-pounder howitzer. The round of spherical case shot passed over the heads of those with Crazy Horse and exploded near the shouting warriors, killing an Indian pony. Another round from the howitzer quickly followed, which was too much for most of the warriors along the creek, who streamed out of the brush and trees and galloped for the safety of nearby ravines leading up into the hills.

Crazy Horse and nine others—five Lakotas, two Cheyennes, and two Arapahos—held back. They'd been selected as the main decoys to draw the Long Knives into the ambush. By pretending that their mounts were lame and tired, seemingly hindering their escape, the decoys hoped to convince the Long Knives they were easy prey. It would be risky, necessarily putting the warriors within the range of the Long Knives' guns, but every trap must have its bait.

Within moments of the firing of the second round from the howitzer, a column of infantry and cavalry, eighty-one men total, left the fort. It was not heading for the wood train, which was no longer under attack. No, it was heading straight for Piney Creek, obviously intent on crossing and pursuing the warriors on the north side. Crazy Horse now turned to his fellow decoys and told them to get ready. Today was a good day to die.

Much had happened in the two years since Killdeer Mountain and the fights in the Badlands, and none of it boded well for future relations between the Plains tribes and the white man. Far to the south, on November 29, 1864, Colorado volunteer cavalrymen under Colonel John M. Chivington had attacked the Southern Cheyenne and Arapaho village of chiefs Black Kettle and Left Hand at Big Sandy Creek. An ardent proponent of cooperation with the whites, Black Kettle had been led to believe, by both territorial and military officials, that his people were safe from an ongoing campaign against marauding Cheyenne and Arapaho warriors. As the surprise attack began, Black Kettle even held aloft a lodgepole with an American flag and a small white flag tied to the end. He might as well have been waving a bull's-eye.

With rifles, carbines, revolvers, and mountain howitzers, the Colorado troopers had blazed away at the terrified Cheyennes and Arapahos. Those who could fought back, while others ran for their lives. But in the end, the Coloradans killed some 150 Indians, mostly women, children, and the elderly. Also numbered among the dead were several Cheyenne and Arapaho leaders who, like Black Kettle, had supported peace with the whites.

In the weeks and months that followed, Southern Cheyenne Dog Soldiers, Arapahos, Northern Cheyennes, and Lakotas made it hot for white travelers and settlers on the central plains, especially along the Platte. Like Sitting Bull and Crazy Horse, the Dog Soldier band wanted nothing to do with the white man and his treaties, and the terrible massacre on Big Sandy Creek gave them even more cause to resist and retaliate. George Bent, a mixed-blood Southern Cheyenne fighting with the Dog Soldiers, said there would be no talk of peace until the U.S. government hanged Colonel Chivington.

In the summer of 1865, Northern and Southern Cheyenne, Arapaho, and Lakota warriors, including Crazy Horse, swooped down on mail carriers and small supply trains on the Oregon-California Trail between Fort Laramie and South Pass. Again and again, they cut and carried off the wires of the Pacific Telegraph Company and tore down numerous telegraph poles. The Indians referred to the telegraph as the "Long Tongue," and they discovered that when they cut the tongue, a repair party soon ventured out to fix it, offering the warriors yet another opportunity to kill white men.

On July 25, as many as two thousand Cheyennes, Arapahos, and Lakotas converged on Platte Bridge Station, about 120 miles above Fort Laramie, where a toll bridge spanned the North Platte

River. Near this bridge, on the river's south side, was a small trader's store and a ramshackle military post that on this day housed a little over one hundred officers and men. Leading the warrior force were such prominent chiefs and headmen as the Northern Cheyenne Roman Nose, Crazy Horse's mentor High Backbone of the Miniconjous, They Fear Even His Horses (now not so friendly toward the whites), and a rising Oglala war chief named Red Cloud, of the Bad Face band. Red Cloud was an uncle of Crazy Horse's friend He Dog.

To plunder and destroy the lightly garrisoned post seemed easily within their grasp, but the warriors dared not get in range of the fort's single mountain howitzer, so they hoped to draw the Long Knives out and across the bridge without revealing their overwhelming numbers.

About 2:00 P.M., fifteen warriors galloped back and forth along the north side of the river, yelling at the top of their lungs. Soldiers in the fort began to shoot at them, and sure enough, a small party of cavalry and infantry, thirty-two men total, raced across the bridge and gave chase. The warriors retreated slowly. After pursuing them for more than two miles, the soldiers saw forty or fifty warriors galloping up on their flanks, prompting them to immediately wheel around. Not only were they outnumbered, but they were in serious danger of being cut off from the bridge. As the Long Knives fought their way back, more and more warriors came racing out of nearby ravines, but the soldiers somehow reached the bridge safely, the cavalrymen trotting across while the infantry stationed themselves at the end of the bridge. The warriors broke off their attack without having shown anything close to their full strength.

Still determined to spill white man blood that day, the warriors spotted a herd of cattle east of the bridge being hurriedly driven to the fort for protection. Forty or so warriors splashed across the river to the south side and started for the herd. A few soldiers on foot assisting the herders began firing at the warriors, all the while feverishly prodding the cattle ahead of them. As the warriors closed in, a dozen troopers from the post joined the foot soldiers. One very brave and highly respected Northern Cheyenne leader named High Back Wolf charged into the Long Knives to count coup. He carried an old, dull sword and began striking one of the troopers in the back. When the soldier cried out for help, two of his comrades spun around and fired their carbines almost simultaneously at the chief, one ball striking the Cheyenne in the wrist and another entering his neck. High Back Wolf flipped off his horse and hit the ground hard, but he immediately jumped up and ran toward a willow thicket, where he collapsed, facedown.

The other warriors now retreated, and the two soldiers who'd shot High Back Wolf rode up to his body and dismounted. One grabbed hold of High Back Wolf's feet and dragged him away from the undergrowth and out into the open, then turned him over to get a good look at his face. Suddenly High Back Wolf sprang to life and grappled with his two startled adversaries. Even with just one useful arm, the powerful warrior put up an incredible fight, nearly exhausting the two troopers, who were unable to reach their firearms. But the blood gushing from High Back Wolf's neck quickly settled the contest. Without uttering a word, the brave Cheyenne slowly released his grasp and slumped to the ground, his dead eyes fixed open, staring at the deep blue sky overhead.

High Back Wolf had given the soldiers the fright of their lives. "We were so crazy mad at the time," one wrote later, "[we] did not think out the proper thing to do, so like a couple of fools that should have known better, scalped the Cheyenne chief, and the memory of it makes me feel ashamed to this day." The two soldiers hurriedly removed the chief's beaded shirt and other trappings and raced to catch up to their comrades with the herd. As they did so, High Back Wolf's followers advanced to retrieve his body. When they discovered that he'd been scalped, the soldiers heard "the real savage yell of a band of Indians maddened almost into blindness rage."

The following morning, as the summer sun lit up the low, yellow bluffs north of the river, a number of mounted warriors, perhaps as many as ninety, made themselves visible on the low slopes, but no more than had revealed themselves the previous day. Their companions remained hidden out of sight and hoped that the Long Knives would again venture out from the stockade. They were about to get their wish. The post's commanding officer knew that a small military wagon train of four wagons with an escort, close to thirty men total, was to arrive shortly from the west. Because of the fighting of the previous day and the Indians now in sight, he ordered a detachment of twenty-six men to ride out and meet them. Mounted on a large gray horse, Lieutenant Caspar Collins, age twenty, led the command out of the post and across the bridge.

Collins's small column kicked up dust for about a mile along the trail when warriors suddenly swarmed them from all sides. "It appeared as though they sprung up out of the ground," wrote one of Collins's men. "We were completely surrounded. Thousands came rushing and yelling from every point. . . . Our only salvation was the bridge or heaven." Collins didn't have to order retreat; all the troopers bolted for the bridge in what became a deadly gauntlet of every-man-for-himself. The lieutenant's horse, which he'd never ridden before this day, became uncontrollable and rushed into a mass of warriors. George Bent saw the lieutenant pass by in a blur. What wasn't a blur was the arrow he saw sticking from the white man's forehead.

Warriors raced alongside the terrified soldiers, swinging their war clubs and trying to pull the men from their mounts. Cavalry horses and Indian ponies bumped and jostled together. Arrows flew so thick that several struck warriors. Some soldiers reached out with their revolvers and actually pressed the muzzles to the heads and upper bodies of the warriors when firing, blowing tiny bits of flesh and bone and spatters of red blood onto the eagle feathers of Indian headdresses. A trooper described it as "one long, long, bloody lane."

The soldiers in the fort witnessed the ambush of Collins's detachment and several ran across the bridge as their comrades galloped toward them, and despite the danger of hitting their friends, they poured a heavy fire into the warriors. When the detachment finally reached safety, they had suffered only five killed. However, fifteen men had been wounded, and blood seeped from wounds on nearly every one of their horses. The warriors now did their best to decoy the soldiers away from the bridge. They led Collins's gray horse with its empty saddle along the bluff for all to see. When that didn't work, the warriors called the soldiers all kinds of vulgar names—in English.

At 11:30 A.M., the expected wagon train came into view about four miles distant, and the fort's howitzer was fired twice to warn it of the danger, but there was no escaping the hordes of warriors, who swarmed the slow-moving train like they had Collins's detachment. The soldiers at the fort heard multiple volleys and then sporadic gunfire that lasted for four hours. Shortly after the shooting stopped, plumes of black smoke boiled up into the sky—the warriors had set the wagons on fire. Only three men from the wagon train escaped with their lives.

The warriors broke up into several raiding parties the following morning and rode off in different directions. They'd counted many coups, but they'd lost more than sixty killed. When the Long Knives found the bodies of their fellow troopers, they got a pretty good idea of just how much they were not wanted there. The skulls were "cut open and brains taken out," one soldier wrote, "in one instance head cut off; heart and liver cut out; sinews taken out of their legs and arms; legs cut off; feet cut off; hands cut off; ears cut off; scalped; the bodies pierced full of barbed arrows. Of those killed at the wagons, many had hot irons run into their bodies. Others were horribly burned—equaling any barbarism ever heard or read of."

Nearly four hundred miles to the northeast, General Sully was once again leading an army into Sioux country. He intended to strike raiding Sioux bands believed to be in the area of Devil's Lake, some 125 miles northeast of Fort Rice. But he was also eager to fight or make peace with any of the Sioux he encountered along the way. The general knew the northern Sioux tribes continued to be divided on whether or not to coexist with the white man on the Upper Missouri. In June, when a large raiding party of Lakotas and Cheyennes threatened Fort Rice, seventy Yanktonai warriors under Two Bears helped the Long Knives drive them away. Sully hoped to use Sioux against Sioux on his campaign as well. He called for the enlistment of a small body of Indians to be paid the same as soldiers but with an added incentive: a $50 "reward" for every fresh Indian scalp they brought in. "I have Indians I know I can trust in this business," Sully assured his commanding officer. "I have so compromised them with their nation that it is to their interest to serve me."

On July 16, 250 hide lodges dotted the prairie around Fort Rice, many of them belonging to Two Bears's Yanktonais and Bear's Rib's Húnkpapas (this Bear's Rib was the son of the chief of the same name who was murdered for being too friendly with the whites). Across the river, hundreds of white tents belonging to Sully's army covered the plain, while inside the fort's stockade walls, Two Bears, Bear's Rib, and several other chiefs met with Sully. More than one chief noted that this was the third time Sully had come to their country with soldiers and guns, and each of the previous two times his men had killed lots of Sioux people. Was he truly earnest when he spoke of peace? Quickly tiring of all the talk, a Sihásapa chief named Fire Heart challenged Sully. "If you are a brave man," he said to the general, "why don't you begin and hang all the [Indian] agents here on this ground in presence of the Indians? It is they who get us into trouble by telling us lies."

Sully and his army of one thousand Bluecoats left Fort Rice nine days later—without killing any Indian agents. He still wanted to "make peace" with the Lakotas, Cheyennes, and Arapahos said to be hunting just east of the Good Horse Grass Country, near the Heart River. These Indian camps stretched for three miles and contained several thousand people, including Sitting Bull's band. Sully sent runners to the camps with a message: come and meet with him or he would conduct war against them. Their reply, which sounded a lot like Sitting Bull, stated they didn't care for peace with the white man and were prepared to fight, that "Gen. Sully with his 'little boys' [could] come and 'pitch in' as soon as he pleased."

Not all the leaders in the camps were as defiant as Sitting Bull, but even those inclined to make peace were suspicious of any overtures coming from Sully. Like the chiefs Sully met at Fort Rice, they had fresh memories of their previous unpeaceful encounters with the general; some suspected he was setting a trap. In fact, a rumor to that effect reached Sitting Bull at this same time. All the Sioux that'd gone to Fort Rice, so the story went, had been massacred. Sitting Bull immediately rode through the camps crying and singing and telling of the Long Knives' treacherous deed. He called for brave warriors to follow him to Fort Rice to avenge the bloody murders.

At 7:00 A.M. on July 28, 1865, approximately fifteen hundred warriors from the Heart River village crested the hills west of Fort Rice. They'd planned their approach with amazing precision so that they surrounded the fort on all sides except that on the east, which faced the Missouri River. The line of warriors curved for a good two miles, their feather headdresses and lances, painted faces, shields, and ponies creating an explosion of colors in the glow of the morning sun. Hearts beating rapidly, Húnkpapas, Oglalas, Miniconjous, Brulés, Sans Arcs, Cheyennes, and Arapahos thrilled at the magnificent sight of so many mounted warriors prepared for battle. And then they were off, quirts slapping against ponies' haunches, pouring down the hills in pell-mell bunches, the wind rushing against their faces as thousands of hooves thundered over the sod.

Because Two Bears's and Bear's Ribs's people were no longer camped at the post, the attacking warriors met no opposition as a group swept down on the herd of horses and mules grazing near the fort. The attack occurred too suddenly for the howitzers in the bastions to be brought into action at the first charge, but mounted Bluecoats quickly stormed out of the fort's gates to give battle. The warriors drew back several hundred yards in the face of the oncoming Long Knives, only to rally and charge again at different points. They did so, one soldier testified, "successively with great bravery. Indians never fought so gallantly before."

Multiple vignettes of combat played out simultaneously on the barren plains and hills in all directions, some of it hand to hand. A surgeon watching from the stockade walls described the fighting as "in the highest degree exciting." Soon the fieldpieces in the fort's parade ground were run out, their crews lobbing shells at groups of warriors in the distance. By midmorning, the Lakotas and their allies had had enough. The warriors retreated behind the hills where they were safe from the balls and shrapnel of the "gun that shoots twice."

The Bluecoats lost one killed, one mortally wounded, and

one seriously wounded, and they were convinced they'd inflicted heavy casualties upon their attackers, as they saw numerous warriors tumble from their horses, all of whom were swiftly carried away by their companions. A captain boasted, "There is many a squaw will bewail her brave killed on the 28th of July, and make night hideous with her howlings, as in the depth of her anguish she pulls her long black hair by the side of some bluff or in some deep ravine of Dakota." The warriors admitted only nine badly wounded, but they also claimed to have killed many whites.

Nine weeks later, a group of Húnkpapas seeking the good graces of Rice's commanding officer (i.e., handouts) reported that Sitting Bull and a warrior named The Man That Has His Head Shaved led the attack of July 28, but that these leaders had acted like cowards. After stealing two horses from the fort herd, the pair had skedaddled, leaving the rest of the warriors to continue the fight. The Húnkpapas claimed everyone was so angry with Sitting Bull that once back in camp, the war chief was flogged. He "only lived by the little end of his finger," they said. As additional punishment for such cowardice, the two captured horses were killed. It was a tale evidently intended to please the commanding officer and absolve them of any blame. But as the editor of the fort's newspaper observed, the Húnkpapas' "stories are very conflicting, and to be received with a grain of salt."

Back along the Oregon-California Trail, Crazy Horse and his fellow Lakotas, along with their allies, had caused considerable mayhem for the white man. In a few weeks' time, they'd destroyed so much of the Pacific Telegraph Company's line that repairs required more than sixty miles of wire and thirty-five hundred telegraph poles. They'd also made life worrisome for the miners, emigrants, and freighters brave enough to travel the Bozeman Cut-off, which left the North Platte approximately sixty miles northwest of Fort Laramie and traversed the length of Powder River country.

That summer of 1865, the U.S. Army got up yet another campaign to "punish" these tribes for what was essentially the crime of defending their territory against white invasion. Called the Powder River Indian Expedition, it consisted of three separate columns. One column was tasked with building a fort on the Bozeman Cut-off while the other two, under Colonel Nelson Cole and Lieutenant Colonel Samuel Walker, were on missions of seek and destroy to the Black Hills and Powder River. The orders to the two colonels were clear and direct: "You will not receive overtures of peace or submission from Indians, but will attack and kill every male Indian over twelve years of age."

The take-no-prisoners order was a reflection of the feelings of nearly all whites in the West, but especially those in the young settlements of Colorado and Montana (the people of Denver were elated over the carnage at Big Sandy Creek). "We deny the Indians' right to the lands," wrote the editor of Virginia City's *Montana Post*. "Robbers and murderers have no such rights, and all the red skins are born and reared for that special trade. . . . The fact is that the Indian is, practically, a wild beast with human cunning. The only sin a commander in an Indian war can commit (except being beaten) is to leave one of the accursed marauders alive, that it is in his power to kill."

Cole and Walker had little luck locating Indians of any age or gender until early September, by which time their two columns had joined forces and were on the Powder River and nearly out of rations. With no wild game to be found, their nineteen hundred men were, in fact, on the brink of starvation. So, too, were their broken-down horses and mules, which were used to being fed grain and now struggled to survive on the sparse grass along the Powder. Then, as was often the case, the Indians found the soldiers before the soldiers could find the Indians, and it would mark the first time Sitting Bull and Crazy Horse fought together in the same battle.

Four hundred warriors briefly skirmished with Cole's command on September 1, capturing a few horses and killing six soldiers. The Long Knives tried to pursue the warriors, but their horses were so used up that the warriors easily outdistanced them. For the next three days, the two commands floundered about looking for Indians, buffalo, and forage, as well as the third column under General Patrick E. Connor that was supposed to be bringing desperately needed supplies. In that time, 225 of Cole's horses and mules died from starvation, exhaustion, and shock induced from a dramatic change in the weather when a fast-moving cold front replaced the blistering heat with freezing temperatures. Cole was forced to destroy most of his wagons.

The commands of Cole and Walker maintained a separation of a few miles in marching and camping. This allowed the warriors' leaders to choose the body of troops and the terrain that offered the best advantage for an attack. They chose Cole's command, which had bivouacked on the west bank of the Powder River on the night of September 4. The following morning, as Cole's men broke camp, they spotted a large body of warriors racing to cut off some teamsters bringing in stray mules. The troopers fired a quick volley at the Indians, and a few ponies galloped away without their riders. Next, scattered groups of warriors appeared on the nearby hills, and Cole started his command after them, but as the Long Knives approached, even more warriors became visible in the surrounding ravines and gulches. Within moments, hundreds of warriors emerged from nowhere and everywhere, blanketing the hills and bluffs on all sides. And with that, the fight was on, the warriors' yips and shouts sounding above the troopers' heavy gunfire.

The large warrior force, two thousand fighters or more, was a combination of the Lakotas, Cheyennes, and Arapahos that'd been harassing Long Knives and telegraph operations on the Oregon-California Trail and those from the Heart River village that'd attacked Fort Rice. Most of the warriors fought with bows and arrows. Sitting Bull, riding a sorrel horse, carried a bow and arrow and a Northwest trade gun, and, as always, the sacred shield given to him by his father. In his hair, Sitting Bull wore two eagle feathers. A scalp dangled from his horse's bridle, which meant that the horse had ridden down an enemy.

The Long Knives were armed with rapid-firing Spencer carbines that shot a .52-caliber metallic cartridge. One soldier on the Powder River that day wrote that "the Indians are brave, but they are afraid of our Spencer carbines, which shoot 7 times without reloading." That was true when a good distance separated the foes, but the carbine could be unwieldy to fire from horseback, and at close quarters the Spencers were, according to Cole, "useless" against warriors who could nock and shoot their arrows in a blur of speed while maneuvering their ponies at a gallop. The problem for the warriors, of course, was getting close without getting dead.

Several groups of from ten to one hundred warriors took turns charging to within 250 yards of the soldier lines before abruptly turning and racing away, trying to tempt some of the troopers to pursue them. After a number of these charges, Crazy Horse wanted to try it alone. "Just keep away for a little while," he said to the warriors closest to him. "These soldiers like to shoot. I am going to give them a chance to do all the shooting they want to do. You draw back and I will make them shoot. If I fall off, then you can do something if you feel like it, but don't do anything until I have run by them."

Crazy Horse galloped into the open and straight for the Long

Knives. The Spencer carbines belched fire and smoke as the soldiers rapidly worked the lever actions of their guns, firing round after round at the Oglala, yet Crazy Horse and his pony returned to his fellow warriors unharmed. After resting his pony for a moment, Crazy Horse again galloped toward the Long Knives, this time extending his course even closer to the soldiers. Once more, the bullets flew thick around Crazy Horse but he wasn't hit. Now everyone was watching to see if Crazy Horse would taunt the soldiers with a third bravery run.

He did. Crazy Horse dashed closer still to the Bluecoats, but, curiously, the soldiers stopped shooting at him and let the warrior gallop by. No one knows why they stopped firing, but perhaps the white men were in awe of the daring Oglala. It was astonishing deeds such as this that reinforced the belief among the Lakotas that Horn Chips's war medicine was incredibly powerful, that Crazy Horse couldn't be killed by a bullet. Sitting Bull may or may not have witnessed Crazy Horse's heroics, but the war chief did not attempt any such dangerous feats himself. Those were for young men thirsty for coups.

From a high hill, war chiefs signaled instructions to their warriors using mirrors and a red flag, and it was apparently through these signals that they alerted their men to a detachment of Bluecoats that'd advanced beyond their lines and crossed to the east side of the Powder. Suddenly hundreds of warriors raced forward to attack. The Bluecoats panicked and whipped their horses around, wildly kicking the poor animals' flanks. But the worn-out cavalry mounts couldn't outrun the Indian ponies. The Húnkpapa warriors Bull Head, Stand Looking Back, and Bull Eagle were among those who overtook the retreating Bluecoats as they splashed into the river. Bull Head and Stand Looking Back each knocked a trooper off his horse, and Bull Eagle counted coup. The entire detachment might have fallen to the swinging war clubs and axes of the warriors had not an alert officer ordered his men forward to drive them off with well-timed volleys from the Spencers. As it was, two troopers were killed and two wounded.

About this time, Colonel Cole noticed the flashing signals coming from the Indians on the hill, and he directed his artillerymen to send the bunch a loud greeting with the three-inch ordnance rifles. The screaming shells from the two cannons didn't kill any Indians, but they did clear the hill, as well as the surrounding terrain within the range of the guns. Having thus toyed with the Long Knives for more than three hours, the warriors withdrew. Cole claimed his men killed scores of warriors in the fight, even though not a single body had been left behind for him to count— army officers unfailingly overestimated enemy casualties. Probably only a handful of warriors were killed and wounded.

Three days later, an even larger force of warriors skirmished with the commands of Cole and Walker. "The whole bottom and hills in advance were covered full of Indians," an officer jotted in his diary, "they were thicker than fiddlers in hell." But the warriors weren't nearly as willing to get close to the Long Knives this time, and not one trooper fell to their arrows. That night, however, as the Lakotas, Cheyennes, and Arapahos slept safely and comfortably in their hide lodges, another storm front, much more violent than the previous, darkened the Powder River Valley. It began with heavy rain, followed by hail, then rain again, and finally alternating bands of sleet and snow. The camp of the Bluecoats was in the open, with no natural barrier to lessen the storm's fury. When the wind and snow ended thirty-six hours later, 414 horses and mules lay dead. Now, as the ragged command limped along looking for General Connor, groups of warriors followed in the distance, just out of gun range, biding their time like vultures circling some beast in its death struggles.

But the warriors would be denied the satisfaction of delivering the coup de grâce to the Long Knives, who'd been reduced to eating mule and horse flesh to stay alive. On September 13, couriers from General Connor reached Cole and Walker's command. Connor had established a fort a few weeks earlier, they said, and it was just upriver, near a crossing of the Bozeman Cut-off. The famished troopers arrived there safely a week later, most of them in bare feet.

The Powder River Indian Expedition had come to an end without accomplishing much except stirring up the Lakotas and their allies. General Connor's column had attacked and destroyed an Arapaho village on the Tongue River, home to five hundred people, and captured six hundred of their ponies. Much more disturbing, though, was the new fort he'd built in the heart of Powder River country. Named Fort Connor (later changed to Fort Reno), its sole purpose was to protect travelers on the Bozeman Cut-off. To the Lakotas, it meant more whites were coming.

For the Plains Indians, the winter season, the months of November to March, was the time to harvest buffalo robes intended for trade. A buffalo's coat was at its woolliest then, but only the robes of cows and calves would do, at least for trade in the eastern markets. A bull's hide was too thick and heavy and was best used for such things as warrior shields and soles for moccasins. The preference for lighter, more pliable robes, then, placed an emphasis on harvesting breeding females and potential breeding females, of which tens of thousands were killed annually on the northern and southern plains. Both Indians and whites clearly saw the effects on the herds—the Lakotas never failed to complain of the scarcity of the buffalo in their conferences with agents and military officers—but the traders' goods were always calling. For just a few cups of sugar, a trader acquired a luxurious, fully tanned robe that he then sold for about fifteen dollars to a fur dealer in St. Louis or New York.

But the buffalo herds enjoyed a slight reprieve during the winter of 1865 to 1866. Storm after storm piled snow on the northern plains deeper than anyone had seen in years, and bitterly cold temperatures lasted for weeks. Their people suffering, several Lakota chiefs were now willing to discuss peace with the commanding officer at Fort Laramie, at least long enough to talk him out of some provisions. Even the war chief Red Cloud, who'd emerged as the most powerful leader of the Oglalas, more so than the hereditary chief They Fear Even His Horses, appeared at Fort Laramie with many of his followers.

The forty-five-year-old Red Cloud stood six feet tall and weighed about two hundred pounds, most of it muscle. One contemporary described him as "a magnificent specimen of manhood." He had a broad face and dark, penetrating eyes, and when he arrived at the fort, he wore an elaborate eagle feather headdress, its trailer reaching to the ground behind him. This great warrior had counted numerous coups.

Red Cloud and other chiefs met with Colonel Henry Maynadier at Fort Laramie in March 1866 and again in June, with treaty commissioners participating in the June council. Before each meeting, Red Cloud carefully filled his pipe, lighted the tobacco in the bowl, and shared the pipe with all those in the council room. "He that smokes this pipe," Red Cloud announced, "never tells lies." And, indeed, many hard truths came out. Maynadier informed the gathered leaders that the Great Father could not prevent the whites from traveling the roads through their country and killing off their game. "The white men will come here," he said, "so long as anything is to be gained by it." Once a treaty was agreed upon, however, the Great Father would make it right by paying for the "damages" caused by the white men. The country was plenty large enough, Maynadier asserted, to hold both whites and Indians without war.

"My tribe want peace," one Lakota chief volunteered, "but as for myself, I prefer war." Red Cloud initially wanted peace, but not if it meant allowing the white man to travel through the Powder River country. He became angry at how the commissioners treated him and his fellow leaders as if they were children. The whites had never acted in good faith with the Indians, he told them. Each year, they crowded the Lakotas back, but no more. The white man must stay out of the Powder River country. If they didn't, the Lakotas and their allies would come together to fight them. It might be a long and painful war, he said, but he would rather die fighting than from starvation.

The June discussions stretched over several days, and during that time a column of Bluecoats, approximately eight hundred men of the Eighteenth U.S. Infantry and three hundred wagons, arrived at Fort Laramie. But Fort Laramie was not the end of their journey. Their actual destination lay in the Powder River country, where they were tasked with establishing two new forts on the Bozeman Cut-off. With the Civil War ended, the migration to the Montana goldfields that summer was expected to be much greater than in previous years, and the U.S. government was determined to protect its citizens. When the chiefs learned the purpose of the recently arrived column, however, one stood before the council and offered another truth: "Great Father sends us presents and wants new road, but white chief goes with soldiers to *steal* road before Indian say yes or no!"

Red Cloud would have voiced his approval for those strong words—had he been present. But he and his warriors had already abandoned the treaty talks and ridden north, and they wasted no time making good on his warning. In isolated surprise attacks, his Bad Faces and other Oglalas preyed upon the weak, vulnerable, and often foolish emigrants and soldiers traveling the Bozeman Cut-off. They killed when they could, gathered booty and fresh scalps, and then vanished into the surrounding hills, as ephemeral as prairie dust devils.

Soon other Lakotas, as well as Cheyennes and Arapahos, joined Red Cloud's followers, and the number of whites who paid with their lives for trespassing on Indian land soared. One newspaper reported in September that the "road from Laramie to Powder River is filled with graves of murdered men." And regardless of how large the size of a wagon train, no one was safe from attack. A train of 256 wagons was reported to have daily battled with Red Cloud's warriors all the way from Fort Laramie to Fort Reno, a distance of more than two hundred miles. The warriors killed twenty-two men from the train and made off with a good portion of their livestock.

Neither were the new forts immune, especially as the warriors far outnumbered the small garrisons. A favorite for harassment was the new post rapidly going up near Piney Creek. Day and night, the warriors probed for any little weakness or a Bluecoat or two letting their guard down, if only for a split second. One day, warriors brazenly slipped up on three men within thirty yards of the fort's gates and shot them. The Indian threat was so bad and terrifying that the post's stockade walls became, from the viewpoint of an officer's wife, more like prison walls. The name given to this beleaguered post was Fort Phil Kearny.

At the same time Red Cloud waged war along the Bozeman Cut-off, Sitting Bull's Húnkpapas and other antitreaty Sioux assailed river traffic on the Upper Missouri, firing from the riverbanks on passing steamboats and Mackinaws. Sometimes they got lucky and killed a white man or two. Even the traders with whom

Sitting Bull occasionally conducted business suffered stolen live-stock and outright attacks.

During one of Sitting Bull's peaceful visit's to the Fort Union trading post, the trader told the war chief that he wished to be considered a friend, but it was always difficult to tell whether Sitting Bull came to trade or to fight. He then presented the Húnk-papa with a bright red shirt and asked him to wear it when he came to the post to make war so he would know the chief's intentions. If this was a joke by the trader, it didn't go over well. Sitting Bull coolly responded that "right now would be a good time to put it on," which he did.

Having finished their trading, the Húnkpapas mounted their ponies and rode off. A short distance from the post, however, the group stopped and turned back to face it. Leveling their Northwest guns, the warriors fired a volley at the post. The lead balls peppered the stockade, sending wood splinters flying. Sitting Bull and his men then calmly continued on their way. The trader now decided he didn't need the Húnkpapa chief's business that bad after all, and he sent word to nearby Fort Buford that if an Indian appeared wearing a red shirt, they should shoot him.

Beginning in the summer of 1866, Fort Buford became the main focus of Sitting Bull's wrath. Located opposite the mouth of the Yellowstone River, and just two miles from the Fort Union trading post, Fort Buford placed an army garrison in the heart of the northern Lakotas' territory. "This country is the finest in the world for buffalo and large game," wrote a Buford soldier. "One can get up most any morning and see the prairie covered with them. I have been out on several buffalo hunts and have killed a great many." And that was exactly why Sitting Bull didn't want more white men there. He vowed to kill every last man of the garrison.

On an almost daily basis, Lakota warriors harassed the fort.

When warriors weren't attacking the woodcutters securing timber for the post's construction, they were trying to stampede the fort's beef herd. When they weren't taking long-range potshots at the Bluecoats, they were taunting them. The simple task of hauling water from the river to the post, a distance of a few hundred yards, became so dangerous that a party of miners wintering at the fort dug a well inside the stockade.

Because of the fort's two twelve-pounder howitzers in corner blockhouses, Sitting Bull's vow to wipe out the garrison was fairly unrealistic. And still, even with his past bad experiences with the gun that shoots twice, the war chief wasn't afraid to test them. In December, he and his warriors twice overran the post's sawmill, which was situated near the river and about five hundred yards from the fort's walls. The second time the Lakotas took possession of the mill, the soldiers heard an odd sound coming from inside. It was like someone ringing a dinner bell. Next they saw a few warriors outside the building dancing to the rhythmic clanging. The soldiers soon realized that someone inside the mill was banging a metal tool against the mill's saw blade.

The dancing warriors seemed to believe the Bluecoats wouldn't risk damaging the mill with a shell from the howitzers, but they were mistaken. A round of spherical case shot exploded overhead, abruptly ending the dance and killing two warriors. An infantry charge followed, and Sitting Bull and his men fled to the cover of the riverbank. As arrows and bullets flew back and forth, the warriors set fire to cords of firewood stacked near the river and then retreated upstream.

Sitting Bull would never again be so bold in attacking Fort Buford, but the harassment continued, with parties of warriors always lurking nearby, just waiting for an opportunity to pounce and relieve a Bluecoat or white civilian of his scalp.

Some 250 miles southwest of Fort Buford, at a village on the Tongue River, the Miniconjou chief White Swan was dying. A beloved hereditary chief in his midfifties, White Swan had a parting message for his people. Try to kill as many white men as you can, he said, because the white men are trying to kill you. Of course, many Lakotas already shared the chief's thinking on the whites, but White Swan's dying words incited the warriors even more as they focused their attentions on the garrison at Fort Phil Kearny.

On December 20, 1866, nearly two thousand warriors—Oglala, Miniconjou, Brulé, Two Kettle, Húnkpapa, Northern Cheyenne, and Arapaho—gathered on a broad plain about ten miles north of the fort. To the west loomed the snow-clad Big Horn Mountains, home to the headwaters of the storied Greasy Grass (Little Big Horn), Powder, and Tongue Rivers. Mounted on their ponies, carrying their weapons (mostly bows), shields, and war medicine, the warriors formed a long, curved line. From that line a lone horseman rode out in full view. The horseman wore a woman's dress, and by all appearances was a woman. But this individual was actually a man.

The Lakotas called such men *winktes*. Not only did *winktes* dress, act, and look like women, but they did the work of women, such as cooking and tanning robes. *Winktes* existed because *Wakan Tanka* wished it so, and they were accepted by their fellow Lakotas for what they were. But because *Wakan Tanka* had brought undue hardships upon these individuals by making them different, he gave *winktes* a gift of great power, usually that of prophecy.

It was for this power of prophecy that the *winkte* was called upon this day. The several chiefs planned to spring a great trap on the Long Knives of Fort Phil Kearny the following morning, and they wished to know what kind of success they could expect. The *winkte* began by blowing a bone whistle and riding his pony about in great zigzags. All the while, he turned his head from side to side, peering into the distance, looking for something: the specters of Long Knives. The warriors watched, mesmerized.

Soon the *winkte* rode up to the chiefs and held out two clenched fists.

"I have ten [white] men, five in each hand; do you want them?"

"No, we do not wish them," a chief answered. "Look at all the people here. Do you think ten men are enough to go around?"

The *winkte* rode off, going through the same ritual and then returning to the chiefs, again holding out his clenched fists.

"I have ten men in each hand, twenty in all. Do you wish them?"

"No," said the same chief, "I do not wish them; there are too many people here and too few enemies."

The *winkte* looked hard for ethereal Bluecoats a third time, leaning far forward in his saddle as he galloped his pony back and forth. When he rode up to the chiefs, he shouted, "I have twenty in one hand and thirty in the other."

"No! There are too many people here. It is not worthwhile to go on for so small a number."

Now came a fourth effort by the *winkte*—the sacred number four—and the chiefs and warriors waited anxiously as the *winkte* approached when suddenly he jumped from his pony and fell to the ground, striking the earth with both fists.

"Answer quickly," he shouted, "I have a hundred or more!"

A roar erupted from the warriors, several of whom clustered around the *winkte*, striking the ground near his hands so as to count coup on the future dead.

That night in camp, the chiefs finalized their plan of attack. Among those gathered around the lodge fire was High Backbone

(Crazy Horse's friend and mentor and now a war chief of the Miniconjous), Red Cloud, They Fear Even His Horses, and several others. These leaders chose ten warriors to serve as decoys to lure as many soldiers as they could over Lodge Trail Ridge, north of the fort, where they would be surrounded and slaughtered like the *winkte* foretold. The decoys, led by Crazy Horse, left in the early-morning darkness to take their positions while the soldiers in the fort slept.

This is how Crazy Horse found himself on Piney Creek, opposite Fort Phil Kearny, on the morning of December 21, 1866, as eighty-one Bluecoats—infantry, cavalry, and a few thrill seekers—crossed the Piney and headed straight for him and his fellow decoys.

The distance from the creek to the top of Lodge Trail Ridge was well over a mile, and because the infantry necessarily slowed the military column's advance, Crazy Horse and the other decoys were forced to give a prolonged and highly convincing performance. One or two warriors at a time got off their ponies and led them, implying their mounts were worn out, and they made several brief halts, as if giving their ponies needed time to rest, thus allowing the Long Knives to keep up. These halts were perilous for the decoys and required incredible nerve. An occasional buzzing bullet from a troopers' carbine sounded so close that it seemed they should be able to glimpse it in flight. Some decoys sang to *Wakan Tanka*, asking him to have mercy on them and vowing to take part in a Sun Dance if they survived.

If it had been a clear day, the sun would have been visible near its highest point in the sky. Instead, the lack of sunlight and absence of hard shadows made the land look bleak and colorless. The warriors hidden on the other side of Lodge Trail Ridge had been waiting for more than an hour when a single shot echoed in the distance. The decoys were coming. After coaxing the soldiers over the crest of the ridge, Crazy Horse and the others continued down the north side and onto a long, high spur, its grassy crest cut with ruts from heavy wagons: the hated Bozeman Cut-off. The gullies and depressions on each side of this spur held hundreds of warriors, who listened intently from their hiding places. Many a warrior clamped a hand over his pony's nostrils to prevent it from whinnying to the soldier horses. More shots rang out, now much closer, then the sound of a bugle, followed by the trampling of horses' hooves on the white man's road.

Eager to overtake the decoys before they could escape, the mounted troops, riding four abreast, had left the fifty-man infantry detail plodding along behind until approximately a mile separated the two detachments. Nevertheless, Crazy Horse and the decoys had successfully delivered all the Bluecoats beyond Lodge Trail Ridge, well within the jaws of the trap and out of view of the garrison at the fort. Suddenly the decoys split into two groups, half riding east, the other half west, then wheeling around and coming together again until they crossed each other on the road. It was a signal to the hidden warrior forces to rise up and smash the Long Knives between them. Shouting and yipping, the warriors rushed forward to attack the cavalry detachment.

Never had these white men seen so many Indians. Disbelief, nausea, and terror flooded over the Long Knives all at once as they realized the next few moments would likely be their last in this world. The mounted detachment numbered just twenty-eight men, plus two civilians who surely regretted their decision to tag along. The cavalrymen carried Spencer repeaters and sixty to seventy cartridges each. The two civilians were armed with prized lever-action Henry rifles. The Henry could fire sixteen times before reloading, but its smaller caliber, .44, didn't have the same punch as a Spencer. Still, the rapid fire of the repeating arms kept the swirling warriors at bay—for a time.

The foot soldiers, carrying heavy Springfield muskets, were exhausted after the long march to the top of Lodge Trail Ridge, but their commander urged them forward. The eruption of shots from the rapid-fire weapons of the cavalry told him the troopers were in some kind of scrape, but they were much farther down the wagon road and out of his line of sight. His confusion as to what was happening ahead disappeared, however, when waves of screaming warriors rolled up and enveloped him and his men. The infantrymen's muzzleloading muskets were no match for the thousands of arrows the warriors loosed from both sides of the hill. The arrows flew so thick, in fact, that it seemed as if a swarm of locusts had descended from the heavens. And more than a few of these arrows struck unintentional targets. "Indians killed each other as well as the soldiers," remembered Fire Thunder, an Oglala. "I saw them shot through the arms and legs."

As foot soldiers dropped right and left, those remaining alive attempted to take shelter behind a cluster of large, flat rocks. These men didn't last long, either. Two officers, one the overall commander of the column, were among those keeping up a steady fire as the warriors closed in. That is, until the commander's companion suddenly raised his revolver and blew his own brains out. Next, American Horse, a Bad Face warrior, charged his pony into the officer, knocking him down. American Horse, knife in hand, jumped to the ground and grabbed the officer's hair, pulled his head back, and viciously cut deep into the man's neck, the knife's blade reaching the cervical spine.

The cavalry detachment retreated steadily up the wagon road, firing their Spencers as they went. Some troopers were on foot, leading their horses—a man could be more accurate shooting from the ground than from the back of a moving horse, and he was also slightly less exposed to the arrows zipping through the air. Warriors made bravery runs around and through the Long

Knives. Crazy Horse, riding a fleet bald-faced bay with white stockings borrowed from his half brother, Little Hawk, was among the most conspicuous. The daring Oglala, an old Lakota recalled, "really was flirting with death." A bravery run by another warrior came to a sudden end when he rode too close to an officer and received a blow from the cavalryman's saber, which separated the warrior's head from his body with near surgical precision. Within moments, however, several arrows toppled the officer from his saddle.

The troopers pushed ahead—or were driven—toward Lodge Trail Ridge, the barrels of their Spencers now hot enough to burn flesh. The men looked frantically to the ridge's crest for a rescue column from the fort, but they saw nothing, and they made their own stand not far from the bunched bodies of the dead infantrymen. In a desperate effort to buy time, the troopers turned their horses loose, hoping the warriors would chase after them. But as Fire Thunder recalled, "I wasn't after horses—I was after white men."

A Lakota chief instructed the warriors to get off their ponies and crawl up on the troopers. As they slowly advanced on the prone Long Knives, a warrior would occasionally rise up on his feet as if he were about to charge, which would prompt a soldier to sit up and try a shot. Other warriors were waiting for this moment, however, and sent several arrows thumping into the soldier's body. Soon the warriors were close enough to hear the heavy breathing of the last, desperate white men.

"Let's go, this is a good day to die!" a warrior shouted. "At home our women are hungry!" At this, the warriors jumped up yelling *"Hóka hé!"* and ran in among the troopers, swinging war clubs and axes. Fire Thunder killed three white men with a revolver. The bugler, apparently out of ammunition, smashed his bugle on the heads of several warriors before he was finally killed.

The entire affair, remembered the Húnkpapa Rain in the Face, lasted "a shorter time than it takes to annihilate a small herd of buffalo."

As the smoke cleared and the warriors began to scalp, strip, and mutilate the Bluecoats, a dog appeared. One of the soldier's pets, it was visibly agitated, running about, and continuously barking. "All are dead but the dog," a warrior said, "let him carry the news to the fort." But another disagreed. "No, do not let even a dog get away."

The dog suddenly yelped and tumbled over, a single arrow protruding from its side.

# Too Many Tongues

*There are a number of chiefs who, I believe, would make*
*peace, but the young men won't let them. In place of chiefs*
*controlling the young men, the young men control them.*

INTERPRETER MITCH BOYER, MIXED-
BLOOD SANTEE, JULY 27, 1867

Women, children, and elders waited anxiously in the Indian
camps on the Tongue River for the return of their warriors from
the white man's fort near Piney Creek. They became even more
worried when a blizzard blew in that evening, the flying snow
obliterating everything more than a few feet away. Finally, late
that night, the village dogs started barking, and groups of snow-
dusted warriors began emerging from the darkness.

Crazy Horse was among the last to arrive back at the camps.
At some point on the homeward journey, he discovered that Lone
Bear, his friend from childhood, was unaccounted for. Crazy
Horse and High Backbone rushed back to the battlefield and
searched for Lone Bear until they found him, badly wounded and
half frozen. The warrior was beyond saving, causing High Backbone to break out in tears, but they did what they could to warm

Lone Bear and otherwise make him comfortable. Lone Bear died in Crazy Horse's arms.

Because of the several tribes involved in the Hundred in the Hand, no one could provide an exact count of all the dead and wounded, but it was believed the Bluecoats had killed at least eight on the battlefield, including two Oglala chiefs and a Northern Cheyenne chief, and seriously wounded fifty. Nearly half the wounded died from their injuries, many of them on the torturous return to their camps. They also lost more than sixty ponies to the soldiers' bullets. The Indian casualties could have easily been much higher, but according to one warrior, the panicked Bluecoats fired their guns wildly at the end.

Rejuvenated by their warm lodges and hearty meals prepared by wives and mothers, the warriors told and retold their individual coups, sang their "kill songs," and otherwise reveled in the great victory. The fight had seen the Plains tribes' decoy-ambush tactic work to near perfection. Never had they killed so many Long Knives all at once. Never had they taken so many scalps. Never had they acquired so many soldier guns and ammunition. And never had so many coups been counted on white men. As for Crazy Horse, his renown as one of the bravest and most fearsome Lakota warriors alive was now firmly established.

Had the warriors known a thing or two about some of the white men they'd "given ears," their satisfaction would've been much the sweeter. The commander of the military column that fell into their trap was Captain William J. Fetterman, a thirty-three-year-old Civil War veteran and scion of a military family. Fetterman found the weather "delightful" at Fort Phil Kearny, and marveled at the game-rich country. But he held deep contempt for the Indians and didn't hesitate to say so. The captain offered that a single company of regulars could easily defeat a thousand warriors, and "no command of good soldiers if handled well could be whipped by ragamuffins of Indians."

Thirty-five-year-old Captain Frederick H. Brown, a hardened veteran of several battles and skirmishes during Sherman's Atlanta campaign, wasn't even supposed to be with Fetterman that day. He'd been transferred to Fort Laramie but delayed starting in the hopes of taking at least one Indian scalp first, preferably Red Cloud's. And unbeknownst to the post's commanding officer, Brown had joined Fetterman's column as a volunteer, armed to the teeth. Brown had said he would always keep a last bullet for himself, and that he did, committing suicide while fighting near Fetterman. His weapons and clothing now belonged to some very happy warrior.

Most of the enlisted men in the different companies had begged their sergeants to choose them to be part of Fetterman's command, calling out, "Let me go." Like Captain Brown, they relished the chance to kill an Indian—any Indian—little imagining the objects of their desire might kill them. Fetterman and his men needed a *winkte* of their own to tell them that if they crossed Lodge Trail Ridge, they would all die on the white man's road and be counted among the Hundred in the Hand.

Weeks passed. Snows became rains. All the while, Lakota men fanned out over the Powder River country and the Upper Missouri, hunting game and enemies. By the light of their lodge fires, they painted their coups in white man ledgerbooks captured from Bluecoats and traders. Women tanned hides and made clothing and footwear as they'd always done. Mothers patiently taught daughters the art of beading and quillwork. Elders mentored boys in the ways of a Lakota warrior, and holy men guided young men in their vision quests.

Leaders such as Sitting Bull and now Crazy Horse prayed to *Wakan Tanka* for protection from enemies, an abundance of buffalo, and wisdom in navigating the uncertainty of the future. In the different tribal camps, chiefs and warrior societies smoked together and delved into deep discussions about the white man threat. Long angered by the concessions, both real and imagined, that chiefs friendly with the whites made on behalf of all Lakotas, many felt the time had come for the antitreaty factions to unite, if possible, under one supreme chief. Granting such status and power to one man went against the Lakotas' preferred political structure of collective leadership, but these were extraordinary times in need of extraordinary measures.

In late June 1867, during the Moon of the Wild Turnip, a great gathering of northern plains tribes occurred deep in the heart of Sioux country. The several camp circles included Húnkpapas, Miniconjous, Oglalas, Sihásapas, Sans Arcs, Yanktonais, and Northern Cheyennes and Arapahos. A Sun Dance was undoubtedly part of this gathering, but one day a massive crowd from the different tribes collected under shade shelters to observe a singular ceremony. Villagers of all ages watched in silence as the four Húnkpapa Shirt Wearer chiefs emerged carrying Sitting Bull on a buffalo robe. Carrying an individual in this way, by human hands, was an act of high tribute to that person. Four Horns, one of the Shirt Wearers, announced that his nephew had been chosen supreme chief over the entire Sioux Nation. Turning to Sitting Bull, he said, "When you tell us to fight, we will raise up our weapons; and if you tell us to make peace, we will lay down our weapons."

Four Horns and the other Shirt Wearers presented Sitting Bull with a white horse, a Northwest trade gun, ten arrows, a bow, and a spectacular bonnet bristling with dozens of eagle feathers. Each feather came from a warrior who'd earned it with a coup. From this moment on, when Sitting Bull wasn't wearing a trailered bonnet, he wore a single eagle feather straight up on his head, signifying he was chief over all other chiefs.

Also recognized before the crowd were the twenty-six-year-old Húnkpapa warrior Gall and Crazy Horse. Gall was named a war chief of the Húnkpapas and Crazy Horse a war chief of the Oglalas and also the Northern Cheyennes and Arapahos. Crazy Horse had fought side by side with the Cheyennes and Arapahos in several fights, most memorably in the Hundred in the Hand, and although these allies had their own war chiefs, they would gladly follow Crazy Horse in battle—a brave, successful leader with many coups always attracted followers, regardless of tribal affiliation. And these northern tribes gathered together shared the same goal of defending their territory against the white man.

Incredibly, a white man was in the tribes' very midst during this time, one whose presence was actually welcomed. But this individual was not just any white man; he was a "Black Gown." Father Jean-Baptiste Marie Genin was a French-born priest of the Missionary Oblates of Mary Immaculate. Twenty-seven years old that summer, he wore his hair long and sported a flowing blondish beard that complemented his unusually fair complexion. It was his twinkling eyes and warm smile, however, that most caught the attention of those who met him. Based out of a modest log cabin mission he'd established on the Red River, Genin described his parish as stretching from that stream's muddy banks all the way to the Rocky Mountains.

The Lakotas had only come to know Father Genin within the last year, but they seemed to have taken an immediate liking to him. Black Gowns such as Genin certainly benefited from the goodwill spread earlier among the various western tribes by the beloved Jesuit Father De Smet. But priests were also seen as spiritual leaders with special powers much like the Lakotas' own holy men. Another name for a Black Gown was "the man who talks to the medicine-chief in the sun," and the sun was *wakan*, sacred. The Catholic religious rituals observed and participated in by many Lakotas, from baptisms to last rites, as well as the priests' rosary beads, silver crucifixes, and black robes, all signified a deeply devout and mystical human being. But perhaps more than that, the various tribes saw in Genin a kind and comforting man genuinely concerned for their well-being, both physically and spiritually. Genin would, in fact, eventually learn to speak the Lakota language.

Sitting Bull's admiration for Genin was so great that he adopted the priest as his brother during this gathering of northern tribes; Chief Black Moon adopted him as a nephew. And the feelings were mutual; Genin never ceased to defend Sitting Bull before the white public. Genin would later claim that because of his influence, the new supreme chief of the Sioux forbade the consumption of "firewater" (alcohol) by his people. However, Genin wasn't expecting the severe penalty Sitting Bull decided upon for violating his decree: death. Sitting Bull also ordered the death penalty for any Lakota who bought or acquired alcohol and refused to reveal the contraband's supplier. There are no known instances when Sitting Bull enforced these new rules, but the threat was there.

A name oddly absent from the accounts of Sitting Bull's ascendancy is Red Cloud. The Oglala war chief had become the face of the Indian resistance in the Powder River country, at least to white Americans. And, not unlike Sitting Bull, Red Cloud was an ambitious and proud man—he'd apparently antagonized some Lakotas by claiming more than his share of the credit for the Hundred in the Hand victory. The Oglala war chief would have welcomed the title of supreme chief if offered, but he also well knew that just because these northern Lakotas had bestowed this rank on Sitting Bull, he wasn't obliged to acknowledge it or obey any of Sitting Bull's commands. According to Sitting Bull's great-grandson, both Red Cloud and Spotted Tail of the Brulés refused to recognize Sitting Bull as their chief.

Yet Sitting Bull's election as "chief of the Sioux nation" demonstrated the Húnkpapa's powerful influence with the antitreaty faction. And influence was far more important than a title. "A chief's authority depended on his wisdom and ability to carry out his wishes," explained a Lakota named Bad Bear. "If he was wise and the people found that his advice was good, then they obeyed him. Or if he was strong, and had many friends who would help him, then all obeyed him."

Red Cloud remained a central Lakota leader, but at the June gathering, Sitting Bull acquired a vital friend and ally in the war against the whites, a celebrated Oglala warrior and now war chief who'd chosen to be present to witness Sitting Bull's coronation. This man was Crazy Horse. The great warrior would continue to join forces with Red Cloud and any other native leader who shared his goal of driving the Long Knives from the Great Plains, but Crazy Horse's future was now inextricably linked with Sitting Bull's. And when Sitting Bull told Crazy Horse it was time to fight, he would fight.


The summer of 1867 saw Lakota warriors earn more eagle feathers along the Bozeman—mail carriers murdered here, a handful of Bluecoats there, wagon trains attacked and stock driven off. The mules, horses, oxen, and beef cattle killed or captured by the Lakotas that summer numbered in the hundreds. Many soldiers at the Bozeman forts suffered from scurvy because of a lack of provisions, particularly the fresh beef the Lakotas and their allies were so adept at stealing. And no private freighters with Montana-bound goods dared travel the Bozeman Cut-off. It was simply too dangerous. Traffic now consisted solely of government columns and the trains of military contractors. The "Indians own, hold, possess, and occupy the [Powder River] country," observed one military contractor, "the white men the Forts."

In late July, following Sun Dances held at a large village near Rosebud Creek by the Northern Cheyennes and the Lakotas, the war leaders of the several antitreaty tribes had a decision to make. With hundreds of warriors at their disposal, they wished to make an all-out attack on one of the Long Knife forts on the Bozeman, and they'd narrowed the choice down to two: Phil Kearny near Piney Creek or C. F. Smith on the Big Horn River. But as sometimes happened, the chiefs couldn't reach a consensus, so most of the Cheyennes and a few Lakotas and Northern Arapahos headed west for the Big Horn, while most of the Lakotas with some Cheyennes rode south for Fort Phil Kearny.

Early on the morning of August 2, at least six hundred warriors, perhaps as many as a thousand, crested Lodge Trail Ridge, not far from the battleground of the Hundred in the Hand. It was the memory of their great victory here over the Long Knives less than eight months earlier, with its great plunder of scalps, weapons, and uniforms, that had influenced their decision to strike again. Maybe these Bluecoats would act as stupidly as had their brothers last winter.

The Lakota contingent, made up of Oglalas, Miniconjous, and Sans Arcs, was led by Crazy Horse, High Backbone, and Thunder Hawk. About fifty Northern Cheyennes rode under a chief named Ice, but the Cheyenne chief and his men had attached themselves to the great Crazy Horse, and they would fight alongside him and his followers. Red Cloud was along, too, but, curiously, he did not have a role in directing this affair. The warriors would not attack the fort itself with its artillery; no warrior was willing to test his war medicine against the gun that shoots twice. Instead, their target was the weakly guarded operations of the civilian woodcutters contracted to supply firewood for Fort Phil Kearny.

Working some five miles west of the fort, the woodcutters had made a large oval corral for their livestock by placing fourteen large wagon beds on the ground, end to end (the running gears were being used for hauling logs). Several tents were pitched on one side of the corral for the woodcutters and their military guards, and the whole was surrounded by a broad, grassy plain. A side camp was situated about a mile to the southwest, in the timber near the foot of the mountains. A military detachment of fifty-one men and two officers, all members of the Twenty-Seventh U.S. Infantry, was divided between these two camps and escort duty for the wood trains going to and from the fort.

Mules grazed contentedly this quiet morning a few hundred yards from the wagon box corral, some herders keeping them from straying too far apart, and woodsmoke curled upward from several breakfast cook fires in both camps. About 9:00 A.M., a single rifle shot rang out, fired by one of the soldier sentries, and where it once seemed there were no Indians for miles, they now seemed to be everywhere. Bodies painted white, green, and yellow, singing their brave songs, they scared the hell out of the soldiers and woodcutters. "Look at the Indians!" one soldier gasped. "My God! There are thousands of them."

Crazy Horse, leading at least half the warrior force, charged into the side camp. Sitting Bull's eighteen-year-old nephew, the Miniconjou White Bull, proudly rode with this party. They easily overran the camp as four woodcutters and their four-man guard scattered. The warriors killed and scalped three soldiers, then set about plundering the tents and setting fire to the wood piled on the running gears. White Bull jumped down from his pony and sampled some molasses and hardtack sitting next to one of the fires where the woodcutters had been enjoying breakfast moments before. But the time Crazy Horse's warriors spent ransacking the side camp allowed the Bluecoats at the corral precious minutes to prepare for the onslaught they knew was coming.

White Bull remounted and hurried to catch up with Crazy

Horse and the others, who were riding hard across the plain toward the wagon box corral, now under attack. The mule herd was long gone, having been driven off by warriors at the start, its herders fleeing to the hills. Soon several hundred Indians galloped around the corral, the staccato popping of gunshots mixing with the sound of thundering hooves. As the warriors tightened the circle, they grabbed their ponies' manes with one hand and dropped to the side opposite the gunfire, clinging to the animals with their legs. A bow and arrow couldn't be used from this position, but a firearm, particularly a handgun, could.

Within the wagon boxes, thirty-two white men, including six civilians, did their best to get a bead on the moving targets while ducking arrows and wood splinters from Indian bullets striking the wagon panels, which were no more than an inch thick. White Bull arrived to see a group of mounted warriors charge close to the corral. Gunfire and black powder smoke erupted from the wagon boxes, and White Bull saw his friend, Hairy Hand, knocked from his horse about a hundred yards from the corral.

White Bull watched anxiously for Hairy Hand to get up, but the warrior remained motionless on the ground. Even if Hairy Hand was dead, White Bull was not about to leave him there. The young Miniconjou got down from his pony and ran as fast as he could to Hairy Hand's side. Blood oozed from a wound in his friend's right breast and also from his nose and mouth, but he was breathing. As bullets kicked up rocks and dust around them, White Bull lifted Hairy Hand up and dragged him to a low area out of sight of the soldiers. The wound, it turned out, wasn't fatal. White Bull had saved his friend's life.

Crazy Horse and the other leaders quickly realized that these Bluecoats were taking no time at all to reload their weapons; the gunfire simply didn't let up. And none of the soldiers were seen using ramrods like they would if they were armed with muzzleloaders. The slow-loading muskets of the Long Knives at the Hundred in the Hand had given the Indians a decided advantage. But that was far from the case this day. What the Lakotas and Cheyennes didn't know was that Fort Phil Kearny's infantrymen had recently been equipped with Model 1866 Springfield breechloading rifles that fired a powerful .50-caliber cartridge. The guns were fast and easy to reload, and the men in those boxes had plenty of ammunition.

The horseback charges having become too dangerous for both warriors and their ponies, the Indians withdrew several hundred yards and dismounted. Many removed their colorful feather bonnets and stripped down to their breechclouts in preparation for the next round of assaults. During this lull, some of the corral defenders jumped out of the wagon boxes and ran over to the several tents and knocked them down to give them a better field of fire.

A small creek cut into the prairie just a hundred yards east of the corral, giving the warriors a protected staging area. From here, Indian sharpshooters crept up and shot wherever they saw a puff of black powder smoke from a soldier gun. The warriors also launched arrows from this area, arcing them high so that they landed within the corral. Some of these projectiles were "fire arrows," which ignited the dried manure inside the corral, causing a great stench for the defenders, who were already miserable from heat and thirst. Fire erupted in the prairie grass outside as well and soon engulfed the scattered bodies of dead warriors, charring them black. The smoke from these fires, combined with the thick black powder smoke, at times enveloped the corral. Scattered flashes of flame from the soldier guns burst through this heavy haze, resembling some kind of fireworks show.

On a nearby hill, Red Cloud and other war leaders watched the battle transpire. One Bluecoat remembered seeing the flashes of signal mirrors from this direction and individual riders, couriers, apparently carrying messages back and forth. Brave up, Crazy Horse encouraged his men, only the earth lasts forever. They charged up a ravine and onto the plain, individuals and bunches, running, crouching, zigzagging, pressing ever closer to the corral, looking for a weak spot. The gunfire from the Bluecoats was deadly, though, and the warriors fell back. But they were hardly done. Certain that they would eventually overrun the defenders with their vastly superior numbers, the charges kept coming, yet each time they were repelled.

A giant Miniconjou warrior named Stings Like Wasp, more than six feet tall, believed his war medicine to be strong. Time and again, he advanced toward the Bluecoats carrying a long lance in one hand and holding a large buffalo-hide shield with the other. When Stings Like Wasp charged, he dropped his shield to his side and took off on a run, occasionally jumping into the air and dodging from side to side. Upon reaching a point so close to the wagon boxes it was nearly suicidal, he retreated. "The sight was fascinating," remembered one of the defenders, "and we could not but admire his superb courage."

On his last charge, Stings Like Wasp approached more slowly, shaking his spear at the defenders and singing his brave song. But his daring had drawn the attention of several Bluecoats on that side of the corral, all of whom now had their rifles trained in that direction. When the big Miniconjou shifted his shield to the side and began his run, several rifle shots cracked at once. How many lead bullets found their mark is not known, but Stings Like Wasp convulsively flipped into the air and landed on the ground in a heap.

The blistering sun was now near its high point in the summer sky. After more fruitless and costly charges on foot, many of the Lakotas and Cheyennes remounted. Hundreds galloped in a wide circle over the plain to the west of the corral. Hoping to catch the defenders on the south side of the wagon boxes off guard, they quickly turned and raced toward the Bluecoats, screaming at the tops of their lungs. The soldier rifles opened up, one bullet ripping into a Cheyenne named Sun's Robe and passing completely through his body. Sun's Robe fell from his pony and tumbled along the ground, the only Cheyenne to die that day.

The hail of bullets from the Bluecoats caused the charging warriors to flare and turn back. Just then a cannon boom echoed. A relief party from the fort was closing rapidly, and with it was one of the dreaded mountain howitzers. Crazy Horse and the other leaders ordered their followers to withdraw. After three and a half hours of intense fighting, warriors and their ponies were tired, and they had wounded to tend to. The Lakotas and Cheyennes melted away as swiftly as they'd first appeared.

The Bluecoats in the corral lost only three killed, including a lieutenant, and two wounded in what would become known as the Wagon Box Fight. Those breechloading Springfields and the steely resolve of the defenders were the only things that saved them from slaughter. Five or six warrior bodies had been left behind; they were so close to the corral that trying to retrieve them would've only resulted in more dead Lakotas. The Bluecoats believed they'd killed, at a minimum, sixty warriors and wounded approximately 120. One of the civilian contractors thought the total wounded wasn't less than two or three hundred, and he believed most of those wounds to be fatal. An old Plainsman who'd been in the fight said he'd fired more than fifty shots from his rifle at Indians who were no more than seventy-five yards away. At that distance, he declared, he could hit a silver dollar every damn time.

The high casualty estimates seemed to be confirmed by what the Bluecoats found when they examined the Indian positions: bloody moccasins and leggings and blood-soaked pieces of cloth that'd been used for bandages. Every few feet, a pool of dark-red blood stained the ground, seemingly marking where a warrior had breathed his last. But as with almost all fights between the Plains tribes and the Long Knives, what the white man believed and what the Indians said were far apart. Remembering decades later, Red Feather, an Oglala warrior, said they suffered five killed and five wounded. White Bull recollected there was a total of six men killed: a Cheyenne, an Oglala, and four Miniconjous. While these figures are almost certainly low, had the warriors suffered a horrific number of casualties, one would expect that fact to be a vivid memory. Instead, Red Feather dismissed the affair as not much of a battle.

One thing the old warriors did distinctly recall were the acts of courage, both their own and those of others. White Bull made a pictograph showing himself in the battle. He wears an eagle-feather bonnet and a bright red cape. In his hand is a long lance ornamented with numerous dangling eagle feathers, and his charging steel-gray steed is adorned with eagle feathers as well. White Bull's fine leggings and moccasins are colorfully decorated. A single set of hoofprints loop in front of the soldiers, telling us that White Bull rode close to the Bluecoats. Smoke comes from the muzzles of the soldier guns, and the bullets flying past the warrior are represented by several dashes. "It was a big running fight," reads part of White Bull's caption to the drawing, "and there was a lot of shooting."

Although they'd not wiped out the Bluecoats, Crazy Horse and his warriors had hurt them. And that was the point, to hit them again and again, to make their very existence so unpleasant that they would abandon the Bozeman Cut-off and its forts. And it was working. War parties of Lakotas and Cheyennes, now broken up into smaller groups, continued to prowl the wagon road, and white men caught napping paid with their lives. Two weeks after the Wagon Box Fight, warriors surprised a Wells, Fargo & Company wagon train waiting at Fort Reno, killing one of the herders, mortally wounding the wagonmaster, and running off three hundred head of oxen. In another attack near the fort a day or two earlier, they killed three men, adding to an ever-growing number of white man graves along the Bozeman.

An exasperated lieutenant recently arrived at Fort Reno wrote on August 16, 1867, that "all who are here think it the greatest folly of the Government to try to hold this route to Montana with the small number of troops now here. We *cannot* hold the country much longer without reinforcements. We are fighting every day." The grizzled mountain man Jim Bridger had actually summed up the situation three months earlier: "The only way to settle the question [of the Powder River county] is to send out a sufficient number of troops to completely whip the hostile Sioux, Cheyennes and Arapahoes, and make them sue for peace. Unless this is done the road had better be abandoned and the country given up to the Indians."

Sitting Bull didn't give Fort Buford on the Missouri a rest, either. His warriors had become masters of the stealth attack, to strike quickly and then gallop away before the garrison could turn out. On the very same day as the Wagon Box Fight, his warriors filtered out of the woods and bluffs northwest of the fort and rapidly approached within a half mile of the post to where its cow herd was grazing. This particular raid was not about running off the cattle. No, this was about causing mayhem. The warriors rode among the herd shooting their Northwest trade guns and bows and arrows at the harmless bovines, killing several outright and wounding others so badly that they had to be killed later. Among the casualties were "three choice cows" that supplied most of the garrison's milk.

Buford's sentries sounded the alarm, an infantry company rushed to arms, and a howitzer belched fire and smoke from one of the blockhouses. An artillery round exploded directly over the warriors, scattering shot and shell fragments into the prairie all around them. Ponies reared and plunged, but the warriors speedily got them under control and raced for the bluffs. Once there, they curiously halted and dismounted. Three or four warriors then spread out and stood as still as tree trunks, facing the fort, daring the artillerymen to fire another shot at them. The gunners obliged, and puffs of dust appeared near the warriors, who promptly skedaddled out of sight.

While Crazy Horse and Sitting Bull preyed upon whites that summer, government peace commissioners sought councils with the various tribes of southern and northern Lakotas and Cheyennes, particularly the antitreaty bands. Two groups of commissioners traveled up the Missouri, the first holding a council at Fort Rice in June and the second getting only as far north as Fort Sully in September. The Indians who came to meet them were mostly "Sticks around the Fort" Lakotas, who of course agreed to remain at peace with the white man, which they did every time they came in for the "presents" offered by the agents.

Sitting Bull and his Húnkpapas didn't attend either council. Chiefs friendly with the whites encouraged him to go, but he told them bluntly, "I have killed, robbed, and injured too many white men to believe in a good peace. They are medicine, and I would eventually die a lingering death. I had rather have my skin pierced with bullets. And, for another thing, I don't want to have anything to do with people who make one carry water on the shoulders and haul manure." When they cautioned the supreme chief that if he didn't make peace, the whites would eventually chase him down and capture or kill him, he replied, "Look at me, see if I am poor, or my people either. The whites may get me at last, as you say, but I will have good times till then. You are fools to make yourselves slaves to a piece of fat bacon, some hardtack, and a little sugar."

Peace commissioners met with various tribes at Fort Laramie throughout May, June, and July, and at North Platte, Nebraska, in September. Among the commissioners at the September meeting was the famed cigar-chomping Civil War hero General William Tecumseh Sherman, commander of the Military Division of the Missouri. It was the first time the Oglalas, Brulés, and Cheyennes laid eyes on the tight-jawed proponent of "total war," a military strategy the Lakotas had been practicing long before the general— just ask the Crows or any white person who wasn't a trader who foolishly ventured into Sioux country.

Several chiefs recognized one of Sherman's fellow commissioners, the white-bearded "Mad Bear" Harney, now retired from military service. They also got a good look at the future that Sitting Bull and Crazy Horse wanted no part of. The "iron road" of the Union Pacific had reached North Platte ten months earlier and, at a rate of one to three miles of track-laying per day, was rapidly approaching Cheyenne, a fast-growing town on the prairie just two months old. North Platte itself wasn't much to look at, having only about twenty houses, but like Cheyenne, it hadn't even existed a year earlier.

An Englishman riding over these new rails along the Platte was struck by the sight of countless, sun-bleached buffalo bones strewn for miles and miles. He also observed many broad, circular depressions absent of any vegetation—old buffalo wallows created by the large beasts rolling and pawing in the sand and dust. Emigrants and gold seekers on the Great Medicine Road of the Whites had chased the buffalo away long ago, but with towns, ranches, and homesteads now springing up along the Union Pacific, it was clear the buffalo would never return to this place.

As for the Indians, the English traveler wrote that "their disappearance will only be a question of time. And the time is now at hand, for the white man has begun to settle on the plains, and the two races cannot exist together in the same region." The Englishman's assertions were not new to Sitting Bull and Crazy Horse, nor were they new to most whites. The Lakota leaders had long concluded that if they allowed the white man to "exist" in their hunting grounds, it would be the end of them. It was why they were fighting.

Red Cloud was a no-show for the council at North Platte, as was Crazy Horse. "We don't want peace," Red Cloud is supposed to have said after getting the invitation, "because when we are at peace, we are poor. Now we are rich." Considering the amount of livestock, weapons and ammunition, and other booty captured from soldiers and civilians in the Powder River country, he had a point.

They Fear Even His Horses did participate in the council, however. So, too, Crazy Horse's uncle, the Brulé chief Spotted Tail, who'd become increasingly accommodating toward the white man. Yet despite Spotted Tail's desire to please the commissioners—he and the other chiefs were expecting gifts of ammunition for their fall buffalo hunt—he told them that peace would come only if the Powder River road and the Smoky Hill road were stopped and "turned in some other direction." The heavily used Smoky Hill route, named for the Smoky Hill River in western Kansas, was the most direct route across the plains to Denver, and steel rails were coming for it, too.

Pawnee Killer, a southern Oglala leader who is said to have more than earned his name, spoke more defiantly to the commissioners. "Who is our Great Father? And has he sent you here? We are not the cause of this trouble. Stop the Powder River road and the Smoky Hill road, and stop the soldiers coming into our country. Tell our Great Father this, and there will be peace."

In a long speech, General Sherman acknowledged the chiefs' demands, but he told them the Bozeman Cut-off would not be given up as long as the Indians continued their attacks along it. And the railroads absolutely could not and would not be stopped. He then revealed that he wished to give the entire Sioux nation a reservation on the Missouri River—far away from the Powder River and Smoky Hill, of course. He also delivered the ominous threats that were de rigueur for all speeches by government officials to Indians: the white men in the East "hardly think of what you call war out here, and if they make up their minds, they will come to these plains as thick as the largest herd of buffalos, and they will kill you all . . . in a war that will be different from any you have ever seen."

The general concluded by asking the chiefs to consider the reservation and to meet the commissioners again in November with a decision. Another commissioner offered an added enticement, saying the Indians would be given all the powder and lead they wanted once they signed off on "a contract of peace."

The peace commissioners arrived at Fort Laramie in November 1867 as promised, but the Lakotas did not appear. The commissioners had especially hoped to meet with Red Cloud, believing him to be the driving force behind the war on the Powder River—the name of Crazy Horse had not yet become known to the whites. Of course, other Lakota leaders opposed the white man's road and forts just as much as Red Cloud, paticularly the young men, but the commissioners thought that if they could get this renowned war chief to agree to terms of peace, the others would fall in line.

Yet Red Cloud refused to meet them. According to one report, his reason for not coming to Laramie was that he was bitter over the death of a nephew, Lone Man, at the Wagon Box Fight. Word also reached the commissioners that he would not discuss peace until the forts (Phil Kearny, Reno, and C. F. Smith) and the Bozeman Cut-off were abandoned. "Money is no object," the messenger stated, "they must have [wild] game."

Red Cloud's actions in the middle of these peace overtures sent a very clear message to the commissioners, no interpreter required. On November 4, some three hundred warriors under Red Cloud, Crazy Horse, and others spotted a large wagon train on the road twenty-two miles south of Fort Phil Kearny. The train, consisting of twenty-six wagons heavily loaded with sutler supplies for Fort C. F. Smith, was attempting to navigate a deep ravine, using ropes to ease the wagons down, one by one. Approximately forty infantrymen served as an escort, and they had a howitzer. Yipping and shouting to one another and whipping their horses, the warriors galloped toward the train.

The howitzer fired one round before being limbered and rushed across the ravine, where the teamsters were forming a defensive corral with the wagons. Three wagons still remained to make the passage, and the escort's rear guard feverishly worked to get them across, but they underestimated the speed of the Indian ponies. Shooting arrows and firing their guns at nearly point-blank range, the warriors killed three Bluecoats outright and mortally wounded two others. One warrior's arrow didn't fly true and struck the commanding officer's left foot, its sharp point pushing all the way through muscle and tendons and out the leather sole of his boot. The miss was a costly mistake, as the officer instantly fired his Colt revolver, striking the warrior in the stomach. The warrior fell from his saddle and bled out within moments.

The surviving soldiers barely made it to the protection of the corral, the warriors close behind them. The Lakotas and Cheyennes speedily captured five vehicles, including the lead wagon, containing a thousand rounds of reserve ammunition for the army Springfields. Its mule team had stampeded during the initial gunfire and commotion. In a near repeat of the Wagon Box Fight, the warriors made several charges against the corral on horseback and on foot. The howitzer broke up some charges, but the Bluecoats had only six rounds for it, so they were forced to use the gun sparingly. Through their own countercharges and the threat of the cannon, the infantrymen eventually recaptured three wagons, leaving the warriors with two. One of these big wagons contained dozens of bundles containing red wool trade blankets, causing the warriors to break off the fight temporarily to ransack it and grab blankets while they lasted. Crazy Horse was among those to claim one.

The fighting continued until dark and started up again at daylight the next morning. The battle was cut short, however, when a rescue column of cavalry from Fort Phil Kearny appeared in the distance. The warriors galloped away, leaving behind the scattered carcasses of a dozen ponies killed in the charges, as well as the booty, mostly ruined, they were unable to pack off. The loss to the sutler at Fort C. F. Smith amounted to $15,000. It was such a memorable battle for the Lakotas that it's represented in a winter count for the Lakota year 1867–68. The pictograph shows a single wagon surrounded by pony hoofprints. Several horizontal dashes denote gunfire. Drawn next to the wagon is a "point blanket," representing the red wool blankets found inside. The picture is captioned, "They captured a train of wagons near the Tongue River."

Determined to bring an end to this warfare if at all possible, the commissioners sent a surprising message to Red Cloud: if they could agree on a lasting peace, his wish that the Bozeman road and forts be abandoned would be granted. It was an immense concession, but it wasn't something that could be done immediately. There was simply too much valuable military property to be removed, and winter wasn't the time to do it. The commissioners insisted that the raiding stop until they could hold a great peace council at Laramie in the spring, when a timeline for the withdrawal would be presented. But, just as General Sherman had said back in September, if the attacks along the Bozeman continued, the whites would "meet war with war."

Only two days after the peace commissioners' proposal for a truce, a band of fourteen Lakotas stole a herd of seventy horses and mules within two miles of Fort Laramie. And sporadic attacks against soldiers and civilians failed to let up along the Bozeman through the winter. A party of Lakotas that came to Fort Laramie from the Powder River in early December reported that Red Cloud was prepared to fight the whites as long as he had a warrior left. But at the same time, the white man's assurances that the Bozeman forts were indeed on the trading block worked powerfully to sway the hard stance of Red Cloud and other leaders.

On January 1, 1868, an event transpired at Fort Phil Kearny that neither the Lakotas, Cheyennes, and Arapahos, nor the Long Knives, would ever have imagined possible. A special agent of the Indian Bureau had invited the headmen and warriors to meet him at the fort, and 260 appeared that day at the fort's gate (the agent's invitation also included the promise of presents). The next morning, 150 Indians walked into the military post they'd been trying to destroy ever since its first log was planted in the ground. Most of the warriors, in fact, had participated in the slaughter of Fetterman's command and the Wagon Box Fight, and their presence outraged the fort's officers, but the officers held their tongues, at least while the delegation was present.

The meeting occurred in a large log structure that served as the post theater, complete with stage and theatrical scenery. Red

Cloud wasn't among those gathered and, not surprisingly, neither was Crazy Horse. When asked why the Bad Face chief wasn't there, a headman replied, "He has sent us, as the Great Father has sent you. When the Great Father comes, Red Cloud will be here." This speaker was likely Red Cloud's brother, Spider, who'd been appointed to represent the war chief's interests.

Spider and the other headmen wanted to know when the Long Knives were leaving. "I want to tell you that we want them to hurry and go," said an Oglala named Stabber. "Send word to the Great Father to take away his warriors with the snow, and he will please us." The chiefs also wanted gifts of powder and lead to shoot buffalo and deer. The special agent didn't give the chiefs an answer about the troop removal. He simply reiterated the words of the peace commissioners: stop the attacks and meet at Laramie in the spring and there would be a treaty that would satisfy all parties. Shortly after the conclusion of the council, the agent presented the Indians with clothing, blankets, bread, sugar, and the precious powder and lead.

According to military officers who observed the meeting, the warriors and headmen left largely dissatisfied, and they'd not promised to stop their war against the white man. The special agent, on the other hand, sent a telegram to the Indian Bureau describing the council as a great success: "They have all pledged themselves to keep the peace, and to prevent all war parties until after the [spring] meeting of the Commission. . . . I believe they are sincere."

A few days later, warriors stole a herd of mules from Fort C. F. Smith and killed the herder. About the same time, another party of warriors attacked woodcutters working some four miles from the post, wounding three and stealing their horses. It's possible these warriors weren't part of the council at Fort Phil Kearny and thus wouldn't have felt obligated to abide by promises made by someone who wasn't one of their chiefs, if promises were indeed made. But while a chief might agree to a truce, it was another matter entirely for that chief to control his young men. Even with peace on the line, horses, mules, booty, and the possibility for coups were just too tempting.

As it turned out, however, the U.S. government's saber-rattling about meeting war with war was essentially a bluff. It wanted the Powder River forts abandoned nearly as much as the Lakotas and Cheyennes. Maintaining the posts was far too expensive, and to adequately reinforce them would come at an even greater cost to the treasury, not to mention the strain on a regular army already stretched thin. And as for the Bozeman Cutoff, it was hardly being used, with emigrants, miners, and other travelers preferring the much safer Missouri River route to Fort Benton, or riding the rails to the terminus of the Union Pacific. The westward-advancing railroads, of course, were key. General Sherman smartly pointed out that although the railroads' remote stations and the farmsteads and ranches that invariably sprang up along the tracks needed military protection, too, at least the warriors couldn't steal the locomotives and cars like they did a wagon train's mules and horses.

In early March, Sherman received the order to withdraw the garrisons from Forts Reno, Phil Kearny, and C. F. Smith. Rumors of Red Cloud's whereabouts and whether or not he would meet the peace commissioners frequently reached Fort Laramie. Meanwhile, Indian attacks on Bluecoats and civilians became more frequent and lethal. During the month of March, several columns of black smoke boiled up from the horizon. Each column marked a ranch warriors had raided and set on fire between Fort Laramie and Fort Fetterman (the Fetterman post had been established the previous summer near the Bozeman Cut-off's southern terminus). Five white men lost their lives to the warriors, one of them an enlisted man, and stolen stock amounted to approximately thirty-five mules and sixty head of cattle.

Peace commissioners arrived at Fort Laramie on April 10, but they found no Indians with which to make peace. So they sent runners with messages to Red Cloud and other chiefs. And they waited. Toward the end of the month, various Lakota groups began to trickle in. On April 29, Spotted Tail and other Brulé headmen, as well as several "Sticks Around the Fort" Lakotas, touched the pen to the prepared treaty the commissioners had brought for the occasion. In early May, bands of Crows, Northern Cheyennes and Arapahos, and southern Oglalas under Little Wound arrived. The Crows, Cheyennes, and Arapahos signed treaties that were separate from the one prepared for the Sioux.

The Washington, D.C., photographer Alexander Gardner, renowned for his Civil War battlefield photography and his images of the execution of the Lincoln conspirators, had come to Fort Laramie to record for history the various participants in the treaty council, both Indians and commissioners. He initially had trouble convincing the Indians to pose for his large box camera, but he eventually captured several stunning images on collodion-coated glass plates. Gardner assumed he would be the first to secure the likeness of the fearsome Red Cloud, but it wasn't to be. Red Cloud sent word that he wouldn't be appearing at Fort Laramie any time soon. "We are on the mountain looking down on the soldiers and the [Powder River ] forts," his message said. "When we see the soldiers moving away and the forts abandoned, then I will come down and talk."

Gardner did obtain several good images of They Fear Even His Horses, who arrived on May 21 with a large group of headmen and warriors. The sixty-year-old Oglala chief wore no feathers in his graying hair, which had a single short braid on the left side of his face. And in each Gardner photograph the chief carries his long-stemmed pipe; one fascinating and rare image shows him smoking it during the council with the commissioners. They Fear Even His Horses had always been inclined toward peace with the whites, but he fought the Long Knives when the circumstances called for it, and, with his blessing, his warriors, including his son, had ridden alongside Crazy Horse at the Hundred in the Hand and the Wagon Box Fight.

On May 25, They Fear Even His Horses and thirty-eight Oglala headmen and warriors signed the treaty. Among those signers was Chief American Horse of Red Cloud's Bad Faces, the same American Horse who'd served as one of the nine decoys under Crazy Horse that led eighty-one Long Knives to their doom, the same fierce warrior who'd personally ended the life of Captain Fetterman with a sharp knife to the throat. "I will sign," American Horse sternly told the commissioners, "and if there is anything wrong afterwards I will watch the commissioners, and they will be the first one that I will whip." The commissioners had no way of knowing American Horse's past deeds, but his threat was unsettling nonetheless.

A group of Miniconjous also touched the pen at this time, but on May 30, the last of the peace commissioners departed Fort Laramie. They placed a copy of the treaty with the post commandant so that it could be signed by Red Cloud if and when he appeared on the North Platte. In July and August, the three contested forts were abandoned by the army and shortly thereafter joyously set aflame by warriors—they didn't want to take a chance, they said, of the Long Knives moving back in. Red Cloud felt no rush to get to Fort Laramie, however. The white man could wait a little longer. Finally, on November 4, 1868, the war chief arrived with approximately 125 other headmen and warriors, some of whom, such as They Fear Even His Horses, had already signed the treaty.

In the previous councils, the treaty provisions were explained to the Indian delegations by an interpreter, after which they were given an opportunity to speak. It was the same now, but what Red Cloud and the earlier signers didn't realize was that none of their concerns or demands voiced during these councils resulted in emendations to the treaty. That document, prepared in advance by the commissioners, was not to be altered. And like other treaties, the Lakotas clearly didn't understand all its provisions, some of which would come back to haunt them.

Although the treaty did call for the removal of the Powder River forts and the closing of the Bozeman Cut-off, it also stipulated that the Lakotas must confine themselves to a new Sioux reservation outlined in the treaty. Known as the Great Sioux Reservation, it comprised all of present-day South Dakota west of the Missouri River. That portion of the sacred Black Hills not contained within those boundaries, as well as the cherished Powder River country, fell within an area designated as "unceded Indian territory." The Lakotas could hunt this region so long as the buffalo remained in sufficient numbers "to justify the chase," a clever phrase on the part of the treaty makers that could be used to restrict the Lakotas to their reservation undoubtedly sooner than later.

No white men, other than government agents and employees with reservation business, were allowed to enter or pass through the Lakotas' lands. An agency would be established within the reservation where the Lakotas would not only receive their annuities, but also where the men could be trained in farming and the children could attend school, all with the aim of transitioning the Lakotas to an agrarian people. No white men were allowed in the unceded territory as well, but at the same time, the treaty obligated the Lakotas to offer no objections to the future construction of railroads, wagon roads, mail stations, and "other works of utility or necessity"—even if they occurred within reservation boundaries.

Red Cloud really didn't care to hear all the provisions of the treaty, particularly those pertaining to the "civilization of the Indian." It was wrong, he said, to ask his people to give up the chase of the buffalo and become farmers. And he was hesitant to make promises he couldn't keep. What he really wanted from this visit was powder and lead and provisions. Nevertheless, on the third meeting with the fort's commandant, Red Cloud, "with a show of reluctance and tremulousness, washed his hands with the dust of the floor" and made his mark. So, too, did the other Lakotas in the delegation. Red Cloud insisted that the whites also touch the pen.

The treaty signing completed, the tension left Red Cloud's face and he seemed to warm to the officers in the room. He told them he was happy to again shake the white man's hand as he and their fathers had done years ago, a time when the land was filled with Indian traders instead of military posts with their Long Knives. Fort Laramie, of course, had started out as a trading post, and its current sutler still carried on a good Indian trade. Red Cloud and the other headmen had been led to believe by both the commissioners and the post commander that once there was peace, they could again trade with the sutler, which they were keen to do. But as an old Lakota once said, "Too many tongues. Many lies." Shortly after Red Cloud's delegation had gone, an order came from the army's Department of the Platte forbidding the Fort Laramie sutler from trading with any Lakotas. The fort was south of the North Platte River, and the Sioux were not allowed to trade off their new reservation.

The 1868 Treaty of Fort Laramie was exactly the kind of finagling and half-truths Crazy Horse expected from the white man. Crazy Horse did not go to Fort Laramie. He did not touch the pen. He called the treaty "False Papers."

# Land of Uncertainty

*My brothers, shall we submit? Or shall we say to them: "First
kill me, before you take possession of my fatherland!"*

SITTING BULL

*Yellowstone River, Four Miles Above the
Mouth of the Powder, June 19, 1868*

An immense village of six hundred lodges is nestled along the
south side of the river, now running high from melting snow
in the mountains and spring rains. The several camp circles are
mostly Húnkpapa, but the sprawling village also contains the
lodges of Miniconjous, Oglalas, Sihásapas, Sans Arcs, Two Kettles,
and Yanktonais. To the whites, the people camped here are simply the "hostile bands." But the whites do know the name of the
bands' leader: Sitting Bull.

Late in the afternoon, village criers announce that the Black
Gown is approaching. Women stop their chores, children stop
their playing, and old men come out of their lodges. Everyone,
some four thousand people, quickly make their way to the edge
of the village to get a look at the Black Gown. What they see is a

magnificent procession slowly moving across the valley. The Black Gown comes with an escort of eighty Sioux warriors friendly with the priest, many of whom have relatives in these camps. But surrounding the priest's entourage are approximately five hundred warriors that had left the village early that morning to meet him. These men, dressed and painted spectacularly, make their ponies prance and race back and forth across the prairie. It's a panorama of action and pomp, and it's glorious.

Sitting Bull also walks out from his lodge to see the Black Gown. A few days earlier, the Húnkpapa leader received a gift of tobacco with a message that the Black Gown was coming and wished to be allowed into his village. But even though Sitting Bull was expecting the Black Gown's visit, he's momentarily startled by a banner held aloft at the head of the priest's column. Only the Long Knives fly large flags, and this flag also has the white man's stars. But Sitting Bull soon realizes it isn't an American flag. On one side is a portrait of the Virgin Mary, surrounded with shiny stars of gilt. On the other is the name of Jesus. The priest calls it his "standard of peace."

The Lakotas crowd around the Black Gown as he's led into the village, and several of them vividly remember the priest, for he is the venerable Father Pierre-Jean De Smet, now sixty-eight years old and looking feeble. But even in this day's hot sun, he wears his black vestments. And, as always, a bronze and ebony crucifix hangs from De Smet's neck. The Lakotas know him as both "Black Gown" and "The Great Holy Man." With De Smet are Charles Galpin, an experienced trader from Fort Rice, and his wife, Eagle Woman That All Look At. Eagle Woman, the daughter of a Two Kettle chief and his Húnkpapa spouse, has much influence among the Lakotas. She's also considered "a very good Catholic." With her husband, Eagle Woman serves as De Smet's interpreter.

Sitting Bull orders De Smet's baggage be placed in a lodge in the center of the camp that's been specially prepared for him and then directs nearby warriors serving as camp soldiers to disperse the throng. Despite the grand welcome shown the priest, there is some concern for his safety. Any Lakota who'd had a relative killed by whites might seek to avenge that death by taking the Black Gown's scalp. One warrior is overhead to say, "Another white man coming to cheat us." As a precaution, then, Sitting Bull places a guard of twenty of his best men around the lodge to keep watch until morning. And when De Smet stretches out on a soft buffalo robe for the night, lying next to him are Sitting Bull's uncle, Four Horns; his cousin, Black Moon; and Sitting Bull himself. Before surrendering to sleep, however, De Smet's mind wanders over the day's events, and he hears again the words spoken to him ominously by an unnamed chief: "Had it been any other man but you, Black Gown, this day must have been his last."


As part of the same peace initiative that sought to end the fighting in the Powder River country and along the Platte, Father De Smet had traveled 350 miles west from Fort Rice to see Sitting Bull and other northern Lakota chiefs. Because Sitting Bull refused to meet with peace commissioners on the Upper Missouri, the U.S. government had prevailed upon the beloved missionary to make this difficult and dangerous journey. The commissioners hoped De Smet would use his goodwill with the tribes to persuade the chiefs to come in and sign the new treaty. The priest's aims were more altruistic: "I have no other motives than the welfare of the Indians and will trust entirely to the kind providence of God."

On the morning of June 20, hundreds of men, women, and children gathered to observe the council. Sitting Bull, Father De Smet, and various chiefs and headmen took their seats on buffalo robes in a large, open-sided shelter made by combining the hides and poles of ten lodges. Planted in the center was De Smet's religious banner. Representatives of several bands sang and danced, after which Four Horns opened the council by lighting his pipe, offering it first to *Wakan Tanka,* then presenting it to the four cardinal directions and to the sun above and the earth below. He next held the pipe's stem up to Father De Smet, who took a few puffs. Four Horns repeated this ritual with each chief until all had smoked.

Many Lakotas believed Father De Smet to be "the only white man who never tells lies," and they were eager to hear the Black Gown's words. After a short prayer, De Smet addressed the hushed crowd. He said the bloodshed must stop, that although he came only as an adviser, he knew the Great Father meant well by them, and his commissioners were waiting to speak to the chiefs at Fort Rice. De Smet then implored the tribes to "bury all your bitterness towards the whites, forget the past, and accept the hand of peace which is extended to you."

Next to speak was Black Moon, who said he would never sell any of his country as others had done. However, he would send some of his young men with the Black Gown on the return journey to Fort Rice to make peace with the whites. When Black Moon took his seat, Sitting Bull stood and addressed the council, although he didn't speak directly to De Smet and his interpreters. In imitation of the white man, he said his words to another Húnkpapa, who then relayed them to the interpreters.

"I am, and always have been, a fool and a warrior," he said, "but my people caused me to be so. They have been troubled and confused for several years past, and they look upon the whites as the cause of their troubles, and they pushed me forward."

Like Black Moon, Sitting Bull agreed to send some of his people to Fort Rice. He shook hands with Father De Smet, trader Galpin, and Eagle Woman and then turned to the onlookers and asked if they'd heard his words. "Hou, Hou!" they answered. Sitting Bull returned to his seat, but only for a moment. He rose again, saying he'd forgotten some things. The great Húnkpapa wanted all to know that he was against selling any part of his country, and he wanted the forts on the Missouri abandoned. He also wanted the woodcutters for the steamboats to stop cutting the timber along the river, especially the oaks. He was very fond of the little groves of oaks, he said. "They stand the wintry storms and the summer's blast and, not unlike ourselves, seem to flourish by them." The crowd of Lakotas cheered as their supreme chief sat back down.

Following the council, Eagle Woman talked privately with Sitting Bull and did her best to convince him to go to Fort Rice and meet the commissioners. "Some of my people will go," he told her, "and that is just the same as if I went; but as for myself, *I will not go!* My great reason is, I hear that they want to arrest me and take me a prisoner."

Neither the peace commissioners nor the military had any intentions of arresting Sitting Bull, but his name had become notorious to most whites and was usually linked with any attacks or killings on the northern plains. And a rumor was current that the authorities of Minnesota and Montana had put a price on his head. Thus, the chief had good reason to be wary. Ultimately, however, Sitting Bull had no desire to visit Fort Rice simply because he had no desire to touch the white man's pen. The free-roaming Lakotas had never gained by a treaty; they had only lost. Moreover, Sitting Bull shared an identical view with Red Cloud that war with the white man brought him and his people wealth.

As soon as Father De Smet returned to his lodge, dozens of children and their mothers appeared. Many of the women cradled babies in their arms. When De Smet walked out to greet them, the children crowded around, holding out their hands. The families didn't leave until the missionary had laid his hands on every baby and child, two of whom were likely Sitting Bull's. The chief had lost his first wife, Light Hair, during childbirth in 1857. The baby boy she'd given birth to lived just four years. Shortly after the death of this son, Sitting Bull married Snow on Her, an Arikara woman, and she bore him two daughters: Her Many Horses in 1865 and Walks Looking, who was only a few months old at the time of De Smet's visit. Sitting Bull had taken a second wife in 1866 named Red Woman, but there had not yet been any offspring.

Not only did Father De Smet bless the Lakota children, but he also blessed Sitting Bull with a precious gift. The priest removed from around his neck his rosary beads and crucifix and placed them around the neck of the Lakota chief and holy man. De Smet didn't convert Sitting Bull to Christianity—no priest did—but Sitting Bull wearing a crucifix gave the all-important impression that he'd accepted the white man's God and that he was, in fact, a Catholic—it was the next best thing for De Smet. And as for Sitting Bull, this talisman of the Great Holy Man clearly held special power, and so he occasionally wore it.

De Smet's party left for Fort Rice the following morning with eight Húnkpapa delegates led by Gall, Sitting Bull's lieutenant. Just a year and a half earlier, Gall had nearly been killed in a botched arrest attempt by Bluecoats near Fort Berthold, so he likely felt some trepidation about visiting Fort Rice as well. But, like Sitting Bull, Gall believed Father De Smet truly cared for the Lakotas and would do nothing that would put him or the other delegates in harm's way.

On July 2, Sitting Bull's and Black Moon's delegates, along with other Sioux leaders, met at Fort Rice with the peace commissioners and De Smet, who was present only as an observer. The commissioners carried the identical treaty presented earlier that year at Fort Laramie. Gall spoke first, reiterating Sitting Bull's demands. But as at Fort Laramie, the treaty had already been written and might as well have been carved in stone. The Missouri River posts would not be removed, one of the commissioners informed the council. The commissioner then gave the chiefs a rather novel explanation of their purpose, saying that the forts were there "to keep the whites out of your country." This was hardly true, of course. The forts had been established to protect an important transportation route of the whites, with some of those posts serving as bases of operation for bloody military campaigns against the Lakotas.

While Gall and the others obviously didn't understand that they hadn't been called to Fort Rice for a negotiation, they did understand that there were presents waiting after they touched the pen. All the Sioux representatives, then, including Gall, signed the document. And this after being told one of Sitting Bull's key demands wouldn't be met. Gall's fellow Lakotas, including Sitting Bull, would criticize him later for succumbing to the white man's bribes. (Similar feelings existed against Crazy Horse's Brulé uncle, Spotted Tail.) But Gall's mark on a treaty meant nothing to Sitting Bull. He'd made no promises to the white man. Sitting Bull's only promise was to his people, to protect their way of life and their land. And for the near future, that could only mean war.

Sitting Bull had now lived thirty-seven years on the buffalo plains. His bravery, his wisdom, his ambition, and his defiance of the white man had seen him anointed supreme chief of the Lakotas. His standing as a revered holy man was also ably earned. And his family was growing. Sitting Bull's mother began to push her son to consider all his responsibilities and not take unnecessary risks. Let the young men fight the battles, she told him; he had a family and a people to look out for. But Sitting Bull wasn't willing to give up just yet that wind-in-your-face thrill of bearing down on an enemy, a hundred or more whooping Lakotas behind him.

Seven weeks after Gall touched the pen, Sitting Bull and approximately two hundred warriors again targeted the cow herd at Fort Buford. Even though the herd's guard of twenty-one men knew to expect attacks at any time, the warriors were still able to creep up on both sides of the herd and surprise the Bluecoats. Blowing eagle-bone whistles, shouting, and flapping blankets, they stampeded the herd of 250 animals. Of the guard, the warriors killed two and wounded five. Soldiers from the fort rushed after the fleeing warriors and, after some brief skirmishing, retrieved only fifty-seven head of cattle. A dispatch describing the attack stated the warriors "fought like trained soldiers." It added the alarming comment that "the whole region between Buford and Benton is being cleared of whites."

Just a month later, in September, Sitting Bull led a combined force of Húnkpapas, Yanktons, Yanktonais, and other northern tribes in an attack on the newly constructed Fort Peck trading post, 267 miles up the Missouri from Fort Buford. The warriors surrounded the post and for six long hours attempted several assaults against its inhabitants, who'd been bolstered by the small crew of a steamboat recently arrived at the fort. Sitting Bull directed the action from a black horse, his eagle-feather bonnet streaming to the ground. By the end of the fight, the warriors had slain one white man, killed several cattle, and driven off several more. They removed the dead man's scalp but left in his mutilated body forty arrows, three knives, and two minié balls.

Long Knives or no Long Knives in the Powder River country, the Lakotas still had their historic rivals—the Crows, Shoshones, and others—to contend with. There were always wrongs to be avenged, hunting grounds to be defended, horses to be stolen, scalps to be taken. Such things were what Lakota warriors lived for. As the holy man Horn Chips put it, the essence of Crazy Horse's existence was to make war, "that was his business"—a business he conducted better than most. And as the stories of Crazy Horse's fearlessness and battlefield successes multiplied, so, too, did the number of his followers.

Crazy Horse refused to allow any of his warriors to ride ahead of him in an attack. The Crows once told the Lakotas, "We know Crazy Horse better than we do you other Sioux. Whenever we have a fight, he is closer to us than he is to you." Crazy Horse also began to do something peculiar during a fight, which only added to a growing list of peculiarities surrounding the man. When Crazy Horse felled an enemy, he didn't immediately count coup as any other warrior would do. Instead, he dropped back and let others take first, second, and third coup, and so on. If Crazy Horse counted coup at all, he did it last. And he stopped taking scalps. Crazy Horse's cousin, Eagle Elk, supposed the war chief did this because he "had such a reputation that he did not have to get more of that."

The high regard with which the Oglalas held the twenty-seven-year-old Crazy Horse resulted in his greatest political advancement within the tribe. It came during the Moon of the Chokecherries (midsummer) in 1868, about the same time as the Fort Rice council. In an elaborate ceremony similar in many respects to the one in which Sitting Bull had been named supreme chief, four men—Crazy Horse, American Horse, Man That Owns a Sword, and Young They Fear Even His Horses (son of They Fear Even His Horses)—were invested as Shirt Wearers. It was a position of tremendous responsibility and usually fell to the son of a chief or headman. Crazy Horse was not descended from a line of chiefs, so his selection was unconventional, but then again, so was Crazy Horse.

The *shirt* in the Shirt Wearer's name, sometimes called a "hair shirt," was made of tanned bighorn sheepskin and always painted, frequently blue for the top and yellow for the bottom, representing the Lakota deities the Sky and the Rock. The shirt was fringed with bunches of long, dark human hair, each bunch wrapped in dyed porcupine quills where it attached to the shirt. These hairlocks were not scalps but hair given and fashioned by village women. The hair represented the tribe's people, those whom the Shirt Wearers were meant to govern and protect. The garment wasn't a war shirt and was to be worn only by the "peacemakers" of the tribe.

Crazy Horse and the other Shirt Wearers were expected to equally govern the tribe in such everyday matters as where to hunt and camp and when to move. It was up to them to maintain peace within the tribe and to ensure that no one's rights were abused. If a rule was broken or a crime committed, the Shirt Wearers were the final arbiters of justice. Not only were they to look out for the welfare of the tribe as a whole, but they were to take special care of the helpless, especially widows and orphans. And they were to be stewards of the land, for only in the preservation of the land, its four-leggeds, and other creatures would the tribe survive. All these responsibilities required a heightened embodiment of the Lakota man's four virtues, and, if necessary, an ultimate sacrifice. "They were elected to give their lives for the people," recalled the holy man Black Elk, "so they may have to die for the people."

That winter saw Sitting Bull's Húnkpapas camped on the Yellowstone, above the mouth of the Powder. In early January 1870, during the Moon of Hard Times, snow blanketed the countryside. Every hunter in winter welcomed snow. Not only did the snow make game easy to track, but the large, dark forms of the buffalo could be spotted at great distances when against a white landscape. But if it was easy to track game, it was also easy to track humans. And that's exactly what happened to two Húnkpapa boys one cold day while returning from a buffalo hunt—their two sets of footprints were discovered by a band of thirty Crow warriors.

The Crows were on foot as well, except for two, who shared a horse. The pair on horseback raced ahead and overtook the boy hunters, killing one. The other boy, however, managed to escape. When the rest of the Crow warriors caught up and learned a Sioux had gotten away, their hearts sank. They well knew that when the boy reached his village—which couldn't be far—the Crows would now become the hunted; it would be *their* tracks warriors were following. Although the sun was sinking in the sky, the Crows did not make camp but pushed themselves through the night in an effort to put as many miles behind them as possible.

In Sitting Bull's village, the news of the attack resulted in swift, concerted action: weapons, ammunition, and shields were retrieved, war medicine prepared, and horses saddled. With Sitting Bull in the lead, some one hundred warriors left that night. The moon cast a greenish hue on the rapidly moving horseback figures and made hard shadows on the snow. It also illuminated the enemy's trail, and because the Lakotas had the advantage of being mounted, they made good time. The warriors caught up to their prey at first light.

Having sensed the closeness of their pursuers, the Crows had taken refuge on top of a sandstone butte rising forty feet above the snow-crusted prairie. With its summit surrounded by caprock about five feet in height, it was a natural fortress. And the Crows had hastily piled up large stones in the gaps to make it even more impregnable. As the Húnkpapas surrounded the butte, one of the Crows shouted down, "We came here to be killed; come on now and kill us!"

The Lakotas dismounted and immediately charged up the

sides of the butte. Gunfire erupted from the rocks, killing some warriors outright and wounding others. Sitting Bull encouraged his men to be brave, and they again rushed up in twos and threes, dodging and weaving, while others waited and shot at any part of a Crow's body that chanced to come into view.

Sitting Bull's adopted brother, Jumping Bull, was the bravest of all that day. He guided his pony up to the fortification and then rode circles around it. He was so close to the wall that none of the Crows could resist taking a shot at him. Soon the shooting decreased dramatically, however, and it was evident the Crows had nearly exhausted their ammunition. Sitting Bull ran up to the summit, reached over the wall, and counted coup on an enemy warrior. Other Lakotas who'd charged with their chief now scrambled over the caprock and fought hand to hand with the defenders, slaying most of them with knives. Scarlet sprays of blood on the snow rapidly turned to large blotches and pools as the Lakotas took their vengeance upon their enemy.

The assault cost Sitting Bull thirteen killed, including one of his uncles, Looks for Him in a Tent, who took a bullet to the belly as he climbed over the rock wall. The Lakota chief also had seventeen wounded, and many of those injuries were grisly—the Crows had sold their lives dearly. The fight went down in Lakota lore as "Thirty Crows Killed." The site of the bloody battle is known to this day as Crow Rock.

Like Sitting Bull, Crazy Horse still considered white men fair game, and many were to be found to the south, on the North Platte. Three months after the battle of Thirty Crows Killed, during the Moon When Leaves Turn Green, Crazy Horse and several of his warriors chanced on three white men a half mile from Fort Laramie. The three were heading for a spot on the river, intent on doing a little duck hunting. Two rode in a wagon and one was on horseback. Crazy Horse, careful to keep himself and his men out of sight, watched as the wagon turned to avoid some rough terrain while the rider continued on a more direct route. When the rider entered a ravine close to Crazy Horse, the war chief kicked his pony in the flanks and dropped into the ravine at a solid gallop.

Crazy Horse had the white man at his mercy, but he struggled to check the momentum of his swift pony. As Crazy Horse swept past the surprised hunter, he managed a snap shot with a revolver, which struck the man just above the ankle joint. The hurt man spurred his mount and made a beeline for the fort, which he reached with a blood-soaked pant leg and absent his hat. The ugly wound would result in the amputation of the man's foot, but he had narrowly avoided death—Crazy Horse didn't miss often.

This brief encounter added nothing to the Shirt Wearer's war record, but Laramie's post chaplain wrote about the April 19 incident in letters published in his hometown newspaper, the Plattsmouth *Nebraska Herald,* and the *Chicago Tribune.* The chaplain stated the Indian who attacked the duck hunter had been identified as "an Ogallalla Chief, by the name of 'Crazy Horse,' a great warrior." It marked the first appearance of Crazy Horse's now-iconic name in print.

Crazy Horse was still single at this time. Though he'd courted girls in his youth, his overwhelming desire to become a great warrior had left little room for the opposite sex, and Crazy Horse had gone longer than most Lakota men in finding a partner. But he'd now settled on an attractive young Oglala, a niece of Red Cloud, named Black Buffalo Woman. He even enlisted Horn Chips to create powerful charms to cause the woman to fall in love with him. Maybe these charms worked, maybe they didn't, but Black Buffalo Woman did return the Shirt Wearer's affections. There was one very serious impediment to this love affair, however: Black Buffalo Woman was already married.

Not only was Black Buffalo Woman married, but she had three small children. Her husband, No Water, was a warrior of Red Cloud's Bad Face band. Nevertheless, one late spring day while No Water was away, Black Buffalo Woman placed her children with relatives and left the village with Crazy Horse and a few followers on a planned raid against the Crows. They reached the Powder River on the second night, where they found several Lakota groups camped. A number of their friends were there, and Crazy Horse and Black Buffalo Woman accepted an invitation to share one of their tipis.

Meanwhile, No Water returned home to discover his wife and his children missing. After a little searching among the lodges, he located the children but not Black Buffalo Woman. When he learned that Crazy Horse had left the camp a short time before, he instantly knew his wife was with the Shirt Wearer. Most everyone knew, actually, as Crazy Horse had been giving Black Buffalo Woman considerable attention for a long time. A furious No Water immediately gathered several warriors and set out on Crazy Horse's trail, which was easily followed to the Powder River camps.

The sun had long set when No Water's party arrived, and the several hide lodges glowed and flickered like paper lanterns from the fires burning inside. Silently scouting about, No Water recognized the tipi of Bad Heart Bull, a relative, whom he knew possessed a cap and ball revolver. No Water entered the lodge and asked Bad Heart Bull if he could borrow the gun. Before Bad Heart Bull had a chance to ask why, No Water said he wanted to go hunting. There was something about No Water's demeanor that didn't seem quite right, but Bad Heart Bull handed him the revolver. After checking to see that the gun was loaded, No Water left the lodge.

In a nearby large, double tipi, Crazy Horse and Black Buffalo Woman sat with several other men and women, including their friends Little Big Man, Little Shield (younger brother of He Dog), and the six-foot, five-inch Touch the Clouds, a Miniconjou. Per custom, the women sat on one side of the tipi and the men on the other. Crazy Horse sat at the back of the lodge, the place of honor. The mood was festive as the warriors told of their recent coups and discussed where they might find their enemy the Crows. Suddenly a dark figure rushed into the lodge, and a collective gasp went up when the light of the fire revealed the face of No Water.

Crazy Horse leapt up and reached for the knife in his belt, but Little Big Man, wishing to prevent bloodshed, locked his arms around the Shirt Wearer, apparently unaware of the revolver at No Water's side. In the same instant, No Water lunged forward, threw up his gun hand, and shouted, "My friend, I have come!" He jerked the trigger of the revolver, and a flash and loud bang filled the lodge. A startled Little Big Man released his grip, and Crazy Horse fell forward into the small fire, knocking sparks and embers into the air. Women screamed. With ears ringing from the closeness of the gunshot, men dragged the wounded Crazy Horse from the fire while Touch the Clouds struggled with No Water, finally prying the revolver out of his hand.

A terrified Black Buffalo Woman pushed up the back of the lodge cover, crawled outside, and ran for a relative's lodge, where she begged to be protected from her deranged husband. No Water, rightly fearing the wrath of Crazy Horse's followers, ran away, jumped on the first pony he came across, and galloped off. Inside the tipi, beneath a haze of black powder smoke from the revolver blast, blood streamed from Crazy Horse's face. A close examination revealed that No Water's bullet had entered just below the left nostril, ripped along the outside of the upper jaw, fracturing it, and exited at the base of the skull. Crazy Horse would likely live, but his friends were enraged. They found the mule No Water had ridden to the village, a fine animal known to be especially fast, and they killed it.

In the initial days of Crazy Horse's convalescence, a real crisis faced all those affected by the shooting of the illustrious leader. Crazy Horse's followers wanted No Water turned over to be punished, threatening vengeance against his people if they didn't comply. "For a while it looked as if a lot of blood would flow," recalled He Dog. A peace was finally brokered, however, with No Water sending three first-rate horses to Crazy Horse as reparation. Crazy Horse agreed to have Black Buffalo Woman turned over to Bad Heart Bull on the condition that she not be punished. Bad Heart Bull then took the responsibility of arranging her return to No Water and their children.

But this was not the end of repercussions for Crazy Horse's adulterous affair. Shirt Wearers were held to the highest standards, which they pledged to uphold. Stealing another man's wife was strictly taboo, and Crazy Horse knew this. The consequence was quick and final: his hair shirt was taken back, and he was never again to be a Shirt Wearer. Although this temporarily brought shame to Crazy Horse, he was never really suited to the position. Crazy Horse was the archetypal man of action. He rarely attended councils, and in those he did, he didn't speak. It was "just his nature," remembered He Dog. "He was a very quiet man except when there was fighting."

Crazy Horse fully recovered from the shooting, but he was left with a pronounced scar, and because of the impossibility of properly repairing the fractured jaw, the left side of his face was slightly disfigured. A white observer said the healed wound gave Crazy Horse's mouth "a drawn and somewhat fierce or brutal expression." Outwardly, Black Buffalo Woman seemed content to return to her life the way it was before Crazy Horse came into it.

Some months later, she gave birth to her fourth child. It was a girl with unusually light hair.

Sometime during the early summer, as Crazy Horse suffered with pain from his slow-healing jaw, word came that Little Hawk, his half brother, was dead. Little Hawk had taken one too many risks and been slain in a raid against one of the ranches along the railroad below Fort Laramie. Crazy Horse obtained the location of the fight from the warriors who'd been on the expedition, and once he felt well enough, left to find his brother's body and give it a proper burial. Tethered behind the war chief's mount was his brother's pony, a beautiful animal that the warriors had brought back from the raid.

Crazy Horse had little trouble locating his brother's remains, and after securing the bones in a shallow grave, he led his brother's pony over the spot and shot it—Little Hawk would have a fine warhorse to ride in the land of ghosts. The death of his brother was yet another sadness for Crazy Horse, but he could at least take some comfort in the fact that Little Hawk had died young and on a field of battle. He hadn't died a bent-over old man with here and there a stray tooth; he'd died a warrior. According to one Lakota account, Crazy Horse took out his grief on a few white men in the area before returning home.

As the days turned shorter, and sunrise came with a crisp chill in the air, Crazy Horse was more than ready to join his old friend High Backbone on an expedition against the Shoshones. This raid, however, wasn't simply about stealing horses; it was revenge for some injury now long forgotten. High Backbone was after Shoshone blood. The Lakota war party numbered just sixteen men, which was small considering that their destination was the Wind River, in the heart of Shoshone territory. If they encountered a superior enemy force, be it Shoshone or Crow, they would have to rely upon the fleetness of their ponies to carry them out of danger.

After several days' travel, the Lakotas located their quarry where Bad Water Creek joins the Wind River (near present-day Shoshoni, Wyoming), but it was a large village, some 150 lodges. And a cold, drizzling rain was beginning to fall. In the waning darkness before dawn, as Crazy Horse, High Backbone, and their men moved into position to attack, the rain turned to sleet and snow. Crazy Horse knew they were about to stir a nest of bees, and with the heavy slush that was now forming on the ground, the speed of their horses would be compromised; their mounts would tire quicker. While the Oglala war chief was not afraid to risk his own life in battle, his goal was always to kill as many of the enemy without losing any of his own warriors. To attack now was chancy.

When High Backbone learned Crazy Horse was considering calling off the attack, the Miniconjou chief was furious. He reminded his friend that he'd done this before, in nearly the same place. "The last time you called off a fight here, when we got back to camp they laughed at us. You and I have our good name to think about. If you don't care about it you can go back. But I'm going to stay here and fight."

"All right," Crazy Horse said, "we fight, if you feel that way about it. But I think we're going to get a good licking. You have a good gun and I have a good gun, but look at our men! None of them have good guns, and most of them have only bows and arrows. It's a bad place for a fight and a bad day for it, and the enemy are twelve to our one."

High Backbone remained unswayed, and once it was light enough to see the faint outlines of the tipis through the falling snow, the Lakotas charged. Several warriors headed for the horse herd while Crazy Horse and High Backbone rode among the

lodges, firing their guns into the tipis indiscriminately, not knowing whether their bullets hit man, woman, or child—they hated
the Shoshones that much. In less than a minute from the first gunshot, Shoshone men were pouring out of their lodges. With such
a large village, it was impossible to round up all the horses, so the
Lakotas gathered what they could and began their retreat. They
thus left plenty of mounts for angry Shoshone warriors to saddle
and start in pursuit.

As Crazy Horse feared, the slush, which reached above their
horses' ankles, slowed them down. The retreat quickly became
a running fight as approximately two hundred Shoshones closed
in. High Backbone, Crazy Horse, and a twenty-five-year-old warrior named Good Weasel fought a rearguard action. The rest were
told to concern themselves only with flight. To break up and slow
their pursuers, the three Lakotas divided, with Crazy Horse and
High Backbone making a wide circle to come up on opposite sides
of the Shoshone force. The two chiefs paused and briefly taunted
the Shoshones, drawing scattered enemy riders and plenty of bullets, before spurring their ponies and again racing in the direction
of their fleeing comrades.

When High Backbone reunited with Crazy Horse and Good
Weasel, he shouted, "We're up against it now; my horse has a
wound in the leg."

"I know it," Crazy Horse said. "We were up against it from
the start."

The three separated once more and Crazy Horse and High
Backbone again made feints on opposite sides of the Shoshones.
But when Crazy Horse afterward met up with Good Weasel, there
was no High Backbone. The two looked back and saw a large
group of Shoshones massed in one area; several had dismounted.
High Backbone had either fallen off his lame horse or been shot
from it. In any event, the Shoshones were gleefully scalping and

otherwise mutilating his body. Crazy Horse and Good Weasel turned their ponies and galloped away.

A few days later, Crazy Horse returned to locate High Backbone's body and bury him. The war chief was accompanied by Red Feather, one of the warriors on the ill-fated raid. When they got to the location of the fight, all they found were the skull and a few bones—the wolves and coyotes had already ravaged the remains of Crazy Horse's mentor.

Although Crazy Horse had lost his hair shirt, no one doubted his devotion to his people and their homeland, nor his resolve to defy the white man and his treaties. That could no longer be said of Red Cloud, however. At the same time Crazy Horse was recuperating from the No Water shooting, Red Cloud was having ice cream and fresh strawberries with President Ulysses S. Grant in the White House. Red Cloud had requested to see the Great Father to discuss treaty concerns, and he and his party of headmen, warriors, and a few of their wives were feted in the capital city. So, too, was Spotted Tail, who was visiting Washington at the same time.

Wishing to impress upon Red Cloud the military might of the United States, Secretary of War William Belknap led the Oglala war chief and Spotted Tail on a tour of the weaponry at the Washington Arsenal. The tour included the firing of a sixty-ton columbiad cannon, its twenty-inch round sailing through the air for three miles before splashing down in the Potomac. The chiefs observed the demonstration with great interest, but it didn't have quite the effect the officials had hoped for. Red Cloud and Spotted Tail argued that their warriors could ride all around the cannon and get away unscathed in the time it took the gunners to load and fire it. Additionally, they said the big gun was far too heavy to be moved. Of course, the monstrous columbiad was intended for placement in a fortification, but the chiefs still wondered why anyone would be foolish enough to come near it and "wait to be killed."

The generally stoic Red Cloud didn't actually exhibit any real surprise until the next-to-last day of his Washington stay, at a meeting with Secretary of the Interior Jacob Cox. At this meeting, Red Cloud reiterated what he'd said more than once during his visit: no roads were to be built across Lakota lands, and he wanted the Northern Pacific's survey stakes removed. Not only that, he also demanded that Fort Fetterman be abandoned. But the secretary had come armed with a copy of the Fort Laramie Treaty containing the chief's mark, as well as a large map showing the Great Sioux Reservation and the unceded Indian territory. Cox explained to Red Cloud that not only did the treaty allow for a railroad, but also the Sioux had promised not to disturb it; the railroad would be built. Then the secretary drew Red Cloud's attention to the map, and he pointed out the boundaries of the reservation and the unceded lands the signers had agreed to.

Red Cloud became agitated. "This is the first time I have heard of such a treaty," he said, "and I do not mean to follow it." He asked for the names of the interpreters at the treaty council; surely they hadn't properly conveyed the treaty's provisions. "The Great Spirit hears me today," his voice now getting louder, "and I tell nothing but what is true when I say that these words of the treaty were not explained. It was only said that treaty was for peace and friendship among the whites. When we took hold of the pen they said they would take the troops away, so we could raise children."

Secretary Cox responded that he'd been careful to make no mistakes: "We simply say this is the agreement made, as we remember." Cox then offered that he had several printed copies of the treaty, and he would give a copy to Red Cloud and the others present so it could be interpreted to them. "I will not take the paper with me," Red Cloud declared. "It is all lies."

Lies or not, Red Cloud was done fighting the white man. That the famous war leader had made the long journey to Washington, D.C., in the first place clearly signified he'd become resigned to diplomacy over war. When Red Cloud returned to Sioux country and told of the vast numbers of whites living east of the Mississippi, their fantastic possessions, and their frightening weaponry, he was "regarded as a sort of Baron Munchausen." The Lakotas who listened to his tales refused to believe them. They said the white people must have put bad medicine over his eyes "to make him see everything and anything that pleased them."

But all that didn't matter so much to the free-roaming Lakotas as the fact that Red Cloud had touched the pen. And just six months after he did so, whites were already violating the treaty. An expedition of more than one hundred miners and fourteen wagons set out from Cheyenne in May 1870, to prospect the Big Horn Mountains, which had been impossible to access previously because of the war in the Powder River country. That access should've still been impossible, for the Fort Laramie Treaty promised that no white men would be allowed in the unceded Indian territory. But that wasn't about to stop the miners who'd been salivating for years over rumors of rich gold deposits in the region. One recent story had it that there was enough gulch gold within twenty miles of the site of Fort C. F. Smith to pay the national debt!

The men of what was called the Big Horn Mining Expedition didn't find nearly that much of the precious metal. In fact, they determined that placer mining in the Big Horns wasn't even worth the effort. But one day while they were in camp, two strangers rode up: a mixed-blood Indian and a trader of French descent who went by "Beaver Joe." When Beaver Joe learned the purpose of the expedition, he reached into his pocket and pulled out a handful of gold nuggets, a few of which were the size of musket balls. This straightaway got the miners' attention, naturally, and a small party convinced Beaver Joe and his friend to lead them to the place that yielded such impressive specimens.

Beaver Joe took the miners to the Black Hills.

# The Act of Thieves

*[Indian] policies are inaugurated and pursued according
to the dictates of the ruling sentiment of the hour.*

D. C. POOLE, INDIAN AGENT

Many a strange story about the Sioux had been published in eastern newspapers, but perhaps the strangest was an 1871 report that Sitting Bull's leading warrior was a "Sandwich Islander." That wasn't true; the young man was actually a native of the South Pacific's Society Islands, some twenty-five hundred miles south of the Sandwich (Hawaiian) Islands. The Lakotas knew him as Grabber, but his birth name was Frank Grouard. He'd been born on the island of Tahiti in 1850, the son of a Mormon missionary and a Polynesian woman. When Frank was two, the missionary brought his family to California. His mother soon returned to the South Pacific with Frank's siblings, leaving Frank in California with his father. Unable or unwilling to care for the boy, the father gave his son up for adoption to a Mormon family, who relocated with Frank to Utah.

At age fifteen, Frank ran away from his Utah family and eventually ended up in Montana Territory. In the spring of 1867, he joined the short-lived Montana territorial militia. It was especially short-lived for Frank, as he deserted his company that August, taking with him several militia horses and guns. Frank's pilfering kept him jumping from one job to another. It also led him to periodically seek refuge with different Upper Missouri tribes. In the winter of 1869–70, an Indian trader named Abe Farwell employed Frank to take a load of presents to Sitting Bull's camp and persuade the Húnkpapa chief to come trade at his Missouri River post, above Fort Buford.

When Frank arrived at Sitting Bull's village, the chief saw a broad-shouldered, long-limbed young man six feet in height with dark, copper-colored skin. His broad face featured a strong nose and high cheekbones. Frank said later that Sitting Bull believed he'd come from some strange, unknown tribe far to the west. In any event, Sitting Bull took a liking to Frank, protected him, and adopted him as a brother. It wasn't until a year later that Grouard finally brought Sitting Bull to Farwell's small post, but it wasn't to trade. Instead, they stole all Farwell's horses.

Frank readily embraced the ways of a Lakota warrior, learning the fighting and hunting skills and also the Lakota language. No one enjoyed their life more with the antitreaty bands and, in time, Frank took an Oglala wife. His ability to read the letters taken from mail carriers ambushed and killed by the Lakotas was especially appreciated, as some were soldier letters with details of army activities. Frank would later claim he remained a captive in the years he rode and raided with Sitting Bull and Crazy Horse, but this was a fabrication intended to absolve himself with the whites he would one day return to. But that was still in the future. For now, Grabber was a valued friend of the two Lakota leaders.

Living in Sitting Bull's village, Frank saw a side of the chief rarely observed by non-Indians. He was "a great practical joker," recalled Grouard, "and even in serious council, he found immense delight in telling a joke on some chief or warrior present. Among his own people he was constantly laughing. He was quick tempered, but soon recovered his good nature."

Grouard was one of several recent changes to Sitting Bull's family life. His two wives, Snow on Her and Red Woman, had bickered and fought so much that Sitting Bull finally sent Snow on Her packing back to her people, the Arikaras. His daughters by Snow on Her, however, remained with their father. Red Woman gave birth to a son in 1870 but she died of an unknown illness a year later. Sitting Bull's mother and a sister helped with the children and other lodge-keeping duties, but Sitting Bull was on the lookout for a wife, and by the spring of 1872, the chief had taken a fancy to a young woman named Whole Tribe Seeing Her.

The brother of this young woman was Gray Eagle, and in the custom of the Lakotas, Sitting Bull approached Gray Eagle and offered him a very fast horse skilled at chasing buffalo for his sister. Gray Eagle accepted, and Whole Tribe Seeing Her moved into Sitting Bull's lodge, along with a small boy from a previous marriage. Sitting Bull also desired the younger sister of his new wife, named Four Robes, but Four Robes, who had a small boy as well, refused. By that fall, however, Gray Eagle wasn't as inclined to respect Four Robes's wishes. As Gray Eagle explained years later, Four Robes had no choice in the matter. "I wanted and needed a horse," he said, "and when I said for her to marry, she had to." Sitting Bull happily provided Gray Eagle a second horse.

Crazy Horse also experienced a major life change during this time. He seems to have been reluctant to marry following his disastrous affair with Black Buffalo Woman, although the experience did not prevent him from having additional liaisons with married women, at least according to stories passed down among the Oglalas. However, Crazy Horse's parents and friends pushed him to take a wife, which he did early in 1871. His bride was an Oglala named Black Shawl, an older sister of the warrior Red Feather. And at twenty-seven years of age, Black Shawl, like Crazy Horse, had remained single much longer than usual. Before the year was out, though, she bore her husband a baby girl. The child was given the name They Are Afraid of Her.

Finding a suitable trade partner, be it a clandestine outfit in Sioux country or the transient Métis (mixed-bloods) with their Red River carts weighted down with goods, was always a desire of Sitting Bull. As much as his people wished to freely wander the prairies in pursuit of buffalo and other game, they had long been dependent upon the white man's manufactured items, his sugar and tobacco—and his guns and ammunition. And the Lakotas had lots of buffalo robes and mules (stolen) to barter, as the bourgeois at the Fort Peck trading post well knew. And even though Sitting Bull and his warriors tried to destroy that post in 1868, the bourgeois had lately been sending gifts of tobacco to Sitting Bull's village, enticing him to bring his people in to trade.

On a September night in 1871, Sitting Bull and a small group of warriors approached the fort's wooden stockade. Sitting Bull halloed from his horse until he roused the bourgeois, who cautiously peered out at the dark forms, their feathered headdresses softly reflecting the moonlight. The chief gave his name and said he came in peace and wished for his people to begin trading there. This was welcome news to the bourgeois, and a truce was agreed upon. Over the next few weeks, several small parties of Húnkpapas brought their robes and skins to the post, and the bourgeois almost certainly provided Sitting Bull's people with the gunpowder, lead, and cartridges they were always in need of. The following month, Sitting Bull appeared again at Fort Peck and said he would like to speak with an Indian agent and continue this peace.

In the meantime, he promised to prevent any war parties from leaving his village.

Sitting Bull made good on his word, with his Strong Hearts violently attacking a group of warriors who attempted to slip out of the village for a raid. The trade had been too good thus far to allow any hostilities to disrupt it, particularly in regard to much-needed powder and lead. When a U.S. special Indian agent arrived at Fort Peck in November, however, Sitting Bull chose not to meet him, instead sending Black Moon and His Horse Looking, a brother-in-law, as emissaries, in company with several tribal headmen. Over the next few days, both sides discussed what it would take to achieve harmony. Black Moon stated that both he and Sitting Bull wanted peace with the white man, and their solution for achieving that end was, if anything, straightforward: keep white men out of their country. That meant, at the least, no Fort Buford and especially no Northern Pacific Railroad.

The agent told Black Moon and the others exactly what Red Cloud had been told in Washington. The Northern Pacific Railroad would be built. The Lakotas "might as well undertake to stop the Missouri River from flowing down stream as to stop the railroad." And if they made war upon the Northern Pacific, the Great Father would send soldiers to punish them. Black Moon didn't get angry upon hearing this. He still expressed to the agent a desire for peace. However, his people "didn't want any civilization," he said, "but wanted something to eat."

In his report to Washington, the agent wrote that he believed Black Moon and the others were sincere about wanting peace, yet Lakota leaders had learned that the more they professed peace in talks with agents and commissioners, the more likely these councils were to end with gifts. Black Moon's party wasn't disappointed in this regard, and they left Fort Peck with flour, sugar, coffee, and other goods purchased by the agent from the bourgeois. The hoped-for peace, however, lasted about as long as the sugar and coffee. By late spring, Lakotas had pulled up the stakes left by Northern Pacific surveyors the previous summer, and information reached the white man forts that Sitting Bull promised to disrupt any further survey work. Sitting Bull again made good on his word.

In the early hours of August 14, 1872, scattered groups of Lakotas, Cheyennes, and Arapahos silently crossed the Yellowstone River to the north side (near present-day Huntley, Montana). The river was running high and swift, but if anyone knew how to swim a western river safely with a horse, it was those who'd been born and raised there. On a large plain opening upon the Yellowstone was the camp of a Northern Pacific survey party and their military escort. The surveyors numbered about twenty while the escort consisted of four companies each of U.S. infantry and cavalry, amounting to 376 Bluecoats. Nearly seventy wagons were parked just outside the area of tents, with several wagons forming a large corral for the livestock. The camp also included about twenty gold seekers.

A slough in the shape of a horseshoe surrounded the camp on all but the river side, its belt of timber and thick willows offering the perfect cover for the stealthily approaching warriors. Many more warriors had yet to cross the river, but those first across had no intention of holding off for a concerted attack, even though that strategy had the best chance of success. Only on rare occasions did Plains Indians have what would be considered a formal battle plan, and when they did have a plan, it was very difficult to make the young men follow it—waiting for a signal to attack didn't lend itself to counting first coup. When White Bull was asked if warriors were ever punished for going off on their own against orders, he answered dismissively, "No, they are not white men."

Getting there first definitely paid off for several warriors who slipped into the prospectors' camp. They cut loose six mules and made off with several saddles and other items without waking the white men. The warriors who attempted to drive off the mule and cattle herd grazing in the middle of the plain, however, weren't so fortunate. Although the herd was a good three hundred yards from the wagon corral, they were guarded by alert herdsmen and four cavalrymen. When a group of warriors galloped out of the timber firing their guns and whooping in an attempt to stampede the animals, the guards quickly returned fire on the shadowy forms. A Húnkpapa named Plenty Lice fell from his saddle dead.

As muzzle flashes punctured the darkness and buzzing bullets crisscrossed the plain, the herders drove the stock into the corral while soldiers poured out of their tents and grabbed their breech-loading rifles and Spencer carbines. Warriors did capture fifteen head of beef cattle that refused to budge for the herders. The number of Indians occupying the timber steadily increased and some charged out from it into the open but were driven back. By the time a yellowish glow began to form on the eastern horizon, the heavy gunfire of the Bluecoats and gold seekers had forced the warriors to abandon the slough and retreat to some high bluffs overlooking the valley. The military escort now advanced and took up positions in the belt of timber.

As the sun's first rays bathed the bluffs in a fiery orange, the Bluecoats got an exceptional view of the warrior force: eight hundred to one thousand prancing Húnkpapas, Oglalas, Brulés, Miniconjous, Sans Arcs, Cheyennes, and Arapahos. Among them were their leaders Sitting Bull and Crazy Horse, who looked down toward the slough on what had become something of a stand-off, with the warriors firing sporadically and ineffectively from the blufftops. Except for the occasional bravery run, the warriors weren't about to charge within the range of the soldier guns.

It was at this moment that Sitting Bull dismounted and started slowly walking down toward the Long Knives, his decorated pipe bag at his side.

Sitting Bull turned and called out to the milling warriors, saying if anyone wanted to smoke with him, to come along. Although they weren't certain of exactly what Sitting Bull had in mind, his nephew White Bull, two Cheyenne warriors, and a Húnkpapa named Gets the Best Of immediately dismounted and followed the chief. When Sitting Bull reached a point about a hundred yards from the blufftop, he and those with him sat down on the ground in a small circle.

The chief now placed a small amount of tobacco in his pipe's bowl, and by striking a firesteel against a small piece of flint, he lit the tobacco and took some long draws on the pipe stem. The spot where Sitting Bull chose to smoke his pipe was less than five hundred yards from the Long Knives, easily within the killing range of their breechloaders, and soon heavy lead bullets began to kick up dirt around the chief's group. And there was no mistaking the sound of flying bullets, each one seemingly closer than the one before it. Nevertheless, Sitting Bull smoked peacefully without saying a word. When he passed the pipe to his companions, however, they each smoked as rapidly as possible. Once the last person had finished, Sitting Bull took a small stick and carefully cleaned the pipe bowl, placed the pipe back in its bag, stood up, and started walking up to the top of the bluff. The others, their nerves in tatters, took off in a sprint. Gets the Best Of was so rattled that he left his bow and arrows behind on the ground. White Bull raced back and retrieved the weapons.

Did Sitting Bull perform this highly dangerous feat to enrage the Long Knives? To flaunt his contempt and defiance? Was it to remind his people of his incredible bravery? Or was it a display of his faith in his war medicine and the power of *Wakan Tanka*? No one knows, and Sitting Bull never said. But White Bull called it "the most brave deed possible," ranking above counting coup.

Sitting Bull remounted his war horse and announced to the warriors, "That's enough. We must quit. That's enough." But Crazy Horse had been inspired by what he'd just witnessed. He challenged White Bull to join him on one last bravery run. White Bull accepted, and the two started their ponies down the bluff to the flat ground facing the soldiers occupying the slough. Crazy Horse wore a white shirt and leather leggings. No feathers hung from his hair, which was unbraided. The Oglala chief's only weapon was a spear, and he held it high in the air. White Bull was completely naked, as he was convinced he could move quicker in a fight without clothing.

The route Crazy Horse chose stretched for several hundred yards in the open and took them very close to the Long Knives, which, of course, was the point of a bravery run. The soldiers saw the two riders coming from a long way off, and the better marksmen attempted to guess the amount of lead required for their weapons—the spot in front of the racing warriors where they needed to place their bullet so as to hit their target. Yet despite the eruption of gunfire from the Long Knives, not a single bullet found its mark. Except one of the last.

As Crazy Horse and White Bull neared the warrior line at the end of their run, Crazy Horse's pony collapsed in a cloud of dust, sending its rider flying through air. The warriors watching let out a gasp but then began cheering as Crazy Horse jumped up from the ground unhurt and ran the final short distance to the warriors.

The bravery run of Crazy Horse and White Bull marked the end of the Battle of the Yellowstone. The day had grown hot, the warriors' horses were tired, and the warriors themselves were hungry. The soldiers suffered one killed and three wounded, and one of the gold seekers had been mortally wounded. Sitting Bull's losses amounted to two killed, several wounded, and at least a dozen dead war ponies. The bodies of the two slain warriors remained on the field.

Most of the Indians soon disappeared from the blufftops, but Sitting Bull remained behind for a short time, together with the Húnkpapa headman Old Bull and the warriors White Bull, Charging Hawk, Running Bear, Two Spears, and Horned Thunder. They watched the Bluecoats pile up a large stack of wood near the camp and ignite it. Once the fire began to burn hot, its flames licking upward, four Bluecoats carried the body of Plenty Lice to the fire and tossed it on top.

The flames leapt even higher.


Although Sitting Bull's warriors had been soundly repulsed, the fight rattled the surveyors and the army major in charge of their escort; they abandoned their work on the Yellowstone six days later. But the camp Sitting Bull's men attacked was actually one of two groups of surveyors laying out the route of the Northern Pacific that summer. On August 16, approximately 165 miles to the northeast of the Yellowstone battleground, some thirty Húnkpapa warriors led by Gall commenced harassing the companion expedition. Gall, now a full-fledged war chief under Sitting Bull, appeared painted from head to foot and wearing a tattered stovepipe silk hat. He was eventually joined by Sitting Bull and an additional two hundred warriors, but their modest force wasn't much of a threat to the surveyors' escort of 586 officers and men—plus artillery.

Other than a tense skirmish that marked the first time a Gatling gun was used against American Indians (several dozen warriors galloped within a hundred yards of the gun and not one was killed), there was no great contest. Sitting Bull climbed a high bluff and yelled to the surveyors and Long Knives that he was going to gather all the Lakotas along the Yellowstone and fight the white men again before they left the Badlands. But his promised big battle never came, and the surveyors were able to complete their work in the coming weeks.

As the *Helena Weekly Herald* saw it, a significant result of the summer's hostilities was that Sitting Bull and his allies had "shown their hand." That is, the antitreaty Lakotas, Cheyennes, and Arapahos had made it abundantly clear that they would not allow the railroad to be built if they could at all help it. Consequently, the next surveying expedition would be even better protected than the last, and so, too, the workers who would build the Northern Pacific line west. Thus, "the Indians will be obliged to do one of two things," the *Herald*'s editor wrote, "make themselves scarce in the vicinity of the line, or get their fill of fight."

Sitting Bull had no intention of making himself scarce on the Yellowstone, and it wasn't just the railroad he was determined to keep away. In early July 1873, his warriors discovered a large village of Crows and visiting Nez Perce on the Yellowstone, near the mouth of Pryor Creek. As Old Bull described it years later, the two tribes were "encamped in Sioux country, killing Sioux meat." The Crows, of course, considered this Crow country. But it really made no difference whose country it belonged to; the fact of the matter was that the Crows and the Lakotas were mortal enemies. They were "like two dogs fighting," said Old Bull; "if you pull them apart and then let them go, they will be at each other's throats again. They will fight; they cannot stop."

Sitting Bull, with a force of Húnkpapa, Cheyenne, and Arapaho warriors, attacked the village on the morning of July 9. Riding a black horse with white stockings, the chief led his men straight in among the tipis. Over the shouts, screams, and gunfire, his voice could be heard "high up in the air" giving commands. After the initial assault, and as hundreds of Crow warriors rallied, the Lakotas and Cheyennes withdrew to a safe distance, and for the next few hours, the fight consisted mostly of bloodless sparring and bantering between the two sides.

Finally, Sitting Bull ordered a stop to the contest, but as his men began to ride away, a mass of Crow and Nez Perce warriors suddenly came pouring out of the village. What had been a stalemate quickly turned into a rout. In a chase of more than fifteen miles, the Crows ran down and killed a number of their enemies. They also shot down many Lakota horses. Sitting Bull sorely needed the fighting prowess of Crazy Horse that day, but the Oglala war chief and his followers were more than five hundred miles to the southeast in the region of Nebraska's Republican River. For the time being, at least, the Crow village would continue to enjoy "Sioux meat," while Sitting Bull turned his attentions to the white man.

Just a few weeks after the debacle with the Crows, a Northern Pacific survey expedition appeared once again on the Yellowstone. And as the *Helena Weekly Herald*'s editor had predicted, its military escort was the largest yet: 1,530 officers and men, both infantry and cavalry, plus thirty-eight Indian and mixed-blood scouts. Two three-inch rifled Rodman guns composed the artillery.

The mounted troops, a total of ten companies, were commanded by a thirty-three-year-old lieutenant colonel who'd exited the Civil War as perhaps the North's most celebrated cavalryman, known to many as the "Boy General." More recently he'd become a celebrated "Indian fighter," having famously captured and destroyed the village of Southern Cheyenne chief Black Kettle in the winter of 1868, although some, particularly the Cheyennes, likened it to a massacre. It was the southern Plains Indians who gave him the name Long Hair. To the American public, he was the dashing George Armstrong Custer, and his regiment was the Seventh U.S. Cavalry.

Custer embraced life on the plains, especially its game animals, which he hunted with a passion. When on campaign, he had a penchant for fringed buckskin jackets and pants. Around his neck, the lieutenant colonel fancied a dapper crimson necktie. And he generally wore his reddish-gold hair long, its curls falling down the back of his neck.

Midmorning on August 4, 1873, approximately 250 warriors, mostly Húnkpapas and a few Miniconjous from Sitting Bull's village, watched from a hidden vantage point as two companies of the Seventh Cavalry, ninety-one officers and men, gradually made their way up the Yellowstone Valley, marching close to the river. The Long Knives were scouting a route for the expedition's main column, its 275 supply wagons following a few miles behind. The cavalry squadron's leader, Long Hair, wore a red shirt (far too hot that day for his leather jacket) and a wide-brimmed hat. His mount was a magnificent Kentucky thoroughbred.

As the warriors watched, they saw Long Hair's command halt in a grove of cottonwood trees and dismount. Custer had decided to make camp and await the arrival of the expedition's slow-moving train. The horses were led to the river to water and then brought back and picketed in the scattered woods to graze. Many of the Long Knives laid down to nap. The Lakotas, screened from view of Custer's men by a thick copse of cottonwoods a quarter mile upstream, quickly decided upon a plan of attack. Six warriors, decoys, would charge the Long Knives' camp as if trying to run off the horses, but they would stop short and retreat, hopefully bringing the cavalrymen with them. The decoys would lead Custer and his men past the cottonwoods hiding the warriors, when the Lakotas would charge out and smash the Long Knives' flank.

The first part of the plan worked to perfection. The troopers hastily mounted and started after the fleeing decoys, with Custer in the lead. But the lieutenant colonel, a veteran of countless hard-fought battles and skirmishes in his short military career, suspected a trap. When he slowed or halted, the six warriors did the same. Custer ordered most of his command to wait behind while he advanced with about twenty troopers. After trotting ahead a short distance, he then instructed this detachment to halt while he rode on with only an orderly. Both were mounted on good horses, and Custer wanted to tempt whatever might be lurking in the heavy woods he was now abreast of and distant only three hundred yards.

He didn't have to wait long. The warriors burst out of the trees and brush, whooping and yelling. They "moved in perfect line," Custer wrote later, "and with as seeming good order and alignment as the best drilled cavalry." Custer spurred his thoroughbred and raced back to his command. A volley broke up the Lakota charge, and the troopers made an orderly withdrawal to their camp in the cottonwood grove, which the warriors rapidly surrounded on all sides except that facing the river. Again and again, warriors made bravery runs along the line of troopers, drawing their fire, until the officers realized the Lakotas were trying to get them to exhaust their ammunition. Instructions went out to the troopers to only shoot to hold the line.

After at least three hours of attempting, unsuccessfully, to inflict casualties on the Long Knives, the warriors resorted to setting the grass on fire in four or five spots around the grove, but the grass was green, and there wasn't the slightest breeze. However, there was a large dust cloud rising on the eastern horizon— the other ten companies of the Seventh rushing to the rescue. The warriors displayed some confusion as they began to slowly pull back, and Custer chose this moment to mount his men and charge the Lakotas, his troopers yelling like demons. Despite their superior numbers, the warriors broke and fled pell-mell up the valley. The Long Knives chased them for three miles before turning back.

At what is sometimes called the Battle of the Tongue River (the fight occurred about six miles above that river's mouth), Custer's command suffered just one wounded cavalryman and two wounded horses. However, two noncombatants (a veterinary surgeon and the cavalry sutler) and a trooper were surprised by warriors between Custer's force and the main expedition column and killed. The Lakotas lost at least two killed, and five dead or badly wounded Indian ponies remained on the battleground. But the Lakotas weren't done fighting Long Hair just yet.

Custer's commander, Colonel David S. Stanley, decided that Sitting Bull and his followers needed to be punished. He ordered Custer to take most of his regiment, eight companies, find the Sioux village, and attack it. Including Indian scouts and staff officers, the attack force numbered 459 men. The Lakotas, fearing just such a movement from the Long Knives, had hurriedly retreated up the Yellowstone Valley more than seventy-five miles to near the mouth of the Big Horn. Here they constructed bullboats out of willow branches and buffalo hides and floated the women and children and family possessions—some four to five hundred lodges and much of their contents—across the river to the south side. Pitching their village a few miles up the Big Horn, Sitting Bull's fighters were soon reinforced by warriors from nearby camps of Sans Arcs, Miniconjous, Oglalas, and Cheyennes.

Custer and his men reached the point where the Lakotas crossed on August 10, but the river was too deep and fast to swim cavalry horses with all their trappings and the heavy weapons and accoutrements of the troopers. Sufficient timber was on the other side to make rafts, and several attempts were made to get a line across that could be used to retrieve the rafts once built, but the line kept snapping in the swift current. Toward the end of the day,

Custer's most trusted scout, the part Húnkpapa and part Arikara Bloody Knife, made two sturdy bullboats, and the lieutenant colonel was confident these would do the trick to get the line over at daylight the next morning. But before daylight came, the crack of gunfire sounded from the opposite bank, and lead balls whistled over the Seventh's campsite. "The Indians!" a trooper cried. "The Indians!"

The distance between the two banks was from five to six hundred yards, a range where only the best marksmen could shoot their weapons with accuracy. But sometimes a man could get lucky, and sporadic gunfire erupted from the brush and timber on both sides for the next two hours. During moments between shooting, Sitting Bull's warriors and Custer's Indian scouts shouted taunts back and forth. "Come, man, why don't you?" a warrior yelled from across the river. "We'll give you all you want. We are bound to have those horses of yours anyhow. We are going to cross and take them in spite of you."

This wasn't all talk. As Sitting Bull, various headmen, and women and children watched from the bluffs opposite, a steady stream of warriors swam the river with their ponies, climbing out of the cool water above and below the Long Knives' position. Then commenced a series of charges and probes on both sides of the regiment while other warriors continued to pour a menacing fire from across the river. The largest bunch of Lakotas and Cheyennes, three hundred or more, gathered on the upstream side of the Seventh. They galloped to and fro, their feather headdresses opening and closing, the trailers dancing in the wind. These warriors became more and more daring until Custer decided it was time to drive them off. After issuing the order for most of his regiment to advance, he shouted, "Strike up Garry Owen!" The regimental band, mounted nearby, at once began playing the jaunty Irish tune. "Custer knew how to avail himself of dramatic effects," recalled a journalist with the expedition.

The warriors, not suspecting the sudden charge (or the music), fled in disarray before the yelling cavalrymen. Gall, wearing a red blanket, was among those fleeing when his horse was shot out from under him. He swiftly jumped on another pony and dug his heels into the animal's flanks. Custer's men chased Gall and the rest of the warriors for several miles until the Indians finally splashed into the Yellowstone and swam to the other side.

Moments after the rout began, a loud boom came from downstream, echoing up and down the river. On the bluffs crowded with Indian observers, a cloud of dust sprayed into the air where an artillery shell slammed into the ground below them. Colonel Stanley had arrived with the Rodman guns. Sitting Bull and the others scattered as two more rounds rapidly followed the first. The Battle of the Big Horn was over.

About the same time Sitting Bull attacked Long Hair on the Yellowstone, approximately two hundred Pawnee Indians were moving camp in southwest Nebraska. The Pawnees were far from their reservation on the Loup River, but they'd been given permission to go on a buffalo hunt. It was morning, and the majority of the men of the village were out hunting. Consequently, those moving camp were mostly women and children. The hunting had been good for the last several days—nearly a thousand of the shaggy beasts had been harvested—and the women, horses, and dogs were loaded down with heavy packs of buffalo meat, robes, and furs.

The Pawnee column moved slowly across low, rolling hills near the fork of Frenchman Creek and the Republican River. Occasionally the column dipped out of sight as it entered a wide ravine or draw, but soon reappeared on the other side. Not a single tree grew on this open prairie; there was no direction where one couldn't see where the blue sky kissed the horizon. And the day matched the beauty of the view—until about one hundred Oglala and Brulé warriors topped a distant rise, coming toward the Pawnees at a full gallop.

The Pawnees sought shelter in a deep ravine while the few men with the caravan rode out singing their brave songs to meet the charging Lakotas. The two age-old enemies skirmished for about an hour with few if any casualties on either side, but additional warriors began arriving on the battleground until the Lakotas numbered six hundred, and they were better armed than the Pawnees. Among the Oglalas, some of whom were members of Red Cloud's Bad Face band, were Crazy Horse, his friend Flying Hawk, and Little Shield. The Brulés were led by a forty-two-year-old chief named Two Strike.

The Lakotas eventually surrounded their quarry on three sides, leaving the open end of the ravine as the only possibility of escape. The Pawnees frantically threw off the meat and robes from the packhorses, placed the women and children on the animals' backs, and raced down the ravine, which led to the Republican three miles away. But the Pawnees fled in a panic, running for their lives, the women and children screaming and crying. They offered no resistance to slow their pursuers, and the result was nothing short of a bloodbath. Those who weren't able to flee as rapidly, primarily the women and children, the warriors easily ran down and killed. Some of the women were raped before being slain.

An army surgeon who arrived on the battleground later that day counted sixty bodies, and the grizzly scene horrified him: "Dead warriors lay grim in death, with bows still grasped in their stiffened fingers. Suckling infants were pinned with arrows to their mothers' breasts. Some lay on the ground, their bowels protruding from ghastly wounds made by knives. Others presented to us their skinless heads, the red blood glazed upon the skull where the scalp had been torn off."

The Lakotas killed twelve Pawnee horses and captured one

hundred. They also made off with some of the buffalo meat, robes, and furs. A total of eleven Pawnees were taken prisoner. The Brulés carried away two girls, a boy, and a woman. The Oglalas' captives were three women and four girls aged two to ten years. The subagent for the southern Oglalas, who also happened to be an agency interpreter, reported the names of those Lakotas who held captives, and in his list appears the name "Mad Horse." Just like English words, Lakota words can have more than one meaning or interpretation, and they can vary depending on the translator. "Mad Horse" was another way of translating *Tasunke Witko*, Crazy Horse. The thirty-two-year-old Crazy Horse might have been renowned in the world of the Lakotas, but he remained a little-known figure in the world of the white man. This would soon change.

Through pressure from the Oglala and Brulé agents, the Pawnee captives were turned over and sent home to their people. Before the prisoners departed, the Lakotas are said to have gifted them horses and many presents. However, this seeming gesture of peace did nothing to quell the bitterness and animosity of the Pawnees, who lost so many friends and loved ones in the massacre. The Pawnee chief Rules His Son, whose wife and son were murdered in the attack, hated the Sioux until his last breath passed from his lips in 1928 at the age of 104.

Crazy Horse and his followers, loaded down with Pawnee booty, rode north to the Powder River country. Their route took them past the rugged Black Hills, rising like its own continent out of a sea of grass. Here the women of the village would have replenished their supply of lodgepoles. They also passed the imposing Bear Butte, where Crazy Horse's father talked to the bear that was *Wakan Tanka* and near where Crazy Horse was born.

This country was the Oglala war chief's homeland, but he saw enemies on all sides. And, treaty or no treaty, the whites were becoming bolder about encroaching on Lakota lands. It's what made his alliance with Sitting Bull so important. Neither leader had enough men to fight the white man alone. Even together, they would need help from other Lakota bands, as well as the Cheyennes and Arapahos. The resistance, however, increasingly centered on Sitting Bull and Crazy Horse, and by all accounts, the two were not just allies but strong friends. According to Sitting Bull's nephew One Bull, Crazy Horse believed in the supreme chief and would do anything for him.

Although not numbering more than two thousand men, the warriors who followed the two leaders and their fellow antitreaty chiefs were arguably the best horseback fighters in the world. Living on buffalo meat and other wild game (and the occasional stolen beef cattle, not to mention village dogs), the young men were mostly muscle and sinew—lean, strong, and agile. Crazy Horse's bodyguards, known as the Last-Born Child Society, were especially impressive. Organized and named by the Oglala war chief, it consisted of more than forty men who were second-born sons or later within their families. As in many cultures, a family's oldest male offspring was favored in a number of ways. But as Eagle Elk, himself a member of the Last-Born Child Society, explained, if a younger brother "did great deeds or something very brave, then they would have greater honor than the first child. They were always making themselves greater."

As someone who'd earned his acclaim and leadership status on the battlefield, Crazy Horse understood what motivated these young men. And he wasn't disappointed. "They were all very brave warriors," Eagle Elk recalled, "and always went out with him and fought with him."

And the warriors of Crazy Horse and Sitting Bull were now fighting with improved weaponry, both captured and acquired in trade. A Crow chief told commissioners in 1873 that the Sioux must have "good white-men friends," as they were far better armed than his warriors. He said the Sioux carried lever-action Henrys and Winchesters, Spencer carbines, and breechloading Springfields. Custer made a similar observation after his fights that summer with Sitting Bull on the Yellowstone and added that "their supply of metallic rifle cartridges seemed unlimited, as they were anything but sparing in its use." In truth, the proper cartridges for their firearms were often in short supply, but the warriors had learned how to reload their spent shell casings.

These modern firearms didn't replace the bow and arrow. They did, however, make Sitting Bull and Crazy Horse's men increasingly formidable opponents. The only thing that intimidated these warriors in a fight was artillery, "thunder iron," as some called it. The trade-off for the Long Knives was that artillery slowed a cavalry column down. Once the Plains tribes learned to fear the artillery, a military force dragging along cannons in a country without roads would find it quite challenging to catch up to and surprise a village.

In the fall of 1873, Crazy Horse's village was nestled along the Little Big Horn River. Frank Grouard, Grabber, was now living in this camp. According to Grouard, his close relationship with Sitting Bull ended bitterly earlier that year when Grouard was caught in a lie: he told Sitting Bull he was going off for a few days to steal horses when he instead visited Fort Peck. "If you ever saw a mad Indian, he was one," Grouard recalled. Grouard believed Sitting Bull intended to kill him. But this is Grouard's version of the incident. Sitting Bull's side of the story—and this episode is likely just that, a story—is unknown. The supreme chief did come to wish Grabber dead, but that was after his adopted brother turned on his Lakota friends.

Grouard's presence in Crazy Horse's village is important,

because it's through him that we know something of the death of Crazy Horse's daughter, They Are Afraid of Her. It occurred while Crazy Horse was on a raid against the Crows. The two-year-old girl came down with an unknown illness and died. Her grieving mother and other close relatives helped dress They Are Afraid of Her in her best beaded outfit and moccasins and, together with her favorite playthings, wrapped the body in a fine buffalo robe. Securely bound with leather thongs, the small bundle was then carried to a burial scaffold erected on a high prominence near the village and placed on top.

The village moved shortly after They Are Afraid of Her's death, and it was some seventy miles from her burial place when Crazy Horse returned to his lodge and a distraught Black Shawl. Crazy Horse, overcome with emotions of pain and disbelief, insisted on visiting his daughter's grave, and he asked his friend Grouard to accompany him. The two traveled for two days to reach the barren hill with the lonely scaffold, and while Grouard made camp, Crazy Horse went to the wooden structure, climbed on top, and sat there silently with his daughter's remains. Crazy Horse remained on the scaffold for three days and nights. No food and no water did he ask for or consume in that time.

At sunrise on the fourth day, Crazy Horse shook Grouard awake and told him it was time to go home. Grouard said Crazy Horse never revealed to anyone where they'd been or what they'd done in their time away. The few words and the brooding were characteristic of the Oglala leader.

The Panic of 1873 put a temporary stop to the Northern Pacific, but it didn't put a stop to the white man's incursions. In February 1874, a heavily armed force of some 150 white men started from the town of Bozeman, in Montana's Gallatin Valley, bound for the

Yellowstone. The name of their organization was the Yellowstone Wagon Road and Prospecting Expedition, which was a fairly apt description of its purpose, especially the word *prospecting*. Although the white men found little gold on Sioux lands, they did find hundreds of angry warriors led by Sitting Bull, Crazy Horse, and others. After four sharp skirmishes, the expedition turned back at the end of April.

Headlines in the *Bozeman Avant Courier* announced that the members of the returning expedition slew one hundred Indians in their fights with the warriors and suffered only one of their own number killed. But while the losses of the Lakotas and their allies were indeed severe, they likely didn't approach one hundred. And the newspaper failed to report that a few of the Indian casualties resulted from poisoning. After capturing a large batch of the warriors' pemmican, the white men "dosed it pretty strong with strychnine" and left it behind for the Indians to recover.

Although the Yellowstone Wagon Road and Prospecting Expedition failed to deliver the hoped-for news of fantastic mineral wealth in the Powder River country, stories of gold in the Black Hills became increasingly tantalizing. One report from Fort Randall on the Missouri River told of a party of Indians who arrived direct from the Black Hills with enough gold nuggets to fill two hands. Another story came from Fort Laramie of an Indian woman who possessed a shiny gold nugget the size of an egg. She said it came from the Black Hills.

At the same time, newspapers spread fear among whites in the West concerning the antitreaty bands. "Crazy Horse is on the warpath," read an Indian agent's letter published in the *Sioux City Journal* and several other papers in March. The agent further reported that the Sioux were trying to entice peaceful Cheyennes to join them in a war against the white man. Even more terrifying to westerners, however, was a rumor that white men working in the interests of the Sioux and Cheyennes were in Denver "for the purpose of spying out the situation and with the ultimate view of buying arms and ammunition." Some of the white men were thought to be "in disguise." This rumor was published in newspapers in Colorado and Montana in April with the warning to expect trouble with the Indians that summer.

Lieutenant General Phil Sheridan, commander of the Division of the Missouri, came up with a plan that would resolve both the question about gold in the Black Hills and possibly lead to a solution for the "trouble" from the free-roaming northern tribes. With the approval of his superiors in Washington, he ordered a military expedition to explore the Black Hills. Sheridan publicly claimed the expedition's objective was a reconnaissance for a military post in the heart of the Hills. Such a post, he said, would allow a garrison to be at the ready to swoop down on villages and livestock of Indians that raided white settlements. Yet the expedition included two experienced miners.

Sheridan and those above him, from General William Tecumseh Sherman, to Secretary of War W. W. Belknap, to President Ulysses S. Grant, well knew what the discovery of gold would mean in these times of financial hardship: hordes of white men invading the Black Hills. And regardless of the provisions formally agreed upon in the Treaty of 1868, the Lakotas would be pushed out and forced to relinquish their claim to the sacred hills. The loss of those lands would be another step closer to the demise of the antitreaty bands' buffalo culture, another step closer to confinement on a reservation.

The man Sheridan chose to lead the expedition was one of his favorite officers in the army, Lieutenant Colonel George Armstrong Custer—Long Hair. Shortly before the expedition departed Fort Abraham Lincoln on July 2, Custer told a reporter that it was "a shame that so vast a region, reputed so rich in minerals and agricultural resources, lying almost in the center of the continent, surrounded except on the north by civilization, should so long remain unexplored."

Custer was forgetting that the Black Hills had previously been partially explored by army personnel, primarily for purposes of mapmaking. The Lakotas hadn't liked the intrusion then and they didn't like it now. A missionary, probably Father Jean-Baptiste Marie Genin, arrived at Fort Abraham Lincoln to warn Custer that the Lakotas were prepared to "contest every foot of the march," and he begged Long Hair to abandon the expedition to avoid bloodshed. But Custer was never one to be frightened off by the prospect of an Indian fight. And he insisted, as did the army's top commanders, that the 1868 treaty gave the U.S. government the right to explore Lakota lands.

The long column that entered the Black Hills that summer made for a wondrous sight. The cavalcade included ten companies of the Seventh Cavalry, two companies of infantry, sixty Indian scouts, 150 wagons, three Gatling guns, several scientists, three newspaper correspondents, a photographer, and the miners. The expected resistance from Sitting Bull never materialized, at least while the column wended its way through the Hills' lush valleys. So while scientists explored among the bluffs and miners worked the earth, Custer hunted to his heart's content and collected specimens of the area's fauna for New York City's Central Park zoo.

Once the expedition started on its homeward journey, the Lakotas finally made their displeasure known. For a stretch of two hundred miles, they set the prairie on fire, creating large swaths of burnt grass that made finding adequate forage for the column's hundreds of horses and mules a challenge. It was nothing, however, compared with the fire that swept the nation's press. Long Hair's miners had found gold. The first news of the discovery came from the *New York Tribune*'s man with the expedition. One of Custer's scouts had ridden hell-for-leather with the correspondent's dispatch to Fort Laramie, where it was transmitted east over the "long tongue." The *Tribune's* scoop appeared on that paper's front page on Monday, August 10, 1874, under the headline "A New Gold Country."

Custer's own report, published in Chicago's *Inter Ocean* ten days later, proclaimed that his miners had found gold from the roots of the grass down. And in the creeks, almost every pan full of earth and sand produced the precious metal. In addition to its incredible mineral riches, Custer painted the Black Hills as a virtual Shangri-la. The rippling streams coursed with the purest water, and the valleys were covered with succulent grasses, perfect for raising stock. The region received plenty of rain, he wrote, and there was no sign of drought. The best-quality building stone was "inexhaustible," and timber for fuel and lumber was "sufficient for all time to come."

Long Hair had still more glowing observations when interviewed by a reporter for the *Bismarck Tribune* on September 1. He also happily provided the best route to the "gold region," which could be reached in only eight days' travel from Bismarck. As for the 1868 treaty with the Lakotas, Custer admitted the Black Hills were currently off-limits to whites, but he planned to urge the extinguishment of the Indian title as soon as possible. Such a move had long been called for by westerners who coveted the Black Hills' resources. "It was bad enough," one Montana newspaper editor commented, "to squander millions ostensibly supplying Indians. But it is worse, if reports of the Black Hills are correct, to keep such a treasure-house barred to all save savages." The editor called the 1868 treaty a "treaty of shame" and "one-sided." Until the government rescinded those provisions of the treaty pertaining to the Black Hills, he wrote, the region would be "as valueless to civilization as though it were in the heart of Africa."

The army pledged to enforce the treaty's terms, but gold-seeking expeditions were already forming. One party of miners left Bismarck that October. By the following summer of 1875, some eight hundred white men crowded the creeks and gullies and scrambled over the rocky outcroppings. "Miners are everywhere," an army officer then in the Black Hills jotted in his journal. The *Bismarck Tribune*'s editor triumphantly declared that "obstructions by [the] military or no obstructions, with or without the consent of the Government, the Hills are being filled up with miners, and within the next three months we shall be surprised if enough do not go there to clean out the whole Sioux Nation."

On a trip to Washington to see the Great Father in May 1875, Red Cloud, Spotted Tail, and several other Lakota chiefs and head-men were asked again and again if they would give up the Black Hills. The invariably obliging Spotted Tail, who said he wanted to live on white man's food and even become a white man himself, was in favor of selling a part of their lands at a good price. So, too, the formerly defiant Red Cloud. There is "no use opposing the whites," Red Cloud explained, "as they will take the country anyway in a few years." The fifty-four-year-old Red Cloud, who, not that long ago, held sway over the Powder River country, was now more concerned with holding sway over the Oglalas at the Red Cloud Agency (located on the White River near present-day Crawford, Nebraska). Seven years earlier, the legendary Oglala war chief had touched the pen, and since that time he'd become exactly what Sitting Bull and Crazy Horse despised.

In August 1875, beneath the looming Big Horn Mountains, the villages of Sitting Bull and Crazy Horse and other antitreaty bands were clustered along the upper Tongue River (present-day Dayton, Wyoming). While those camps were on the Tongue, a large party of approximately eighty-five Lakotas, Cheyennes, and Arapahos under Young They Fear Even His Horses arrived from the Red Cloud Agency. It was quite common for Indians from the reservation to visit the antitreaty bands in the summer—they had relatives and friends in the camps, and with their access to goods and ammunition sold by traders at the agencies, these visits were also opportunities for trade. But this party had a special mission. They came with news of a council to be held the next month with white commissioners from Washington. The Great Father wanted to buy the Black Hills, and the commissioners wished to invite the chiefs of the antitreaty bands to the council.

For Sitting Bull, the news of yet another proposed treaty council wasn't surprising. The white man was always wanting something more. What did surprise him, however, was to see his adopted brother Grabber, Frank Grouard. Grouard was there on behalf of the commissioners, too. It was the beginning of a long career as an interpreter and scout, one in which Grouard had no qualms about using his knowledge of the Lakotas against them. "Knowing all they do themselves, [I am] able to meet them at every step and to foil all their designs," he wrote his mother, "and all was learnt by my close application to the study of their character." Sitting Bull would later say that only one white man ever fooled him, and that was Grouard.

The village leaders gathered to decide if any should go meet the commissioners. Several dozen spoke. Big Breast stood and said, "All those that are in favor of selling their land from their children, let them go." Sitting Bull followed with a long speech and, looking directly at Grouard and a fellow interpreter, said, "Are you the Great God that made me, or was it the Great God that made me who sent you? If He asks me to come see him, I will go, but the Big Chief of the white men must come see me. I will not go to the reservation. I have no land to sell. There is plenty of game here for us. We have enough ammunition. We don't want any white men here."

A number of those in the delegation from the Red Cloud

Agency encouraged the chiefs and headmen to see what the commissioners had to say, but after Sitting Bull's strong statement, none were ready to admit any thought of accepting the invitation. Crazy Horse refused to speak at the meeting, instead having his uncle, Little Hawk, speak for him. (Not to be confused with Crazy Horse's half brother, also named Little Hawk.) "My friends," Little Hawk said, "the other tribes have concluded not to go in, and I will have to say the same thing."

Many warriors in the villages were angry at the delegation. They viewed the agency Indians, and also Grouard, as cooperating with the whites to take their lands. Rumors circulated that an attack was planned that night on the emissaries. When the rumor got to Crazy Horse, however, he immediately let it be known that no bullets were to be fired into the camp. Anyone who came to his village in peace would be fed and watered, he said, and they would smoke together. "My friends," Crazy Horse announced, "whoever attempts to murder these people will have to fight me, too." No one dared defy Crazy Horse, and the delegation was allowed to return to the Red Cloud Agency unmolested. Grouard always credited Crazy Horse as having saved their lives.

Jealousy between Red Cloud and Spotted Tail nearly ended the council with the commissioners before it began. And even though the antitreaty bands had denounced the council and made it clear they wouldn't attend, more than three hundred warriors showed up to disrupt and intimidate the chiefs and headmen who sat down with the commissioners. Crazy Horse's comrade Little Big Man arrived completely naked, his skin covered from head to toe in bright paint and his long hair unbraided. Small but muscular, the warrior brought to mind "a bronze statue of some ancient gladiator," reported a correspondent.

Little Big Man came with a gladiator's fierce demeanor that

didn't bode well, especially as he'd already threatened to kill a commissioner. In an especially tense moment, the Oglala warrior and several scantily clad followers rode in a circle around the council place as Little Big Man shook his lever-action rifle high in the air and shouted that he would shoot any chief who advocated selling the Black Hills.

The histrionics of Little Big Man frightened many of those present, both Indians and whites, but they didn't result in ending the talks on the sale of the Black Hills. Nor did an angry speech from the Miniconjou Lone Horn, who rode up and disrupted the council much like Little Big Man. From his saddle, Lone Horn yelled at the Brulés and Oglalas present for trying to sell his country. "Red Cloud, Spotted Tail, and you people," he said, "you are doing the act of thieves!" Such angry dissent didn't help, of course, but what actually ended the talks was the high price Red Cloud and Spotted Tail placed on the Hills. The "old plan of getting Indian land for a few beads and cheap trinkets," commented one newspaper, "will no longer work."

The chiefs' selling price steadily increased over the course of the negotiations until it finally reached $70 million. And on top of the fixed selling price, Spotted Tail believed they should be paid for the gold taken out of the Hills by the miners over the summer. An offer from the commissioners to "borrow" or lease the Black Hills for $400,000 annually was considered too small. Thus the commissioners departed without an agreement, and the Black Hills council, in the eyes of the commissioners and newspapers across the United States, was considered a complete failure. But for the antitreaty bands, it appeared as a complete victory. "Our hearts are happy when we are away from the whites," said the Oglala warrior Moon Eagle to a correspondent, "and we are glad our brothers have not sold the Hills, for they do not own them."

And yet, the miners weren't going anywhere. And many more

were on the way, along with town builders, ranchers, and other settlers, infiltrating every valley, gulch, and streambed, shooting game and cutting timber. Consequently, the U.S. government would persist in its efforts to extinguish the Lakotas' title to the lands, treaty be damned. In speaking of the failed council, the *Inter Ocean* offered that "the extravagant demands of these savages, made in a most insolent way, will likely result in a total change of method in treating with the Sioux." The statement was prescient. Attempts at peaceful negotiations, particularly when it came to those Indians deemed "troublesome" (i.e., the antitreaty bands), had come to an end.

# Soldiers Coming with Heads Down

*I fought for my people. My people said I was right.*
*I will answer to my people. The friends of the dead*
*palefaces must answer for those who are dead.*

SITTING BULL

*Powder River, Moon When Ducks Come Back (March) 1876*

Some one hundred lodges of Northern Cheyennes and a few Miniconjous and Oglalas hug a grove of cottonwoods and willows near the river's west bank. The Cheyennes are followers of chiefs Old Bear, Box Elder, and Black Eagle. The Oglalas are led by Crazy Horse's friend He Dog. A late-winter storm has left a heavy blanket of snow on the ground, and the temperature is well below freezing. Near the camp, on both sides of the river, hundreds of ponies paw at the crunchy snow and push it around with their muzzles to find the dry grass underneath.

Shortly before 9:00 A.M., the sun begins to burn off the low blue-gray clouds and mist. Most of the village inhabitants, about 735 people, remain snug in their warm lodges, but a few individuals venture outside to check on their horses, perform some chore, or visit a relative. An old holy man climbs a knoll about two hundred yards from the village to offer his morning prayers to *Wakan Tanka*. Though the snow and cold is an uncomfortable reminder that winter is not yet ready to surrender to spring, the valley and village stretching out below the holy man are a beautiful, tranquil sight. And then the holy man sees them—galloping, thundering Long Knives, their revolvers held high, their horses' flaring nostrils shooting bursts of condensation into the frigid air.

"The soldiers are right here!" he yells, running back to the lodges. "The soldiers are right here!"

His cry is followed by a single, terrifying shout from one of the Bluecoats: "Charge, my boys!"

The cavalrymen come crashing into the village, dashing among lodges, firing at everything that moves. Warriors fight back as screaming women and children run for safety. Some escape by cutting a slit in the back of their tipis. Wooden Leg, a young Northern Cheyenne, starts for the closest ponies, which the troopers are beginning to round up. He catches a horse belonging to Old Bear, quickly bridles it, and jumps on its back. His only weapons are a bow and arrows, but he makes good use of them, sending several sharp arrows singing through the air.

Even with the Long Knives overrunning the village, Wooden Leg wants his shield and war medicine from his lodge, and he gallops toward it, only to see the women and old people struggling to get away with whatever they can pack. He comes upon a mother carrying a little girl under one arm and dragging a ten-year-old girl. All three are crying. "Let me take one of the children," he says.

Wooden Leg pulls the older girl up behind him. She reaches her arms around his waist and they ride off. Hardly have they started, however, when Wooden Leg sees a woman with a baby on her back and two small children under her arms. Stumbling behind is an eight-year-old boy. Wooden Leg reaches down for the boy and seats him in front. They ride until Wooden Leg finds a place where the children are out of danger. Then Wooden Leg gallops back to the village to join the fight.

But the camp is in the hands of the Long Knives, who've also captured most of the horse herd. The warriors pour a heavy fire from behind rocks on a high bluff overlooking the village and watch angrily as the Long Knives loot and burn their lodges and possessions: eagle-feather bonnets, dresses heavy with beadwork, painted and embroidered buffalo robes, brightly colored wool blankets, a ledger book brimming with drawings of various coups, bar lead for casting bullets, thousands of pounds of dried and fresh meat, pots and kettles, knives, hatchets, sewing kits, and more than 125 saddles. Here and there, the flames find a cache of gunpowder, and the resulting small explosion and cloud of white smoke causes the Bluecoats to pause and look. A splendidly dressed chief, perhaps He Dog, rides back and forth along the cliff, exhorting the warriors.

About 2:00 P.M., with the village mostly destroyed, the Long Knives mount their horses and begin to withdraw, glad to get away from the warriors' withering fire. But a wounded trooper is unable to follow. Wooden Leg points the man out to Chief Two Moons and a fellow Cheyenne named Ridge Bear. Two Moons shoots first but misses. Next Ridge Bear takes steady aim with his muzzleloading Northwest gun, squeezes the trigger, and the speeding round ball strikes the Bluecoat in the back of the head. The three Cheyennes and another warrior dash through the hanging smoke from Ridge Bear's gun. They find the trooper still alive and beat and stab him to death. Wooden Leg strips the dead man of his nice but bloody blue coat and puts it on.

For three days and three nights, the Cheyennes and Oglalas

from the village trudge through the cold with very little to eat and hardly any warm clothing until they reach Crazy Horse's village, situated on a tributary of the Powder. From every tipi in the camp can be heard the voices of the patriarchs: "Cheyennes, come and eat here." All the refugees are welcomed, fed, and sheltered. No one is turned away; it was an unpardonable sin to let anyone go hungry. In the evening, Two Moons goes to Crazy Horse's lodge.

"I'm glad you are come," Crazy Horse says. "We are going to fight the white man again."

"All right. I am ready to fight," says Two Moons to the war chief. "I have fought already. My people have been killed, my horses stolen; I am satisfied to fight."

After President Ulysses S. Grant took office in 1869, he implemented a so-called Peace Policy that emphasized restricting the various tribes in the West to reservations, where they would undergo a process of acculturation overseen by white agents and various Christian religious organizations. The policy of "civilizing" the Plains tribes wasn't all that new, but it was hoped that with the Indians content on their reservations—and distant from white settlers—peace would prevail. The pressing issue of the Black Hills, however, caused Grant to radically rethink his dealings with the Lakotas.

On November 3, 1875, behind closed doors at the White House, Grant discussed his strategy for the coming months with Generals Sheridan and George Crook, Secretary of War Belknap, and others in his administration. The army would no longer attempt to keep miners out of the Black Hills, he said. As for the antitreaty bands, he'd had enough of Sitting Bull and Crazy Horse's followers; they were hindering a deal to acquire the Hills. For these bands, Grant issued an ultimatum: they must "go upon their proper reserves or be whipped." However, military action would be portrayed as punishment for the unruly Sioux, not as a means to remove Indian title to the Black Hills. Support for this ploy came from an Indian Bureau inspector, who gladly gave an interview to Chicago's *Inter Ocean*, in which he talked at length on what a scourge Sitting Bull and his warriors were to both white settlers and friendly Indians on the northern plains. Very few spoke up in defense of the Lakotas, and, as Father Genin observed, the Indians had no newspapers of their own to tell their side.

Upon instructions from the secretary of the interior, Lakota and Cheyenne couriers left the various Indian agencies in December to inform Sitting Bull, Crazy Horse, and the other antitreaty chiefs and headmen that they must remove with their people to a reservation by January 31. Those who didn't come in would be reported to the War Department as "hostile Indians," and they would be hunted down by the army and crushed. It was the way the white man had dealt with North America's native inhabitants from time immemorial: accept subjugation or risk extermination.

Grant and his generals assumed the most defiant chiefs, particularly Sitting Bull and Crazy Horse, wouldn't obey the secretary's directive. It was an outcome they actually desired. The January 31 deadline, coming in the dead of winter, was intentional and completely unrealistic. Some Indian agents didn't receive the order to contact the antitreaty bands until the third week of December, and for those Lakotas and Cheyennes inclined to obey it, heavy snows made the prospect of moving families, lodges, and possessions extremely daunting. Meanwhile, army quartermasters began buying up hundreds of mules and amassing stacks of pack saddles to transport ammunition and other supplies for the coming campaign in Sioux country.

Wooden Leg remembered his village receiving the warning to leave the unceded territory, where they had every right to be according to the 1868 Fort Laramie Treaty. The instructions to relocate to the reservation puzzled the Northern Cheyenne leadership. They hadn't seen any white men for months and were, in fact, trying to stay away from the whites. "We were rich, contented, at peace with the whites so far as we knew," Wooden Leg recalled. "Why should soldiers come out to seek for us and fight us?" Nevertheless, the village of Cheyennes, Miniconjous, and He Dog's Oglalas slowly began to make its way eastward to report at an agency—until the late-winter storm delayed them on the Powder River. It was there, on the morning of March 17, 1876, that the Long Knives—six cavalry companies from a force under General George Crook—found them. Although the Cheyennes and Lakotas lost, at the most, two or three killed, it was the destruction of their homes that hurt most. It "broke the friendly feeling we had for [the whites]," recalled Two Moons. "And our hearts were bad when our babies and children cried in the cold."

The Battle of Powder River, as the surprise attack came to be known, was the army's de facto declaration of war on the free-roaming Lakotas and Cheyennes. And there was considerable jubilation in the army and in the press at the time, as the village was identified by Frank Grouard as belonging to Crazy Horse—the dusky scout led them right to it. But Grouard was mistaken. No matter, more Long Knives would soon be taking the field. And once the followers of Sitting Bull, Crazy Horse, and the other antitreaty chiefs were defeated and forced onto the Great Sioux Reservation, the Grant administration believed it could more easily cow the Lakotas into signing away the Black Hills—a singular provision in the Fort Laramie Treaty stipulated that any land cessions required the signatures of three-fourths of all adult male Lakotas.

For the moment, however, upholding the treaty's provisions didn't seem to be a concern of the U.S. government. And, ironically enough, neither was it for Sitting Bull and Crazy Horse.

Their marks were not to be found anywhere on the "False Papers." In fact, the two chiefs had never touched the pen in their lives. And now, after the Powder River fight, where their Cheyenne friends were made poor, the stupidity and treachery of this treaty business was even more palpable.

Crazy Horse led his people and the Powder River refugees northeast to Sitting Bull's encampment of Húnkpapas and Miniconjous. They found it a few miles from the Powder in a broken country of chalky white buttes rising above scattered ponderosa pines. More than a hundred tipis and a large pony herd crowded the valley of a small creek. Sitting Bull's people received the refugees just as warmly as Crazy Horse's Oglalas, offering a bounty of gifts: "Who needs a blanket? Take this one." "Who wants this tipi? It is yours." "Who wants a horse? You may have this one."

"Oh what good hearts they had!" recalled Wooden Leg. "I never can forget the generosity of Sitting Bull's Húnkpapa Sioux on that day."

Throughout the months of April and May, as the village moved from one campsite to the next, it saw a steady stream of new arrivals: Sans Arcs, Sihásapas, Brulés, Two Kettles, and Southern Cheyennes. The Lakotas also welcomed a small party of their eastern cousins, Santees and Yanktonais, comprising about fifteen lodges. Leading the Santees was a chief who, much like Sitting Bull, had spent his life resisting the white man. This chief had fought valiantly at Killdeer Mountain twelve years earlier and managed to stay one step ahead of the Long Knives ever since. He was Inkpaduta, now sixty years old but no less defiant.

Also joining Sitting Bull that spring were agency Indians simply wanting to visit relatives, harvest fresh buffalo meat to supplement their meager government rations, and participate in the annual Sun Dance. But Sitting Bull's reputation also had a lot to do with attracting various bands to his side. As Wooden Leg recalled, the supreme chief had "come into notice as the most consistent advocate of the idea of living out of all touch with white people." He was admired as a man "whose medicine was good—that is, as a man having a kind heart and good judgment as to the best course of conduct. . . . He was strong in religion—the Indian religion. He made medicine many times. He prayed and fasted and whipped his flesh into submission to the will of the Great Medicine."

The chiefs and headmen in the big village were well aware of the threat of attack from the Long Knives. Troops were already marching down the Yellowstone from Fort Ellis, and soon the army would initiate a three-pronged invasion of Sioux country intended to ensnare the antitreaty bands. The Long Knives hoped to do to Sitting Bull's village what it had done to the Cheyennes and Lakotas on the Powder River in March. They would make them poor, and those of Sitting Bull's followers who survived would have no choice but to go to the agencies and live off what the U.S. government provided.

But like a buffalo herd on the prairie surrounded by predators, those gathering around Sitting Bull felt safety in numbers. "We supposed the combined camps would frighten off the soldiers," recalled Wooden Leg. "Then we could separate again into the tribal bands and resume our quiet wandering and hunting."

At each village campsite, the various chiefs convened for a council. After passing a pipe, they listened to the reports of their scouts, who fanned out for miles in all directions looking for game and any evidence of the Long Knives. Based on these reports, much of their discussions centered on where they would move next. The growing number of lodges and horses exhausted food, wood, and forage at any one place in just a few days. In addition to such everyday matters, Sitting Bull's thoughts were also on the Black Hills. In the latter part of May, the supreme chief learned

that a Brulé named Bear Stands Up was about to escort some relatives to the Spotted Tail Agency (on Beaver Creek in northwestern
Nebraska). He asked the Brulé to take a message to the Indian
agent.

He didn't intend to molest any whites south of the Black Hills,
Sitting Bull told Bear Stands Up, but he would fight those now
occupying the Hills as long as any question remained regarding
Lakota title. "When the rascality about the Black Hills is settled,"
Sitting Bull said, "then [I] will stop [my] rascality." The supreme
chief also let it be known that he wasn't happy with how the miners were desecrating sacred land. The whites killed each other, he
claimed, and all these dead men made the Hills "stink."

Sitting Bull didn't want to fight the whites, "only steal from
them as they have done." But if the Long Knives came out to fight,
his warriors would meet them in battle. However, if the soldiers
didn't come, Sitting Bull promised to visit the agency and counsel
his people for peace.

Bear Stands Up dutifully reported Sitting Bull's words to the
agent at Spotted Tail. About this same time, prospectors and settlers in the Black Hills claimed to have also received a message
from the Lakota leader, one that was shorter and to the point: the
miners must leave or he would "make a graveyard of that particular part of his domain." And someone, or several someones, was
already making good on that threat.

From different parts of the Hills came shocking reports of
killings of white men and women. In northwestern Nebraska,
droves of horses and cattle were being run off. "The wind sown
by the excursion against Crazy Horse last winter," proclaimed
one Black Hills correspondent, "is now being reaped in the shape
of a whirlwind of murder." It's unlikely these depredations were
the handiwork of warriors from Sitting Bull's camp, however;
the big village was some two hundred miles away. The actual

perpetrators, in fact, were probably Oglalas living at the nearby Red Cloud Agency, with contributions from a white outlaw or two.

But such distinctions mattered little now. The army had declared war against Sitting Bull and Crazy Horse, a war wholeheartedly supported by westerners. As far as these whites were concerned, the destruction of the "hostiles" and extinguishment of Indian title to the Black Hills couldn't come soon enough.

As the Moon When Leaves Turn Green gave way to the Moon of the Wild Turnip (the end of May), Sitting Bull became more worried for his people. A party of Cheyennes just arrived from one of the agencies confirmed that lots of soldiers were being sent to fight the antitreaty bands. This news spread through the camps, and the following morning, Sitting Bull called to his side White Bull, his adopted brother Jumping Bull, and one of Chief Black Moon's sons. He led them to the top of a small butte overlooking the village, now located on the Rosebud, near the mouth of Greenleaf Creek. Sitting Bull wanted these warriors as witnesses to his prayer to *Wakan Tanka.*

The supreme chief and holy man, his hair unbraided and free of feathers, turned toward the sun and lit his pipe, which was wrapped in sage. He held the pipe vertical with the stem up, the bowl turned to face his body. As the three witnesses stood silent, Sitting Bull cried out:

> *Wakan Tanka,* save me and give me all my wild game animals, and have [them] close enough so my people will have food enough this winter, and also [let] the good men on earth have more power so their tribes get along better and be of good nature so all Sioux nations get along well. If you do this for me, I will Sun Dance two days and two nights and will give you a whole buffalo.

When the smoke ceased to curl out of the pipe bowl, Sitting Bull wiped his face with sage, and the four men returned to the village.

The Sun Dance began two days later, after the big village moved to a new camping spot eleven miles farther up the Rosebud near a sacred sandstone formation known as the Picture Rock. The various ceremonies, feasting, and singing lasted for four days. On the day Sitting Bull honored his promise to *Wakan Tanka*, throngs of Lakotas and Cheyennes watched from the shade arbors. The chief entered the circular dance area wearing only a breechclout and some sage around his wrists and ankles. He walked to the painted medicine pole in the center and sat down with his back against it, his arms relaxed at his side, his legs straight out. Jumping Bull followed his brother and sat down, cross-legged, next to him.

With a steel awl, a common trade item, Jumping Bull pricked the skin of Sitting Bull's left arm, pulled the skin up, and, using a knife, cut off the small piece of flesh at the point of the awl. Jumping Bull repeated this procedure until fifty wounds oozed blood up and down the arm, then he switched to Sitting Bull's right arm. The pieces were no bigger than a match head, but the tiny wounds caused swelling and bleeding nonetheless. The giving of flesh consumed an hour, with tears running down Sitting Bull's face the entire time. The chief wasn't sobbing in pain, however; it was a cry of humility before *Wakan Tanka*.

Sitting Bull stood up and began to slowly dance while staring just below the sun. He wasn't skewered and tethered to the medicine pole as in his previous Sun Dances. Glistening with sweat, the blood on his arms turning dark as it dried and scabbed, he danced for hours. Day became night, and still Sitting Bull danced. Like all Sun Dancers, Sitting Bull fasted prior to the ceremony, and the loss of blood, combined with a lack of nourishment and dehydration, put his body under extreme stress. But he'd made a promise to *Wakan Tanka*.

The following morning, as the sun's fiery orb rose above the horizon, Sitting Bull again fixed his eyes just beneath it. The shuffling of his feet was much slower now; his arms hung at his side like lead weights. The world around him was no more—no spectators, no movement, no sounds, no colors. Just the sun. Then, from the place where he was staring, many figures on horseback appeared. Long Knives! But something was wrong; the soldiers' heads were down, their hats falling off. More and more fell from the sky, like so many grasshoppers. A few Indian riders swirled among the Long Knives, and they, too, rode with heads down.

From above, a powerful voice spoke to Sitting Bull: "These white men have no ears, so I give them to you." Sitting Bull understood. Long Knives would attack his followers, but the soldiers would suffer a great loss. However, the voice warned, Sitting Bull's people must not touch the spoils of their victory—not the soldiers' guns, ammunition, clothing, saddles, or personal items. Nothing. If his people violated this command, the free-roaming Lakotas "will be in [the] white man's clutches, at mercy of [the] white man." And last, Sitting Bull was not to personally shed blood in this fight. He could carry a bow and arrows for protection, but he was not to take part in the battle.

The Lakotas and Cheyennes watching from the shade arbors saw Sitting Bull suddenly falter. The chief looked ill, as if he was about to faint. Several men rushed to his side and eased Sitting Bull to the ground while others brought water. Among those hovering over Sitting Bull was Black Moon. In a voice weak and hoarse, Sitting Bull told Black Moon of his incredible vision, and he asked his cousin to announce it to the people. Black Moon stood and turned to face the spectators. As he told of the supreme chief's vision, everyone listened in awe. The truth of a Sun Dance vision was never questioned. "Whatever you foresaw," said the holy man Black Elk, "it always came true." And Sitting Bull had proved his closeness to *Wakan Tanka* and the gift of prophecy too many times to be doubted.

When the sun crested the horizon on June 16, approximately a thousand lodges, comprising at least six large camp circles, occupied both sides of a small tributary of the Little Big Horn called Ash Creek (known today as Reno Creek). As serene as the sprawling village appeared, the surprise attack on the Powder River back in March remained brutally fresh on the minds of many of these Lakotas and Cheyennes. They also knew Long Knives were massing on the Yellowstone; a few warriors had even been north to harass them. And only recently, an army of Bluecoats was discovered to the south, on the Tongue River. Clearly, Long Knives were on the hunt for them—Sitting Bull saw them in his vision.

The tips of the poles splayed at the tops of the lodges were just beginning to glow in the morning sunlight, the lodges themselves still in the shadows, when a party of Cheyenne and Lakota warriors came thundering into the camps howling like wolves. This party had been charged with keeping an eye on the army to the south, and their howling indicated they brought significant news.

"What is it?" someone asked the leader of the scouting party, a Cheyenne warrior named Little Hawk.

"Pretty near to the head of the Rosebud, where it bends to turn into the hills, as we were roasting meat, we saw soldiers—I think there are many Indians with them, too. They may come right down the Rosebud."

This latest information on the Long Knives, who were now less than a day's ride away, quickly spread through the large village, causing near chaos. Women began to pack family possessions and strike their lodges; men retrieved their war medicine, donned their best shirts, leggings, and moccasins, and painted their faces.

Boys rushed to the large horse herd and fetched war ponies for their fathers and uncles. But the village elders cautioned against any action until they could meet in council, which they did as soon as all the chiefs and headmen could gather.

Sitting Bull's uncle, Four Horns, often advised his nephew to think carefully when considering a foray against the Long Knives. "Be a little against fighting," he said. "But when anyone shoots, be ready to fight him." The problem with Four Horns's defensive strategy was that the white man wouldn't leave the Lakotas or their lands alone—he kept invading and taking, weaving his suffocating web tighter and tighter. The southern plains had already been lost to the white man. Now he wanted the Black Hills and probably something else after that.

The army to the south was accompanied by a large auxiliary of Crow and Shoshone warriors, long the enemies of the Lakotas. This expedition was anything but a goodwill mission, and it was now an immediate threat to the village. Thus, following a quick meeting of the elders, village heralds announced, "The scouts have returned and they have reported that the soldiers are now camping on the Rosebud River, so young warriors, take courage and get ready to go meet them."

The warriors didn't leave the village en masse. As soon as one group was ready, it rode off; they would all meet up somewhere near the Rosebud. However, the chiefs made sure that a number of fighting men remained behind to protect the village—a nagging fear was that a village would be attacked while most of the men were out hunting or raiding. Crazy Horse led a large contingent of both Oglalas and Brulés. Riding at his side was Good Weasel, a favored lieutenant ever since the ill-fated raid on the Shoshone village six years earlier that cost High Backbone his life. Others with Crazy Horse included Short Bull, Bad Heart Bull, Black Deer, and Kicking Bear, all good warriors.

Sitting Bull rode in the same large group as Crazy Horse. His arms remained swollen and tender from the Sun Dance, and his eyesight hadn't completely recovered from the hours of staring below the sun. But as the supreme chief and a holy man, he knew his presence would inspire the warriors. Not far from Sitting Bull were Chief Gall and his nephews White Bull and One Bull. The different warrior parties rode throughout the night, silently navigating the rolling hills and hidden draws flanking the valley of the Rosebud. As the sun rose the following day, its rays danced upon the warbonnets, painted shields, feathered lances, and glistening guns of some eight hundred warriors.

Sitting Bull reined in his horse on a high prominence overlooking a wide gap leading down to the valley. Crazy Horse rode up next to him. The Rosebud, where they expected to find the Long Knives, was just over a mile to the south. "Be of steady mind," Sitting Bull called out to the warriors. "Remember how to hold a gun [well] and shoot them. Brace up!"

The warriors started off, singing their brave songs and praying to *Wakan Tanka*. They were eager to count coup, eager to defend their homeland against the white invader and his Indian mercenaries.


At approximately 8:00 A.M. on June 17, the long army column halted its march along the Rosebud, about a mile west of where the creek makes a big bend to the north. Horses were unsaddled and allowed to graze, and men stretched out and relaxed in the lush grass within hearing of the Rosebud's gurgling waters. The Bluecoats (cavalry and mounted infantry) numbered approximately 975 men, and the Crows and Shoshones counted some 250 warriors. Including the large pack train and a pony herd belonging to the auxiliaries, the column was scattered out along the creek for nearly two miles. Its commander was the big-bearded George Crook, known to the Indians as Three Stars.

Hardly thirty minutes passed when several distant gunshots echoed from the hills rising to the north, but the Bluecoats surmised that some of the Indian scouts had come upon a few buffalo. The popping became more frequent and closer, however. Suddenly, twenty or more Crows and Shoshones appeared over a rise, riding like hell in the direction of the column. As they reached the safety of the Bluecoats, the warriors pointed feverishly behind them, shouting, "Heap Sioux! Heap Sioux!" A quick glance to the north revealed the Lakotas and Cheyennes silhouetted against the sky in a jagged and scattered line. Bullets whistled over the heads of the soldiers as officers shouted commands and bugles sounded.

It took several minutes for the Bluecoats to organize—Three Stars was at the tail of the column—but once they advanced on the warriors, thus began a series of charges, countercharges, and flanking movements lasting nearly four hours and covering a battlefield encompassing well more than a dozen square miles. "Valley full," remembered Northern Cheyenne Louis Dog. "Three fights going on." Wooden Leg told of how he and his fellow warriors "fought and ran away, fought and ran away. The soldiers and their Indian scouts did the same. Sometimes we chased them, sometimes they chased us."

Bravery runs, defiant antics, and memorable feats of heroism were the order of the day for the warriors—and also for one Cheyenne woman. She was a sister of Comes in Sight, a Cheyenne chief, and her name was Buffalo Calf Road Woman. Riding a gray pony, she'd accompanied her brother and the other Cheyenne warriors to the Rosebud, the only woman to do so. From a hidden vantage point, she watched as her brother led an early charge, and when a shot brought down his mount, Buffalo Calf Road Woman raced through the bullets to her brother's rescue. White Elk, a Northern Cheyenne, witnessed this deed. If it wasn't for the sister, he said, Comes in Sight would've surely been killed by Crows and Shoshones, who were rapidly closing in on the chief.

Crazy Horse's legendary courage and leadership was again on full display in this fight with Three Stars. When the Oglala war chief's men fell back, he held his Winchester repeater high and yelled to his warriors. And for a man who often declined to speak in councils, or even speak at all, his voice was readily recognized by his men, and his words roared above the sounds of battle like a voice from on high: "Hold on, my friends! Be strong! Remember the helpless! *This is a good day to die!*"

Ignoring the many bullets whizzing past him, Crazy Horse spurred his pony, dashing up and down and in large circles before the Bluecoats. Crook's chief of scouts, Captain George Randall, recognized Crazy Horse from Frank Grouard's description of his old friend and his favorite warhorse. Randall ordered some nearby Crow warriors to direct their fire at the notorious chief, but they might as well have been trying to hit a ghost. Another scout, Baptiste "Big Bat" Pourier, testified to Crazy Horse's strange invincibility that day. "You can call it medicine or anything you want to," said Pourier, "but I saw Crazy Horse . . . charge straight into Crook's army, and it seemed every soldier and Indian we had with us took a shot at him and they couldn't even hit his horse."

One of the newspaper correspondents with Three Stars couldn't help but admire the ferocity of the Lakota and Cheyenne charges. Their fighting, he wrote, was "little less than savage frenzy or the fighting of demons." But by midafternoon, heavy sweat was foaming on their fatigued horses, and the warriors themselves were famished. A larger concern, however, was the big village. Seeing the great numbers of Crows and Shoshones with Crook, the war chiefs grew worried that perhaps more of these enemies were on the way to their camps. Consequently, as was so often the case, the warriors just disappeared into the hills. Their casualties were surprisingly light, probably less than two dozen killed, especially so considering the Long Knives burned through more than ten thousand rounds of ammunition! It would seem Crazy Horse wasn't the only warrior whose war medicine was strong that day.

Three Stars lost nine men killed and twenty-one wounded. The Indian auxiliaries suffered two killed and eleven wounded. Certain that the Lakota and Cheyenne warriors were protecting a nearby village, Crook was eager to pursue them that evening and surprise the village at dawn. But he couldn't persuade his Crow and Shoshone allies to accompany him. They expressed concerns about the safety of their own villages, and they seemed quite happy with the few fresh scalps they'd added to their belts. Thus, low on ammunition and rations, and with wounded to attend to, Crook made the decision to return to his base camp on Goose Creek (near present-day Sheridan, Wyoming), where he would await reinforcements. As an officer later wrote of Crook, "The Sioux had proved more numerous than he expected."

The retrograde movement by Three Stars didn't go unnoticed by scouts from the big village. And after three days of mourning, a large victory dance was held the night of the fourth. Once again, Sitting Bull's prophecy had come true, or so it seemed. The antitreaty bands had triumphed over the Long Knives. But the Rosebud fight wasn't what Sitting Bull saw in his vision. What appeared to him were many soldiers falling from the heavens—dead soldiers. Only a few Bluecoats had been killed on the Rosebud. Was an even greater victory still to come?

Sitting Bull and Crazy Horse had parried one of the three strike forces that were part of the army's carefully planned summer campaign. The two remaining columns were now on the Yellowstone River, preparing to march south. Four companies of cavalry and six of infantry under Colonel John Gibbon would advance up the valley of the Big Horn River, at least as far as its juncture with the Little Big Horn. General Alfred H. Terry, commander of the Department of Dakota, would accompany Gibbon's force. The third column was Custer's Seventh U.S. Cavalry, twelve companies consisting of 566 troopers and thirty-one officers. Custer's column also included thirty-five Crow and Arikara scouts, seven civilian scouts, and six civilian mule packers.

Long Hair, who'd shorn his famous locks, would lead his men up the Rosebud, and if he found evidence the antitreaty bands were on the Little Big Horn, he would take his regiment over the divide to that watercourse. The Seventh started out at noon on June 22, with no knowledge of Three Stars's stunning setback. "Everybody was in excellent spirits," remembered a lieutenant of the Seventh, "and we all felt the worst that could happen would be the getting away of the Indians." Custer, however, was determined to run down the "hostiles." "We can't get Indians without hard riding and plenty of it!" he told his officers. And though the weather was unbearably hot, he set a brisk pace for both men and animals. Just two days later, the regiment arrived at the site of Sitting Bull's Sun Dance, and what the Arikara scouts discovered there spooked them.

On the floor of one of the sweat lodges was a drawing the Arikaras were convinced revealed the future. The drawing covered a long mound or ridge made of sand. A distinctive set of hoofprints had been drawn on each side of the ridge. The scouts believed one set represented Custer's men and the other set, Lakota warriors. On the ridge between the hoofprints were figures of dead men; their heads pointed toward the Lakotas. The Arikaras believed this drawing showed that the Lakotas' medicine was too strong for Custer, and he and his men would be whipped.

The following morning, Custer gazed northwest into the valley of the Little Big Horn from a prominence known as the Crow's Nest. One of the scouts instructed Custer to look at a spot along the river about fourteen miles away where light smoke hung in the air from an enormous village. Custer nodded when he finally saw the smoke, then took a pair of field glasses and studied the same spot. He nodded again.

Sitting Bull and his followers were now within Custer's grasp; he could feel it. However, the men and animals needed rest. Custer had taken his regiment eighty-four miles in under seventy-two hours. Best to bivouac for the remainder of the day and set out early in the morning for a dawn attack on the village. But then the scouts gave Custer some disturbing information: they believed the Lakotas had discovered the presence of the regiment. This seemed to be confirmed when Custer subsequently learned that troopers sent on the back trail that morning to retrieve a fallen load of hardtack had surprised a group of Indians rummaging through the pack. The troopers fired upon the Indians but they fled unscathed. This, of course, changed everything. To delay the attack risked the Indians scattering to the winds.

The Seventh moved out shortly before noon, Custer at the head. The little relief the early-morning coolness provided was gone, and the heat from the sun now high in a perfectly clear sky was stifling. After advancing about a mile, Custer called a halt and proceeded to divide his force into three battalions. Major Marcus Reno, the regiment's second-in-command, was assigned three companies. Custer took five companies. Three companies went to Captain Frederick W. Benteen, and one company was delegated to escort the slow-moving pack train. Custer ordered Benteen to take his battalion toward some high bluffs about a mile to the southwest and attack any Indians he might encounter and stay in contact. If he failed to turn up any villagers, Benteen was to

A drawing by Sitting Bull depicting his duel with a Crow chief in 1856. Sitting Bull killed the chief, but the Crow wounded Sitting Bull in two places. The wound to his left foot caused him to walk with a slight limp for the rest of his life.

BUFFALO BILL CENTER OF THE WEST

Sitting Bull captures an Assiniboine boy, 1857. Sitting Bull adopted this boy as his brother and eventually gave him the name Jumping Bull, the name of Sitting Bull's father. The two remained close for the rest of their days. Drawing by Sitting Bull.

BUFFALO BILL CENTER OF THE WEST

Sitting Bull's fight with Corporal Jefferson Dilts, September 2, 1864. In this work, a copy made by Four Horns of a now-missing Sitting Bull drawing, Dilts bleeds from an arrow shot by the Húnkpapa chief while the corporal shoots and wounds Sitting Bull in the left hip.

NATIONAL ANTHROPOLOGICAL ARCHIVES

"SITTING BULL"
(Ta-Ton-ka-I-yo-ton-ka,)
The Sioux Chief in command at the Custer Massacre.
ZIMMERMAN BROS., Publishers.    Photographed by O. S. GOFF.
Copyright applied for.

Sitting Bull, photographed by Orlando S. Goff at the Standing Rock Agency in early August 1881, less than a month after the chief's surrender to the U.S. Army.

Gall (*Phizí*)—Húnkpapa war chief, Little Big Horn veteran, and Sitting Bull's onetime lieutenant. During the reservation years, Gall was a strong "progressive" and a favorite of Standing Rock Indian agent James McLaughlin.

NEWBERRY LIBRARY

One Bull, nephew of Sitting Bull and Little Big Horn veteran, photographed at Fort Randall in 1882. The vivid recollections of One Bull and his brother, White Bull, were obtained by author Walter Campbell (pen name Stanley Vestal) in the late 1920s and early '30s.

COURTESY OF THE AUTHOR

Frank Grouard, the son of a Mormon missionary and a Polynesian woman, lived for several years with the northern Lakotas, becoming a trusted friend of both Sitting Bull and Crazy Horse. Grouard later became a scout for the U.S. Army and betrayed that friendship by helping the Long Knives hunt down the free-roaming Sioux and Cheyennes.

NEWBERRY LIBRARY

*Left:* Horn Chips, famed Oglala holy man and cousin of Crazy Horse, with his wife, Feels All Around It, 1907. Horn Chips made protective "war medicine" and other charms for his cousin.

He Dog, lifelong friend of Crazy Horse and Little Big Horn veteran. Photographed here as part of a Sioux and Arapaho delegation to Washington, D.C., in September 1877.

Little Big Man, onetime lieutenant of Crazy Horse and Little Big Horn veteran. Little Big Man later played a despicable part in the war chief's death. Photographed in Washington, D.C., September 1877.

Scalping, committed by both Indians and whites, came to symbolize the warfare on the Great Plains. "My people took scalps," explained Luther Standing Bear, "only to prove their stories that they had met the enemy and overpowered him." This 1868 engraving appeared in the French journal *Le Tour du Monde*.

The mutilation of dead enemies ensured that they would enter the land of ghosts in that same condition. This unfortunate victim, Sergeant Frederick Wyllyams of the Seventh U.S. Cavalry, was killed June 26, 1867, in western Kansas. The dead of Custer's men at the Little Big Horn were treated much the same way.

*Above left:* Red Cloud, fierce Oglala war chief and leader of the Bad Face band. He vowed to fight to the death until the forts in the Powder River country were abandoned, which happened in 1868. Red Cloud subsequently signed the Treaty of Fort Laramie and never again went to war against the whites.

NATIONAL ANTHROPOLOGICAL ARCHIVES

*Above right:* They Fear Even His Horses, hereditary chief of the Oglalas, smokes his pipe in a council with peace commissioners at Fort Laramie, May 1868. Photograph by Alexander Gardner.

NATIONAL ANTHROPOLOGICAL ARCHIVES

*Left:* Spotted Tail, head chief of the Brulé tribe and uncle of Crazy Horse. Like Red Cloud, he fell into disfavor with both Sitting Bull and Crazy Horse for not joining them in their war against the white man and for signing away Lakota lands.

NEWBERRY LIBRARY

This drawing is believed to depict the August 5, 1873, "Battle" of Massacre Canyon, in which Crazy Horse was a participant. The drawing is one of ten contained in a small ledger book that Crazy Horse presented to a journalist in May 1877. Crazy Horse said the drawings represented the life of a famous warrior, but he wouldn't say whether or not that warrior was himself.

DENVER ART MUSEUM

Last Stand Hill at Little Big Horn Battlefield, Montana. "The people in the States blame me for having killed Custer and his army," Sitting Bull said in 1878. "He came to attack me, and in sufficient numbers to show me that they wanted to destroy me and my children."

PHOTOGRAPH BY THE AUTHOR

Looking west from Last Stand Hill to the valley of the Greasy Grass (Little Big Horn). On June 25, 1876, the valley held a thousand lodges, homes to more than five thousand Sioux and Cheyennes. The village stretched along the stream for a mile and a half.

PHOTOGRAPH BY THE AUTHOR

Two Moons, Northern Cheyenne chief. In describing the Little Big Horn battle, Two Moons said the "smoke was like a great cloud, and everywhere the Sioux went the dust rose like smoke. We circled all round [Custer]—swirling like water around a stone. We shoot, we ride fast, we shoot again. Soldiers drop, and horses fall on them."

Wooden Leg, Northern Cheyenne, holding a Springfield carbine captured at the Little Big Horn. His autobiography, published in 1931 as *A Warrior Who Fought Custer*, is one of the best accounts of the Cheyennes' and Lakotas' last years of freedom and their warfare with the Long Knives.

Hunts the Enemy (George Sword). A former warrior under Crazy Horse and a nephew of Red Cloud, Hunts the Enemy traveled to Crazy Horse's camp in the spring of 1877 and helped persuade the chief to go to the Red Cloud Agency and surrender with his people. Hunts the Enemy is pictured here as a Metal Breast (Indian policeman) at the Pine Ridge Agency.

Camp Robinson and the Red Cloud Buttes in 1877, the year of Crazy Horse's death.

Lieutenant William Philo Clark and Little Hawk, uncle of Crazy Horse, 1877. Clark, head of the Indian scouts at Camp Robinson, failed in his efforts to manipulate or "work" Crazy Horse, and later commented that the chief's death "will save trouble."

Camp Robinson interpreters Baptiste "Big Bat" Pourier (*left*) and William "Billy" Garnett (*right*), circa 1877. Pourier was at Crazy Horse's deathbed and recalled the warrior's last words.

Ellen "Nellie" Larabee proposed to Crazy Horse in the summer of 1877 and subsequently shared his lodge with Black Shawl, the chief's first wife. The multilingual Nellie kept Crazy Horse informed of the news and gossip circulating through the villages and at Camp Robinson.

COURTESY OF THE AUTHOR

The killing of Crazy Horse as imagined by Oglala artist Amos Bad Heart Bull (1869–1913).

UNIVERSITY OF CINCINNATI ARCHIVES AND RARE BOOKS LIBRARY

The reconstructed Camp Robinson guardhouse. Crazy Horse was bayonetted just outside the guardhouse door.

PHOTOGRAPH BY THE AUTHOR

An engraving based on German artist Rudolf Cronau's sketch of Sitting Bull made at Fort Randall on October 25, 1881.

James McLaughlin, Standing Rock Indian agent and Sitting Bull's greatest adversary during his reservation years. A Jesuit priest at Standing Rock wrote that McLaughlin had "the cunning of Satan."

*Left:* Sitting Bull and William F. "Buffalo Bill" Cody, photographed by William Notman & Son in Montreal, Canada, August 1885. Sitting Bull toured with Cody's Wild West for only one season.

COURTESY OF THE AUTHOR

*Below:* Ghost Dance at Sitting Bull's camp, Grand River, December 1890. This photograph was taken by *Chicago Herald* correspondent Sam T. Clover with a small Kodak box camera. Clover wrote that one of Sitting Bull's wives "eyed my black box very suspiciously and vented a grunt of disapproval as she caught the sharp click of the button."

MINNESOTA HISTORICAL SOCIETY

Kicking Bear—Little Big Horn veteran, cousin of Crazy Horse, nephew of Sitting Bull, and Ghost Dance holy man. At Sitting Bull's request, Kicking Bear taught the Ghost Dance religion to the Lakotas on Grand River.

NEWBERRY LIBRARY

The arrest and death of Sitting Bull, December 15, 1890, painted by Thomas Stone Man, circa 1920. Stone Man, a Yanktonai, was a member of the Metal Breast detachment that came to arrest the holy man.

Second Sergeant Red Tomahawk of the Standing Rock Metal Breasts. Red Tomahawk put a bullet in Sitting Bull's head after the holy man had been fatally shot in the chest by Lieutenant Bull Head.

Crow Foot, Sitting Bull's son by Whole Tribe Seeing Her. At the conclusion of the fight with Sitting Bull's followers, the Metal Breasts discovered the sixteen-year-old boy hiding underneath his metal bed and murdered him.

This painting by Caroline Weldon hung in the cabin behind Sitting Bull's. It was not painted from life but is copied from one of the photographs made of Sitting Bull in Montreal in 1885. The large gash in the left side of the canvas was made by a Metal Breast who tried to destroy the painting but then was stopped by an army lieutenant.

STATE HISTORICAL SOCIETY OF NORTH DAKOTA

These bloodstained cabinet card portraits were found in Sitting Bull's clothing after his death. The photograph on the left is a portrait of "Captain Jack" Crawford and is inscribed by Crawford to Sitting Bull. The photograph on the right is identified only as "Sitting Bull's 'pet.'" The holy man loved children and this white child is undoubtedly someone he knew.

SOUTH DAKOTA STATE HISTORICAL SOCIETY

Sitting Bull's wives and daughters pose in front of his cabin shortly after his death. *Left to right:* Lodge in Sight, Four Robes, Whole Tribe Seeing Her, and Standing Holy.

COURTESY OF THE AUTHOR

Sitting Bull's Log Cabin now on Exhibition at World's Fair, Chicago, 1893, owned by Sitting Bull Log Cabin Co., Mandan, North Dakota.

SITTING BULL'S LOG CABIN MORNING OF THE FIGHT.

This photograph was sold as a souvenir at the Sitting Bull cabin exhibit at the 1893 World's Columbian Exposition. It purports to be a reenactment of Sitting Bull's arrest but is wholly inaccurate. The image does picture the cabin at its original location on Grand River before it was disassembled. The timbers and bent saplings in the foreground are the framework for a sweat lodge, used by the Ghost Dancers to purify themselves before participating in the dance.

COURTESY OF THE AUTHOR

*Above:* Standing Rock Metal Breasts, survivors of the fight at Sitting Bull's camp, taken five days after the botched arrest attempt. The man on horseback on the left is Agent McLaughlin.

COURTESY OF THE AUTHOR

*Above left:* Sitting Bull's death made front pages and headlines around the world. The garish illustration at the bottom of this December 31, 1890, *Christian Herald* is supposed to depict Sitting Bull's "last campfire."

AUTHOR'S COLLECTION

Sitting Bull's grave at Fort Yates, circa 1910, from a photographic postcard.

COURTESY OF THE AUTHOR

Sitting Bull's original grave site at Fort Yates as it appears today.

PHOTOGRAPH BY THE AUTHOR

Sitting Bull's grave site overlooking the Missouri River opposite Mobridge, South Dakota. Whether all of Sitting Bull's remains, some of his remains, or none of his remains are buried here is unknown.

PHOTOGRAPH BY THE AUTHOR

return and find the main command. Custer and Reno would proceed toward the big village. There would be no "Garry Owen" to rouse the men this day, however, as the regimental band had been left behind at a camp on the Powder River.

As Custer gave the orders for the company assignments, a Crow scout named Half Yellow Face asked one of the interpreters to explain what was happening. The interpreter did so, and Half Yellow Face reacted with a look of concern. The Crow requested to speak to Long Hair, so the interpreter got Custer's attention and translated Half Yellow Face's words.

"Do not divide your men," Half Yellow Face warned. "There are too many of the enemy for us, even if we all stay together. If you must fight, keep us all together."

Custer, visibly perturbed at the interruption and unwanted advice, snapped back: "You do the scouting, and I will attend to the fighting."

A few moments later, Custer noticed that Half Yellow Face had stripped down to his breechclout and painted his face. Curious, Custer wanted to know why, and he instructed his interpreter to ask the Crow.

"Because you and I are going home today," Half Yellow Face replied, "and by a trail that is strange to us both."


The battalions of Custer and Reno proceeded along Ash Creek toward its juncture with the Little Big Horn. After about ten miles, Custer could see ahead into the valley. The village was still two to three miles downstream and out of sight, but a large cloud of dust was clearly visible in that direction. That dust cloud suggested the Indians were indeed fleeing. Custer ordered Reno to take his battalion down the valley and attempt to overtake the villagers. It was already understood that the Seventh wasn't here to parley with the tribes or force a surrender. When Reno encountered the villagers, he was to attack, plain and simple.

Reno led his battalion to the Little Big Horn and forded to the west side, emerging from the cottonwoods along the stream onto open ground. Custer had promised to support Reno's advance, but for some reason he didn't follow Reno's three companies across the river. Instead, Custer took his battalion north and ascended the blufftops overlooking the valley. There, Custer and his troopers got a first glimpse at the immense village, and the men burst out in cheers. This excited some of the horses, and a few bolted from the ranks, their riders struggling to control them. "Hold your horses in boys," Custer shouted, "there are plenty of them down there for all of us." Custer sent a messenger back to recall Benteen and fetch the pack train—he was going to need the extra men and ammunition.

Not only could Custer see the village, but the heights also offered a good vantage to observe Reno's charge—or, rather, Reno's failure to charge. A few hundred yards short of the first camp circle, the major abruptly stopped his advance and ordered his men to dismount and form a skirmish line. Reno said later he was fully expecting the Indians to stampede before his men, but instead, "they came back at me like a nest of hornets." In no more than fifteen minutes, so many warriors threatened to overwhelm Reno's 150 men that he withdrew his battalion to the timber near the river. Moments later, a thoroughly rattled Reno ordered a retreat, although only some of his men heard it.

As the panicked procession streamed out of the timber and back up the valley, screaming warriors charged in among them, cutting down Bluecoats right and left. And the slaughter continued as Reno and his men splashed across the Little Big Horn to the steep east bank and climbed the bluff. Those who reached the top were in a state of shock, especially their commander. Reno lost forty killed and several wounded in the debacle, and some of his troopers were still holed up in the timber. Yet hardly any warriors followed the soldiers to the top of the bluff, and the shooting mostly ceased except for a few scattered gunshots in the bottom. But from downstream, some of the men heard gunfire. Not just a few shots, but volleys.

Custer's battalion, approximately 210 men strong, trotted north along the bluffs for only a few minutes before veering away from the river and down a long gulch to where it joined a larger ravine or coulee. Here, Custer pulled up. The coulee obviously led to the river, and Custer ordered two companies down it, either to scout a ford for an attack on the village or as a feint to draw pressure off Reno. Perhaps both. Custer also sent written orders back to Benteen. Scrawled in pencil on a small piece of paper, it read, "Benteen. Come on. Big Village. Be quick. Bring packs. P.S. Bring pacs." Those all-important packs carried the extra ammunition.

As the two companies galloped down the coulee to the river, Custer's men fired at a large party of warriors that appeared to the north, causing the warriors to temporarily scatter. Custer then led his men in that same direction, riding up and down hills for about two miles. Halting on a high hill, Custer was able to get a good look at the north end of the huge village. In the river bottom to the west, he could see lodges dropping to the ground as women frantically packed up their camps to flee. He also saw women, children, and old men rushing through the village, escaping downstream and to the west. Looking to his back trail, Custer anxiously scanned the horizon for any sign of Benteen, but the captain and his battalion was nowhere to be seen.

At the river, the two companies met resistance from warriors intent on preventing the Long Knives from crossing to the village side. After briefly trading gunfire in which two or three men were shot from their horses, the two companies turned and slowly made their way northeast on the shoulder of another large coulee. They rejoined Custer on the high hill (known today as Calhoun Hill), about a half mile from the river. At the same time, warriors fresh from routing Reno splashed across the stream and galloped up the same coulee. Keeping at a distance, they began to snipe at the troopers with an assortment of weapons, from Springfield carbines just taken from Reno's dead to bows and arrows. Warriors pulled their bowstrings nearly to the breaking point, releasing their arrows high into the air.

Demonstrating his interminable offensive mindset, Custer took the two companies just returned from the river, approximately eighty men, and trotted north along a connecting hogback ridge for about a half mile before angling back toward the Little Big Horn. He wanted to get a close look at the north end of the village and locate a good ford. Once his reinforcements arrived, he could cross the river and quickly round up some of the fleeing noncombatants. A key to Custer's success at the Battle of the Washita in 1868 was that he'd taken prisoner a number of Southern Cheyenne women and children. When a superior force of warriors rallied to challenge Custer, the warriors were afraid to shoot for fear of harming their own people. If Custer could secure a number of prisoners here, the fighting would almost certainly come to an end, or at least swing decidedly in his favor.

The other three companies of Custer's battalion remained behind to wait for Benteen and the pack train. But Lakota and Cheyenne warriors were arriving on the field in alarming numbers. Dismounting and deploying as skirmishers, two companies defended the hill while one company, acting as a reserve, was positioned about five hundred yards north, along the hogback ridge. All the while, warriors stealthily crawled up ravines and ditches on all sides, creeping ever closer with a seemingly endless supply of cartridges and arrows. Efforts to drive the warriors back simply saw them regroup and come again with even more fighters. An expanding haze of black powder smoke turned sweaty, scared men into gray silhouettes, horses kicked and plunged with arrows sticking out of their bleeding rumps, and soldiers fell.

Custer's predicament was little better. The warriors had made it hot for him, but he'd gotten the information he needed. He withdrew his men back to high ground and eventually stopped at the far north end of the hogback. Once Benteen's men finally arrived, he would lead them and the rest of his battalion to the village over the route he'd just scouted. A half mile away, heavy gunfire and smoke rising into the blue sky told Custer the rest of his battalion was heavily engaged, but, clearly, Benteen and the packs were not anywhere close—a messenger would have informed him if they were.

As the minutes passed, more warriors closed in on Custer's position, sending a flurry of bullets and arrows from draws and clumps of sagebrush. One company charged downhill to push the warriors back and out of a ravine and then dismounted to form a skirmish line. Meanwhile, Custer shouted orders for the placement of his remaining troopers on the slope of the ridge, just below the crest. His window for an attack hadn't just closed, it'd slammed shut. With absolutely nothing for cover on the hillside that would stop a bullet, he was forced to resort to a cavalryman's last, desperate act. He ordered several of the horses shot to form breastworks.

For the three companies Custer had left behind to wait for Benteen, desperation turned to utter and pitiful collapse. Warriors targeted the horse holders with their bullets and arrows and waved blankets to stampede the horses. The roar of gunfire became deafening. The soldiers defending the hill panicked and ran for their lives. Those men who stood their ground found themselves fighting hand to hand with ferocious warriors swinging war clubs, thrusting knives, and shooting pistols point-blank. The few troopers who managed to outrun the slaughter found safety with the reserves on the hogback, but they were chased by a mass of determined warriors, who now joined those fighters already surrounding the reserve company. The men from the hill had exchanged one hell for another.

Warrior shouts and the distinctive sound of eagle-bone whistles on the east side of the hogback caught the attention of these soldiers. A split second later, a lone Indian rider emerged from the smoke, galloping straight toward a dip or gap in the hogback that cut through the troopers' position. In a sudden explosion of gunfire, soldier guns blasted away at the daring rider as he raced through the gap and over to the other side. But not one bullet grazed the warrior or his horse. Most of the troopers needed to reload, but as they reached for more cartridges, hordes of warriors rushed in. A few troopers, less than a dozen, broke free and escaped north to Custer, but the rest were annihilated. Their demise had come at the hands of the greatest Lakota warrior to ever live, Crazy Horse.

Crazy Horse now led his Oglalas and several Cheyenne followers to the fight raging around Long Hair at the north end of the hogback (known today as Last Stand Hill). Warriors crawled on their stomachs, popped up to quickly shoot, and then disappeared again in the prairie grasses and sagebrush. Farther out, mounted warriors circled the besieged Bluecoats, "swirling like water round a stone," recalled Two Moons. "We shoot, we ride fast, we shoot again." To the thirteen-year-old Black Elk, watching from a distance, the warriors looked "like a bunch of swallows flying all around."

The heat was suffocating. Trampling warrior ponies kicked

up considerable dust that, combined with the thick gunsmoke, dimmed the sun enough so that the muzzle flashes from the Bluecoats' guns were easily seen. Men screamed in pain, officers yelled commands, warriors shouted *"Hóka hé!"* And out of this tremendous den of battle came the sound of a bugle. The bugle calls continued for a long time, it seemed, and the warriors thought the bugler a very brave man.

Lakotas and Cheyennes, all mixed together, steadily crawled closer, shouting and yipping. One by one, Long Knives dropped their guns and rolled in the dirt, grabbing at arrow shafts sticking from their bodies or clutching at a bullet hole leaking their lifeblood. Warriors fell, too, some accidentally hit by their own tribesmen in the cross fire. As the soldiers saw comrades knocked out of the fight, a terrifying realization set in: they were all about to die, perhaps tortured first. A few of the Long Knives began to act strange, firing their guns wildly in the air. More than one put a revolver to his head and blew his brains out.

The shooting from the troopers noticeably slackened, and the warriors became bolder, some rushing forward to count coup before running back. Finally, ten or so soldiers jumped up and fled downhill, prompting an avalanche of warriors to pour in from all sides and give chase. The Bluecoats made it to the ravine that held a few of their surviving comrades from the earlier skirmish line. But it wasn't long before they were all wiped out, too. Reflecting back on the intense battle, one old warrior said, "There was a great deal of shooting. Then all was still."

The sudden quiet after so much chaos was surreal, made even more so by the low moaning of wounded and dying Long Knives. Most of these were finished off by women and boys from the village, who arrived on the killing ground very soon after the last shots were fired. Black Elk said that when he and the other boys came across a wounded trooper writhing in agony, they grabbed the arrow shafts sticking out of the man and pushed them further in. They also shot their own arrows into the dying and wounded.

Women plunged knives into soldiers' bodies to make sure they were dead before stripping them of clothing. Two women neglected to stab one body and only realized the soldier was still alive after they'd removed his uniform. The naked trooper jumped up and grappled with them, swinging the two around as they screamed and hollered and tried to cut him with their knives. Finally, another woman rushed up and stabbed the man, causing a stream of bright red blood to spew out of the wound. The trooper collapsed, and this time he truly was dead.

The warriors did very little scalping this day, as most of the Long Knives had close-cropped hair—there was little glory in taking a scalp with short hair. But that didn't stop the young boys from securing a white man scalp. The bodies were further mutilated by wives and other relatives mourning a loved one killed in the fight. They mashed in skulls with stone clubs; cut off hands, noses, and other body parts; and, in a few instances, severed heads. Young Black Elk soon got his fill of the butchering and left the hill. "I could smell nothing but blood and gunpowder," he said, "so I got sick of it pretty soon."

The scramble for plunder occupied warriors and women and children alike, but it was cut short, for the men at least, when a large dust cloud indicated Long Knives to the south, distant about three miles. These were the remaining seven companies of the Seventh. Captain Benteen had indeed received Custer's urgent message about the big village and to "be quick," but when he and his men reached the survivors of Reno's shell-shocked battalion, Reno pleaded with Benteen to stop and help him. Benteen stopped. The appearance of the Long Knives now was a belated effort to march to the sound of the guns, to reach Custer, but it was far too late.

As many as a thousand warriors, perhaps more, galloped off, intent on destroying the remaining Bluecoats. Meanwhile, the women, old men, and boys continued to gather booty: horses, guns, ammunition, saddles, clothing, paper money, jewelry, pocket watches—whatever struck their fancy or could be put to good use. And the disfiguring of the soldier bodies continued as well. Two Southern Cheyenne women searching for plunder stopped suddenly at the body of a white man with a bushy mustache. As they stood there, intensely discussing the naked figure stretched out on the ground at their feet, some Lakota men walked toward them, intent on cutting up the body. But the women strongly objected. They explained that the white man was a relative of theirs, so the Lakotas only cut off part of a finger.

None of the warriors knew who they were fighting that day, only that they were enemy soldiers who came to destroy them. But the two Cheyenne women definitely recognized this dead white man. The body they protected was that of Long Hair, George Armstrong Custer. However, the women knew him as the husband of Monahsetah, or Morning Walker. Years earlier, a young Monahsetah was among Custer's fifty-three prisoners from the attack on Black Kettle's village on the Washita River. Rumors hinted at sexual relationships between the officers of the Seventh and the female captives, but for the Southern Cheyenne women, they weren't rumors at all. This happened. Monahsetah claimed Custer as her husband, and she later gave birth to a child the Cheyennes understood was Long Hair's.

Four months after the Washita fight, Custer met with a Southern Cheyenne chief named Rock Forehead, keeper of the Cheyennes' Sacred Arrows. In a ceremony invoking the power of the Arrows, the chief compelled Custer to smoke a peace pipe until all the tobacco in the bowl turned to ash. Rock Forehead then emptied the pipe's ashes on Custer's boots, saying, "Thus will the

Great Spirit destroy the White Soldier Chief if ever he walks contrary to the peace pipe again."

Custer understood nothing of the ceremony's import, but the Southern Cheyenne women staring at his body knew the story well. They kneeled down next to Long Hair's head and took a sewing awl and pushed its rigid metal needle deep into one ear and then the other. Perhaps this would help him hear, they thought, for when Long Hair smoked the pipe under the Sacred Arrows, he'd apparently been a poor listener.

It was a sobering, if not terrifying, sight for the remnants of the Seventh Cavalry: a thousand warriors fresh from obliterating Custer's battalion—and the Indians were heading straight for them. The cavalry column retreated to the original position of Major Reno and his survivors, a large natural depression on a high blufftop (known today as Reno Hill). There they formed a defensive perimeter with troopers on their bellies, everyone trying his best to melt into the hard ground. Wounded men were placed in the center of the basin, surrounded by pack mules and cavalry mounts.

The Lakotas and Cheyennes thundered up near the perimeter and made several charges, but flared each time in the face of withering fire from the defenders. Finally, the warriors settled in behind nearly every ridge and hill within sight. And as some of these ridges offered an advantage in elevation, the warriors—many with newly acquired Springfields and plenty of ammunition—wreaked havoc on the Long Knives. Buzzing bullets slammed into horses, mules, and men. And the heavy gunfire rarely let up. One trooper recalled an occasional lull, but then "it would start again, and the bullets came like hail." By the time darkness ended the fighting about 9:00 P.M., the warriors had added twelve dead Bluecoats and twenty-one wounded to the day's total carnage. More than forty horses and mules lay dead.

The Long Knives were in no condition to sneak away in the night, but the warriors didn't know this. To keep the soldiers under siege, the leaders came up with a plan whereby their men would take turns going to the camps for food and rest. The officers of the Seventh developed a strategy for the night as well—dig in. Using cups, tin plates, butcher knives, and their bare hands, the men worked feverishly for hours to carve out depressions in the earth. Saddles and packs from the horses and mules were brought up to the line and fashioned into crude breastworks. Even dead horses and mules were dragged to the perimeter and dirt scraped up around their bodies—troopers were more than happy to put up with the stench on the chance the carcasses might stop a bullet.

In the village, Sitting Bull announced, "We shall not celebrate tonight. There are too many of our warriors killed." That loss was approximately thirty-one killed and at least twice that number wounded. The relatives of the dead warriors could take some comfort in the fact that their loved ones had died heroes' deaths, protecting the woman and children from the Long Knives. And they'd died in battle, as warriors, not as shriveled and bent over old men, waiting for the end of their time.

Sitting Bull also had something to say about the plundering on the battlefield that day. He'd warned everyone not to touch the spoils, but only Sitting Bull and his band had refrained from taking the Long Knives' booty. Sitting Bull didn't even go across the river to view Custer's dead. He scolded those within hearing, saying the Lakotas and Cheyennes would now "starve at [the] white man's door, they will be scattered and crushed by troops."

Whether it was Sitting Bull's ominous words, the excitement of the day's victory, the wailing of the mourners, or all these things, hardly anyone in the camps slept that night. Large bonfires were built all through the village, and people stayed up talking and moving to and from the different camp circles. Stephen Standing Bear remembered trying to get a little sleep sometime before morning, but it was no use. He simply couldn't cleanse his mind of all "the horrible things" he'd seen.

As the sky began to lighten in the east, criers went to the different camp circles shouting, "The remainder of the soldiers shall perish today." And once it was light enough to see the sights on their guns, the warriors began shooting. They were surprised, however, to discover the Long Knives had dug rifle pits. Somehow, with their flimsy utensils and knives, the soldiers had scraped pits deep enough so that the warriors could hardly see them. But see them they could, and the warriors blazed away at the Bluecoats.

A long line of dense smoke rose above the warrior positions, which were five to eight hundred yards out from the entrenchments. At least one warrior possessed a long-range Sharps "buffalo gun," and he knew how to use it. Any soldier who exposed a part of his body for more than a moment chanced receiving a gift of 425 grains of lead traveling at more than a thousand feet per second. But the warriors weren't content to fight at long range. They made several charges throughout the morning hours, on horseback and on foot. Each time, however, the alert and determined defenders were ready for them. During one approach, a Miniconjou named Dog's Backbone yelled to the warriors near him: "Be careful, it's a long way from here, but their bullets are coming fierce." The words hardly passed his lips when one of those fierce bullets punched through his forehead, just above the eyebrow. He pitched forward dead.

Women and old men watched the fight from a safe distance, and some of the old men advised the warriors that the Long Knives would eventually need water. Watch the gulches leading to the Greasy Grass, they said, for sooner or later, the Long Knives were sure to attempt a run to the river. The old men were right. Just before midday, a party of a dozen Bluecoats, packing multiple canteens and camp kettles, slipped down a brush-filled ravine to the river, five hundred yards away. The most dangerous part of their mission came at the bottom of the gulch, where they had no choice but to race across thirty feet of open space to the water's edge. The brave troopers made the dash in small groups as comrades on the bluff provided cover fire. But even though the warriors were watching for the water carriers and got several shots at them, the entire party miraculously reached the river and returned with its precious cargo. One Bluecoat took a serious hit in the leg, and a few of the containers came back leaking water from bullet holes.

Early in the afternoon, scouts arrived from the north and alerted the village to more soldiers approaching from downstream. This was the column of cavalry and infantry under Colonel Gibbon and General Terry, the third prong of the U.S. Army's summer campaign. The column was still miles away, but many warriors wanted to go and fight them, too. The chiefs counseled against it, and Sitting Bull believed it was time to break off the fight with the Long Knives on the hill as well. "Leave 'em go now so some can go home and spread the news," he said.

Women began taking down lodges while boys fetched ponies from the horse herd. Warriors set fire to the grass in the valley so the Long Knives would find little forage for their mounts. The billowing smoke drifted over the camp circles buzzing with activity. Within a few hours, the entire village was on the move. The troopers on the bluff, puzzled by the long lull in the fighting, watched in awe as the mass of Indians and animals emerged from the cloud of smoke, slowly snaking up the valley. With the sun sinking to the west, the smoke and dust turning the enormous sky to a blood-red hue, the incredible procession seemed like it would never end.

The column stretched for more than two miles. The horse herd alone numbered some twenty thousand animals. Warriors rode at the front and on the flanks of the column. Countless ponies dragged tipis and travois loaded with children, puppies, cooking utensils, meat-stuffed parfleches, and other necessities.

The travois also bore wounded warriors, and a few horses carried the blanket-wrapped bodies of the dead. Several dead warriors were left behind on burial scaffolds and in standing lodges. Nestled alongside their immaculately clothed bodies were the warriors' treasured possessions, as well as parting gifts from loved ones: beautiful beaded moccasins, guns, bows and arrows, war medicine, tobacco, pipes, and firesteels. A few bodies of women and children were also to be found, killed by the Long Knives' Arikara scouts at the outset of the fight. (Among these were Gall's wives and children.) Many of the belongings of families in mourning were left behind at the village site as well.

The Cheyennes led the cavalcade, with the Húnkpapas bringing up the rear. At different times as the column moved along, the sound of singing carried across the valley and to the top of the bluffs. It was made up of shrill female voices. The women were joyous and singing victory songs. But the singing soon faded away as the last free Plains Indians receded out of sight, and the stillness of the evening settled over the Greasy Grass.

The besieged Seventh cavalrymen were rescued by Gibbon's column on the morning of June 27, and the first thing out of the mouths of the survivors was, "Where is Custer?"

Wishing to put as many miles as possible between them and the Long Knives, the people of the big village traveled late into the night. They stopped just once to rest for a few hours but began moving again early in the morning, heading south and southwest, toward the Big Horn Mountains. Camp that night was up Wood Louse Creek, a pretty, meandering stream that flows into the Greasy Grass. It was at this camp that the much-anticipated victory celebration was held.

Most of the Oglalas were just finishing a late-day meal when a commotion started in their camp circle. The heralds shouted, "The soldiers are coming!" Everyone turned and was startled to see a line of Long Knives galloping toward the tipis. But then the people broke out in smiles and laughed in delight. The "Long Knives" were actually warriors dressed in the uniforms of Custer's dead. The warriors wanted to give the villagers a little scare, if only for an instant.

Several "kill dances" took place throughout the village that night. Men, women, and children participated in these dances, which celebrated the killing of an enemy. However, some women were unable to dance—the deep "mourning cuts" in their legs were too fresh. Warriors took turns recounting their exploits in the battle, but only if they had a witness to verify their feat. As a warrior danced, he would brandish a gun or war club and loudly announce, "I killed a white man soldier." The warriors also created and sang kill songs, which were often addressed to their vanquished foe. One man's song went,

> *When you came attacking, why did not*
> *you have more men?*
> *Why didn't you bring more men so that*
> *you would be a little stronger?*

Another warrior sang,

> *I had no guns and you brought them to me.*
> *You charged us and gratified us—*
> *Made us thankful.*

All through the evening, the names of chiefs and warriors who'd distinguished themselves in the battle were talked about around the fires: Gall, He Dog, Crow King, Rain in the Face, Low Dog, White Bull, One Bull, Flying Hawk, Kicking Bear, Lame Deer, Little Big Man, and dozens more. Most who fought on the Greasy Grass only reaffirmed their bravery, while others had their names recognized in such a manner for the first time. All agreed, however, that Crazy Horse had been the greatest warrior, the true leader in the fight. "After the battle," remembered Stephen Standing Bear, "I heard a lot about Crazy Horse."

So, too, did the world to the east. The shocking news of the "Custer Massacre" burned up telegraph wires and spilled across the pages of newspapers in America and Europe. The name "Custer" was on the lips of every schoolchild, minister, maid, blacksmith, barkeep, merchant, politician, and railroad worker. And it was followed closely by the names "Sitting Bull" and "Crazy Horse." With those names came a nagging question: How could such a catastrophe have occurred to George Armstrong Custer, Civil War hero and darling cavalryman of the army?

Major Reno would soon get a good share of the blame. Had he charged the village instead of stopping short, his critics argued, the battle would have had a different outcome. But even taking Reno's failings into consideration, many still found it difficult to believe that Custer, the famed Indian fighter, and more than two hundred men under his command, could be wiped out. Surely there was something more that tipped the odds in the Indians' favor.

That "something," according to the *New York Herald*, was "the Napoleonic tactics and strategy of Sitting Bull." And for anyone wondering where Sitting Bull might have learned those tactics, the *Chicago Daily Tribune* ran an interview with an Upper Missouri steamboat captain who said Sitting Bull was quite the French scholar. He'd been taught to read and write that language by Father De Smet and had somehow obtained a copy of a French history of Napoleon's wars, which the Húnkpapa chief read cover to cover. Other news reports, even more incredible, portrayed Sitting Bull as having received formal military training—from the best in the land. The *Baltimore Gazette* revealed that the chief was likely a West Point graduate, known to his fellow cadets by the nickname "Bison" for his stocky build and bushy hair.

All these sensational stories were soon shown to be false, but they were emblematic of the overpowering desire to make sense of the army's disaster on the Little Big Horn. For the Indians, however, there was no mystery. "The Long Haired Chief was very brave," they said, "but very foolish to get killed the way he did." The warriors were simply too many, Crazy Horse explained later, and Custer divided his regiment one too many times. And as for Reno, Crazy Horse thought him a wise man. He "saved his men," the Oglala leader said. "If he had reached into our village, we would have eaten him up."

# A Winter War

*We were not bothering any white people. We*
*did not want to see any of them.*

WOODEN LEG

The initial shock of Custer's defeat was followed by demands to settle the "Indian problem" once and for all. "If the Indian will not submit to civilization," opined one newspaper, "let us cage him as we would a tiger or a wolf." General Sherman assured the public that the army would be pursuing its hard line toward the antitreaty bands with a vengeance. The followers of Sitting Bull and Crazy Horse would be driven down on the reservation, he told a reporter. "You can say that we will do it now, or exterminate them."

In this climate of national mourning and outrage, Christian and humanitarian organizations that had long advocated for Indian rights were scorned as "Indian lovers," particularly one group called the Connecticut Peace Society. Just weeks after the news of the massacre, the society passed an inflammatory resolution declaring Custer's death "a just retribution for the slaughter of friendly Indians," which was rather ironic coming from a "peace" organization. The society also passed resolutions denouncing the white invasion of the Black Hills and calling for the withdrawal of the army from Indian country. Clearly, that wasn't going to happen.

Instead, more troops, artillery, and military supplies headed to Sioux country. Two new military posts were authorized, one on the upper Powder River and one at the mouth of the Tongue, to keep troops within easy striking distance of Sitting Bull's and Crazy Horse's favorite haunts. The army was now given total control of the various Indian agencies, and Indians arriving from the unceded territory were to have their arms, ammunition, and ponies confiscated. The returning Indians themselves were to be held as prisoners of war.

Meanwhile, Congress passed an "Indian Appropriation Bill" that disallowed future funding for subsistence rations until the Lakota nation gave up its right to the unceded territory and agreed to allow up to three roads across their permanent reservation. These roads, unsurprisingly, were intended to link the Black Hills. And to take care of the annoying legal issue of the hills belonging to the Lakotas, the same bill allowed the president to appoint a commission to negotiate the hills' purchase. But there would be no true "negotiating" this time. That the Lakotas would lose the Black Hills was a foregone conclusion. The commission hadn't even begun collecting the signatures on the new treaty when a railroad upstart announced its steel rails would reach the Black Hills the next year.

None of the uproar in the states and machinations of the government were known to Sitting Bull and Crazy Horse. In the weeks following their victory over Long Hair, the big village gradually dispersed, with the different chiefs and headmen leading their bands in pursuit of buffalo. In that time, messages from Sitting Bull periodically arrived at different agencies. About August 1,

1876, the Fort Peck agent received a verbal message from the chief via an Indian courier. Sitting Bull said he planned to visit before the fall to trade. He wanted the agent to know he didn't commence the current war. "I am getting old. I do not want to fight the whites, but the whites rush on me and I am compelled to defend myself." Sitting Bull was willing to come in and make peace, he said, but he and the other chiefs had conditions: the Great Father must promise protection, and the whites must abandon the Black Hills.

A few weeks later, a message was delivered to the Standing Rock Agency by a Húnkpapa with the curious name The Man That Smells His Hand. Sitting Bull professed that he was tired of fighting, and he wanted the Long Knives to stop fighting his people. Nevertheless, it was the duty of the Lakotas to defend their country. "Perhaps the whites think they can exterminate us," Sitting Bull said, "but the Great Spirit will not permit them to do so."

Crazy Horse sent no messages, other than the occasional dead bodies of white men he and his followers left in and around the northern Black Hills. To be sure, Crazy Horse wasn't ready to make peace, and he wasn't interested in teasing peace like his friend Sitting Bull, either. A surge of killings and depredations in the Black Hills began in mid-August, with eleven white men slaughtered in a span of a few days, plus a herd of some sixty horses driven off. A warrior slain in one of these run-ins was found to have an army Springfield and a horse marked with a Seventh Cavalry brand. The warrior's head was promptly cut off and taken to Deadwood, where it was paraded around town, earning its keeper enough whiskey to get him falling-down drunk.

In early September, during the Moon When Plums Are Ripe, villages of Oglalas, Northern Cheyennes, Sans Arcs, Miniconjous, and Húnkpapas were spread apart over the prairies of northwest South Dakota, near a miles-long chalky, pine-clad escarpment known as Slim Buttes. The Lakotas and Cheyennes were mostly engaged in buffalo and deer hunting. The weather had been rainy and overcast for several days, turning the ground into an annoying muck. And with the fog and rain came cool temperatures; a light frost settled on the lodges one night, early for that part of the country.

Crazy Horse's camp of Oglalas and Cheyennes was one of the larger villages, consisting of some three hundred lodges. On the morning of September 9, the calm of this village was interrupted by shouting. "Trouble in one of the camps," someone yelled. "A lot [of our people] are getting killed!" Crazy Horse learned that Long Knives had surprised a camp of thirty-five lodges of Sans Arc and Miniconjous under Iron Plume, about twenty miles away. Warriors immediately called for their horses, gathered their weapons, and prepared war medicine. Excited for the prospects of a fight, as well as the chance to rescue their relatives, the warriors rapidly formed outside the village, then galloped off. Riding with Crazy Horse were some of his best men: He Dog, Kicking Bear, Brave Wolf, and Wears the Deer Bonnet.

Late that afternoon, scattered shots rang out as approximately six hundred boldly painted and befeathered warriors burst into view, scattered among the castlelike buttes and dark pines just west of Iron Plume's camp. Below them, eighteen hundred Bluecoats belonging to Three Stars occupied the open slopes surrounding the village. The first reports to Crazy Horse said it was a small force of Long Knives that attacked the village, only about 150 men. That estimate was accurate, but those soldiers had only been a detachment from Three Stars's main column, and now the entire force was united. There would be no repeat of the Little Big Horn this day, but as with most of the warriors' skirmishes with the Bluecoats, there was always a chance of picking off a white man or two and counting coup.

Puffy balls of gray smoke from the warriors' guns floated in the air in front of the sculpted crags and deep crevices while the cracks of their gunfire echoed off the bluffs. Over the next two hours, the Long Knives advanced on foot on the warrior positions. With bullets buzzing over their heads, the Bluecoats executed a heavy fire of their own and steadily forced the warriors back. In a last-ditch effort to inflict some kind of damage on the enemy, Crazy Horse, mounted on a fast white horse, led a contingent of at least 250 warriors out of a small gap in the bluffs. Despite the muddy slickness and the narrowness of the path—no wider than a game trail—they galloped down the steep incline single file, yelling at the top of their lungs.

The feat of horsemanship was awe-inspiring to the troopers who witnessed it. Crazy Horse and his warriors raced near the skirmish line of the Bluecoats, dropping down to the off-side of their ponies and firing their guns as they galloped past. But the soldiers held firm, and with dark shadows now covering the captured village, the warriors broke off the fight and disappeared into the nearby ravines. The only indication Crazy Horse had suffered any casualties were a few pools of blood found on top the bluffs.

The contents of the village were gathered into three piles, each as large as a small cabin, and set afire, the flames licking the villagers' possessions throughout the night and into the next morning, when more goods were piled on. Watching the beautiful clothing, hides, and lodge poles burn was Frank Grouard, General Crook's favorite scout. It was Grouard who'd discovered the camp, making it the second village the old friend of Sitting Bull and Crazy Horse had led the Long Knives to so they could destroy it.

A brief skirmish between warriors and the rear of Three Stars's column occurred the next day, and five or six warriors were seen to fall. This dismal last act of the Battle of Slim Buttes seemed to match the day's heavy clouds and drizzling rain.

"Now General, how is the Indian question going to be settled?" It was a query put to General Sherman by a reporter for the *Leavenworth Times*.

"The army will clean them out this winter," Sherman replied. "We are only waiting for winter to come. They will be powerless then."

The interview took place on September 11, 1876, just a day after the conclusion of the Battle of Slim Buttes. A severe winter, Sherman knew, was one of the best weapons the army could have. With the green grasses of spring and summer brown and covered with snow, the Indian ponies would be weak, surviving mostly on cottonwood bark. The tribes would be settled into their winter camps. And there was nothing like a good snow for tracking a village on the run. The army, on the other hand, was well equipped to march and fight in the cold and snow, with vast stores of provisions for its soldiers and grain to feed horses and mules. For Sherman's army in Sioux country, harsh weather was a friend, not an enemy.

Another weapon was starvation. The Lakotas and their allies might elude the army forever if they had a steady food supply. They didn't. White Bull believed the white man purposely slaughtered the buffalo to get rid of the Indians. But while the whites were certainly killing buffalo, they did it for sport, meat, and to line their pockets, not as some grand scheme to force the Indians onto reservations. And the Plains tribes contributed to their own hardships by continuing to harvest buffalo beyond their own needs so as to have robes for trade. A Fort Benton fur trader was paying $5.50 a robe in 1876, and buffalo tongues were on menus and in meat markets across the United States. Thus, Sherman rested easy, knowing that if his soldiers didn't get the Lakotas first, sooner or later, starvation would.

A few days after Sherman's interview, news arrived that would give the army's winter pursuit of the antitreaty bands the stamp of legality, at least in the eyes of the Grant administration. Several chiefs of the Lakotas, Cheyennes, and Arapahos had signed away the Black Hills and the unceded Indian territory. Sitting Bull and Crazy Horse's followers were now not only roaming outside the boundaries of the Sioux reservation, but the country where they hunted, raised their families, gave flesh at the Sun Dance, and buried loved ones was no longer Indian land.

Among the Oglala chiefs to touch the pen were Red Cloud, Young They Fear Even His Horses, Little Wound, American Horse, and Fire Thunder, all of whom signed at the Red Cloud Agency on September 20. Fire Thunder found the treaty so shameful that when he approached the table to touch the pen, he held his blanket up over his eyes and made his mark blind. The chief walked back to his seat without uttering a word.

The Brulés' turn came three days later at the Spotted Tail Agency, approximately forty-three miles to the northeast, but Spotted Tail was hesitant. And if Spotted Tail didn't sign, the other Brulé headmen wouldn't touch the pen, either. However, an old Indian trader knew exactly how to get Spotted Tail to accept the treaty. If the chief didn't sign, the white man said, "Red Cloud would get ahead of him, and derive all the advantages to be had from the treaty." Spotted Tail couldn't touch the pen fast enough.

No effort was made to obtain the signatures of three-fourths of all adult male Lakotas, as required by the 1868 Fort Laramie Treaty to validate any land sessions. The chiefs had seemingly forgotten about that significant treaty provision, if they even understood it at the time, which is doubtful. One thing is certain, though. No one with the U.S. government was going to remind them of it.

Sometime after the leaves on the cottonwoods turned a golden yellow, but before the first snow, Crazy Horse led his warriors on a raid against the Crows. He rode back to his village on the Rosebud with several scalps, a feat that surprised no one. In the meantime, Sitting Bull and his Húnkpapas, along with bands of Miniconjous and Sans Arcs, had moved north of the Yellowstone. It was there the chief got in a fight with Man with the Bear Coat.

Man with the Bear Coat, or just Bear Coat, was the name the Lakotas gave to thirty-seven-year-old Colonel Nelson A. Miles. Standing six feet tall with a handsome, soldierly bearing, he was, now that Custer was gone, probably the most ambitious, attention-seeking officer in the army. But, like Custer, he was a real fighter and absolutely relentless in the face of the enemy. He bore the scars of several wounds from his service in the Civil War. His heroics at the Battle of Chancellorsville in 1863 had earned him the Medal of Honor. And he'd had experience fighting Indians, campaigning against the Comanches, Kiowas, and Southern Cheyennes in the Texas Panhandle during the Red River War. The name Bear Coat, however, came from his time on the northern plains, for he favored a greatcoat trimmed in bear fur during the chill of fall and winter.

Miles, leading nearly four hundred riflemen of the Fifth Infantry regiment and one artillery piece, caught up with Sitting Bull and his followers on Cedar Creek (northwest of present-day Terry, Montana) the third week of October. Wishing to avoid a fight with the village so close, Sitting Bull decided to meet with the commander of the Long Knives under a flag of truce. Together with Chiefs Gall, Pretty Bear, Standing Bear, and his nephew White Bull, the supreme chief of the antitreaty bands actually held two parleys with Bear Coat, one in the afternoon and one the following morning. Neither went well.

The chiefs listed off several demands, including the usual "get out of Sioux country," but none of which mentioned surrendering, while Miles countered with just one demand: unconditional surrender. Toward the end of the second meeting, a warrior walked forward and whispered in White Bull's ear: "You better get your uncle Sitting Bull away from the soldier. They are both mad."

Moments later, Sitting Bull stormed off, shouting orders to nearby headmen and warriors as he went. "Immediately the prairie was alive with Indians dashing in every direction," remembered Miles. The fight that followed, however, wasn't much of a contest, especially once the artillerymen began to "fire the wagon," a three-inch ordnance rifle. The warriors were soon driven from the field, less six men, whose bloodied bodies lay contorted on the ground. Also left behind were tons of dried buffalo meat and considerable camp equipage at the village site, a severe loss, especially with winter aching to wrap the plains in snow and ice.

Bear Coat followed the trail of the fleeing village, pushing his regiment for more than forty miles. He finally caught up to the camps at the Yellowstone River, and on October 26, the Lakotas, four hundred lodges of mostly Miniconjous and Sans Arcs, agreed to surrender and return to one of the agencies. The people were starving. Once Miles provided the Lakotas with rations, however, it remained to be seen how many would actually follow through with their promise. As for Sitting Bull, Miles learned the chief had broken away with thirty Húnkpapa lodges a day or two previous, heading for the Missouri.

The antitreaty bands were more vulnerable than ever. Forced to split up because of limited resources of game, fuel, and forage, each village or lodge group could be hunted down and picked off piecemeal by the Long Knives. The smaller villages naturally contained fewer numbers of warriors to fend off attacks. And, of course, those invading armies of Bluecoats weren't encumbered with their own families and lifelong possessions trailing behind.

The mental stress of the Long Knives' ongoing pursuit also wore on the tribes and their leaders. Sleep is difficult when one worries about being awakened early in the morning by gunfire and screaming. Even Sitting Bull was feeling the effects of the constant struggle to protect his people and elude the soldiers, at least according to Bear Coat. After his parleys with the chief, Miles wrote his wife that "I think [Sitting Bull] feels that his strength is somewhat exhausted and he appeared much depressed, suffering from nervous excitement and loss of power."

The next village to suffer a terrifying dawn attack was that of Dull Knife, a Northern Cheyenne chief. On November 25, more than a thousand cavalrymen and Pawnee and Shoshone Indian scouts belonging to Three Stars surprised the village, tucked away in the Big Horn Mountains. In the desperate fight that followed, a Cheyenne yelled out, "We can fight the white men, but we cannot fight the white men and Indians, too!" Thirty warriors were killed, and 175 lodges and all their contents were consigned to the flames. Frank Grouard, demonstrating that he'd learned well in the time he spent with Sitting Bull and Crazy Horse, separated a Cheyenne from his scalp. Some of the soldiers tied bloody scalps to their belts as well.

Without warm robes and shelter, nearly a dozen suckling Cheyenne infants froze to death that night. And because the Long Knives had captured the village's horse herd (more than five hundred ponies), most of Dull Knife's survivors were left to escape on foot. They trudged east, looking for Crazy Horse's village, believed to be on the Tongue. "Travel and sleep, travel and sleep, we kept going," recalled Wooden Leg. Not until eleven torturous days later did they finally arrive at the Oglala camps, and once again, Crazy Horse's people welcomed the refugees. Several Oglala men went about collecting clothes and lodge skins. "We helped the Cheyennes the best we could," remembered Short Bull. "We hadn't much ourselves." But the little the Oglalas had meant everything to the famished Cheyenne families. Wooden Leg warmly recalled that "not any Cheyenne was allowed to go to sleep hungry or cold that night."

More than 160 miles to the north, Sitting Bull remained in the vicinity of the Missouri River, his camp growing to 170 lodges. He kept close to Fort Peck, within thirty miles or so. Its trading post and Indian agency offered the possibility of acquiring ammunition—illicitly, of course. The ammunition came through agency Indians camped nearby and even post employees, a number of them mixed-bloods, who acquired cartridges they claimed were needed for hunting purposes. They would then turn around and make a tidy profit trading these to Sitting Bull's people. The camp was also well within the range of Sitting Bull's old trade partners the Métis, and he was less than a hundred miles from Wood Mountain in Canada, the site of another trading post. Sometime during the fall, Sitting Bull traded buffalo robes and a herd of mules to the Métis for cartridges, powder, and balls.

The chief explained to those who'd listen that he needed ammunition not because he wanted to make war on the whites, but because the soldiers were making war on him. The Húnkpapa leader was being a little disingenuous, however. He may not have intended to make war now, but he'd spent most of his life warring on the white man. And if given the chance to defeat him and force him off Lakota lands, he wouldn't hesitate. But also for most of his life, the white man had tried to contain and subjugate Sitting Bull's people and steal their homeland. And maybe, for the first time, it seemed to Sitting Bull the white man was winning.

The whereabouts of Sitting Bull's camp was hardly a well-kept secret, and at daybreak on December 7, his scouts spotted soldiers approaching the village, its dusky lodges spread out near the banks of the Missouri opposite the mouth of Bark Creek. Most of the Húnkpapas were able to escape across the ice to the south bank before the morning light revealed the Bluecoats, 112 men of the Fifth Infantry under Lieutenant Frank Baldwin, a thirty-four-year-old Civil War veteran. The soldiers sent bullets whizzing in the direction of the retreating villagers while warriors put up a cover fire to allow the women and children to slip away through the timber. Fortunately, the women had time to also rescue their lodges and possessions. The warriors then withdrew to commanding positions on the bluffs overlooking the river bottom, where they eagerly waited for Baldwin's small force to follow. More gunfire cut the chilly air, but as Baldwin estimated the warriors to number at least five hundred, he wisely thought it best to fight the Húnkpapa chief another day and marched off.

That "another day" came less than two weeks later and approximately sixty-five miles south of the Missouri, on Ash Creek. This time, Sitting Bull's village was caught napping, believing that the deep, drifted snow that now covered the country and temperatures that plummeted well below zero at night would dissuade the Long Knives from leaving their posts. No one saw the line of charging Bluecoats until they were less than a mile from the camp, nor did they see the gun that shoots twice until it boomed, sending a shrieking shell over the tipis. The artillery fire started a stampede out of the village. And as most of the men were out hunting buffalo, any kind of challenge to Baldwin's three companies was impossible.

The Bluecoats rushed into the abandoned village and set about destroying it. They burned the lodgepoles and skins of ninety tipis and plundered the dried buffalo meat and hundreds of warm buffalo robes and blankets. They also killed sixty horses and mules captured from the village herd. The Bluecoats believed Sitting Bull and his followers were left with what little they could pack on their backs, which was mostly true. But somehow, Sitting Bull was able to flee with the precious ammunition he'd obtained from the Métis.

Good communication was kept up between Sitting Bull's camp and Crazy Horse, and when the war chief learned of the devastating loss on Ash Creek, he sent a message to Sitting Bull to join him, adding that he had plenty of warriors and ammunition. But Crazy Horse had worries, too. Some in the antitreaty bands were wavering in their allegiance, mostly among the Miniconjou leadership. How many villages had to burn, they thought, before they sought peace with the Long Knives? And Crazy Horse was fast tiring of Lakota emissaries sent from the agencies to persuade him and his followers to surrender. All these outsiders did was sow dissent and spy on the camps, passing to the white man information on Crazy Horse's location and strength.

Two Miniconjou emissaries from the Cheyenne River Agency crossed a very dangerous line when they slipped out of the camps with thirteen families, headed east. Crazy Horse had warned these men that they wouldn't be allowed to take anyone from the camp, and as soon as he learned of the defection, he and Little Big Man gathered several warriors and immediately took up their trail. The pony tracks and drag marks from lodgepoles were easily followed in the snow, and when the war chief caught up to the deserters, he was in a rage. Crazy Horse ordered his warriors to kill the families' horses, confiscate their guns and knives, and take all their robes and other possessions. The war chief then allowed that if the defectors still wanted to go to the whites, to go on.

When Crazy Horse returned to the village, he sent heralds to the different camp circles to announce that Indians living at the agencies would now be considered enemies and the same as white men. And no Indian messengers or visitors from the agencies would be allowed in the camps. Crazy Horse was undoubtedly aware by then that several Oglalas and Brulés from the Red Cloud and Spotted Tail agencies had enlisted as scouts for Three Stars. These scouts weren't expected to fight their relatives; their role was to help the Long Knives hunt down Crazy Horse's and Sitting Bull's followers. Nevertheless, just like Frank Grouard, they would be helping the white man to destroy the villages of the antitreaty bands and end their freedom.

In early January 1877, the smoke of nearly eight hundred lodge fires hung low over the valley of the Tongue, some one hundred miles south of the Yellowstone. Making up the camp circles were Miniconjous, Sans Arcs, Northern Cheyennes, and Crazy Horse's Oglalas. Snow blanketed the ground and bitter cold air settled around the village at the end of short winter days. "This was a good place to stay," recalled Black Elk.

As the Lakotas and Cheyennes went about their usual hunting and village activities, Bear Coat marched up the Tongue toward their camps with 436 officers and men of the Fifth and Twenty-Second Infantries and two artillery pieces. Crazy Horse was well aware of this. In fact, warriors had skirmished with Miles's men on the first day of 1877 and also on the third. Many leaders would have taken their people far away from an approaching army of Bluecoats, but Crazy Horse saw this as an opportunity. The challenge to fighting Long Knives had always been figuring out a way to draw an inferior force away from a post or separate it from a larger command, where it could be surrounded and overwhelmed. Such scenarios had brought great victories at the Hundred in the Hand and against Long Hair on the Greasy Grass. And with the combined tribes now at his disposal, Crazy Horse had many more men than Bear Coat.

Most looked to the Oglala war chief for decisions on when and where to fight, but on January 7, debate sprang up over whether to strike Bear Coat at his camp eighteen miles downstream or to allow him to come closer and ambush him where the valley was narrower and surrounded by more broken country. The question was settled when word came that Bear Coat's men had captured a small party of Cheyenne women and children. More than two hundred Cheyenne warriors galloped out of the village and reached Bear Coat's force at dusk and skirmished with the Bluecoats until nightfall. If there'd ever been a chance for a surprise, the Cheyennes had spoiled it.

The following morning, Crazy Horse and from five hundred to six hundred headmen and warriors emerged from a whitish haze of falling snow to see the Bluecoats' camp in the cottonwoods along the Tongue. Bear Coat spotted the warriors as well and barked orders for the deployment of his men, some of whom had already prepared breastworks the night before. For the next several hours, the warriors used the bluffs and hills on each side of the valley to threaten the positions of the Bluecoats. "The Indians moved back and forth, down and up, fighting the soldiers at different times all day," remembered Wooden Leg. Distances between the opposing forces varied from seven hundred yards or more to the length of a carbine when warriors swung their guns as clubs to beat back advancing soldiers. Seven hundred yards was long range for the rifles of the infantry, but what was considered long range for a rifle was like shooting point-blank for the artillery, and their exploding shells kept the warriors hopping.

Unlike in other battles with the Long Knives, the warriors fought mostly dismounted, using their ponies only to carry them from ravine to ravine and from ridge to ridge. These warriors were smartly using the rocks, scattered cedars, and terrain for cover. The rattle of gunfire and the booming of the cannons was, at times, ferocious. Previous information that the Lakotas and Cheyennes were short of ammunition had been greatly exaggerated, observed one officer, for they "used it rather lavishly."

Eagle-bone whistles cut the air, and the distinctive cry of Crazy Horse could be heard as he shouted encouragement and issued commands. Many brave deeds were performed, but like previous encounters with the Long Knives, the warriors had no answer for the gun that shoots twice. The warriors were pushed back, one hill at a time, until a furious snowstorm enveloped the valley in the afternoon, making visibility virtually nonexistent. Crazy Horse broke off the fight, and the warriors returned upstream, with the Oglala war chief and several warriors trailing behind as a rear guard. Despite the intensity of the battle, the Lakotas and Cheyennes lost but three men killed and a few wounded. One of those killed was a renowned Cheyenne holy man named Big Crow, who claimed no bullet could go through him. The warriors killed one of Bear Coat's men and wounded nine.

Bear Coat Miles led a short reconnaissance up the Tongue the next day before turning the command around; his men were worn out, and he was short of rations. Once back at his cantonment at the mouth of the Tongue (later Fort Keogh), Miles wrote his official report, in which he portrayed the engagement, soon dubbed the Battle of Wolf Mountains, as a complete victory. The warriors, he stated, were "swept from the field," and the result of his campaigning had "broken the strength and prestige of both Sitting Bull and Crazy Horse." But one of Miles's own officers held a contrary view. In a letter written to a friend, Lieutenant Cornelius C. Cusick reported that "our offensive operations were ended, our advance was checked, and we were forced on the defensive. Crazy Horse seeing us checked at the close of the day's battle quietly withdrew his warriors from our front."

A week or so after the battle, during the Moon of Frost in the Lodge, the large village had relocated to near the juncture of Prairie Dog Creek and the Tongue River (a little more than two miles southeast of present-day Decker, Montana). Here, Crazy Horse welcomed the arrival of Sitting Bull and fifty lodges of Húnkpapas (half his band). The ammunition Sitting Bull brought was welcomed, too, especially as so much had been expended during the recent fight with Bear Coat. Once the supreme chief and his people were settled in camp, the two friends met—privately and with other headmen in the camps—to discuss the future. Should they continue to fight the Long Knives? Surrender? Or should they abandon their homeland and find refuge in Grandmother's Country (Canada).

If they surrendered, the antitreaty bands would be forced to relinquish their weapons and ponies. The possibility of imprisonment and even execution was also a grave concern. As for Grandmother's Country—a reference to Queen Victoria—Sitting Bull knew that U.S. troops would not cross the "holy line," the international border. Crazy Horse and Sitting Bull never respected any kind of boundary; they went where they pleased. But they weren't opposed to using the white man's boundaries against him.

Continuing to fight, especially after the relentless campaigning of the Bluecoats of the last few months, didn't seem the best course, at least in Sitting Bull's mind. The tribes were scattered, Sitting Bull pointed out. Some five hundred families, mostly Húnkpapas, Black Moon among them, had already crossed the holy line into Canada. Old Inkpaduta and his Santee followers were there, too. Sitting Bull believed that if he and his Húnkpapas were to remain, the odds were they would eventually be captured or killed—in just the last three months he'd seen his camp decimated twice. If they went north, Sitting Bull suggested, they might be able to persuade the Métis to join forces with the antitreaty bands. Thus reinforced, they could drive the Long Knives from Indian country.

In the end, Sitting Bull's visit to Crazy Horse's village wasn't so much about deciding what was to be done as it was to convince Crazy Horse to go north with him. But Crazy Horse was ever a warrior, in both spirit and body. And he wasn't so willing to leave the country that was rightfully theirs. Maybe it was simply his time to die, Crazy Horse said. Perhaps he would go south and settle the question. At the same time, the Oglala leader recognized his responsibility for the well-being of the women and children and old men. Balancing his desire to wage war against the white invaders with the suffering that his people had endured thus far, and the likelihood of more suffering to come, was trying. He would pray to *Wakan Tanka* for guidance, and he would call on the power the Thunder Beings had given him to protect his people—in life and in death. And he would try to hold the land for Sitting Bull, the Lakotas, and the Cheyennes.

Disappointed but respectful of Crazy Horse's decision, Sitting Bull left his friend behind on the Tongue, promising to inform Crazy Horse of their reception in Grandmother's Country. In the winter count of the Húnkpapa Long Soldier, the Lakota year 1876 to 1877 is represented by a drawing of Sitting Bull shaking hands with a man wearing a red coat and black knee-high boots, the uniform of the North-West Mounted Police. It is titled the "Year Sitting Bull made peace with the Englishman."

# Father, I Want to See You

*It is not possible to change the nature of
any race of men in a moment.*

PIERRE-JEAN DE SMET

With the departure of Sitting Bull, so too went some of the sense of unity and purpose that formerly drove these Lakotas and Cheyennes to resist, to defend their traditional lifestyle, to refuse to be confined to a reservation drawn up by white men. Crazy Horse was in no way defeated, but the same couldn't be said for those among his followers who were hungry and poor, whose horses were weak or dead. Many in the camps had simply lost the will to fight, and it was only the fear of Crazy Horse and his camp soldiers that'd kept them from leaving for the agencies. But now even that wasn't enough to stop the exodus, and Crazy Horse soon became resigned to letting those leave who wished to. It was a deeply disheartening time; after everything he'd done to preserve the Lakotas' freedom, Crazy Horse couldn't help but feel his own people were turning against him.

Word of the cracks in the resolve of the antitreaty bands prompted the army to step up its "policy of persuasion," sending new emissaries to Crazy Horse to convince him to surrender. The first to arrive at Crazy Horse's camp, now located on the Powder River, was a party from the Red Cloud Agency under Hunts the Enemy, a nephew of Red Cloud and a member of his Bad Face band. Hunts the Enemy fought bravely under his uncle and Crazy Horse in the war over the Bozeman Cut-off, but he'd joined the white man in friendship, he later explained, after becoming convinced the white man's God was more powerful than *Wakan Tanka*.

Hunts the Enemy and his two companions went straight to Crazy Horse's lodge, where they were relieved to be met with a kind reception from the war chief. Crazy Horse listened in silence as Hunts the Enemy spoke. The Oglala emissary told Crazy Horse he'd been sent by Three Stars, who wanted to end the fighting and have peace. If Crazy Horse and his followers would come to one of the agencies and turn themselves in, nothing bad would happen. No one would be punished for the death of Long Hair or for any of the fights with the Bluecoats. And the agent would issue the people blankets, clothes, and rations.

Crazy Horse didn't speak for some time. He didn't want to go to an agency, and he likely was regretting his decision not to join Sitting Bull. Crazy Horse knew that his most loyal followers would abide by whatever course he chose, but he simply couldn't bear to be the one to tell his people to surrender. Surrender, as Luther Standing Bear explained, "meant submission to a people whom [Crazy Horse] did not consider his equal; it meant the doom of his race."

Finally, without having revealed his thoughts on surrendering, the war chief indicated the meeting was over. Such a weighty matter would require a second council, which was held the following day. At this second meeting, Crazy Horse instructed Hunts the Enemy and his companions to visit the main Oglala and Cheyenne village, about a day's travel to the west. Whatever the headmen there wished to do, he would do the same. Hunts the Enemy had brought colorful cloth-wrapped packages of tobacco as a token of peace from Three Stars. But Crazy Horse declined the gift and instructed Hunts the Enemy to take it to the other village. Refusing a gift, no matter how politely, was considered bad mannered, if not an act of ill will. Nevertheless, Hunts the Enemy felt confident he'd secured a promise from Crazy Horse.

At the main village, Hunts the Enemy presented the packages of tobacco, after which he imparted to the headmen the same message from Three Stars he'd delivered to Crazy Horse. Iron Hawk, an Oglala elder, acted as overall spokesperson. "You see all the people here are in rags," he said to Hunts the Enemy; "they all need clothing, we might as well go in." And if Three Stars was offering peace, he added, "Well, it shall be a big peace! . . . whoever brings good to me will not outdo me." However, Iron Hawk cautioned it was still very much winter, with a deep snow then covering the plains and foothills. It would be some time before they could come in. But come in they would.

Before Hunts the Enemy could return to the Red Cloud Agency with the good news, another delegation left for Crazy Horse's camp to persuade him to surrender, this one led by his uncle Spotted Tail. It amounted to the same old game between Spotted Tail and Red Cloud of who could be viewed as the bigger friend of the white man—and thus reap the most favors and recognition. Well aware of this bitter rivalry, the army was happy to take advantage of it. Red Cloud had been deposed as chief by Three Stars the previous October. Adding insult to injury, Three Stars named Spotted Tail chief over all the Lakotas. But if Red Cloud brought Crazy Horse in, he was promised reinstatement as chief and even an appointment as first sergeant in the Indian scouts, the highest rank available and higher than any other enlisted chief. It was with Red Cloud's blessing, naturally, that his nephew Hunts the Enemy undertook his important mission.

Spotted Tail with a large entourage of two hundred Brulés met in council with several Lakota and Cheyenne bands on the Little Powder River, but Crazy Horse wouldn't see him. Crazy Horse's father, who'd taken the name "Worm" after giving his former name to his son, told Spotted Tail that Crazy Horse was out hunting alone. Crazy Horse was the ultimate prize, of course, and Spotted Tail sent two runners with tobacco to find him, but they returned empty-handed.

Crazy Horse didn't want to be found, especially by his uncle Spotted Tail, whom he considered the same as a white man. And more councils were unnecessary; Crazy Horse had already told Hunts the Enemy he would follow the decision of the Oglala headmen, and they'd agreed to surrender. Worm assured Spotted Tail that he spoke for his son when he said they would come in and make peace. The Brulé chief arrived back at his agency on Beaver Creek on April 5 and reported to the agent that three hundred families from the antitreaty bands were only eight or nine days out, but he couldn't say definitely when Crazy Horse would be in. Without Crazy Horse, however, Spotted Tail's mission could be viewed as something of a failure; at the least, disappointing. Undoubtedly Spotted Tail sensed this, as the agent reported the chief wasn't "very communicative" upon his return.

As families and bands slowly began the trek from the Powder River country to the agencies, Crazy Horse continued to stay away from the main camps. "He was a queer man," remembered his cousin Black Elk. "He had been queer all of this winter." On their way to the Red Cloud Agency, Black Elk's family encountered Crazy Horse and Black Shawl camped near a small creek. Crazy Horse spoke to Black Elk's father: "Uncle, you might have noticed me, how I act, but it is for the good of my people that I am out alone. Out there I am making plans—nothing but good plans—for the good of my people. I don't care where the people go. They can go where they wish." Crazy Horse didn't owe Black Elk's father an explanation, but he was family and a holy man, and he wanted him to know. "This country is ours," Crazy Horse added emphatically, "therefore I am doing this."

A week after Spotted Tail's return, Red Cloud started out with a delegation to meet Crazy Horse and accompany him and his followers in (and to make sure they came in). Like his Brulé rival, Red Cloud had touched the pen, and he was complicit in giving away the Black Hills as well, but Red Cloud was also a fellow tribesman, an Oglala. Red Cloud's party located Crazy Horse and his band eighty miles northwest of the agency, and their appearance was alarming: the women and children were starving and the ponies were thin and weak. The last few months of warfare and bitter weather had taken a harsh toll. It was little wonder so many of his people were ready to surrender.

Red Cloud had a simple message for the war chief: "All is well; have no fear; come on in." He of course meant the Red Cloud Agency, not Spotted Tail. Red Cloud then sent a runner to the agency with an urgent request for rations. Those rations—ten wagons of hard crackers and one hundred head of beef—reached the procession on May 1, and such a feeding frenzy ensued that nearly all the women and children became ill, forcing a two-day delay before the caravan could resume its journey. On the morning of May 6, 1877, however, Crazy Horse reached a point five miles from the Red Cloud Agency, where the formalities of surrendering his people would begin.

Overseeing the surrender for the army was a handsome thirty-two-year-old lieutenant named William Philo Clark, a West Point graduate who'd recently served as aide-de-camp to General Crook.

Based out of the military post of Camp Robinson (a mile and a half from the Red Cloud Agency), Clark was in charge of recruiting and leading Three Stars's Indian scouts. Having a keen interest in Plains Indian culture—he'd mastered Indian sign language—the lieutenant was generally well liked by his scouts and agency Indians alike. They knew him as White Hat.

Crazy Horse sent a messenger ahead to Clark informing the lieutenant he would be approaching with his warriors abreast in a line, and he would be riding alone out in front. He asked Clark to meet him the same way, riding in advance of his Indian scouts. If Clark didn't grasp that an epoch was coming to an end, that the world of the Lakotas was about to change forever, Crazy Horse did, and the occasion demanded a certain formality.

As promised, Crazy Horse appeared on the edge of a long, sloping bluff riding a white horse, followed by ten Oglala headmen— He Dog, Little Big Man, Little Hawk, Bad Road, Old Hawk, and others. Behind the headmen rode three hundred warriors on brightly painted ponies. All except Crazy Horse were adorned in their finest warbonnets, blankets, beaded and painted shirts, leggings, and moccasins. The morning sunlight shimmered off brass-framed Henrys and Winchesters, silver hair plates, abalone shells, and brass armbands. Crazy Horse rode slowly down into a small valley and halted, his headmen and warriors about a hundred yards behind. As he did this, the long bluff darkened with hundreds of women, children, old men, ponies pulling travois, and barking dogs.

Crazy Horse dismounted, and Clark rode up and did the same. The war leader sat upon the ground and motioned to Clark to sit also. Then Crazy Horse filled his pipe with tobacco and they smoked. They sat while smoking the pipe of peace, Crazy Horse explained, because he wanted the peace to last forever. After Crazy Horse put down the pipe, he held out his left hand, saying, *"Kola*

[friend], I shake with this hand because my heart is on this side."
The headmen now came forward and shook hands with Clark
and others of his party. He Dog removed his ornately beaded hair
shirt and laid it over Clark's shoulders. Then he took off his warbonnet and placed it on Clark's head. Thus, He Dog signified his
submission to the white man's authority.

Clark gave a short speech reminding Crazy Horse and the
headmen that he would be collecting their firearms and ponies
when they reached the agency. The surrender ceremony concluded by noon, when the entire cavalcade, Red Cloud in the
lead, started for the agency. Suddenly, Crazy Horse's men began
singing. An interpreter explained that the warriors were singing a
"peace song." One white observer described it as a "rude and slow-
measured chant." The men's voices, all in unison, lent the colorful
procession an air of triumph—they'd surrendered, but their spirit
remained undefeated.

At 2:00 P.M., Crazy Horse's band arrived at a campsite near
the Red Cloud Agency, and the agency clerk immediately began
a tally: 217 men, 312 women, 186 boys, and 184 girls for a total of
899 individuals. They arrived with 146 lodges, some nearly in tatters, and their immense herd of livestock counted more than two
thousand horses and mules. Many of the women and children had
never seen white men, and they were fairly timid around Clark and
the few other whites in the camp. Once the lodges were erected,
Clark asked the warriors to surrender their guns, and they piled
up forty-six long guns and seventy-six pistols at his feet. This was
far short of what they actually possessed, and Clark knew it. He
confronted Crazy Horse, telling him he must have all the guns
in the camp. Crazy Horse just stared blankly, so the lieutenant
got an army wagon and some interpreters and Indian scouts and
went through the camp searching every lodge. Clark found firearms rather plentiful, most of them being lever-action repeaters

and army Springfields. From Crazy Horse's lodge the lieutenant recovered three nice Winchester rifles.

Including Crazy Horse's followers, nearly four thousand members of the antitreaty bands—Northern Cheyennes, Sans Arcs, Miniconjous, and Oglalas—had turned themselves in at Spotted Tail and Red Cloud during the last ten weeks. The only holdouts now were Sitting Bull and his people and the Miniconjou Lame Deer with sixty-one lodges. The day after Crazy Horse surrendered, Bear Coat caught up to Lame Deer's village along Little Muddy Creek (near present-day Lame Deer, Montana). Miles and his Bluecoats killed Lame Deer and several followers, destroyed the village, and captured 450 horses.

Sometime during the evening of May 6, Lieutenant John G. Bourke, a member of General Crook's headquarters staff at Camp Robinson, chronicled in his diary the day's momentous events. "This surrender [of Crazy Horse]," he wrote, "terminates the Indian war, so far as Genl. Crook's forces are concerned. If the Government will only keep its promises and treat these red men with justice, we shall have no more Indian wars."

On May 7, the agency issued Crazy Horse's band a small herd of Texas longhorns for butchering. The animals would normally be slaughtered in the corral, but several warriors saw no sport in that, and they asked that some of the steers be let loose to be hunted down on horseback with bows and arrows. Permission was granted, and about twenty animals were released from the corral. The longhorns were somewhat wild, so it only took a few yips from the warriors to get them to break into a run and scatter. The warriors dashed alongside, letting their arrows fly. More than once, an angry longhorn turned on his pursuers, which thrilled the warriors—they yearned for the inherent risks of a buffalo chase. In twenty minutes, however, the killing was over, and several women and boys began the work of skinning and butchering.

Beef for buffalo was just one of many abrupt adjustments for Crazy Horse's band. The same day as the longhorn "hunt," the Lakota women were instructed on how to make a bread of sorts out of their flour rations. Crazy Horse observed these happenings around him with little visible emotion, and he hardly spoke, all of which were aspects of his personality well known to his followers. The white officers and civilians who interacted with Crazy Horse, however, interpreted his strange and quiet ways as being sullen, gloomy, aloof, even defiant. And it seemed to them the only non-Indian Crazy Horse enjoyed seeing was, oddly enough, Frank Grouard.

At first, the Oglala leader probably knew little of Grouard's role in bringing an end to his peoples' days of freedom. The two had once been close, however, and Grouard offered a much-needed window into the white man's world, allowing Crazy Horse to get answers about the workings of the agencies without going to Red Cloud, Spotted Tail, or other leaders whom he considered either rivals or beneath him. Whether or not Grouard was the best person for Crazy Horse to depend upon remained to be seen.

An important status symbol for warriors at the agencies was White Hat's unit of Indian scouts. For Lakota and Cheyenne men, becoming a soldier for an enemy that had killed and maimed your women and children wasn't as incongruous as it sounds. They'd been raised since birth to become warriors; their culture celebrated warrior deeds, which in turn led to prestige and, for those who weren't born into a line of chiefs (Crazy Horse, for example), leadership positions in their tribes. In essence, by becoming scouts for the army, they were perpetuating their roles as warriors. This new warrior identity was made complete by the issuing of weapons: Indian scouts received Sharps carbines and Colt revolvers.

Thus, on May 12, Crazy Horse and fifteen of his headmen held up their right hands and pledged they would "bear true faith and allegiance to the United States of America." Lieutenant Clark promoted Crazy Horse, Red Cloud, and Spotted Tail to the rank of first sergeant. Crazy Horse, looking after his warriors' interests, said he'd like to enlist a hundred of his men.

Clark did his best to befriend the Oglala war chief, but the times he sat in Crazy Horse's lodge partaking of a pot of dog meat were only attempts to "work him," as Clark readily admitted. White Hat was like so many white men who claimed to be a friend of the Indians: they were wonderful friends as long as the Indians did what the white man wanted. Another individual who claimed friendship with Crazy Horse was Camp Robinson's assistant post surgeon, Doctor Valentine T. McGillycuddy. McGillycuddy gave medical care to Crazy Horse's wife, Black Shawl, who suffered from tuberculosis, as well as members of Crazy Horse's band. From this frequent contact, McGillycuddy wrote later, Crazy Horse "became a warm personal friend." McGillycuddy didn't speak Lakota, nor did he have the benefit of knowing Indian sign language like White Hat. That he developed a close friendship with Crazy Horse seems highly doubtful, and whether or not those feelings were mutual is a legitimate question.

A new Indian agent, sixty-year-old James Irwin, doesn't seem to have even tried to be Crazy Horse's friend, let alone understand him. Irwin arrived at the Red Cloud Agency in early July and just four weeks later reported that Crazy Horse wasn't "acting in good faith with the Army. He has all the time been silent, sullen, lordly and dictatorial." Irwin was upset that Crazy Horse and several of his followers either refused or were extremely leery of signing receipts for weekly distributions of rations. It was their old fear of what they might be signing away, of course. The Lakotas had been persuaded far too often to touch the pen, only to be told later that what they thought they were agreeing upon wasn't what the white man's document actually said. Irwin was either oblivious to this sordid history or just unsympathetic. Crazy Horse also refused to receive his band's annuity goods but finally relented after Irwin declared that Crazy Horse's people would receive nothing in the future if the goods weren't accepted.

But it wasn't just Irwin Crazy Horse was having trouble with. The Oglala leader believed he'd been promised his own reservation if he surrendered. Whether or not such an offer was actually conveyed and by whom is unclear, but Crazy Horse was certain of it. When he later met in council with Three Stars, he told the general that on his way to Red Cloud, he'd picked a place for the reservation in the Powder River country. "I put a stake in the ground to mark the spot," he said. "There is plenty of game in that country. All these relatives of mine that are here approve my choice of place, and I would like them all to go back there with me and stay there together."

Yet the weeks passed, and the agent, Three Stars, and other officials did their best to forget Crazy Horse's request. At one point, an angry and frustrated Crazy Horse threatened to take his people north to the place he'd selected. Nothing created a scare for the agent and the military quite like the thought of Crazy Horse's band leaving the agency and heading north, but even this threat failed to get an answer regarding a home for him and his people.

Sometime in July or early August, another dramatic change came for Crazy Horse, this one within his own lodge. An attractive twenty-four-year-old woman named Nellie Larabee approached him as he returned from a meeting with White Hat and stunned the Oglala leader with a marriage proposal. Nellie told Crazy Horse she'd already talked the matter over with his wife, Black Shawl.

Black Shawl, very aware of how her poor health was affecting her ability to properly maintain Crazy Horse's lodge, graciously consented to Nellie joining their union. As the two women seemed to have settled the matter for him, a bemused Crazy Horse told Nellie to fetch her things and put them in his tipi.

Nellie's father was a trader and government interpreter of French descent known as "Long Joe" Larabee; her mother was a Southern Cheyenne. History has not been kind to Nellie, whom the Lakotas called "Brown Eyes." Interpreter William "Billy" Garnett defamed her as a "half-blood woman, not of the best frontier variety" and, apparently not satisfied with that slander, also described her as an "insidious and evil woman." At some point, a rumor emerged of a possible romantic relationship between Nellie and White Hat. The only voice missing from this chorus, though, is Nellie's own. We have nothing from Brown Eyes herself about her life or her time with Crazy Horse, only the recollections of those who knew her.

That Nellie had a profound influence on Crazy Horse is indisputable. Having grown up in a multilingual household, she had the ability to absorb the gossip and news circulating through the camps and the agency—in Lakota, Cheyenne, and English—and relay it to her spouse. Not only was an army officer trying to "work" him, and a new agent striving to bend Crazy Horse to his will, but alliances among his own people were shifting. Crazy Horse could easily identify an enemy on the battlefield, but it was much more difficult to tell who remained a friend and who only professed to be. He'd recently had a falling-out with his old comrade and follower Little Big Man, who came to resent Crazy Horse's authority and was suddenly disposed to working with the white man. And White Hat's spies were always present, one of whom was, unsurprisingly, Frank Grouard. Having the insights of Brown Eyes, then, was a godsend, even if her information wasn't always accurate.

Red Cloud and Spotted Tail, increasingly jealous of Crazy Horse's fame and influence, actively sowed doubt in the minds of the agents and army officers about the war chief's intentions. They warned that a communal buffalo hunt that'd recently been approved by General Crook was a dangerous idea, that Crazy Horse would avail himself of the opportunity to escape with his warriors and join Sitting Bull in Canada. Ammunition and arms issued for the hunt would surely be used to kill whites. They considered Crazy Horse an "unreconstructed Indian." He was "tricky and unfaithful to others, and very selfish as to the personal interests of his own tribe." The buffalo hunt was canceled.

Tricky or not, General Crook was eager to have Crazy Horse as part of a delegation of Lakota leaders he wanted to visit President Rutherford B. Hayes in September. Talked about since the surrender, the Washington trip was something Crazy Horse was initially agreeable to. He quizzed those who'd been east about what such a journey entailed, and he told Billy Garnett that in preparation for the trip, he wanted to learn to eat at a table with a fork. But now Clark stepped up the pressure on Crazy Horse to make a decision, explaining that it was critical the Oglala leader go to Washington to help determine the future of the agency. What White Hat was referring to was the future locations of the Red Cloud and Spotted Tail agencies. Both agencies were in Nebraska and thus outside the Great Sioux Reservation. One suspects, however, that Three Stars was just as interested in parading before the American public the renowned Crazy Horse, the victor over Custer, as his war prize.

Crazy Horse did not like to be pushed, and not only were Clark and Agent Irwin pushing, but Clark enlisted Frank Grouard and several headmen to use any influence they had with the war chief. All this talk of the Washington trip appeared suspicious. Nellie feared the trip was a trap to get Crazy Horse away from his people and that he would never return. Others close to Crazy

Horse agreed, believing the war chief would be imprisoned on some ocean island, if not killed outright. On August 18, then, Crazy Horse told Clark he wouldn't be going to Washington. Instead, he'd selected several of his headmen to go in his place. He'd already said where he wanted *his* agency, he informed Clark, and if the Great Father wanted to know anything more, his headmen would tell him.

Clark, clearly frustrated and annoyed, explained to Crazy Horse that the other chiefs were going and that he, the chief of his Hunkpatila band, was the one who was requested to meet with the president and Three Stars, not his headmen. Crazy Horse curtly replied that he'd said he wasn't going, and when Clark continued to press, the Oglala leader became angry. Crazy Horse told Clark he wasn't hunting for any Great Father. *His* father was with him, and there was no Great Father between Crazy Horse and *Wakan Tanka*.

There were too many tongues. Crazy Horse sought quiet on solitary walks on the prairie, away from his village. On one of these walks, he chanced upon a dead eagle, and it deeply disturbed him. Crazy Horse returned to his lodge and sat in silence for several hours. The war chief was often immersed in his own thoughts, but those close to him sensed something was different. When asked what troubled him, Crazy Horse's answer was startling. He said he'd found his dead body on the prairie.

A short time after this incident, Crazy Horse experienced a terrifying dream. In the dream, he rode a white pony on an elevated plain. On all sides were enemies and even cannons. Crazy Horse said he was killed in this dream, but how he met his fate he didn't know. All he knew was that he didn't die from a bullet. For a man guided by visions and dreams, this powerful nightmare could only be a foreboding.

Close on the heels of these bad omens came another meeting with White Hat at Camp Robinson on the morning of August 31. Present were Crazy Horse's old friend, the Miniconjou leader Touch the Clouds, a Sans Arc named High Bear, and several members of Crazy Horse's band. Serving as interpreter was Frank Grouard, who'd come to be a little afraid of Crazy Horse—it hadn't taken long for Crazy Horse to learn of Grouard's treachery in helping Three Stars hunt down Lakota and Cheyenne villages. White Hat wanted to send some of the Indian scouts north to help the army corral the Nez Perce, who'd refused to move to a new reservation in Idaho and were fighting their way to Montana Territory and their allies the Crows.

The meeting didn't go well. The request to help chase the Nez Perce was confusing. As Crazy Horse's brother-in-law, Red Feather, explained, when the war chief came to the agency, "the soldiers had him promise not to go on the warpath any more. They told him not to fight, and then to fight." Crazy Horse reminded Clark that even though they'd enlisted as Indian scouts, they'd been assured they wouldn't be asked to go to war with another nation. The chief also brought up the canceled buffalo hunt, which remained a major sore point. The lodges of Crazy Horse's people were in poor shape, as was their clothing; they needed a supply of buffalo robes.

Clark insisted it was their duty as scouts to go where they were ordered, to which Crazy Horse responded that he would go, but he would also bring his band so his people could hunt, after which his warriors would help fight the Nez Perce. What Crazy Horse didn't reveal to Clark was that by taking his village along, it would allow the Oglala leader to remove to the place he'd selected for a reservation, on the other side of the Black Hills.

Clark flatly refused this proposition, and the exchange became heated. Grouard, who wasn't the most proficient interpreter, garbled the translations and said Crazy Horse and Touch the Clouds now threatened to take their bands north and go to war against the whites. (Some would later accuse Grouard of purposely mistranslating Crazy Horse's statements to cause the war chief trouble.) Finally, overwhelmed by the flurry of strong language and his nerves in tatters, Grouard bolted from the room. Outside, the interpreter saw Billy Garnett and frantically waved him over. "Billy, go back to Lieut. Clark's office," he said, "it is too hot for me."

"What's the matter?"

"Crazy Horse is up there with his people."

Garnett took over the translating and Clark instructed him to again ask Crazy Horse if he would go out with his men as part of the scout force and fight the Nez Perce.

"No," Crazy Horse said, forcefully. "I told [White Hat] what I wanted to do. We are going to move; we are going out there to hunt." Then, looking at White Hat, he said, "You are too soft; you can't fight."

Garnett translated Crazy Horse's words, including the insult.

"You can't go out there," Clark said. "The trouble is I don't want anybody to go out there. That is the reason I am trying to get the scouts to go out there, to head [the Nez Perce] off from that country."

"If you want to fight Nez Perce, go out and fight them," Crazy Horse snapped, "we don't want to fight; we are going to hunt."

"You cannot go out there, I tell you!"

Crazy Horse turned to Touch the Clouds and his own people in the room, saying, "These people can't fight; what do they want to go out there for? Let's go home; this is enough of this!"

Crazy Horse and all the Lakotas stormed out of the room. Clark, in an equally foul mood, immediately alerted Camp Robinson's commanding officer, Colonel Luther P. Bradley, of the war chief's intent to take his people away. Bradley in turn telegraphed

General Crook, and the news was forwarded as well to Crook's superior in Chicago, General Sheridan. Sheridan ordered Crook to Camp Robinson to take charge and hopefully calm things down with Crazy Horse and his followers. As a precaution, more troops were ordered there as well. In a comment reflecting just how little Sheridan knew about the situation for the Oglala leader, he opined that the trouble had come about because "Crazy Horse has been treated too well."

Three Stars arrived at Camp Robinson on September 2, 1877. He originally planned to send troops to surround and disarm Crazy Horse's village, but the remnants of Lame Deer's band were due to surrender at the agency, and he worried that any violence at Crazy Horse's camp might scare the Miniconjous away. So he proposed a council with Crazy Horse and other leaders for the next day, a Monday. Crazy Horse agreed, and the council was all set to take place at White Clay Creek, about two miles southeast of the agency, where most of the Oglalas were camped. That is, until Three Stars learned Crazy Horse was going to *murder him.*

The shocking details of the plot were brought to Camp Robinson that morning by an Oglala named Woman Dress, a cousin of Red Cloud and a member of his Bad Face band. Woman Dress was also one of White Hat's spies. Woman Dress said Crazy Horse planned to walk up to the general with the apparent friendly intent of shaking hands, but instead of a handshake, the general would receive several deep knife stabs to the heart. While Crazy Horse was busy scalping Three Stars, his followers would kill White Hat and all others in the party.

Woman Dress's incredible tale was an outright lie. Who put him up to the despicable act is unknown to this day, although his connection to Red Cloud shouldn't be overlooked. To Crook and White Hat, Woman Dress's story was actually quite believable. Every Indian-fighting army officer knew about the murder of white peace commissioners during negotiations with Modoc headmen in 1873. One of those slain was a brigadier general. Crook asked if Woman Dress was reliable and truthful, and the interpreter, "Big Bat" Pourier, said he was. That decided it; Crook would not go to the council site. The Oglala leader had instantly gone from a worrying concern to someone absolutely dangerous, a renegade. (General Sherman frequently described both Sitting Bull and Crazy Horse as "outlaws.")

White Hat quickly came up with a new plan. He instructed Billy Garnett to go to the different camps and announce that Three Stars was suddenly called away. After that, Garnett was to secretly approach several known leaders "of the loyal brand" and tell them to come to post headquarters. Within three hours, Three Stars sat in a room with more than a dozen Oglala chiefs and headmen, including Red Cloud, Young They Fear Even His Horses, American Horse, Little Wound, Red Dog, and an old Crazy Horse antagonist, No Water, the man responsible for the scar on Crazy Horse's face. Also present was White Hat and interpreters Billy Garnett, "Big Bat" Pourier, and Frank Grouard.

Three Stars and White Hat got right down to business. They explained how Crazy Horse and his men had plotted to kill the general. All those present acted surprised at this news, but no one disputed it. Three Stars said Crazy Horse must be stopped. Several of his followers were enrolled as Indian scouts, so a good number of arms and ammunition were present among his people. Three Stars asked the gathered chiefs and headmen how they might take care of this threat to the peace. After a short deliberation, the leaders suggested that four of the bravest men be selected from each band. These men would go to Crazy Horse's village that night, quietly surround it, and call out to Crazy Horse to surrender all the carbines and revolvers in the camp, after which they would take Crazy Horse prisoner. If he refused, they would rush the camp and take Crazy Horse and the weapons by force.

The Oglala leaders believed Crazy Horse would likely resist and thus have to be killed. If that was the case, White Hat spoke up, so be it. White Hat then offered $300 and a good sorrel race-horse he owned to the man who killed the famous war chief. Such an offer from Clark basically ensured that Crazy Horse would not live to see the sunrise and is exceedingly strange considering Crook supposedly professed to wanting Crazy Horse as a prisoner. Nevertheless, the general ordered Clark to issue ammunition to the leaders to distribute to their men. The Oglalas were told to return to their villages, keep quiet, and prepare for the night's mission. Satisfied that everything was well in hand, General Crook retired to his quarters.

But everything wasn't well in hand. Late in the day, Crazy Horse's old friend and lieutenant, He Dog, along with Agent Irwin and an agency interpreter, appeared at the quarters of Colonel Bradley. He Dog was troubled by rumors of a planned offensive against Crazy Horse's village and, even more disturbing, a price on Crazy Horse's head. For some reason, Crook and Clark had neglected to inform Bradley of the results of the day's council, so this was all news to the colonel. Bradley sent for Garnett, who confirmed what He Dog had heard, and the colonel didn't like it at all. He said "it was too bad to go after a man of the standing of Crazy Horse in this manner in the nighttime without his knowing anything about it."

Bradley conferred with General Crook and Lieutenant Clark and pointed out that the element of surprise was clearly gone. They would need a much larger force than just the friendly Oglala scouts to successfully contain Crazy Horse's village and disarm his men. He recommended putting off the expedition until the morning and adding a large command from the post. Crook agreed. Now their allies in the camps needed to be alerted to the change in plans. Clark sent a messenger to fetch Garnett. The interpreter found White Hat in his quarters, visibly agitated; his operation had been spoiled. "These Indians can hold nothing," he said in frustration. Clark instructed Garnett to go to the camps right away. "When you go down," he said, "tell those Indians not to disturb Crazy Horse, but tell all to report to Camp Robinson before sunup in the morning."

Nellie Larabee heard the rumors, too. She'd been busy listening at the agency and the fort for the last few days and reporting everything she learned to her husband. Bad voices were telling lies, she said. Soldiers were coming to take him, either that night or in the morning. Red Feather came to Crazy Horse's lodge with the same information. Garnett had tipped him off, Red Feather said, so it must be true. Crazy Horse was stunned. "I came here for peace," he said. "No matter if my own relatives pointed a gun at my head and ordered me to change that word I would not change it." And yet somehow the Long Knives believed he'd done something terribly wrong and were coming for him.

Crazy Horse gave his Sharps carbine and its scabbard to Red Feather and sat down in his lodge to await the soldiers. But Nellie pleaded with Crazy Horse not to let the Bluecoats take him. She reminded her husband of what Crazy Horse himself believed to be true, that if he was ever arrested for any reason, he would probably lose his life, and if not that, most certainly his freedom. Take Black Shawl and go to the Spotted Tail Agency, Nellie urged, and she would come later. Crazy Horse listened to Nellie's words. His father, Worm, lived at Spotted Tail, as did several of Black Shawl's relatives. So, too, Horn Chips. He wouldn't be surrounded by enemies there. And one of Black Shawl's arms had become swollen, causing her considerable pain. It was said a Lakota healer resided at Spotted Tail who could cure such ailments.

For a long time, Crazy Horse was silent, thinking. Was this what *Wakan Tanka* had planned for him? Were the Thunder Beings through protecting him? Would his dead body lie cold and alone on the prairie, like that of the eagle?

The following morning, around 9:30 A.M., a large cloud of dust rose near Crazy Horse's village, about five miles down the White River. Soon, six hundred cavalrymen and four hundred Indian scouts and "friendlies" stormed into view. Led by American Horse, Young They Fear Even His Horses, and He Dog, the agency Indians began to encircle the village. Simultaneously, a line of approximately seventy of Crazy Horse's men, dressed in full war regalia, appeared on a hilltop a few hundred yards away. One of their number, obviously a headman, fearlessly galloped forward on a buckskin pony until abruptly reining up in front of American Horse, who'd quickly retrieved a pipe and was holding it with outstretched arms. American Horse recognized the headman as Black Fox, a cousin of Crazy Horse.

"I have been looking all my life to die," Black Fox shouted. "I see only the clouds and the ground; I am all scarred up."

"Think of the women and children behind you [and] come straight for the pipe," American Horse said. "The pipe is yours."

The two men smoked and talked. The warriors on the hill raced back and forth and made sham charges until Black Fox suddenly called out for them to stop. "All over. Go back," he said. White Hat now learned that Crazy Horse wasn't in the village. Actually, most of the families had scattered and only a few lodges remained. Crazy Horse and Black Shawl were on their way to the Spotted Tail Agency.

Clark immediately ordered a detachment of Indian scouts in

pursuit of the war chief. He also sent couriers racing to the acting agent at Spotted Tail, Jesse M. Lee, a thirty-four-year-old infantry lieutenant. Lee was to arrest Crazy Horse if he appeared there. A short time later, in a sign of how desperately Clark wanted Crazy Horse contained, he ordered another ten men after the fugitive chief, this party led by No Water. If Crazy Horse somehow got away, it would represent an embarrassing failure for Clark and his handling of Crazy Horse's band, not to mention his Indian scouts and his network of spies. Clark once boasted, "Crazy Horse can't make a move without my knowing it, and I can have him whenever I want him." Now the war chief's escape had made a fool of White Hat, who'd not forgotten how Crazy Horse insulted him just days earlier. If White Hat harbored a hatred for the famed chief, as some believed, this turn of events only made it worse.

No Water swore to White Hat he would finish the job he started seven years earlier when Crazy Horse stole his wife, and it was said that No Water rode two horses to death in his attempt to overtake Crazy Horse and Black Shawl. But the couple had too much of a head start. However, the first scout detachment did eventually catch up to the war chief and his wife, close to the Spotted Tail Agency. Crazy Horse did not stop for them but calmly rode ahead with Black Shawl. The scouts came abreast of the pair and told Crazy Horse he must return to Red Cloud with them. The Oglala leader flatly refused. "I am Crazy Horse!" he said. "Don't touch me! I'm not running away!" This completely cowed the Indian scouts—Crazy Horse's many brave deeds and invincibility in battle gave him the aura of something like a supernatural being. They held back and allowed Crazy Horse and Black Shawl to continue unmolested.

The couple arrived at Touch the Clouds's camp, three miles from Camp Sheridan, late that afternoon, and their presence instantly caused tremendous excitement. Numerous warriors in the village had fought under Crazy Horse and won great victories with him. News of the pursuit of the Oglala leader enraged them. They believed he was being persecuted for no good reason. Of course, Crazy Horse knew he couldn't remain at the Spotted Tail Agency without permission, and runners shortly arrived requesting his presence at the Sheridan post. Soon some three hundred armed warriors, dressed in their finest beaded buckskin shirts and many wearing warbonnets, assembled to escort Crazy Horse to the post. They would fend off any of Clark's Indian scouts foolish enough to cause trouble. Touch the Clouds rode beside the chief.

About halfway to Sheridan, a mule-drawn army ambulance rolled up and stopped in front of Crazy Horse and the long line of warriors. Seated inside were Lee, Camp Sheridan's commander, Captain Daniel W. Burke, interpreter Louis Bordeaux, and the post surgeon. After a round of handshakes, the entire cavalcade continued to Sheridan. Just as they entered the post's small parade ground, Spotted Tail and three hundred of his Brulés trotted onto the yard from the opposite end, many brandishing Winchester repeaters. The two groups formed facing the other, a narrow path between them. Crazy Horse dismounted but his warriors remained on their ponies, glaring at the Spotted Tail faction. The tension was nearly unbearable as everyone waited to see what would happen between Crazy Horse and his uncle.

Spotted Tail stepped to within touching distance of Crazy Horse, who remained silent and unflinching. "You have come to this agency, and you have got to listen to me," Spotted Tail said. "I am chief here. We have no trouble here. The Brulés listen to me and we get along good, and any Indian who comes here must listen to me! That's all." These words were followed by shouts of "Hou! Hou!" from Spotted Tail's followers.

Crazy Horse had no respect for his uncle, but the man was an intimidating presence, and Crazy Horse wouldn't be able to transfer his band to this agency without recognizing Spotted Tail's supremacy. It was something he'd simply have to accept. Crazy Horse told Spotted Tail there were "bad winds blowing" at Red Cloud, that there was a feeling against him he didn't understand. He wanted to come to Spotted Tail because it was quiet and there were no ill winds. If Crazy Horse and his band were allowed to transfer to this agency, he promised they would find him and his followers peaceable. Captain Burke and Lee now invited Crazy Horse into Burke's quarters to talk. The excitement largely over, and the late-summer sun sinking in the sky, the warriors gradually dispersed from the parade ground.

Once inside with Crazy Horse, Agent Lee could plainly see the nervous strain of the last several hours on the chief's face. "I want to get away from the trouble at Red Cloud," Crazy Horse explained. "They have misunderstood and misinterpreted me there. . . . They gave me no rest at Red Cloud. I was talked to night and day, and my brain is in a whirl. I want to do what is right."

To Lee, Crazy Horse reminded him of a cornered wild animal, trembling and unpredictable. Even cornered, though, Crazy Horse scared the hell out of almost everyone. A recurring nightmare of whites was that he would indeed break away with his followers and wash the plains with the blood of hundreds of settlers. In fact, when Crazy Horse arrived at Touch the Clouds's village, dozens of women began taking down their lodges, believing Crazy Horse was there to lead them back to a life of following the buffalo.

Lakota leaders like Spotted Tail, Red Cloud, American Horse, and others feared Crazy Horse because he was a threat to their status at the agencies. These chiefs believed they had a good thing going with the white man, and the last thing they wanted was a defiant Crazy Horse shaking up agency politics. Feeding their anxiety was a rumor that said the Great Father intended to make Crazy Horse chief over all the Lakotas.

All this fear put Crazy Horse in extreme danger. Many whites and Lakotas would sleep much more soundly if Crazy Horse no longer lived. When an early report from White Hat's failed attempt to corral Crazy Horse's band claimed the war chief had been killed, one of the officer's wives wrote that it was "considered good news."

Lee and Captain Burke assured Crazy Horse they meant him no harm and that he was safe at the Spotted Tail Agency. Lee was willing to consider a transfer of Crazy Horse's band, but it was something that would have to be worked out with the authorities at the Red Cloud Agency and Camp Robinson. In the meantime, Crazy Horse would be under the protection of his friend Touch the Clouds during the night. Lee instructed Crazy Horse to report at Sheridan the following morning, when Lee would accompany the war chief back to Red Cloud to see what could be arranged. No troops would be part of the escort, Lee promised.


Crazy Horse arrived at the post the next day as requested but informed Agent Lee he'd changed his mind about going to Red Cloud. He said "he feared some trouble would happen." The war chief asked Lee to make the trip without him and settle the matter about the transfer. Lee made it clear, however, that that wouldn't do. The agent stressed to Crazy Horse that no one intended to harm him and that he would have to return peaceably to Red Cloud as planned. But Crazy Horse wanted additional assurances. Accordingly, Lee promised a meeting with the Soldier Chief, Colonel Bradley, in which he would explain everything they'd discussed at Camp Sheridan. Crazy Horse would then have a chance to give his side of the events that led to his flight. If Crazy Horse was truthful, Lee would tell Bradley that he, Captain Burke, and Spotted Tail were agreeable to the transfer of Crazy Horse's band to the Spotted Tail Agency. Lee and Crazy Horse also agreed that both would travel to Red Cloud unarmed.

Now that Crazy Horse was going to make the forty-three-mile journey, he decided he wanted a saddle; he'd ridden bareback from his village to Spotted Tail. Crazy Horse started back to Touch the Clouds's camp to get one. Lee planned to meet him there with the ambulance. Two Sheridan Indian scouts were ordered to follow Crazy Horse to the camp. Even though Lee and Captain Burke told Crazy Horse several times not to worry about being harmed, they weren't about to take a chance of the war chief escaping. If Crazy Horse tried to flee, the scouts were instructed to shoot his mount. If that didn't work, they were to shoot Crazy Horse.

When the mule-drawn ambulance arrived at Touch the Clouds's camp, Crazy Horse seemed in no hurry to leave. Eager to get going, though, was Lee, who sent the interpreter Bordeaux after the chief. But just as the interpreter found Crazy Horse, Touch the Clouds invited the war chief to his lodge for a breakfast of bread, meat, and coffee. The two friends took their time eating, seemingly trying to put off the inevitable as long as possible. Finally, having finished their leisurely meal, Crazy Horse said he was ready to go.

As promised, no troops appeared to escort the party, but a number of warriors and headmen came along, some friends of Crazy Horse whom he requested and others there to make sure the Oglala leader didn't try to get away. Seated in the ambulance with Lee were Bordeaux, Touch the Clouds, and three other chiefs. Crazy Horse, a bright red trade blanket draped around his upper body, rode horseback.

After the procession was about fifteen miles out, it became obvious Crazy Horse wasn't going to get away even if he'd wanted to. Small groups of scouts from Spotted Tail began to come up on their back trail. By the halfway point to Red Cloud, some forty scouts had joined the party. This sudden increase of strength had all been planned. Crazy Horse tested the escort just once by suddenly spurring his pony ahead and galloping over a rise a hundred yards away and out of sight. The scouts gave chase and brought the chief back to the ambulance. Crazy Horse said he'd only gone ahead to find water for his horse. Lee instructed him to ride behind the ambulance for the remainder of the trip. Crazy Horse now grew very serious and uneasy, more uncertain than ever as to what awaited him. This prompted Lee to reassure Crazy Horse and his friends that he would do exactly as promised, and Crazy Horse would be allowed to state his case to the Soldier Chief and request a transfer.

When within fifteen miles of Red Cloud, Lee sent a runner ahead with a message to Lieutenant Clark asking if he should bring Crazy Horse to the agency or to Camp Robinson. Lee also mentioned his promise to Crazy Horse of an audience with Colonel Bradley and asked that this be arranged. After going another eleven miles, a rider delivered Clark's written response: take Crazy Horse directly to the adjutant's office at the post. Clark said not a word about the requested meeting with the colonel, and as the adjutant's office was next to the post guardhouse, Lee figured that was where Crazy Horse was going to end up. Lee still hoped for a brief talk with Bradley, however; he'd given Crazy Horse his word.

The procession passed the Red Cloud Agency at a good clip. Groups of Indians stood silently near their lodges to catch a glimpse of Crazy Horse as he passed. They'd been warned not to approach the party; it could be confused as a rescue attempt. The Indian scouts were already on edge, leery of a possible ambush from Crazy Horse's people. A mile and a half more and the col-

Robinson. The time was approximately 6:00 P.M.;
han an hour, sunset would bring a close to this

...o the war chief's approach, a crowd of several hundred had gathered at the post: Crazy Horse's people, agency Lakotas, Cheyennes, Arapahos, and Bluecoats. Crazy Horse rode in
front of the ambulance as it crossed the parade ground. Among
those waiting to see the war chief was He Dog, who rode up on
the left side of Crazy Horse and shook hands. He Dog leaned
close to his friend. "Look out," he whispered, "watch your step.
You are going into a dangerous place."

The ambulance stopped in front of the adjutant's office, on the
south side of the parade ground. Here several artillery pieces
were arranged in a line, not unlike in Crazy Horse's dream. As
Lee stepped down from the vehicle, the post adjutant met him
and said Crazy Horse was to be turned over to the officer of the
day. This meant the guardhouse for the chief. "No, not yet!" Lee
blurted out. He requested that Crazy Horse be allowed to speak
to Colonel Bradley first. Only the colonel could decide that, the
adjutant replied, so Lee had Crazy Horse dismount and go into
the adjutant's office to wait. Crazy Horse was joined by his friends
Touch the Clouds, High Bear, and other Lakotas who'd made the
journey from Spotted Tail.

Lee rapidly walked the 175 yards across the parade ground to
Bradley's quarters, passing through throngs of Lakotas on horse-
back and on foot, all wondering what was transpiring with Crazy
Horse. But to Lee's utter dismay, Bradley refused to see the chief.
General Crook, who'd departed Robinson the morning previ-
ous, had telegraphed orders to send Crazy Horse under guard to
Omaha. From there, the chief was destined for exile at Fort Mar-

ion, Florida, the War Department's prison of choice for American Indians who dared resist the loss of their lands and freedom.

Lee tried to delicately reason with his superior, explaining that the only way he'd been able to convince the Oglala leader to come was by promising he could have a hearing before the Soldier Chief. But Bradley was unsympathetic and firmly told Lee it was too late for any talk. Orders were orders. Turn Crazy Horse over to the officer of the day, he said, and tell the chief "not a hair of his head should be harmed." Desirous of somehow finding a way to honor his pledge to Crazy Horse, Lieutenant Lee asked the colonel if it would be possible to meet with the chief in the morning. Bradley gave Lee a glance that signaled their talk was over.

This was a disconcerting turn of events for Lee; he'd betrayed Crazy Horse's trust. Nevertheless, a promise to an Indian, one his fellow officers considered a troublemaker and a murderer, definitely wasn't worth risking his career over. Lee walked back to the adjutant's office and told Bordeaux to bring out a few of Crazy Horse's friends. Through the interpreter, Lee told them he'd done all he could for Crazy Horse and that Colonel Bradley would take care of him for the night. Then Lee, who wished to avoid any uncomfortable questions from Crazy Horse, told Bordeaux to go in and tell the Oglala leader that night was coming, and thus it was too late to talk to the Soldier Chief. Instead, he was to go with the officer of the day, Captain James Kennington, who would get him settled and keep him from any harm.

Crazy Horse appeared satisfied with Bordeaux's words and walked out with Kennington, followed by the Lakotas who'd been waiting with him. Suddenly appearing near the door was Little Big Man, who roughly took Crazy Horse by the left arm. "So you are the brave man," he sneered. "Come on you coward." Crazy Horse was both astonished and taken aback. Little Big Man had seized this moment when Crazy Horse was at his most vulnerable to demonstrate how big a friend he was to the white man. Two soldiers of the guard followed close behind the war chief. Several Indian scouts watched with weapons at the ready.

A distance of sixty feet separated the adjutant's office from the guardhouse. Like many structures at the post, both buildings were constructed of pine logs. The guardhouse, one story high, contained two rooms, and from the outside, there was little to suggest its purpose. Its main door opened into the guardroom; to the right was the prison room, and it currently held a number of inmates, the chains of their leg irons clinking and rattling on the wood floor every time the men moved.

Crazy Horse stepped through the door of the guardhouse with Kennington and Little Big Man, followed by a cluster of allies, among whom were Touch the Clouds and Horn Chips, Crazy Horse's friend and holy man. Neither Crazy Horse nor his friends realized what they were walking into until Touch the Clouds heard the sound of the chains and saw the door to the prison room with its barred window. In a startled voice, Touch the Clouds said the place was a jail. Crazy Horse instantly sprang back, careening into bodies of guards and Indians. Even though the war chief had promised Lee he would not come armed, he wore a revolver and a knife beneath his blanket. In a blur of movement, he yanked his knife from its sheath. Seeing a knife on Little Big Man's belt, he seized that, too, and began slashing wildly in all directions while moving toward the outside doorway.

Kennington drew his saber. Little Big Man grabbed one of Crazy Horse's arms. "Let me go! Let me go! Let me go!" the chief shouted. Stunned onlookers in the parade ground saw flashes of polished steel and heard sounds of chaos: shouts, stomping feet, chairs tumbling. Crazy Horse spun around so his back faced the doorway and lunged for the outside, dragging Little Big Man with him. Several Indian scouts raised their revolvers, causing Kennington to yell, "Don't Shoot! Don't Shoot!"

Crazy Horse brought the sharp blade of his knife down on Little Big Man's hand, cutting deeply into his thumb and forefinger. Little Big Man howled in pain and jerked his hand back, blood spurting from the wound. Indian scouts and guards grappled with the chief, who violently pulled in all directions, trying to break free. Kennington hovered near the frenzied mass of bodies looking for an opportunity to deal a blow with his saber, yelling, "Kill the son of a bitch! Kill the son of a bitch!"

A sentry next to the door, intently watching the scuffle, already had his Springfield rifle lowered, an eighteen-inch bayonet blade affixed to the gun's muzzle. He swiftly guided the sharp point of the bayonet between those struggling with the chief and made a sudden jab, pushing the triangular steel blade deep into Crazy Horse's abdomen, just above the hip. Crazy Horse stiffened for an instant and gasped as the sentry withdrew the blade. "Let me go, you've got me hurt now," he cried. The sentry thrust again but missed the squirming chief and struck the doorframe, the rigid bayonet sinking deep into the pine wood. The soldier jerked the Springfield back to make another stab, accidentally slamming the butt of the gun into Horn Chips, dislocating the holy man's shoulder.

Nauseated from pain, Crazy Horse stopped fighting and sank to the ground. An Indian scout grabbed the grip of the war chief's revolver and jerked it out of its scabbard; Crazy Horse had never tried to use it. The scout held the gun triumphantly in the air. As the Indian scouts and guards stepped back from the war chief, Crazy Horse was seen to be writhing on the ground in a fetal position, moaning loudly. Crazy Horse's father, Worm, had watched in horror as his son fought with Little Big Man and the soldiers. He now jumped off his pony and ran toward Captain Kennington, a cocked revolver in one hand and a bow and arrows in the other. The Indian scouts knocked the old man down and disarmed him.

Doctor McGillycuddy also witnessed the melee, and he pushed

his way through to Crazy Horse's side. The war chief was frothing at the mouth, and his pulse in both arms was weak and inter-
mittent. The doctor searched for the wound and found it on Crazy
Horse's right side, where blood trickled from a small puncture
on the upper edge of the war chief's hip. The entry wound didn't
look bad, but the doctor assumed the bayonet's long blade had
traversed the entire width of Crazy Horse's body, slicing through
vital organs and causing internal bleeding. The Oglala leader had
but a short time to live.

Meanwhile, Crazy Horse's friends and followers in the crowd
began shouting angrily and brandishing their weapons. The Indian scouts fled across the parade ground to the front of Colonel
Bradley's quarters. Kennington ordered his guards to take Crazy
Horse back inside the guardhouse, but when they attempted to
pick up the wounded chief, the crowd became more threatening,
chambering rounds and cocking hammers. At this point, the interpreters Bordeaux, Billy Garnett, and Frank Grouard decided to
make themselves scarce. Kennington and McGillycuddy became
increasingly anxious and uncertain as what to do, neither one being able to speak or understand Lakota. All it would take was one
gun going off to commence an all-out firefight.

After several tense moments, a mixed-blood Lakota offered to
translate and informed the crowd that McGillycuddy wanted to
move Crazy Horse inside the guardhouse so he could be treated.
"Don't take him in the guardhouse," someone shouted, "he is a
chief."

"What shall I do with him?" said McGillycuddy.

Several in the crowd motioned to the adjutant's office. "Take
him there," they said.

Crazy Horse was carefully removed to the adjutant's office and
placed on a pallet of blankets on the floor. McGillycuddy made a
more thorough examination of Crazy Horse's wound, confirm-

ing his earlier assessment. The doctor gave the war chief a hypo-dermic injection of morphine to ease his pain and bandaged the swollen puncture on his side. Touch the Clouds and Crazy Horse's father were allowed to stay with the chief. Others in the room included post surgeon Charles E. Munn, Captain Kennington, and officer of the guard Lieutenant Henry R. Lemly. Louis Bordeaux had gotten over his fright and was there for the next few hours as interpreter.

As darkness settled on Camp Robinson, the crowd of Indians gradually melted away. Most didn't know exactly how Crazy Horse had been hurt, whether it was from a knife or a bayonet. And they didn't know the culprit, either. The bayonet thrust had been so quick that very few saw it, and the soldier who skewered the war chief was immediately relieved by a new sentry. Some strongly suspected Little Big Man stabbed Crazy Horse to gain favor with the Long Knives. Another theory was that Crazy Horse stabbed himself. This fantastical theory involved Little Big Man, too, for he claimed afterward that when Crazy Horse cut his hand, the blade glanced off and entered the war chief's body. The Crazy Horse-killed-himself scenario was especially liked by White Hat. He telegraphed General Crook that he was "trying to persuade all [the] Indians" that was indeed what happened.

Under the warm glow of kerosene lamps, Crazy Horse slipped in and out of consciousness. McGillycuddy shot morphine into the war chief's veins as needed. Lucid moments were far apart and brief. During one of these, Crazy Horse told Bordeaux the soldiers shouldn't have stabbed him. "I had no desire to do injury to any of them," he said. "The only man to whom I wished to do harm was Little Big Man, for his insolent treatment of me, but he got away. I don't know why they stabbed me."

Worm sat on the floor next to his son. Crazy Horse looked up at him and said, "Father, it is no use to depend upon me; I am going to die." Worm and Touch the Clouds began to sob uncontrollably.

Late in the evening, about 11:00 P.M., "Big Bat" Pourier relieved Bordeaux as interpreter so Bordeaux could get some rest. Crazy Horse's face had become very pale, and his body was growing cold. The war chief, as if speaking from a dream, began a sort of chant: "Father, I want to see you." He repeated this several times. It was the last that Crazy Horse's voice was heard in this world. He died at approximately 11:40 P.M. Touch the Clouds pulled Crazy Horse's blanket over his face and pointed to his body. "There lies his lodge," he said. The Miniconjou then motioned toward the heavens and said, "The chief has gone above."

Crazy Horse, Tasunke Witko, was with the Thunder Beings.

# The End of Freedom

*I yield by necessity, not by choice. It is vain to resist; but if I had an army, I would forever remain in the field against you.*

SITTING BULL

*Fort Buford, Dakota Territory, July 19, 1881*

Moisture-laden, dark gray clouds hovered over the Missouri River Valley. A cold front had blown through the day before, providing the fort's garrison a little relief from the usual ninety-degree-plus summer temperatures. Bands of rain and gusty winds kept most soldiers indoors. Shortly before noon, however, many fort residents braved the weather to view a long column approaching in the distance across the treeless river bottom. They heard the column long before they could distinguish individuals—it was the obnoxious squeaking coming from the ungreased wheels of more than thirty Red River carts. Six army mule wagons also traveled with the column.

A group of Húnkpapa headmen and warriors rode at the front of the procession. The wagons were crammed with women and children, and the carts carried camp equipage, lodge skins, and personal possessions belonging to this Lakota band of thirty-five families. As the cavalcade marched past the west side of the post, headed for a camping area near the river landing, the soldiers and civilians watching from the buildings couldn't help but be astonished at the appearance of these Indians. What clothing they wore was in tatters, falling off a piece at a time; some of the Húnkpapas were naked. One of the shabbiest-looking of the bunch was actually their chief: Sitting Bull.

Understandably, the whites stationed at Fort Buford weren't familiar with the Lakota virtue of generosity, which resulted in the greatest leaders often being the poorest among their people. But in Sitting Bull's band, everyone was now poor and hungry. It was the reason they were here at this place where Sitting Bull had, years earlier, harassed and taunted the garrison on nearly a daily basis. The supreme chief of the antitreaty bands, the terror of whites across the West, was surrendering to the U.S. government.

The years in Grandmother's Country had not gone well for Sitting Bull and his people. Twelve months after the defeat of Long Hair, some eight hundred lodges of Lakotas were living in Canada. And soon after Crazy Horse's death, most of his followers crossed the holy line to join the Húnkpapa leader. But the Canadian government didn't really want the Lakotas, who competed for game and caused tension with the Blackfeet, Piegans, Crees, and other resident tribes. The government tolerated the Lakotas' presence and allowed them to roam freely as long as they obeyed the laws, but the Lakotas were not Canadian "treaty Indians," so officials refused to feed or clothe them. And this is what eventually settled the matter, for just like elsewhere on the northern plains, the herds of buffalo on the Canadian side of the holy line were declining at a frightening rate.

The largest exodus of Lakotas returning to face surrender occurred in 1880. Black Elk said his people were "tired of being in

Canada." What he meant was that his family was tired of starving in Canada. Many of their horses had died of disease, and nearly all those that survived had been traded for food, leaving Black Elk and his relatives to travel south afoot. In a bitter break with Sitting Bull, Gall deserted the chief in late November and led approximately three hundred followers south and across the holy line to the Missouri River. Bluecoats attacked Gall's band on January 2 and, after a sixty-minute firefight, forced their surrender. Gall and his followers watched as the Bluecoats burned many of their lodges and possessions. Their herd of two hundred ponies was confiscated, as were sixty-nine firearms. Eight Húnkpapas, including at least one woman, were killed in the fight. Such were the consequences of resisting the inevitable.

By the start of 1881, what had once been a population of as many as four thousand Lakotas in Grandmother's Country had dwindled to roughly five hundred destitute people. When Sitting Bull reluctantly concluded he would either have to trust to the benevolence of the U.S. government or see his women and children perish from malnutrition and the elements, his village counted only 187 individuals (44 men and 143 women and children).

Upon arriving at Fort Buford, Sitting Bull was tired and sullen. An officer recalled that the chief "did not appear to be a well man, showing in his face and figure the ravages of worry and hunger he had gone through." And he was in no mood for an official surrender ceremony. Instead, the formal surrender occurred at 11:00 A.M. the following day, July 20, in the quarters of the post's commanding officer, Major David H. Brotherton. Sitting Bull appeared with Crow Foot, his seven-year-old son by Whole Tribe Seeing Her. The chief wore a soiled and heavily worn calico shirt, black leggings, and a ratty blue trade blanket. A calico handkerchief was tied on his head so that it partially covered his eyes, which were swollen and sore. Cradled in his arm was a Model 1866 Winchester carbine, its buttstock decorated with brass tacks.

Before a tightly packed audience of Húnkpapas, army officers, an interpreter, a newspaper correspondent, and other guests, Brotherton briefly outlined what Sitting Bull could expect in the coming days as he and his people were transferred to the Standing Rock Agency at Fort Yates, 280 miles down the Missouri. It was then Sitting Bull's turn to speak, and he motioned to Crow Foot to take the Winchester and present it to Major Brotherton.

"I surrender this rifle to you through my young son, whom I now desire to teach in this manner that he has become a friend of the Americans," Sitting Bull said. "I wish him to learn the habits of the whites and be educated as their sons are educated. I wish it to be remembered that I was the last man of my tribe to surrender my rifle. This boy has given it to you, and he now wants to know how he is going to make a living."

No one in the room seemed to grasp that Sitting Bull didn't actually surrender; Crow Foot had "surrendered" Sitting Bull's Winchester. Even at the complete mercy of his enemy, Sitting Bull resisted. He told Brotherton he wished to roam both sides of the holy line, hunting and trading as he saw fit. With a broad sweep of his hand, Sitting Bull said, "This is my country, and I don't wish to be compelled to give it up." But it didn't matter what the chief wanted. The "Americans" hardly considered Sitting Bull and his followers friends. They were now prisoners of war.

Early in the morning of July 29, 1881, a Friday, Sitting Bull and his band tromped up the gangplank of the stern-wheeler *General Sherman*, which pushed off from the Fort Buford landing at 6:00 A.M. It was the Húnkpapas' first ride on a fireboat. Previously, they'd only taken potshots at the Missouri's smoke-belching steamers. Two days later, the *Sherman* snugged up to the dock at Bismarck, whose citizens stopped just short of giving Sitting Bull the keys to the city. The chief and a small entourage that included his uncle Four Horns were given an informal reception at the spacious Sheridan House, billed as the largest hotel in Dakota Territory. Hundreds came to gawk at the victor over Custer and shake his hand. Later, at another Bismarck hotel, a lavish dinner was served the Húnkpapas. Scores of townspeople pressed their faces against the hotel's wavy glass windows and marveled to see how gracefully the Lakotas dined with knives and forks.

At Fort Buford, Sitting Bull had complained of curious whites visiting his camp wanting a good look at him. Some of the bolder ones even attempted to follow him into his lodge. But here at Bismarck, the first town Sitting Bull had ever set foot in, he patiently accepted his newfound celebrity and discovered a way to profit from it. He'd learned to write his name from a trader in Canada, and the chief now collected two to five dollars for his autograph. (Free to pretty ladies.) He also sold his pipe for $100 and a small pair of green-lensed goggles he wore for five dollars. Both were easily replaced. At the river landing that evening, shortly before the *Sherman* continued its voyage to Fort Yates, a thousand citizens gathered to see the chief. Through an interpreter, Sitting Bull answered several questions from the crowd. But Sitting Bull was also putting on a brave face for the whites and his followers. The next day, after the *Sherman* reached Fort Yates, the Húnkpapa chief was found on the boat crying and wiping away his tears with a silk handkerchief recently gifted him.

Sitting Bull's band settled in at Standing Rock, elated to be reunited with their fellow tribesmen—Standing Rock was home to some three thousand Lakotas who'd formerly been in Canada with Sitting Bull. Sometime after August 3, the chief was persuaded to enter Orlando S. Goff's makeshift Standing Rock studio, where Goff took the first formal portraits of the chief. Photographing Indians was a major business for western photographers, although not all Indians were willing to go before the camera. Crazy Horse supposedly objected to having his image made, and he was asked more than once after his surrender. Doctor Valentine T. McGillycuddy was one of those who asked, and the doctor claimed the war chief responded by saying, "My friend, why should you wish to shorten my life by taking from me my shadow?" Maybe Crazy Horse said this, but if indeed his likeness was never refracted through a camera lens, it was surely due to his modesty and reclusiveness.

Sitting Bull didn't allow Goff to steal his shadow—he sold it to him. For the price of $100, Goff exposed two glass-plate negatives of the chief, seated and holding his pipe. Sitting Bull arrived wearing goggles, replacements for the ones he'd sold to a Bismarck souvenir hunter. The goggles gave the chief a strange, bug-eyed look, but they were practical. They kept the dust out of his sensitive eyes, and their colored lenses were soothing. However, Goff asked Sitting Bull to remove the goggles for his second exposure. In the coming years, Sitting Bull would allow his photograph to be made several times, but none of these images are as natural and timeless as Goff's second portrait, nor do they succeed as well in conveying the chief's dignity.

Sitting Bull had been promised his band would reside near the Standing Rock Agency, which, among other Lakotas, served the rest of the Húnkpapas, including Gall and his followers. But despite that promise, the army wasn't so certain of the wisdom of releasing him to the Indian Bureau just yet. And impertinent statements Sitting Bull gave to the press didn't help. In speaking with one reporter, the chief declared he hadn't surrendered at Fort Buford, and he didn't want a white man over him. Nor did he want an agent. "I never stood in the white man's country," Sitting

Bull informed the reporter. "I never committed any depredations in the white man's country. . . . The white man came on to my land and followed me. The white men made me fight for my hunting grounds. The white man made me kill him or he would kill my friends, my women, and my children."

When asked about a Húnkpapa chief named Running Antelope, long friendly to the whites, Sitting Bull called him a fool. Running Antelope had signed treaties that allowed the white man to occupy Lakota lands, primarily the 1868 Fort Laramie Treaty and the 1877 treaty stealing the Black Hills. "Ever since that time," Sitting Bull said, "there has been trouble." Sitting Bull viewed Crazy Horse's uncle, Spotted Tail, with equal contempt. On August 6, news arrived at Fort Yates that Spotted Tail had been shot and killed near the Rosebud Agency. The killing was supposedly the climax to a personal feud, but some Lakotas thought the motive was revenge for Crazy Horse's death. The Oglala war chief's relatives accused the army of paying Spotted Tail to bring Crazy Horse in so he could be murdered. No evidence exists for such a scenario, but Spotted Tail's killer, a Brulé named Crow Dog, was a relative of Crazy Horse.

Sitting Bull bluntly said Spotted Tail's death was "a fit ending for a fool." Spotted Tail surrendered when he "should have kept the warpath." It was plain to Sitting Bull, as it had been to his dead friend Crazy Horse, that had all the Lakotas united, they could have held off the white man. But Red Cloud and Spotted Tail had refused to recognize Sitting Bull as the supreme chief. They and other "tame Indians" touched the pen. By siding with the white man and against their fellow Lakotas, these chiefs had doomed the antitreaty bands.

Of course, it was one thing for Sitting Bull to *think* Spotted Tail was a fool for not going to war, but his words were published in newspapers across the country, including the *New York Times*.

Another news story out of Fort Yates quoted a "prominent official" who speculated that Sitting Bull had secreted a cache of firearms in the mountains, which was guarded by the chief's best warriors. Upon the heels of this story came a dispatch reporting that two Húnkpapa women were caught carrying guns and ammunition into Sitting Bull's camp. He "undoubtedly means mischief," the dispatch read. Consequently, the army decided that Sitting Bull and his band would remain prisoners of war and be transported 350 miles downstream to Fort Randall, where it would be impossible for the chief and holy man to assert any influence over the Standing Rock Lakotas.

The army's decision, opined an eastern newspaper, was "the same old story of contracts violated and pledges broken like glass." When Sitting Bull learned of the impending move, he was furious. He vowed his people wouldn't go. The chief said he preferred to die resisting, like Crazy Horse. Hearing this, the Fort Yates commanding officer not only mobilized his infantry and cavalry units, but he armed the musicians of the marching band and the fort's civilian employees. He also ordered the fort's artillery trained on the Húnkpapa camp, which had been moved to the riverbank to better guard.

At 11:00 A.M. on September 10, two companies of infantry with long bayonets affixed to their rifles pushed and prodded Sitting Bull's band toward the *General Sherman*'s gangplank. The Lakotas were very agitated because of a rumor that they were being sent away to be executed. Another rumor had it that their destination was far to the south in Indian Territory. One Húnkpapa woman became so distraught that she drew a knife from her belt and killed her small child and then attempted to commit suicide. Sitting Bull's nephew, One Bull, refused to move, causing an angry infantryman to slam the butt of his Springfield into One Bull's back, between the shoulder blades. Sitting Bull balked upon reaching the gangplank, and several soldiers instantly grabbed the chief and carried him aboard and into the boat's cabin. He would not die like Crazy Horse this day.

For a week, the *Sherman*'s big paddles churned through the Missouri's muddy, eddying waters, its banks lined with an endless grove of cottonwood trees. Fort Randall came into view late on September 17, its numerous buildings clustered on a broad plateau on the west side of the Missouri. For the next nineteen months, the thirty-two lodges of Sitting Bull's band would camp within sight of the post. Officers took a head count of the prisoners each morning, but that was the only time all the Húnkpapas were required to be present in the village. Men, women, and children were free to come and go, although there was little to see or do outside the normal village routine other than collect their food rations and visit the post trader's store.

Boredom wasn't as much of a concern for Sitting Bull as it was his followers. The chief frequently entertained visitors: newspaper correspondents, army officers, photographers, tourists, and Lakota leaders from different agencies who came to Sitting Bull for advice, as well as to reminisce. These visits of headmen, who usually came in groups of five or six, were arranged in advance, and the men carried passes signed by their agents. Second Lieutenant George P. Ahern, who gained Sitting Bull's friendship at Fort Randall, attended several of these gatherings in Sitting Bull's lodge and found them fascinating. The headmen related such pressing issues as their dealings with agency officials, the challenges in farming in poor soil, and troubles raising livestock. The conferences, Ahern recalled, showed "the deep respect in which Sitting Bull was held by his people."

Ahern, twenty-two years old and fresh out of West Point, was detailed to translate the many French and German letters received by Sitting Bull. The chief's fame had spread overseas with the spectacular defeat of Custer at the Little Big Horn, and the surrender of Sitting Bull's band was big international news as well. He even received a sympathetic French biography in 1879: *Sitting Bull, The Hero of the Desert: Scenes from the Indian War in the United States.* The French and German letters were usually requests for his autograph, but some letter writers sought a pipe, tomahawk, or other artifact. Sitting Bull seldom instructed Ahern to pen a reply—unless the requests came with cash.

"Sitting Bull was a very remarkable man," remembered Ahern, "such a vivid personality. He stood before you square-shouldered, deep chested, fine head, and [in] the manner of a man who knew his ground. He looked squarely into your eyes, and spoke deliberately and forcefully."

Another friendship Sitting Bull formed at Fort Randall was with a German correspondent and artist, Rudolf Cronau. Cronau visited Standing Rock and Fort Randall to sketch Indian portraits and scenes of traditional Lakota life. Fortunately for the young artist, the Lakotas took a liking to him and his work. Because he wore wire-framed spectacles, they gave him the name "Iron Eyes." Over several weeks, Cronau produced drawings of such prominent leaders as Rain in the Face, Red Thunder, Crow King, and Sitting Bull's uncle Four Horns. One of the first portraits he made at Fort Randall was of Sitting Bull. However, being cognizant of his European audience, Cronau added a large eagle-feather warbonnet and a bone breastplate to the famous Húnkpapa so he would better fit the popular stereotype of an Indian chief.

While at Fort Randall, Cronau was often in Sitting Bull's company. His artistic renderings seem to have influenced Sitting Bull's own efforts at drawing, and Cronau very likely gave his friend a supply of pencils, colored crayons, and paints before returning east. Art was one way for a prisoner of war to kill time, and Sitting Bull soon immersed himself in creating vivid, color images on paper.

Sitting Bull produced three sets of pictographs while at Fort Randall that we know of, all at the request of whites living at the fort. One set was made for the post trader, possibly in exchange for store credit; another was created for a lieutenant, who obtained them for his former commander during the Civil War; and the third was a gift to a captain's wife, with whose family Sitting Bull had become close. All the drawings Sitting Bull made at Fort Randall depict his personal war deeds, his coups—absent, of course, any heroics that involved attacks on whites.

The Húnkpapa chief, eager to return to Standing Rock and have a place set aside for his band, frequently told his white captors what he thought they wanted to hear. He said he was done with war and "wished to settle down to civilized ways," that he wanted his men to make their living through farming and his children taught in schools the same as whites. "I want my people to dress up like white people and live like they do," he said. Perhaps Sitting Bull was indeed sincere about some of these things—he did want his people taught to read "in our language." But his many drawings from Fort Randall reveal what most often occupied his thoughts: the glory days of the past, of freedom, and of victory over enemies.

In December 1882, Secretary of War Robert Todd Lincoln received an unusual letter regarding Sitting Bull. It came from a Yankton chief named Strike the Ree. The Yankton Agency was across the Missouri from Fort Randall. Strike the Ree wanted to know "what has Sitting Bull been convicted of doing that you hold him prisoner for so many long moons. . . . I speak for him because he is kept in prison just across the river from me, and his moaning cry comes to my ear. There is no one else to speak for him so I plead his case."

Actually, a number of people had been pushing the army to act on Sitting Bull's case, including Fort Randall's commanding officer and the Indian agent at Standing Rock. The wait continued a few more weeks, but by mid-March 1883, the army and the Indian Bureau agreed to sending Sitting Bull and his people to Standing Rock. On the afternoon of April 28, the former prisoners boarded the stern-wheeler *W. J. Behan* and began a twelve-day journey upriver. Five of their number died before reaching Standing Rock, three of them children. No one bothered to record the children's names, but the parents of one child, a boy, lovingly placed his body high in the branches of a tree on an island in the Missouri, where his spirit could watch the fireboats going up and down the river.

News that Sitting Bull was traveling upstream on the *Behan* preceded the steamboat, and at the different river landings, large crowds gathered to see the chief. Sitting Bull again did a booming business in autographs. And he was willing to spend some of his sudden wealth on a beautifully carved wooden pipestem belonging to the boat's captain, Grant Marsh. But as the pipestem had been a gift, Marsh wasn't interested in selling. Sitting Bull kept pressing for a price, however, until Marsh jokingly said $50. When the interpreter translated Marsh's price, Sitting Bull reacted with a look of indignation. That amounted to a lot of autographs and was far too much for the pipestem.

"Well," Marsh said to the interpreter, "tell him he has kept me scared for twenty years along the river and he ought to give me something for that."

"I did not come on your land to scare you," Sitting Bull quickly retorted. "If you had not come on my land, you would not have been scared, either."

Marsh recognized he'd been bested by the chief, but he still wasn't selling the pipestem.

The *Behan* tied up at Fort Yates on the afternoon of May 10. Shortly after Sitting Bull and his followers debarked, the chief requested a meeting with James McLaughlin, Standing Rock's Indian agent. McLaughlin, in his first not-so-subtle show of authority, sent a message to Sitting Bull the following morning that they could meet sometime that afternoon, when he wasn't "too busy."

Born in Canada to an Irish father and a Scottish mother, the forty-one-year-old McLaughlin was a blacksmith by trade. His work for the Indian Bureau began in 1871, when he was employed as a blacksmith at the Devil's Lake Agency, which served the Eastern Sioux in the vicinity of Fort Totten (present-day North Dakota). Five years later, he received the appointment of Indian agent at Devil's Lake. McLaughlin's wife, Marie Louise, was one-quarter Santee and spoke the Sioux language fluently; she served as agency interpreter.

In September 1881, McLaughlin took over duties as Indian agent at the larger Standing Rock Agency, having stepped off the *General Sherman* moments before Sitting Bull and his band were forced up its gangplank for their journey to Fort Randall. If Sitting Bull glimpsed Standing Rock's new agent that day, he would have seen a short man, five feet, six and a half inches tall, with graying hair and dark eyes. On his upper lip McLaughlin sported a bushy mustache, and on his lower, a scraggly imperial beard. An imposing figure he was not, but an imposing will he had in spades.

A devout Catholic, McLaughlin was a fierce proponent of acculturation as the only future for the American Indian. When he first sought to be an Indian agent, he couldn't have been any clearer about his plans for his wards, or his belief in the superiority of his own religion: "I will do my best to abolish polygamy & eradicate from my agency all kinds of Superstitions there existing, viz., *medicine dances or feasts, Sundances, &c.*, for I know that polygamy & Superstitious practices are not only adverse to political but also to Christian civilization, this last being the only true, real & efficacious civilization." It was an opinion shared by the vast majority of whites, and for the U.S. government, it was policy. The Indian Bureau banned the Sun Dance and other "pagan practices" in 1882.

At his first meeting with Sitting Bull, McLaughlin seems to have enjoyed putting the Húnkpapa chief in his place. The rules of the agency would be strictly enforced, he said. Sitting Bull would get no special treatment, no recognition as a chief over other chiefs. He and his people were to begin their lives as farmers the next morning, he informed Sitting Bull, when they would plant twelve acres. And that they did, with Sitting Bull working a hoe in the fresh-plowed ground along with the rest.

But McLaughlin wasn't impressed with Sitting Bull from the start, and within three months' time, he'd formed a low opinion of the chief. In his annual report, written on August 15, the agent described Sitting Bull as a man of "very mediocre ability, rather dull, and much inferior of Gall and others of his lieutenants in intelligence." Of course, McLaughlin's praise for the intelligence of Gall, Crow King, and others had more than a little to do with the fact that those individuals willingly cooperated with the agent and pushed their followers to accept his policies. But this was just the beginning of McLaughlin's harangue. "I cannot understand how [Sitting Bull] held such sway over or controlled men so eminently his superiors in every respect," he continued, "unless it was by his sheer obstinacy and stubborn tenacity. He is pompous, vain, and boastful, and considers himself a very important personage."

McLaughlin, according to One Bull, refused to consider Sitting Bull anything more than a common man. Yet Sitting Bull was anything but. No matter how much McLaughlin didn't want to admit it, Sitting Bull *was* an important personage, one of the greatest leaders the Lakotas had ever known. Always, even as a prisoner of war, he strove to conduct himself as a chief and to look out for his people. And while McLaughlin did his best to quash Sitting Bull's influence at Standing Rock, with some success, outside the reservation was a different story. Sitting Bull remained the most famous living Lakota, "the warrior chief who planned the massacre of the brave and gallant Custer and his Spartan band," and the defiant Indian leader who'd thwarted the U.S. Army for years.

It wasn't hard for anyone to see that money could be made off Sitting Bull's fame—few celebrities in the 1880s could command two dollars for an autograph. In 1882, the scout and performer William F. "Buffalo Bill" Cody proposed to add Sitting Bull and his nephew One Bull to his troupe, called the Buffalo Bill Combination (he hadn't yet formed his iconic Wild West exhibition). Cody's planned route for the troupe would take them to Milwaukee, Chicago, St. Louis, Louisville, Cincinnati, Nashville, and the East Coast. The scout was reported to have letters of support from President Chester A. Arthur and General Sheridan, but, for reasons unknown, Cody's proposition fell through and Sitting Bull remained at Fort Randall.

Once Sitting Bull arrived at Standing Rock, McLaughlin received several inquiries about exhibiting the chief. A St. Paul businessman proposed sending around the country what amounted to a Sitting Bull village, with thirty or so men and women, tipis, and ponies. The Iowa State Fair also believed Sitting Bull would make a fine attraction. Nearly all these proposals McLaughlin peremptorily rejected. On September 5, 1883, however, Sitting Bull participated in the laying of the cornerstone of the Dakota territorial capitol, sixty-seven miles away in Bismarck. Among the several distinguished guests who spoke that day were Governor Nehemiah Ordway, Secretary of the Interior Henry Teller, former president Ulysses S. Grant, and Sitting Bull, who said he was glad to meet the governor and his friends and that the Great Spirit had inspired him to shake their hands. Sitting Bull didn't need any inspiration to sell his autograph, and there was no lack of buyers.

In March 1884, McLaughlin took Sitting Bull and One Bull with him on a business trip to St. Paul. McLaughlin explained to his superior in Washington that by exposing Sitting Bull to the wonders of the white man's world, it would "add very considerably to the object of civilization now engaged in" at Standing Rock. But McLaughlin seems to have been guided by his own interests as well, for there were perks and recognition that came with being the famed chief's custodian. The Northern Pacific Railroad supplied passes over its line; the party would stay in one of the city's top hotels; McLaughlin's oldest son, Harry, would come along as a paid interpreter; the agent would meet the same prominent officials and businessmen who wanted to meet the chief; and wherever Sitting Bull and One Bull were wined and dined, well, the McLaughlins would be wined and dined, too.

The Minnesota visit wasn't intended as an exhibition, but no one bothered to tell that to the people of St. Paul. Newspaper telegrams announced the coming of Sitting Bull, and thousands flocked to the Merchant's Hotel during his weeklong stay, hoping to see him. The local press covered his every move, giving him as much attention as it would a visit by the president or a member of royalty. The *St. Paul Daily Globe* called him "the great lion of the hour." The Húnkpapa chief was given tours of the city's public schools, churches, its fire department, post office, banks, and several businesses and factories. He also sat for a series of fourteen portraits in a local photography studio.

In the offices of the *Pioneer Press,* Sitting Bull and One Bull experienced their first telephone conversation, though rather one-sided. While the chief remained in one room, One Bull was taken into another office about a hundred feet distant, the two rooms being connected by a telephone line. Sitting Bull, who was usually rather stoic, was visibly startled when he heard his nephew's voice through the phone, but then his face broke into a grin. "*Wakan,*" he said. The telephone was a mysterious, magical thing.

Sitting Bull's and his nephew's evenings were taken up with a St. Patrick's Day concert and related festivities at Armory Hall, a musical comedy at the Grand Opera House, and a vaudeville show at the Olympic Theater. Among the latter's several acts were the Wertz Brothers, acrobats, and a husband-and-wife team of trick shot artists who went by the name Butler & Oakley. This was Frank Butler and a twenty-three-year-old Annie Oakley. Sitting Bull was very impressed with young Oakley and clapped enthusiastically at the petite woman's feats of marksmanship, which included shooting the ends off cigarettes pursed between Butler's lips.

The next day, Sitting Bull sent a carriage to bring the "little sharpshooter" and Butler to the Merchant's Hotel, where he "adopted" Annie as his daughter and presented her with several gifts, among which was "the original pair of moccasins he wore in the Custer fight." Annie apparently didn't question how Sitting Bull managed to have an eight-year-old pair of moccasins, especially after his village was destroyed by Bluecoats in December 1876. It was too good a story, which she repeated often.

The well-heeled and influential proprietor of the Merchant's Hotel, Alvaren Allen, witnessed the throngs that crowded his establishment to see the chief and came to the same conclusion as several other money-grubbers before him: Sitting Bull was a walking gold mine. Allen began using his political connections to obtain permission from the secretary of the interior to send Sitting Bull on a multicity tour. Working hand in hand with Allen to bring about the tour was a man who'd told a St. Paul reporter he didn't want Sitting Bull lionized, that he didn't want the chief to "become impressed with the idea that he was a great man." The individual who spoke those words was none other than Agent McLaughlin, who'd oddly had a change of heart about displaying the chief, undoubtedly after Allen offered certain incentives.

Over most of the summer, McLaughlin pressured Sitting Bull to agree to the tour. In a letter to Allen, the agent complained that Sitting Bull "is such an ignorant and vain man that his ideas are very crude and he talks of 'millions' as you or I would talk of 'hundreds' and he says that he is worth untold fortunes and that he will not go without taking some more of his people."

While McLaughlin worked on Sitting Bull, he blocked other suitors. Father Joseph A. Stephan, McLaughlin's predecessor as agent at Standing Rock, wished to take Sitting Bull on tour that year. Now the director of the Bureau of Catholic Indian Missions in Washington, Stephan presumably hoped to use Sitting Bull to raise money for Catholic education efforts on the reservations.

Also trying to get Sitting Bull was Buffalo Bill Cody, this time as part of his Wild West exhibition. But McLaughlin wasn't going to allow either one to interfere with his arrangement with Allen. In what amounted to a bald-faced lie, McLaughlin wrote Cody that he simply couldn't disrupt the "late hostiles" when they were just settling in to their new lives as farmers. Cody must have gotten quite the shock when he saw the newspaper notices for the Sitting Bull Combination, which began a two-month tour in September.

The Combination consisted of Sitting Bull and his wife, Whole Tribe Seeing Her; Spotted Horn Bull and his wife, Pretty White Buffalo Woman; Gray Eagle (Sitting Bull's brother-in-law); Long Dog; Flying By; Crow Eagle; and the six-foot-tall "Princess" Winona Red Spear, "a beautiful Indian girl of sixteen years, with coal black hair, snow-white teeth, and a ravishing smile." The princess wore a buckskin dress covered with beadwork and a white plume in her hair. Three paid interpreters accompanied Sitting Bull's party and, not surprisingly, two of them were McLaughlin's wife and son, who received an expense-free trip on top of their salaries. If this was the only pecuniary incentive Allen offered Agent McLaughlin, it was significant.

Billing itself as a performance of Indian songs, war dances, and speeches, the show featured a stage decorated as a traditional camp, complete with buffalo robes and a faux tipi covered with white canvas. Sitting Bull's party occupied a line of chairs in front. The presentation began with a lecture by T. M. Newson, a St. Paul newspaperman and author, who justified Sitting Bull's role in the hero Custer's death by explaining to the audience that the Lakotas were only defending themselves. Newson also talked at length about the problems of the reservation system, that the way whites treated the Indian was "a blanked outrage." Among the many wrongs Newson recited, interestingly enough, was corrupt Indian agents.

Dances and songs followed Newson's introduction, and the entire program concluded with a "feeling speech" from Sitting Bull, who told the audiences his people were through roaming and wanted to be self-sufficient, and for that they needed more teachers. The government, Sitting Bull complained, "does nothing but feed us." The chief was exaggerating somewhat the situation at Standing Rock, which operated agricultural and industrial boarding schools for the children and supplied agricultural equipment and employed white farmers as instructors (albeit certainly not enough instructors for such a large reservation). Some at Standing Rock definitely took to farming better than others, though, with Agent McLaughlin blaming the lack of progress with the "late hostiles" on "Sitting Bull's retarding influence."

The Sitting Bull Combination garnered generally positive reviews, although some in the press were appalled that audiences showered applause on a man they viewed as nothing more than a red-handed murderer. In its notice of the show, Philadelphia's *The Times* thought the chief "ought to have been hanged long ago." But others who came to the performances were like-minded with the California poet Joaquin Miller, who caught the Combination in New York. Following Newson's introduction, Miller spoke out from the audience: "There is usually a damn sight of nonsense about this Indian question," he said, "but you talk good sense—go on, I'm with you."

The grandiose plan of the Combination's investors was to send Sitting Bull's party to the major eastern cities and then to Europe, the tour lasting perhaps two years. But the show came to an abrupt end after appearances in just New York, Philadelphia, and Brooklyn. It seems that Father Stephan, miffed about being cut out of the exhibition business, complained to the secretary of the interior, who subsequently ordered the Lakotas back to Standing Rock.

A stated goal of the show's promoters was to use the profits for houses and tools for Sitting Bull's people, but how much money the Combination made, if any, depended on whom one asked. Allen's son, Ehle, the show's treasurer, told a reporter they cleared $12,000, while the show's assistant manager said the concern made no money at all. T. M. Newson bragged that he'd lectured to more than eighty thousand people in New York and ten thousand each in Philadelphia and Brooklyn. If Newson's figures aren't grossly inflated, the show couldn't have helped but make a profit. And yet, no new houses sprang up on the reservation.

Buffalo Bill Cody remained obsessed with thoughts of the profits Sitting Bull would bring to his Wild West, and the crowds the chief drew on his short tour, especially in New York, only made Cody want him that much more. "If we can manage to get him," he'd written a friend, "our everlasting fortune is made." In the spring of 1885, again armed with letters of support from prominent individuals such as General Sherman and Brevet Major General Eugene A. Carr, he applied for permission to tour Sitting Bull. Cody's timing was excellent, for there was a new administration in the nation's capital and, consequently, a new secretary of the interior. This time Cody succeeded, but a final challenge awaited: Sitting Bull himself.

Cody dispatched his show manager, John M. Burke, to Standing Rock to negotiate with the chief. According to Burke, it took four weeks of "pleading, coaxing, and bartering" to reach an agreement. But there really wasn't much bartering to speak of, for the shrewd Sitting Bull saw how eager, even desperate, Burke was to sign him. The chief simply held out for all his demands. Top among those was a visit with the new Great Father, Grover Cleveland. Sitting Bull also required he be accompanied by several Húnkpapas of his choosing. And he retained the right to sell his photographs and autographs. As for the important matter of remuneration, Sitting Bull would receive $50 per week and an initial bonus of $125.

Sitting Bull scrawled his name on the two-page contract on June 6, and six days later, in front of a packed grandstand at Buffalo, New York, he shook hands with the tall, long-haired Cody for the first time. Sitting Bull's role for the duration of the tour was, as on this day, to be seen. Dressed in a leather shirt and leggings heavily decorated with blue-and-white beadwork, and wearing an iconic eagle-feather bonnet, he rode in a carriage in the opening processional parade and then took a seat with his retinue on the judges' stand for the remainder of the show. Neither Sitting Bull, nor those with him, would be called upon to participate in Cody's thrilling reenactments of Indian attacks on the Deadwood stage and a settler's cabin—no one wanted to see Sitting Bull "killing" any more white people.

On June 23, the chief got to meet the Great Father. First, though, Sitting Bull, Cody, and fifteen other Lakotas visited the State, War, and Navy Building, where they met one of their former antagonists, General Phil Sheridan, after which they were escorted to the State Department library and shown the original Declaration of Independence. It's not known what Sitting Bull was told about the extraordinary freedom document, but if its preamble was interpreted for him correctly, one can't help but wonder if he might have asked why its "truths" didn't apply to his people as well.

Sitting Bull's party went next to the White House to see President Cleveland. This was the moment the chief had been eagerly awaiting. He told a reporter he had "nothing but justice to ask" of the Great Father. In Sioux country, the white man wanted everything, even the sky, Sitting Bull said, but all he wanted for his people was a section of broad prairie where his village would be safe and the white man wouldn't bother them, where he could "die in peace, and let his people bury him undisturbed." Sitting Bull was stunned and upset, however, when, after a short round of handshakes with the portly, forty-eight-year-old Cleveland, his party was ushered away. The chief had traveled eighteen hundred miles to *speak* to the Great Father, but the Great Father apparently had no ears to listen.

The interpreter attempted to placate the chief by explaining that the president was very busy and that hundreds of men came to Washington to see him and often stayed for months without getting an audience, to which Sitting Bull snapped back, "White man one great damned fool!"

Sitting Bull remained with the Wild West through its final engagement of the season at St. Louis in early October and arrived back at Standing Rock on the seventeenth. Buffalo Bill and his partners did indeed make a fortune that year, although no amount of money with Cody was "everlasting." In just one Saturday afternoon in Philadelphia, the show admitted 46,582 people, with the receipts totaling more than $24,000. Cody was so pleased with Sitting Bull that, as a parting gift, he presented the chief with a large white horse (sixteen hands high), said to be "the finest riding pony in the show." It'd been purchased in New Orleans the previous winter from "a distinguished French family." Lakotas savvied horseflesh better than most, and the animal could not have been a more fitting and impressive gift.

Money didn't last long with Sitting Bull, either, but it wasn't a matter of extravagances. It was a matter of generosity. One oft-told story from his time with the Wild West involved the chief's encounter with an old woman begging on the street. Sitting Bull had just sold three autographs for a dollar each, and he promptly dropped all three silver dollars into the woman's hand. He commented to his interpreter that it was a shame that white people let their poor beg—he didn't let his Húnkpapas beg. At Standing Rock, Sitting Bull's Wild West earnings paid for feasts for his followers and other Lakotas. In three weeks' time, he went through all his money. McLaughlin, in addition to considering this a great waste, believed the feasts were all about Sitting Bull trying to impress upon the Indians his importance. But Sitting Bull was sharing his great fortune and feeding his people, as was expected of a chief.

On November 2, 1885, James McLaughlin penned his monthly report to the commissioner of Indian affairs, most of which was devoted to how much of a problem Sitting Bull had been since his return two weeks earlier. The chief, he wrote, "is so inflated with the public attention he received that it is next to impossible to do anything with him." According to McLaughlin, Sitting Bull spewed all kinds of nonsense among the Indians at Standing Rock: the Great Father had made him the head of the Sioux nation, he was now above Agent McLaughlin, and the traditional Lakota religious practices that'd been banned, such as the Sun Dance, must be revived. However, McLaughlin assured the commissioner that 95 percent of those living on the reservation had no respect for Sitting Bull, "knowing him to be the most non-progressive, arrogant, vain, and untruthful Indian living."

And yet, in the very same report, McLaughlin contradicted himself regarding Sitting Bull's influence, writing that the chief was "pernicious and very dangerous to his people." Sitting Bull's "haughty manner, and disobedience, if persisted or to go longer unpunished may have a tendency to contaminate and demoralize others." McLaughlin warned the commissioner that upon Sitting Bull's next "offence," he would throw the chief in the Fort Yates guardhouse.

All this is McLaughlin's side of the story. We have nothing from Sitting Bull that might serve as an answer to the agent's damning charges. What's quite obvious, though, is the hostility McLaughlin held for the chief. And the agent didn't think much of his 225 followers, either, whom he described as "of the most worthless and non-progressive elements."

McLaughlin got over his initial impulse to lock Sitting Bull up, but for the next few years, the relationship between the two was rocky. Sitting Bull, intent on preserving what he could of his people's culture and what remained of Lakota lands, was generally wary of most things the agent advocated. "Sitting Bull was a thinker and didn't take anything up until he thought it was good," said Robert Higheagle, a Húnkpapa tribal historian and interpreter. "He was for the Indians and was for protecting their rights. . . . He was never known to betray his tribe."

Sitting Bull did want to see his people educated, but he apparently assumed the curriculum of the white man's schools would include learning to read and write in Lakota. He assumed wrong. The missionary and government schools on the reservation were prohibited by the Indian Bureau from teaching students to read and write in their native language, what the bureau referred to as "their barbarous dialects." Agent McLaughlin wholeheartedly supported this policy. The use of the Lakota language in reservation schools, he wrote, served only to "encourage Indians to adhere to their time-honored customs and inherent superstitions, which the government has in every way sought to overcome."

The schools were part and parcel, then, of the government's efforts to erase Lakota culture, to "civilize" the Indians, which no one had to tell Sitting Bull. In 1884, while touring with his Combination, Sitting Bull and Whole Tribe Seeing Her visited the Lincoln Institute, an Indian boarding school in Philadelphia. They saw Indian boys with their black hair cropped short and clothed in tight suits or uniforms. The Indian girls wore long dresses with checked calico aprons. One of the female students, a young girl named Iron Owl, was a niece of Whole Tribe Seeing Her. Nine months after the visit of her relatives, Iron Owl was trotted out before a reporter for Philadelphia's *The Times* as an example of the school's handiwork. "I don't no more like a blanket," she said, referring to the universal garment of the Plains Indians. "It is bad dress. . . . When I go back to my people, I say to all: Indian way not good. Live like white people."

For a time, at least, Sitting Bull kept his children out of the day school on the reservation, and he encouraged his followers to do the same, which naturally irritated McLaughlin. Thus, Sitting Bull made it easy for the agent to deny a request from John M. Burke asking that the chief rejoin Cody's Wild West for the 1886 season. McLaughlin explained to Burke that he didn't "think it advisable for [Sitting] Bull to travel again, as he is such a consummate liar and too vain and obstinate to be benefitted by what he sees."

There would be no more touring for Sitting Bull, although, amazingly enough, McLaughlin did include the chief in a delegation of fourteen leaders from Standing Rock that traveled to Washington in October 1888. The Standing Rock contingent joined forty-three chiefs from the other five Sioux agencies to discuss the government's desire to break up the Great Sioux Reservation into much smaller reserves. Nearly half of the existing reservation, some nine million acres, would be opened to settlers—lands westerners had had their eyes on for some time.

In addition to a good deal of speechmaking, the Sioux leaders visited the usual tourist attractions, shook hands with President Cleveland and other officials, and were photographed on the steps of the Capitol. In the photo, Sitting Bull stands a bit apart from the main group, wearing a suit of clothes purchased during a stopover in St. Paul. The new suit was undoubtedly McLaughlin's doing, as it suggested the agent was making great strides in his efforts to rehabilitate the "late hostiles." The clothing store that sold the suit took out a large advertisement in the *St. Paul Daily Globe* claiming credit for "adding the last finishing touch of civilization to that great and renowned chief of all Indians, the famous Sitting Bull." McLaughlin apparently didn't bother to take Sitting Bull to a shoe store, for the chief is seen in the photo wearing beaded moccasins.

No agreement on the sell-off of reservation lands was reached in Washington, but some of the chiefs' conditions for a sale were worked into the Sioux Act of 1889, and commissioners arrived at the different agencies that summer to get the required signatures from three-fourths of the adult male population. In a council with the leaders at Standing Rock, one of the commissioners urged the Lakotas to sign using the old argument that it was inevitable they would lose the lands in question. "In some way," he said, "the white man is going to make a hole through this reservation." However, it wasn't the talk of the commissioners so much as Mc-Laughlin's influence over leaders such as Gall, the Sihásapa chief John Grass, and others that secured the needed signatures.

As McLaughlin wrote later, he took it upon himself to get these chiefs "into line." Working behind the scenes in secret one-on-one meetings, the master manipulator convinced the chiefs it was in their best interests to go along with the agreement. It likely didn't take much effort on McLaughlin's part, though, as many of these Indian leaders had earned the derogatory name "ration chiefs," meaning they hadn't gained their status in the traditional way but by accommodating government agents and officials. However, there was one bona fide chief McLaughlin ignored completely.

On August 3, 1889, Sitting Bull and approximately twenty men mounted on horseback and sporting their finest war dress thundered up to the council grounds, where several hundred Lakotas were meeting with the commissioners. Sitting Bull entered the circle and asked to speak, but his request was refused. Enraged, Sitting Bull and his followers charged their ponies through the crowd in an attempt to break up the council, shouting at the men to leave the chiefs "who had sold them out." Lakotas scattered right and left, but McLaughlin's Indian police quickly put a stop to

Sitting Bull's antics and arrested some of his men. The chief and his remaining followers hovered just back of the circle of Indians, and when Chief John Grass announced his intention to sign, they yelled "Shame!" "Coward!" "Woman Heart!" and other epithets.

It made no difference. By the end of the day, the commissioners had four hundred signatures, with more to come. Chief Gall signed on August 6. Even Sitting Bull's nephew, One Bull, signed, and so, too, his brother-in-law, Gray Eagle. The signatures obtained at Standing Rock, combined with those from the other agencies, were more than enough to ratify the agreement. A newspaper correspondent found Sitting Bull stewing about the turn of events and asked the chief how the partial opening of the reservation might affect the Indians. "Don't talk to me about Indians!" he growled. "There are no Indians left! Excepting my band of Húnkpapas, they are all dead, and those wearing the clothing of warriors are only squaws. I am sorry for my followers who have been defeated and their lands taken from them."

# Ghosts

*Who would have thought that dancing could make such trouble?*

SHORT BULL, BRULÉ HOLY MAN

One of the greatest Lakota holy men to ever live was named Drinking Cup. According to Black Elk, Drinking Cup was unique in that his power came straight from *Wakan Tanka*. Like Sitting Bull, Drinking Cup foretold things, and sometime in the early 1860s, the holy man experienced a dark vision of the Lakotas' future. In that vision, *Wakan Tanka* revealed to the holy man that the four-leggeds would disappear back into the earth. And "all over the universe there shall be a spider's web woven all around the Sioux," Drinking Cup said, "and then when it shall happen you shall live in gray houses [sod-roofed cabins], but that will not be the way of your life and religion and so when this happens, alongside of those gray houses you shall starve to death."

Sitting Bull and his followers resided on Grand River, about forty miles southwest of agency headquarters, adjacent to Fort Yates. The chief's home was an eighteen-by-thirty-six-foot cabin, eight feet high, with one door at the front and simple six-over-six-light windows on each end. It was constructed of hewn cottonwood logs chinked with mud, and its roof consisted of poles covered with a heavy layer of dirt. The rustic cabin's interior was one large room, and spread around its pine floor were two beds, tables, and several chairs. A wood-fired cooking stove was at one end of the room, along with blackened pots, pans, and kettles of different sizes. Sharing the cabin with Sitting Bull were his two wives, Whole Tribe Seeing Her and Four Robes, and their children. In a second cabin, a few feet away, lived Sitting Bull's deaf stepson, John Sitting Bull. This cabin would also be used by Sitting Bull's wives and children from time to time.

Nothing in Sitting Bull's home indicated this was the residence of the legendary leader of the antitreaty bands and close friend of the great Crazy Horse. Guns, bows, and war clubs were nowhere to be seen. No mementos of past coups. Not even the sacred shield made by his father. The shield's power had protected Sitting Bull many times in battle, but he was no longer at war, and the shield remained safely stored away. Hanging from a peg on the wall was the crucifix given to him by Father De Smet, but Sitting Bull remained a non-Christian, despite the occasional rumor he'd been baptized.

Outside, the Sitting Bull place had all the appearances of a sodbuster's outfit, with a corral, stable, sheds, chicken coops, root cellar, corncrib, and haystacks. He owned about twenty horses (including the prized show horse from Buffalo Bill), forty-five head of cattle, and some eighty chickens. For crops, he raised oats, corn, and potatoes—when the weather cooperated, which wasn't often. But regardless of how "civilized" the place looked, the fifty-eight-year-old Sitting Bull still talked to the meadowlarks, listened to the wind for messages, and prayed often to *Wakan Tanka* to protect him and his people. Sitting Bull would always be a Lakota chief and holy man foremost.

Down near the river, a white cross marked the grave of a favorite daughter, Walks Looking. She died of unknown causes in 1887, just nineteen years old. The loss devastated Sitting Bull and other relatives, and on the next ration day after her death, several women from the chief's camp were seen with deep cuts on their arms and legs from grieving. Walks Looking's husband, a Húnkpapa named Andrew Fox, was a former student at the missionary-run Hampton Institute and could speak English well. He sometimes acted as a secretary for Sitting Bull, translating messages from agency headquarters, reading the chief his mail, and penning necessary replies.

Because Sitting Bull's home was fairly remote, twenty miles west of the Missouri River, the chief didn't receive nearly the visitors he did while a prisoner of war at Fort Randall. Distance, however, wasn't the problem in seeing Sitting Bull. It was Agent McLaughlin, who was obsessed with maintaining complete control over his wards, as well as the reservation itself. In June 1889, a Mrs. Catherine Weldon of Brooklyn, New York, discovered firsthand just how much of an impediment the feisty agent could be.

A Swiss immigrant in her early forties, Weldon was an amateur artist, poet, and passionate member of the National Indian Defense Association, an organization established in Washington in 1885 to advocate for Indian rights. The nation's press referred to the group derogatorily as "Sioux Sentimentalists" and "Meddlesome Philanthropists." Many in Washington believed the group was responsible for the failure of the Sioux chiefs to come to an agreement in October 1888 over the opening of the reservation to settlers. The association's legitimate concern that the Indians weren't being justly compensated for their lands was seen as "interfering." The group also objected to the Sioux Act of 1889, and Weldon was on a mission that summer to visit Sitting Bull and caution the Lakotas against signing. Traveling with her was her eleven-year-old son, Christie.

A white female activist was hardly an everyday sight on the reservation, but Weldon also stood out because of her forceful, self-assured personality. At a time when women were expected to manage the household, to avoid the sun so their skin would remain China-doll white, and, above all, to keep their opinions to themselves, most people didn't know quite what to make of her. She was described variously as a "female crank," "a peculiar character," and an "adventuress." Father Bernard Strassmaier of the Standing Rock Catholic Mission wrote that Weldon's fascination for Sitting Bull "seemed funny to me, that a lady of her education should make such ado about him—she a cultured woman and he a perfect dragon of doubtful moral standing."

Weldon had written Sitting Bull several times before their first meeting at Fort Yates, where she claimed she made him and several other Húnkpapas members of the association. It's doubtful the men knew exactly what they were joining. However, Sitting Bull took a fancy to the indomitable Weldon, who appeared younger than her age—she was "not bad looking," commented one Fort Yates man. Weldon wanted Sitting Bull to accompany her to the Rosebud Agency, where she planned to visit with the Brulé leadership, and the chief readily agreed. For Sitting Bull to visit another agency, however, he would need a pass from McLaughlin.

McLaughlin was well aware of the work of the National Indian Defense Association and also Mrs. Weldon's purpose at Standing Rock—like other agents, he had his spies, too. Before she even had a chance to inquire about a pass, he informed her that Sitting Bull was selfish, of no importance, and "a burden on the younger men, who were more progressive." When she said that Sitting Bull had offered to escort her to Rosebud, he refused to let him go. McLaughlin explained that the commissioners were coming to Standing Rock to get signatures for the Sioux Act, and Sitting

Bull's presence—suddenly important again—was needed. What he didn't say was that he wasn't about to let Sitting Bull go to Rosebud and stir up opposition to the commissioners.

The agent's gatekeeper mentality angered Weldon, and she accused McLaughlin of being afraid of a woman's influence. She also threatened to report him to his superiors at the Indian Bureau. McLaughlin, never keen on having his authority challenged, and by a woman no less, blew up. In something of an understatement, Weldon later wrote that "high words passed between us both." Not only did McLaughlin refuse to issue a pass for Sitting Bull, but he also forbade Weldon from passing through the reservation. The volatile exchange finally ended when Weldon jumped up and stormed out of the agent's office, her long dress swishing behind her.

Sitting Bull drove Weldon and Christie down to the river landing in a wagon and saw them off. She was gone no more than a day or two, however, when an ugly story appeared in the *Sioux City Journal* claiming that Weldon had traveled all the way from New York to make Sitting Bull her husband. Weldon was furious and blamed McLaughlin for planting the story, which he may very well have done. Father Francis M. Craft, a Jesuit priest who battled the agent's attempts to control him and the work of the other Catholic missionaries, commented in his diary that "McLaughlin has the cunning of Satan."

By making Weldon look ridiculous, if not delusional, McLaughlin could rest assured the Indian Bureau wouldn't take her seriously if she made good on her threat to report him. "The agent fears my presence," she wrote shortly afterward, "and did all he can to destroy me."

Weldon sent a scathing letter to the *Sioux City Journal* threatening to sue the paper for publishing such "unparalleled untruths." And yet, Weldon harbored some untruths of her own. Her name

wasn't actually Mrs. Catherine Weldon; it was Caroline Schlatter, although she'd been divorced from her physician husband,
Claude B. Schlatter, since 1883. Her son, Christie, was fathered by
another man, and that extramarital affair was the cause of her
very public divorce. Caroline apparently believed the family scan-
dal would hinder her efforts to help the Lakotas, so she took an
assumed name. Her personal history wouldn't be revealed until a
couple of years later.

Caroline's mother died in 1887, leaving her $2,000, which gave
Caroline the independence to travel to Dakota Territory and help
the Indians she'd befriended. After being rebuffed by McLaughlin
at Standing Rock, she returned to Brooklyn, but only temporarily. Caroline was determined to make her home in Sioux country. Over the next few months, she settled her affairs in the East,
and, with young Christie in tow, started back west, arriving on
the Cannonball River, the reservation's northern boundary, late
in the spring of 1890. Caroline had written McLaughlin about living for a short time on the reservation. Because she needed his
permission, she had no choice but to put aside her bitter feelings.
There is no record of a response from McLaughlin, however, but
it seems telling that Caroline and Christie initially settled in at a
ranch at the mouth of the Cannonball, about twenty-five miles
north of agency headquarters.

Soon McLaughlin's spies informed him of Sitting Bull's frequent visits to Caroline's residence, where she counseled the
chief on the government's treaty obligations to his people. In Mc-
Laughlin's view, every visit Sitting Bull made to Caroline resulted
in the chief becoming "more insolent and worthless." After a few
weeks, Caroline chose to ignore whatever objections McLaughlin might have and went to live on Grand River. She and Christie
moved into Sitting Bull's cabin, sharing the small space with him
and his large family.

Caroline is said to have cooked and cleaned for Sitting Bull right alongside his wives. The Húnkpapas called her Woman Walking Ahead. The Catholic women on the reservation sneeringly called her Sitting Bull's third wife, although Caroline strongly insisted that Sitting Bull was like a father to her. The chief became especially fond of Christie. On ration day, Sitting Bull would put the boy on one of his ponies while he mounted the Buffalo Bill horse, and they would ride side by side to agency headquarters and back.

With food purchased by Caroline's inheritance, Sitting Bull held numerous feasts and councils. McLaughlin viewed this in the same way he did Sitting Bull squandering his Wild West earnings on feasts: it was influence-peddling and allowed the chief to perpetuate the Lakotas' "old-time customs," customs the agent was trying his best to obliterate. But it was also true that many Húnkpapas at Standing Rock were hungry. "Rations are always short," said one agent, and cattle issued by the government in the fall lost weight dramatically during the cold and lean winter months so that the Indians ended up with less meat when they needed it most.

Caroline calculated that the Indians were receiving only one-fifth of the supplies the government allowed them, and she accused McLaughlin and his fellow agents of taking goods intended for their wards. The pilfering of Indian goods by crooked agents was indeed a long-standing problem, but there is no evidence McLaughlin was ever guilty of stealing. However, some Húnkpapas claimed later that any who professed sympathy for Sitting Bull or were outspoken in his behalf "were told there were no rations for them, or they had some other trouble put upon them."

Sitting Bull and his followers, then, were fortunate to have Caroline's generosity, as the Indians had little or no money with which to buy food. A severe drought along the Missouri resulted in almost a total crop failure, with most of the fields not worth the cost of harvesting. In fact, the Indians of Standing Rock experienced a good growing season only once every four years or so. Writing in November 1889, McLaughlin explained to the governor of Dakota Territory that the "recurring droughts with blighting hot winds, which seem to prevail throughout this section of the country, makes farming too precarious and unprofitable to encourage even the hardy white pioneer, much less the Indian who is a new beginner, and who needs paying results to stimulate him."

McLaughlin believed his wards would be much better off devoting their efforts to stock raising. However, while the Standing Rock agent concerned himself with plotting a future for his progressives, a holy man from the Cheyenne River reservation arrived at Grand River with the knowledge of a new religion that promised a return to halcyon days, when buffalo blackened the prairies and the Lakotas were fearsome rulers of the northern plains. The religion involved specific rituals and clothing, but mostly, its devotees simply had to dance.

The holy man was Crazy Horse's cousin and friend Kicking Bear. A renowned Oglala warrior, Kicking Bear had fought at his cousin's side in several battles and skirmishes with the Long Knives, including the Rosebud and Little Big Horn. He'd married the daughter of a Miniconjou chief, Big Foot, and subsequently became a band leader within that tribe. In the fall of 1889, Kicking Bear and nine other Lakotas traveled to Nevada to visit a thirty-three-year-old Northern Paiute holy man who'd reportedly received a powerful vision. Stories of his vision and what it meant had quickly spread among the western Indian nations, from the Shoshones of Wyoming to the Southern Cheyennes and Arapahos of Oklahoma Territory. The Lakota delegation was tasked with learning what it could about this mysterious holy man and his claims.

Named Wovoka (the Messiah to his disciples), the Paiute holy man said he'd visited God in his vision, and God had shown him how to make the world over again. But for this momentous change to occur, certain ceremonies must be performed, and God had instructed Wovoka to teach them. Awed by Wovoka and his prophecy, the Lakota delegation remained several weeks as the holy man instructed them in the new religion. The Lakota delegates returned to Sioux country in the spring and immediately introduced the new religion on the different reservations. They rapidly gained converts.

Sitting Bull had known of Wovoka's vision for months, and once he learned Kicking Bear was back and overseeing the new religion's prescribed dance at Cheyenne River, he invited him to the Grand River settlement. Kicking Bear was not only a cousin of Crazy Horse, but he was also Sitting Bull's nephew, his mother being a sister of one of Sitting Bull's wives. The Húnkpapa chief liked and trusted him.

Kicking Bear arrived at Sitting Bull's camp on October 9, and what he told his uncle about Wovoka and his vision was even more incredible than the tales and rumors that'd made their way to Standing Rock. The Indian Messiah was coming in the spring, Kicking Bear said. And with the arrival of the Messiah, all their dead relatives would arise, also the buffalo, antelope, deer, and other prairie creatures. The earth would be covered in a layer of new earth, and a mystical, unnamed black man would stand from morning to night making new buffalo, gold, and light wagons. All the white people would be sent across the ocean or turned into dogs or fish, and a deep gulf would form to prevent the whites from ever coming onto Sioux lands again. Those Indians who doubted the prophecy of the Messiah would themselves be turned into dogs.

For these things to come to pass, however, the Messiah stressed that the Indians must remain at peace and not fight the white man, they must love one another, and, above all, they must dance. The dance, which the Lakotas conducted in a large circle around a tall, holy pole, was to be performed for five days in a row and then repeated. The more they danced, the Messiah said, the sooner they would be reunited with their dead family and friends. It was this promise of bringing the dead back from the spirit world that earned the new religion the name Ghost Dance.

Kicking Bear told all those who wished to dance—and nearly all of Sitting Bull's followers were eager to bring about the Messiah's prophecy—that they must wear "blessed white robes." These "robes" were shirts and dresses made of unbleached muslin and decorated with painted symbols: stars, crosses, crescent moons, bows and arrows, and almost always a large eagle. Fringe ran along the seams and hems of both the shirts and dresses, and some were further decorated with hair locks and feathers. The Ghost Dancers prayed over the shirts and dresses to make them *wakan*, holy, after which it was said that no bullet could penetrate them.

Sitting Bull didn't dance. The Húnkpapa holy man wasn't one to question another man's vision, nor did he question the sincerity of his nephew's words. But the new doctrine clearly incorporated elements of Christianity, a religion Sitting Bull had rejected numerous times. His devotion was always to *Wakan Tanka* and the old ways. The chief didn't need Wovoka to communicate with the winged peoples and four-leggeds or to receive visions of the future. If the Messiah indeed appeared as Kicking Bear promised and the prophecy came true, no one would welcome the new world sans the white man more than Sitting Bull. But until then, he would wait and see what the dancing brought.

As for his people, Sitting Bull recognized that the Ghost Dance gave them hope and purpose. So he sat in the sacred tent near the two dance circles (one for adults and one for small children) and made the dancers *wakan*. With a finger dipped in blue paint, he traced crescents and crosses on their vermillion-covered faces. Then, one by one, the dancers left the tent and joined the circles.

Sitting Bull's support of the Ghost Dancers also allowed him to strengthen his position as chief, gain additional followers, and thus thwart Agent McLaughlin's efforts to destroy his influence. "I will be chief," he said emphatically to a missionary who visited the Ghost Dance camp. Sitting Bull believed his supremacy hinged on his peoples' resistance to the government's plans for them. "If they become civilized," Sitting Bull said, "I shall go down."

Predictably, McLaughlin considered the Ghost Dance "demoralizing, indecent, and disgusting." As soon as his spies alerted him that Kicking Bear was leading a Ghost Dance at Sitting Bull's camp, he ordered a detachment of thirteen Metal Breasts (Indian policemen) to Grand River to arrest Kicking Bear and escort him off the reservation. One of those Metal Breasts was One Bull, who received ten dollars a month for his service, and his family didn't go hungry. It was said One Bull received other incentives from McLaughlin for his allegiance, including the promise he would one day replace Sitting Bull as chief. Maybe. That the thirty-seven-year-old One Bull became a key informer for McLaughlin, however, seems fairly evident.

A strange thing happened when the Metal Breasts arrived at the Ghost Dance site. The captain and his second lieutenant sensed something powerful emanating from Kicking Bear and the dancers. It was very *wakan,* and it spooked them. A few of the privates urged the two officers to make the arrest of Kicking Bear as they'd been ordered, but the officers refused. Instead, the captain spoke to Sitting Bull and told him the Ghost Dance must stop and that it was McLaughlin's orders that Kicking Bear leave Standing Rock. The Metal Breasts then started back for Fort Yates. The two officers arrived at headquarters in what McLaughlin described as a "dazed condition." The agent immediately dispatched a second party of Metal Breasts to Grand River, and this time Kicking Bear was successfully removed from the reservation. But the dancing continued.

Across Grand River and a short distance west of Sitting Bull's place lived his brother-in-law Gray Eagle. Like One Bull, Gray Eagle had aligned himself with McLaughlin, who'd rewarded his ally by appointing Gray Eagle a judge on the reservation's court of Indian offenses. McLaughlin now asked Gray Eagle to talk to Sitting Bull and get him to stop the dancing. So Gray Eagle went to the Ghost Dance grounds, and while dancers sang and drummers beat a steady rhythm with taut rawhide-covered drums, he tried to reason with Sitting Bull.

"Brother-in-law, we're settled on the reservation now," Gray Eagle said, "and we're under [the] jurisdiction of [the] government now, and we must do as they say—we must cut out the roaming around and live as they say and [you] must cut out this dancing."

Sitting Bull acknowledged the truth of Gray Eagle's words. They were indeed living on a reservation, one now smaller than it used to be thanks to Gray Eagle and others who signed the land away. But he would not give up the traditional ways of his people; they were central to their existence. "You go and follow what [the] white man says," Sitting Bull told Gray Eagle, "but for my part, leave me alone."

"If you're not going to obey and not do as the whites say," Gray Eagle warned, "you are going to cause a lot of trouble and cost your life." They had been friends a long time, Gray Eagle continued, but he'd sworn to stand by the white government. If Sitting Bull refused to stop the Ghost Dance, he said, "we will not be together anymore."

The new religion drove a wedge not only between Sitting Bull and Gray Eagle but also between the chief and his strongest white advocate, Caroline (a.k.a. Catherine) Weldon. In a rare letter to Agent McLaughlin, she wrote disparagingly of Kicking Bear. "This false prophet and cheat claims to have spoken to 'Christ' who is again upon the earth and who has come to help the Indians defeat the whites. . . . It is heart-rending to see how zealous they are in their faith of this false Christ, and reject the true Christ about whom I spoke to all the Indians explaining our faith."

Caroline pleaded with Sitting Bull to stop the dances. Troops were sure to come, she said, and when they did, there would be a battle. But the chief calmly explained that the dancing was not his doing, and he would actually be glad if the Long Knives killed him; he wanted to die. "If you want to die, kill yourself," Caroline snapped, "and do not bring other people into trouble." So strongly and passionately did Caroline speak against Kicking Bear and the Ghost Dance that many in the Grand River settlement considered her an enemy, and she came to believe her life was in danger.

In early November, Caroline packed up her paints, books, papers, clothing, carpets, and "beautiful Indian trinkets," and, with Christie at her side, boarded a Missouri steamer bound downriver. She now saw her work to defend and educate Sitting Bull and his people as a failure. "It was money, health, and heart thrown away," she wrote. She still thought of Sitting Bull as her friend, though, and she left with him one of four paintings she'd made of the chief. The painting showed him standing in profile and wearing an immaculate eagle-feather bonnet, its trailer touching the ground. His hands grasped a lever-action Winchester. Caroline based the painting on a photograph made of the chief in 1885, when he was touring with Cody's Wild West. Sitting Bull hung it on the wall inside his second cabin.

The chief escorted Caroline and Christie to Fort Yates, and

when he said good-bye to the boy, tears rolled down his cheeks. Those who caught a glimpse of Sitting Bull's sad face were astonished, as the chief rarely showed emotion when among white people. Three weeks later, Sitting Bull received a letter from Caroline that hit him like a thunderbolt. Her beloved Christie was dead. The boy had stepped on a nail sometime before they left, and tetanus soon set in. After much suffering, twelve-year-old Christie died on their Missouri River steamer. Grief-stricken, Sitting Bull abruptly left the Ghost Dance and didn't reappear until some days later.

On the morning of November 16, 1890, a Sunday, Agent McLaughlin drove a team and wagon out of Fort Yates, his interpreter sitting at his side. Their destination was the Grand River settlement. McLaughlin wanted to see the Ghost Dance for himself and also confront Sitting Bull, who'd failed to respond to McLaughlin's request to visit him at agency headquarters. The agent had already recommended to Washington that the chief be removed to a military prison far from Sioux country, preferably before the spring. But until that time came, he was determined to remind Sitting Bull and his followers just who was in charge at Standing Rock.

McLaughlin kept his planned visit a secret and even detoured off the main road so that his approach would be undetected until the last moment, which came that afternoon at about 3:00 P.M. As the settlement came into view, McLaughlin noticed numerous lodges and tents scattered among the cottonwoods on both sides of Grand River, with another cluster of lodges just north of the Ghost Dance grounds. Many of these lodges belonged to visiting Lakotas, but some of Sitting Bull's followers had vacated their cabins to be nearer the dance and to socialize with friends and relatives. Several sweat lodges stood near Sitting Bull's home—before one participated in the dance, purification with a sweat bath was necessary.

If McLaughlin expected his sudden appearance to disrupt the dance, he was disappointed. He drove his team near the circle and halted, but the Ghost Dancers and spectators paid little attention to him. Forty-five men, twenty-five women, twenty-five boys, and ten girls made up the large dance circle. Among the youths, Mc-Laughlin recognized several who, up until a few weeks previous, had been students in the settlement's day schools. The dancers held hands and circled to the left while facing the fifteen-foot-tall holy pole, which was painted red and blue and festooned with colorful flags at the top.

All the while, the dancers stared at the sun and chanted. At times, they stopped moving around the pole and raised their hands high, stretching themselves upward on their toes and then back down. They raised themselves like this several times, always gazing at the sun, before again joining hands and moving to the left. The dancers kept this up until, one by one, they fell into a trance. Some collapsed to the ground, rolling in the dirt and frothing at the mouth. Others broke free from the circle and ran about, whooping and madly waving their arms. When the dancers returned to their senses, they described their visions. And everyone, old and young, experienced a vision.

The approximately two hundred Indian spectators were mesmerized by the spectacle, but McLaughlin could only take so much. He wisely concluded it was not the time to try talking to Sitting Bull. Instead, he drove three miles to the house of one of his Metal Breasts, First Lieutenant Henry Bull Head, where he and his interpreter spent the night. The following morning, the agent was back at Sitting Bull's cabin shortly after daylight, along with his interpreter and the lieutenant. McLaughlin wasted no time in lecturing the chief. "Look here, Sitting Bull," he said, "I want to know what you mean by your present conduct and utter disregard of department orders."

Some of the chief's followers now began to gather, rubbing the sleep from their eyes as McLaughlin went into a long harangue about how well the government had treated Sitting Bull and his people. They'd been granted full amnesty for all their past offenses, McLaughlin said, and much effort and money had been expended in teaching them to be farmers, as well as to educate their children. These dances were abusing the confidence the government had placed in Sitting Bull's band, and if they weren't stopped soon, McLaughlin warned, they would all be punished.

When the agent finally finished, Sitting Bull presented him with a proposition. He suggested they take a trip together to trace the source of the Messiah story. They would go west, from tribe to tribe, until they reached the man who started the story. And if they didn't find the Messiah and see with their own eyes the dead Indians and buffalo returning to repopulate the earth as promised by the Messiah's prophecy, then Sitting Bull would report to his people that they'd been deceived, that there was no Messiah. Such a statement coming from him, the chief believed, would put an end to the movement. However, if he and McLaughlin found evidence the prophecy was true, then Sitting Bull wanted his people to be allowed to continue dancing around the holy pole.

McLaughlin scoffed at the proposition. It would be like trying to catch the wind that blew last year, he said. Besides, the Indian Bureau hadn't authorized any money for such an expedition, and he was unwilling to spend money out of his own pocket. Sitting Bull offered that they could use his team and camping outfit, but still McLaughlin objected. He instructed Sitting Bull to come to his house at the agency, where he would set aside a whole day to talk about the false Messiah and the Ghost Dance religion. That was plenty of time, McLaughlin thought, to convince Sitting Bull "of the absurdity of this foolish craze." Disappointed that the agent so quickly dismissed his idea for a fact-finding mission, however, Sitting Bull didn't make any promises, only that he'd consider a visit.

As McLaughlin and Sitting Bull talked, their words translated by the interpreter, Bull Head stood nearby, watching and listening. The forty-three-year-old lieutenant didn't like Sitting Bull. He partly didn't like the chief because McLaughlin didn't like him. Sitting Bull was a nonprogressive, a troublemaker. But Bull Head was also jealous of Sitting Bull, and he'd been humiliated by the chief more than once. Years previous, during a buffalo hunt, Sitting Bull and a longtime friend, Catch the Bear, did something that angered Bull Head. He responded by calling the pair old women, a highly offensive insult to a Lakota warrior. Sitting Bull and Catch the Bear rode up to Bull Head and struck him repeatedly with small clubs until he tumbled from his saddle.

On becoming a Metal Breast, Bull Head took advantage of his newfound authority to exact some revenge. At a ration day, Bull Head took several beef tongues from Catch the Bear simply because he could. And recently, when Catch the Bear was given several used flour sacks by the agency issue clerk, Bull Head stepped in and snatched them away, accusing Catch the Bear of intending to make Ghost Dance shirts out of the cloth. Nothing would have given Bull Head greater pleasure than to arrest the great Sitting Bull in front of his followers. However, McLaughlin would never attempt such a move without a large armed force, and he wanted to give Sitting Bull a chance to visit him at the agency. He still planned to have the chief removed to a military prison before the spring, but for now, McLaughlin was confident he could break up the Messiah movement by simply withholding rations from the dancers, and he reported as much to the Indian Bureau.

McLaughlin may have believed he could easily handle the Ghost Dancers, but white settlers in the Dakotas and elsewhere were beginning to panic. Upon his return to Fort Yates, McLaughlin found several telegrams on his desk. One came from a man who wanted to know, "Am I safe in keeping my wife at the ranch?" Another was sent by David Carey, the father of seventeen-year-old Delia Carey, a new teacher at one of the Standing Rock day schools. "If there is any sign of danger," he wrote, "please tell my daughter to close school [and] come home, her mother anxious." The sheriff of neighboring Morton County also telegraphed the agent: "There is great excitement here about the Indians. What is there to it? If you think it necessary, I will call on the governor for military [assistance]."

The rising fear among the white population was perplexing to many Lakotas. At a council held at the Pine Ridge Agency, Chief American Horse spoke out in frustration: "We are hungry; and when we get hungry, the white people are afraid of us," he said. "Now they begin to say we are going to 'break out.' We do not intend to break out; we want peace, but we are very hungry."

Newspapers were partly to blame. Seldom did a story on the Ghost Dance appear without a sensational—and usually false— headline: "Trouble Is Expected . . . Young Bucks Eager to Fight," "Sioux Take the Warpath Today," "Six to Eight Thousand Redskins Prepared to Re-enact the Custer Massacre," and others of the same ilk. And newspapers were quick to publish unsubstantiated reports of Lakotas murdering whites, all of which turned out to be untrue. Consequently, a flood of settlers abandoned homes and towns and fled east as far as a hundred miles the other side of the

Missouri River. To some Ghost Dancers, this exodus seemed to be confirmation that the Messiah was coming, with the whites leaving the land of the Sioux to avoid being turned into fish.

Not only were settlers panicking so too were officials in Washington. President Benjamin Harrison handed over the responsibility for containing the Ghost Dance movement to the military. That meant the fate of Sitting Bull and other Indian "fomenters of disturbances" was largely in the hands of the chief's old adversary, Bear Coat Miles, now a major general and commander of the army's Military Division of Missouri. Although headquartered in Chicago, hundreds of miles from the Sioux reservations, Miles was convinced the Ghost Dancers were on the verge of becoming violent, and when that happened, their most dangerous leader would be the victor over Custer. As the general explained later, "I concluded that if the so-called Messiah was to appear in that country, Sitting Bull better be out of it, and I considered it of the first importance to secure his arrest and removal from that country."

And Miles believed he had just the man to bring Sitting Bull in. That individual was none other than Buffalo Bill Cody, who'd briefly served alongside Miles as a scout fourteen years earlier during the so-called Sioux Wars. Buffalo Bill, thanks to his outrageously popular Wild West exhibition, was now one of the country's leading celebrities, but Miles greatly respected the showman for his skills as a savvy Plainsman. That the former army scout—and Medal of Honor recipient—could acquit himself well in just about any situation with Indians or whites, the general had no doubt. And the good feelings between Sitting Bull and Cody formed during the months the chief toured with the Wild West couldn't help but offer an advantage. Cody himself was confident the chief would at least listen to him.

On the afternoon of November 28, then, the forty-four-year-old Cody and several companions arrived at Fort Yates. His long hair flowing from beneath a wide-brimmed Stetson, Cody called for whiskey as Fort Yates's commanding officer, Lieutenant Colonel William F. Drum, read over the orders from Miles. Cody's mission came as a shock to both Drum and McLaughlin, who were not consulted beforehand. McLaughlin didn't like it one bit. Ironically, the agent who was always quick to characterize Sitting Bull as vain chafed at the idea of Buffalo Bill coming on *his* reservation and getting all the glory for corralling his most famous ward. If anyone was to bring Sitting Bull in, McLaughlin wanted it to be his Indian police force, which he was exceedingly proud of.

Thus, as a number of conspirators did their best to get Cody liquored up at the officers' club, McLaughlin and Drum rushed to the telegraph office and burned up the wires with requests to have Miles's order rescinded. The hours slowly slipped by without an answer, and the following morning, Cody surprised nearly everyone by appearing bright and chipper and raring to get started for Grand River—the man could hold his liquor. Cody's entourage, which included a wagon loaded with presents Cody had purchased for the chief, departed Fort Yates at 11:00 A.M. But the cunning McLaughlin wasn't yet defeated. Two routes led to Sitting Bull's camp, and the agent sent a man ahead on each route to await the showman's party. Whichever man encountered Cody, he was to tell him the Húnkpapa chief was already on his way to the agency—by the other route. It was hoped this information would cause Cody to turn around and thus buy time to receive an answer from Washington, preferably one ordering Cody to abort his mission.

The subterfuge worked to perfection. Having no reason to suspect McLaughlin's man would lie to him, Cody decided to try and catch up to Sitting Bull by striking out overland to the other road, about five miles distant. He then followed that road back toward the agency until reaching a point five miles out, where he and his companions camped for the night. Cody sent his interpreter to the agency that evening to confirm that Sitting Bull was indeed there. But the interpreter arrived back at camp early the next morning with the news that no one had seen the chief. The showman's party now started again for Grand River but were soon overtaken by a breathless courier from Lieutenant Colonel Drum with orders to abandon their mission and return to Fort Yates.

Agent McLaughlin's telegram to the commissioner of Indian affairs, it turns out, had caused considerable fretting in the interior and war departments. Buffalo Bill's mission, the agent warned, was unnecessary, unwise, and it was bound to lead to a fight. McLaughlin assured the commissioner that he had matters on the reservation well in hand, and when the time came to remove Sitting Bull, his Indian police could do it "in such a way that not a drop of blood need be shed." McLaughlin's plea made it all the way to President Harrison who, despite General Miles's earnest request that Cody be allowed to carry out his mission, believed that a strong force of troops should be close by when an arrest was made. The president wired a message to Fort Yates countermanding Miles's order.

Years later, McLaughlin gave himself a tremendous pat on the back for having foiled the efforts of Miles and Cody. "My telegram," he wrote, "saved to the world that day a royal good fellow and most excellent showman." It did nothing of the sort. None of the Ghost Dancers at Grand River had acted in the least bit hostile, and Sitting Bull actually liked Cody. The showman was far too smart than to try kidnapping the holy man; he simply intended to shower his gifts on the chief and sweet-talk him into leaving the Ghost Dance and coming to the agency, where the Metal Breasts would surprise Sitting Bull and take him into custody. It's doubtful Cody would have succeeded, but to not let him at least try was a regrettable missed opportunity.

In the midst of the fear and hand-wringing over the Ghost Dance, the *Brooklyn Daily Eagle* asked two profound questions: "So long as the Indians abstain from crime, why should they not be permitted to indulge in religious enthusiasm for their Messiah? What business has the government to interfere unless overt acts of a hostile character are committed?" For the Indian Bureau, the answer was simple, if legally questionable. The Ghost Dance was a step back to paganism and threatened to destroy the ongoing work of agents and missionaries to civilize the Indian. Right or wrong, it must be stopped. For McLaughlin, however, there was another, infuriating aspect: the Ghost Dancers' loss of respect for his authority and, conversely, the rising influence the movement gave to Sitting Bull, the proverbial thorn in McLaughlin's side.

Speaking to a reporter on December 1, 1890, McLaughlin complained that Sitting Bull had broken his promise to send his children to school and that he'd disobeyed McLaughlin's order to come to the agency on the last ration day. "Sitting Bull should be captured and confined," the agent continued. "Of that there is no doubt. His influence is strongly and constantly for evil, and while he does not participate in the Ghost Dances to the extent of jumping about and yelling, he is present all the time and keeps the frenzy at the highest pitch." McLaughlin informed the reporter that ten of his Metal Breasts under Sergeant Shave Head were then patrolling the roads leading from Sitting Bull's camp to the agency. "If the old recalcitrant comes within the power of these scouts," he said confidently, "they will bring him in instantly."

Before his men had a chance to nab Sitting Bull, however, McLaughlin received word from Washington that he was to make no arrests except under orders of the military. This caused the agent to suddenly downplay any concerns about the chief and the Ghost

Dance. In a December 6 telegram to the army's commander of the Department of Dakota, Thomas H. Ruger, McLaughlin advised that there was no need for an immediate arrest. More winterlike temperatures had finally arrived at Standing Rock, he wrote, and each day of cold weather dampened the fervor of the Ghost Dancers. He further stated that his Metal Breasts would have no problem keeping the chief on the reservation until it was time for an arrest. And he again reminded General Ruger that when that time came, his Metal Breasts were more than up to the task.

As always, McLaughlin's communications were about maintaining total control over affairs at Standing Rock. He didn't want any more surprises like the Buffalo Bill mission, and he especially didn't want Bluecoats whisking Sitting Bull away. It would be more humiliating for the chief if he was arrested by his own people. And, most importantly, McLaughlin could take more than a little credit for the success of the operation. The Metal Breasts were all good progressives, handpicked by him.

What Ruger thought of McLaughlin's report is unknown, but over Ruger was General Miles, who was well aware of McLaughlin's role in sabotaging his plan for Buffalo Bill. The agent was undoubtedly the last person Miles wanted advice from. Miles hadn't changed his mind about removing Sitting Bull from the reservation, the sooner the better. Thus, on December 12, orders to "secure the person of Sitting Bull" arrived at the Fort Yates telegraph office. The orders also instructed Lieutenant Colonel Drum to cooperate with McLaughlin on how best to accomplish the arrest.

McLaughlin suggested they wait until the twentieth, a Saturday. That was the next biweekly ration day, and many of Sitting Bull's followers would be away at the agency. Drum agreed, but they both worried about the possibility that Sitting Bull might leave the reservation before they were ready to act. McLaughlin, however, had increased his force of Metal Breasts on Grand River, and with these, as well as his spies, the agent was kept well informed of Sitting Bull's nearly every move. Even so, a letter from Sitting Bull that arrived at agency headquarters late on the twelfth showed that McLaughlin and Drum had every reason to worry.

In that letter, written on behalf of the chief by his son-in-law Andrew Fox, Sitting Bull tried to explain to McLaughlin why his people were dancing despite the agent's stern warnings to stop. He and McLaughlin shared the same God, Sitting Bull said. His people were praying to God to let them live and to help them follow the good road and do nothing wrong. Sitting Bull didn't look down upon the way McLaughlin prayed, he further pointed out, so why should the agent question the way his people prayed? Sitting Bull concluded his letter by saying he needed to learn more about the Ghost Dance and planned to visit the Pine Ridge Reservation, where Kicking Bear and other holy men were leading a large gathering of Oglala, Brulé, and Miniconjou Ghost Dancers. The chief wanted McLaughlin's permission to make the visit, but he was going whether he got the permission or not.

McLaughlin responded with a long letter of his own in which he again reminded the chief of all the government had done for him and his people. The Ghost Dance, he wrote, was "in open violation of department regulations and contrary to the wishes of all friends of the Indians." Nothing good would come from it. He warned Sitting Bull not to visit any other reservation for the time being and, incredibly, closed by telling Sitting Bull *not to feel that he disliked him.* No lie was too big for McLaughlin if it kept the "old recalcitrant" at Grand River until ration day.

One of McLaughlin's spies was the teacher at the Grand River day school, four and a half miles from Sitting Bull's camp. Formerly the clerk in Fort Yates's post sutler store, twenty-five-year-old John M. Carignan began teaching at the day school on September 1, just in time to serve as point man for McLaughlin. Couriers and Metal Breasts brought their messages and instructions to the school, and Carignan, who could speak Lakota tolerably well, made sure those messages were delivered to the appropriate parties.

Just after midnight on December 14, Lieutenant Bull Head awakened Carignan with an urgent report for the agent. Sitting Bull was definitely preparing to leave, the lieutenant said. He understood the chief met in council with his followers the day before concerning an important letter from Pine Ridge. The letter, likely sent by Kicking Bear, said the Messiah was soon to appear before the Ghost Dancers there and invited Sitting Bull to join them. It was this letter that'd prompted Sitting Bull to write McLaughlin for permission to leave Standing Rock. In the council, Sitting Bull's followers had pressed him to go. Consequently, Bull Head strongly advised they arrest the chief now. He feared that if Sitting Bull got a head start, it would be impossible to overtake him. Carignan dutifully wrote down Bull Head's information and gave it to a courier later that morning.

McLaughlin received Bull Head's report that afternoon and immediately shared it with Lieutenant Colonel Drum, who now became alarmed. Drum's orders from Miles were clear, and with the imminent threat of Sitting Bull fleeing—if he hadn't already gotten away—waiting for ration day was no longer an option. Drum ordered that they proceed with the arrest at once. He agreed to McLaughlin's plan to let the Metal Breasts enter the camp and make the arrest. However, to prevent the Ghost Dancers from rallying and attempting to rescue the chief on the road to Fort Yates, two companies of the Eighth Cavalry with a Gatling gun and a breechloading steel Hotchkiss gun would be waiting about eighteen miles from Grand River.

Drum watched McLaughlin hurriedly write out orders in English and Lakota for Lieutenant Bull Head and Sergeant Shave Head. The agent specified that the arrest should take place in the morning, before daylight. The darkness would allow the Metal

Breasts to slip into the settlement unseen as Sitting Bull's follow-ers slept. The agent also penned a short letter to Carignan explain-ing the plan for the arrest so that he could clarify the orders to Bull Head in case of any confusion. McLaughlin placed the letters in an envelope and then handed it to Red Tomahawk, a forty-one-year-old sergeant of the Metal Breasts.

"Now you have something to do," the agent said. "You give this to Bull Head, sure. You are all to arrest Sitting Bull before morning. You say to Bull Head to arrest him and not let him get away or be rescued."

At 5:45 P.M., Red Tomahawk galloped out of Fort Yates.

Sunday, December 14, began no different from any other day for Sitting Bull. As he often did, the chief walked to a high bluff over-looking his place and the Grand River. Here the holy man found the quiet and solitude he needed to think and to pray to *Wakan Tanka*. And Sitting Bull had much to think about, particularly his upcoming trip to Pine Ridge. What would happen to his family and followers while he was away? Would McLaughlin make good on his threat to punish the Ghost Dancers?

Sitting Bull sat upon the ground, and as the sun's rays warmed his body against the cold air, the chief dozed off. While he slept, a dream came to him. In his dream, Sitting Bull learned he would die the next day. After waking up and returning to his cabin, he told several followers of the disturbing premonition. Sitting Bull had known for a long time that he would not die peacefully. He vividly remembered when a meadowlark told him he would die at the hands of his own people. But would death really come on the morrow, just as he was preparing to meet the Messiah?

That evening, Sitting Bull entertained guests, two old men whose names have been lost to time. It became so late that the two men spread their blankets on the floor of the cabin and spent the night. Sitting Bull retired to a pallet of blankets in a corner with his favorite of the two sisters, Whole Tribe Seeing Her. Crow Foot, now sixteen, had an iron bed, the only actual bed in the home. Sleeping in the cabin just behind Sitting Bull's were Four Robes, John Sitting Bull, and other children. A few feet from these cabins stood a tipi that was being used by One Bull's wife, Scarlet Whirlwind Woman, who was pregnant, and Scarlet's aunt.

One Bull was away hauling freight from Mandan to Fort Yates but was expected home at any time. No longer was One Bull a Metal Breast, however. It seems that Sitting Bull's nephew had recently thrown off his white man clothes and joined in the dancing. Despite his previous efforts on McLaughlin's behalf, One Bull was promptly booted from the police force and his uniform taken away. In a November 28 report to the commissioner of Indian affairs, McLaughlin briefly stated the reason for One Bull's removal as, "Believing in the Ghost Dance & sympathizing with its members."

Early the next morning, everyone at Sitting Bull's camp was deep in sleep. Only glowing embers remained in the cabin's lone woodstove. Outside, an overcast sky was just beginning to turn gray, and a drizzling rain was falling, at times mixed with sleet. From the west, however, the sound of thundering hooves came out of the predawn silence, growing louder by the second. Dogs in the Ghost Dance camps began to bark furiously, rousing the occupants of the numerous lodges along the river and on the flat beyond the dance circle.

The sound of the hooves stopped at Sitting Bull's cabin. If the chief and the other occupants were not yet awake, a loud bang on the door from a kick, quickly followed by a sharp rap from a rifle butt, startled them out of their slumbers. The door flew open, and Sitting Bull made out the silhouettes of several figures entering.

The chief next heard the striking of a match. The match's initial bright glow was nearly blinding, but it illuminated the face of a Metal Breast, Red Tomahawk. Sitting Bull saw Red Tomahawk's eyes searching the room until they rested upon the chief, and then the Metal Breast quickly blew out the match. The room again in darkness, Sitting Bull heard the approach of shuffling feet on the wood floor. A hand roughly took hold of his arm.

"The Government sent me," Red Tomahawk said to Sitting Bull. "You are arrested. You can either walk or ride. If you fight, you shall be killed."

Whole Tribe Seeing Her jumped up and rushed outside; she wasn't wearing much. The two guests of Sitting Bull ran out behind her, dragging their blankets. Red Tomahawk and other Metal Breasts pulled Sitting Bull from his warm blankets, making him angry. Sitting Bull asked why they couldn't have come later in the morning, when he was awake. The Metal Breasts didn't answer but pushed him to the door and outside. "This is a great way to do things," Sitting Bull snapped, "not give me a chance to put on my clothes in winter time." Sitting Bull was indeed naked. It wouldn't do to bring the chief to the agency without any clothes on, so Lieutenant Bull Head allowed him to go back in the cabin and get dressed, but under a strong guard.

Inside, Metal Breasts threw Sitting Bull's clothes at him while others held his wrists. "I want to put on my clothes," the chief shouted in frustration, "but you are holding me!" Sitting Bull took his time dressing, and with each passing minute, the sky became lighter, and the chief's followers, awakened by the commotion of dogs, horses, and voices, began converging on the chief's camp.

The squad of Metal Breasts that came to arrest Sitting Bull numbered forty-three men, including four volunteers. Among those volunteers was Gray Eagle, Sitting Bull's brother-in-law. The two hadn't been on good terms ever since their argument over the Ghost Dance. The Metal Breasts were all dismounted, most of their horses tied to a shade shelter a short distance behind the cabin. Each man was equipped with a Springfield carbine and Colt revolver. Around their waists they wore a cartridge belt and holster, and around their necks they sported bandannas of white cloth so as to distinguish them from Sitting Bull's followers.

Five or six Metal Breasts attended to Sitting Bull in the cabin, while the remainder, more than thirty-five men, gathered in a loose semicircle facing the cabin door. Just beyond this line of Metal Breasts was another line, one made up of Sitting Bull's people. It rapidly grew to at least 150 agitated and vocal men, women, and children who strongly objected to their chief being arrested.

All eyes were on the doorway when Sitting Bull finally appeared. He spread his arms and legs, wedging himself in the doorframe until a Metal Breast kicked the chief's legs from behind to force him outside. Lieutenant Bull Head and Sergeants Shave Head, Red Tomahawk, Little Eagle, and Eagle Man—all the leaders of the Metal Breasts—clustered around Sitting Bull and led him a few steps from the cabin. Red Tomahawk walked behind the chief. The sergeant had discovered a fine revolver, a gift from Caroline Weldon, inside the cabin, and he now held it to the back of Sitting Bull's head as they walked along. He poked the gun's muzzle against the chief and said, "You have no ears, you have no ears."

"What are you holding that gun to my head for?" said a defiant Sitting Bull. "Do you think to scare me into this?"

Sitting Bull's followers shouted profanities at Bull Head and his Metal Breasts. Tears streaked down the cheeks of the women and children. Pretty White Buffalo Woman, the wife of Spotted Horn Bull, yelled "Here are a multitude of jealous men!" referring to the police. And then she added the insult, "Jealous women!" One or two in the crowd shouted, "Kill! Kill!"

Bull Head could plainly see he and his men were in trouble, and it was primarily his own fault. Not only had he and his men made a serious mistake by loudly galloping into Sitting Bull's camp, but they'd arrived late, quickly losing the advantage of darkness. And now the lieutenant confronted another critical error. He was supposed to have brought along a light wagon. The idea was to throw the chief in the wagon and whisk him away before his followers knew what'd happened. But upon receiving McLaughlin's order, Bull Head was so eager to arrest his old nemesis that he started without one. The chief would have to be taken away on horseback. Someone had supposedly been sent to the corral to saddle the chief's horse, the one given him by Buffalo Bill, but that someone and the horse were nowhere in sight.

Four men now emerged from the ring of Sitting Bull's followers and pushed through the line of Metal Breasts. Leading was Catch the Bear, who'd long waited for an opportunity to exact revenge for the times Bull Head had mistreated him. The others in the group were Spotted Horn Bull, Black Bird, and Strikes the Kettle. They wore their blankets wrapped around in front of them, obviously for the purpose of concealing weapons.

"Now, here are the Metal Breasts," sneered Catch the Bear, "just as we had expected all the time. You think you are going to take him. You shall not do it!"

Bull Head, facing Sitting Bull, said, "Come now, do not listen to anyone."

Over the shouts of the crowd, Sitting Bull recognized the voice of Whole Tribe Seeing Her. She was singing a brave song. Whole Tribe Seeing Her believed her husband would be better among the dead than to be exiled or imprisoned far from his homeland, and her song was meant to encourage him to resist. She sang, "Sitting Bull, you have always been a brave man. What is going to happen now?"

Upon hearing his wife's words, Sitting Bull announced, "I am not going. Do with me as you please, but I am not going!"

Sitting Bull's brother Jumping Bull rapidly approached the knot of Metal Breasts around the chief. He was unarmed. Jumping Bull had remained fiercely loyal to Sitting Bull ever since that day, now more than three decades ago, when the chief spared his life and adopted him as a brother. He didn't want to see Sitting Bull harmed. "Brother, [you] ought to go with the police and not cause any trouble," he said. "If you go, I go with you."

Before Sitting Bull could respond, Catch the Bear rushed forward, yelling, "Let him go!" In a flash of movement, his blanket swept open and he raised a Winchester rifle and fired at Bull Head. The bullet struck the lieutenant at the waistline on his right side and passed entirely through his body. Bull Head stiffened and let out a grunt. As he began to crumple, Bull Head jerked the trigger of his carbine, sending a bullet into Sitting Bull's chest. The .45-55 bullet plowed upward through the chief's body and exited at the base of his neck, leaving a jagged, two-inch hole. Sitting Bull was dead in his moccasins but staggered and started to lean. Red Tomahawk held his revolver close to Sitting Bull's face and shot the chief below his open right eye. Sitting Bull's lifeless body hit the ground with a thud.

A split second after Catch the Bear fired, Strikes the Kettle shot Sergeant Shave Head in the gut. The sergeant collapsed near Sitting Bull and Bull Head. A relative of the lieutenant, a private named He Alone Is a Man, ran toward the fallen Metal Breasts. Catch the Bear aimed his Winchester at the oncoming private and pulled the trigger but the gun misfired. The two men scuffled, and He Alone Is a Man wrested the Winchester away and used it to club Catch the Bear, knocking him senseless. The Metal Breast then took his own gun and put a bullet in Catch the Bear's limp body, killing him.

Sitting Bull's followers mobbed the Metal Breasts with clubs, knives, and guns. Even some of the women joined in the brief hand-to-hand fighting. "Bullets came so thick," recalled Private Swift Hawk, "some made me dizzy, they were so close." At least one bullet hit Jumping Bull, who fell dead near Sitting Bull's body. The pregnant Scarlet Whirlwind Woman ran back to her tipi and threw herself flat on the ground to avoid being struck. Like a thick fog, acrid black powder smoke from the gunfire hung in the chilly, moisture-laden air. Several Metal Breasts retreated to Sitting Bull's cabin, others sought cover behind sheds and anything else that might stop a bullet. Some fled to the brush near the river.

With Bull Head and First Sergeant Shave Head down, the Metal Breast command fell to Second Sergeant Red Tomahawk, who was now inside the cabin. He ordered his men to knock out the mud chinking from between the logs to create openings for their gun barrels. Just a hundred feet away, Sitting Bull's followers occupied the stable, from which they peppered the cabin and tried to pick off those Metal Breasts trapped outside. To the surprise of these followers, several Metal Breasts suddenly poured out of the cabin and charged the stable, firing their guns as they advanced. Those in the stable fled and took new positions at the river.

The Metal Breasts were still surrounded, however, and greatly outnumbered. They were also running low on ammunition, and from the heavy fire coming from Sitting Bull's people, it appeared they didn't have the same problem. A Metal Breast named Hawk Man volunteered to ride the Buffalo Bill horse to the cavalry command supposed to be waiting eighteen miles away. But when Hawk Man entered the corral, there wasn't a bridle or saddle to be found, only a rope. He tied the rope around the horse's neck and led it to the gate, but the gate's sliding rails were tight, and try as he might, Hawk Man couldn't free them. All the while, bullets buzzed around him, popping and splintering the wood of the corral and stable. Seeing Hawk Man's troubles, Red Tomahawk ran to the corral and got the rails unstuck, allowing the anxious private to finally gallop away. Miraculously, neither Hawk Man, Red Tomahawk, nor the horse received even a scratch.

The two companies of the Eighth Cavalry with field artillery under the command of Captain Edmond G. Fechet arrived at the rendezvous point that morning as planned, but after waiting several minutes without word from Bull Head, they proceeded toward the Grand River settlement. When three miles from the camp, they encountered Hawk Man on the famed white horse, which was dripping sweat. The Metal Breast was highly excited. "I am the only policeman alive," he panted, and which he had good reason to believe. "We attempted to take [Sitting] Bull at dawn," he continued, "but there were too many for us. We killed Bull but his friends have killed us all. There are a hundred and twenty of Bull's men."

This alarming news caused Captain Fechet to question the need to continue, considering that Sitting Bull and all the Metal Breasts were dead. Close on the heels of Hawk Man, however, galloped up another Indian private. He reported that many Metal Breasts were indeed still alive and their situation desperate. There was no hesitation now; the cavalry and artillery moved out at a trot. Thirty minutes later, the command arrived on the brow of the bluffs overlooking the valley of the Grand River. The time was approximately 7:30 A.M. The cavalrymen could easily see the fight in progress below them. Fechet ordered his artillerymen to begin dropping shells from the Hotchkiss gun into the woods along the river.

The distance to Sitting Bull's cabin from the Hotchkiss measured approximately a thousand yards. Whether intentionally or by a miscalculation of the range, at least two rounds fell far short of the timber and struck very close to Sitting Bull's cabins, the exploding projectiles killing a horse and maiming other mounts. Red Tomahawk frantically tied a white cloth to the barrel of his carbine and stuck it out one of the cabin windows, its glass panes already shattered by flying bullets. Subsequent Hotchkiss shells fell where they were supposed to, eliciting yells of rage from the followers in the woods.

As the artillerymen fired the Hotchkiss, one cavalry company moved into the valley on foot, the deadly shells shrieking over their heads. Steadily advancing their skirmish line, the troopers kept up a constant fire with their carbines, and Sitting Bull's people were soon seen fleeing upstream. The other cavalry company remained mounted and rode up the valley to cut off the retreat, but, as Sergeant George DuBois wrote later, the Ghost Dancers "disappeared like magic." The retreat had been so panicked, however, that some women and children were left stranded behind in the camps. DuBois observed one Metal Breast about to shoot a six-year-old child. "I knocked his pistol up and talked him out of it," DuBois wrote. The police, he explained, had their blood up.

The battle over, the wounded and dead Metal Breasts were carried into Sitting Bull's cabin and placed on the floor. Both Bull Head and Shave Head were alive, although their wounds were mortal. As the Metal Breasts gathered quilts and bedding for the wounded, Crow Foot was discovered hiding beneath his iron bed. "There's another one in here!" a Metal Breast shouted. The men dragged Crow Foot out and asked their lieutenant what should be done with Sitting Bull's son.

Bull Head, in tremendous pain from his wounds, answered sternly, "Kill him, they killed me."

"Uncles, I want to live," pleaded Crow Foot.

Red Tomahawk sharply struck the youth's head with the

butt of his revolver, sending him tumbling toward the doorway. Crow Foot fell across the threshold, and as he struggled to rise, two Metal Breasts put bullets in him. They grabbed his twitching body and tossed it outside.

Several Metal Breasts, and also relatives of their dead comrades, took out their anger and grief on Sitting Bull's corpse. One grabbed an ax and chunked its blade into the chief's face. Others bashed his head repeatedly with a club. Sergeant DuBois witnessed a Metal Breast cut Sitting Bull "with a knife till his own wife wouldn't know him." The chief's dead followers received similar treatment. They "looked horrible cut and shot and the blood and brains lay around in all shapes."

Soldiers and Metal Breasts searched through Sitting Bull's buildings, mostly looking for spoils and souvenirs. Second Lieutenant Matthew F. Steele heard the wailing of women and children coming from the chief's second cabin and entered it with a squad of troopers. Whole Tribe Seeing Her and Four Robes sat on top of thick bedding on the floor. Lieutenant Steele thought they sat rather rigidly, and they refused to budge. Steele ordered his men to pull the women up. They next jerked up the bedding and discovered two young men lying facedown. They were Henry Growler, twenty-one-year-old nephew of Sitting Bull, and Protecting Others While Running, the twenty-one-year-old son of Jumping Bull. Both were taken prisoner. Jumping Bull's oldest son, Chase Wounded, lay dead outside, not far from his father.

While Lieutenant Steele was occupied with the chief's family, a Metal Breast had quietly slipped into the cabin. Upon seeing Caroline Weldon's painting of Sitting Bull on the wall, the Metal Breast took the butt of his carbine and smashed the frame, knocking the painting to the floor. He quickly struck it again, punching a hole in the canvas. Steele rushed over and snatched the painting away, saving it from further damage. The lieutenant took the painting back to Fort Yates and subsequently purchased it from Sitting Bull's wives for two dollars.

Later that morning, a train of four wagons came rattling down the road. This was One Bull's freighting outfit. He was halted by a Metal Breast a good distance from Sitting Bull's cabins and instructed not to come closer. "They have killed Sitting Bull," the Metal Breast said, "and we have killed each other, and it looks awful."

"Have you killed my wife and children?"

"All the women are safe," said the Metal Breast.

Sergeant Tomahawk approached, whom One Bull knew, and One Bull asked him if he could come in.

"No," Red Tomahawk answered. "The police are mad now. They will kill you. Go get your wife and go to Fort Yates."

One Bull jumped off his wagon, quickly located Scarlet Whirlwind Woman, and made a hasty exit. His arrival had been fortuitous, though, in that a wagon was needed to haul Sitting Bull's body and those of the dead Metal Breasts to Fort Yates. (The wounded Bull Head and Shave Head were transported in an army ambulance.) When it came time to load the bodies, however, several Metal Breasts strongly objected to placing their four dead comrades in the same wagon with the man who'd been the cause of their demise. They only agreed to allow the bodies to be transported together on the condition that Sitting Bull's body be placed on the bottom and the dead Metal Breasts on top. No one asked Sitting Bull's wives what their wishes were.

Before the Bluecoats and Metal Breasts left Grand River, a lone rider approached through the drizzling haze. He rode a black horse and carried a long staff. As the rider came closer, he was seen to be wearing a fringed Ghost shirt painted red—his blessed robe. The Metal Breasts opened fire on him, and he dashed into the willows near the river. But the Ghost Dancer quickly reappeared, racing his horse nearer, daring the troopers and police to shoot. The bullets flew thick, but when the smoke of the gunfire cleared, the mysterious rider was seen galloping away in the distance. Not one bullet had struck him.

Some of those who witnessed the Ghost Dancer's feat said they heard him singing.

He sang, "Father, I thought you said we were all going to live."

# Epilogue

*But I think I understand him, for I know his story now.*

HENRY HERBERT KNIBBS

As with Crazy Horse, Sitting Bull's last act was one of resistance. He would not suffer the ignominy of being imprisoned. As Húnkpapa historian Josephine Waggoner commented, "Sometimes death can defeat disgrace." Sadly, however, there was nothing to prevent further disgrace to Sitting Bull's corpse. At 4:30 P.M. on December 16, 1890, his body arrived at Fort Yates's "dead house," a small building behind the post hospital. There, the post surgeon cut off a small braid from the chief's scalp that held his eagle feather. The surgeon also took possession of Sitting Bull's blood-soaked leggings. His breechclout, shirt, additional items of clothing, and what remained of his hair were snatched up by other souvenir hunters before the following morning.

The fort's hospital steward retrieved two cabinet card photographs from Sitting Bull's coat pocket. One was an autographed portrait of "Captain Jack" Crawford, a Buffalo Bill protégé who went by the sobriquet "The Poet Scout." The other was a photograph of a white child wearing a dress or gown, identified only as

"Sitting Bull's 'pet.'" The child could be anyone. Even its sex is uncertain, for it was the norm at this time for both young boys and girls to wear dresses. But the word *pet* suggests much more than a passing acquaintance. Sitting Bull loved children, and this may be the offspring of an officer stationed at Fort Randall or Fort Yates. It could even be a young Christie Weldon—the photographer's imprint bears a New York City address. To this day, the thick streaks of Sitting Bull's blood, now crystallized and turned a deep brown and black, are unmistakable.

Sitting Bull's naked body was sewn up in canvas and placed in a simple pine coffin fabricated by the agency carpenter. Relatives of the dead Metal Breasts didn't want his remains in the Catholic cemetery with their fallen, and those consecrated grounds were no place for a "pagan" anyway. So the chief was relegated to the northwest corner of the fort's graveyard, his grave dug by prisoners from the guardhouse. There was no funeral, no words spoken over the grave, and hardly anyone to witness the burial. Agent McLaughlin walked up as clods of dirt were being shoveled into the grave. He didn't remain long.

Two months after the death of Crazy Horse, a small party that included the chief's aged parents, his wife Black Shawl, and the holy man Horn Chips disappeared with his blanket-wrapped corpse into the broken Pine Ridge country. Crazy Horse's father, Worm, and Horn Chips buried the chief's remains in a spot where no one would find them, and Horn Chips made certain of that by returning in subsequent years and moving the chief's bones to a different location—three times. Crazy Horse's final resting place is an enduring mystery. Unfortunately, there was no mystery as to the location of Sitting Bull's grave, and his bones had no such protector.

In 1903, the U.S. Army abandoned Fort Yates, and five years later, the bodies in the military cemetery were disinterred and removed to the national cemetery at Keokuk, Iowa—except for Sitting Bull's. However, the man superintending the removal of the remains, Frank Ecker, was aware that some people doubted the chief had actually been buried in the cemetery. Among the doubters was the current Standing Rock agent, William Belden. Frank had also heard stories about quicklime and acid being put in the grave to destroy any trace of the chief. Curious to learn the truth, Frank ordered Sitting Bull's grave opened.

The chief's bones were discovered easily enough, and Frank detected no damage from quicklime or any other foreign substance. The skull was in several pieces, and some of the ribs were snapped, as if cut by a bullet. Frank placed the bones in a wooden box and informed Agent Belden he could now see the chief's remains for himself. The news nearly gave Belden a stroke. As Frank recalled, the agent "told me to put him back in the grave so no one would know anything, as it might cause trouble in many ways." Frank obliged, but he made sure to snap some photographs of the bones first. He later had some photographic postcards made from the negatives, although no examples have surfaced to date.

Not all of Sitting Bull was returned to the earth, however. Some bones went missing from the box before Frank could bury it, including a piece of the skull, a shoulder blade, and a rib, maybe more. Frank claimed the bones were stolen when he had his back turned for a few minutes attending to other cadavers. These stolen bones haven't surfaced, either.

Sitting Bull's remains again saw the light of day in 1931. After grazing horses broke the chief's simple marble headstone that summer, the decision was made to overhaul the grave site. As part of that work, it seems the Standing Rock superintendent thought it would be a good idea to open the grave, presumably to confirm Sitting Bull was still there. Diggers unearthed a box, inside of which were the bones Frank Ecker had placed there years earlier. Whether or not any bones were pilfered this go-around is unknown. The remains were given a new box (the box possibly placed in a coffin) and reburied. The grave was then covered by a concrete slab with a rock cairn rising from one end and a new marker on the other.

Fast-forward more than twenty years. Shortly after 1:00 A.M. on April 8, 1953, a tow truck dragged chunks of the concrete slab to the side, allowing a group of men to begin digging. Sitting Bull's descendants, including three granddaughters, had long been upset with the neglect shown their ancestor's grave, and they'd been fighting to get the remains relocated to South Dakota. Thirty miles to the south, city leaders of Mobridge imagined they would see some tourist dollars if the famous chief's grave was nearby. They promised the family a memorial to Sitting Bull overlooking the Missouri River with a suitable monument for his grave. Frustrated with "the white man's red tape and delays," the chief's family and some Mobridge businessmen decided to take matters into their own hands.

The diggers found no remains directly beneath where the slab formerly rested, but they did strike bones and fragments of wood off to a corner of the plot. Under the tow truck's spotlight, they quickly fished out a partial skeleton, including a skull that was, according to one account, crushed in the back but otherwise intact. The bones were placed in a box and speedily transported across the state line. By noon that same day, the remains were in a new grave on a high bluff across the river from Mobridge. But it was no ordinary grave. To dissuade any future tampering with the chief's remains, they'd been buried in a heavy black burial vault surrounded by twenty tons of concrete.

Sitting Bull's sudden change of address made national headlines and was met with outrage in North Dakota. Many questioned if the "Mobridge raiders," as they became known, actually got all the remains, especially after a Lakota from Fort Yates named John Plenty was selling bones from the grave in Bismarck the next day—four dollars each. "They did a pretty sloppy job of digging up Sitting Bull," said Plenty. "Lots of Indians have been picking up bones that were left." A list of the chief's bones provided to the press by the retired mortician who assisted the diggers revealed they'd come away with "only a small portion of the skeletal remains" of Sitting Bull.

Some also wondered if the Mobridge party had even gotten the correct skeleton. A coffin accidentally unearthed by the Corps of Engineers in 1962 strongly suggests they didn't. While constructing embankments to prevent flooding from the Missouri River's Oahe Reservoir, the corps disturbed the earth very close to Sitting Bull's original grave site, exposing the coffin. Inside was a box containing "17 hand and foot bones, 9 fragments of ribs, 4 fragments of skull, 3 vertebra including the atlas, 2 patella, and 1 clavicle." There were no long bones. Were these the remains originally dug up and reburied by Frank Ecker in 1908 and then given a new box when the grave was opened in 1931? The skull being in fragments as opposed to intact closely fits what Ecker found and also fits the accounts of the brutal treatment of the chief's corpse at his death.

In 2007, Sitting Bull's four surviving great-grandchildren sought to move the remains yet again. Although a substantial monument had been erected over the grave, the promise to maintain and care for their grandfather's burial site, they said, had not been honored. The place had become a late-night hangout for youths from Mobridge and the reservation, who left beer bottles and other trash strewn around the grave site. The descendants wanted to move the remains to Little Bighorn Battlefield National

Monument. A year later, however, the family changed their mind. They decided their grandfather should be buried in a secret location with nothing to mark his final resting place—like Crazy Horse. "Basically remains should go back to the earth and not be commercialized and marked with headstones," said Sitting Bull's great-grandson, Ernie LaPointe. "Our people never had headstones in the old days."

As of 2022, however, the concrete entombed bones near Mobridge, whether they belong to Sitting Bull or not, remain undisturbed. On still summer mornings, the grave site is a good place to listen to meadowlarks.

Agent McLaughlin penned no mea culpa for Sitting Bull's death. Instead, he blamed the Indian Bureau for not taking his advice on diffusing the Ghost Dance. And he blamed Sitting Bull. Nevertheless, while he deeply regretted the loss of life among the Metal Breasts, he found "the great good accomplished by the ending of Sitting Bull's career . . . most gratifying." His greatest adversary would trouble him no more, and the Ghost Dance movement at Standing Rock was finished, never to return. Two weeks later, it was pretty much finished for all of Sioux country.

On December 29, 1890, as Custer's old regiment, the Seventh Cavalry, searched for weapons in the Ghost Dance camp of the Miniconjou Big Foot, a single gunshot rang out. The sharp crack of the gun triggered a horrific firefight—the Wounded Knee Massacre. No less than two hundred Lakotas were slaughtered, at least half of these women and children. Among the dead were some of Sitting Bull's Húnkpapas, who'd fled to Big Foot's band for protection.

Whole Tribe Seeing Her, Four Robes, and their children were not among those at Wounded Knee. They temporarily moved in with their brother, Gray Eagle. It was said that the wives were afraid to return to their old home, believing it was haunted by Sitting Bull's spirit. Unable to resist the chance to make a ghost story scarier, a news correspondent out of Bismarck reported that Sitting Bull's bloodstains on the cabin's threshold turned a "sort of phosphorus hue at night." Of course, Sitting Bull wasn't killed in the cabin's doorway. If there was blood, and undoubtedly there was a good amount, it belonged to Crow Foot and the wounded Metal Breasts who were carried into the cabin. Spooky bloodstains or not, though, the chief's wives made it known that they intended to move the cabin about a mile from its original location and settle back in. That is, until a group of businessmen from Mandan approached them with a wad of cash.

The four businessmen believed there was good money to be made exhibiting the famed chief's cabin, and they'd set their sights on the World's Columbian Exposition in Chicago, just two years away. In a long negotiation with Whole Tribe Seeing Her and Four Robes, they purchased the cabin for $1,000 in cash, four blue silk dresses and four red silk dresses (one of each for the two wives and daughters Standing Holy and Lodge in Sight), eight red-checked shawls, eight dollars in groceries for each widow, and, finally, a two-year-old steer to match one being raised by Runs Away from Him, the thirteen-year-old son of the chief by Four Robes.

The purchase also included the holy pole from the Ghost Dance and numerous "trinkets, Indian relics, and curiosities." Among these latter were fourteen painted buffalo robes with depictions of animals, coups, and even the Battle of the Little Big Horn. At least some of these drawings, maybe all of them, were created by Sitting Bull.

The cabin was taken apart and each log marked so that it could be reassembled just like it was on the day of the "Battle of Standing

Rock." It required ten wagons to transport the cabin and another four for the cabin's simple furnishings and all the curiosities. With the cabin safely in storage in Mandan, the owners finalized their plans for the World's Fair. In February 1893, they signed a contract with Buffalo Bill's Wild West to display the cabin within the Wild West's enclosure, just a block away from the fairgrounds. When the fair opened that May, however, the cabin didn't get the foot traffic the owners hoped for. Although Cody's Wild West did a booming business, the cabin's owners felt their attraction wasn't in a good location within the enclosure, and they were drawing only on fairgoers who chose to visit the Wild West. That July, then, they secured a spot for the cabin on the fair's extremely popular Midway Plaisance, next to such exotic attractions as the Ostrich Farm and the Brazilian Music Hall.

An enormous screen surrounded the cabin on three sides, preventing a free view of Sitting Bull's home by those strolling the Plaisance. Painted on the screen were iconic western scenes: Custer's Last Stand, a brutal Indian attack on a homesteader's family, an Indian village, among others. A stuffed buffalo surmounted the entrance. For a ten-cent admission, visitors could scrutinize three bullet holes in the cabin door, listen to a guide provide historical information on Sitting Bull and his fight with the Metal Breasts, and observe real Lakotas from Standing Rock perform a "war dance." The star attraction among the Lakotas was the old war chief Rain in the Face. A salacious story widely circulated in the years following the Little Big Horn claimed that Rain in the Face cut out the heart of Tom Custer, the general's brother. He was also often identified as the general's killer. Neither story was true, but many late nineteenth-century Americans were well familiar with the chief's name, and a large banner outside the exhibit made sure to connect the Húnkpapa with the famous battle.

Among the many "curiosities" to be seen was one of Caroline

Weldon's oil paintings of the chief (not the one vandalized the day of the chief's death), but a tour was mostly an opportunity to buy Indian handicrafts, and these items were so popular that the stock had to be replenished several times before the fair ended. Chicago's *Inter Ocean* observed that early on, "visitors insisted on having war clubs, saddlebags, necklaces, and other trappings that had been used and sort of reeked with blood, smoke, and prairie sand, but now, since the new stocks of white buckskin with the pretty beadwork have come they have gone to the other extreme and are buying the articles for house furnishings as well as relics."

The fair closed on October 30, but the cabin exhibit was again before the public less than five months later, this time at Coney Island. At the height of the summer, the popular Brooklyn amusement park could see as many as fifty thousand visitors a day. The Coney Island version of the cabin display, which the proprietors advertised as a "Historic Sioux Indian War Village," was considerably more elaborate (and more carnival sideshow) than what appeared in Chicago. It featured fifty "Ghost Dancers" from Standing Rock, tipis, Indian ponies, a "female Sioux dwarf . . . said to be the only dwarf in the tribe," and a "magnificent taxidermic display."

Rain in the Face was there, too, and he made a deep impression on at least one visitor that summer, a young man who thought he'd show his girlfriend how funny he could be by presenting the chief with a "loaded cigar." When the cigar exploded after a few puffs, Rain in the Face nearly toppled backward out of his chair. The chief looked at the tattered and smoldering cigar butt, screamed in anger, and instantly brought his cane down on the young man's head, making a cut that required stitches at a nearby drugstore.

In early September 1894, on the day the Lakotas broke up their Coney Island camp in preparation for returning to North

Dakota, George B. Forrester, an excise commissioner for the City of Brooklyn, struck a deal to purchase the log cabin. Forrester had been a frequent visitor to the exhibit over the summer and never failed to leave without purchasing some artifact or curio. The cabin itself, he thought, would be the perfect place to display what had become a rather large personal collection. The cabin's owners were apparently ready to get out of the exhibition business, and selling the cabin would avoid the shipping costs for getting it back to Mandan—if they were even considering shipping it back.

Forrester, who lived in a brownstone at 382 Degraw Street, proposed to his next-door neighbor that they take down the fence separating their backyards and place the cabin there. If that wasn't feasible, Forrester had in mind the park next to Brooklyn's Borough Hall—with the city aldermen's approval, that is. Where the cabin actually went after Forrester took possession, however, is a mystery. The commissioner died in 1906, and none of his obituaries mention him as the proud owner of Sitting Bull's last home. The cabin doesn't rest behind the brownstone at 382 Degraw Street today, nor is it in any park in Brooklyn. Cottonwood rots rather quickly if left unprotected in a humid environment, and the logs may have rotted away long ago, or perhaps they were cut up for firewood. But what of that door with the bullet holes? Was it saved and incorporated into a house somewhere? Might there be a piece of wood in Brooklyn that gives off a phosphorus hue at night?

In 1895, James McLaughlin was promoted to U.S. Indian inspector, a position that took him to reservations across the country, from Standing Rock to Round Valley, California. He would continue to serve as an inspector, under various titles, until his death twenty-eight years later. And in all that time, he never lost his hatred for

Sitting Bull, and he was loath to show any compassion for the chief's family as well. In 1907, William Sitting Bull (formerly Runs Away from Him) sought a transfer for himself, his wife and two children, and his mother from the Pine Ridge Agency, where they then resided, to Standing Rock. Sitting Bull's widows had gone to Pine Ridge with their children shortly after selling their cabin. According to Ernie LaPointe, the move was prompted by a spirit that appeared to Whole Tribe Seeing Her. The spirit said they must leave Standing Rock and the influence of Agent McLaughlin to "preserve the heritage and bloodline" of the chief.

William had done well the last few years touring with various Wild West shows. Why he wanted to return to the reservation he'd left as a child is unknown. But his request was forwarded to Indian inspector McLaughlin for an opinion, and the inspector certainly had one. Chief Sitting Bull's "attitude throughout his life was detrimental to the advancement of the Indians among whom he lived," wrote McLaughlin, "and should this son of his be transferred to Standing Rock Agency I am fearful that the former adherents of his father would make an effort to install him their leader, thereby fostering disaffection among the former followers of Sitting Bull who are now well disposed and steadily advancing in civilization. . . . I believe that it would be better for the Sitting Bull family and decidedly better for the Standing Rock Indians if William Sitting Bull be required to remain at Pine Ridge." The transfer request was denied.

In 1910, Houghton Mifflin Company published McLaughlin's memoir, titled *My Friend the Indian*. In it, he spewed the same old vitriol regarding Sitting Bull that he'd related in his reports to Washington and interviews with journalists. "Naturally, Major McLaughlin would not . . . praise the man who never sold the rights of his people for a mess of pottage," explained Frank Zahn, a government interpreter of Yanktonai heritage at Fort Yates.

"The Major would have been faithful to himself had he written another book entitled 'My Enemy Sitting Bull.'"

For whatever reason, another of McLaughlin's enemies, Caroline Weldon, failed to earn a mention in his book. When Sitting Bull's cabin was searched by Metal Breasts shortly after his death, three of Weldon's letters to the chief were found, as well as some random penciled notes she'd left behind. Sitting Bull received lots of correspondence, but no other papers are mentioned. These letters he saved.

Caroline's reaction to the news of Sitting Bull's violent end is unknown. In fact, she's something of an enigma once she returned to Brooklyn. One can't help but wonder if she visited Sitting Bull's cabin at Coney Island and thought back to the pleasant times she had there, when her darling boy Christie was still alive and before the Ghost Dance movement took hold of the chief's followers.

"No one in the world was as happy as I, and I wish that all might have shared that happiness," Weldon wrote of her time on the reservation. "A city seems a prison to me. One must work hard to get along in the city, and I enjoyed the freedom of the wilderness. I enjoyed the trees, and the hills, and the clouds. The flowers and the birds made me happy."

And yet, Weldon seems to have remained in the city for the rest of her days, never returning to her beloved Sioux country. Her name is missing from newspapers until her tragic death in 1921. Living alone at the time, her clothing caught fire from a candle and she quickly became engulfed in flames. By the time she managed to extinguish the fire, she'd suffered ghastly burns to her face and body. Caroline died less than ten hours later. At least two of her paintings of Sitting Bull have survived to the twenty-first century. The one vandalized at the time of Sitting Bull's death now hangs at the North Dakota State Museum, the long gash in its canvas bearing witness to that day's brutality.

Sitting Bull's former right-hand man, Chief Gall, of whom Custer's widow once said she'd never seen "as fine a specimen of a warrior," grew so fat he was unable to mount a horse. Nevertheless, he was one of McLaughlin's favorite progressives. "On all occasions [Gall] advises his people to adopt the white man's ways," commented an agency clerk, "and says that the Indians need never again resist the Government." And he was a Christian, too. In other words, Gall was Sitting Bull's exact opposite.

For Gall's loyalty during the Ghost Dance movement, Agent McLaughlin asked that he be allowed to purchase a wagon for the chief, seeing as how he could no longer ride horseback. Instead, a brand-new spring wagon made at the Carlisle Indian School was sent to Standing Rock. Gall didn't get to enjoy his new conveyance for long, however. He died in December 1894, just fifty-four years old.

Little Big Man, Crazy Horse's onetime ally, didn't get a wagon, but he did get a medal and a silver-headed cane from President Rutherford B. Hayes. The inscription on the medal's reverse read "A Token of Regard for Gallant Services Rendered to the Whites at the Death of Crazy Horse." The medal was almost certainly the doing of White Hat (Lieutenant Clark), who singled out Little Big Man for praise in his initial report on Crazy Horse's bungled arrest. Little Big Man wore the medal proudly. The Oglala also liked to show—"with great satisfaction"—the scar on his hand made by Crazy Horse's knife. He even boasted to whites that it was he who fatally stabbed the legendary chief—but only when none of his fellow Lakotas were around to hear. Little Big Man died in 1888, his cause of death unknown. His final resting place is an unmarked grave in the Holy Cross Cemetery on the Pine Ridge Reservation.

Had Little Big Man lived longer, he may have enjoyed the same undeserved celebrity bestowed upon Red Tomahawk. As the years passed, Red Tomahawk took more and more credit for the killing of Sitting Bull, eventually claiming it was he who fired both shots into the chief with his revolver, with no bullet coming from Bull Head's gun. Newspapers seldom questioned Red Tomahawk's version; it made a better story if they could refer to the old Lakota as "the man who killed Sitting Bull." As a result, Red Tomahawk would eventually have audiences with three presidents, Theodore Roosevelt and Woodrow Wilson when they visited Bismarck in 1903 and 1919, respectively, and at the White House with Herbert Hoover in 1929.

Both the press and the public couldn't get enough of Red Tomahawk during his trip east in 1929, which was actually more like a grand tour. His many stops included the Tomb of the Unknown Soldier (where he placed a warbonnet), Mount Vernon, Valley Forge, Philadelphia, and the Atlantic City Boardwalk. Whirring newsreel cameras followed him everywhere. So, too, large crowds curious to see the slayer of the slayer of Custer and his men. In Washington alone, Red Tomahawk was said to have shaken hands with as many as four thousand people. And seldom did a stop not come with a lavish reception or banquet.

Sitting Bull was Red Tomahawk's claim to fame, his identity, but there was one thing about the dead chief he wanted nothing to do with: the Fort Yates grave site. When an interviewer once asked to be shown the holy man's final resting place, Red Tomahawk refused. He said he was afraid to go there. "There are mysterious flowers upon his grave every year," explained Red Tomahawk. "We do not know where they come from. They are *wakan*." Red Tomahawk died in 1931, and his passing was duly noted by the nation's press.

Frank Grouard also had plenty of stories to tell in his later years. And in what should hardly come as a surprise, some of those stories fell far short of the truth. In 1891, a Wyoming newspaperman named Joe DeBarthe arranged with Grouard to write and publish the scout's biography. The book was printed three years later in St. Joseph, Missouri, under the title *The Life and Adventures of Frank Grouard, Chief of Scouts, U.S. A.* Nowhere in the 545-page tome (a result of some padding by DeBarthe) does Grouard reflect on his betrayal of the antitreaty bands, although he does mention more than once the money he made by cooperating with the whites.

While overseeing the book's production with DeBarthe in St. Joseph, Frank fell in love with the sister of the book's printer. They married in the spring of 1895, and Frank subsequently split his time between Wyoming and Missouri. Whether Frank ever informed his Missouri wife of his two (some say three) marriages in Sioux country is unknown, but they certainly aren't to be found among the "life and adventures" in his book.

At the outbreak of the Spanish-American War in 1898, Grouard made headlines when he proposed to lead several hundred Lakotas against the Spaniards. "They are ready to go to war with Spain at a moment's notice," Grouard told a correspondent. "They have no ties to bind them at home like the bravest and best of the white men. They would be glad of an opportunity to go to war, and, while their fighting is of a peculiar kind, it is effective in its way." The news story ended with the statement, "All the ill-feeling between the Sioux and Grouard has died out, and he will lead them if they go to war." "Died out" was quite literally true, as most of those who had reason to hate him, Crazy Horse and Sitting Bull especially, were dead.

Frank's life ended from complications from pneumonia in August 1905, at a St. Joseph hospital where he was a "charity patient." He'd been separated from his wife for a few years, and, as his classification at the hospital implies, he was broke. Friends pitched in to pay for his burial. His grave in Ashland Cemetery is marked with the standard government headstone for veterans. Except for a history buff or two, no one who visits the cemetery today has the slightest clue that it contains the remains of a man who played a singular role in the Lakota and Cheyenne peoples' loss of freedom.

Much more reliable when it came to telling the history of Crazy Horse, Sitting Bull, and the Plains Indians' struggle to preserve their homeland were the old warriors and the women who shared in that struggle. Crazy Horse's friend He Dog, his young cousin Black Elk, Sitting Bull's nephews White Bull and One Bull, and numerous others recounted their memories in interviews with historians and writers. Those interviews, many conducted in the late twenties and early thirties, are the bedrock upon which all modern scholarship on the Lakotas of the nineteenth century must be built.

It wasn't just the historians who had questions, though. Walter Campbell, who published under the pen name Stanley Vestal, conducted extensive interviews on the Standing Rock and Cheyenne River reservations as background for biographies of Sitting Bull and White Bull. Campbell recalled that the old warriors peppered him with questions about the "white man's motives. . . . Those old men wanted to know why the white men came against them; most of them had not the faintest idea what the wars were all about."

Those questions should have been easy for Campbell to answer. The Lakotas had what the white man wanted, and the white man took it—often by force. Even today, though, some writers have trouble comprehending just what was done to the Lakotas. In a recent history of the "Indian Wars," the author opines that the white conquest of the northern plains was actually "a displacement of one immigrant people by another, rather than the destruction of a deeply rooted way of life," which comes across as a white-centric justification for the taking of Lakota lands. Why this author doesn't consider the free will of the Plains Indians "deeply rooted" is also rather hard to understand.

It shouldn't be forgotten that the immigrant people, Euro-Americans, who displaced the Plains Indians always held themselves up as "civilized," as vastly superior to the Lakotas and other native tribes. And yet there was nothing civilized in the way the U.S. government, its Indian agents, and its citizens lied to and stole from the Lakotas. There was nothing civilized in the way the U.S. Army attacked Indian villages, killing and maiming women and children. There was nothing civilized in the deaths of Crazy Horse and Sitting Bull.

The Battle of the Little Big Horn—popularly known as Custer's Last Stand—is often viewed as the last stand of the free-roaming Plains Indians. The Ghost Dance can also be seen as a last stand, a resistance to reservation life, to being controlled by white men. But when it comes to justice for the Lakotas, there is no such thing as a last stand.

"We owned the Black Hills," the old warrior Iron Hawk told a newspaper reporter in 1948. "We still do, and I wish we had the power to get them back." Thirty-two years later, the U.S. Supreme Court agreed with Iron Hawk. In a landmark case known as *United States v. Sioux Nation of Indians,* the court affirmed that the Black Hills had been wrongfully taken from the Lakotas. The 1868 Fort Laramie Treaty plainly stated that land cessions required the signatures of three-fourths of all adult male Lakotas. The government had obtained only the signatures of chiefs and headmen when it took Lakota lands in 1877, and chiefs friendly to the government at that.

The Lakotas were awarded more than $100 million in 1980. That figure was based on the value of the land in 1877, the 1877 value of the gold stolen by miners from the Hills, and 5 percent interest per year for a century. But the worth of the Black Hills was much higher than that figure in 1980 and even more so today, to say nothing of the Hills' spiritual significance for the Lakotas. Like Iron Hawk, modern-day Lakotas want to get their sacred Black Hills back. They refuse to accept the payment, and it supposedly sits gathering interest in a Bureau of Indian Affairs account. With that interest accruing annually, the award has reportedly grown to nearly $2 billion.

Lakotas today live in some of the poorest places in the country, but as an Oglala leader explained in 2011, "If we accept the money, then we have no more of the treaty obligations that the federal government has with us for taking our land, for taking our gold, all our resources out of the Black Hills . . . we're poor now, we'll be poorer then when that happens."

The refusal of the money is also about honoring the many ancestors who lived and died defending Indian lands and culture. "I want you to hold these grounds," Sitting Bull once said to his people. "I want you to follow me. I want you to pledge yourselves to what I ask of you." Crazy Horse and Sitting Bull never signed a treaty. They resisted the white invaders to the end. If these great leaders were alive today, they would shout "Hou, Hou!" in approval of the words spoken by one Lakota man in regard to the effort to return the Black Hills; they are the words of a warrior: "We won the battle against Custer," he said, "but the war continues."

# ACKNOWLEDGMENTS

It's said that the spirit of Sitting Bull occasionally leaves the land of ghosts and visits Standing Rock, the Húnkpapa holy man's final home. He comes riding in on an elk spirit. As for Crazy Horse, some believe his "warrior power" never left Sioux country. In his 1972 book, the Miniconjou holy man John Lame Deer told of how this force or spirit could become volatile during certain ceremonies, breaking dishes and causing other damage. This Crazy Horse power, Lame Deer said, was "like two flintstones clashing."

In my own journeys through Lakota lands researching this book, I felt the presence of Crazy Horse's and Sitting Bull's spirits on many occasions. It was in the glow of the cottonwood leaves in the early-morning sunlight at Fort Robinson, in the wind as it danced with the tall grasses at the Rosebud and Little Big Horn, and in the calm stillness at Fetterman battlefield, where the *winkte* foretold the hundred in the hand. These places and others once intimately familiar to Crazy Horse and Sitting Bull remain little changed since the days when these two great leaders roamed the vastness of the High Plains, and I encourage you to visit them. You will understand even better why these Lakota chiefs fought so hard to keep what was theirs.

In addition to exploring Crazy Horse's and Sitting Bull's old haunts, I spent weeks researching in archives and museums, from Chicago's Newberry Library to Cody's Buffalo Bill Center of the West. I'm an independent author/historian, so these research trips were paid for out of my own pocket. I did apply for a grant of $994 from BYU's Charles Redd Center for Western Studies to cover the expense of a trip to BYU's Harold B. Lee Library. No one ever said, but I have to assume the folks at the Redd Center didn't feel my book project was very worthwhile, for I failed to get the grant. As luck would have it, though, I found the information I needed from the Lee Library elsewhere, thus saving me a long road trip through the mountains to Utah. Just thought I would mention that.

As with all my books, I conducted my own research for *The Earth Is All That Lasts*. A few scholars kindly shared information with me, but I don't hire researchers or assistants as some authors do, and not being a university professor, I don't have graduate students to press into service. Except for considerations of time, I've never really understood why an author would want someone else to do their research. It's the research—particularly the thrill of discovering new information—that's one of the most enjoyable parts of writing a book. And even though there are many top-notch professional researchers out there, I simply couldn't help but worry that someone working for me might accidentally overlook some enlightening nugget in a document or book.

Of course, the above doesn't mean I didn't have help—I had plenty. Among the many archivists, librarians, and curators who have my thanks are Julia Strunk, curatorial assistant, Denver Art Museum; Karen McWhorter, Scarlett Curator of Western American Art, Whitney Western Art Museum, Cody; Nicole Harrison, curatorial assistant, Whitney Western Art Museum; Lori J. Terrill, special collections librarian/archivist, Black Hills State University; Clint Pumphrey, curator, special collections and archives, Utah State University; Randy Kane, research associate, Museum of the Fur Trade; Elizabeth Cisar, Center for Western Studies, Augustana University; Kellen Cutsforth, archivist, Denver Public Library; Wade Popp, archives specialist, National Archives at Kansas City; Elizabeth Burnes, archivist, National Archives at Kansas City; Lori Cox-Paul, director of archival operations, National Archives at Kansas City; Josh Caster, Archives & Special Collections, University of Nebraska-Lincoln Libraries; Matthew T. Reitzel, manuscript/photo archivist, South Dakota State Historical Society; Ann B. Jenks, director, state archives, State Historical Society of North Dakota; Sarah Walker, North Dakota State Archives; Chris Cialdella, stacks coordinator, the Newberry Library; Mark J. Halvorson, curator of collections research, State Historical Society of North Dakota; and, finally, the helpful staff of the Interlibrary Loan Department, Pikes Peak Library District, Colorado Springs.

For countless kind favors—whether it was simply offering enthusiasm for the book, giving valuable time to answer a query, or providing important source material—I must thank Jeffrey Pearson, Chris Dixon, Vincent Heier, Ernie and Sonja LaPointe, Philip Burnham, Kingsley M. Bray, Lance J. Dorrel, James Hanson, Judy and Jerry Crandall, Mike Koury, Michael O'Keefe, Doug Ellison, Brian Naschel, Mark Fitzgerald, "Putt" Thompson, Brad Hamlett, Jerry Greene, Lisa Haight, James Mills, Roy B. Young, Kurt House, Richard Forry, Connie Dover, Gloria Ballton, all my followers on Instagram, and, last but not least, four old compadres with whom I've shared many fine adventures: Marc Simmons, Ron Kil, Rex Rideout, and Andy Morris.

My literary agent and good friend, Jim Donovan, sent me a big box of his research files from his landmark 2008 book on the Battle of the Little Big Horn, *A Terrible Glory*. It remains the definitive work on this iconic fight, not only because of his exhaustive use of far-flung primary sources but because the book is engagingly written with many a fresh insight.

Historians Paul Hedren and Eli Paul, both leading scholars of Indian–white relations on the Great Plains, have been keen on this book from the moment I told them it was to be my next writing project. Eli gave me excellent advice on archival collections and online resources to pursue, and Paul invited me to join his annual walking tour/march of the Rosebud battlefield, which I gladly accepted and survived. Paul's book *Rosebud, June 17, 1876* is the last word on the subject.

Paul and Eli gladly answered my numerous questions, and Paul graciously shared significant findings from his current book project, which is also set on the northern plains of the nineteenth century, on nearly a daily basis. On top of all this, Paul and Eli read my manuscript and provided thoughtful comments. So, too, did the Museum of the Fur Trade's Randy Kane. The insights of all three have made this a better book. It's nice to have friends, especially ones who know your book's subject inside out.

D. W. Groethe, a fine western poet and musician living in Bainville, Montana, grew up near the sites of Fort Buford and Fort Union. He spent a few hours with me at Fort Buford, sharing his rich memories of the place. D. W. recalled the community picnics held at the site when he was a kid and how he and other children would comb the area for artifacts. (Only a portion of the original Fort Buford grounds is a protected state historic site.) A short time after our visit, I received a small box in the mail from D. W. Imagine my surprise to find inside a cache of relics that included patinaed .45-70 shell casings, rusted square-cut nails, and fragments of glass and china. D. W. described them as "the final remnants of stories long ago told and lost in time." For me, they are a special reminder of a special day.

I'll also never forget my visit to the home of Larry Belitz outside Hot Springs, South Dakota. Larry is an expert on brain tanning and the making of Plains Indian hide tipis and has supplied museums and film companies with authentic reproductions. For most of a day, Larry showed me a collection of dozens of exquisitely crafted hide charms or protections, explaining to me the meaning of each little effigy. These charms had come from the family of Horn Chips, Crazy Horse's holy man, and according to the family, they were the ones Horn Chips made for the Oglala warrior. They'd been returned to Horn Chips after Crazy Horse's death. The collection is now owned by the Crazy Horse Memorial, near Custer, South Dakota.

This book took me a good five years to research and write, the longest of any of my books. Sadly, I lost a number of family and friends during that time whom I know would have been excited to see the finished product. These include my dad, Missouri logger C. W. Gardner; my mother-in-law, Mary Ann Davis, a revered local historian of Green Mountain Falls, Colorado; Nelda Forry, an old friend of Arrow Rock, Missouri, and a voracious reader; and my cousin, Tim Gardner, a history lover who raved about all my books. It's a strange world indeed to no longer have them in it.

Fortunately, I was often able to combine research trips with visits to my old Missouri stomping grounds. My uncle Curly Gardner of Pattonsburg, Missouri, always had a Model 12 Winchester and plenty of shotgun shells handy for the local trap shoot. And thanks to David Greenwood, Ivan Greenwood, Teri Gardner, and David Wayne Gardner, my son and I had some wonderful places to chase gobblers in the spring. My mom, Venita Gardner, made sure to have a bed or air mattress available whenever needed.

At HarperCollins, I have two primary editors to thank: Henry Ferris, the editor of my previous titles at William Morrow, and Peter Hubbard, my present editor at Mariner Books. Henry acquired *The Earth Is All That Lasts* for the William Morrow imprint, and when he left HarperCollins, Peter asked to take me on. Changing editors can be pretty worrisome for an author, but I'm pleased to say that Peter made the transition absolutely painless, and he and I were of the same mind on what this book should be. Others at HarperCollins to whom I owe thanks are assistant editor Molly Gendell, editor Nick Amphlett, senior production editor Dale Rohrbaugh, marketing director Andrea DeWerd, publicist Taryn Roeder, interior design director Lucy Albanese, and cover designer Mumtaz Mustafa. My copy editor, Laurie McGee, has been a lifesaver as usual. She's edited four of my books now, and there's a very good reason for that: her eagle eye and mastery of the very latest *Chicago Manual of Style* are simply unparalleled. My thanks to cartographer Jeffrey L. Ward for his beautiful map.

As always, I can't close without acknowledging my family: wife, Katie; daughter, Christiana, and her partner, Eric Hailey; and son, Vance. One of my greatest pleasures is bringing my family along on field trips to historic places. This book took us across the holy line to Canada, where we spent perfect days at Cypress Hills Interprovincial Park and Fort Walsh National Historic Site. At Fort Phil Kearny State Historic Site, near Banner, Wyoming, Vance and I made the long hike to the top of Pilot Hill, where soldiers manning a small picket post signaled the movements of Lakota and Cheyenne warriors threatening the daily wood train. And on my first visit to the Rosebud battlefield, Vance served as my cameraman, allowing me to take notes as Paul Hedren held forth on the intricacies of that swirling engagement.

I say to my family, then, that I'm deeply grateful for your love and support. And I apologize for all the times I had to skip or postpone a get-together with the words, "I have to work on my book." But, really, you should be well used to that by now.

Mark Lee Gardner
Ute Pass Wagon Road
Cascade, Colorado

# AMERICAN INDIAN INFORMANTS

*If the white historians were half as careful in their statements as these Indians, history would be a nobler thing.*

WALTER CAMPBELL (STANLEY VESTAL), STANDING
ROCK RESERVATION, SEPTEMBER 6, 1929

In researching and writing this book, I consulted dozens of interviews (i.e., oral histories) of Indian contemporaries of Crazy Horse and Sitting Bull, both published and unpublished, as well as the known words and sayings of the two Lakota leaders themselves. The interviews were conducted, transcribed, and preserved over many years by a number of farsighted and dedicated men and women, including Walter Mason Camp, Eli Ricker, Thomas Marquis, Walter Campbell, John G. Neihardt, James R. Walker, E. A. Brininstool, Eleanor Hinman, Mari Sandoz, and David Humphreys Miller, among others. A very few accounts were written and preserved by the Lakotas themselves, Josephine Waggoner being a prime example. These first-person accounts are fully cited in my endnotes. However, because not every reader consults a book's endnotes, and because many of the informants' names do not appear in my main narrative, I am recognizing those individuals again here. I have also included informants who, though living after the time of Crazy Horse and Sitting Bull, had knowledge of these men and their times passed down through tribal elders and/or family members.

## Brulé

Hollow Horn Bear
Susan Bordeaux Bettelyoun
William J. Bordeaux
Bear Stands Up
Short Bull

## Húnkpapa

Sitting Bull
Circling Hawk
Gall
Gray Eagle
Grover Eagle Boy
Four Horns
Four Robes
Her Eagle Robe (Mary Crawler)
Little Soldier
Crow King
Pretty White Buffalo Woman
Josephine Waggoner
Ernie LaPointe
Old Bull
One Bull
Scarlet Whirlwind Woman (Mrs. One Bull)
Shoots Walking
Otter Robe
Rain in the Face
One Elk
Two Bull
White Bird

## Miniconjou

White Bull
Dewey Beard (Iron Hail)
Iron Thunder
Standing Bear
Eagle Shield
Swelled Face

## Oglala

Crazy Horse
Red Feather
William "Billy" Garnett
He Alone Is a Man
Frank Kicking Bear
Luther Standing Bear
He Dog
Iron Hawk
Iron Horse
Eagle Hawk
Little Wound
Low Dog
Mathew H. King
Horn Chips
Eagle Elk
Mark Spider
Black Elk
Fire Thunder
Wide Road
Chasing Hawk
Flying Hawk
Joseph White Cow Bull

John No Ears
Short Bull
Little Killer
They Fear Even His Horses
Thomas Tyon
Rocky Bear
Thunder Bear
Frank Kicking Bear
Red Sack
Red Hawk
Victoria Conroy

## Santee

Charles A. Eastman

## Sihásapa

Crawler
Red Tomahawk

## Two Kettle

Runs the Enemy
Eagle Woman That All Look At
   (Matilda Galpin)

## Yanktonai

Bear's Ghost
Francis Benjamin "Frank" Zahn

## Northern Cheyenne

John Stands in Timber
Young Two Moons
Two Moons
Wooden Leg
James Tangled Yellow Hair
Little Hawk
White Elk

## Southern Cheyenne

Antelope Woman (Kate Bighead)
George Bent

## Cheyenne River Sioux

Little Wounded

## Arickara

Red Star

## Tribal Affiliation Uncertain

Shot in the Face
Iron Bull

# NOTES

## Abbreviations

CC:      Walter Stanley Campbell Collection, University of Oklahoma, Western History Collections

NA:      National Archives documents accessed at https://catalog.archives .gov

NA-KC:  National Archives at Kansas City, Missouri

RG 75:  Record Group 75, Records of the Bureau of Indian Affairs, 1793–1999


## 1 / Hóka Hé!

I    *"A charger, he is coming"*: Raymond J. DeMallie, ed., *The Sixth Grandfather: Black Elk's Teachings Given to John G. Neihardt* (Lincoln: University of Nebraska Press, 1984), 198.

I    *Sitting Bull carefully dressed:* Sitting Bull's offering was related by One Bull, a nephew of Sitting Bull, to Robert Higheagle. See Robert Higheagle, "Twenty-Five Songs Made by Sitting Bull," typescript in CC, box 104, folder 18. An example of a Lakota offering stick was collected by Frances Densmore on the Standing Rock Reservation in the early 1900s. It's part of the collections of the National Museum of the American Indian, Washington, D.C., catalog number 6/7988.

I    *about five feet, ten inches tall:* The estimate of Sitting Bull's height is from the *New York Herald* journalist James Creelman, who met Sitting Bull at Fort Randall in 1881. His report of that encounter is reprinted in the *Abbeville Press and Banner,* Abbeville, SC, November 30, 1881. Artist De Cost Smith, who got to know Sitting Bull well at Standing Rock, described him as "above middle height." De Cost Smith, *Red Indian Experiences* (London: George Allen & Unwin Ltd., 1949), 184.

1  *walked with a slight limp:* One Bull interview, CC, box 104, folder 11; and Circling Hawk interview, CC, box 105, folder 13.

2  *more than five thousand souls:* The size of the Indian village on the Little Big Horn in June 1876 has captured the attention of scholars for decades, with some estimates as high as 15,000 people! In recent years, numbers have been revised down to more conservative estimates, actually falling in line with the careful analysis made by famed Santee (Eastern Sioux) author Charles A. Eastman 120 years ago. See his "The Story of the Little Big Horn (Told from the Indian standpoint by one of their race)," *The Chautauquan* 31 (July 1900): 354, and his letter of September 30, 1914, in Warren K. Moorehead, *The American Indian in the United States, Period 1850–1914* (Andover, MA: The Andover Press, 1914), 199. In an interview with Major Marcus A. Reno in 1885, Sitting Bull and his interpreter came up with an estimate of more than seven hundred lodges and between five and six thousand people in the village. "Questioning Sitting Bull About Custer's Defeat," *Wheeling Sunday Register*, WV, June 28, 1885. See also Gregory F. Michno, *Lakota Noon: The Indian Narrative of Custer's Defeat* (Missoula, MT: Mountain Press Publishing Company, 1997), 4–20.

2  *"Great Spirit, pity me":* As quoted by One Bull in Higheagle, "Twenty-Five Songs Made by Sitting Bull," CC. For additional descriptions of Sitting Bull's offering, see Ernie LaPointe, *Sitting Bull: His Life and Legacy* (Salt Lake City: Gibbs Smith, 2009), 67; One Bull interview, David Humphreys Miller, "Echoes of the Little Bighorn," *American Heritage* 22 (June 1971): 30; and Stanley Vestal, *Sitting Bull: Champion of the Sioux* (Norman: University of Oklahoma Press, 1957), 158.

3  *"where the girl saved her brother":* John Stands in Timber and Margot Liberty, *A Cheyenne Voice: The Complete John Stands in Timber Interviews* (Norman: University of Oklahoma Press, 2013), 422.

3  *Crazy Horse urged them on:* David Humphreys Miller, *Ghost Dance* (New York: Duell, Sloan and Pearce, 1959), 289.

4  *Box Elder had the gift:* Peter J. Powell, *Sweet Medicine: The Continuing Role of the Sacred Arrows, the Sun Dance, and the Sacred Buffalo Hat in Northern Cheyenne History*, 2 vols. (Norman: University of Oklahoma Press, 1998), 1: 94.

4  *disturbed by a dream:* Young Two Moons interview, CC, box 105, folder 15.

4  *"We had driven away the soldiers":* Thomas B. Marquis, interpreter, *A Warrior Who Fought Custer* (Minneapolis: The Midwest Company, 1931), 214.

4  *sitting on the banks fishing:* Thomas B. Marquis, interpreter, *She Watched Custer's Last Battle* (1933; reprint: Scottsdale, AZ: Cactus Pony, c. 1969), 2.

4  *women were out digging turnips:* Dewey Beard interview, Miller, "Echoes of the Little Bighorn," 38.

4  *village would be moving soon:* Marquis, *She Watched Custer's Last Battle*, 2.

5  *Iron Hail:* In later years, Iron Hail would go by the name Dewey Beard. See Philip Burnham, *Song of Dewey Beard: Last Survivor of the Little Bighorn* (Lincoln: University of Nebraska Press, 2014).

5  *"When you finish eating":* Beard interview, Miller, "Echoes of the Little Bighorn," 38.

5   *the wind carried messages:* Luther Standing Bear, *Land of the Spotted Eagle* (Boston: Houghton Mifflin Company, 1933), 50.

5   *"Soldiers are here!":* Marquis, *A Warrior Who Fought Custer,* 217.

5   *women and children struggled to catch:* Low Dog and Iron Thunder interviews in *Jamestown Alert,* Jamestown, ND, August 19, 1881; and Gall interview in the *Republican Journal,* Belfast, ME, June 24, 1897.

6   *old clothes exchanged for fancy dress:* Marquis, *A Warrior Who Fought Custer,* 218.

6   *grabbed his trade gun:* One Bull interview, Miller, "Echoes of the Little Bighorn," 30–31.

6   *shield held tremendous significance:* Sitting Bull's shield is well documented, including its depiction in drawings made by Sitting Bull illustrating his warrior exploits. See One Bull interviews, CC, box 104, folder 11, and box 105, folder 19; Stanley Vestal, *New Sources of Indian History, 1850–1891* (Norman: University of Oklahoma Press, 1934), 154–55; and Four Horns drawings (copies of autobiographical drawings made by Sitting Bull), Manuscript 1929A, National Anthropological Archives, Smithsonian Institution (available for online viewing here: https://learninglab.si.edu/search?st=Four%20Horns).

6   *"Go right ahead":* One Bull interview, CC, box 105, folder 19. In his interview with David Humphreys Miller, One Bull claimed that Sitting Bull instructed him to meet the attacking soldiers and "parley with them, if you can. If they are willing, tell them I will talk peace with them." This is highly unlikely. For one thing, it was clear that the village was already under attack, and it was just as clear that the Lakotas and the U.S. Army were presently at war—the Lakotas had attacked General George Crook's army on the Rosebud eight days earlier. The Long Knives were not on the Greasy Grass to make peace, which would have been quite obvious to Sitting Bull. See Miller, "Echoes of the Little Bighorn," 31.

6   *left to find his aged mother:* One Bull interview, Miller, "Echoes of the Little Bighorn," 31.

6   *"old man chief":* Marquis, *A Warrior Who Fought Custer,* 57 and 211; and James Tangled Yellow Hair interview in Ronald H. Limbaugh, ed., *Cheyenne and Sioux: The Reminiscences of Four Indians and a White Soldier* (Stockton, CA: Pacific Center for Western Historical Studies, 1973), 45. Crow King, one of Sitting Bull's lieutenants, said, "Sitting Bull did not himself fight, but he gave orders." *Jamestown Alert,* August 19, 1881. One Bull also remembered his uncle "telling his men what to do" during the battle. One Bull interview, Charles Edmund DeLand, "The Sioux Wars," *South Dakota Historical Collections* 15 (1930): 653.

7   *"Brave up, boys":* White Bull interview, CC, box 105, folder 24.

7   *many warriors flocked to him:* One Bull interview, Miller, "Echoes of the Little Bighorn," 31.

7   *sang to the shield:* One Bull interview, CC, box 105, folder 19.

7   *"I am Two Moons":* Hamlin Garland, "General Custer's Last Fight as Seen by Two Moon[s]," *McClure's Magazine* 11 (September 1898): 446. The Northern Cheyenne chief's name is sometimes given as "Two Moon." However, most contemporary newspaper accounts, including his 1917 obituary, use "Two Moons." His fellow Cheyennes knew him as Ree Roman Nose. "Two Moons, Greatest Indian Survivor of Custer Battle, Dies," *The Billings Gazette,*

MT, May 19, 1917; and James C. Clifford to Olin D. Wheeler, Tongue River Agency, MT, October 17, 1901, Olin Dunbar Wheeler Papers, 1892–1924, The Newberry, Chicago, Illinois.

7  *air was so full of dust:* Marquis, *A Warrior Who Fought Custer,* 219.

7  *impatient warriors:* Standing Bear interview, Kenneth Hammer, ed., *Custer in '76: Walter Camp's Notes on the Custer Fight* (Provo, UT: Brigham Young University Press, 1976), 215.

7  *a warrior was also meant to suffer:* Robert Higheagle manuscript, CC, box 104, folder 22.

7  *Horn Chips, a legendary holy man:* See William K. Powers, *Yuwipi: Vision and Experience in Oglala Ritual* (Lincoln: University of Nebraska Press, 1982), 90–95.

8  *A "Stone Dreamer":* Standing Bear, *Land of the Spotted Eagle,* 208; and ibid., 91–92.

8  *a black stone:* He Dog interview with Mari Sandoz and John Colhoff, June 30, 1931, Mari Sandoz Collection (MS 0080), Archives & Special Collections, University of Nebraska-Lincoln Libraries. See also He Dog's description of Crazy Horse's medicine in Eleanor Hinman, *The Eleanor H. Hinman Interviews on the Life and Death of Crazy Horse,* edited by John M. Carroll (New Brunswick, NJ: The Gary Owen Press, 1976), 23. John G. Bourke wrote in his diary that Crazy Horse "wears a charm, made of a piece of white rock." However, Bourke probably obtained this information from Frank Grouard and certainly not from personal observation. See John Gregory Bourke, *The Diaries of John Gregory Bourke,* ed. Charles M. Robinson III, vol. 2 (Denton: University of North Texas Press, 2005), 212.

8  *never to wear a warbonnet:* Horn Chips and William Garnett interviews, *Voices of the American West,* 2 vols., *The Settler and Soldier Interviews of Eli S. Ricker, 1903–1919* (vol. 1), and *The Indian Interviews of Eli S. Ricker, 1903–1919* (vol. 2) (Lincoln: University of Nebraska Press, 2005), 1: 277 and 117, respectively.

8  *Crazy Horse drew a zigzag line:* Horn Chips interview, Jensen, *Voices of the American West,* 1: 274. White Bull, a nephew of Sitting Bull, stated that Crazy Horse painted his face with white dots before a fight, but neither Horn Chips, Crazy Horse's holy man, nor He Dog, who was a close friend of Crazy Horse, mention this detail when describing how Crazy Horse prepared himself for battle. And Eagle Elk, a cousin of Crazy Horse, told John G. Neihardt that Crazy Horse "did not paint" himself when preparing for a fight. See White Bull account in Vestal, *New Sources,* 320; and Eagle Elk interview, 1944, John G. Neihardt Papers (C3716), The State Historical Society of Missouri Research Center-Columbia. The white dots mentioned by White Bull represented hail. See Helen Blish notes on the Thunder Cult, Sandoz Collection.

8  *lightning of the Thunder Beings:* Mathew H. King interview, Edward Kadlecek and Mabell Kadlecek, *To Kill an Eagle: Indian Views on the Last Days of Crazy Horse* (Boulder, CO: Johnson Books, 1981), 126.

8  *spotted eagle's dried heart:* Horn Chips interview, Jensen, *Voices of the American West,* 1: 277.

8  *medicine for Crazy Horse's pony:* Ibid., 274.

8  *dirt of a gopher hill:* William Garnett interview, *Voices of the American West,* 1:

117; and Eagle Elk interview, Neihardt Papers. Mark Spider, a Lakota veteran of the Little Big Horn, stated in 1936 that Crazy Horse also sprinkled this dirt on about ten of the younger warriors with him. See Joseph G. Masters, *Shadows Fall Across the Little Horn* (Laramie: University of Wyoming Library, 1951), 41.

8    ***no bullet could touch him:*** Horn Chips interview, *Voices of the American West,* 1: 277; and Dewey Beard (Iron Hail), "Dewey Beard: The Last Survivor," interview typescript (1955), in *Black Hills Nuggets, Commemorative Edition, 1776-1876-1976* (Rapid City, SD: The Rapid City Society for Genealogical Research, Inc., 1975), 19.

8    ***white-faced pony:*** Black Elk interview, *The Sixth Grandfather,* 182.

8    ***Just under six feet tall:*** White Bull stated that Crazy Horse was just about his own height, which was five feet, ten inches when White Bull was in his eighties. Short Bull, who also knew Crazy Horse, said the famed warrior was "a trifle under six feet tall." See Walter S. Campbell to Eleanor Hinman, Norman, OK, October 13, 1932, CC, box 117; and Short Bull interview, *Hinman Interviews,* 43.

9    ***eight horses shot out:*** Red Feather interview, *Hinman Interviews,* 36; and Standing Bear, *Land of the Spotted Eagle,* 180.

9    ***The battle had commenced:*** The three companies—A, G, and M—formed a battalion of the Seventh U.S. Cavalry under the command of Major Marcus Reno. Reno's commanding officer, was, of course, Lieutenant Colonel George Armstrong Custer. There are numerous histories of the Battle of the Little Big Horn, but see James Donovan's masterful *A Terrible Glory: Custer and the Little Bighorn—The Last Great Battle of the American West* (New York: Little, Brown and Company, 2008), and my *Little Bighorn Battlefield National Monument* (Tucson: Western National Parks Association, 2005).

9    ***shot down ten women and children:*** Richard G. Hardorff, *Hokahey! A Good Day to Die! The Indian Casualties of the Custer Fight* (Spokane, WA: The Arthur H. Clark Company, 1993), 34–35.

9    ***formed a skirmish line:*** Garland, "General Custer's Last Fight," 446.

9    ***"Crazy Horse is coming!":*** Black Elk interview, *The Sixth Grandfather,* 182.

10   ***"Here are the soldiers":*** Nick Ruleau interview, Jensen, *Voices of the American West,* 1: 312. Ruleau, an interpreter at Pine Ridge, stated that he got his information on the valley fight from Lakotas Red Hawk, Shot in the Face, Big Road, and Iron Bull.

10   ***At that same moment:*** He Dog interview, Hammer, ed., *Custer in '76,* 206.

10   ***resembled buffalo fleeing:*** Two Moons interview, Garland, "General Custer's Last Fight," 446.

10   ***a soldier riding a sorrel horse:*** Red Hawk interview with Edmond S. Meany, July 19, 1907, Meany Papers, 1877–1935, University of Washington Libraries, Special Collections, transcription at http://amertribes.proboards.com /thread/803/red-hawk#ixzz4YM9nyPRN. In his account of the Little Big Horn battle, Red Hawk starts with this incident, which suggests that it occurred in the valley against one of Reno's men. His mention of the trooper's sorrel horse supports this supposition, as only three companies of the Seventh

were mounted on sorrel horses. One of these, Company G, was part of Reno's battalion. Lawrence A. Frost, *General Custer's Thoroughbreds: Racing, Riding, Hunting, and Fighting* (Mattituck, NY: J. M. Carroll & Co. 1986), 251.

11 **pulling troopers off their floundering mounts:** M. I. McCreight, *Chief Flying Hawk's Tales: The True Story of Custer's Last Fight as Told by Chief Flying Hawk* (New York: The Alliance Press, 1936), 27–28. Flying Hawk and Kicking Bear were brothers.

11 **"We killed many":** One Bull interview, Miller, "Echoes of the Little Bighorn," 31.

11 **grass was set on fire:** Eagle Elk interview, Neihardt Papers.

11 **"Lots of Indians were hunting":** Marquis, *A Warrior Who Fought Custer,* 224–25.

12 **"Boy, get off":** Black Elk interview, *The Sixth Grandfather,* 183.

12 **"After I did this":** Ibid.

12 **"Would you see me":** Ibid.

12 **named Her Eagle Robe:** In later years, she was known as Mary Crawler. See her interviews in the Joseph G. Masters Collection, Kansas Historical Society, Topeka; and Richard G. Hardorff, ed., *Lakota Recollections of the Custer Fight: New Sources of Indian-Military History* (Spokane, WA: The Arthur H. Clark Company, 1991), 91–96.

13 **bullet-riddled horse:** Runs the Enemy interview, Joseph K. Dixon, *The Vanishing Race: The Last Great Indian Council* (Garden City, NY: Doubleday, Page & Company, 1913), 173.

13 **knew him by the name Teat:** Teat's English name was Isaiah Dorman. For a biographical sketch, see Kenneth Hammer, *Men with Custer: Biographies of the 7th Cavalry,* ed. Ronald H. Nichols (Hardin, MT: Custer Battlefield Historical and Museum Association, Inc., 1995), 92–93.

13 **oozing from his chest:** Bear's Ghost interview, CC, box 104, folder 4. Bear's Ghost claimed that Sitting Bull approached the Black man, recognized him as a friend, and ordered that he not be harmed. Not only this, but Bear's Ghost also said that Sitting Bull gave the dying man a drink of water. However, Sitting Bull was never on this part of the field. Bear's Ghost also claimed that the thoroughbred ridden by George Custer during the Little Big Horn fight, Vic, had been sold to Custer by Bear's Ghost! Clearly, Bear's Ghost is not the most reliable informant.

13 **"Do not kill me":** Eagle Elk interview, Neihardt Papers.

13 **with stone clubs:** George Herendeen interview, Hammer, ed., *Custer in '76,* 223.

13 **shooting arrows into the body:** Hammer, *Men with Custer,* 93. This form of counting coup is referenced in Henry B. Carrington, *The Indian Question* (1884; reprint: New York: Sol Lewis, 1973), 19–20. See also William Philo Clark, *The Indian Sign Language* (Philadelphia: L. R. Hamersly & Co., 1885), 128–29.

13 **penis cut off:** Hardorff, ed., *Lakota Recollections,* 102 n. 7. In an interview with a newspaper correspondent shortly after the battle, George Herendeen, a scout, said he was convinced Isaiah Dorman had been tortured before he was killed. Dorman had "small pistol balls in his legs from the knees down, and I believe they were shot into him while alive." See "Narrative of a Scout," *The New York Herald,* July 8, 1876.

13  *retrieve possessions and food:* Marquis, *A Warrior Who Fought Custer*, 227; and Two Moons interview, Jensen, *Voices of the American West*, 1: 322.
13  *"Other soldiers are coming!":* Marquis, *She Watched Custer's Last Battle*, 3.
14  *Two companies of cavalry:* These were Companies E and F of the Seventh, and the large, dry gulch is today known as Medicine Tail Coulee.
14  *to encircle the village:* Pretty White Buffalo Woman interview, James McLaughlin, *My Friend the Indian* (Boston: Houghton, Mifflin Company, 1926), 171; and Young Two Moons interview, CC, box 105, folder 15.
14  *they were now in danger:* Iron Thunder interview, *Jamestown Alert*, August 19, 1881.
14  *knocking as many as three:* Joseph White Cow Bull interview, Miller, "Echoes of the Little Bighorn," 33.
14  *"It appeared there would be no end":* Marquis, *She Watched Custer's Last Battle*, 3. Antelope Woman was later known to whites as Kate Bighead.
14  *"You have been brave":* Marquis, *A Warrior Who Fought Custer*, 227–28.
15  *Leading a group of Oglalas and Cheyennes:* Pretty White Buffalo Woman interview, McLaughlin, *My Friend the Indian*, 174; and Gall interview, Usher L. Burdick, ed., *David F. Barry's Indian Notes on "The Custer Battle"* (Baltimore: Wirth Brothers, 1949), 25–27.
15  *"No good soldiers":* McCreight, *Chief Flying Hawk's Tales*, 30.
15  *reins to Flying Hawk:* Ibid., 28.
16  *"The bullets flew past":* Chasing Hawk interview, Elmo Scott Watson, "Stirring War Tales Told in the Soft Syllables of Ogallalas by Big Chief," *The Colorado Springs Gazette*, August 13, 1922.
16  *shoot from the ground:* He Dog interview, *Hinman Interviews*, 25.
16  *shot several rounds:* McCreight, *Chief Flying Hawk's Tales*, 28.
16  *stuck in their rumps:* Marquis, *A Warrior Who Fought Custer*, 230.
16  *aim for the horse holders:* Valentine McGillycuddy, "That 'Suicide' of Gen. George A. Custer, U.S. Army," typescript, Elmo Scott Watson Papers, The Newberry; and Gall interview, Burdick, ed., *David F. Barry's Indian Notes*, 27.
16  *waved blankets and yelled:* Gall interview, *The Republican Journal*, June 24, 1897.
16  *"brave songs":* Standing Bear, *Land of the Spotted Eagle*, 217.
16  *"It is a good day to fight":* As quoted in McGillycuddy, "That 'Suicide' of Gen. George A. Custer."
17  *"He rode closest":* Waterman interview, Col. W. A. Graham, *The Custer Myth: A Source Book of Custeriana* (Harrisburg, PA: The Stackpole Company, 1953), 110.
17  *known to the Lakotas as a "bravery run":* Also called a "brave-heart run."
17  *through the gauntlet:* Crazy Horse's ride through the soldiers took place in the middle of what is now known as Battle Ridge. The troopers were men from Captain Miles Keogh's Company I, as well as men from Companies L and C, who'd fled north from "Calhoun Hill" moments before when those companies collapsed under the assault of overwhelming numbers of warriors. For specific warrior references to Crazy Horse's daring bravery run, see He Dog interview, Hammer, ed., *Custer in '76*, 207; Red Feather interview, Hardorff, ed., *Lakota Recollections of the Custer Fight*, 87–88; Mark Spider interview, Masters, *Shadows Fall Across the Little Horn*, 41–42; and White Bull interview,

CC, box 105, folder 24. White Bull told Walter Campbell (Stanley Vestal) that Crazy Horse charged through the "infantry" and that White Bull followed him. He would tell a different and more elaborate tale to David Humphreys Miller in 1939. In this latter interview, reportedly conducted through Indian sign language, White Bull claimed he dared Crazy Horse to make a charge at the soldiers but Crazy Horse refused. Additionally, White Bull said he made a bravery run through the troopers—twice. And last but not least, he took the credit for killing Custer. I find this version of White Bull's experiences in the battle highly questionable. See Joseph White Bull interview, Miller, "Echoes of the Little Bighorn," 35–36.

## 2 / Becoming Warriors

19    *"Son, I never want to see"*: Standing Bear, *Land of the Spotted Eagle*, 40.

19    *a series of colorful drawings:* These drawings are split among three institutions: the Buffalo Bill Center of the West, Cody, Wyoming; the Niles History Center, Niles, Michigan; and the National Anthropological Archives, Smithsonian Institution, Washington, D.C. Another set of forty autobiographical drawings was created by Sitting Bull sometime prior to 1870. They were last in the possession of Sitting Bull's adopted brother, Jumping Bull, but are now lost. However, Sitting Bull's uncle, Four Horns, made at least two sets of copies. The only known surviving set of copies is in the National Anthropological Archives. See the excellent articles by Ron McCoy: "Sitting Bull: A Hunkpapa Lakota Chronicles His Life of Dauntless Courage," *American Indian Art Magazine* 40 (Winter 2014): 34–45; and "Four Horns: A Hunkpapa Lakota Warrior-Artist Commemorates His Relative's Valor," *American Indian Art Magazine* 39 (Spring 2014): 42–51.

19    *depictions of white victims:* Although Sitting Bull did not create drawings depicting violence against whites while a prisoner at Fort Randall, the drawings he made prior to 1870—at a time when he and his people lived free on the northern plains—do show several violent encounters with white soldiers and civilians. At Fort Randall, in December 1881, Sitting Bull was shown the Four Horns set of copies mentioned above, and he "immediately recognized the pictures as scenes from his early life." When asked to elaborate on the specific events depicted, however, Sitting Bull wasn't particularly forthcoming, especially when it came to those drawings that showed Sitting Bull killing or counting coup on whites. A Presbyterian missionary who assisted with the interview of Sitting Bull about the drawings wrote, "We could see that any mention he gave of the several events was colored by the circumstances of his present situation." John P. Williamson to Col. George L. Andrews, Fort Randall, Dakota Territory, December 12, 1881, Manuscript 1929A, National Anthropological Archives, Smithsonian Institution, Washington, D.C.

20    *settled on 1831, possibly in March:* See LaPointe, *Sitting Bull*, 21; Vestal, *Sitting Bull*, 3; Robert M. Utley, *The Lance and the Shield: The Life and Times of Sitting Bull* (New York: Henry Holt and Company, 1993), 335 n. 2; and White Bull interview, CC, box 105, folder 4.

20  *"I don't know where I was born":* "A Chat with the Chief," *The Omaha Daily Bee,* Omaha, NE, August 9, 1881, quoting the *St. Paul Pioneer Press.*

20  *born at a camp on Willow Creek:* Ibid.; and E. H. Allison, "Sitting Bull's Birthplace," *South Dakota Historical Collections* 6 (1912): 271.

20  *a pictograph showing two wagons:* Candace S. Greene and Russell Thornton, eds., *The Year the Stars Fell: Lakota Winter Counts at the Smithsonian* (Lincoln: University of Nebraska Press, 2007), 188.

21  *several tons of gunpowder and lead:* Lonis Wendt, "Fort Pierre Looking Back 200 Years—the 1830s," *Capital Journal,* Pierre, SD, November 18, 2016.

21  *a thousand gallons of whiskey:* Donald Jackson, *Voyages of the Steamboat* Yellow Stone (New York: Ticknor & Fields, 1985), 2.

21  *forbidden by law:* Francis Paul Prucha, *The Great Father: The United States Government and the American Indians* (Lincoln: University of Nebraska Press, 1995), 100–101. In 1832, a new law strictly forbade the introduction of alcohol into Indian country with no exceptions. The fur companies then resorted to smuggling whiskey to their posts.

21  *ten thousand pounds of salted buffalo tongues:* Daily National Intelligencer, Washington, D.C., August 1, 1831.

22  *a particularly shocking instance:* George Catlin, *Letters and Notes on the Manners, Customs, and Conditions of the North American Indians,* 2 vols. (1844; reprint: New York: Dover Publications Inc., 1973), 1: 256. Catlin accurately predicted the demise of the buffalo from the excesses of the robe trade, faulting both the Indians and the white traders who enticed them with goods and alcohol.

22  *When a man killed a buffalo:* John No Ears interview, James R. Walker Collection, History Colorado, Denver, reel 4, frame 358.

22  *A gift to the Lakotas:* Short Bull interview, James R. Walker, *Lakota Belief and Ritual,* edited by Raymond J. DeMallie and Elaine A. Jahner (Lincoln: University of Nebraska Press, 1991).

22  *"is ruled by his senses":* Black Elk, *The Sacred Pipe: Black Elk's Account of the Seven Rites of the Oglala Sioux,* recorded and edited by Joseph Epes Brown (Norman: University of Oklahoma Press, 1989), 7 n. 10.

23  *"There is no tribe on the Continent":* Catlin, *Letters and Notes,* 1: 210.

23  *"very fine and prepossessing":* Ibid., 1: 208.

23  *bow and arrow was easier:* White Bull interview, CC, box 105, folder 8. One Bull told Walter Campbell that he took ten arrows when buffalo hunting. It was "hard to get arrows, so when One Bull killed, would jump off horse and get them to shoot again." One Bull interview, CC, box 104, folder 6.

23  *"Life and activity everywhere":* Stephen S. Witte and Marsha V. Gallagher, eds., *The North American Journals of Prince Maximilian of Wied,* 3 vols. (Norman: University of Oklahoma Press, 2008–2012), 2: 142.

24  *"They have to do all the work":* Ibid., 2: 159.

24  *"They were mostly strong":* Ibid., 2: 193.

25  *Bodmer sketched in watercolor:* See David C. Hunt and Marsha V. Gallagher, eds., *Karl Bodmer's America* (N.p.: Joslyn Art Museum and University of Nebraska Press, 1984).

25  *"Forsakes His Home":* One Bull interview, CC, box 105, folder 19.

25  *a holy man himself:* White Bull interview, CC, box 105, folder 24.

25  *four identical shields:* My discussion of Returns Again's vision and the making of the shields comes from One Bull interview, CC, box 105, folder 19; White Bull interview, CC, box 105, folder 24; and White Bull, Old Bull, and One Bull interviews, CC, box 105, folder 4. In speaking of the shield Sitting Bull's father had passed to his son, Robert M. Utley writes that it was constructed by a "specially skilled craftsman" and painted by a holy man to represent Returns Again's vision. While it is true that shield-making and decorating were often entrusted to others with recognized skills and powers, White Bull informs us that Returns Again himself "was [a] medicine [holy] man in early days." Both White Bull and One Bull are very clear that the shields were personally made by Returns Again. See Utley, *The Lance and the Shield*, 15. For shield-making as the domain of holy men, see Robert Higheagle manuscript, CC, box 104, folder 22; and James R. Walker, *Lakota Society*, ed. Raymond J. DeMallie (Lincoln: University of Nebraska Press, 1982), 100–101.

25  *The number four was sacred:* See Walker, *Lakota Society*, 62; Black Elk, *The Sacred Pipe*, 65 and 100 n. 5; and Standing Bear, *Land of the Spotted Eagle*, 122.

26  *knowledge of nature's medicines:* White Bull interview, CC, box 105, folder 8.

26  *not a "big chief":* Ibid.; Robert Higheagle manuscript, CC, box 104, folder 22; and "General notes on Sitting Bull," CC, box 105, folder 42.

26  *commonly inherited:* Sister H. Inez Hilger, ed., "The Narrative of Oscar One Bull," *Mid-America: An Historical Review* 28 (July 1946), 151; and Valentine T. McGillycuddy to Elmo Scott Watson, San Francisco, CA, February 10, 1922, Watson Papers.

26  *A lodge group:* The lodge group (*tiospaye*) and band is discussed in numerous sources, but I have relied primarily on Kingsley M. Bray, "Sitting Bull and Lakota Leadership," *English Westerners' Society Brand Book* 43 (Summer 2010), 13–15. See also Josephine Waggoner, *Witness: A Húŋkpapȟa Historian's Stong-Heart Song of the Lakotas*, ed. Emily Levine (Lincoln: University of Nebraska, 2013), 40–52; and Royal B. Hassrick, *The Sioux: Life and Customs of a Warrior Society* (Norman: University of Oklahoma Press, 1964), 107–8.

26  *make people laugh:* White Bull interview, CC, box 105, folder 24. According to White Bull, Her Holy Door was first known by the name Mixed Day.

26  *manhood was planned in babyhood:* Standing Bear, *Land of the Spotted Eagle*, 2. Standing Bear describes the nightly ritual of cleansing and massage as he experienced it.

26  *Jumping Badger:* McLaughlin, *My Friend the Indian*, 181; and LaPointe, *Sitting Bull*, 21.

26  *connection to that animal's traits or powers:* Joseph Epes Brown, *Animals of the Soul: Sacred Animals of the Oglala Sioux* (Rockport, MA: Element Books, 1997), 66–67.

27  *"Slow" or "Slow-Moving":* One Bull account in Frank Bennett Fiske, *Life and Death of Sitting Bull* (Fort Yates, ND: Pioneer-Arrow Print, 1933), 4; LaPointe, *Sitting Bull*, 22; and Charles A. Eastman, *Indian Heroes and Great Chieftains* (Boston: Little, Brown, and Company, 1918), 108. In an interview with William Campbell, One Bull said Sitting Bull's childhood name translated as "Slow Runner." One Bull interview, CC, box 104, folder 6. What may be the earliest

printed reference to Sitting Bull's nickname of "Slow" appears in "The Great Powwow," *The New York Herald*, August 26, 1875.

27   *"was always last in everything"*: Waggoner, *Witness*, 397.

27   *a certain deliberateness*: LaPointe, *Sitting Bull*, 22; and Vestal, *Sitting Bull*, 3.

27   *called him by his nickname*: According to Joseph Epes Brown, speaking sacred personal names too frequently could diminish the power acquired from the creature named. (In Sitting Bull's case, the badger.) This may explain why the nickname was preferred over his given name. See Brown, *Animals of the Soul*, 66.

27   *"There was no such thing"*: Standing Bear, *Land of the Spotted Eagle*, 14.

27   *"most cowardly tribe"*: White Bull interview, CC, box 105, folder 4.

27   *Crows had lots of horses*: Eagle Elk interview, Neihardt Papers.

27   *"bad men"*: Charles Augustus Murray, *Travels in North America During the Years 1834, 1835, and 1836*, 2 vols. (New York: Harper & Brothers, 1839), 2: 306.

28   *universal hand sign for the tribe*: Ibid., 1: 286; and Clark, *The Indian Sign Language*, 341.

28   *a son of the lodge group*: Standing Bear, *Land of the Spotted Eagle*, 5.

28   *his uncle Four Horns*: One Bull interview, CC, box 105, folder 19. According to Sitting Bull's great-grandson, Four Horns took the young Slow into his lodge, where he lived for much of his youth as Four Horns trained and educated his nephew in the ways of a hunter and warrior. See LaPointe, *Sitting Bull*, 23. For biographical information on Four Horns, see Waggoner, *Witness*, 676 n. 2; and McCoy, "Four Horns: A Hunkpapa Lakota Warrior-Artist Commemorates His Relative's Valor."

28   *four virtues of Lakota men*: John Lame Deer (Fire) and Richard Erdoes, *Lame Deer: Seeker of Visions* (New York: Simon & Schuster, 1972), 116. According to this same source, the four virtues of Lakota women were bravery, generosity, truthfulness, and the bearing of children. John Colhoff, a mixed-blood Lakota interpreter, stated the four virtues were bravery, generosity, fortitude, and integrity. "Sioux Indian Ways Explained," *Rapid City Journal*, SD, May 9, 1944.

28   *"You must be brave"*: Standing Bear, *Land of the Spotted Eagle*, 68.

28   *nothing hurt so much*: Fiske, *Life and Death of Sitting Bull*, 4.

28   *a "brave heart"*: Hilger, ed., "The Narrative of Oscar One Bull," 169.

29   *tied to his pony's back*: Standing Bear, *Land of the Spotted Eagle*, 11.

29   *retrieving mounts from the camp herd*: White Bull interview, CC, box 105, folder 8.

29   *help train ponies for warfare*: Ibid.

29   *"The greatest brave was"*: Standing Bear, *Land of the Spotted Eagle*, 15.

29   *well known for his kindness*: Robert Higheagle manuscript, CC, box 104, folder 22.

29   *prepared feasts for them*: Hilger, ed., "The Narrative of Oscar One Bull," 152.

30   *"Here, take my blunt point arrow"*: One Bull, "Sitting Bull's Skill with Bow and Arrow," CC, box 104, folder 21.

30   *creatures they shared the world with*: Brown, *Animals of the Soul*, xi–xiii.

30   *the bull speak four names*: There are many variations of this story. See One Bull and Mrs. One Bull interview, CC, box 105, folder 19; One Bull account in

Fiske, *Life and Death of Sitting Bull*, 4–5; LaPointe, *Sitting Bull*, 26–27; and Vestal, *Sitting Bull*, 15–17.

31 ***"My father gave me this nation"***: Hilger, ed., "The Narrative of Oscar One Bull," 152.

31 ***few were as adept:*** My discussion of Sitting Bull's mastering of various skills is drawn from Waggoner, *Witness*, 397; and White Bull interview, CC, box 106, folder 53.

31 ***"When I was ten years old"***: "A Chat with the Chief," *The Omaha Daily Bee*, August 9, 1881. White Bull said Sitting Bull was the best hunter he ever knew. See White Bull interview, CC, box 105, folder 8.

31 ***That came when he was fourteen:*** My description of Sitting Bull's first coup and the bestowing of his adult name is drawn primarily from the White Bull interview in the CC, box 106, folder 53; "Sitting Bull" by Josephine Waggoner, typescript, Josephine Waggoner Papers, Museum of the Fur Trade, Chadron, NE; and Sitting Bull's drawing of the episode as copied by Four Horns, National Anthropological Archives (drawing #1). See also One Bull, "Why Sitting Bull Wears a White Eagle Feather as a Head Ornament," CC, box 104, folder 18; LaPointe, *Sitting Bull*, 27–29; McLaughlin, *My Friend the Indian*, 181; Vestal, *Sitting Bull*, 11–13; and Utley, *The Lance and the Shield*, 14–15. Utley writes that Sitting Bull's father presented him with his shield at the time he gave him his name. However, White Bull states that Sitting Bull was in "lots of fights before shield given him." See White Bull interview, CC, box 105, folder 56. Interestingly, the Sitting Bull/Four Horns drawing of this first coup depicts Sitting Bull carrying the famous shield of his father.

33 ***to be known as Sitting Bull:*** For another version of how Sitting Bull received his adult name, see Eastman, *Indian Heroes and Great Chieftains*, 108–9.

33 ***a five-year-old Lakota boy:*** Crazy Horse's father gave the date of his son's birth as the fall of 1840. See the *Sun* (NY), September 14, 1877. Horn Chips provided the same date, stating that Crazy Horse was born the year identified on winter counts as when the Oglalas "stole One Hundred Horses, and in the fall of that year," which was 1840–41. See Horn Chips interview, Jensen, *Voices of the American West*, 1: 273.

33 ***The boy's grandfather:*** Information on Crazy Horse's grandfather and father is so scant that one hesitates to make any definitive statement about them. Horn Chips informs us that the name of the grandfather was Makes the Song. In a 2004 interview, the Lakota informants of the Crazy Horse biographer Kingsley Bray told him Makes the Song was a holy man. He Dog stated that Crazy Horse's father "wasn't a chief, but he was a very prominent man among the people." Horn Chips interview, Jensen, *Voices of the American West*, 1: 273; Kingsley M. Bray, "Notes on the Crazy Horse Genealogy: Part 1," http://www.american-tribes.com/Lakota/BIO/CrazyHorse-Part1.htm; and He Dog narrative, Crazy Horse File, Museum of the Fur Trade. For Crazy Horse's father as a holy man, see Montana Lisle Reese, ed., *Legends of the Mighty Sioux* (Chicago: Albert Whitman & Company, 1941), 110–11.

33 ***translated as His Horse Foolish:*** Oglala winter count by No Ears, James R. Walker Collection, reel 4, frame 41. William J. Bordeaux, a onetime govern-

ment interpreter as well as a Crazy Horse biographer, wrote that the proper translation was His Foolish Horse. According to William Philo Clark, who knew Crazy Horse, the Oglala leader's name was "improperly interpreted" and should be His Horse Is Crazy. See "Sioux Translation," *The Daily Argus-Leader*, Sioux Falls, SD, July 10, 1948; and Clark's *The Indian Sign Language*, 267 and 422.

33   **Rattle Blanket Woman:** Also given as Rattling Blanket Woman.

33   **light-colored or "yellow" hair:** He Dog narrative, Crazy Horse File, Museum of the Fur Trade, Chadron, NE; and He Dog interview, June 30, 1931, Sandoz Collection.

33   **find on a white man:** Little Killer interview, *Hinman Interviews*, 46.

33   **fathered by a white man:** Kingsley M. Bray, *Crazy Horse: A Lakota Life*, 10. Army scout and interpreter Frank Grouard stated that Crazy Horse was "remarkably white for an Indian, and many who met him imagined he was not a full-blooded Sioux." Joe DeBarthe, *The Life and Adventures of Frank Grouard, Chief of Scouts, U.S.A.* (St. Joseph, MO: Combe Printing Company, 1894), 347.

33   **nickname, Curly:** In a letter to Mari Sandoz, Louis Roubideaux wrote that his grandfather, Blunt Arrow, told him the nickname was actually *Gu-Gu-La*, which he translated as "Kinky, like a negro's head." Roubideaux to Sandoz, Hot Springs, SD, January 26, 1944, Sandoz Collection.

34   **"didn't miss much":** Short Bull interview, *Hinman Interviews*, 43.

34   **in love with her husband's younger brother:** Bray, *Crazy Horse: A Lakota Life*, 10 and 402 n. 21; Victoria Conroy statement in Richard G. Hardorff, *The Oglala Lakota Crazy Horse: A Preliminary Genealogical Study and an Annotated Listing of Primary Sources* (Matituck, NY: J. M. Carroll and Company, 1985), 29–32; Cleve Walstrom, *Search for the Lost Trail of Crazy Horse* (Crete, NE: Dageford Publishing, Inc., 2003), 7–8; and Richard G. Hardorff, ed., *The Surrender and Death of Crazy Horse: A Source Book About a Tragic Episode in Lakota History* (Spokane, WA: The Arthur H. Clark Company, 1998), 75 n. 3.

34   **dangling from a tree:** Larry Belitz, an authority on Plains Indian material culture who has worked closely with the Horn Chips family, maintains that Rattle Blanket Woman did not commit suicide but was murdered for having a mixed-blood child. See his *Chips Collection of Crazy Horse Medicines* (Hot Springs, SD: privately printed, n.d.), 8.

34   **Curly's generous invitation:** This story from Crazy Horse's childhood is from Santee author Charles A. Eastman, who was the agency doctor at the Pine Ridge Reservation from 1890 to 1893. At Pine Ridge, Eastman became personally acquainted with many individuals who knew Crazy Horse, so I am inclined to take his information seriously. However, Eastman writes that Crazy Horse was four or five years old when he rode through the village offering fresh pronghorn. I doubt Crazy Horse was that young. See Eastman, *Indian Heroes and Great Chieftains*, 85–86.

35   **an astonishing event:** This episode, including quotes, is drawn from Chris Dixon, "Crazy Horse and the Cheyenne," in Ronald H. Nichols, ed., *The Brian C. Pohanka 32nd Annual Symposium, Custer Battlefield Historical & Museum Assn., Inc., held at Hardin, Montana, on June 22, 2018* (Fort Collins, CO: Citizen

Printing Company, Inc., 2019), 54–55. My description of how the Lakotas caught wild horses is from Luther Standing Bear, *My People the Sioux* (Boston: Houghton Mifflin Company, 1928), 77–81; and Edwin Thompson Denig, *Five Indian Tribes of the Upper Missouri*, ed. John C. Ewers (Norman: University of Oklahoma Press, 1961), 17 n. 20.

35  *"Watch the horses are come dancing":* This song is from Frank Kicking Bear, as quoted in Kadlecek, *To Kill an Eagle*, 119.

36  *His Horse Stands Looking:* Additional names associated with a juvenile Crazy Horse include Yellow Hair, Light-Haired Boy, Crusher, and Owns Bad Woman. He Dog narrative, Crazy Horse File, Museum of the Fur Trade; Horn Chips interview, Hardorff, ed., *Surrender and Death*, 74; and personal correspondence with Chris Dixon, September 18, 2019.

36  *With boyhood friends:* He Dog account, as told to Eagle Hawk, his son, Robert A. Clark, ed., *The Killing of Chief Crazy Horse, Three Eyewitness Views . . .* (Glendale, CA: The Arthur H. Clark Company, 1976), 68; and DeBarthe, *Life and Adventures*, 348.

36  *High Backbone:* References to High Backbone (also known as Hump) and his relationship with young Crazy Horse are few and scattered, but see the He Dog and Red Feather interviews in *Hinman Interviews*, 24, and 36–37; Bray, *Crazy Horse: A Lakota Life*, 13; and Mari Sandoz, *Crazy Horse: The Strange Man of the Oglalas* (New York: Alfred A. Knopf, 1942), 18. The role of older Lakota boys as mentors is discussed by Standing Bear in his *Land of the Spotted Eagle*, 32.

36  *"the grizzly and his cub":* Eastman, *Indian Heroes and Great Chieftains*, 90.

37  *"had some power":* Ibid., 87–88.

37  *those who were worthy:* Black Elk, *The Sacred Pipe*, 44.

37  *"did not understand the Indian's touch":* Standing Bear, *Land of the Spotted Eagle*, 209.

37  *struck by their lightning:* William K. Powers, *Oglala Religion* (Lincoln: University of Nebraska Press, 1977), 93.

38  *"There was a trail nearby":* As quoted in M. I. McCreight, *Firewater and Forked Tongues: A Sioux Chief Interprets U.S. History* (Pasadena, CA: Trail's End Publishing Co., Inc., 1947), 139.

38  *the water's great power:* Black Elk interview, *The Sixth Grandfather*, 123.

38  *Death would come:* Horn Chips interview, Jensen, *Voices of the American West*, 1: 277. According to William Garnett, the prediction that Crazy Horse would die while being held and stabbed came from a vision in which a man on horseback emerged from a lake and told this to the warrior. Jensen, *Voices of the American West*, 1: 117. Horn Chips, on the other hand, said, "There is no truth in the story of the horseman coming out of the pond and telling Crazy Horse what to do."

38  *"If anything happens to myself":* As quoted in Kadlecek, *To Kill an Eagle*, 126.

39  *age-old foes of the Lakotas:* See Witte and Gallagher, *The North American Journals of Prince Maximilian of Wied*, 2: 202–3; and J. N. B. Hewitt, ed., *Journal of Rudolph Friederich Kurz: An Account of His Experiences Among Fur Traders and American Indians on the Mississippi and the Upper Missouri Rivers During the Years 1846 to 1852* (Washington: Government Printing Office, 1937), 81 and 184.

39   *the two Lakotas could not be caught:* The only source for the story of the fight with the Hidatsas is Eastman, *Indian Heroes and Great Chieftains*, 88–89. During Eastman's time and earlier, the Hidatsas were commonly known as the Gros Ventres and the "Gros Ventres of the Missouri." Eastman uses the shorter "Gros Ventres." Some writers have suggested that Eastman is referring to the Atsina tribe, also known as the "Gros Ventres of the Prairies," but the Hidatsas were suffering terribly at the hands of the Lakotas during this period. Their Indian agent wrote in 1855 that the complaints of the Hidatsas "against the Sioux for stealing their horses and murdering their people were anything but pleasant." See Alfred J. Vaughan, Indian agent, to Col. Alfred Cumming, Fort Clark, September 12, 1855, *Report of the Commissioner of Indian Affairs*, S. Exec. Doc. No. 1, 34th Cong., 1st Sess., 393. In the 1947 book *Chief Flying Hawk's Tales*, a similar account of the fight with the Hidatsas is given and attributed to Flying Hawk. However, it is clearly taken from Eastman's earlier work. See McCreight, *Chief Flying Hawk's Tales*, 132–33.

40   *He Dog remembered the story well:* He Dog interview, *Hinman Interviews*, 21–22.

40   *"All tried to get their names up":* Horn Chips interview, Hardorff, ed., *Surrender and Death*, 76.

40   *"I throw away [my son's] old name":* As quoted in Elmo Scott Watson, "Crazy Horse—The Greatest Among Them," in Roderick Peattie, ed., *The Black Hills* (New York: The Vanguard Press, 1952), 131.

## 3 / Native Ground

41   *"Most of our troubles":* Standing Bear, *Land of the Spotted Eagle*, 40.

41   *Once they lived hundreds of miles east:* There are many works that discuss early Sioux history and migrations, but I have found most useful Guy Gibbon, *The Sioux: The Dakota and Lakota Nations* (Oxford, UK: Blackwell Publishing, 2003); and George E. Hyde, *Red Cloud's Folk: A History of the Oglala Sioux Indians* (Norman: University of Oklahoma Press, 1957).

41   *a corruption by French traders:* Gibbon, *The Sioux*, 2; and Raymond J. DeMallie, "The Sioux in Dakota and Montana Territories: Cultural and Historical Background of the Ogden B. Read Collection," in Glenn E. Markoe, ed., *Vestiges of a Proud Nation: The Ogden B. Read Northern Plains Indian Collection* (Burlington, VT: Robert Hull Fleming Museum, 1986), 20.

42   *trade networks with their Eastern Sioux cousins:* Raymond J. DeMallie, Douglas R. Parks, and Robert Vézina, eds., *A Fur Trader on the Upper Missouri: The Journal and Description of Jean-Baptiste Truteau, 1794–1796* (Lincoln: University of Nebraska Press, 2017), 93 and 261.

42   *"are the terror and in fact lordly masters":* William H. Thomas journal in David A. White, ed., *News of the Plains and Rockies, 1803–1865*, 8 vols. (Spokane, WA: The Arthur H. Clark Company, 1996–2001), 1: 99.

42   *He wished for others to see it:* This event was recorded in the winter count of American Horse. See Greene and Thornton, eds., *The Year the Stars Fell*,

97; and Mike Cowdrey, "A Winter Count of the Wajaje Lakota, 1758–59 to 1885–86," *Tribal Art* 19 (Autumn 2015): 132.

42 *"as a child to its mother's arms":* Standing Bear, *Land of the Spotted Eagle*, 43.

43 *They called him vèho:* Rev. Rodolphe Petter, *English–Cheyenne Dictionary* (Kettle Falls, WA: Valdo Petter, 1915), 999.

43 *In November 1841:* This episode was recorded in the journal of David Adams, who traded with the Lakotas from "Fort Adams," a post very near Fort Laramie. At this time, Laramie was commonly known as Fort John, for trader John B. Sarpy. Charles E. Hanson Jr., *The David Adams Journals* (Chadron, NE: The Museum of the Fur Trade, 1994), 19.

43 *They Fear Even His Horses:* The name They Fear Even His Horses has been translated incorrectly since the 1840s, most often as Man Afraid of His Horse. A variant translation is The Man Whose Horses Are a Terror to His Foes. See James A. Hanson, *Little Chief's Gatherings: The Smithsonian Institution's G. K. Warren 1855–1856 Plains Indian Collection and the New York State Library's 1855–1857 Warren Expeditions Journals* (Crawford, NE: The Fur Press, 1996), 110.

45 *an estimated five thousand emigrants:* Emigrant estimates for each year from 1841 to 1866 are given in Merrill J. Mattes, *The Great Platte River Road* (Lincoln: Nebraska State Historical Society, 1969), 23.

45 *"blackened the land":* Lieutenant J. Henry Carleton, *The Prairie Logbooks: Dragoon Campaigns to the Pawnee Villages in 1844, and to the Rocky Mountains in 1845*, ed. Louis Pelzer (Lincoln: University of Nebraska Press, 1983), 250.

46 *"Your great father has learned":* White, ed., *News of the Plains and Rockies*, 4: 126.

46 *"the gun that shoots twice":* George Bent, "Forty Years with the Cheyennes," part four, *The Frontier: A Magazine of the West* 4 (January 1906): 6.

46 *what Kearny wrote in his report:* White, ed., *News of the Plains and Rockies*, 4: 123.

47 *The Broken Hand:* John C. Fremont, *The Exploring Expedition to the Rocky Mountains* (Washington, D.C.: Smithsonian Institution Press, 1988), 41.

47 *"I consider them a doomed race":* Thomas Fitzpatrick to Thomas W. Harvey, Bent's Fort, Arkansas River, October 19, 1847, Thomas Fitzpatrick Letters, 1846–1853, Bent's Old Fort National Historic Site, La Junta, Colorado.

47 *"a great struggle for the ascendancy":* Thomas Fitzpatrick to Lieutenant Colonel Clifton Wharton, Fort Leavenworth, KS, January 7, 1847, ibid.

47 *In May 1849, he wrote:* Thomas Fitzpatrick to D. D. Mitchell, St. Louis, MO, May 22, 1849, ibid.

48 *"Great Medicine Road of the Whites":* Pierre-Jean De Smet, *Western Missions and Missionaries: A Series of Letters* (New York: James B. Kirker, 1863), 98.

48 *left strewn in their wake:* Hiram Martin Chittenden and Alfred Talbot Richardson, eds., *Life, Letters and Travels of Father Pierre-Jean De Smet, S. J., 1801–1873*, 4 vols. (New York: Francis P. Harper, 1905), 2: 726.

48 *the stench of death from decomposing bodies:* Waggoner, *Witness*, 69.

48 *"Many died of the cramps":* Greene and Thornton, eds., *The Year the Stars Fell*, 226. Smallpox and measles, again introduced by emigrants, also proved deadly to the Lakotas.

48 *purposely introducing the disease:* Report of D. D. Mitchell, Superintendent of Indian Affairs, St. Louis, September 14, 1850, *Message from the President of the*

United States to the Two Houses of Congress, H. Exec. Doc. No. 1, 31st Cong., 2nd Sess., 49.

48    *no ordinary treaty:* Superintendent of Indian Affairs Mitchell outlined his ideas for the treaty in letters to William Medill and Thomas Fitzpatrick of June 1, 1849, and August 1, 1849, respectively. Both are in Thomas Fitzpatrick Letters, 1846–1853.

49    *The only thing more surprising:* Fur trader Charles Larpenteur described the 1851 treaty as the most absurd he had ever heard of, "though gotten up by men who should have known better." Elliott Coues, ed., *Forty Years a Fur Trader on the Upper Missouri: The Personal Narrative of Charles Larpenteur, 1833–1872,* 2 vols. (New York: Francis P. Harper, 1899), 2: 419.

49    *The "Great Indian Council":* The New York Herald, October 6, 1851. A good account of the council and resulting treaty is Burton S. Hill, "The Great Indian Treaty Council of 1851," *Nebraska History* 47 (1966): 85–110.

49    *Comanches, Kiowas, and Apaches:* Report of Thomas Fitzpatrick, Indian Agent, Upper Platte Agency, November 24, 1851, *Message from the President of the United States to the Two Houses of Congress,* H. Exec. Doc. No. 2, 32nd Cong., 1st Sess., 333.

50    *men "ignorant and weak minded":* Thomas Fitzpatrick to Thomas W. Harvey, Bent's Fort, Arkansas River, October 19, 1847, Thomas Fitzpatrick Letters, 1846–1853.

50    *"Father, this is the third time":* As quoted in Hill, "The Great Indian Treaty Council of 1851," 101. The Yankton chief was named Painted Bear.

50    *put down a few more buffalo: The Daily Crescent,* New Orleans, November 1, 1851.

50    *each band's chief represented:* See the statement of Blue Earth, a Brulé chief, in Raymond J. DeMallie, "Touching the Pen," in Roger L. Nichols, ed., *The American Indian, Past and Present* (Norman: University of Oklahoma Press, 2008), 176–77.

51    *$50,000 worth of goods:* D. D. Mitchell to Luke Lea, St. Louis, November 11, 1851, *Message from the President of the United States to the Two Houses of Congress,* H. Exec. Doc. No. 2, 32nd Cong., 1st Sess., 289. The original terms of the treaty specified $50,000 worth of goods for fifty years, but that number was later changed to ten by the U.S. Senate.

51    *a colorful military uniform:* Chittenden and Richardson, eds., *Life, Letters and Travels of Father Pierre-Jean De Smet,* 2: 683.

51    *payment for all past claims:* D. D. Mitchell to Luke Lea, St. Louis, November 11, 1851, *Message from the President,* 289.

51    *"no epoch in Indian annals":* De Smet, *Western Missions and Missionaries,* 108.

52    *baptized 1,194 Indian children:* Chittenden and Richardson, eds., *Life, Letters and Travels of Father Pierre-Jean De Smet,* 2: 678–79.

52    *"In future, peaceable citizens may":* Ibid., 684.

52    *"some untoward misfortune":* D. D. Mitchell to Luke Lea, St. Louis, November 11, 1851, *Message from the President,* 290.

52    *promptly killed and butchered:* James Bordeaux account, August 21, 1854, *The New York Herald,* September 18, 1854.

53  *"with thirty men":* As quoted in John D. McDermott, R. Eli Paul, and Sandra J. Lowry, eds., *All Because of a Mormon Cow: Historical Accounts of the Grattan Massacre, 1854–1855* (Norman: University of Oklahoma Press, 2018), 188–89.

53  *"white man's arms":* Ibid.

53  *Riding along with Grattan:* I have relied heavily on the eyewitness testimony of They Fear Even His Horses, February 13, 1855, which is reproduced ibid., 167–72. See also the eyewitness account of Rocky Bear, an Oglala, in "Brule Sioux, Chief Actors," *The Salt Lake Herald*, September 16, 1907.

54  *"You tell the Bear":* Obridge Allen account, November 19, 1854, as quoted in *All Because of a Mormon Cow*, 124.

54  *"For all I tell you":* They Fear Even His Horses account, 171.

54  *"You are talking":* Ibid.

54  *Behind their blankets, they held guns:* George Bent to George Hyde, Colony, OK, March 19, 1906, George Bent Papers, 1904–1926, WA MSS 32, Beinecke Rare Book and Manuscript Library, Yale University, New Haven, CT.

55  *"Yes," the Oglala replied:* They Fear Even His Horses account, 171.

55  *three lead balls struck the Brulé chief:* Sefroy Iott account in the *New York Herald*, September 18, 1854.

55  *"would not listen to anything":* George Bent to George Hyde, March 19, 1906, George Bent Papers.

55  *stuffed into the muzzle of the fieldpiece:* The *New York Herald*, October 20, 1854.

55  *"They killed thirty white men":* Joseph S. Karol, ed., *Red Horse Owner's Winter Count: The Oglala Sioux, 1786–1968* (Martin, SD: The Booster Publishing Co., 1969), 35 and 61. The names of those killed is found in the *New York Herald*, October 22, 1854.

56  *increasingly hostile toward whites:* Denig, *Five Indian Tribes of the Upper Missouri*, 27.

56  *"that they preferred the liberty":* Alfred J. Vaughan, Indian agent, to Col. Alfred Cumming, Fort Pierre, October 19, 1854, *Report of the Commissioner of Indian Affairs*, S. Exec. Doc. No. 1, 33rd Cong., 2nd Sess., 297.

56  *the most dreaded Indians:* Ibid., 295.

57  *seven fur company employees:* Alfred J. Vaughan, Indian agent, to Col. Alfred Cumming, Fort Clark, September 12, 1855, *Report of the Commissioner of Indian Affairs*, S. Exec. Doc. No. 1, 34th Cong., 1st Sess., 394.

57  *"murders, robberies, and horse stealing":* Ibid., 396.

57  *Poised to attack those camps:* George Rollie Adams, *General William S. Harney: Prince of Dragoons* (Lincoln: University of Nebraska Press, 2001), 128.

58  *rifled and fired conical minié balls:* Louis A. Garavaglia and Charles G. Worman, *Firearms of the American West, 1803–1865* (Albuquerque: University of New Mexico Press, 1984), 159–60.

58  *"he had not come out here for nothing":* Gouverneur K. Warren journal, September 3, 1855, in Hanson, *Little Chief's Gatherings*, 104.

58  *shooting at any living thing that moved:* 1855 letter of Lieutenant Marshall K. Polk in R. Eli Paul, ed., *The Frontier Army: Episodes from Dakota and the West* (Pierre: South Dakota Historical Society Press, 2019), 16–17.

58  *Those caves became death traps:* Ibid.

58    *Long Knives climbed onto an outcropping:* Account of Nathan A. M. Dudley,
       August 26, 1909, in R. Eli Paul, ed., "The Battle of Ash Hollow: The 1909–1910
       Recollections of General N. A. M. Dudley," *Nebraska History* 62 (1981): 392.
58    *"heart rending—wounded women & children":* Warren journal, September 3,
       1855, 106.
59    *showed no signs of surrendering:* Account of Nathan A. M. Dudley, January 29,
       1909, 382.
59    *eighty-six Lakotas lay dead and about seventy women and children:* R. Eli Paul,
       *Blue Water Creek and the First Sioux War, 1854–1856* (Norman: University of Okla-
       homa Press, 2004).
59    *Lakota attack on a mail train:* The New York Herald, December 7, 1854.
59    *"there were plenty of bad Indians in Camp":* Warren journal, September 3,
       1855, 106.
59    *It's said that a young Crazy Horse:* Mari Sandoz, in her biography of the Oglala
       leader, describes a young Crazy Horse visiting the destroyed village. Be-
       cause her book contains no endnotes, it's impossible to know if Sandoz had
       a specific source for this episode or whether she invented it for the sake of
       her narrative. Most scholars today consider her book to contain far too much
       invention (including created dialogue) for it to be of any value as a reference.
       However, Sandoz did participate in interviews with several Pine Ridge Lako-
       tas who knew Crazy Horse. Those 1930 and 1931 interviews are the foundation
       stones for anyone studying Crazy Horse's life. And Sandoz claimed a personal
       connection to Crazy Horse's people from her childhood. In a 1958 letter, she
       wrote, "I grew up among the Oglalas, so to speak, with many of the hostiles,
       the old Crazy Horse people, often camped across the road from our house
       on the river, the Niobrara. From these I heard the great stories told over and
       over—by men who had been in the fights." So, while scholars are certainly
       justified in looking at Sandoz's book with a wary eye, they should not be too
       quick to dismiss the various events of Crazy Horse's life she recounts. See
       Sandoz, *Crazy Horse: The Strange Man of the Oglalas,* 76–77; Sandoz to Elias
       Jacobsen, New York, NY, August 20, 1958; and Sandoz to Bonnie Lee O'Dell,
       n.p., November 10, 1951, Sandoz Collection.
59    *lodges plundered by the Long Knives:* Lieutenant Gouverneur K. Warren, a
       topographer with Harney's expedition, gathered at least one hundred items
       from the battlefield—dresses, moccasins, leggings, pad saddles, decorated
       buffalo robes, weapons, etc.—and donated the collection to the Smithsonian
       Institution in 1856, where the majority remain to this day. Many of these arti-
       facts are illustrated in Hanson, *Little Chief's Gatherings.*
59    *"some as pretty tepees as I ever saw":* As quoted in Paul, *Blue Water Creek,* 107.
59    *exterminate the entire Yanktonai:* Interview with Alfred J. Vaughan, *Washing-
       ton Sentinel,* Washington, D.C., April 26, 1856; and Doreen Chaky, *Terrible
       Justice: Sioux Chiefs and U.S. Soldiers on the Upper Missouri, 1854–1868* (Norman,
       OK: The Arthur H. Clark Company, 2012), 52.
60    *the Lakotas named Harney "Mad Bear":* Utley, *The Lance and the Shield,* 45,
       and 342 n. 9. Susan Bordeaux Bettelyoun, a mixed-blood Lakota, wrote that
       because of the women and children killed at Blue Water Creek, the general

became known as "Squaw Killer Harney." Susan Bordeaux Bettelyoun and Josephine Waggoner, *With My Own Eyes: A Lakota Woman Tells Her People's History*, ed. Emily Levine (Lincoln: University of Nebraska Press, 1998), 57. A Lakota winter count identified Harney as "White Beard." Research correspondence with Judge Frank Zahn, CC, box 107, folder 5.

60 *presenting a set of demands:* "A Report of the Proceedings of a Council Held at Fort Pierre by General Harney," S. Exec. Doc. No. 94, 34th Cong., 1st Sess., 2–4.

60 *"I am going to tell you something":* As quoted in ibid., 26.

61 *angrily told Warren to turn back:* Warren journal, September 16, 1857, 162–64.

61 *"only to see what was in their country":* Ibid., 162.

61 *Bear's Rib warned, it was a rule:* Ibid., September 24, 1857, 165.

61 *the four Sacred Arrows:* Ben Clark, "Cheyenne History and Dictionary," 1887 manuscript in the Francis W. Cragin Collection, Colorado Springs Pioneers Museum, Colorado Springs, Colorado.

61 *in the form of a bear:* Reese, ed., *Legends of the Mighty Sioux*, 110–12. According to this same source, the butte received the name *Mato Paha* (Bear Mountain) because of Crazy Horse's father's encounter at that place with the bear that was *Wakan Tanka*.

62 *Black Hills were rich with timber:* Frank N. Schubert, ed., *Explorer on the Northern Plains: Lieutenant Gouverneur K. Warren's Preliminary Report of Explorations in Nebraska and Dakota, in the Years 1855-'56-'57* (Washington: Government Printing Office, 1981), 31.

62 *"there would soon spring up":* Ibid., 30.

62 *"I almost feel guilty of crime":* From a Warren letter draft dated January 27, 1858, quoted in ibid., xxvi.

## 4 / Visions of the Future

63 *"What we see":* Elaine Goodale Eastman, "Justice to the Indian," *Frank Leslie's Illustrated Newspaper*, June 27, 1891.

63 *fight for survival with other tribes:* De Smet, *Western Missions and Missionaries*, 53–54.

63 *"Sticks around the Fort":* Black Elk interview, *The Sixth Grandfather*, 159.

64 *his most famous fight:* There are several versions of Sitting Bull's duel with the Crow chief. And it's not even certain that his opponent was indeed a chief. For my narrative, I've relied primarily on the account of Circling Hawk and Sitting Bull's own drawing of the encounter. Circling Hawk interview, CC, box 105, folder 13; and Sitting Bull drawing, #11, Pratt-Evans-Pettinger-Anderson Collection, Buffalo Bill Center of the West, Cody, Wyoming.

64 *Only the four bravest Strong Hearts:* White Bull interview, CC, box 105, folder 4.

65 *one of two "sash-wearers":* White Bull interview, box 106, folder 53; and LaPointe, *Sitting Bull*, 32.

65 *why the medicine failed:* As explained by Robert Higheagle to Walter Campbell, "If a man was wounded, he didn't blame the charm. If he had done his part in the battle, he didn't think that he should be successful every time.

There were times when a warrior had to suffer." Robert Higheagle manuscript, CC, box 104, folder 22.

65   *no woman was allowed to touch:* White Bull interview, CC, box 5, folder 4.

66   *One of those pictographs:* The drawing I'm referencing is marked #9 in the Pratt-Evans-Pettinger-Anderson Collection, Buffalo Bill Center. However, Sitting Bull depicted this same event in at least two additional drawings; one is part of his pictographic autobiography held by the National Anthropological Archives and the other is a Four Horns copy of a Sitting Bull drawing, also at the National Anthropological Archives.

66   *there is much more to the story:* As with several episodes in Sitting Bull's life passed down through oral history, there is more than one version of this event, but see White Bull interview, CC, box 106, folder 53; One Bull interview, CC, box 104, folder 11; One Bull and Mrs. One Bull interview, CC, box 105, folder 19; and Circling Hawk interview, CC, box 105, folder 13. Although Circling Hawk claimed to be a witness, it appears he may be confusing two different events involving the Assiniboines. Circling Hawk's account describes a major battle between the Húnkpapa raiding party and the Assiniboines where eight Húnkpapas were killed. Such a battle is not part of One Bull's and White Bull's stories of Sitting Bull's capture of the Assiniboine boy. Another problem with the Circling Hawk version is that he has the Húnkpapas swimming their horses across a lake during a running fight. Because we know that the episode I describe occurred in the dead of winter (Sitting Bull's own drawings show him wearing a blanket coat), any lake in Assiniboine country would've been frozen over.

67   *"Big brother, save me!":* As quoted in LaPointe, *Sitting Bull,* 34.

68   *Rainy Butte:* For my account of the Rainy Butte fight, I have relied upon Brian L. Keefe, *The Battle at Rainy Butte: A Significant Sioux-Crow Encounter of 1858* (London: The English Westerners Society, 2006); White Bull interview, CC, box 105, folder 8; Old Bull interview, CC, box 105, folder 11; Circling Hawk interview, CC, box 105, folder 13; Waggoner, *Witness,* 397–98; and Vestal, *Sitting Bull,* 43–49.

68   *In 1858, during the Moon of Changing Leaves:* There is disagreement on when the Rainy Butte engagement occurred. The only full-length work devoted to the fight, Keefe's *The Battle at Rainy Butte,* places it in 1858 and in September or early October. Stanley Vestal also gives the year as 1858 but has the battle occurring in June. Robert Utley gives the year as 1859. Keefe had access to Crow oral history for his narrative; Vestal and Utley did not. And while there is no reason to give more weight to the Crow sources, because Keefe's is the most recent and most detailed study of the fight, I have gone with his dates.

69   *"You are like old women":* As quoted in Keefe, *The Battle at Rainy Butte,* 38.

69   *"Leave him to me":* Old Bull interview, CC, box 105, folder 11.

70   *thrust his lance into the Crow's side:* Some Lakota accounts identify this Crow warrior as the slayer of Jumping Bull, and Sitting Bull may have believed this as well, but Keefe provides compelling evidence that this was not the case. See his *The Battle at Rainy Butte,* 41.

71   *"Take good care of":* Old Bull interview, CC, box 105, folder 11; and Waggoner,

*Witness*, 398 (last sentence of quote). Sitting Bull's compassion for enemy captives was legendary. "Sitting Bull was a very humane chief," recalled Frank Desjarlais, an interpreter, "and . . . he always ordered his men to spare the women and children of their enemies." As quoted in Charles De Noyer, "The History of Fort Totten," *Collections of the State Historical Society of North Dakota* 3 (1910): 216.

71 *For four days Sitting Bull mourned:* Waggoner, *Witness*, 398. For Sitting Bull's method of mourning, see White Bull interview, CC, box 105, folder 8.

72 *"soldier chief":* In Walter Campbell's interviews with Lakota informants, "soldier chief" is interpreted variously as "chief of police" and "peace officer." See White Bull and Circling Hawk interviews, CC, box 105, folders 4 and 13.

72 *Sitting Bull fully earned:* "Whatever Sitting Bull attained was through his own personal efforts." Robert Higheagle manuscript, CC, box 104, folder 22.

72 *the heart of Lakota existence:* Literature on the Lakota Sun Dance is considerable. For my brief description, I have drawn from the following: Standing Bear, *Land of the Spotted Eagle*, 220–25; White Bull interview, CC, box 105, folder 8; Delphine Red Shirt, *George Sword's Warrior Narratives: Compositional Processes in Lakota Oral Tradition* (Lincoln: University of Nebraska Press, 2016), 214–46; Darcy Paige, "George W. Hill's Account of the Sioux Indian Sun Dance of 1866," *Plains Anthropologist* 25 (1979): 99–112; William Garnett interview in Jensen, *Voices of the American West*, 1: 55–56; Alice C. Fletcher, "The Sun Dance of the Ogalalla Sioux," *Proceedings of the American Association for the Advancement of Science, Thirty-First Meeting* (1883): 580–84; Little Wound interview, Walker, *Lakota Belief and Ritual*, 67–68; and James R. Walker, "The Sun Dance and Other Ceremonies of the Oglala Division of the Teton Dakota," *American Museum of Natural History Anthropological Papers* 16, pt. 2 (1917): 50–221.

74 *a tenet existed that no man:* Belitz, *Chips Collection of Crazy Horse Medicines*, 95; and Chris Dixon interview with the author, Hardin, MT, June 23, 2017. Belitz's informant on the Sun Dance rule was Dwight Good Voice Boy, a step-great-grandson of Crazy Horse's holy man Horn Chips.

74 *The man is Crazy Horse's father:* Greene and Thornton, eds., *The Year the Stars Fell*, 216.

74 *strove to become a holy man:* Standing Bear, *Land of the Spotted Eagle*, 39.

74 *everything in the world has a spirit:* Walker, *Lakota Belief and Ritual*, 118.

74 *a holy man hoped to please them:* Thomas Tyon interview, ibid., 119.

74 *mentored by other holy men:* George Sword interview, ibid., 79–80.

75 *"He was a man medicine seemed":* Robert Higheagle manuscript, CC, box 104, folder 22.

75 *a blue speckled bird was singing:* One Bull and Mrs. One Bull interviews, CC, box 105, folder 19.

75 *prayed more often than anyone else:* White Bull interview, CC, box 105, folder 4.

75 *had plenty of food that year:* One Bull and Mrs. One Bull interviews, CC, box 105, folder 19.

76 *"Friends, we must honor these bones":* As quoted in Vestal, *Sitting Bull*, 33.

76 *a gift for Wakan Tanka:* White Bull interview, CC, box 105, folder 4.

76 *Sitting Bull's greatest power:* Ibid. Black Elk related to John G. Neihardt four

ways that Indians could see into the future, the first two of which were the Sun Dance and "lamenting," or crying for a vision. See Black Elk interview, *The Sixth Grandfather*, 376.

76   *told the future by a meadowlark:* One Bull, "Prophesy of Sitting Bull," CC, box 104, folder 21.

76   *the songs of the yellow-throated bird:* Robert Higheagle manuscript, CC, box 104, folder 22.

77   *so fearful of the Lakotas:* James I. Patten, Indian agent, to the Commissioner of Indian Affairs, Shoshone and Bannock Agency, Wyoming Territory, August 25, 1878, *Report of the Secretary of the Interior*, H. Exec. Doc. No. 1, Part 5, 45th Cong., 3rd Sess., 645.

77   *One of Crazy Horse's early exploits:* Short Bull interview, *Hinman Interviews*, 38; McCreight, *Firewater and Forked Tongues*, 139; White Bull recollections in Walter S. Campbell to Eleanor Hinman, Norman, OK, October 13, 1932, CC, box 117, folder 27; and Horn Chips interview, Jensen, *Voices of the American West*, 1: 275. The above are the only sources for this fight. They are brief, and they do not entirely agree with one another on specifics. None provide us with the weapon Crazy Horse used to kill the Shoshone. I'm assuming it was a bow and arrow.

77   *a little too foolhardy:* He Dog interview, *Hinman Interviews*, 25.

78   *a nephew through his stepmothers:* Chris Dixon to the author, August 12, 2019. Professor Dixon explains that the stepmothers of Crazy Horse were Spotted Tail's biological first cousins, but in Lakota terms he called them "sisters." Thus, Crazy Horse would be Spotted Tail's nephew through marriage.

78   *"I was told":* He Dog interview, *Hinman Interviews*, 21.

79   *"Wiping of Blood from the Hands":* Belitz, *Chips Collection of Crazy Horse Medicines*, 95.

79   *"best and last home":* The Kansas Herald of Freedom, Lawrence, KS, October 2, 1858.

80   *"This is the white man's money":* St. Louis Globe-Democrat, MO, August 14, 1876. Eagle Woman (1820–1888) was the daughter of Chief Two Lance and the wife, first, of Indian trader Honoré Picotte and, second, Charles Galpin. She was also known as Matilda Galpin. See John S. Gray, "The Story of Mrs. Picotte-Galpin, a Sioux Heroine: Eagle Woman Learns About White Ways and Racial Conflict, 1820–1868," *Montana The Magazine of Western History* 36 (Spring 1986): 3–21.

## 5 / The Invasion of Good Horse Grass Country

81   *"At present [the Indians] are":* The American Phrenological Journal (January 1864), as quoted in the *St. Cloud Democrat*, St. Cloud, MN, January 7, 1864.

81   *all claims to their lands:* Pierre-Jean De Smet to Charles E. Mix, Washington, D.C., September 6, 1862, in *Report of the Commissioner of Indian Affairs for 1862* (Washington: Government Printing Office, 1863), 214.

81   *"We beg of you for the last time":* Feather Tied to His Hair, The Bald Eagle, The

Red Hair, The One That Shouts, The Little Bear, The Crow That Looks, The Bear Heart, The Little Knife, and The White at Both Ends to "the agent," Fort Berthold, July 25, 1862, ibid., 372–73.

82    *A Bannack City prospector's letter:* "Letter from the New Gold Mines," *Sioux City Register*, IA, April 11, 1863.

83    *"and they say it is a good route":* Ibid.

83    *Bozeman Cut-off:* *The Missouri Republican*, August 5, 1865. Today known as the Bozeman Trail.

83    *chronicle their conflicts:* Greene and Thornton, eds., *The Year the Stars Fell*, 250–55.

83    *"First fight with white men":* Red Horse Owner's winter count identifies the year 1864 as "They were fighting with the white man." Karol, ed., *Red Horse Owner's Winter Count*, 37 and 61.

84    *"one awful holocaust of blood and fire":* As quoted in the *Cleveland Morning Leader*, May 18, 1863.

84    *reorganize and strike again:* In February 1863, newspapers published rumors of a planned spring attack on Minnesota's white settlements based on "private information" from the Upper Missouri trading posts. See "Hostile Indians," *Sioux City Register*, February 28, 1863.

84    *seven hundred Long Knives:* A recent history of the "Dakota War" and the subsequent U.S. military campaigns against the Sioux is Paul N. Beck, *Columns of Vengeance: Soldiers, Sioux, and the Punitive Expeditions, 1863–1864* (Norman: University of Oklahoma Press, 2013).

85    *fathered a child by a Yankton woman:* Soldier Woman, later known as Mary Sully Deloria (1858–1916), was the mother of anthropologist, ethnographer, and author Ella Deloria (1889–1971), and the grandmother of American Indian historian and activist Vine Deloria Jr. (1933–2005). See Philip J. Deloria, *Becoming Mary Sully: Toward an American Indian Abstract* (Seattle: University of Washington Press, 2019), 27–35.

85    *destroyed three hundred lodges:* Report of Brig. Gen. Alfred Sully, September 11, 1863, *The War of the Rebellion*, ser. 1, vol. 22, pt. 1 (Washington: Government Printing Office, 1888), 559.

85    *Black Moon, a cousin to Sitting Bull:* Some sources identify Black Moon as Sitting Bull's uncle. See Robert Higheagle manuscript, CC, box 104, folder 22; and letter of J. B. M. Genin to the editor of *Freeman's Journal*, Bismarck, Dakota Territory, September 8, 1876, in Linda W. Slaughter, "Leaves from Northwestern History," *Collections of the State Historical Society of North Dakota* 1 (1906): 258.

85    *"clear out all the whites":* As quoted in P. Chouteau & Co. to Maj. Gen. H. W. Halleck, St. Louis, March 26, 1864, *The War of the Rebellion*, ser. 1, vol. 34, pt. 2 (Washington: Government Printing Office, 1891), 743. See also "An Arrival from Fort Union on the Missouri," *Sioux City Register*, April 23, 1864.

86    *"This whole section":* Ibid.

86    *"savage demons":* *St. Cloud Democrat*, March 24, 1864.

86    *"must be broken to pieces":* Maj. Gen. John Pope to Newton Edwards, Milwaukee, WI, June 30, 1864, *The War of the Rebellion*, ser. 1, vol. 34, pt. 4 (Washington: Government Printing Office, 1891), 605.

86    *a train of gold seekers:* Rev. Louis Pfaller, "Sully's Expedition of 1864, Featuring

the Killdeer Mountain and Badlands Battles," *North Dakota History* 31 (January 1964): 32; and Beck, *Columns of Vengeance*, 191.

87     **some eight thousand Sioux:** Beck, *Columns of Vengeance*, 204.

87     **a party of returning Montana miners:** Contemporary accounts of this episode are found in the *Weekly Pioneer and Democrat*, St. Paul, MN, September 1, October 30, and December 25, 1863; and the *Sioux City Register*, January 9, 1864. These news reports identify the Sioux involved as Yanktonais, but Josephine Waggoner, in her biographical sketch of Inkpaduta, writes that it was the Santee chief and his men who perpetrated the attack, which she states was provoked by the miners shooting and killing an old Sioux man fishing at the river's edge. Joseph No Two Horns, a Húnkpapa, gave a slightly different version of the episode to A. B. Welch sometime in the early 1920s. He said that a number of Indians had waved at the miners in the boat to come to shore, as they wished to trade, but the miners opened fire on them, killing his father, Black Eyes. After killing all the whites and plundering their possessions, the Indians burned the boat to the waterline. No Two Horns made no mention of the woman and children killed with the miners. Considering that the Húnkpapas had already announced their intention to stop all whites from traveling through their country, No Two Horns's claim that they wished to trade with the miners is rather dubious. See Waggoner, *Witness*, 272; and "Death of Montana Miners and Burning of the Boat," in A. B. Welch, "War Drums" (1924), Welch Dakota Papers, https://www.welchdakotapapers.com/2013/10 /war-drums-genuine-war-stories-from-the-sioux-mandan-hidatsa-and-arikara -written-by-col-a-b-welch-a/

88     **their scouts shadowed Sully's column:** White Bull interview, CC, box 105, folder 24; and Martin Williams, "Narrative of the Second Regiment of Cavalry," in Board of Commissioners, *Minnesota in the Civil and Indian Wars, 1861–1865*, 2 vols. (St. Paul, MN: Pioneer Press Company, 1891), 1: 544.

89     **"If they shoot at me":** White Bull interview, CC, box 105, folder 24.

89     **waving a war club:** Lieut. Col. John Pattee recalled a warrior, undoubtedly Lone Dog, who rode close to their lines before the battle's first shots were fired. He was "very gayly dressed, carrying a large war club gorgeously ornamented . . . and called loudly to us and gesticulated wildly about one-half mile away." Soon Pattee received this order from General Sully: "The general sends his compliments and wishes you to kill that Indian for God's sake." Pattee directed his two best marksmen to fire at the warrior, but Pattee believed they overshot their target. General Sully claimed to have witnessed the warrior ride a short distance and then fall from his horse. John Pattee, "Dakota Campaigns," *South Dakota Historical Collections* 5 (1910): 308.

90     **"the imps of hell let loose":** David L. Kingsbury, "Sully's Expedition Against the Sioux in 1864," *Collections of the Minnesota Historical Society* 8 (1898): 449–62.

90     **warriors fired up into the sky:** Pattee, "Dakota Campaigns," 309.

90     **The artillerymen specifically targeted:** Frank Myers, *Soldiering in Dakota, Among the Indians, in 1863-4-5* (1888; reprint: Pierre, SD: State Historical Society, 1936), 15.

90     **When a Sioux fell:** Ibid., 16.

91     **man named Bear's Heart:** White Bull interview, CC, box 105, folder 24; and

Circling Hawk interview, CC, box 105, folder 13. White Bull provided an additional name for Bear's Heart: Man Who Never Walked.

91   *"I am shot!":* White Bull interview, CC, box 105, folder 24.

91   *made a last, desperate attempt:* Isaac Botsford, "Narrative of Brackett's Battalion of Cavalry," in Board of Commissioners, *Minnesota in the Civil and Indian Wars,* 1: 581–82; and Report of Alfred J. Brackett, August 1, 1864, *The War of the Rebellion,* ser. 1, vol. 41, pt. 1 (Washington: Government Printing Office, 1893), 161.

92   *tallied up their casualties:* Report of Brig. Gen. Alfred Sully, July 31, 1864, *The War of the Rebellion,* ser. 1, vol. 41, pt. 1, 144: and *Milwaukee Daily Sentinel,* October 6, 1864.

93   *dropped into his stomach:* White Bull interview, CC, box 105, folder 24.

93   *tons of dried buffalo meat:* Report of Col. Robert N. McLaren, July 29, 1864, *The War of the Rebellion,* ser. 1, vol. 41, pt. 1, 172; *Milwaukee Daily Sentinel,* October 6, 1864; and Kingsbury, "Sully's Expedition Against the Sioux," 455–56.

93   *"worth little to a white man":* Botsford, "Narrative of Brackett's Battalion of Cavalry," 581.

93   *"was wicked to destroy the work":* A. N. Judd, *Campaigning Against the Sioux* (1906; reprint: New York, Sol Lewis, 1973), 11.

93   *"could not interpret the meaning":* McLaren Report, 173; and Sully Report, July 31, 1864, 144.

93   *set fire to the surrounding timber:* Ibid., and *Milwaukee Daily Sentinel,* October 6, 1864.

94   *proper mourning for those slain:* Fanny Kelly, *Narrative of My Captivity Among the Sioux Indians* (Hartford, CT: Mutual Publishing Company, 1873), 106.

94   *"live very fat":* Caspar Collins to Catherine Collins, Fort Laramie, September 20, 1862, in Agnes Wright Spring, *Caspar Collins: The Life and Exploits of an Indian Fighter of the Sixties* (New York: Columbia University Press, 1927), 133.

94   *soon joined by Brulés:* Report of Brig. Gen. Alfred Sully, August 13, 1864, *The War of the Rebellion,* ser. 1, vol. 41, pt. 1, 147.

94   *Sioux scouts alerted their people:* White Bull interview, CC, box 105, folder 24.

95   *some immense ancient city:* Sully Report, August 13, 1864, 145.

95   *Over three days:* The skirmishing between the Indians and Sully's men from August 7 to 9 is known as the Battle of the Badlands. See Sully's official report, cited above, and Beck, *Columns of Vengence,* 220–38; and Pfaller, "Sully's Expedition of 1864," 56–66.

95   *"We are about thirsty to death":* As quoted in White Bull interview, CC, box 105, folder 24.

96   *"Let them go":* Ibid.

96   *empty a few saddles:* Sully Report, August 13, 1864, 147.

97   *the Indian campsites:* The village camps were located on Andrews Creek near present-day Sentinel Butte, North Dakota.

97   *dead bodies of several warriors:* Nicholas Hilger, "General Alfred Sully's Expedition of 1864," in *Contributions to the Historical Society of Montana* 2 (1896): 319.

97   *Sully's casualties:* Sully does not give his casualties in his report of August 13, which covers his combat in the Badlands, and there does not appear to be an official tally. However, a letter written by a member of the expedition on

August 21 reported a total of nine wounded, all but one by Indian arrows. See
"The Indian Expedition," *The Weekly Pioneer and Democrat,* October 7, 1864.
See also the *Milwaukee Daily Sentinel,* October 6, 1864.

97    *"I don't think the Indians will ever again":* Alfred Sully to John Pope, Fort
Union, August 18, 1864, *Report of the Adjutant General and Acting Quartermaster
General of the State of Iowa, January 11, 1864, to January 1, 1865* (Des Moines: F. W.
Palmer, 1865), 1366.

98    *another group of gold seekers:* This caravan is known as the Fisk wagon train
for its leader, James L. Fisk. I have based my narrative on the accounts of members of the train, Lakota oral histories, and contemporary newspaper reports,
primarily the following: Charles F. Sims to L. G. Sims, Sioux City, Iowa, November 6, 1864, in "Expeditions of Captain James L. Fisk to the Gold Mines of
Idaho and Montana, 1864–1866," in *Collections of the State Historical Society of
North Dakota* 2 (1908): 431–39; Ethel A. Collins, "Pioneer Experiences of Horatio H. Larned," *Collections of the State Historical Society of North Dakota* 7 (1925):
1–58; J. H. Drips, *Three Years Among the Indians in Dakota* (Kimball, SD: Brule
Index, 1894); White Bull interview, CC, box 105, folder 8 and folder 24; Circling
Hawk interview, CC, box 105, folder 13; "Capt. Fisk's Expedition," *The Weekly
Pioneer and Democrat,* October 7, 1864; "The Fisk Expedition," *The Weekly Pio-
neer and Democrat,* November 18, 1864; "Return of Captain Fisk," *The St. Cloud
Democrat,* November 17, 1864; "Fisk's Expedition: Official Report of Col. Dill,
Commander of the Party Sent to Its Relief," *The Weekly Pioneer and Democrat,*
November 25, 1864; and "Philanthropy and Strychnine," *The Weekly Pioneer
and Democrat,* December 2, 1864.

99    *Corporal Jefferson Dilts:* The Lakota accounts of this fight do not, of course,
mention Dilts by name, but we know from the white accounts that Dilts
charged alone and engaged several warriors at once, receiving three arrow
wounds. We also know from the white accounts that, during the fighting,
Dilts recovered the revolver that belonged to the emigrant who'd gone back
to look for an ox. Circling Hawk, an eyewitness, specifically states that the
soldier who wounded Sitting Bull had wrested a revolver from Fool Buffalo.
Additionally, Sitting Bull made a drawing showing the moment he was shot
in the hip (copied by Four Horns). The white man who wounds him in this
drawing has an arrow protruding from his body that's been shot by Sitting
Bull. Circling Hawk tells us that the soldier who wounded Sitting Bull got
away, as was the case with Dilts. In addition to the references previously cited,
see the Four Horns copy of Sitting Bull, drawing #13, National Anthropological Archives.

102   *"had many killed by the goods":* Kelly, *Narrative of My Captivity Among the Sioux
Indians,* 275–77.

103   *"They say this is their ground":* Ibid.

104   *"I can see in her face":* As quoted by White Bull, CC, box 106, folder 53.

104   *"My friend, I have come":* Crawler interview in Doane Robinson, "The Rescue
of Frances Kelly," *South Dakota Historical Collections* 6 (1908): 114–15.

104   *"My friend," Sitting Bull said:* As quoted by White Bull, CC, box 106, folder 53.
See also Old Bull interview, CC, box 105, folder 12.

105   *Sihásapas delivered her safely:* According to an 1866 news item, President

Andrew Johnson ordered that the Sihásapa chief responsible for rescuing Fanny Kelly be forwarded "a testimonial in the shape of a parchment letter of transmittal, handsomely ornamented with the American coat of arms in colors, accompanied by a large silver medal and one hundred silver dollars." See *The Evening Telegraph*, Philadelphia, October 1, 1866.

105    *"The youth are very fond of war"*: Kelly, *Narrative of My Captivity Among the Sioux Indians*, 188.

## 6 / The Hundred in the Hand

107    *"So, like wolves we travel"*: As quoted in Paul I. Manhart, *Lakota Tales and Texts in Translation* (Chamberlain, SD: Tipi Press, 1998), 639.

107    *December 21, 1866:* For the opening phase of the so-called Fetterman fight, I've relied upon several military and civilian eyewitness accounts, as well as Indian accounts, some of which have been rarely sourced. These include an undated letter of Horace D. Vankirk, 27th U.S. Infantry, Fort Phil Kearny, *The Janesville Daily Gazette*, Janesville, WI, January 30, 1867; undated letter of C. M. Hines, Fort Phil Kearny, *Chicago Tribune*, February 2, 1867; letter of unnamed sergeant, 2nd U.S. Cavalry, Fort Phil Kearny, January 21, 1867, *Rutland Daily Herald*, VT, April 24, 1867; Henry B. Carrington, "Official Report of the Phil Kearney Massacre," January 3, 1867, in Carrington, *The Indian Question*, 22–23; Margaret Carrington, *Ab-Sa-Ra-Ka, Home of the Crows, Being the Experience of an Officer's Wife on the Plains* (Philadelphia: J. B. Lippincott & Co., 1868), 200–205; Frances C. Carrington, *My Army Life on the Plains and the Fort Phil Kearney Massacre* (Philadelphia: J. B. Lippincott Company, 1910), 142–46; "Fort Phil Kearny Massacre," *The Omaha Daily Bee*, December 22, 1907; and the warrior accounts gathered in John H. Monnett, ed., *Eyewitness to the Fetterman Fight: Indian Views* (Norman: University of Oklahoma Press, 2017).

107    *weather was actually unseasonably mild:* Numerous authors and historians have mistakenly written that the weather on the day of the Fetterman fight was bitterly cold (they love to include a good blanket of snow as well). However, the available eyewitness accounts clearly tell us it was exactly the opposite. The wife of Fort Phil Kearny's commanding officer wrote that the morning was "quite pleasant," the men of the garrison going about in their shirtsleeves. And George Webber of Company C, 27th U.S. Infantry, wrote, "There was no snow on the ground. . . . I am very certain there was no snow at that time." See Carrington, *Ab-Sa-Ra-Ka*, 200; and letter of George Webber as quoted in the *National Tribune*, Washington, D.C., October 28, 1897.

109    *Crazy Horse and nine others:* John D. McDermott, *Red Cloud's War: The Bozeman Trail, 1866–1868*, 2 vols. (Norman: The Arthur H. Clark Company, 2010), 1: 207. There's been much hand-wringing in recent years over whether or not Crazy Horse was part of the famed decoy party. Credible evidence exists that he was. Rocky Bear, an Oglala veteran of the Fetterman fight, stated that Crazy Horse and eight warriors were assigned the task of drawing the soldiers out of the fort. The historian George E. Hyde reports that the Northern

Cheyenne Two Moons "stated in 1912 that Crazy Horse led the decoy party." A transcript of this particular Two Moons interview hasn't been located to date, but we know the chief was interviewed a number of times during this period. And Charles A. Eastman, who personally knew and interviewed numerous old Lakota warriors, wrote that "Crazy Horse was chosen to lead the attack on the woodchoppers, designed to draw the soldiers out of the fort." This last reference gives Crazy Horse a different role in the overall plan for the trap but reinforces our understanding that he played a key part in the day's events. See John R. Brennan, "Red Cloud – Marpiyaluta: A Brief History of the Most Celebrated Sioux Chief," *The Oglala Light* 3 (June 1907): 3; Hyde, *Red Cloud's Folk*, 146–48; and Eastman, *Indian Heroes and Great Chieftains*, 94.

109  *lodgepole with an American flag:* Testimony of John S. Smith, March 8, 1865, in *Condition of the Indian Tribes: Report of the Joint Special Committee Appointed Under Joint Resolution of March 3, 1865* (Washington: Government Printing Office, 1867), 41; and George Bent, "Forty Years with the Cheyennes," part one, *The Frontier: A Magazine of the West* 4 (October 1905): 6.

110  *hanged Colonel Chivington:* Maj. Gen. G. M. Dodge to Maj. Gen. John Pope, Horse Shoe, North Platte River, September 15, 1865, *The War of the Rebellion*, ser. 1, vol. 48, pt. 2 (Washington: Government Printing Office, 1896), 1229.

110  *cut and carried off the wires:* Letter of William F. Boardman, Sweetwater Bridge, Dakota Territory, August 1, 1865, in *The Highland News*, Hillsborough, Ohio, August 31, 1865.

110  *the "Long Tongue":* *Proceedings of the Great Peace Commission of 1867–1868* (Washington, D.C.: The Institute for the Development of Indian Law, 1975), 65.

110  *converged on Platte Bridge Station:* My account of the fighting at Platte Bridge Station is taken from letter of William F. Boardman, Sweetwater Bridge, Dakota Territory, August 1, 1865, *The Highland News*, August 31, 1865; letter of Sergeant Isaac B. Pennock, Platte Bridge Station, in *Gold Hill Daily News*, Gold Hill, NV, September 29, 1865; diary of Isaac B. Pennock, in Grace Raymond Hebard and E. A. Brininstool, *The Bozeman Trail: Historical Accounts of the Overland Routes into the Northwest and the Fights with Red Cloud's Warriors*, 2 vols. (Cleveland, OH: The Arthur H. Clark Company, 1922), 1: 167–71; diary of Lieutenant William I. Drew, in Hebard and Brininstool, *The Bozeman Trail*, 1: 179–200; Operator Mowberry dispatch, Sweetwater Bridge, August 3, 1865, in *Gold Hill Daily News*, August 3, 1865; "The Indian Butcheries," *The Leavenworth Times*, August 31, 1865; "Indian Troubles in the Far West," Fort Laramie, July 27, 1865, *Bradford Reporter*, Towanda, PA, August 3, 1865; George Bent, "Forty Years with the Cheyennes," part four, *The Frontier: A Magazine of the West* 4 (January 1906): 3–4; and John Hart, ed., *Bluecoat and Pioneer: The Recollections of John Benton Hart, 1864–1868* (Norman: University of Oklahoma Press, 2019).

112  *"We were so crazy":* Hart, ed., *Bluecoat and Pioneer*, 49 and 51. Trooper Hervey Johnson mentions the removal of High Back Wolf's leather war shirt. See William E. Unrau, ed., *Tending the Talking Wire: A Buck Soldier's View of Indian Country, 1863–1866* (Salt Lake City: University of Utah Press, 1979), 273.

113  *"the real savage yell":* Ibid.

113  *"It appeared as though"*: Pennock letter, *Gold Hill Daily News*, September 29, 1865.

114  *"one long, long bloody lane"*: Ibid.

115  *"cut open and brains taken"*: "The Indian Butcheries."

115  *warriors under Two Bears:* Maj. Gen. Alfred Sully to Brig. Gen. H. H. Sibley, June 27, 1865, *The War of the Rebellion*, ser. 1, vol. 48, pt. 2, 1013; and *Frontier Scout*, June 22, 1865.

115  *"I have Indians I know I can trust"*: Maj. Gen. Alfred Sully to Maj. Gen. John Pope, Sioux City, Iowa, June 10, 1865, *The War of the Rebellion*, ser. 1, vol. 48., pt. 2, 852.

116  *"If you are a brave man"*: As quoted in Maj. Gen. Alfred Sully to Maj. Gen. John Pope, Fort Rice, July 17, 1865, ibid., 1091. For the words spoken by other chiefs at their meeting with Sully, see the *Frontier Scout*, July 20, 1865.

116  *camps stretched for three miles:* Report of Maj. Gen. Alfred Sully, Fort Berthold, August 8, 1865, *The War of the Rebellion*, ser. 1, vol. 48., pt. 2, 1173.

116  *"Gen. Sully with his 'little boys'"*: "From Fort Rice," *Junction City Weekly Union*, Junction City, KS, August 19, 1865.

116  *rode through the camps crying:* One Bull interview, CC, box 104, folder 11; and Report of Maj. Gen. Alfred Sully, Fort Berthold, August 8, 1865, *The War of the Rebellion*, ser. 1, vol. 48., pt. 2, 1173.

116  *At 7:00 A.M. on July 28:* Accounts of the Battle of Fort Rice are nearly all from the soldiers' perspective. See "Ft. Rice Attack By Indians," *Sioux City Register*, August 12, 1865; *Frontier Scout*, issues of August 3, August 10, and October 12, 1865; Pattee, "Dakota Campaigns," 340–42; and Report of Maj. Gen. Alfred Sully, Fort Berthold, August 13, 1865, *The War of the Rebellion*, ser. 1, vol. 48, pt. 2, 1181.

116  *approximately fifteen hundred warriors:* The size of the warrior force in the available primary sources ranges from three hundred to three thousand. In the *Frontier Scout* of August 10, 1865, the editor, an eyewitness, estimated the warriors numbered at least fifteen hundred. Considering that the warriors' line is said to have stretched for more than a mile and surrounded the fort on three sides, it is hard to imagine this could be done with less than a thousand men.

117  *"successively with great bravery"*: *Frontier Scout*, August 3, 1865.

117  *"in the highest degree exciting"*: "Ft. Rice Attack by Indians," *Sioux City Register*, August 12, 1865.

118  *"There is many a squaw"*: *Frontier Scout*, August 3, 1865.

118  *"only lived by the little end"*: Ibid., October 12, 1865.

118  *"stories are very conflicting"*: Ibid.

118  *sixty miles of wire:* *Chicago Tribune*, September 25, 1865.

119  *"You will not receive overtures"*: Brig. Gen. P. Edward Connor to Col. Nelson Cole, Fort Laramie, July 4, 1865, *The War of the Rebellion*, ser. 1, vol. 48, pt. 2, 1049.

119  *"The only sin a commander"*: The *Montana Post*, Virginia City, MT, June 10, 1865.

119  *the Indians found the soldiers:* For my narrative of the fighting on the Powder River, I've relied upon Col. Nelson Cole's official report in *The War of the Rebel-*

*lion*, ser. 1, vol. 48, pt. 1, 366–80; "Account of the Late Expedition, under Gen. P. E. Connor, against the Indians of the North-west," *The Weekly Free Press*, Atchison, KS, November 18, 1865; "The Indian War," *The Kansas Chief*, White Cloud, KS, October 19, 1865; Eagle Elk interview, Neihardt Papers; and White Bull interview, CC, box 105, folder 24.

121    *Sitting Bull, riding a sorrel horse:* White Bull interview, CC, box 105, folder 24.

121    *horse had ridden down an enemy:* Joseph White Bull, *Lakota Warrior*, translated and edited by James H. Howard (Lincoln: University of Nebraska Press, 1998), 73.

121    *"the Indians are brave":* As quoted in Garavaglia and Worman, *Firearms of the American West*, 202.

121    *"useless" against warriors:* Col. Nelson Cole report, *The War of the Rebellion*, ser. 1, vol. 48, pt. 1, 374.

121    *"Just keep away for a little while":* Eagle Elk interview, Neihardt Papers.

123    *"The whole bottom and hills":* Lieut. Charles H. Springer as quoted in David E. Wagner, *Powder River Odyssey: Nelson Cole's Western Campaign of 1865: The Journals of Lyman G. Bennett and Other Eyewitness Accounts* (Norman, OK: The Arthur H. Clark Company, 2009), 178.

124    *destroyed an Arapaho village:* See H. E. Palmer, "History of the Powder River Expedition of 1865," *Transactions and Reports of the Nebraska State Historical Society* 2 (1887): 213–20; and Maj. Gen. G. M. Dodge to Maj. Gen. John Pope, Central City, CO, September 27, 1865, in Grenville M. Dodge, *The Battle of Atlanta and Other Campaigns, Addresses, Etc.* (Council Bluffs, IA: The Monarch Printing Company, 1911), 98.

125    *now willing to discuss peace:* Report of E. B. Taylor, Superintendent of Indian Affairs, October 1, 1866, *Message of the President of the United States . . . to the Two Houses of Congress*, H. Exec. Doc. No. 1, 39th Cong., 2nd Sess., 211.

125    *Red Cloud stood six feet tall:* Letter dated Fort Sedgwick, CO, February 10, 1867, *Gold Hill Daily News*, March 8, 1867.

125    *"a magnificent specimen of manhood":* Brennan, "Red Cloud—Marpiyaluta," 1.

125    *"He that smokes this pipe":* "From Dakota Territory," *New Orleans Daily Crescent*, LA, April 6, 1866. Additional accounts of the Fort Laramie conferences with the Sioux in March and June are found in "Interesting Letter from Dacotah," *The Pittsfield Sun*, MA, April 19, 1866; "The Peace Commission at Fort Laramie," *Rocky Mountain News*, June 18, 1866; "From Fort Laramie," *The Montana Post*, July 7, 1866; "The Indian Treaty Commission," *Chicago Tribune*, July 8, 1866; "Indian Treaties," *Chicago Tribune*, July 21, 1866; and William Murphy account in Carrington, *My Army Life on the Plains*, 291–92.

125    *"The white men will come here":* As quoted in "The Far West," *The Philadelphia Inquirer*, March 31, 1866.

126    *"My tribe want peace":* *The Montana Post*, July 7, 1866. The chief was Roman Nose, a Miniconjou.

126    *He became angry at how:* Carrington, *My Army Life on the Plains*, 292.

126    *"Great Father sends us presents":* Carrington, *Ab-Sa-Ra-Ka*, 78–79.

126    *abandoned the treaty talks:* Ibid., 79; and Murphy account in Carrington, *My Army Life on the Plains*, 292.

127    *"road from Laramie to Powder River":* "The Indians," *The Evening Telegraph*,

September 26, 1866. See also "From Leavenworth," *Daily Ohio Statesman*, Columbus, August 30, 1866; and "Death of Lieut. Daniels," *Burlington Daily Times*, VT, September 14, 1866.

127    *more like prison walls:* Carrington, *Ab-Sa-Ra-Ka*, 180.

127    *Sioux assailed river traffic:* Reports of the several Missouri River attacks are found in the *Muscatine Evening Journal*, IA, June 12, 1866; the *Montana Post*, June 30, 1866; the *Sioux City Register*, August 18, 1866; the *Louisville Daily Courier*, KY, October 12, 1866; and the *Philadelphia Inquirer*, PA, November 29, 1866.

128    *"right now would be a good time":* As quoted in Nelson A. Miles, *Personal Recollections and Observations of General Nelson A. Miles* (Chicago: The Werner Company, 1896), 194. Another version of the red shirt episode is found in the affidavit of Charles W. Hoffman, December 3, 1902, James Boyd Hubbell Papers, 1865–1906, A/.H876, Minnesota Historical Society, St. Paul. Although Miles and Hoffman differ on some key details, I've done my best to combine the two accounts.

128    *nearby Fort Buford:* "Military Order in Nebraska," *The Evening Star*, Washington, D.C., August 3, 1866.

128    *"This country is the finest":* Charles W. Hoffman to George Hoffman, Fort Buford, January 10, 1867, in *Union and Dakotaian*, Yankton, SD, February 23, 1867.

129    *twice overran the post's sawmill:* For Sitting Bull's December attacks on Fort Buford, see Miles, *Personal Recollections*, 194–95; Joseph Henry Taylor, *Sketches of Frontier and Indian Life on the Upper Missouri and Great Plains* (Washburn, ND: published by the author, 1895), 109–10; and Utley, *The Lance and the Shield*, 72.

130    *Try to kill as many white men:* White Bull interview, CC, box 105, folder 4; and Mitch Boyer testimony in John S. Gray, *Custer's Last Campaign: Mitch Boyer and the Little Bighorn Reconstructed* (Lincoln: University of Nebraska Press, 1991), 403.

130    *called such men* winktes: Lame Deer (Fire) and Erdoes, *Lame Deer: Seeker of Visions*, 117 and 149. Some *winktes*, a "half man-half woman kind of being," were intersex individuals. See also Stands in Timber and Liberty, *A Cheyenne Voice*, 346.

131    *"I have ten [white] men":* As quoted in George Bird Grinnell, *The Fighting Cheyennes* (New York: Charles Scribner's Sons, 1915), 228–29.

131    *"Answer quickly":* Ibid.

132    *highly convincing performance:* Joseph M. Marshall III writes that Crazy Horse halted, dismounted, and "calmly scraped ice from the bottom of his horse's hooves" as bullets whizzed around him. Marshall provides no source for this extremely doubtful detail. An equally dubious claim put forth by modern authors is that Crazy Horse mooned Fetterman. See Marshall's *The Journey of Crazy Horse: A Lakota History* (New York: Viking, 2004), 148; and Bob Drury and Tom Clavin, *The Heart of Everything That Is: The Untold Story of Red Cloud, An American Legend* (New York: Simon & Schuster, 2013), 329 and 371–72.

133    *clamped a hand over his pony's nostrils:* Fire Thunder account in John G. Neihardt, *Black Elk Speaks, Being the Life Story of a Holy Man of the Ogalala Sioux as told to John G. Neihardt* (New York: William Morrow & Company, 1932), 11.

133   *the decoys split into two groups:* Grinnell, *The Fighting Cheyennes,* 232.

133   *sixty to seventy cartridges each:* McDermott, *Red Cloud's War,* 1: 216.

134   *"Indians killed each other":* Fire Thunder account, *The Sixth Grandfather,* 103. Eagle Elk stated to John G. Neihardt that the warriors "shot over the top of the hill and killed some of their own people." See Eagle Elk interview, Neihardt Papers. These friendly fire casualties were also mentioned in one of the early published Indian accounts of the fight. See "The Indian Campaign," *The Montana Post,* March 16, 1867.

134   *American Horse, knife in hand:* American Horse interview, Jensen, *Voices of the American West,* 1: 280–81.

134   *on foot, leading their horses:* Grinnell, *The Fighting Cheyennes,* 233.

135   *riding a fleet bald-faced bay:* Stanley Vestal, *Warpath: The True Story of the Fighting Sioux Told in a Biography of Chief White Bull* (Boston: Houghton Mifflin Company, 1934), 54.

135   *"really was flirting with death":* As quoted in William J. Bordeaux, *Custer's Conqueror* (Sioux Falls, SD: Smith and Company, 1951), 23.

135   *separated the warrior's head:* "The Fort Phil Kearny Massacre," *The United States Army and Navy Journal,* New York, NY, April 6, 1867.

135   *bodies of the dead infantrymen:* White Bull stated that the remaining cavalrymen reached the infantrymen while some were still alive, and they fought together until they were all killed. However, Grinnell's Cheyenne informants clearly indicated that the infantry detachment was wiped out before the cavalry. Mixed-blood interpreter Mitch Boyer learned from a Lakota veteran of the fight that the two detachments were destroyed separately. White Bull interview, CC, box 104, folder 12; Grinnell, *The Fighting Cheyennes,* 232–34; and Mitch Boyer interview, Gray, *Custer's Last Campaign,* 403.

135   *"I wasn't after horses":* Fire Thunder account, *The Sixth Grandfather,* 104.

135   *as if he were about to charge:* Grinnell, *The Fighting Cheyennes,* 234.

135   *"Let's go, this is a good day to die!":* Fire Thunder account, *The Sixth Grandfather,* 104.

135   *smashed his bugle on the heads:* "The Fort Phil Kearny Massacre," *The United States Army and Navy Journal,* April 6, 1867.

136   *"a shorter time than it takes":* Charles A. Eastman, "Rain-In-The-Face: The Story of a Sioux Warrior," *The Outlook* 84 (October 27, 1906): 509.

136   *"All are dead but the dog":* As quoted in Grinnell, *The Fighting Cheyennes,* 234. Fire Thunder claimed that the dog *wasn't* killed because "he looked too sweet." Fire Thunder account, *The Sixth Grandfather,* 104.

## 7 / Too Many Tongues

137   *"There are a number of chiefs":* As quoted in Gray, *Custer's Last Campaign,* 403.

137   *blizzard blew in that evening:* Fire Thunder account, *The Sixth Grandfather,* 104; and Carrington, *My Army Life,* 150.

137   *Lone Bear, his friend:* DeBarthe, *Life and Adventures,* 348–49.

138   *all the dead and wounded:* Estimates of Indian casualties in the Hundred in the

Hand engagement vary greatly, and no two agree. Fort Kearny's commanding officer, Colonel Henry B. Carrington, counted sixty-five pools of blood on
the battlefield, which he believed represented Indian fatalities, but these pools
could just as easily have been created by wounded Indian ponies. I've followed
the estimates provided in 1867 by Mitch Boyer in Gray, *Custer's Last Campaign*,
402. See also George Sword interview, Jensen, *Voices of the American West*, 1:
329; "The Indian Campaign," *The Montana Post*, March 16, 1867; and John B.
Sanborn to O. H. Browning, Washington, D.C., July 8, 1867, in "Letter of the
Secretary of the Interior . . . touching the origin of Indian hostilities on the
frontier," Sen. Exec. Doc. No. 13, 40th Cong., 1st Sess., 66.

138   *fired their guns wildly:* American Horse interview in Jensen, *Voices of the American West*, 1: 281.

138   *his renown as one of the bravest:* See American Horse interview in Monnett,
ed., *Eyewitness to the Fetterman Fight*, 59.

138   *found the weather "delightful":* William J. Fetterman to Dr. Charles Terry, Fort
Phil Kearny, November 26, 1866, in John D. McDermott, ed., "Documents
Relating to the Fetterman Fight," *Annals of Wyoming* 63 (Spring 1991): 68.

138   *"no command of good soldiers":* As quoted in McDermott, *Red Cloud's War*, 1:
173 n. 29.

139   *taking at least one Indian scalp:* Carrington, *Ab-Sa-Ra-Ka*, 209; and Carrington,
*My Army Life*, 143.

139   *keep a last bullet for himself:* Carrington, *Ab-Sa-Ra-Ka*, 248.

139   *"Let me go":* As quoted in William Haymond Bisbee, *Through Four American
Wars: The Impressions and Experiences of Brigadier General William Henry Bisbee*
(Boston: Meador Publishing Company, 1931), 174.

140   *under one supreme chief:* Bray, "Sitting Bull and Lakota Leadership," 21–22.

140   *to observe a singular ceremony:* My discussion of this event is primarily drawn
from One Bull interview, CC, box 104, folder 11; White Bull interview, CC,
box 105, folder 8; the account of Father Jean-Baptiste Marie Genin as sourced by
Linda W. Slaughter, "Leaves from Northwestern History"; and Robert Higheagle, "How Sitting Bull Was Made a Chief," CC, box 104, folder 22. Several
sites have been offered as the location of this gathering. One Bull said it was
near Rainy Butte. White Bull claimed the camps were on the Rosebud. Linda
Slaughter, based on the notes of Father Genin, identified variously the region
of Lake Traverse and Big Stone Lake and also the area of Fort Abercrombie,
all on the Minnesota River. Another possibile location is suggested by a letter
written at Fort Ransom that summer. It stated that a scout from the James
River reported "an abundance of Indians on this side of the Missouri River, in
consequence of the buffalo having come this way." Letter by "Montana," Fort
Ransom, Dakota Territory, July 19, 1867, "The Minnesota Expedition," *The
Montana Post*, August 31, 1867

140   *an act of high tribute:* Waggoner, *Witness*, 384.

140   *over the entire Sioux Nation:* Father Genin always insisted that Black Moon
was the supreme chief of all the Sioux and that this ceremony named Sitting
Bull as head war chief of the Sioux. However, there does not appear to be a
clear distinction between the two titles. In the One Bull interview, he states

that Sitting Bull was elected "as our war chief—leader of the entire Sioux nation."

140    *"When you tell us to fight":* As quoted in LaPointe, *Sitting Bull,* 51.

140    *Each feather came from a warrior:* Ibid.

141    *Crazy Horse a war chief:* One Bull interview, CC, box 104, folder 11; Waggoner, *Witness,* 384; and Usher L. Burdick, *The Last Battle of the Sioux Nation* (Stevens Point, WI: Worzalla Publishing Co., 1929), 79.

141    *fought side by side with the Cheyennes:* Dixon, "Crazy Horse and the Cheyenne," 55. Crazy Horse's close relationship with the Cheyennes is also referenced in Stands in Timber and Liberty, *A Cheyenne Voice,* 245 and 445.

141    *Genin was a French-born priest:* J. Fletcher Williams, *History of the Upper Mississippi Valley* (Minneapolis: Minnesota Historical Company, 1881), 686; and Genin biographical sketch at https://www.omiworld.org/lemma/genin-jean -baptiste/. My description of Genin's physical appearance is from Slaughter, "Leaves from Northwestern History," 243; and the *New York Herald,* July 2, 1879.

141    *Genin described his parish:* "Engineering in the Northwest," *Vermont Watchman and State Journal,* Montpelier, VT, January 4, 1871.

141    *Father Genin within the last year:* In a letter dated September 8, 1876, Genin stated that he had been a missionary to the Sioux "for the last ten years." A news story from 1878 reported that Genin had been with the Sioux since 1867 "and almost has become one of them." Slaughter, "Leaves from Northwestern History," 257; and *The Daily Journal,* Ogdensburg, NY, June 20, 1878.

141    *"the man who talks to the medicine-chief":* Clark, *The Indian Sign Language,* 310.

142    *adopted the priest as his brother:* Slaughter, "Leaves from Northwestern History," 227 and 247; and "In Sitting Bull's Camp," *The New York Herald,* June 10, 1878. Genin's relationship with Sitting Bull and the northern Lakotas has been oddly overlooked by previous biographers and historians. At the time of Genin's death in 1900, he was gathering material for a planned book of his experiences in the West. His "voluminous notes," in both French and English, were left to his old friend Linda W. Slaughter, for her to compose the book. She did borrow heavily from these notes for her "Leaves from Northwestern History," but the book, with a working title of "The Sun and the Cross," never appeared. Unfortunately, Genin's original manuscripts are unaccounted for. References to Genin's notes and the planned book are found in the *Bismarck Daily Tribune,* ND, February 5, April 10, and June 2, 1900.

142    *forbade the consumption of "firewater":* Slaughter, "Leaves from Northwestern History," 232; and Linda W. Slaughter, "Fort Abercrombie," *Collections of the State Historical Society of North Dakota* 1 (1906): 421. One Bull seems to confirm Sitting Bull's harsh penalty. See interview of One Bull and Mrs. One Bull, CC, box 105, folder 19.

142    *claiming more than his share:* Bray, *Crazy Horse,* 103.

142    *refused to recognize Sitting Bull:* LaPointe, *Sitting Bull,* 52.

142    *"chief of the Sioux nation":* One Bull, CC, box 105, folder 19.

143    *"A chief's authority depended on":* Bad Bear as quoted in Walker, *Lakota Society,* 25.

143 *"Indians own, hold, possess, and occupy":* James R. Whitehead, "The Indian War," *Leavenworth Daily Commercial*, August 14, 1867.

144 *their target was the weakly guarded operations:* The best single source on the Wagon Box Fight is Jerry Keenan's *The Wagon Box Fight: An Episode of Red Cloud's War* (Conshohocken, PA: Savas Publishing Company, 2000), which reproduces the after-action reports of the Fort Kearny officers involved, as well as the recollections of three soldier participants. Accounts by the Indian participants are few, the most detailed being White Bull in his interview with Walter Campbell, box 104, folder 12. Father Peter John Powell incorporates the recollections of three Cheyennes in his story of the fight in *People of the Sacred Mountain: A History of the Northern Cheyenne Chiefs and Warrior Societies, 1830–1879, with an Epilogue, 1969–1974*, 2 vols. (San Francisco: Harper & Row, 1981), 2: 752–54.

145 *"Look at the Indians!":* As quoted in the account of Samuel Gibson, Keenan, *The Wagon Box Fight*, 67.

145 *They easily overran the camp:* "Was in Wagon Box Fight," *The Nebraska State Journal*, Lincoln, March 12, 1911; and Eagle Elk interview, Neihardt Papers.

146 *grabbed their ponies' manes:* This famous warrior feat of horseback fighting is described in White Bull interview, CC, box 105, folder 8.

147 *dead warriors, charring them black:* Young Little Wolf, a Cheyenne participant, told the historian George Bird Grinnell that the fire that charred the warrior bodies had been set by the soldiers, presumably to thwart the Indian charges. See "Clarence Reckmeyer Delves Deeply for the Truth About the 'Wagon Box Fight,'" *The Nebraska State Journal*, June 19, 1927.

148 *named Stings Like Wasp:* Both White Bull and George Sword give this warrior's Lakota name as Ji pa la. White Bull identifies him as a Miniconjou. See White Bull interview, CC, box 104, folder 12; and George Sword interview, Jensen, *Voices of the American West*, 1: 329.

148 *"The sight was fascinating":* Samuel Gibson account, Keenan, *The Wagon Box Fight*, 77.

149 *a Cheyenne named Sun's Robe:* Powell, *People of the Sacred Mountain*, 2: 754.

149 *One of the civilian contractors:* This was J. R. Porter, and his account of the Wagon Box Fight was published in the *Chicago Tribune*, August 26, 1867. For another estimate of Indian losses, see "Indian Affairs," *Gold Hill Daily News*, September 6, 1867.

150 *bloody moccasins and leggings:* "The Fight at Fort Phil Kearney," *Chicago Tribune*, August 26, 1867.

150 *Red Feather dismissed:* Doane Robinson, "The Education of Red Cloud," *South Dakota Historical Collections* 12 (1924): 171 n. 21.

150 *"It was a big running fight":* James H. Howard, ed., *Lakota Warrior: White Bull* (Lincoln: University of Nebraska Press, 1998), 39. The pictograph is reproduced as plate six.

151 *surprised a Wells, Fargo & Company:* *The Manhattan Nationalist*, September 21, 1867. According to the newspaper report, the three men were killed at Crazy Woman's Fork, on the road to Fort Reno.

151 *"all who are here think it":* Jerome A. Greene, "'We Do Not Know What the

Government Intends to Do . . .": Lt. Palmer Writes from the Bozeman Trail, 1867–68," *Montana The Magazine of Western History* 28 (Summer 1978): 19.

151     *"The only way to settle the question"*: As quoted in McDermott, *Red Cloud's War*, 2: 362.

152     *"three choice cows"*: Letter dated Fort Buford, Dakota Territory, August 3, 1867, in the *New York Herald*, August 23, 1867. One of these cows belonged to the post's colonel. See Maria B. Kimball, *A Soldier-Doctor of Our Army: James P. Kimball, Late Colonel and Assistant Surgeon-General, U.S. Army* (Boston: Houghton Mifflin Company, 1917), 43–44.

152     *"I have killed, robbed, and injured"*: As quoted in Coues, ed., *Forty Years a Fur Trader on the Upper Missouri*, 2: 429–30.

153     *countless, sun-bleached buffalo bones*: F. Barham Zincke, *Last Winter in the United States* (London: John Murray, 1868), 208.

154     *"their disappearance will only be"*: Ibid., 238.

154     *"We don't want peace"*: "The Indian War," *The Chicago Tribune*, September 20, 1867.

154     *"turned in some other direction"*: "The Indian Troubles," *The Brooklyn Union*, NY, September 27, 1867.

154     *"Who is our Great Father?"*: Ibid. Slightly different translations of the chiefs' speeches at North Platte, based on the handwritten minutes of the peace commission, are found in *Proceedings of the Great Peace Commission*, 57–65.

155     *"hardly think of what you call war"*: "The Indian War," *The Evening Telegraph*, Philadelphia, PA, September 26, 1867.

155     *"a contract of peace"*: *Proceedings of the Great Peace Commission*, 63.

156     *a nephew, Lone Man*: Both White Bull and George Sword remembered that Lone Man (also translated as Only Man) was killed charging the corral at the Wagon Box Fight.

156     *"Money is no object"*: *The Lancaster Intelligencer*, Lancaster, PA, November 9, 1867.

156     *spotted a large wagon train*: Much of my information for this engagement is from McDermott, *Red Cloud's War*, 2: 463–66; and "Indian News," *The Leavenworth Times*, December 1, 1867.

157     *among those to claim one*: Bordeaux, *Custer's Conqueror*, 24.

157     *carcasses of a dozen ponies*: George P. Belden, *Belden, the White Chief, or Twelve Years Among the Wild Indians of the Plains* (Cincinnati: C. F. Vent, 1871), 378.

157     *"They captured a train of wagons"*: The winter count was created by American Horse. See Greene and Thornton, eds., *The Year the Stars Fell*, 261.

158     *"meet war with war"*: "The Indians," *The Chicago Tribune*, November 23, 1867. See also "Report of the Indian Peace Commission," *New York Tribune*, January 9, 1868.

158     *stole a herd of seventy horses*: "Indian News," *The Leavenworth Times*, December 1, 1867.

158     *Red Cloud was prepared to fight*: "From the Plains," *The Chicago Tribune*, December 13, 1867.

158     *outraged the fort's officers*: "Dakota," *The Chicago Tribune*, February 15, 1868. This news item is a letter written by Lieut. George Henry Palmer at Fort Phil Kearny on January 2, 1868.

159    *"He has sent us":* As quoted in Belden, *Belden, the White Chief,* 393.

159    *represent the war chief's interests:* Bray, *Crazy Horse,* 115.

159    *"I want to tell you":* As quoted in Belden, *Belden, the White Chief,* 390.

159    *headmen left largely dissatisfied:* Ibid., 393; and "Dakota," *The Chicago Tribune,* February 15, 1868.

159    *"They have all pledged themselves":* Telegram of H. M. Mathews, Fort Phil Kearny, January 13, 1868, in *The Philadelphia Inquirer,* January 22, 1868.

159    *warriors stole a herd of mules:* "Dakota," *The Chicago Tribune,* February 15, 1868.

160    *far too expensive:* James C. Olson, *Red Cloud and the Sioux Problem* (Lincoln: University of Nebraska Press, 1965), 71.

160    *preferring the much safer Missouri River:* "Indian Affairs in the Far West," *The Philadelphia Inquirer,* March 12, 1868.

160    *couldn't steal the locomotives:* W. T. Sherman to General U. S. Grant, Fort Laramie, Dakota Territory, May 8, 1868, in "Subsistence of Indian Tribes," H. Exec. Doc. No. 239, 40th Cong., 2nd Sess., 3.

160    *withdraw the garrisons:* "Indian Affairs in the Far West," *The Philadelphia Inquirer,* March 12, 1868; and McDermott, *Red Cloud's War,* 2: 484.

160    *During the month of March:* "The Indians," *The New York Herald,* April 9, 1868; *The Courier-Journal,* Louisville, KY, April 19, 1868; "The Northwestern Fort," *The Border Sentinel,* Mound City, KS, May 15, 1868; and McDermott, *Red Cloud's War,* 2: 485–88. The attacks on the Horse Shoe Ranch and Twin Springs Ranch of March 19–21, 1868, have been attributed by some authors to Crazy Horse and his followers. Crazy Horse's name is not mentioned in the contemporary reports of these depredations. In fact, no leader of the war party involved is named. However, an 1894 account by one of the raid's survivors, John R. Smith, names Crazy Horse as the leader. Smith doesn't explain how he knew Crazy Horse, but his identification of the Oglala war leader loses credibility when he writes about a negotiation with Crazy Horse for the lives of himself and his companions. Smith claimed Crazy Horse "could talk fair English." The Smith account is published in DeBarthe, *Life and Adventures,* 525–40.

161    *they found no Indians:* Agnes Wright Spring, ed., "Old Letter Book Discloses Economic History of Fort Laramie, 1858–1871," *Annals of Wyoming* 13 (October 1941): 253.

161    *He initially had trouble:* "The Indian Commission," *The New York Herald,* May 14, 1868.

161    *"We are on the mountain":* As quoted in Olson, *Red Cloud and the Sioux Problem,* 74–75. When Red Cloud traveled to Washington in 1872, poor Alexander Gardner missed being the first to photograph the Oglala war chief by two days. That distinction belongs to Gardner's competitor and former employer Mathew Brady, who photographed Red Cloud on May 28, 1872. See Frank H. Goodyear III, *Red Cloud: Photographs of a Lakota Chief* (Lincoln: University of Nebraska Press, 2003), 18–25.

161    *Gardner did obtain several good images:* See Jane L. Aspinwall, *Alexander Gardner: The Western Photographs, 1867–1868* (Kansas City: The Hall Family Foundation and The Nelson-Atkins Museum of Art, 2014).

162    thirty-eight Oglala headmen and warriors: "Official Announcement of Treaties Concluded with Indians," *The New York Herald*, June 3, 1868.

162    "I will sign": Proceedings of the Great Peace Commission, 117.

162    They placed a copy: Ibid., 118–19.

162    set aflame by warriors: McDermott, *Red Cloud's War*, 2: 522–25.

163    That document, prepared in advance: The original Fort Laramie Treaty of 1868 is available for viewing online at https://americanindian.si.edu/nationtonation /fort-laramie-treaty.html.

164    "with a show of reluctance": Proceedings of the Great Peace Commission, 174.

164    again trade with the sutler: Spring, ed., "Old Letter Book," 287.

164    "Too many tongues": White Bull interview, CC, folder 105, box 24.

164    "False Papers": Bordeaux, *Custer's Conqueror*, 24.

## 8 / Land of Uncertainty

165    "My brothers, shall we submit?": As quoted in Eastman, *Indian Heroes and Great Chieftains*, 120–21.

165    the Black Gown is approaching: My sources for Father De Smet's visit to Sitting Bull's village are Charles Galpin's journal, De Smet's own letters, and the reminiscences of Matilda Galpin (Eagle Woman). These are found in Gilbert J. Garraghan, ed., "Father De Smet's Sioux Peace Mission of 1868 and the Journal of Charles Galpin," *Mid-America: An Historical Review* 13 (October 1930): 141–63; Chittenden and Richardson, eds., *Life, Letters and Travels of Father Pierre-Jean De Smet*, 3: 890–922; and Frances Chamberlain Holley, *Once Their Home, or Our Legacy from the Dahkotahs* (Chicago: Donohue & Henneberry, 1891), 303–11.

166    "a very good Catholic": Catholic Telegraph, Cincinnati, OH, July 29, 1868.

167    "Another white man coming to cheat us": One Bull interview, CC, box 105, folder 19.

167    Sitting Bull places a guard: Although White Bull wasn't present, he recalled the perceived danger to Father De Smet and his uncle's actions to protect the priest. See White Bull interview, CC, box 105, folder 4.

167    "Had it been any other man": As quoted in the *Catholic Telegraph*, July 29, 1868.

167    "I have no other motives": Chittenden and Richardson, eds., *Life, Letters and Travels of Father Pierre-Jean De Smet*, 3: 896.

168    "the only white man who never tells lies": Catholic Telegraph, July 29, 1868.

168    "bury all your bitterness": Proceedings of the Great Peace Commission, 131.

168    "I am, and always have been": Ibid., 133.

169    "They stand the wintry storms": Ibid.

169    "Some of my people will go": Holley, *Once Their Home*, 310.

169    a rumor was current: Lucile M. Kane, ed., *Military Life in Dakota: The Journal of Philippe Régis de Trobriand* (St. Paul, MN: Alvord Memorial Commission, 1951), 289.

169    identical view with Red Cloud: Ibid., 289–90.

170    The chief had lost his first wife: LaPointe, *Sitting Bull*, 40–41. LaPointe's book

has a helpful genealogical chart of Sitting Bull's family, which serves as the frontispiece.

170     **this talisman of the Great Holy Man:** One Bull and Mrs. One Bull interview, CC, box 105, folder 19; Walter S. Campbell to Lloyd M. Smith, Norman, OK, February 18, 1957, author's collection; and Karl Van Den Broeck, "Everything We Know About Sitting Bull's Crucifix Is Wrong," *True West* 65 (November 2018): 20–24. Walter Campbell acquired this crucifix from Sitting Bull's nephew, One Bull. It's currently on display in the visitor center at Little Bighorn Battlefield National Monument, Crow Agency, Montana.

170     **a botched arrest attempt:** Robert W. Larson, *Gall: Lakota War Chief* (Norman: University of Oklahoma Press, 2007), 55–57; Lewis F. Crawford, *Rekindling Camp Fires: The Exploits of Ben Arnold (Connor)* (Bismarck, ND: Capital Book Co., 1926), 167–69; "An Incident in Chief Gall's Life," *The Washburn Leader*, Washburn, ND, December 15, 1894; and Chittenden and Richardson, eds., *Life, Letters and Travels of Father Pierre-Jean De Smet*, 3: 918–19.

171     **"to keep the whites out of your country":** *Proceedings of the Great Peace Commission*, 143.

171     **succumbing to the white man's bribes:** Vestal, *New Sources*, 229–30; and "An Illustrious Sioux: The Gall Relates Some of the Incidents of the Past Fifteen Years of His Life," part 1, *Rocky Mountain Husbandman*, Diamond City, MT, May 5, 1881. Gall's name appears on the treaty as Man That Goes in the Middle.

171     **Similar feelings existed against:** Waggoner, *Witness*, 48–49.

171     **Let the young men fight:** White Bull interview, CC, box 105, folder 24; and LaPointe, *Sitting Bull*, 69.

172     **targeted the cow herd at Fort Buford:** *Message from the President of the United States to the Two Houses of Congress at the Commencement of the Third Session of the Fortieth Congress* (Washington: Government Printing Office, 1869), 358–59; and Rodenbaugh and Haskin, eds., *The Army of the United States*, 682–83.

172     **"fought like trained soldiers":** *The Representative*, Fox Lake, WI, September 18, 1868.

173     **"that was his business":** Horn Chips interview, Jensen, *Voices of the American West*, 1: 274.

173     **the number of his followers:** In a recent history of the Lakota people, the author asserts that warriors wanted to follow Crazy Horse because he was a "child of privilege." In other words, it was his lineage that was the attraction. Not only is everything about this assertion incorrect—Crazy Horse's father was a respected holy man, not a chief—but the author demonstrates an utter lack of understanding of what drove young Lakota men, and that was personal glory, the counting of coups. Crazy Horse "was beloved for his bravery," said Iron Horse, his brother-in-law. Iron Horse's brother, Red Feather, said that "some Indians take their high position in their tribe from their fathers and some win theirs by fighting. Crazy Horse became known through the wars in which he took part." Sitting Bull, who also won his position through his deeds, commented that "an Indian may be an inherited chief, but he has to make himself chief by his bravery." The more courageous and victorious a warrior or chief, the more others wanted to follow him, for that leader's successes increased the

opportunities for achieving their own battle honors. See Pekka Hämäläinen, *Lakota America: A New History of Indigenous Power* (New Haven, CT: Yale University Press, 2019), 184–85; Iron Horse as quoted in Standing Bear, *Land of the Spotted Eagle*, 180; "Emil Red Feather, Aged Indian, Tells Vivid Story of Custer Massacre," *The Daily Argus-Leader*, July 18, 1925: and "A Chat with the Chief," *The Omaha Daily Bee*, August 9, 1881.

173    *Crazy Horse refused to allow:* Eagle Elk interview, Neihardt Papers; He Dog interview, *The Hinman Interviews*, 23; and *The Diaries of John Gregory Bourke*, I: 299.

173    *"We know Crazy Horse better":* William Garnett statement on the death of Crazy Horse, Pine Ridge Agency, SD, August 19, 1920, typescript, James McLaughlin Letter, 1920, H74-115, SDSHS.

173    *"had such a reputation that":* Eagle Elk interview, Neihardt Papers.

173    *invested as Shirt Wearers:* He Dog interview, *Hinman Interviews*, 22; William Garnett interview, Jensen, *Voices of the American West*, I: 4–5; Short Bull interview, Sandoz Collection; and William Garnett to V. T. McGillycuddy, Pine Ridge, South Dakota, March 6, 1922, Watson Papers. For the date of the ceremony, I've followed the well-reasoned timeline of Kingsley Bray, *Crazy Horse*, 423 n. 3.

173    *position of tremendous responsibility:* See the above references, as well as Hassrick, *The Sioux*, 26–27.

173    *shirt in the Shirt Wearer's name:* Hassrick, *The Sioux*, 26–27; Standing Bear, *Land of the Spotted Eagle*, 185; Clark Wissler, "Societies and Ceremonial Associations in the Oglala Division of the Teton-Dakota," *American Museum of Natural History Anthropological Papers* 11, pt. 1 (1912): 39; Walker, *Lakota Society*, 99; Emma I. Hansen, *Plains Indian Buffalo Cultures: Art from the Paul Dyck Collection* (Norman: University of Oklahoma Press, 2018), 110–11; and Markoe, ed., *Vestiges of a Proud Nation*, 94.

174    *"They were elected to give":* Black Elk interview, *The Sixth Grandfather*, 322.

175    *"We came here to be killed":* As quoted by Little Swan, a Miniconjou, who brought the news of the fight to the Cheyenne agency, near Fort Sully. His account was published in several newspapers, but see the *Chicago Tribune*, February 26, 1870.

176    *"Thirty Crows Killed":* For Húnkpapa accounts of this battle see Circling Hawk interview, CC, box 105, folder 13; Old Bull interview, CC, box 106, folder 50; and White Bull interview, CC, box 105, folder 8. Another account, far less reliable, is found in DeBarthe, *Life and Adventures*, 103–5. Oglala artist Amos Bad Heart Bull depicted this fight in three drawings. See Amos Bad Heart Bull and Helen Blish, *A Pictographic History of the Oglala Sioux* (Lincoln: University of Nebraska Press, 1967), 185–87.

177    *"an Ogallalla Chief":* Alpha Wright to the editor, Fort Laramie, Wyoming Territory, April 19, 1870, in the *Nebraska Herald*, Plattsmouth, NE, May 5, 1870. Wright's letter in the *Chicago Tribune* appears in the issue of May 3. This incident was reported in other newspapers as well, including the *Philadelphia Age*, April 20, 1870; the *Buffalo Express*, NY, April 22, 1870; and the *Philadelphia Inquirer*, April 22, 1870, which reproduced Crazy Horse's name as "Crazy

George." See also R. Eli Paul, "An Early Reference to Crazy Horse," *Nebraska History* 75 (1994): 189–90.

177     **Black Buffalo Woman:** The most detailed account of Crazy Horse's affair with Black Buffalo Woman comes from He Dog in *Hinman Interviews*. In addition to this seminal source, I've relied upon the Horn Chips interview, Jensen, *Voices of the American West*, 1: 274; the Eagle Elk interview, Neihardt Papers; the William Garnett interview, Jensen, *Voices of the American West*, 1: 75; and Bordeaux, *Custer's Conqueror*, 41–43.

177     **enlisted Horn Chips to create powerful charms:** Belitz, *Chips Collection of Crazy Horse Medicines* (Hot Springs, SD: privately printed, n.d.), 58–65.

178     **cap and ball revolver:** At two different times, He Dog stated that the gun No Water used to shoot Crazy Horse was a revolver. Crazy Horse's biographer Kingsley Bray favors an account by Lone Eagle, who claimed the weapon used was a derringer. However, "Lone Eagle" was a fiction created by Floyd Shuster Maine (1889–1971). Maine's book, *Lone Eagle . . . The White Sioux* (Albuquerque: University of New Mexico Press, 1956), is a complete fabrication, one that has fooled many a historian. There is not space to elaborate here, but I encourage anyone with an interest to look up Maine in the U.S. census records, as well as his World War I draft registration card, and compare that information to what he writes about himself in his book.

180     **"For a while it looked":** He Dog interview, *Hinman Interviews*, 26 and 23.

180     **"just his nature":** Ibid.

180     **"a drawn and somewhat fierce":** "The End of the Sioux War," *The Sun*, May 23, 1877.

181     **his half brother, was dead:** A number of Lakota accounts mention Little Hawk's death and how he was killed, but none of them completely agree on the details. See He Dog interview, *Hinman Interviews*, 25; He Dog interview, Sandoz Collection; Eagle Elk interview, Neihardt Papers; McCreight, *Chief Flying Hawk's Tales*, 21; and Eastman, *Indian Heroes and Great Chieftains*, 91.

181     **a raid against one of the ranches:** These isolated ranches were favorite targets of the Lakotas and Cheyennes. See the *Philadelphia Daily Evening Bulletin*, May 24, 1870; and the *Winona Daily Republican*, MN, May 2, 1870.

181     **Crazy Horse took out his grief:** Eagle Elk interview, Neihardt Papers.

181     **expedition against the Shoshones:** The most detailed accounts of this raid and High Backbone's death are from He Dog, *Hinman Interviews*, 24; and John Colhoff in William K. Powers, "A Winter Count of the Oglala," *American Indian Tradition* 9 (1963): 32. The event is also recorded by Red Feather, *Hinman Interviews*, 37; Stephen Standing Bear interview, *The Sixth Grandfather*, 158; and Frank Grouard in DeBarthe, *Life and Adventures*, 349. The winter counts of American Horse, Cloud Shield, and Battiste Good also depict High Backbone's death. See Green and Thornton, eds., *The Year the Stars Fell*, 266.

182     **"The last time you":** As quoted by He Dog, *Hinman Interviews*, 24.

183     **"I know it":** Ibid.

184     **feted in the capital city:** The visit of Red Cloud's party to Washington was widely covered in the press. See the *New York Tribune*, June 2, 1870; the *Baltimore Sun*, June 2 and 7, 1870; the *New York Times*, June 4, 1870; the *New York Herald*, June 8 and 12, 1870; and the *Chicago Tribune*, June 6 and 11, 1870.

185   *"wait to be killed"*: D. C. Poole, *Among the Sioux of Dakota: Eighteen Months' Experience as an Indian Agent, 1869–1870* (1881; reprint: St. Paul, MN: Minnesota Historical Society Press, 1988), 176.

185   *"This is the first time"*: As quoted in the *Chicago Tribune*, June 11, 1870.

186   *"I will not take"*: Ibid.

186   *"regarded as a sort of"*: *Bangor Daily Whig and Courier*, ME, July 3, 1871.

186   *"to make him see everything"*: "The Indians," *The Chicago Tribune*, July 4, 1871. According to Indian agent D. C. Poole, Spotted Tail and his men avoided referring to any of the wonders they had seen in Washington, "fearing that they would lose caste among their less enlightened associates." Poole, *Among the Sioux of Dakota*, 224.

186   **Big Horn Mining Expedition:** "A New El Dorado," *Western Reserve Chronicle*, Warren, OH, May 4, 1870; "Big Horn Expedition," "The Plains," *The Chicago Tribune*, June 13, 1870; and *The Harrisburg Telegraph*, PA, August 1, 1870.

186   *"Beaver Joe"*: "The Big Horn Expedition," *The Chicago Tribune*, July 29, 1870.

## 9 / The Act of Thieves

189   *"[Indian] policies are inaugurated"*: Poole, *Among the Sioux of Dakota*, 226.

189   *"Sandwich Islander"*: *The Chicago Tribune*, July 4, 1871.

189   *Frank Grouard:* The earliest sketches of Grouard's life are found in the *New York Herald*, September 22, 1875, the *Advertiser-Courier*, Hermann, MO, July 28, 1876 (reprinted from the *Kansas City Times*), and the *Bismarck Weekly Tribune*, November 8, 1876. The first two sketches are based on information obtained directly from Grouard. The third is a long letter from George Boyd, a Montana scout and Indian trader, revealing Grouard as a horse thief and scoundrel. I find Boyd's damning account more believable than the tales spun by Grouard. See also DeBarthe, *Life and Adventures*, 31–33.

190   *Frank arrived at Sitting Bull's village:* I've gone with George Boyd's account of how Grouard ended up in Sitting Bull's village. As alluded to above, I believe Frank's versions are largely fiction. In the interview published in the *Advertiser-Courier*, cited above, Frank said he was captured by a band of Crows while working as a Pony Express rider between Bozeman and Gallatin City. The Crows, he claimed, held him captive for several days as they traveled east. When they finally released him, he was left nearly naked on Clark's Fork of the Yellowstone, a good hundred miles from Bozeman. Frank said he wandered the vicinity for several days, scrounging what nourishment he could from berries, cactus, and frogs until he was discovered by a group of Húnkpapa warriors. These kind Húnkpapas clothed and fed him and took him to Sitting Bull's big village on the Musselshell River. In a letter Frank wrote to his adoptive mother in the winter of 1876, he provides yet another account of how he came to live with the Lakotas. The Lakotas also have their own versions of their first encounter with Frank. Take your pick. See Grouard to Louisa Barnes Pratt, Camp on Belle Fourche River, W. T., Powder River Expedition, December 16, 1876, Addison Pratt family papers, 1830–1931, box 4, folder 39, Special Collections and Archives Division, Merrill-Cazier Library, Utah

State University, Logan; John Colhoff notes on Frank Grouard, Mari Sandoz Collection; Powers, "A Winter Count of the Oglala," 33; Old Bull interview, CC, box 105, folder 41; and Josephine Waggoner to W. S. Campbell, Keldron, SD, October 21, 1929, CC, box 108, folder 18.

190    *adopted him as a brother:* White Bull interview, CC, box 105, folder 8.

190    *His ability to read the letters:* Louis Bordeaux interview, Jensen, *Voices of the American West,* 1: 296.

190    *"a great practical joker":* DeBarthe, *Life and Adventures,* 386.

191    *Sitting Bull's family life:* White Bull interview, CC, box 105, folder 24; Gray Eagle interview, CC, box 106, folder 54; and LaPointe, *Sitting Bull,* 41–43. The boy Whole Tribe Seeing Her brought to the marriage was born circa 1870. He was deaf and would later be known by the name John Sitting Bull. Four Robes's son, born circa 1868, was known in adulthood as Henry Little Soldier. According to Gray Eagle, both boys were fathered by Flees Bear, who died of an unknown illness. Henry Little Soldier should not be confused with Little Soldier, son of Long Soldier or Tall Soldier, who fought at the Little Big Horn and later served with the Indian police who killed Sitting Bull in December 1890. See Henry Little Soldier in Indian census rolls for Pine Ridge, SD, 1929, 1933, and 1934; Ephriam D. Dickson III, *The Sitting Bull Surrender Census* (Pierre: South Dakota State Historical Society Press, 2010), 23; "Sitting Bull's Son Visits Photographer of Famous Father," *Wausau Daily Herald,* Wausau, WI, July 23, 1926; "And Thus It Was That Tatanka i-Yotanka, (Sitting Bull) Chief of the Sioux, Died," *The Chadron Tribune,* NE, December 6, 1940; Robert Gessner, *Massacre: A Survey of Today's American Indian* (New York: Jonathan Cape and Harrison Smith, 1931), 14–15; and "Indians of the Sioux Tribe Soon to Select a New Chief," *The Minneapolis Journal,* MN, September 26, 1903.

191    *liaisons with married women:* David Humphreys Miller, *Custer's Fall: The Indian Side of the Story* (New York: Duell, Sloan and Pearce, 1957), 231.

192    *an Oglala named Black Shawl:* Also known as Black Robe Woman. Red Feather interview, *Hinman Interviews,* 36; Bordeaux, *Custer's Conqueror,* 41; and Hardorff, *The Oglala Lakota Crazy Horse,* 34.

193    *much-needed powder and lead:* White Bull interview, CC, box 105, folder 24.

193    *"might as well undertake":* A. J. Simmons to J. A. Viall, Fort Browning, Montana Territory, December 5, 1871, in "Appropriations for Sioux Indians," H. Exec. Doc. No. 102, 42nd Cong., 2nd Sess., 5–9. For another account of Sitting Bull's views on the Northern Pacific and the possibility of peace, see "The Indians," *The Buffalo Commercial,* NY, November 3, 1871.

193    *"didn't want any civilization":* Ibid.

194    *disrupt any further survey work:* "The Hostile Indians," *Harrisburg Telegraph,* May 27, 1872.

194    *"No, they are not white men":* White Bull interview, CC, box 105, folder 4.

197    *"the most brave deed possible":* White Bull interview, CC, box 105, folder 24. White Bull's brother, One Bull, stated he was among those who smoked with Sitting Bull and that it was he who raced back and retrieved the bow and arrows. See "Norwich Couple Returns to the Land of the Eastern Ocean After

Dancing and Living with Sioux Indians of the Dakotas," *Hartford Courant*, CT, November 18, 1934.

197 *"That's enough"*: White Bull interview, CC, box 105, folder 24.

198 *a tattered stovepipe silk hat*: Thomas Rosser in Lubetkin, ed., *Before Custer*, 115.

198 *escort of 586 officers and men*: David S. Stanley, ibid., 65.

198 *galloped within a hundred yards*: Thomas Rosser, ibid., 117.

198 *Sitting Bull climbed a high bluff*: "N.P.R.R. Surveys and the Indian Troubles," *Helena Weekly Herald*, MT, October 10, 1872; and "Captain Kellogg's Expedition," *Bozeman Avant Courier*, MT, November 7, 1872.

199 *"shown their hand"*: "Justification," *Helena Weekly Herald*, October 17, 1872.

199 *"the Indians will be obliged"*: Ibid.

199 *"encamped in Sioux country"*: Old Bull in Vestal, *New Sources*, 172–73.

199 *"like two dogs fighting"*: Ibid.

199 *on the morning of July 9*: This fight is known as the Battle of Pryor Creek. For Crow accounts, see Thomas Marquis, as told by Thomas Leforge, *Memoirs of a White Crow Indian* (New York: The Century Company, 1928), 90–96; Frank B. Linderman, *American: The Life Story of a Great Indian* (Yonkers-on-Hudson, NY: World Book Company, 1930), 256–61; and the testimony of Blackfoot, a Crow chief, in *Report of the Secretary of the Interior*, H. Exec. Doc. No. 1, Part 5, 43rd Cong., 1st Sess., 492.

199 *"high up in the air"*: Ibid.

200 *escort was the largest yet*: David S. Stanley in M. John Lubetkin, ed., *Custer and the 1873 Yellowstone Survey: A Documentary History* (Norman, OK: The Arthur H. Clark Company, 2013), 95–96.

200 *thirty-three-year-old lieutenant colonel*: For a short biography, see my *George Armstrong Custer: A Biography* (Tucson, AZ: Western National Parks Association, 2005).

201 *Midmorning on August 4, 1873*: For the Battle of the Tongue River, I've relied upon George Armstrong Custer, "Battling with the Sioux on the Yellowstone," in Paul Andrew Hutton, ed., *The Custer Reader* (Lincoln: University of Nebraska Press, 1992), 201–19; Report of G. A. Custer, Pompey's Pillar, Yellowstone River, MT, August 15, 1873, in *Army and Navy Journal*, September 13, 1873; "Barrows with Custer," *The Boston Sunday Globe*, March 28, 1897; "[Gillman] Norris One of Few Survivors of Stanley's Expedition on Yellowstone in 1873," *The Conrad Independent*, Conrad, MT, May 19, 1921; White Bull interview, CC, box 105, folder 24; and M. John Lubetkin, *Custer and the 1873 Yellowstone Survey: A Documentary History* (Norman, OK: The Arthur H. Clark Company, 2013).

201 *Húnkpapas and a few Miniconjous*: Several authors and historians have given Crazy Horse a prominent role in this engagement (e.g., see Bray, *Crazy Horse*, 166–67). However, White Bull stated that Crazy Horse wasn't there and that Custer's attackers were Húnkpapas and Miniconjous. Furthermore, as will be shown, I've made a strong case (the first scholar to do so) that Crazy Horse and his warriors took part in the Battle of Massacre Canyon in southwest Nebraska in early August 1873. The confusion over the Oglala chief's whereabouts during this time stems from a 1934 piece by author Thomas Marquis. Citing "various old Cheyennes" as his source, Marquis claimed that Crazy

Horse, along with a few Cheyennes, participated in the Tongue River fight. However, a newspaper article by Clyde McLemore published the following year and overlooked by modern historians argues convincingly that the skirmishes the Cheyennes described to Marquis actually occurred in the spring of 1874, when they fought a civilian outfit known as the Yellowstone Wagon Road and Prospecting Expedition. See White Bull interview, CC, box 105, folder 24; Thomas B. Marquis, "Indian History Writings Not Thoroughly Reliable; Some Flaws Evident in Reports," *The Mineral Independent,* Superior, MT, June 28, 1934; and Clyde McLemore, "Conflicting Data Presented in Custer-Sioux Skirmish, August 11, 1873," *The Great Falls Tribune,* August 11, 1935.

203 *Sioux village, and attack it:* My sources for the Battle of the Big Horn are White Bull interview, CC, box 105, folder 24; Report of G. A. Custer, August 15, 1873; "Barrows with Custer": DeBarthe, *Life and Adventures,* 114–16; and Lubetkin, *Custer and the 1873 Yellowstone Survey.*

204 *"The Indians!":* Lubetkin, ed., *Custer and the 1873 Yellowstone Survey,* 247.

204 *"Come, man, why don't you?":* Ibid., 247–50.

204 *"Strike up Garry Owen!":* Ibid., 254.

204 *"Custer knew how to avail":* "Barrows with Custer."

205 *two hundred Pawnee Indians:* There are many accounts describing the Battle of Massacre Canyon. I prefer those reported within days of the event. These are found in "Indian Warfare," *The Chicago Daily Tribune,* August 21, 1873; "The Recent Indian Massacre," *New York Times,* August 21, 1873; and "The Sioux-Pawnee War," *The Chicago Daily Tribune,* August 30, 1873. A special issue of *Nebraska History Magazine* devoted to the massacre and a monument dedication at the site reproduces several official documents from the Indian Bureau. See issue number 3, volume 16 (July–September 1935). A very good article on the episode is Paul D. Riley, "The Battle of Massacre Canyon," *Nebraska History* 54 (1973): 220–24. Although rather fanciful, see also Eli Paul, ed., "Lester Beach Platt's Account of the Battle of Massacre Canyon," *Nebraska History* 67 (1986): 381–407.

206 *easily ran down and killed:* In May 1877, Crazy Horse presented a ledger book with several drawings to a newspaperman, George P. Wallihan. He stated through an interpreter that the drawings "pictured the life of a famous warrior but would not say that it was himself." One of the drawings depicts a Lakota on horseback killing two Pawnee women and a warrior. This drawing very likely portrays an episode from the 1873 massacre, and while we can't say that Crazy Horse created this drawing, the fact of its presence within his band can be viewed as additional evidence of Crazy Horse and his followers' participation in the massacre. The ledger book is in the collections of the Denver Art Museum. For the connection to the Pawnee massacre, see Thomas Powers, *The Killing of Crazy Horse* (New York: Alfred A. Knopf, 2010), 509 n. 12.

206 *"Dead warriors lay grim":* Assistant Surgeon David F. Powell as quoted in "The Sioux-Pawnee War."

207 *subagent for the southern Oglalas:* This was Antoine Janis (1824–1890).

207 *Pawnee captives were turned over:* Barclay White to Edward P. Smith, Omaha, NE, September 27, 1873, in *Report of the Secretary of the Interior,* H. Exec. Doc.

No. 1, Part 5, 43rd Cong., 1st Sess., 554; Waggoner, *Witness*, 458; and Bettelyoun and Waggoner, *With My Own Eyes*, 81.

207     **Pawnee chief Rules His Son:** "Famed Chief of Pawness, Hero of Many Indian Battles, Dies," *The Indianapolis Times*, IN, October 4, 1928.

208     **Crazy Horse believed in:** One Bull interview, CC, box 105, folder 41.

208     **"did great deeds":** Eagle Elk interview, Neihardt Papers.

209     **lever-action Henrys and Winchesters:** This was reported by Blackfoot, a Crow chief, in *Report of the Secretary of the Interior*, H. Exec. Doc. No. 1, Part 5, 43rd Cong., 1st Sess., 492.

209     **"their supply of metallic rifle":** Report of G. A. Custer, August 15, 1873. For an interesting description of how the warriors reloaded centerfire and rim-fire cartridges, see Father Genin's letter of December 13, 1877, in Slaughter, "Leaves from Northwestern History," 274.

209     **"thunder iron":** "Custer's Anabasis," *The Inter Ocean*, Chicago, September 8, 1874.

209     **"If you ever saw a mad Indian":** DeBarthe, *Life and Adventures*, 112. Although newspaperman Joe DeBarthe obtained the information for his book directly from his subject, the work is problematic because of DeBarthe's own embellishments and Grouard's frequent twisting of the truth in his favor. Neither Sitting Bull nor Crazy Horse were alive to challenge Grouard's version of events as published in 1894.

210     **came down with an unknown illness:** Ibid., 350; and He Dog interview, *Hinman Interviews*, 23.

210     **150 white men:** "Yellowstone Wagon Road and Prospecting Expedition," *Bozeman Avant Courier*, January 23, 1874; "The Yellowstone Expedition," *The New North-West*, February 28, 1874; and Addison M. Quivey, "The Yellowstone Expedition of 1874," *Contributions to the Historical Society of Montana* 1 (1876): 269–70.

211     **slew one hundred Indians:** *Bozeman Avant Courier*, May 1, 1874.

211     **"dosed it pretty strong with":** James Gourley as quoted in French L. MacLean, *Sitting Bull, Crazy Horse, Gold, and Guns: The 1874 Yellowstone Wagon Road and Prospecting Expedition and the Battle of Lodge Grass Creek* (Atglen, PA: Schiffer Publishing, Ltd., 2016), 150.

211     **report from Fort Randall:** *Helena Weekly Herald*, March 21, 1872.

211     **nugget the size of an egg:** *The Bismarck Tribune*, June 24, 1874.

211     **"Crazy Horse is on the warpath":** J. J. Saville to John E. Smith, Red Cloud Agency, Dakota Territory, February 20, 1874, *The Sioux City Journal*, IA, March 6, 1874.

212     **"for the purpose of spying":** *The New North-West*, April 18, 1874.

212     **Sheridan publicly claimed:** Donald Jackson, *Custer's Gold: The United States Cavalry Expedition of 1874* (New Haven, CT: Yale University Press, 1966), 14.

212     **"a shame that so vast":** *The Bismarck Tribune*, June 24, 1874.

213     **"contest every foot of the march":** "Black Hills Expedition," *The Inter Ocean*, July 4, 1874; and "To the Black Hills," *The Minneapolis Tribune*, MN, July 4, 1874.

213     **The cavalcade included:** "Black Hills Expedition"; and *The Bismarck Tribune*, June 24, 1874.

213    *collected specimens:* Robert M. Utley, *Cavalier in Buckskin: George Armstrong Custer and the Western Military Frontier* (Norman: University of Oklahoma Press, 1988), 137–38.

213    *they set the prairie on fire:* Lawrence A. Frost, ed., *With Custer in '74: James Calhoun's Diary of the Black Hills Expedition* (Provo, UT: Brigham Young University Press, 1979), 82–86; and "Custer's Anabasis."

214    *more glowing observations:* "Custer Interview," *The Bismarck Tribune*, September 2, 1874.

214    *"It was bad enough":* "The Black Hills Prohibition," *The New North-West*, September 5, 1874.

215    *eight hundred white men:* Jackson, *Custer's Gold*, 114.

215    *"Miners are everywhere":* Wayne R. Kime, ed., *The Black Hills Journals of Colonel Richard Irving Dodge* (Norman: University of Oklahoma Press, 1996), 134.

215    *"obstructions by [the] military":* "Black Hills," *The Bismarck Tribune*, June 30, 1875.

215    *become a white man himself:* "The Black Hills Gold Fields," *The New York Herald*, August 26, 1875.

215    *"no use opposing the whites":* "The Black Hills," *The Inter Ocean*, May 11, 1875.

215    *party of approximately eighty-five:* "The Indian Council," *The Chicago Daily Tribune*, October 16, 1875; and DeBarthe, *Life and Adventures*, 172.

216    *"Knowing all they do themselves":* Grouard to Pratt, Camp on Belle Fourche River, W. T., Powder River Expedition, December 16, 1876.

216    *"All those that are in favor":* As quoted in DeBarthe, *Life and Adventures*, 173.

216    *"Are you the Great God":* These words of Sitting Bull were reported by the mixed-blood Louis Richard and quoted in John G. Bourke, *On the Border with Crook* (New York: Charles Scribner's Sons, 1891), 245. Grouard's accounts of Sitting Bull's response are found in DeBarthe, *Life and Adventures*, 174; and "The Grand Council," *The New York Herald*, September 22, 1875.

217    *"My friends":* As quoted in DeBarthe, *Life and Adventures*, 174.

217    *"a bronze statue":* "The Black Hills," *The New York Herald*, October 7, 1875.

218    *he would shoot any chief:* "A Plot to Massacre the Black Hills Commission," *New York Tribune*, September 27, 1875; and Robert Higheagle manuscript, CC, box 104, folder 22.

218    *Miniconjou Lone Horn:* "Nothing Accomplished," *New York Tribune*, October 1, 1875.

218    *"Red Cloud, Spotted Tail":* Iron Hawk interview, *The Sixth Grandfather*, 171.

218    *"old plan of getting Indian land":* *St. Louis Globe-Democrat*, September 27, 1875.

218    *finally reached $70 million:* "Nothing Accomplished," *New York Tribune*, October 1, 1875.

218    *paid for the gold taken out:* "The Black Hills," *The Inter Ocean*, August 16, 1875.

218    *"Our hearts are happy":* "The Indian Council," *The Chicago Daily Tribune*, October 16, 1875.

219    *"the extravagant demands":* "The Black Hills," *The Inter Ocean*, October 11, 1875.

## 10 / Soldiers Coming with Heads Down

221   *"I fought for my people":* As quoted in *The Brooklyn Union*, NY, June 13, 1885.

221   *Old Bear, Box Elder, and Black Eagle:* Paul L. Hedren, *Powder River: Disastrous Opening of the Great Sioux War* (Norman: University of Oklahoma Press, 2016), 50. Hedren's is the definitive work on the Powder River battle of March 17, 1876.

222   *"The soldiers are right here!":* As quoted in Marquis, *A Warrior Who Fought Custer*, 164. Wooden Leg is the best Cheyenne account of the battle, but see also Powell, *People of the Sacred Mountain*, 2: 942–45.

222   *"Charge, my boys!":* As quoted by Robert Strahorn, "The Fight With Crazy Horse," *Rocky Mountain News*, April 7, 1876. Strahorn, who used the nom de plume Alter Ego, was a correspondent with the force that attacked the Powder River village. Frank Grouard, who led the nearly four hundred cavalrymen to the village, mistakenly identified it as belonging to Crazy Horse.

222   *"Let me take one of the children":* Marquis, *A Warrior Who Fought Custer*, 166.

223   *loot and burn their lodges:* John Gregory Bourke, *The Diaries of John Gregory Bourke*, ed. Charles M. Robinson III, vol. 1 (Denton: University of North Texas Press, 2003), 253; Strahorn, "The Fight With Crazy Horse"; and "Trophies from Crazy Horse's Camp – A Book of Battle Scenes," *St. Louis Globe-Democrat*, April 26, 1876.

223   *A splendidly dressed chief:* The Diaries of John Gregory Bourke, 1: 255.

223   *Wooden Leg strips the dead man:* Marquis, *A Warrior Who Fought Custer*, 167. Hedren identifies this trooper as Private Lorenzo Ayers. See *Powder River*, 183–93.

224   *"Cheyennes, come and eat here":* As quoted in Marquis, *A Warrior Who Fought Custer*, 170. See also Thomas B. Marquis, *The Cheyennes of Montana* (Algonac, MI: Reference Publications, Inc., 1978), 71.

224   *it was an unpardonable sin:* Miller, *Custer's Fall*, 229.

224   *"I'm glad you are come":* Two Moons interview, Garland, "General Custer's Last Fight," 445.

224   *behind closed doors:* "Indian Affairs," *The Inter Ocean*, November 4, 1875; "A Campaign Against the Sioux," *The Inter Ocean*, November 17, 1875; and John S. Gray, *Centennial Campaign: The Sioux War of 1876* (Ft. Collins, CO: The Old Army Press, 1976), 25–27.

224   *"go upon their proper reserves":* The Diaries of John Gregory Bourke, 1: 273.

225   *portrayed as punishment:* "Punishment for the Sioux," *Helena Weekly Herald*, December 2, 1875.

225   *interview to Chicago's* Inter Ocean: "A Campaign Against the Hostile Sioux," *The Inter Ocean*, November 17, 1875.

225   *the Indians had no newspapers:* Genin letter, September 8, 1876, in Slaughter, "Leaves from Northwestern History," 259. Some in the press did see through the machinations of the Grant administration. For example, see "The Black Hills Scheme," *The Times*, Philadelphia, PA, May 27, 1875.

225   *Lakota and Cheyenne couriers:* Zachariah Chandler to William Belknap,

Washington, D.C., December 3, 1875, and extract from letter of John Burke, Standing Rock Agency, December 31, 1875, in "Military Expedition Against the Sioux Indians," H. Exec. Doc. No. 184, 44th Cong., 1st Sess., 10 and 17. White Bull said no couriers reached the village he was in that winter, which was located at the mouth of the Tongue. White Bull interview, CC, box 105, folder 24.

225 *quartermasters began buying:* "A Campaign Against the Hostile Sioux," *The Inter Ocean,* November 17, 1875.

226 *"We were rich, contented":* Marquis, *A Warrior Who Fought Custer,* 161.

226 *report at an agency:* Short Bull interview, *Hinman Interviews,* 39; and Two Moons interview in "True Account of the Fatal Massacre of General Custer and his Men on the Big Horn," *The Billings Gazette,* July 2, 1911.

226 *"broke the friendly feeling":* Two Moons interview in "True Account of the Fatal Massacre of General Custer."

226 *belonging to Crazy Horse:* Strahorn, "The Fight with Crazy Horse"; and DeBarthe, *Life and Adventures,* 192–93.

227 *"Who needs a blanket?":* As quoted in Marquis, *A Warrior Who Fought Custer,* 171–72.

227 *"Oh what good hearts":* Ibid.

227 *He was Inkpaduta:* "The Agencies," *The Chicago Daily Tribune,* July 15, 1876. The leader of the Yanktonais was identified as White Face.

228 *"come into notice":* Marquis, *A Warrior Who Fought Custer,* 178–79.

228 *"Then we could separate":* Ibid.

229 *"When the rascality":* The account of Bear Stands Up was published in several newspapers. I'm quoting from that which appeared in the *Chicago Daily Tribune,* July 15, 1876.

229 *"only steal from them":* Ibid.

229 *"make a graveyard":* St. *Louis Dispatch,* MO, May 17, 1876.

229 *shocking reports of killings:* Ibid.; "Blood Money," *St. Louis Dispatch,* May 19, 1876; and "The Indians," *The Chicago Daily Tribune,* May 9, 1876.

229 *"The wind sown by":* "Blood Money," *St. Louis Dispatch,* May 19, 1876.

229 *The actual perpetrators:* Crazy Horse's biographer Kingsley Bray has the Oglala war chief traveling alone from the big village to the Black Hills and singlehandedly attacking a party of eight travelers on the Fort Laramie-Black Hills road at Red Cañon, killing three outright (a married couple named Metz and their Black female servant) and mortally wounding two others. Bray's evidence for this feat by Crazy Horse is underwhelming. Besides the fact that it's very unlikely Crazy Horse would have left his followers, as well as Sitting Bull, at this particular juncture, the white survivors of this incident said it was a *party* of Indians that attacked them. See Bray, *Crazy Horse,* 201; and Paul L. Hedren, *Rosebud, June 17, 1876: Prelude to the Little Big Horn* (Norman: University of Oklahoma Press, 2019), 64. For a contemporary report of the attack, which occurred midmorning on April 16, see "Indians Attack Black-Hillers," *The New North-West,* May 12, 1876.

230 *confirmed that lots of soldiers:* Marquis, *A Warrior Who Fought Custer,* 190.

230 **"Wakan Tanka,** *save me":* As quoted by White Bull, CC, box 105, folder 24.

231     *Picture Rock:* This formation is more commonly known today by its Cheyenne name: Deer Medicine Rocks. A National Historic Landmark, Deer Medicine Rocks is on private property near Jimtown, Montana.

231     *Sitting Bull honored his promise:* My sources for Sitting Bull's prophetic Sun Dance vision are primarily One Bull and White Bull. See One Bull interviews, CC, box 105, folders 19 and 41, and Hilger, ed., "The Narrative of Oscar One Bull, 165; and White Bull interviews, CC, box 105, folders 8 and 24. Also worthwhile are Raymond J. DeMallie, "'These Have No Ears': Narrative and the Ethnohistorical Method," *Ethnohistory* 40 (Autumn 1993): 515–38; and LaPointe, *Sitting Bull,* 63–65. Stephen Standing Bear (1859–1933) depicts this Sun Dance as part of a large watercolor painting on muslin (circa 1899) that also includes the Battle of the Little Big Horn. See Peter J. Powell, "Sacrifice Transformed into Victory: Standing Bear Portrays Sitting Bull's Sun Dance and the Final Summer of Lakota Freedom," in Even M. Mauer, *Visions of the People: A Pictorial History of Plains Indian Life* (Minneapolis, MN: The Minneapolis Institute of Arts, 1992), 81–101.

232     *like so many grasshoppers:* Time and time again, historians and authors have written that the soldiers Sitting Bull saw in his vision were "falling into camp" (i.e., the big village). It began with the first publication of Stanley Vestal's *Sitting Bull* in 1932, which was based on the extensive interviews Vestal (Walter Campbell) conducted with White Bull, One Bull, Old Bull, and others. However, nowhere in Vestal's notes of these interviews do his informants state that the soldiers of the vision were "falling into camp." Neither is this feature of the vision mentioned by Pretty White Buffalo Woman, who was either a cousin or niece of the Húnkpapa holy man. Her brief account of Sitting Bull's Sun Dance vision is the earliest known, first appearing in print in 1883. It's my belief that Vestal added the part about "falling into camp" to more directly connect the prophecy to the Little Big Horn battle. David Humphreys Miller does quote One Bull as stating the soldiers in the vision were falling upside-down into camp, but this interview wasn't published until 1971, after the legendary vision of Sitting Bull had become firmly entrenched in Little Big Horn lore. I strongly suspect we are seeing the heavy hand of Miller in this instance. In fact, Vestal accused Miller of lifting material from his works. Transcripts of Miller's interviews with his Lakota informants are currently held by a Great Falls, Montana, art gallery, but I was not granted access to study them. See Miller, "Echoes of the Little Bighorn," 30. For Pretty White Buffalo Woman, see "The Narrative of Mrs. Spotted Horn Bull," in Graham, *The Custer Myth,* 83; and Captain Charles King, "Custer's Last Battle," *Harper's New Monthly Magazine* 81 (August 1890): 387. Vestal's criticisms of Miller are found in W. B. Campbell to Joseph Balmer, October 16, 1957, CC, box 109, folder 12.

232     *"These white men have":* One Bull interview, CC, box 105, folder 41. Additional descriptions of Sitting Bull's visions are in One Bull interview, CC, box 104, folder 6. One Bull reported another Sitting Bull vision that foretold the Custer fight, supposedly occurring some two weeks before the Sun Dance. Curiously, White Bull does not mention this earlier vision, nor is it referenced

in any of the contemporary Indian accounts extant. See "Prophecy of Sitting Bull," CC, box 110, folder 8.

232 *"will be in [the] white":* Ibid.

232 *"Whatever you foresaw":* Black Elk interview, *The Sixth Grandfather,* 376. See also White Bull interview, CC, box 105, folder 8, where he says "very often at the Sun Dances someone had a vision which was the truth."

233 *a thousand lodges:* From intelligence gathered later from Lakotas and Cheyennes, Lieut. William Philo Clark estimated the village contained 1,200 lodges. Thomas R. Buecker, "Lt. William Philo Clark's Sioux War Report," *Greasy Grass* 7 (May 1991): 17.

233 *"What is it?":* Young Two Moon interview in Jerome A. Greene, ed., *Lakota and Cheyenne: Indian Views of the Great Sioux War, 1876–1877* (Norman: University of Oklahoma Press, 1994), 26.

234 *"Be a little against fighting":* White Bull interview, CC, box 105, folder 8.

234 *"The scouts have returned":* Stephen Standing Bear interview, *The Sixth Grandfather,* 174. Many historians quote Wooden Leg in regard to the meeting of the village elders on the morning of June 16. According to Wooden Leg, the elders instructed the heralds to announce that the warriors were to "leave the soldiers alone unless they attack us." He then claims this order was ignored and the warriors slipped away from the village after dark to battle the Long Knives. However, no other Lakota or Cheyenne account mentions this June 16 directive forbidding an offensive movement. I believe Wooden Leg, or his translator, Thomas B. Marquis, erroneously repeated an order of the chiefs issued a few days earlier, when Crook's troops were first spotted on the Tongue. The decision at that time was not to attack, but to send scouts to keep track of Crook's movements. Charles A. Eastman adds that the chiefs also agreed they would fight Crook if he approached within a day's march of the village. And that is exactly what happened, for on June 16, Crook's men were just twenty-four miles away. Crook was thus close enough for his mounted troops and Crow and Shoshone axillaries to execute a sudden strike on the big village, which the chiefs wished to prevent at all costs. See Marquis, *A Warrior Who Fought Custer,* 196–99; and Eastman, "The Story of the Little Big Horn," 356.

234 *protect the village:* Eastman claims that half the fighting force was left behind to protect the village, but this number seems far too high. See his "The Story of the Little Big Horn," 356; and Stephen Standing Bear interview, *The Sixth Grandfather,* 174.

234 *Riding at his side:* Short Bull interview, *Hinman Interviews,* 40.

235 *Sitting Bull rode in:* White Bull interview, CC, box 105, folder 8.

235 *Chief Gall and his nephews:* Eastman, "The Story of the Little Big Horn," 356.

235 *"Be of steady mind":* Ibid.

235 *approximately 975 men:* For numbers of combatants, I've followed Hedren's definitive study, *Rosebud, June 17, 1876.*

236 *"Heap Sioux!":* John F. Finerty, *War-Path and Bivouac, or the Conquest of the Sioux* (1890; reprint: Norman: University of Oklahoma Press, 1961), 84.

236 *"Valley full":* As quoted in Jack Keenan, "Wrinkled Cheyenne Warriors Tell

of Battle with Crook and His Soldiers on the Rosebud," *The Billings Gazette*, June 24, 1934.

236    *"fought and ran away"*: Marquis, *A Warrior Who Fought Custer*, 200.

236    *Buffalo Calf Road Woman*: Little Hawk and Young Two Moons interviews, Greene, ed., *Lakota and Cheyenne*, 25 and 27; and Stands in Timber and Liberty, *A Cheyenne Voice*, 434. The rescue of Comes in Sight may be the incident that started a story that Sitting Bull had been killed during the Rosebud battle. Frank Grouard had described to Crook's Indian scouts what Sitting Bull looked like, and in the first charge a warrior with similar trappings as Sitting Bull was in advance of his comrades when a volley sent him rolling to the ground. The warrior was quickly retrieved by his men, who are said to have exhibited such a commotion that it must have been a leader who was killed. Little Hawk's account places Comes in Sight in the first charge and states that he rode a horse faster than those of his fellow warriors, putting him in the lead. Comes in Sight wasn't killed, of course, but this story of the possible death of Sitting Bull came second- or third-hand to the correspondent John F. Finerty, who reported it. See "The Sioux War," *The Chicago Daily Tribune*, July 11, 1876.

237    *"Hold on, my friends!"*: As quoted by Frank Kicking Bear in Miller, *Ghost Dance*, 289. Short Bull also spoke of Crazy Horse rallying the warriors that day. See his interview in *Hinman Interviews*, 40.

237    *recognized Crazy Horse*: "In Crook's Camp," *The New York Herald*, July 13, 1876.

237    *"You can call it medicine"*: As quoted in Eddie Herman, "Noted Oglala Medicine Man Kept Crazy Horse's Secret," *Rapid City Journal*, February 11, 1951. Mixed-blood interpreter Charles Tackett claimed that General Crook told him he'd once shot deliberately at Crazy Horse more than twenty times without hitting him. If this actually occurred, it more likely would have been in a skirmish with Crazy Horse and his warriors at the Battle of Slim Buttes in September 1876. See Edward S. Curtis, *The North American Indian*, vol. 3 (Cambridge, MA: The University Press, 1908), 21 n. 1. Crazy Horse wasn't the only fighter who was "bulletproof" that day. Iron Hawk recalled seeing two warriors, a Lakota and a Crow, whom bullets couldn't touch. The Lakota wore a "sacred ornament" that Iron Hawk believed protected the warrior. See *The Sixth Grandfather*, 176.

237    *"little less than savage frenzy"*: "The Battle of the Rosebud," *Rocky Mountain News*, July 4, 1876.

237    *war chiefs grew worried*: He Dog interview, Hammer, ed., *Custer in '76*, 205; and Iron Hawk interview, *The Sixth Grandfather*, 176.

238    *less than two dozen*: Buecker, "Lt. William Philo Clark's Sioux War Report," 17; White Bull interview, CC, box 105, folder 24; and Old Bull interview, CC, box 105, folder 7. Second Lieutenant Frederick Schwatka, Company M, Third Cavalry, wrote his father that he believed they'd killed fifty or sixty warriors: "They left thirteen on the field, whose scalps were taken by the friendly Indians." Schwatka to Frederick Gustavus Schwatka Sr., Camp near Big Horn Mountains on Middle Creek, Wyoming Territory, July 23, 1876, photocopy in author's collection.

238     *more than ten thousand rounds:* "The Battle of the Rosebud," *Rocky Mountain News,* July 4, 1876. Finerty provided an estimate of 25,000 rounds. *War-Path and Bivouac,* 93.

238     *Three Stars lost nine men:* Finerty, *War-Path and Bivouac,* 340–42; "On the War-Path," *The Inter Ocean,* June 24, 1876; "The Indian War," *The New York Herald,* June 24, 1876; and Hedren, *Rosebud,* 297.

238     *Crook made the decision:* "The Indian War," *The New York Herald,* June 24, 1876; Finerty, *War-Path and Bivouac,* 93, 95, and 340; and Hedren, *Rosebud,* 301–2.

238     *"The Sioux had proved":* H. R. Lemly, "The Fight on the Rosebud," *Proceedings of the Annual Meeting and Dinner of the Order of Indian Wars of the United States* (1917), 41.

238     *three days of mourning:* Old Bull interview, CC, box 105, folder 7.

239     *"Everybody was in excellent":* Second Lieutenant Winfield Scott Edgerly, as quoted in Marguerite Merington, ed., *The Custer Story: The Life and Intimate Letters of General Custer and His Wife Elizabeth* (New York: The Devon-Adair Company, 1950), 310.

239     *"We can't get Indians":* Ibid., 309.

239     *what the Arikara scouts discovered:* Red Star interview, O. G. Libby, ed., "The Arikara Narrative of the Campaign Against the Hostile Dakotas, June 1876," *North Dakota Historical Collections* 6 (1920): 78.

240     *The following morning:* I've based my narrative of the movements of Custer and the Seventh Cavalry on Donovan, *A Terrible Glory,* and my *Little Bighorn Battlefield National Monument* (Tucson: Western National Parks Association, 2005).

240     *took a pair of field glasses:* Red Star interview, "The Arikara Narrative," 91.

240     *Custer took five companies:* These Seventh Cavalry companies were C, E, F, I, and L.

241     *"Do not divide your men":* As quoted in Linderman, *American,* 175.

241     *"Because you and I":* Ibid.

242     *"Hold your horses":* Daniel Kanipe, "A New Story of Custer's Last Battle," *The Deadwood Daily Pioneer-Times,* SD, July 26, 1914.

242     *"they came back at me":* McGillycuddy, "That 'Suicide' of Gen. George A. Custer."

243     *men heard gunfire:* Edward Davern testimony in Robert M. Utley, ed., *The Reno Court of Inquiry* (Fort Collins, CO: Old Army Press, 1983), 291–92.

244     *two companies defended the hill:* The two Seventh Cavalry companies positioned here were L and C.

246     *Oglalas and several Cheyenne:* Arthur Chapman, "Chief Two Moons' Story of the Fateful Day When Custer's Men Met Death," *The Evening Star,* January 18, 1908. As previously noted, some Cheyennes considered Crazy Horse as one of their war chiefs. In this interview, Two Moons states, "Crazy Horse and his Sioux were with the Cheyennes."

246     *"We shoot, we ride":* Two Moons interview, Garland, "General Custer's Last Fight," 448.

246     *"like a bunch of swallows":* Black Elk interview, *The Sixth Grandfather,* 183.

247 **sound of a bugle:** Two Moons interview, Garland, "General Custer's Last Fight," 448.

247 **hit by their own tribesmen:** Stephen Standing Bear interview, *The Sixth Grandfather*, 187; and Frank Zahn interview, Joseph G. Masters Collection.

247 **began to act strange:** Two Moons interviews in "True Account," *The Billings Gazette*, July 2, 1911, and "Indian Tells of Custer," *The Washington Post*, November 28, 1911. Two Moons believed many of Custer's men were drunk and claimed to have discovered whiskey in their canteens. Several other veteran warriors also believed the soldiers were drunk. See Frank Zahn and Little Soldier interviews, Joseph G. Masters Collection; and Marquis, *A Warrior Who Fought Custer*, 246.

247 **"There was a great deal":** As quoted in Don Carlos Seitz, *The Dreadful Decade: Detailing Some Phases in the History of the United States from Reconstruction to Resumption, 1869–1879* (Indianapolis: Bobbs-Merrill Company, 1926), 257. The warrior was Two Bears, son of the Yanktonai chief of the same name mentioned earlier in my narrative.

247 **they grabbed the arrow shafts:** Black Elk interview, *The Sixth Grandfather*, 193.

248 **The naked trooper jumped:** Iron Hawk interview, ibid., 192; and Joseph White Bull interview, Miller, "Echoes of the Little Bighorn," 36.

248 **a scalp with short hair:** Comment by Frank Zahn in Little Soldier interview, Joseph G. Masters Collection.

248 **The bodies were further mutilated:** Statement of George R. Herendeen, scout with Reno's battalion, in "Narrative of a Scout," *The New York Herald*, July 8, 1876; and Thomas Marquis, *Custer, Cavalry and Crows: The Story of William White* (Fort Collins, CO: The Old Army Press, 1975), 78–79.

248 **"I could smell nothing but":** Black Elk interview, *The Sixth Grandfather*, 194.

249 **Two Southern Cheyenne women:** This story is from Kate Bighead in Marquis, *She Watched Custer's Last Battle*, 1 and 8.

249 **cut off part of a finger:** In addition to bullet wounds in his left temple and left breast, Custer's right thigh had been slashed with a knife and an arrow was pushed up his penis. He wasn't scalped.

249 **husband of Monahsetah:** The most detailed study of Monahsetah (also Me-you-zah and Me-o-tzi) and her relationship with Custer is Peter Harrison, *Monahsetah: The Life of a Custer Captive*, ed. Gary Leonard (London: The English Westerners' Society, 2014).

249 **"Thus will the Great Spirit":** As quoted in Charles J. Brill, *Custer, Black Kettle, and the Fight on the Washita* (Norman: University of Oklahoma Press, 2001), 228.

250 **thundered up near the perimeter:** "One of Custer's First Sergeants Tells Story of Reno's Part in Fight on Little Big Horn," *The Billings Gazette*, June 25, 1923.

250 **"it would start again":** Lieutenant George D. Wallace testimony in Utley, ed., *The Reno Court of Inquiry*, 78.

251 **men would take turns:** Stephen Standing Bear interview, *The Sixth Grandfather*, 187.

251 **Using cups, tin plates:** "Custer's Death: The Herald's Special Report from the Field of Battle," and "Narrative of a Scout," both in the *New York Herald*, July 8, 1876.

251    *Even dead horses and mules:* Captain Myles Moylan testimony, Utley, ed., *The Reno Court of Inquiry*, 211.

251    *"We shall not celebrate":* Mary Crawler interview, Joseph G. Masters Collection. This interview was conducted in 1936. Oddly, some years earlier, Mary Crawler insisted to Frank Fiske that the village *did* celebrate the night of the battle. She said the families of the dead warriors mourned, "but the rest of us danced." Frank Bennett Fiske, *Life and Death of Sitting Bull* (Fort Yates, ND: Pioneer-Arrow Print, 1933), 16. One Bull, Two Bull, Frank Zahn, Stephen Standing Bear, and Wooden Leg all said there was no celebration the night of June 25. See their interviews and correspondence in CC, box 104, folder 6; box 105 folder 35; box 107, folder 5; *The Sixth Grandfather*, 189; and Marquis, *A Warrior Who Fought Custer*, 256.

251    *approximately thirty-one killed:* Hardorff, *Hokahey! A Good Day to Die!*, 130; and "Sitting Bull's Letter," *The Sioux City Journal*, August 19, 1876.

251    *only Sitting Bull and his band:* One Bull and Mrs. One Bull interview, CC, box 105, folder 19.

251    *"starve at [the] white man's door":* One Bull interview, CC, box 104, folder 6.

252    *"the horrible things":* Stephen Standing Bear interview, *The Sixth Grandfather*, 189.

252    *"The remainder of the soldiers":* Ibid.

252    *could hardly see them:* White Bull interview, CC. box 105, folder 24.

252    *A long line of dense smoke rose:* Lieutenant Charles Varnum testimony, Utley, ed., *The Reno Court of Inquiry*, 166.

252    *possessed a long-range Sharps:* Ibid., 184; Glendolin Damon Wagner, *Old Neutriment* (Boston: Ruth Hill, 1934), 169–70; and "One of Custer's First Sergeants."

252    *"Be careful, it's a long way":* Old Bull interview, CC, box 105, folder 11; and Stephen Standing Bear interview, *The Sixth Grandfather*, 189.

253    *The old men were right:* Marquis, *A Warrior Who Fought Custer*, 259.

253    *returned with its precious cargo:* Wooden Leg claimed he wounded one of the water carriers, who fell into the river and was swept downstream and finally overtaken by two Lakota warriors and killed. However, Seventh Cavalry regimental records have all the water carriers accounted for, none of whom failed to rejoin their comrades on the hill. See ibid., 259–60.

253    *go and fight them, too:* Ibid., 269.

253    *"Leave 'em go now":* Old Bull interview, CC, box 105, folder 11. In an interview given shortly after his surrender, Sitting Bull explained that "I did not want to kill any more men. I did not like that kind of work. I only defended my camp. When we had killed enough, that was all that was necessary." "A Chat with the Chief," *The Omaha Daily Bee*, August 9, 1881.

254    *The column stretched for:* Lieutenant Winfield Scott Edgerly testimony, Utley, ed., *The Reno Court of Inquiry*, 343; and E. S. Godfrey in Graham, *The Custer Myth*, 145.

254    *warriors' treasured possessions:* Marquis, *Custer, Cavalry and Crows*, 73–74. These items were subsequently looted by men from the Terry-Gibbon column.

254    *Among these were Gall's wives and children:* "Custer Battlefield," *The Evening Star*, September 25, 1903; "Anent Chief Gall," *Bismarck Weekly Tribune*, December 21, 1894; and Hardorff, *Hokahey! A Good Day to Die!*, 32.

254    *singing victory songs:* James Willard Schultz, *William Jackson, Indian Scout: His True Story, Told by His Friend* (Boston: Houghton Mifflin Company, 1926), 150.

254    *"Where is Custer?":* "Custer's Last Battle," *The Evening Star*, July 14, 1876.

255    *Wood Louse Creek:* The creek is known today as Lodge Grass Creek.

255    *"The soldiers are coming!":* Black Elk interview, *The Sixth Grandfather*, 196.

255    *the deep "mourning cuts":* Marquis, *A Warrior Who Fought Custer*, 274.

255    *"I killed a white man":* Ibid., 277.

255    *"When you came attacking":* Black Elk interview, *The Sixth Grandfather*, 197.

255    *"I had no guns":* Mary Crawler as quoted in Fiske, *Life and Death of Sitting Bull*, 16.

256    *"After the battle":* Stephen Standing Bear interview, *The Sixth Grandfather*, 188.

256    *"the Napoleonic tactics":* "The Disastrous Indian Campaign," *The New York Herald*, July 7, 1876.

256    *quite the French scholar:* "History of the Hostile Sioux Warrior, Sitting Bull," *The Chicago Daily Tribune*, July 15, 1876.

257    *a West Point graduate:* "The Sioux West Pointer," reprinted from the *Baltimore Gazette* in *The Lancaster Intelligencer*, August 9, 1876.

257    *soon shown to be false:* "What Mrs. Galpin Knows About Sitting Bull," *The Times*, September 1, 1876.

257    *"The Long Haired Chief":* Eagle Shield statement in Col. W. H. Wood to Asst. Adj. Gen., Cheyenne Agency, Dakota Territory, February 16, 1877, M234 - Letters Received by the Office of Indian Affairs, 1824–1881, Dakota Superintendency, 1861–1880, roll 262, NA.

257    *The warriors were simply too many:* Valentine T. McGillycuddy to Elmo Scott Watson, Berkeley, CA, May 28, 1927, Watson Papers.

257    *"saved his men":* McGillycuddy, "That 'Suicide' of Gen. George A. Custer."

## 11 / A Winter War

259    *"We were not bothering":* Marquis, *A Warrior Who Fought Custer*, 294.

259    *"If the Indian will not":* "The Indian Question," *The New York Herald*, July 9, 1876.

259    *"You can say that":* "Interview with General Sherman," *The New York Herald*, July 7, 1876.

259    *"a just retribution":* "Peace Society Resolutions," *The New York Herald*, August 19, 1876; and "Indian Lovers," *The Sioux City Journal*, August 19, 1876.

260    *control of the various Indian agencies:* Gray, *Centennial Campaign*, 259; and Standing Rock Reservation correspondence, 1876, Welch Dakota Papers, https://www.welchdakotapapers.com/2011/12/little-big-horn-sioux-life-in-1876-standing-rock-reservation-microfilm-roll/#ltr-55-col-carlin.

260    *"Indian Appropriation Bill":* "The Sioux in the Indian Appropriation Bill," *The New York Herald*, August 21, 1876.

260    *a railroad upstart:* "New Railroad," *The Daily Journal of Commerce*, Kansas City, MO, September 16, 1876.

261    *"I am getting old":* "The Sentiments and Opinions of Sitting Bull," *The New York Herald*, August 19, 1876.

261    *"Perhaps the whites":* "Suing for Peace," *St. Louis Globe-Democrat*, September 19, 1876; and statement of The Man that Smells his Hand, Standing Rock Agency, Sept 6, 1876, Welch Dakota Papers, https://www.welchdakotapapers .com/2011/12/little-big-horn-sioux-life-in-1876-standing-rock-reservation -microfilm-roll/#ltr-55-col-carlin. According to this courier, Sitting Bull's Húnkpapas were camped on the Tongue River as of August 30.

261    *surge of killings and depredations:* "Bloody Work" and "Black Hills," *The Chicago Daily Tribune*, September 9, 1876; "Indian Depredations," *The Black Hills Pioneer*, Deadwood, SD, August 28, 1876; "The Black Hills," *Helena Weekly Herald*, September 21, 1876; and Annie D. Tallent, *The Black Hills; or, The Last Hunting Ground of the Dakotahs* (St. Louis: Nixon-Jones Printing Co., 1899), 370–73.

261    *Moon When Plums Are Ripe:* Old Bull interview, CC, box 105, folder 11.

262    *a light frost settled:* Agnes Wright Spring, ed., "Dr. McGillycuddy's Diary," *The Denver Brand Book* 9 (1953): 291.

262    *"Trouble in one of the camps":* Old Bull interview, CC, box 105, folder 11.

262    *some of his best men:* Short Bull interview, *Hinman Interviews*, 41.

262    *approximately six hundred:* One officer in the fight estimated the warrior force at seven to eight hundred. Charles King, "Daring Red Riders," *The Pittsburgh Dispatch*, PA, January 20, 1889.

263    *Over the next two hours:* Eyewitness accounts for the Battle of Slim Buttes I've consulted include "Crook's Victory," *The New York Herald*, September 17, 1876; "Crook's Campaign," *The New York Herald*, October 2, 1876; "Details of the Fight," *St. Louis Globe-Democrat*, September 19, 1876; "Capture of the Village," *New York Tribune*, September 18, 1876; Finerty, *War-Path and Bivouac*, 186–99; Charles King, *Campaigning with Crook and Stories of Army Life* (New York: Harper & Brothers, 1890), 123–32; DeBarthe, *Life and Adventures*, 300–311; Paul L. Hedren, ed., *Ho! For the Black Hills: Captain Jack Crawford Reports the Black Hills Gold Rush and Great Sioux War* (Pierre: South Dakota State Historical Society, 2012), 218–23; and Indian accounts in Greene, ed., *Lakota and Cheyenne*, 86–92.

263    *mounted on a fast white horse:* Finerty, *War-Path and Bivouac*, 196. Stanley Vestal writes that it was Sitting Bull and not Crazy Horse who was the leader riding the white horse. He bases this on his interview with Old Bull, who has Sitting Bull playing a very prominent role in the battle. However, Lakotas taken prisoner from the village stated that Sitting Bull and his Húnkpapas were north of the Yellowstone at this time. See Old Bull interview, CC, box 105, folder 11; and "Crook's Victory."

263    *The feat of horsemanship:* King, "Daring Red Riders."

263    *each as large as a small cabin:* Little Wounded interview, CC, box 106, folder 53.

264    *"Now General, how is":* "Gen. Sherman," *The Leavenworth Times*, September 12, 1876.

264    *White Bull believed:* White Bull interview, CC, box 106, folder 53.

264    *A Fort Benton fur trader:* The Benton Record, Fort Benton, MT, March 25, 1876.

265    *Fire Thunder found the treaty:* "The Indians," *St. Louis Globe-Democrat*, September 23, 1876.

265    *"Red Cloud would get ahead":* "Indians," *The Chicago Daily Tribune*, Septem-

ber 27, 1876. The white trader, who also benefited from government contracts with the Indian Bureau, was Enoch Wheeler Raymond.

266 *with several scalps:* Black Elk interview, *The Sixth Grandfather*, 199.

266 *a greatcoat trimmed in bear fur:* White Bull remembered the details of the coat quite well. See his interview, CC, bow 105, folder 24.

266 *Together with Chiefs Gall:* "Sitting Bull," *Bismarck Weekly Tribune*, November 1, 1876.

267 *"You better get your uncle":* White Bull interview, CC, bow 105, folder 24.

267 *"Immediately the prairie":* Nelson A. Miles, *Serving the Republic: Memoirs of the Civil and Military Life of Nelson A. Miles* (New York: Harper & Brothers, 1911), 151.

267 *soon driven from the field:* "Sitting Bull," *The New York Herald*, November 6, 1876.

267 *agreed to surrender:* Ibid.; "Surrender of Hostiles," *Bismarck Weekly Tribune*, November 8, 1876; and Jerome A. Greene, *Yellowstone Command: Colonel Nelson A. Miles and the Great Sioux War, 1876–1877* (Lincoln: University of Nebraska Press, 1991), 107–11.

268 *"I think [Sitting Bull] feels":* As quoted in Utley, *The Lance and the Shield*, 173.

268 *belonging to Three Stars:* The attacking force was led by Colonel Ranald S. MacKenzie, an officer under General Crook's command. For various Cheyenne accounts of the engagement and aftermath, see Grinnell, *The Fighting Cheyennes*, 346–68; Powell, *People of the Sacred Mountain*, 2: 1058–71; and Greene, ed., *Lakota and Cheyenne*, 113–24.

268 *"We can fight the white men":* As quoted in Thomas M. Anderson, "Army Episodes and Anecdotes," chapter 10, unpublished manuscript, WA MSS 6, Beinecke Rare Book and Manuscript Library, Yale University.

268 *Frank Grouard, demonstrating:* "General MacKenzie's Fight," *The New York Herald*, December 11, 1876.

268 *Cheyenne infants froze to death:* Buecker, "Lt. William Philo Clark's Sioux War Report," 19.

268 *"Travel and sleep":* Marquis, *A Warrior Who Fought Custer*, 287.

269 *collecting clothes and lodge skins:* Black Elk interview, *The Sixth Grandfather*, 201.

269 *"We helped the Cheyennes":* Short Bull interview, *Hinman Interviews*, 42. Some Cheyennes later complained that Crazy Horse and his people were not as giving as they should have been, but other Cheyennes realized that there were simply too many of them for the little the Oglalas had. See Anderson, "Army Episodes and Anecdotes," chapter 10; and William Garnett interview, Jensen, *Voices of the American West*, 1: 51.

269 *"not any Cheyenne":* Marquis, *A Warrior Who Fought Custer*, 288.

269 *growing to 170 lodges:* "Buford Notes," *Bismarck Weekly Tribune*, December 27, 1876.

269 *even post employees:* "The Hostiles," *The New North-West*, December 8, 1876. General William Hazen attempted to put a stop to this illicit trade by confiscating all the ammunition at the trading posts of Fort Peck and Wolf Point (down the Missouri from Fort Peck), leaving a maximum of fifty rounds to each white resident. The trader at Fort Buford turned over all the ammunition

in his possession to the post's commanding officer. "Fort Peck," *Bismarck Weekly Tribune*, November 22, 1876; and "Buford Notes," *Bismarck Weekly Tribune*, December 27, 1876

269 **Wood Mountain in Canada:** "Notes from Buford," *Bismarck Weekly Tribune*, October 18, 1876, and December 20, 1876. Sales of arms and ammunition to the Sioux at Wood Mountain were soon shut down by the North-West Mounted Police. See "Old Fort Walsh Letter," *The Benton Weekly Record*, Fort Benton, MT, December 1, 1876.

269 **buffalo robes and a herd of mules:** "The Indians," *The Chicago Daily Tribune*, May 3, 1877; "Sitting Bull," *The Chicago Daily Tribune*, January 27, 1877; and Eagle Shield statement in Col. W. H. Wood to Asst. Adj. Gen., Cheyenne Agency, Dakota Territory, February 16, 1877.

269 **making war on him:** "Sitting Bull," *The New York Herald*, December 30, 1876.

269 **at daybreak on December 7:** Frank D. Baldwin, "Winter Campaigning Against Indians in Montana in 1876," in Peter Cozzens, ed., *Eyewitness to the Indian Wars, 1865–1890: The Long War for the Northern Plains* (Mechanicsburg, PA: Stackpole Books, 2004), 446–47; "Notes from Buford," *Bismarck Weekly Tribune*, December 20, 1876; "Sitting Bull," *Helena Weekly Herald*, December 28, 1876; "Sitting Bull," *The Chicago Daily Tribune*, January 27, 1877; and "Sitting Bull," *The New York Herald*, December 30, 1876.

270 **village was caught napping:** "Sitting Bull: Particulars of His Defeat by Lieut. Baldwin," *Helena Weekly Herald*, January 25, 1877; "From the Yellowstone Command," *The New North-West*, January 19, 1877; "Miles' Campaign," *The New York Herald*, January 16, 1877; "Winter Campaigning," *The New York Herald*, February 19, 1877; Baldwin, "Winter Campaigning Against Indians in Montana," 449–50; "A Little Sketch of the Life of Joseph Culbertson, Ex-Scout of the United States Army," *The Glasgow Courier*, MT, May 5, 1922; and Greene, *Yellowstone Command*, 141–43.

271 **the precious ammunition:** None of the contemporary reports I've consulted mention ammunition left behind in the camp, and a Lakota who was in Sitting Bull's village after the fight stated that "the Indians were not so destitute of ammunition as was generally supposed." "Notes from Buford," *Bismarck Weekly Tribune*, January 17, 1877.

271 **sent a message to Sitting Bull:** Col. Miles learned of the message and its contents from his Indian informants. See "Gen. Miles' Report of a Year's Work," *Army and Navy Journal*, May 18, 1878.

271 **sow dissent and spy:** William Garnett interview, Jensen, *Voices of the American West*, 1: 43.

271 **Two Miniconjou emissaries:** These men were Fool Bear and Important Man.

271 **Crazy Horse ordered his warriors:** Col. W. H. Wood to Asst. Adj. Gen., Cheyenne Agency, Dakota Territory, January 24, 1877, Eleanor Hamlin Hinman Papers, Nebraska State Historical Society, Lincoln; and Eagle Shield statement in Col. W. H. Wood to Asst. Adj. Gen., Cheyenne Agency, Dakota Territory, February 16, 1877.

271 **now be considered enemies:** "Indians," *The Chicago Daily Tribune*, February 16, 1877.

272    *scouts for Three Stars:* The Diaries of John Gregory Bourke, 2: 154–55 and 168; De-
       Barthe, *Life and Adventures,* 324; and *The Benton Record,* January 19, 1877.

272    *"This was a good place":* Black Elk interview, *The Sixth Grandfather,* 201.

272    *436 officers and men:* Miles, *Serving the Republic,* 153.

272    *January 7, debate sprang up:* Eagle Shield interview, Greene, ed., *Lakota and
       Cheyenne,* 128.

273    *Cheyennes had spoiled it:* Black Elk interview, *The Sixth Grandfather,* 202; and
       Edmond Butler, "General Miles' Expedition Against Crazy Horse," *The Leav-
       enworth Times,* March 24, 1877.

273    *For the next several hours:* A good synopsis of the battle, based on an analysis
       of artifacts found on the battlefield as well as primary accounts, is Keith T.
       Werts, *The Crazy Horse and Colonel Nelson Miles Fight of 1877: New Discoveries at
       the Battle of the Butte* (Spokane, WA: Werts Publishing, 2014). See also Greene,
       *Yellowstone Command,* 166–77.

273    *"The Indians moved back":* Marquis, *A Warrior Who Fought Custer,* 292.

273    *"used it rather lavishly":* Butler, "General Miles' Expedition Against Crazy
       Horse."

274    *distinctive cry of Crazy Horse:* Letter of Lieut. Cornelius C. Cusick, Canton-
       ment at Mouth of Tongue River, Montana Territory, January 20, 1877, in *De-
       troit Free Press,* MI, February 14, 1877.

274    *Crazy Horse broke off the fight:* Ibid. Cusick wrote, "The battle fairly opened at
       9 o'clock and continued with unabated fury until 4 p.m."

274    *three men killed and a few wounded:* Wooden Leg account in Werts, *The Crazy
       Horse and Colonel Nelson Miles Fight of 1877,* 146; Marquis, *A Warrior Who Fought
       Custer,* 292–93; Eagle Shield interview, Greene, ed., *Lakota and Cheyenne,*
       128; and Red Sack account in "The Hostiles," *The Chicago Daily Tribune,* Feb-
       ruary 14, 1877. Miles and other members of his expedition claimed to have
       inflicted much higher casualties among the warriors. For example, see But-
       ler, "General Miles' Expedition Against Crazy Horse"; and "Beats Any Dime
       Novel: The Simple but Thrilling Story which John Bruguier Tells," *The Sioux
       City Journal,* March 8, 1897.

274    *no bullet could go through him:* Swelled Face statement in Col. W. H. Wood to
       Asst. Adj. Gen., Cheyenne Agency, Dakota Territory, February 21, 1877, M234
       - Letters Received by the Office of Indian Affairs, 1824–1881, Dakota Superin-
       tendency, 1861–1880, roll 262, NA.

274    *his men were worn out:* "Miles' Fight on Tongue River," *The New North-West,*
       February 16, 1877.

274    *"swept from the field":* Nelson A. Miles to Assistant Adjutant General, Canton-
       ment on Tongue River, Montana, January 23, 1877, in *Report of the Secretary of
       War,* vol. 1 (Washington: Government Printing Office, 1877), 495.

274    *"our offensive operations":* Letter of Lieut. Cornelius C. Cusick. Lieut. Cusick
       (1835–1904), a Civil War veteran, was a member of the Tuscarora Indian tribe.
       His obituary is found in the *Rochester Democrat and Chronicle,* NY, January 5,
       1904.

275    *fifty lodges of Húnkpapas:* Some sources state Sitting Bull arrived at the camps
       of Lakotas and Cheyennes with Crazy Horse on January 15, 1877. However,

two Brulés named Makes Them Stand Up and Charging Horse left Crazy Horse's village on January 16 and said Sitting Bull and his people were just then marching to join Crazy Horse on the Tongue. In a 1928 interview, Wooden Leg said Sitting Bull participated in the Battle of Wolf Mountains on January 8, although he doesn't repeat that claim in his account of the fight given to Thomas B. Marquis. Lieut. William Philo Clark to Lieut. John G. Bourke, Camp Robinson, NE, February 24, 1877, Hinman Papers; "Suing for Peace," *The Inter Ocean*, February 15. 1877; "Indian," *The Chicago Daily Tribune*, February 16, 1877; Jesse M. Lee to Lieut. John G. Bourke, Spotted Tail Agency, March 6, 1877, Copies of Letters Sent, Spotted Tail Agency, 1876–78, RG 75, NA-KC; Francois C. Boucher to Maj. Horace Neide, Little Missouri River, March 25, 1877, Hinman Papers; and Wooden Leg account in Werts, *The Crazy Horse and Colonel Nelson Miles Fight of 1877*, 147.

275    **The ammunition Sitting Bull brought:** Eagle Shield said Sitting Bull brought fifty boxes of needle gun cartridges. The term "needle gun" was often used for the U.S. army's breechloading Springfield carbines and rifles. If Eagle Shield was referring to a standard "box" of .45-70 ammunition, each box contained twenty cartridges. Eagle Shield statement in Col. W. H. Wood to Asst. Adj. Gen., Cheyenne Agency, Dakota Territory, February 16, 1877; and Swelled Face statement in Col. W. H. Wood to Asst. Adj. Gen., Cheyenne Agency, Dakota Territory, February 21, 1877.

275    **The tribes were scattered:** White Bull interview, CC, box 106, folder 53.

275    **Some five hundred families:** "Sitting Bull," *Bismarck Weekly Tribune*, January 24, 1877; "Major Walsh Among the Hostile Sioux," *Winnipeg Free Press*, Manitoba, Canada; and "The Sioux," *The Helena Independent*, MT, January 17, 1877.

275    **Old Inkpaduta:** *Winnipeg Free Press*, February 19, 1877; and "The Indians," *The Chicago Daily Tribune*, December 30, 1876.

275    **persuade the Métis to join forces:** Swelled Face statement in Col. W. H. Wood to Asst. Adj. Gen., Cheyenne Agency, Dakota Territory, February 21, 1877.

276    **convince Crazy Horse to go north:** Francois C. Boucher to Maj. Horace Neide, Little Missouri River, March 25, 1877, Hinman Papers.

276    **simply his time to die:** White Bull interview, CC, box 106, folder 53.

276    **try to hold the land:** Sitting Bull refers to Crazy Horse as "still holding" the land in a speech delivered in Canada in early June 1877. Mark Diedrich, ed. *Sitting Bull: The Collected Speeches* (Rochester, MN: Coyote Books, 1998), 98.

276    **Crazy Horse's decision:** Bordeaux, *Custer's Conqueror*, 61.

276    **Lakota year 1876 to 1877:** Green and Thornton, eds., *The Year the Stars Fell*, 276.

## 12 / Father, I Want to See You

277    **"It is not possible to change":** Chittenden and Richardson, eds., *Life, Letters and Travels of Father Pierre-Jean De Smet*, 3: 886.

277    **the fear of Crazy Horse:** Eagle Shield statement in Col. W. H. Wood to Asst. Adj. Gen., Cheyenne Agency, Dakota Territory, February 16, 1877.

277    **turning against him:** "Red Cloud Agency," *The Chicago Daily Tribune*, May 3, 1877.

277     *"policy of persuasion"*: William Garnett interview, Jensen, *Voices of the American West*, 1: 43.

278     **the white man's God:** "Story of George Sword," Walker Collection, History Colorado, reel 3, frame 58. Hunts the Enemy would acquire the name George Sword that summer.

278     **a kind reception:** I've based my account of Hunts the Enemy's mission on the following: Red Feather interview, *Hinman Interviews*, 33; George Sword account in DeMallie, "These Have No Ears," 529–30; George Sword interview, Jensen, *Voices of the American West*, 1: 328; William Garnett interview, Jensen, *Voices of the American West*, 1: 45–46; "Crazy Horse," *The Chicago Daily Tribune*, March 8, 1877; Lieut. William Philo Clark to Lieut. John G. Bourke, Camp Robinson, NE, March 3, 1877, in Hardorff, ed., *Surrender and Death*, 159–60; and Clark to Bourke, Camp Robinson, NE, March 8, 1877, Hinman Papers.

278     *"meant submission to a people"*: Standing Bear, *Land of the Spotted Eagle*, 179.

279     *"You see all the people here"*: As quoted in Red Feather interview, *Hinman Interviews*, 33.

279     *"Well, it shall be a big peace!"*: As quoted in DeMallie, "These Have No Ears," 530.

279     **led by his uncle Spotted Tail:** "Spotted Tail's Mission," *The New York Herald*, February 23, 1877; "The Red Man," *The Chicago Daily Tribune*, February 12, 1877; and Second Lieutenant Frederick Schwatka to Frederick Gustavus Schwatka Sr., Camp Sheridan, Nebraska, February 5, 1877, photocopy in author's collection.

279     **deposed as chief:** *The Diaries of John Gregory Bourke*, 2: 147–48; "The Sioux Braves," *The New York Herald*, January 5, 1877; and "The Sioux," *Evening Bulletin*, San Francisco, August 18, 1882. Red Cloud told the *Herald* reporter that Spotted Tail "could never be a chief only in name over his people. He [Red Cloud] was still their chief, and they would obey him though the government had made Spotted Tail chief."

280     **something of a failure:** When Crazy Horse surrendered, some reports incorrectly credited Spotted Tail for bringing it about. As explained in my narrative, it was hunger and fatigue from fighting the army through the winter that primarily led to capitulation. However, Red Cloud and his nephew Hunts the Enemy (George Sword) did play an important role by assuring Crazy Horse that no harm would come to him and his followers if he surrendered. The acting agent at the Red Cloud Agency gave full credit to Red Cloud for the surrender, and both Red Cloud and Hunts the Enemy believed they'd been instrumental in convincing Crazy Horse to come in. Red Cloud stated later that "I sent some of my young men to capture Crazy Horse and bring him in and turn him over to the soldiers." Interpreter Louis Bordeaux also said it was Hunts the Enemy who persuaded Crazy Horse to come in. Report of Jesse M. Lee, Spotted Tail Agency, August 10, 1877, Copies of Letters Sent, Spotted Tail Agency, 1876–78, RG 75, NA-KC; C. A. Johnson to J. Q. Smith, Red Cloud Agency, May 6, 1877, Pine Ridge Agency, Copies of Miscellaneous Letters Sent, RG 75, NA-KC; "What Red Cloud Asks For," *The Council Fire and Arbitrator* 6 (January 1883): 3; George Sword affidavit, Pine Ridge, October 1909,

John R. Brennan Family Papers, folder 25, H72-002, State Historical Society of South Dakota; A. F. Johnson, "Career of Captain George Sword," *The Oglala Light* 11 (November 1910): 22; "Story of George Sword," Walker Collection; and Louis Bordeaux interview in Bruce R. Liddic and Paul Harbaugh, eds., *Custer and Company: Walter Camp's Notes on the Custer Fight* (Lincoln: University of Nebraska Press, 1998), 137.

280 *wasn't "very communicative":* Jesse M. Lee to acting assistant adjutant general, Spotted Tail Agency, April 5, 1877, Copies of Letters Sent, Spotted Tail Agency, 1876–78, RG 75, NA-KC.

280 *"He was a queer man":* Black Elk interview, *The Sixth Grandfather*, 202.

281 *"This country is ours":* Ibid.

281 *Red Cloud started out:* C. A. Johnson to J. Q. Smith, Red Cloud Agency, April 30, 1877, Pine Ridge Agency, Copies of Miscellaneous Letters Sent, RG 75, NA-KC; "The Indians," *Memphis Daily Appeal*, TN, April 14, 1877; Garnett interview, Jensen, *Voices of the American West*, 1: 47; Bourke, *On the Border with Crook*, 402; *The Diaries of John Gregory Bourke*, 2: 266; "The Indians," *The Chicago Daily Tribune*, May 3, 1877; and *The Sixth Grandfather*, 203.

281 *appearance was alarming:* "The Indians," *The Chicago Daily Tribune*, April 28, 1877; and "Indians," *The Chicago Daily Tribune*, May 2, 1877.

281 *"All is well; have no fear":* Short Bull interview, *Hinman Interviews*, 42.

281 *women and children became ill:* "The Aborigines," *The Chicago Daily Tribune*, May 4, 1877; *The Diaries of John Gregory Bourke*, 2: 293; and Garnett interview, Jensen, *Voices of the American West*, 1: 47.

282 *Clark to meet him the same way:* See Clark, *The Indian Sign Language*, 295–96.

282 *Crazy Horse appeared:* I've consulted several sources for my details on the Crazy Horse surrender. One of the best is a report of a *Chicago Times* correspondent who was present. His account appeared in the *Times* issue of May 7, 1877. This news item is reproduced in Hardorff, ed., *Surrender and Death*, 200–203, as are several other newspaper reports on the surrender. See also *The Diaries of John Gregory Bourke*, 2: 297–98; Garnett interview, Jensen, *Voices of the American West*, 1: 47–48; and "Crazy Horse," *The Chicago Daily Tribune*, May 8, 1877.

283 *"rude and slow-measured chant":* "Crazy Horse's Band," *The New York Herald*, May 28, 1877.

283 *immediately began a tally:* Thomas R. Buecker and R. Eli Paul, eds., *The Crazy Horse Surrender Ledger* (Lincoln: Nebraska State Historical Society, 1994), 14 and 164; and C. A. Johnson to J. Q. Smith, Red Cloud Agency, June 4, 1877, Pine Ridge Agency, Copies of Miscellaneous Letters Sent, RG 75, NA-KC.

283 *never seen white men:* "Northern Indians," *Denver Daily Tribune*, May 20, 1877.

283 *surrender their guns:* *The Diaries of John Gregory Bourke*, 2: 298; and "Cleaned Out By Crook," *St. Louis Globe-Democrat*, May 7, 1877. In later years, Charles P. Jordan, the Red Cloud Agency clerk, claimed that it was he who received the surrender of Crazy Horse on behalf of the agency. Jordan also claimed that Crazy Horse presented him with his gun at that time, which Jordan still owned as of 1910. See Charles P. Jordan manuscript in Charles Philander Jordan Papers, RG2095.AM, Nebraska State Historical Society; "After the Cattle

Rustlers," *The Sioux City Journal*, August 10, 1900; Bailey Millard, "The Man Who Captured Crazy Horse: Colonel Charles P. Jordan, To Whom all Indians take off Their Hats," clipped article from *Human Life* magazine, Watson Papers; and Bailey Millard, "The Squaw Man as He Is," *Everybody's Magazine* 22 (March 1910): 369 and 372.

284 **nearly four thousand members:** "The Indian Campaign," *New York Tribune;* Bourke, *On the Border with Crook*, 417; and "Crazy Horse," *The Chicago Daily Tribune*, May 8, 1877.

284 **"This surrender":** *The Diaries of John Gregory Bourke*, 2: 300.

284 **small herd of Texas longhorns:** "The Indians," *Rocky Mountain News*, May 20, 1877; and notebook recording issues of stocks and annuity goods, 1877, Pine Ridge Agency, RG75. Lakotas on the Pine Ridge Reservation were still killing their allotted beeves in this manner more than ten years later. See "A Day at Pine Ridge Agency," *The Omaha Daily Bee*, July 12, 1888.

285 **make a bread of sorts:** Bourke, *On the Border with Crook*, 415.

285 **oddly enough, Frank Grouard:** *The Diaries of John Gregory Bourke*, 2: 299; and "Northern Indians," *Denver Daily Tribune*, May 20, 1877.

286 **on May 12, Crazy Horse:** "Crazy Horse Sick," *Cheyenne Daily Leader*, May 16, 1877; and Garnett interview, Jensen, *Voices of the American West*, 1: 49.

286 **attempts to "work him":** William Philo Clark to Gen. Crook, Camp Robinson, August 18, 1877, in Hardorff, ed., *Surrender and Death*, 171.

286 **"a warm personal friend":** McGillycuddy, "That 'Suicide' of Gen. George A. Custer"; and McGillycuddy to Elmo Scott Watson, San Francisco, CA, April 1, 1922, Watson Papers.

286 **"acting in good faith":** James Irwin to J. Q. Smith, Red Cloud Agency, August 4, 1877, Pine Ridge Agency, Copies of Miscellaneous Letters Sent, RG 75, NA-KC.

287 **promised his own reservation:** Garnett interview, Jensen, *Voices of the American West*, 1: 53. Red Feather said, "When we came in we were promised that we might go back, but after we were there we were not allowed to go back." Red Feather interview, *Hinman Interviews*, 33.

287 **"I put a stake in the ground":** As quoted in "An Indian Council," *The Chicago Daily Tribune*, May 26, 1877.

287 **threatened to take his people:** James Irwin to J. Q. Smith, Red Cloud Agency, August 4, 1877, in Hardorff, ed., *Surrender and Death*, 167.

287 **a marriage proposal:** Nellie's first name, as given in U.S. census records from 1910 and 1920, as well as her death record, was Ellen. She later married a Brulé named Greasy Hand who took the name Crazy Horse, so she appears in the above records as Ellen Crazy Horse. Nellie died on July 8, 1928, and is buried in the Catholic Mission Cemetery, Wanblee, South Dakota. The story of her proposal to Crazy Horse comes from an account told by Julia Iron Cedar Woman (Mrs. Clown), who claimed to be an eyewitness. This account is reproduced in Bordeaux, *Custer's Conqueror*, 70. Additional information on the marriage comes from Nellie's brother, Tom, given to William Bordeaux in a 1943 interview. Bordeaux recounted the interview in a letter to George Philip, a copy of which is in the Hinman Papers. Will G. Robinson interviewed Nellie's sister, brother, and daughter in a successful effort to confirm her identification in a

photographic portrait. See his "Story of Crazy Horse's Picture," September 12, 1947, typescript, Crazy Horse Biography File, SDSHS.

288 *"Long Joe" Larabee:* In 1931, He Dog described Larabee as a "half breed French-man." A June 2, 1894, Department of Justice report on Indian depredations claims states that Larabee, who had since died, "was a white man." He Dog interview, June 30, 1931, Sandoz Collection; and *Hearings Before Subcommittee of House Committee of Appropriations* (Washington: Government Printing Office, 1894), 139.

288 *"half-blood woman":* Garnett interview, Jensen, *Voices of the American West,* 1: 58–59.

288 *possible romantic relationship:* Baptiste Pourier interview, *Voices of the American West,* 2: 271; and Mari Sandoz to Eleanor Hinman, November 27, 1947, Hinman Papers; and Sandoz to Hinman, December 10, 1947, Sandoz Collection. Pourier claimed that Lieut. Clark persuaded Crazy Horse to wed Nellie, a story I find doubtful. Even Pourier's interviewer, Eli Ricker, found the claim questionable.

288 *Little Big Man, who came to resent:* "Light on Border Mystery," *The Omaha Daily Bee,* April 11, 1903; Horn Chips interview, Hardorff, ed., *Surrender and Death,* 86, 88, and 88 n. 10; and Clark to Gen. Crook, Camp Robinson, August 18, 1877, in Hardorff, ed., *Surrender and Death,* 172.

288 *White Hat's spies:* Clark, *Indian Sign Language,* 130; and DeBarthe, *Life and Adventures,* 337–39. Grouard was quite proud of his spying on his old friend.

289 *increasingly jealous of Crazy Horse's fame:* Susan Bordeaux Bettelyoun, a sister of the interpreter Louis Bordeaux, stated that "everyone knew that Spotted Tail and Red Cloud were jealous of Crazy Horse and wished him out of the way." Bettelyoun and Waggoner, *With My Own Eyes,* 109. In later years, many Lakotas spoke of jealousy as a major factor in Crazy Horse's death. See, for example, "Dewey Beard: The Last Survivor," 21.

289 *"unreconstructed Indian":* Benj. K. Shipp, special agent, to J. Q. Smith, Washington, D.C., August 15, 1877, in Hardorff, ed., *Surrender and Death,*169–70; Col. Luther P. Bradley to Gen. Crook, Camp Robinson, July 16, 1877, Hinman Papers; and and Jesse M. Lee, "The Capture and Death of an Indian Chieftain," *Journal of the Military Service Institution of the United States* 54 (May–June 1914): 326–27.

289 *to eat at a table with a fork:* Garnett interview, Jensen, *Voices of the American West,* 1: 59.

289 *Grouard and several headmen:* Clark to Gen. Crook, August 18, 1877, in Hardorff, ed., *Surrender and Death,* 172.

289 *feared the trip was a trap:* Garnett interview, *Voices of the American West,* 1: 59–60; and He Dog interview, *Hinman Interviews,* 32.

290 *told Clark he wouldn't be going:* Clark to Gen. Crook, August 18, 1877, in Hardorff, ed., *Surrender and Death,* 172; and Billy Hunter [Garnett] statement ibid., 61.

290 *between Crazy Horse and Wakan Tanka:* Lee, "The Capture and Death of an Indian Chieftain," 327.

290 *found his dead body on the prairie:* Clark, *Indian Sign Language,* 155.

291    *a little afraid of Crazy Horse:* Louis Bordeaux interview, Jensen, *Voices of the American West*, 1: 292.

291    *"the soldiers had him promise":* Red Feather interview, *Hinman Interviews*, 36.

291    *go to war with another nation:* Louis Bordeaux affidavit, White River, SD, October 9, 1914, Crazy Horse Biography File, SDSHS.

291    *What Crazy Horse didn't reveal:* Billy Hunter [Garnett] statement, Hardorff, ed., *Surrender and Death*, 61.

291    *garbled the translations:* Jesse M. Lee to Commissioner of Indian Affairs, Spotted Tail Agency, September 30, 1877, Copies of Letters Sent, Spotted Tail Agency, 1876–78, RG 75, NA-KC; and Louis Bordeaux interview, *Voices of the American West*, 1: 296.

292    *"Billy, go back to Lieut.":* Garnett interview, Jensen, *Voices of the American West*, 1: 60–61.

292    *"These people can't fight":* Ibid.

293    *Sheridan ordered Crook:* P. H. Sheridan to Crook, Chicago, September 1, 1877, in Hardorff, ed., *Surrender and Death*, 175–76.

293    *"Crazy Horse has been treated too well":* P. H. Sheridan to Gen. E. D. Townsend, Chicago, September 1, 1877, ibid., 176.

293    *might scare the Miniconjous away:* L. P. Bradley to Adjutant General, Camp Robinson, September 7, 1877, in Hardorff, ed., *Surrender and Death*, 184.

293    *Woman Dress's incredible tale:* The best source for Woman Dress's falsehood is Billy Garnett, who heard it firsthand. See Garnett interview, Jensen, *Voices of the American West*, 1: 61–62 and 67–68; Garnett statement on the death of Crazy Horse, SDSHS; and Billy Hunter [Garnett] statement, Hardorff, ed., *Surrender and Death*, 62. In 1893, when Woman Dress applied for a pension for his service as an Indian scout, a local newspaper credited him with saving General Crook's life by reporting the "plot" to kill the general. *Dawes County Journal*, Chadron, NE, August 18, 1893.

294    *"of the loyal brand":* Garnett interview, Jensen, *Voices of the American West*, 1: 61.

295    *White Hat then offered $300:* Clark's offer of a reward for killing Crazy Horse is described in detail by Garnett in his 1920 statement, but it's not mentioned in the other two accounts we have from him, all of which are cited above. However, Red Feather clearly remembered White Hat's offer of a monetary reward and the sorrel horse "to any Indian who would kill Crazy Horse" (Red Feather interview, *Hinman Interviews*, 34).

295    *"it was too bad to go after a man":* Garnett interview, Jensen, *Voices of the American West*, 1: 62.

296    *"These Indians can hold nothing":* Garnett statement on the death of Crazy Horse, SDSHS.

296    *Garnett had tipped him off:* Red Feather interview, *Hinman Interviews*, 34.

296    *"I came here for peace":* He Dog interview, *Hinman Interviews*, 32.

296    *gave his Sharps carbine:* Red Feather interview, *Hinman Interviews*, 34.

296    *Nellie pleaded with Crazy Horse:* Nellie Larabee's role in Crazy Horse's escape to the Spotted Tail Agency was passed down in the family to her half brother Tom. William J. Bordeaux to George Philips, May 4, 1943, copy in Hinman Papers.

296   *what Crazy Horse himself believed:* Bordeaux, *Custer's Conqueror*, 75.

296   *Worm, lived at Spotted Tail:* Bray, *Crazy Horse*, 366.

296   *swollen, causing her considerable pain:* Red Feather interview, *Hinman Interviews*, 34; Bettelyoun and Waggoner, *With My Own Eyes*, 109; and Lee, "The Capture and Death of an Indian Chieftain," 334.

297   *six hundred cavalrymen:* Lucy Lee, Camp Sheridan, September 18, 1877, in Hardorff, ed., *Surrender and Death*, 251; and L. P. Bradley to Adjutant General, Camp Robinson, September 7, 1877, in Hardorff, ed., *Surrender and Death*, 184.

297   *a headman, fearlessly galloped forward:* Garnett interview, Jensen, *Voices of the American West*, 1: 63–64; and He Dog account, Clark, ed., *The Killing of Chief Crazy Horse*, 62–63.

297   *"I have been looking all my life":* As quoted by Garnett, Jensen, *Voices of the American West*, 1: 63–64.

297   *Clark immediately ordered a detachment:* Ibid., 64–65; and Clark to Gen. Crook, Camp Robinson, September 4, 1877, in Hardorff, ed., *Surrender and Death*, 177.

298   *"Crazy Horse can't make a move":* As quoted in Lee, "The Capture and Death of an Indian Chieftain," 331.

298   *White Hat harbored a hatred:* Bordeaux, *Custer's Conqueror*, 73.

298   *No Water swore to White Hat:* "The Death of Crazy Horse," *The Sun*, September 14, 1877.

298   *rode two horses to death:* Clark to Commissioner of Indian Affairs, Camp Robinson, September 10, 1877, in Hardorff, ed., *Surrender and Death*, 187.

298   *Crazy Horse and Black Shawl:* Garnett told Eli Ricker that Crazy Horse and Black Shawl traveled with Kicking Bear and Shell Boy. However, other accounts do not mention these two companions, including the other accounts from Garnett. See Garnett interview, Jensen, *Voices of the American West*, 63.

298   *"I am Crazy Horse!":* As quoted in Lee, "The Capture and Death of an Indian Chieftain," 334. Louis Bordeaux confirms that the Indian scouts who chased Crazy Horse were afraid of the war chief. Bordeaux interview, Jensen, *Voices of the American West*, 1: 292. Garnett claimed the scouts got only as close as seeing Crazy Horse and Black Shawl in the distance, but Garnett admitted this was secondhand information. Garnett interview, Jensen, *Voices of the American West*, 65.

298   *a supernatural being:* "Bayonetted by a Soldier," *The Omaha Daily Bee*, September 2, 1888. Although this article doesn't contain a byline, an August 27, 1888, article in the *Bee* states that Jordan, the Red Cloud Agency clerk, promised to give that paper an account of Crazy Horse's death, "an event to which he was an eyewitness. Mr. Jordan's statement will appear in another letter." This, then, is Jordan's account. See "Among the Rosebud Sioux," *The Omaha Daily Bee*, August 27, 1888.

298   *caused tremendous excitement:* Garnett interview, Jensen, *Voices of the American West*, 1: 68.

299   *persecuted for no good:* Lee, "The Capture and Death of an Indian Chieftain," 332.

299   *some three hundred armed warriors:* Ibid., 333; and Louis Bordeaux affidavit, Crazy Horse Biography File, SDSHS.

299     *"You have come to this agency"*: As quoted in Jesse M. Lee to Commissioner of Indian Affairs, Spotted Tail Agency, September 30, 1877, Copies of Letters Sent, Spotted Tail Agency, 1876–78, RG 75, NA-KC.

300     *"bad winds blowing"*: Louis Bordeaux interview in Liddic and Harbaugh, eds., *Custer and Company*, 143.

300     *"I want to get away from the trouble"*: As quoted in Lee to Commissioner of Indian Affairs, Spotted Tail Agency, September 30, 1877, Copies of Letters Sent, Spotted Tail Agency, 1876–78, RG 75, NA-KC.

300     *a cornered wild animal*: Lee, "The Capture and Death of an Indian Chieftain," 334.

301     *make Crazy Horse chief over all*: Little Killer interview, *Hinman Interviews*, 46.

301     *"considered good news"*: Lucy Lee, Camp Sheridan, September 18, 1877, in Hardorff, ed., *Surrender and Death*, 251.

301     *"he feared some trouble would happen"*: Lee to Commissioner of Indian Affairs, Spotted Tail Agency, September 30, 1877, Copies of Letters Sent, Spotted Tail Agency, 1876–78, RG 75, NA-KC.

301     *promised a meeting with the Soldier Chief*: Lee, "The Capture and Death of an Indian Chieftain," 335; and Anderson, "Army Episodes and Anecdotes," chapter 10.

302     *If Crazy Horse tried to flee*: Louis Bordeaux interview, Jensen, *Voices of the American West*, 1: 298.

303     *Crazy Horse tested the escort*: Lee, "The Capture and Death of an Indian Chieftain," 335.

304     *a crowd of several hundred*: Estimates of the crowd range from fifty to several hundred. See "The Death of Crazy Horse," *The Sun*, September 14, 1877; "Crazy Horse," *Army and Navy Journal*, September 15, 1877; and Garnett statement on the death of Crazy Horse, SDSHS.

304     *"Look out"*: He Dog interview, *Hinman Interviews*, 29.

304     *"No, not yet!"*: Lee, "The Capture and Death of an Indian Chieftain," 336.

304     *exile at Fort Marion, Florida*: H. R. Lemly, "The Passing of Crazy Horse," *Journal of the Military Service Institution of the United States* 54 (May–June 1914): 321.

305     *"not a hair of his head"*: Lee, "The Capture and Death of an Indian Chieftain," 337. In an interesting letter by Col. Bradley to his mother of September 8, he writes, "I told [Crazy Horse] and his friends that no harm would be done to him, but that he was a prisoner and would be confined." Bradley is implying that he personally spoke to Crazy Horse that evening when plainly he did not. Lee makes it clear that Bradley refused to see the war chief. Bradley's letter, in a private collection, may be viewed online here: https://historical.ha.com /itm/autographs/historic-autograph-letter-signed-by-luther-p-bradley-5pp -5-x-775-dated-september-8-1877-just-three-days-after-cra/a/658-25205.s?ic4= GalleryView-Thumbnail-071515.

305     *done all he could for Crazy Horse*: Louis Bordeaux interview, Jensen, *Voices of the American West*, 1: 299.

305     *"So you are the brave man"*: Louis Bordeaux account in Bordeaux, *Custer's Conqueror*, 88; and Bordeaux interview in Liddic and Harbaugh, eds., *Custer and Company*, 147.

306    *Touch the Clouds heard the sound:* Baptiste Pourier interview, Jensen, *Voices of the American West,* 2: 271.

306    *he wore a revolver and a knife:* Clark to Crook, Camp Robinson, September 5, 1877, in Hardorff, ed., *Surrender and Death,* 181.

306    *a knife on Little Big Man's belt:* "The Death of Crazy Horse," *The Sun,* September 14, 1877; and McGillycuddy to Watson, San Francisco, April 13, 1922, Watson Papers.

306    *"Let me go! Let me go! Let me go!":* Garnett interview, Jensen, *Voices of the American West,* 1: 70.

306    *"Don't Shoot! Don't Shoot!":* Garnett statement on the death of Crazy Horse, SDSHS.

307    *his thumb and forefinger:* Baptiste Pourier interview, Jensen, *Voices of the American West,* 2: 271.

307    *Indian scouts and guards:* Louis Bordeaux interview, Jensen, *Voices of the American West,* 1: 299.

307    *"Kill the son of a bitch!":* Louis Bordeaux interview in Liddic and Harbaugh, eds., *Custer and Company,* 149. There are several variations of what Kennington actually shouted, but there's no question he wanted Crazy Horse dead at this point. See "Tragic End of Noted Indian Chief Told by Gen. Jesse M. Lee Retired," *El Paso Morning Times,* TX, March 5, 1911.

307    *"Let me go, you've got me hurt now":* Garnett interview, Jensen, *Voices of the American West,* 1: 71.

307    *struck the doorframe:* Louis Bordeaux interview, Jensen, *Voices of the American West,* 1: 300; and Bourke, *On the Border with Crook,* 422–23.

307    *dislocating the holy man's shoulder:* Horn Chips interview, Jensen, *Voices of the American West,* 1: 276; and Louis Bordeaux interview, ibid., 1: 300.

307    *jerked it out of its scabbard:* Louis Bordeaux interview, Liddic and Harbaugh, eds., *Custer and Company,* 149; and Garnett interview, Jensen, *Voices of the American West,* 1: 71.

307    *writhing on the ground in a fetal position:* "The Death of Crazy Horse," *The Sun,* September 14, 1877; Lucy Lee, Camp Sheridan, September 18, 1877, in Hardorff, ed., *Surrender and Death,* 253; and Bourdeaux account in Bordeaux, *Custer's Conqueror,* 88.

307    *knocked the old man down:* "The Death of Crazy Horse," *The Sun,* September 14, 1877; and Charles P. Jordan, "Crazy Horse: The Death of the Indian Chieftain," *The Chicago Daily Tribune,* September 11, 1877. Jordan signed this story using his pen name, Philander, which was also his middle name.

308    *frothing at the mouth:* McGillycuddy to Watson, San Francisco, April 13, 1922, Watson Papers; and Clark to Gen. Crook, Camp Robinson, September 5, 1877, in Hardorff, ed., *Surrender and Death,* 181.

308    *The Indian scouts fled:* Lucy Lee, Camp Sheridan, September 18, 1877, in Hardorff, ed., *Surrender and Death,* 253.

308    *decided to make themselves scarce:* Jordan, "Crazy Horse," *The Chicago Daily Tribune,* September 11, 1877.

308    *"Don't take him in":* As quoted in Anderson, "Army Episodes and Anecdotes," chapter 10. Years later, McGillycuddy claimed he made two trips across the

parade ground to Col. Bradley's quarters to request permission to place Crazy Horse somewhere other than the guardhouse. No other eyewitness accounts mention this.

308 *"Take him there"*: Ibid.

309 **hypodermic injection of morphine:** McGillycuddy to Watson, San Francisco, April 13, 1922, Watson Papers; and "The Death of Crazy Horse," *The Sun*, September 14, 1877.

309 **relieved by a new sentry:** Jordan, "Bayonetted by a Soldier," *The Omaha Daily Bee*, September 2, 1888. The soldier who bayoneted Crazy Horse has been identified as William Gentles. See Paul L. Hedren, "Who Killed Crazy Horse: A Historiographical Review and Affirmation," *Nebraska History Magazine* 101 (Spring 2020): 2–17.

309 **Little Big Man stabbed Crazy Horse:** Jordan, "Bayonetted by a Soldier," *The Omaha Daily Bee*, September 2, 1888; and Anderson, "Army Episodes and Anecdotes," chapter 10.

309 **the blade glanced off:** Jordan, "Crazy Horse," *The Chicago Daily Tribune*, September 11, 1877. In Jordan's 1888 account, cited above, he wrote that many believed Crazy Horse hurt himself with his own knife while trying to stab Captain Kennington. However, Garnett stated that "the points of his own knives did not touch his body." Billy Hunter [Garnett] statement, Hardorff, ed., *Surrender and Death*, 64.

309 *"trying to persuade all [the] Indians"*: Clark to Gen. Crook, Camp Robinson, September 5, 1877, in Hardorff, ed., *Surrender and Death*, 181. See also Clark to Commissioner of Indian Affairs, Camp Robinson, September 10, 1877 in *Surrender and Death*, 187.

309 *"I had no desire to do injury"*: Louis Bordeaux interview, Liddic and Harbaugh, eds., *Custer and Company*, 150. Bordeaux quoted Crazy Horse similarly in his 1907 interview with Eli Ricker. See Jensen, *Voices of the American West*, 1: 300.

309 *"Father, it is no use"*: Louis Bordeaux interview, Jensen, *Voices of the American West*, 1: 300. There are several accounts giving what are purportedly statements made by Crazy Horse on his deathbed. Agent Jesse M. Lee, who did briefly visit Crazy Horse in the adjutant's office, naturally claimed Crazy Horse absolved him of any fault. In a 1914 account, Lieut. Lemly has Crazy Horse spouting a lengthy soliloquy, which is rather interesting considering that Lemly reported to *The Sun* in 1877 that Crazy Horse "never rallied, and only once spoke indistinctly about bayonets." Lee, "The Capture and Death of an Indian Chieftain," 338; Lemly, "The Passing of Crazy Horse," 321–22; and "The Death of Crazy Horse," *The Sun*, September 14, 1877.

310 **Pourier relieved Bordeaux:** Louis Bordeaux interview, Jensen, *Voices of the American West*, 1: 300.

310 *"Father, I want to see you"*: As quoted in James H. Cook to John G. Neihardt, The Agate Springs Ranch, Agate, Neb., July 8, 1924, Neihardt Papers. Cook stated he obtained this quote directly from Pourier, who told him they were "the only words used by the old warrior when dying." In a 1907 interview, however, Pourier stated Crazy Horse "never spoke afterwards." That is, after receiving his mortal wound. Pourier interview with Edmond S. Meany,

1907, Meany Papers, 1877–1935, University of Washington Libraries, Special Collections, transcription at https://amertribes.proboards.com/thread/468/baptiste-gene-pourier-aka-big#ixzz4YM9JmPbr.

## 13 / The End of Freedom

311 *"I yield by necessity":* As quoted in Fred M. Hans, *The Great Sioux Nation* (Chicago: M. A. Donohue and Company, 1907), 564.

311 *A cold front had blown through:* Paul L. Hedren, *Sitting Bull's Surrender at Fort Buford: An Episode in American History* (Williston, ND: Fort Union Association, 1997), 3 n. 1.

311 *more than thirty Red River carts:* F. C. Wade, "The Surrender of Sitting Bull: Jean Louise Legaré's Story," *Canadian Magazine* 24 (February 1905): 342; and Usher L. Burdick, *Tales from Buffalo Land: The Story of Fort Buford* (Baltimore: Wirth Brothers, 1940), 38.

312 *clothing they wore was in tatters:* Garrett Wilson, *Frontier Farewell: The 1870s and the End of the Old West* (Regina, SK, Canada: Canadian Plains Research Center, University of Regina, 2007), 409; and Burdick, *Tales from Buffalo Land,* 34.

312 *The years in Grandmother's Country:* Sitting Bull's exile in Canada was essentially four long years of struggling to feed his people in a country where neither he nor his followers were wanted. For those wishing to pursue that part of his life, see Robert M. Utley, *The Last Sovereigns: Sitting Bull and the Resistance of the Free Lakotas* (Lincoln: University of Nebraska Press, 2020); David G. McCrady, *Living with Strangers: The Nineteenth-Century Sioux and the Canadian-American Borderlands* (Toronto, Canada: University of Toronto Press, 2010); Grant MacEwan, *Sitting Bull: The Years in Canada* (Edmonton, Canada: Hurtig Publishers, 1973); and Joseph Manzione, *"I Am Looking to the North for My Life": Sitting Bull, 1876–1881* (Salt Lake City: University of Utah Press, 1991).

312 *eight hundred lodges of Lakotas:* Wade, "The Surrender of Sitting Bull," 337.

312 *crossed the holy line:* White Bull interview, CC, box 106, folder 53; Olson, *Red Cloud and the Sioux Problem,* 255; DeMallie, ed., *The Sixth Grandfather,* 204; and "The Sioux Question," *The Evening Star,* December 12, 1877.

312 *didn't really want the Lakotas: Annual Report of the Commissioner of Indian Affairs to the Secretary of the Interior for the Year 1877* (Washington: Government Printing Office, 1877), 16–17; Cecil E. Denny, *The Law Marches West* (1939; reprint: Moreton-in-Marsh, UK: Denny Publishing Limited, 2000), 118–21; and Cy Warman, "The Flight of Sitting Bull," *The Indian School Journal* 7 (March 1907): 42–43.

312 *competed for game and caused tension:* "Threatening Tetons," *The New York Herald,* April 12, 1878.

312 *refused to feed or clothe them:* "The Hostile Sioux," *The Chicago Daily Tribune,* July 10, 1879; and Warman, "The Flight of Sitting Bull," 43.

312 *"tired of being in Canada":* Black Elk interview, DeMallie, ed., *The Sixth Grandfather,* 210.

313 **In a bitter break with Sitting Bull:** E. H. Allison, *The Surrender of Sitting Bull, Being a Full and Complete History of the Negotiations Conducted* (Dayton, OH: The Walker Litho and Printing Co., 1891), 49–50.

313 **Bluecoats attacked Gall's band:** For the Battle of Poplar River, see Report of Maj. Guido Ilges, Headquarters Camp Poplar Creek, MT, January 31, 1881, *Annual Report of the Secretary of War for the Year 1881*, vol. 1 (Washington: Government Printing Office, 1881), 102–3; and "Chief Gall Captured," *The Times*, January 5, 1881. Gall later claimed he'd personally surrendered to Major Ilges prior to his village being attacked and that he rushed through the gunfire to the camp and persuaded his people to stop shooting. "An Illustrious Sioux: The Gall Relates Some of the Incidents of the Past Fifteen Years of His Life," part 2, *Rocky Mountain Husbandman*, May 12, 1881.

313 **five hundred destitute people:** Wade, "The Surrender of Sitting Bull," 338; and "The Starving Sioux," *The Bismarck Tribune*, January 28, 1881.

313 **his village counted only 187 individuals:** "The Fallen Chief," *The Omaha Daily Bee*, August 2, 1881.

313 **"did not appear to be a well man":** Col. William H. C. Bowen to W. S. Campbell, Portland, OR, October 10, 1929, CC, box 108, folder 2.

313 **the formal surrender:** My account of the ceremony, including the Sitting Bull quotes, comes from the description provided by the *Saint Paul Pioneer Press*'s correspondent, as printed in the *Black Hills Pioneer*, July 26, 1881.

314 **a Model 1866 Winchester carbine:** This carbine, serial number 124335 F.S., is in the collections of the Smithsonian Institution. Among the firearms surrendered by Sitting Bull's band at Fort Buford was a Northwest trade gun belonging to Black Moon. It is believed that Black Moon acquired this weapon from Sitting Bull—Sitting Bull's distinctive signature is carved into the stock. On June 9, 2018, this gun sold at Heritage Auctions, Dallas, Texas, to a private buyer for $162,500.

314 **the stern-wheeler General Sherman:** "Sitting Bull," *The Minneapolis Tribune*, July 30, 1881.

315 **given an informal reception:** "Sitting Bull," *The Bismarck Tribune*, August 5, 1881; and *Army and Navy Journal*, August 6, 1881.

315 **follow him into his lodge:** Burdick, *Tales from Buffalo Land*, 33.

315 **two to five dollars for his autograph:** *Army and Navy Journal*, August 6, 1881; "Sitting Bull," *The Bismarck Tribune*, August 5, 1881; and Judson Elliott Walker, *Campaigns of General Custer in the North-West, and the Final Surrender of Sitting Bull* (New York: Jenkins and Thomas, 1881), 135.

315 **found on the boat crying:** "At Fort Yates," *The Bismarck Tribune*, August 5, 1881.

315 **persuaded to enter Orlando S. Goff's:** An ongoing nerdy debate has focused on whether Goff photographed Sitting Bull at his studio in Bismarck on July 31 or later at Standing Rock. Sources missed by other historians and authors can now settle the matter. A news article from Fort Yates tells us that on Wednesday, August 3, Sitting Bull canceled an appointment to have his picture taken, for which he was to be paid. According to the article, the chief canceled the appointment so he could accept an invitation to visit a large village of surrendered Lakotas three miles from Fort Yates. The name of the photographer

isn't provided, but Goff is the only professional photographer known to operate at the Standing Rock Agency at this time. That the appointment with Goff was soon rescheduled comes from author Judson Elliott Walker. Walker was quite eager to secure an image of Sitting Bull for his forthcoming book, *Campaigns of General Custer in the North-West, and the Final Surrender of Sitting Bull*. In that book, Walker credits Goff for obtaining the desired portrait, commenting that "little did the old chief think while in the hands of Professor Goff at 'Standing Rock Agency,' that his photo would be in the hands of an engraver in New York City within the space of four days." See "Bull's New Pasture," *The Omaha Daily Bee*, August 11, 1881; and Walker, *Campaigns of General Custer*, 134–35. The engraving based on Goff's Sitting Bull portrait appears in Walker's book opposite page 66.

316   *Crazy Horse supposedly objected:* Sioux City, Iowa, photographer James H. Hamilton operated a temporary studio next to Camp Robinson's post trader's store during the summer of 1877. In Hamilton's *Catalogue of Stereoscopic Views of the Northwest*, which included "Indian Scenes Representing Distinguished Chiefs and Prominent Characters," view number 104 is titled "Crazy Horse." Unfortunately, no example of this view has been located to date. Although one can't rule out the possibility that Crazy Horse was photographed while residing at the Red Cloud Agency, none of the photos put forward over the years as depicting the Oglala leader are accepted as legitimate by knowledgeable historians, myself included.

316   *"My friend, why should you wish":* McGillycuddy account in E. A. Brininstool, ed., *Crazy Horse: The Invincible Ogalalla Sioux Chief* (Los Angeles, CA: Wetzel Publishing Co., Inc., 1949), 48.

316   *For the price of $100:* Walker, *Campaigns of General Custer*, 135. A news item in *The River Press*, Fort Benton, MT, August 17, 1881, stated that Sitting Bull secured a written agreement for a percentage of the sales of his photograph before allowing Goff to make the image. I find this doubtful.

316   *Goff exposed two glass-plate negatives:* Markus H. Lindner, "Family, Politics, and Show Business: The Photographs of Sitting Bull," *North Dakota History* 72 (2005): 3–5; and Louis N. Hafermehl, "Chasing an Enigma: Frontier Photographer Orlando S. Goff." *North Dakota History* 81 (Summer 2016): 19. Sitting Bull reportedly wasn't pleased with Goff's portraits. He said his face was too light, making him look like a white man. "News from Sitting Bull," *The Bismarck Tribune*, August 26, 1881.

316   *colored lenses were soothing:* Walker, *Campaigns of General Custer*, 90. It was not uncommon for Plains Indians to wear goggles, which seem to have been a popular trade item. See "Sitting Bull: The First Accurate Portrait Ever Published of the Great Chief," *The Bismarck Tribune*, August 12, 1881.

316   *Sitting Bull had been promised:* "Sitting Bull's Removal," *The Sun*, September 17, 1881.

316   *"I never stood in":* "A Chat with the Chief," *The Omaha Daily Bee*, August 9, 1881.

317   *"Ever since that time":* Ibid.

317   *revenge for Crazy Horse's death:* Waggoner, *Witness*, 48–49 and 480; Susan Bordeaux Bettelyoun, "Spotted Tail," Pioneer Biography Files, Native American

Biographies, Box 30, State Historical Society of North Dakota; and Bettelyoun and Waggoner, *With My Own Eyes,* 110.

317    *"a fit ending for a fool":* "Sitting Bull Yet Belligerent," *New York Times,* August 12, 1881.

317    *"tame Indians":* Josephine Waggoner interview, CC, box 104, folder 14.

318    *secreted a cache of firearms:* "Bull's New Pasture," *The Omaha Daily Bee,* August 11, 1881. The prominent official was Major Guido Ilges, stationed at Fort Keogh.

318    *"undoubtedly means mischief":* "Sitting Bull Yet Belligerent," *New York Times,* August 12, 1881.

318    *"the same old story of contracts violated":* "Sitting Bull's Removal," *The Sun,* September 17, 1881.

318    *preferred to die resisting, like Crazy Horse:* "Sitting Bull," *The Bismarck Tribune,* September 9, 1881.

318    *pushed and prodded Sitting Bull's band:* "A Very Mad Bull," *Army and Navy Journal,* September 17, 1881; "Sitting Bull's Band," *The Boston Daily Globe,* MA, September 12, 1881; and "Sitting Bull Quiescent," *Army and Navy Journal,* October 8, 1881.

318    *very agitated because of a rumor:* "Sitting Bull," *The Chicago Daily Tribune,* October 1, 1881.

319    *Officers took a head count:* George P. Ahern to W. S. Campbell, Washington, D.C., July 31, 1929, CC, box 107, folder 4.

319    *These visits of headmen:* Ibid.; and Jerome A. Greene, *Fort Randall on the Missouri, 1856–1892* (Pierre: South Dakota State Historical Society, 2005), 146.

319    *"the deep respect in which Sitting Bull":* George P. Ahern to Gen. Charles J. Summerall, Washington, D.C., June 20, 1929, CC, box 107, folder 4.

320    **Sitting Bull, The Hero of the Desert:** Joseph Bournichon, *Sitting-Bull, Le Héros du Désert: Scènes de la Guerre Indienne aux Étas-Unis* (Tours, France: Cattier, 1879). A second edition was issued in 1885.

320    *letter writers sought a pipe, tomahawk:* Ahern to Campbell, Washington, D.C., July 12, 1929, and February 16, 1930, CC, box 107, folder 4.

320    *"Sitting Bull was a very remarkable man":* Ahern to Campbell, Washington, D.C., July 31, 1929.

320    *gave him the name "Iron Eyes":* Rudolf Cronau, "My Visit Among the Hostile Dakota Indians and How They Became My Friends," *South Dakota Historical Collections* 22 (1946): 413.

320    *added a large eagle-feather warbonnet:* In his drawing of Sitting Bull, dated October 25, 1881, Cronau has the chief wearing a warbonnet identical to one worn by Buffalo's Hump in a drawing dated Standing Rock, September 24, 1881 (note particularly the pattern of the beaded brow band in each drawing). Additionally, Sitting Bull appears in a number of photographs made at Fort Randall, none of which picture him wearing a warbonnet or breastplate. Gerold M. Wunderlich, *Rudolf Cronau, 1855–1939, in "Wilden Westen": Views of the American West* (New York: Gerold Wunderlich & Co., 1996), 2 and 6; Lindner, "Family, Politics, and Show Business," 8; and Greene, *Fort Randall on the Missouri,* 149–64.

320 *gave his friend a supply of pencils, colored crayons:* Cronau gave pencils, colored crayons, and paper to the Lakotas at Standing Rock to "interest the Indians in my doings." Cronau, "My Visit Among the Hostile Dakota Indians," 414.

321 *Sitting Bull produced three sets of pictographs:* See McCoy: "Sitting Bull: A Hunkpapa Lakota Chronicles His Life of Dauntless Courage"; and William John Armstrong, "Legacy of an Unlikely Friendship: Sitting Bull and a Michigan Family," *Michigan History Magazine* 79 (January–February 1995): 28–35.

321 *"wished to settle down":* As quoted in Dennis C. Pope, *Sitting Bull, Prisoner of War* (Pierre: South Dakota State Historical Society Press, 2010), 54–55. Also, "Sitting Bull: The Redoubtable Indian Chief Described, He Makes a Speech," *The Abbeville Press and Banner,* Abbeville, SC, November 30, 1881; and Vestal, *New Sources,* 271.

321 *"I want my people":* Ibid.

321 *"in our language":* Mary C. Collins, "The Autobiography of Mary C. Collins, Missionary to the Western Sioux," ed. Richmond L. Clow, *South Dakota Historical Collections* 41 (1982): 10.

321 *"what has Sitting Bull been convicted of":* As quoted in Pope, *Sitting Bull, Prisoner of War,* 123.

322 *the Indian agent at Standing Rock:* James McLaughlin to Hiram Price, Standing Rock Agency, April 18, 1882, Standing Rock Agency, Copies of Correspondence Sent to the Commissioner of Indian Affairs and Others, 1881–1903, RG 75, NA-KC.

322 *army and the Indian Bureau agreed:* "Sitting Bull to be Allowed to Return to Standing Rock," *The Chicago Daily Tribune,* March 19, 1883; and Hiram Price to James McLaughlin, Washington, D.C., March 20, 1883, Standing Rock, Misc. Correspondence Received, 1864–, RG 75, NA-KC.

322 *On the afternoon of April 28:* Lieut. Col. Peter T. Swaine to Adjutant Gen. of the Dept. of Dakota, Fort Randall, April 28, 1883, photocopy in Tim Nowak Collection, H2010-094, SDSHS.

322 *Five of their number died:* Swaine to Adjutant Gen. of the Dept. of Dakota, Fort Randall, September 6, 1883 (Swain's annual report), ibid., "Sitting Bull," *The Sioux City Journal,* May 17, 1883; and "Sitting Bull as Speculator," *The Bismarck Tribune,* May 18, 1883.

322 *"Well," Marsh said to the interpreter:* As quoted in Joseph Mills Hanson, *The Conquest of the Missouri, Being the Story of the Life and Exploits of Captain Grant Marsh* (Chicago: A. C. McClurg & Co., 1909), 416–17.

323 *Sitting Bull and his followers debarked:* At this time, Sitting Bull's band numbered 147: thirty-five men, fifty-one women, twenty-three children over six years of age, and thirty-eight children under six years of age. Receipt by James McLaughlin, Standing Rock Agency, May 10, 1883, Standing Rock, Misc. Correspondence Received, 1864–, RG 75, NA-KC; and "Sitting Bull at Home Again," *Sacramento Daily Record-Union,* CA, May 12, 1883.

323 *when he wasn't "too busy":* As quoted in Pope, *Sitting Bull, Prisoner of War,* 132.

324 *"I will do my best to abolish polygamy":* As quoted in Louis L. Pfaller, *James McLaughlin: The Man with an Indian Heart* (New York: Vantage Press, 1978), 28.

324 *Indian Bureau banned the Sun Dance:* Hiram Price to Henry M. Teller, Washington, D.C., October 10, 1883, *Annual Report of the Commissioner of Indian Affairs to the Secretary of the Interior for the Year 1883* (Washington, D.C.: Government Printing Office, 1883), xiv–xv.

324 *"very mediocre ability, rather dull":* James McLaughlin to Hiram Price, Standing Rock Agency, August 15, 1883, ibid., 49. McLaughlin's first draft of this report is in Standing Rock Agency, Annual Statistical Reports, RG 75, NA-KC.

324 *McLaughlin, according to One Bull:* One Bull interview, CC, box 105, folder 19.

325 *strove to conduct himself as a chief:* Robert Higheagle manuscript, CC, box 104, folder 22.

325 *"the warrior chief who planned the massacre":* Fremont Tri-Weekly Tribune, NE, August 11, 1882.

325 *William F. "Buffalo Bill" Cody proposed: The Sioux City Journal,* August 6 and 9, 1882; and *Fremont Tri-Weekly Tribune,* NE, August 11, 1882.

325 *A St. Paul businessman proposed:* E. D. Comings to James McLaughlin, St. Paul, MN, August 24, 1883, Standing Rock, Misc. Correspondence Received, 1864–, RG 75, NA-KC.

325 *The Iowa State Fair:* James McLaughlin to William T. Smith, Fort Yates, August 28, 1883, Standing Rock Agency, Copies of Corres. Sent to the Commissioner of Indian Affairs and Others, 1881–1903, RG 75, NA-KC.

325 *McLaughlin peremptorily rejected:* James McLaughlin to Schayler Wyman, Standing Rock, June 30, 1883, ibid.

325 *the laying of the cornerstone: The Bismarck Tribune,* September 7, 1883; "North Pacific," *Chicago Tribune,* September 6, 1883; and Oswald Garrison Villard, *Fighting Years: Memoirs of a Liberal Editor* (New York: Harcourt, Brace and Company, 1939), 55.

326 *there was no lack of buyers:* "Sitting Bull's Return," *The Bismarck Tribune,* September 7, 1883.

326 *"add very considerably to the object of":* McLaughlin to Hiram Price, Standing Rock, March 7, 1884, Standing Rock Agency, Copies of Corres. Sent to the Commissioner of Indian Affairs and Others, 1881–1903, RG 75, NA-KC. In this letter, McLaughlin writes that it was "at the solicitation of Sitting Bull" that he arranged to take the chief and One Bull to St. Paul. However, I find this very doubtful. One wonders how Sitting Bull learned that McLaughlin was planning a trip to St. Paul. Additionally, McLaughlin was asked by a reporter with the *St. Paul Daily Globe* what his reason was for bringing Sitting Bull to the city, and the agent made no mention of a request from the chief, only that he wanted to show Sitting Bull "the difference between the whites and the Indians." Unfortunately, we don't have Sitting Bull's version of how this excursion came about.

326 *local press covered his every move:* See, for example, "Mr. Sitting Bull," *The St. Paul Daily Globe,* March 15, 1884; "The Harp of Erin," *The St. Paul Daily Globe,* March 18, 1884; "Mr. S. Bull," *The St. Paul Daily Globe,* March 19, 1884; and "Another Bull-y Day," *The St. Paul Daily Globe,* March 20, 1884. T. M. Newson includes an account of Sitting Bull's visit in his *Thrilling Scenes Among the Indians* (Chicago: Belford, Clarke & Co., 1884), 194–200. See also Paul D.

Nelson, "'A Shady Pair' and 'An Attempt on His Life': Sitting Bull and His 1884 Visit to St. Paul," *Ramsey County History* 38 (Spring 2003): 4–12.

326    *"the great lion of the hour":* "The Harp of Erin," *The St. Paul Daily Globe,* March 18, 1884.

326    *a series of fourteen portraits:* The photography studio was operated by Palmquist & Jurgens, corner of Seventh and Robert Streets. For two of the portraits, Sitting Bull was pictured with his nephew. Lindner, "Family, Politics, and Show Business," 18–19.

327    *their first telephone conversation:* "Sitting Bull," *The Canton Advocate,* SD, March 27, 1884, quoting the *St. Paul Pioneer Press.*

327    *a husband-and-wife team of trick shot artists:* "Olympic Theater," *The St. Paul Daily Globe,* March 20, 1884; and Nelson, "'A Shady Pair' and 'An Attempt on His Life,'" 10.

327    *"the original pair of moccasins":* Butler and Oakley advertisement in the *New York Clipper,* April 5, 1884.

327    *The well-heeled and influential proprietor:* Allen had important political connections and obtained letters of support for touring Sitting Bull from U.S. Senator Dwight M. Sabin of Minnesota and U.S. Senator John A. Logan of Illinois. W. L. Berry to "Friend Jerome," Chicago, July 31, 1884, private collection but available for viewing online at https://historical.ha.com/itm/autographs/-sitting-bull-circus-promoter-w-l-berry-autograph-letter-signed/a/6182-47267.s?ic4=GalleryView-Thumbnail-071515. For a biographical sketch of Allen, see "Col. Alvaren Allen," *The St. Paul Daily Globe,* May 23, 1886.

328    *"become impressed with the idea":* "Mr. Sitting Bull," *The St. Paul Daily Globe,* March 15, 1884.

328    *"is such an ignorant and vain man":* As quoted in Pfaller, *James McLaughlin,* 102.

328    *Father Joseph A. Stephan, McLaughlin's predecessor:* "Father Stephan to Go to Washington," *The St. Paul Daily Globe,* April 20, 1884; "Father Stephan," *Jamestown Weekly Alert,* August 8, 1884; and "The Champion Murderer," *Press and Dakotaian,* Yankton, SD, September 5, 1884.

328    *simply couldn't disrupt the "late hostiles":* Pfaller, *James McLaughlin,* 101; and Utley, *The Lance and the Shield,* 263.

329    *"a beautiful Indian girl of sixteen":* "Sitting Bull in Town," *Savannah Morning News,* GA, September 15, 1884, quoting the *New York Herald;* and Shoots Walking interview, CC, box 104, folder 5.

329    *pecuniary incentive:* "Statements Prepared by Mrs. J. F. Waggoner," CC, box 104, folder 14.

329    *Billing itself as a performance of:* See, for example, the advertisements for the Combination in the *New York Times,* September 28, 1884, and the *Philadelphia Inquirer,* October 7, 1884. My description of the performance comes primarily from the following: "All the Rage," *The Courier-Journal,* September 28, 1884; "Sitting Bull and His Friends," *The Brooklyn Union,* October 21, 1884; and "That Indian Exhibition and Address by Major Newson," *The St. Paul Daily Globe,* November 26, 1884. Luther Standing Bear attended one of the Philadelphia performances. His account, written years later, is at odds with what was published in the contemporary press. See his *My People the Sioux,* 184–86.

330    *"Sitting Bull's retarding influence"*: Annual Report of James McLaughlin, Standing Rock Agency, August 26, 1885, *Annual Report of the Commissioner of Indian Affairs to the Secretary of the Interior for the Year 1885* (Washington: Government Printing Office, 1885), 56.

330    *"ought to have been hanged long ago"*: The Times, October 12, 1884. The *Buffalo Sunday Morning News*, dumbfounded that audiences were applauding the chief who "killed" Custer, stated, "Such a lack of true feeling is almost inconceivable." See the issue of September 21, 1884.

330    *"There is usually a damn sight of"*: "That Indian Exhibition and Address by Major Newson," *The St. Paul Daily Globe*, November 26, 1884.

330    *Father Stephan, miffed*: "Why They Returned," *The Bismarck Tribune*, October 31, 1884; "Return of the Sitting Bull Show," *The Sioux City Journal*, October 31, 1884; "Current Notes," *The Chicago Daily Tribune*, November 7, 1884; and James McLaughlin to Merritt L. Joslyn, Standing Rock, October 14, 1884, Standing Rock Agency, Copies of Corres. Sent to the Commissioner of Indian Affairs and Others, 1881–1903, RG 75, NA-KC.

330    *T. M. Newson bragged*: "Return of the Sitting Bull Show." According to a newspaper report, the Sitting Bull Combination broke the single-day attendance record at its New York City venue, the Eden Musée, with over 7,000 people. *The Northern Pacific Farmer*, Wadena, MN, September 25, 1884.

331    *couldn't have helped but make a profit*: A news report dated October 15 quoted Sitting Bull's "agent" as saying "the Indian warriors are making money and have cleared $30,000 since he came to New York." Admission prices were fifty cents for adults and twenty-five cents for children, although the venues would have received a healthy share of that. "Sitting Bull's Wealth," *Harrisburg Daily Independent*, PA, October 15, 1884.

331    *"If we can manage to get him"*: As quoted in Louis S. Warren, *Buffalo Bill's America: William Cody and the Wild West Show* (New York: Alfred A. Knopf, 2005), 219.

331    *individuals such as General Sherman*: Pfaller, *James McLaughlin*, 103; and "Major General Eugene A. Carr, United States Army, Calls Him 'King of Them All,'" *Morning Journal and Courier*, New Haven, CT, July 2, 1885.

331    *"pleading, coaxing, and bartering"*: "How 'Arizona John' Succeeded in Capturing Sitting Bull," *The Philadelphia Inquirer*, June 26, 1885; and "Sitting Bull and Braves," *The Boston Daily Globe*, July 26, 1885.

331    *the two-page contract*: The original 1885 contract was sold by Heritage Auctions, Dallas, to a private collector on June 10, 2012, for $155,350. It's available for viewing online here: https://historical.ha.com/itm/autographs/sitting-bull-the -original-1885-contract-for-him-to-appear-in-buffalo-bill-s-wild-west-signed-by -the-great-sioux-chiefandlt-/a/6079-44121.s?ic4=GalleryView-Thumbnail-071515.

331    *in front of a packed grandstand*: Sitting Bull's first meeting with Cody is described in detail in "Greek Meets Greek," *Buffalo Courier*, NY, June 13, 1885. A good description of a typical performance of Cody's show is "The Wild West," *Hartford Courant*, CT, July 18, 1885.

332    *the chief got to meet the Great Father*: "Sitting Bull in War Paint," *The Sun*, June 24, 1885.

332    *"die in peace"*: "Greek Meets Greek," *Buffalo Courier*, June 13, 1885.

333    *"White man one great damned fool!":* "Sitting Bull in War Paint," *The Sun,* June 24, 1885.

333    *the show admitted 46,582 people:* "Buffalo Bill's Big Audience," *The Weekly New Era,* Lancaster, PA, July 11, 1885. Another news report claimed Cody made a profit of $80,000 on the season. *The Sioux City Journal,* October 20, 1885.

333    *"the finest riding pony in the show":* "Sitting Bull's Return," *Bismarck Weekly Tribune,* October 16, 1885; *Emmons County Record,* Linton, ND, November 4, 1885; One Bull interview, CC, box 104, folder 11; and James McLaughlin to W. M. Camp, Washington, D.C., January 15, 1919, Robert S. Ellison/Walter Camp Papers, Denver Public Library, box 1, folder 53.

333    *encounter with an old woman begging:* "Custer's Mistake," *The Times,* July 5, 1885; and "Memories of Bull," *The St. Paul Daily Globe,* September 13, 1886.

333    *feasts for his followers:* James McLaughlin to John M. Burke, Fort Yates, April 16, 1886, in Pfaller, *James McLaughlin,* 106.

334    *"is so inflated":* James McLaughlin to J. D. C. Atkins, Standing Rock, November 2, 1885, Standing Rock Agency, Copies of Corres. Sent to the Commissioner of Indian Affairs and Others, 1881–1903, RG 75, NA-KC.

334    *"of the most worthless":* Ibid.

335    *"Sitting Bull was a thinker":* Robert Higheagle manuscript, CC, box 104, folder 22.

335    *"their barbarous dialects":* "Indian Education," *The Inter Ocean,* August 20, 1887.

335    *"encourage Indians to adhere to":* James McLaughlin to J. D. C. Atkins, Standing Rock, September 22, 1887, Standing Rock Agency, Copies of Corres. Sent to the Commissioner of Indian Affairs and Others, 1881–1903, RG 75, NA-KC.

335    *visited the Lincoln Institute:* "Sitting Bull at Wayne," *The Times,* October 9, 1884.

335    *"I don't no more like a blanket":* "Indians at Play," *The Times,* July 5, 1885.

336    *Sitting Bull kept his children out:* James McLaughlin to J. D. C. Atkins, Standing Rock, April 14, 1886, Standing Rock Agency, Copies of Corres. Sent to the Commissioner of Indian Affairs and Others, 1881–1903, RG 75, NA-KC. McLaughlin—or resident missionaries—seems to have eventually talked Sitting Bull into sending his children to school, for a circa 1888 Húnkpapa census shows four of the chief's children (unidentified) as enrolled in agency schools. One Bull also remembered that Sitting Bull had four children in the day school, which he named as Standing Holy, Captures Horses (Her Many Horses), Crow Foot, and William Sitting Bull (Runs Away from Him). Additionally, an 1888 newspaper profile of Sitting Bull stated that the chief had "five children, all of whom attend the Indian schools on the reservation." The Húnkpapa census is in the Frank Zahn Papers, 1869–1948, #10162, State Historical Society of North Dakota; and One Bull interview, CC, box 104, folder 11. The quote is from Utley, *The Lance and the Shield,* 275.

336    *"think it advisable for [Sitting] Bull":* James McLaughlin to John M. Burke, Fort Yates, April 16, 1886, in Pfaller, *James McLaughlin,* 105.

336    *Washington in October 1888:* The visit of Sitting Bull and the other Sioux chiefs was well covered by the Washington press. See the *Evening Star* for October 13, 15, 17, 18, 19, and 20, 1888.

336  *"adding the last finishing touch"*: The St. Paul Daily Globe, October 11, 1888. The store was the Manhattan Clothing Company, located at 161 to 167 East Seventh Street. Suits were also purchased for Gall, John Grass, Gray Eagle, Bear's Rib, and interpreter Louis Primeau. The chiefs' clothing is described in "The Sioux Chiefs," *The Evening Star*, October 13, 1888.

337  *the Sioux Act of 1889*: See Herbert T. Hoover, "The Sioux Agreement of 1889 and Its Aftermath," *South Dakota History* 19 (1989): 56–94.

337  *"In some way"*: Message from the President of the United States Transmitting Reports Relative to the Proposed Division of the Great Sioux Reservation, and Recommending Certain Legislation, Sen. Exec. Doc. No. 51, 51st Cong., 1st Sess., 189.

337  *get these chiefs "into line"*: McLaughlin, *My Friend the Indian*, 284–85; and John M. Carignan narrative in Fiske, *Life and Death of Sitting Bull*, 26–27.

337  *entered the circle and asked to speak*: "Bull Makes a Break," *The St. Paul Daily Globe*, August 4, 1889; Thomas W. Foley, ed. *At Standing Rock and Wounded Knee: The Journals and Papers of Father Francis M. Craft, 1888–1890* (Norman, OK: The Arthur H. Clark Company, 2009), 268; and Martin F. Schmitt, ed., *General George Crook, His Autobiography* (Norman: University of Oklahoma Press, 1946), 288.

337  *"who had sold them out"*: "Sioux Are Signing Now," *The Chicago Tribune*, August 4, 1889.

338  *"Don't talk to me about Indians!"*: "Gall Says It's a Go," *The St. Paul Daily Globe*, August 6, 1889.

## 14 / Ghosts

339  *"Who would have thought"*: As quoted in Natalie Curtis, ed., *The Indians' Book* (New York: Harper and Brothers, 1907), 45.

339  *"all over the universe"*: Black Elk interview, DeMallie, ed., *The Sixth Grandfather*, 290.

339  *The chief's home*: "A Great Domain," reprinted from the *Chicago Herald* in *Friendship Weekly Register*, Friendship, NY, June 27, 1889; "The Relics of Bull," reprinted from an 1891 issue of *The Minneapolis Journal* in the *Mandan Pioneer*, April 27, 1969; "The Indians in Dakota," *The Chicago Tribune*, December 26, 1888; and diagram of cabin by One Bull, CC, box 105, folder 41. Sitting Bull's cabin was originally half the size stated in my text. Photographs of the cabin taken in the 1890s show the later log addition. The original, smaller cabin is described in "The Autobiography of Mary C. Collins," 7–8.

340  *Hanging from a peg*: One Bull interview, CC, box 105, folder 41.

340  *rumor he'd been baptized*: "Sitting Bull Will Not Baptize," *The Bismarck Tribune*, June 1, 1883.

340  *a sodbuster's outfit*: One Bull interview, CC, box 104, folder 11.

341  *deep cuts on their arms and legs*: "Death of Sitting Bull's Daughter," *The Billings Gazette*, June 15, 1887.

341  *Andrew Fox*: "Letter from the Secretary of the Interior in response to Senate Resolution of February 28, 1891, Forwarding Report Made by the Hampton

Institute Regarding Its Returned Indian Students," Sen. Exec. Doc. No. 31, 52nd Cong., 1st Sess., 13; and Foley, ed. *At Standing Rock and Wounded*, 84.

341 *National Indian Defense Association:* For the founding and goals of the organization, see "The Red Man's Friends," *Springfield Daily Republic*, OH, November 29, 1885; "Indian Affairs," *The Kansas City Star*, February 20, 1886; and *The Kansas City Star*, August 27, 1886.

341 *"Sioux Sentimentalists":* "Sioux Sentimentalists," *The Topeka State Journal*, KS, May 28, 1889; and "Meddlesome Philanthropists," *The Omaha Daily Bee*, May 29, 1889.

342 *"female crank"* and *"a peculiar character":* W. J. Godfrey to Major Roberts, Sioux, NE, July 11, 1889, in Vestal, *New Sources*, 92; and Bernard Strassmaier to W. S. Campbell, Fort Yates, August 2, 1929, CC, box 108, folder 2.

342 *"seemed funny to me":* Bernard Strassmaier to W. S. Campbell, Fort Yates, January 25, 1929, CC, box 108, folder 2.

342 *members of the association:* C. Weldon to Chief Red Cloud, Yankton Indian Agency, July 3, 1889, in Vestal, *New Sources*, 93.

342 *"not bad looking":* "A New York Widow," *The Sioux City Journal*, July 2, 1889.

342 *a pass from McLaughlin:* My narrative of the heated encounter between Weldon and McLaughlin is based on their own accounts, which, unsurprisingly, don't agree on certain specifics, although both agree it was a disaster. See C. Weldon to Chief Red Cloud, July 3, 1889, Vestal, *New Sources*, 94; "The Widow Was Wild," *The St. Paul Daily Globe*, July 1, 1889; and Pfaller, *James McLaughlin*, 120.

343 *an ugly story appeared:* "A New York Widow," *The Sioux City Journal*, July 2, 1889.

343 *"McLaughlin has the cunning of Satan":* Foley, ed. *At Standing Rock and Wounded*, 42.

343 *"The agent fears my presence":* C. Weldon to Chief Red Cloud, July 3, 1889.

343 *"unparalleled untruths":* "An Error Corrected," *The Sioux City Journal*, July 6, 1889.

344 *it was Caroline Schlatter:* My information on Caroline's personal history comes primarily from a lengthy exposé of sorts titled "Rejected By Reds," reprinted from the *World*, NY, in the *St. Paul Daily Globe*, March 23, 1891. There is some confusion regarding Caroline's date of birth. Her age is given as twenty-four in the 1870 U.S. census, which indicates a birth year of 1846. Her obituary states she was seventy-eight at the time of her death in 1921, placing her birth three years earlier. Caroline Schlatter in the 1870 U.S. census, Sixth Ward, City of Brooklyn, New York, page 348; and Caroline Weldon obituary, *The Standard Union*, Brooklyn, NY, March 16, 1921.

344 *Caroline had written McLaughlin:* Mrs. C. Weldon to Major McLaughlin, Brooklyn, NY, April 5, 1890, in Vestal, *New Sources*, 98–100.

344 *settled in at a ranch:* Smith, *Red Indian Experiences*, 199.

344 *"more insolent and worthless":* James McLaughlin to T. J. Morgan, Standing Rock Agency, October 17, 1890, in Pfaller, *James McLaughlin*, 131.

344 *went to live on Grand River:* Frank Zahn to W. S. Campbell, Fort Yates, June 1, 1932, CC, box 107, folder 5.

345 **Woman Walking Ahead:** Vestal, *Sitting Bull*, 266–67. In going through Vestal/ Campbell's massive collection of interview notes, I've been unable to find his source for Weldon's Lakota name.

345 **Sitting Bull's third wife:** Josephine Waggoner interview, CC, box 104, folder 6. This folder is identified as the "statement of Little Soldier." However, in addition to Little Soldier, it contains statements from One Bull and Waggoner. Among a cache of Caroline's letters and other papers left behind in Sitting Bull's cabin was a cryptic note that some have interpreted as evidence that Sitting Bull suggested she had indeed become one of his wives. See Vestal, *New Sources*, 116.

345 **especially fond of Christie:** "Where's Bull's Body?," *Bismarck Weekly Tribune*, December 26, 1890.

345 **"Rations are always short":** "Interview with Ex-Indian Agent McGillycuddy," *Dawes County Journal*, December 5, 1890. From 1888 to 1890, beef rations were drastically reduced at the Pine Ridge, Rosebud, and Cheyenne River reservations. Standing Rock's beef rations were not cut. Jeffrey Ostler, *The Plains Sioux and U.S. Colonialism from Lewis and Clark to Wounded Knee* (New York: Cambridge University Press, 2004), 237 n. 63.

345 **one-fifth of the supplies:** "Among the Ghost Dancers," *The Sun*, December 28, 1890.

345 **"were told there were no rations":** James Tangled Yellow Hair interview, Limbaugh, ed., *Cheyenne and Sioux*, 45.

346 **"recurring droughts with blighting":** James McLaughlin to Arthur C. Mellette, Standing Rock Agency, November 4, 1889, Standing Rock Agency, Copies of Corres. Sent to the Commissioner of Indian Affairs and Others, 1881–1903, RG 75, NA-KC.

346 **Kicking Bear and nine other Lakotas:** Rani-Henrik Andersson, *A Whirlwind Passed Through Our Country: Lakota Voices of the Ghost Dance* (Norman: University of Oklahoma Press, 2018), 7; James Mooney, *The Ghost-Dance Religion and the Sioux Outbreak of 1890* (1896; reprint: Lincoln: University of Nebraska Press, 1991), 820; and Black Elk interview, DeMallie, ed., *The Sixth Grandfather*, 257–58.

347 **the Paiute holy man said:** Interviews with Wovoka in which he describes his vision are found in Mooney, *The Ghost-Dance Religion*, 771–72; and A. I. Chapman to Gen. John Gibbon, San Francisco, December 6, 1890, in *Report of the Secretary of War*, vol. 1 (Washington: Government Printing Office, 1892), 193.

347 **known of Wovoka's vision for months:** Mrs. C. Weldon to T. C. Bland, Cannonball, ND, October 8, 1890, in "Indian Delusions," *Rock Island Daily Argus*, IL, October 30, 1890.

347 **Sitting Bull's nephew:** "Among the Ghost Dancers," *The Sun*, December 28, 1890; and McCreight, *Chief Flying Hawk's Tales*, 14 and 30. Kicking Bear was a brother of Flying Hawk and a half brother of Black Fox.

347 **arrived at Sitting Bull's camp:** "Sioux May Make Trouble," *The Inter Ocean*, October 28, 1890.

347 **told his uncle about Wovoka:** Wovoka's prophecy as interpreted and preached by Kicking Bear and the other Lakota disciples is considerably more elaborate

and detailed than the simple version Wovoka later provided white interviewers. And no two descriptions of the prophecy reported by the Lakota disciples are exactly alike. My account of what Kicking Bear claimed concerning the coming of the Messiah is from a letter by Mary C. Collins, a Congregational missionary who ran a small mission on Grand River near Sitting Bull's settlement. She spoke Lakota and obtained her information directly from Sitting Bull and his followers. Her letter is printed under the title "Sitting Bull's Plans," in the *Inter Ocean*, December 17, 1890. Another version of Kicking Bear's message was reported to Agent McLaughlin by One Bull. It's found in "Coming of the Messiah," *Black Hills Weekly Times*, Deadwood, SD, November 8, 1890.

348     *the name Ghost Dance:* Mooney, *The Ghost-Dance Religion*, 791. Also translated as Spirit Dance. An individual who witnessed a Ghost Dance one night on the Cheyenne and Arapaho Reservation in Oklahoma Territory wrote that the name Ghost Dance came from the white shirts and dresses worn by the dancers. C. C. Painter, *Cheyennes and Arapahoes Revisited* (Philadelphia: The Indian Rights Association, 1893), 10.

348     *"blessed white robes":* Josephine Waggoner interview, CC, box 104, folder 14.

348     *decorated with painted symbols:* "Waiting for the Earth to Move: The 1890 Ghost Dance," museum exhibition, 2017–present, Yellowstone County Museum, Billings, MT; Richard E. Jensen, R. Eli Paul, and John E. Carter, *Eyewitness at Wounded Knee* (Lincoln: University of Nebraska Press, 2011), 7–10; and George Sword account in Mooney, *The Ghost-Dance Religion*, 798.

348     *prayed over the shirts and dresses to make them* **wakan:** Josephine Waggoner interview, CC, box 104, folder 14; and Short Bull interview, Walker, *Lakota Belief and Ritual*, 143.

349     *made the dancers* **wakan:** "Sitting Bull's Plans," *The Inter Ocean*, December 17, 1890.

349     *"I will be chief":* Ibid.

349     *"demoralizing, indecent, and disgusting":* McLaughlin to Morgan, October 17, 1890, in Pfaller, *James McLaughlin*, 132.

349     *detachment of thirteen Metal Breasts:* "Sioux May Make Trouble," *The Inter Ocean*, October 28, 1890.

349     *ten dollars a month: Official Register of the United States, Containing a List of the Officers and Employés in the Civil, Military, and Naval Service on the First of July, 1889*, vol. 1 (Washington: Government Printing Office, 1889), 633.

349     *One Bull received other incentives:* Josephine Waggoner to W. S. Campbell, Keldron, SD, September 19, 1929, CC, box 108, folder 18.

349     *The captain and his second lieutenant:* Captain Crazy Walking and Second Lieutenant Antoine Clement.

349     *the officers refused:* McLaughlin to Morgan, October 17, 1890, in Pfaller, *James McLaughlin*, 131.

349     *the Ghost Dance must stop:* One Bull interview, CC, box 104, folder 11.

350     *as a "dazed condition":* "Kicking Bear and the Ghost Dance," *The Chicago Tribune*, October 28, 1890.

350     *Kicking Bear was successfully removed:* McLaughlin to Morgan, October 17,

1890, in Pfaller, *James McLaughlin,* 132; and McLaughlin, *My Friend the Indian,* 191.

350 *"Brother-in-law, we're settled":* Gray Eagle interview, CC, box 106, folder 54.

351 *"This false prophet and cheat":* C. Weldon to McLaughlin, Cannonball, October 24, 1890, in Vestal, *New Sources,* 102.

351 *"If you want to die":* "Among the Ghost Dancers," *The Sun,* December 28, 1890.

351 *her life was in danger:* Ibid.

351 *"beautiful Indian trinkets":* C. Weldon to Sitting Bull, Kansas City, December 1, 1890, in Vestal, *New Sources,* 110.

351 *"It was money, health, and heart":* C. Weldon to McLaughlin, Cannonball, October 24, 1890, ibid., 103.

351 *based the painting on a photograph:* The iconic photograph was made in the Montreal, QC, studio of William Notman & Son in August 1885. Lindner, "Family, Politics, and Show Business," 12.

352 *tears rolled down his cheeks:* "Where's Bull's Body?," *Bismarck Weekly Tribune,* December 26, 1890.

352 *received a letter from Caroline:* C. Weldon to Sitting Bull, Kansas City, November 20, 1890, in Vestal, *New Sources,* 103.

352 *Grief-stricken, Sitting Bull abruptly left:* "Where's Bull's Body?," *Bismarck Weekly Tribune,* December 26, 1890.

352 *On the morning of November 16:* My account of McLaughlin's visit to Sitting Bull's Grand River settlement is based almost entirely on his November 19 report to the commissioner of Indian affairs. His visit is also described in *My Friend the Indian,* 201–8, but this version is highly embellished and, as with the rest of the book, he presents Sitting Bull in the poorest light possible. We have no account of the visit from Sitting Bull or any of his followers. James McLaughlin to T. J. Morgan, Standing Rock Agency, November 19, 1890, "Letter from the Secretary of the Interior, Transmitting, in Response to a Senate Resolution of 2d Instant, a Communication from the Commissioner of Indian Affairs Relative to the Alleged Armament of Indians in Certain States," S. Exec. Doc. No. 9, 51st Cong., 2nd Sess., 24–26.

352 *the chief be removed to a military prison:* McLaughlin to Morgan, October 17, 1890, in Pfaller, *James McLaughlin,* 132.

353 *Several sweat lodges stood near:* James Tangled Yellow Hair interview, *Cheyenne and Sioux,* 43; and Short Bull interview, Walker, *Lakota Belief and Ritual,* 143.

353 *The dancers held hands:* My description of the dance is from the Short Bull interview, Walker, *Lakota Belief and Ritual,* 143, and Mary C. Collins letter in "Sitting Bull's Plans," in the *Inter Ocean,* December 17, 1890.

354 *"Look here, Sitting Bull":* McLaughlin, *My Friend the Indian,* 205.

355 *calling the pair old women:* Frank Zahn to W. S. Campbell, Fort Yates, SD, November 3, 1929, CC, box 107, folder 5.

355 *took several beef tongues:* Fiske, *Life and Death of Sitting Bull,* 50; and Grover Eagle Boy interview, CC, box 106, folder 54.

355 *intending to make Ghost Dance shirts:* Zahn to Campbell, November 3, 1929, CC, box 107, folder 5. Another version of the incident with the flour sacks is found in Josephine Waggoner, "Sitting Bull at the Agency," CC, box 104, folder 14.

356    *several telegrams on his desk:* John H. Hager to James McLaughlin, Mandan, ND, November 17, 1890; David Carey to James McLaughlin, Mandan, ND, November 18, 1890; and George H. Bingenheimer to James McLaughlin, Mandan, ND, November 17, 1890; all in the Frank Zahn Papers. Delia Carey was employed as a teacher at Standing Rock from November 1 to December 6, when she heeded her parents' advice to return home to Mandan. *Bismarck Weekly Tribune,* December 19, 1890.

356    *"We are hungry":* As quoted in Elaine Goodale, "An Indian's View of the Indian Question," 1890 clipping, Watson Papers.

356    *"Trouble Is Expected":* The *Sioux City Journal,* November 20, 1890.

356    *"Sioux Take the Warpath Today":* The *Pittsburgh Post,* November 22, 1890.

356    *"Six to Eight Thousand Redskins":* The *St. Joseph Herald,* MO, November 22, 1890.

356    *Lakotas murdering whites:* For example, see "Turbulent Reds," *Daily Inter Mountain,* Butte, MT, November 22, 1890; and "Sanguinary Sioux," *St. Louis Globe-Democrat,* November 23, 1890.

356    *a flood of settlers abandoned homes:* Ibid.; "They Buy Papers," *The St. Paul Daily Globe,* November 30, 1890; "Still Excited," *Bismarck Weekly Tribune,* November 21, 1890; and Pfaller, *James McLaughlin,* 136.

357    *"fomenters of disturbances":* R. V. Belt to McLaughlin, Washington, November 20, 1890, in *Sixtieth Annual Report of the Commissioner of Indian Affairs, 1891* (Washington: Government Printing Office, 1891), 331.

357    *"if the so-called Messiah":* Miles, *Serving the Republic,* 238.

357    *for his skills as a savvy Plainsman:* Ibid., 145.

357    *would at least listen to him:* William F. Cody, *An Autobiography of Buffalo Bill* (New York: Cosmopolitan Book Corporation, 1920), 306.

357    *On the afternoon of November 28:* I've drawn upon numerous sources for Cody's mission. These include "Bill and Bull," *The Bismarck Tribune,* December 2, 1890; "Why Buffalo Bill Did Not Arrest Old Sitting Bull," *The Sioux City Journal,* December 4, 1890; America Elmira Collins to Ethel Warner Collins, December 9, 1890, Eric C. Jacobsen Papers, 1883–1939, #10898, State Historical Society of North Dakota; Frank Fiske, "When Buffalo Bill Was at Fort Yates," *Sioux County Pioneer,* Fort Yates, ND, January 25, 1917; Peter E. Traub, "The First Act of the Last Sioux Campaign," *Journal of the United States Cavalry Association* 15 (April 1905): 872–79; Matthew F. Steele, "Buffalo Bill's Bluff," *South Dakota Historical Collections* 9 (1918): 475–85; Fiske, *Life and Death of Sitting Bull,* 37–40; and Pfaller, *James McLaughlin,* 139–46, which includes McLaughlin's telegram to the commissioner of Indian affairs and Lieut. Col. Drum's official reports on Cody's visit.

359    *"in such a way that not a drop":* "Blocked by Benjamin," *The St. Paul Daily Globe,* December 1, 1890.

359    *"My telegram," he wrote:* McLaughlin, *My Friend the Indian,* 211.

359    *he simply intended to shower his gifts:* Some believed that Cody accepted the assignment from General Miles in the hopes of re-signing Sitting Bull to his Wild West. See Matthew F. Steele, "The Death of Sitting Bull: A Reminiscence," typescript, Matthew Forney Steele Papers, 1871–1936, #10115, box 4, folder 20, State Historical Society of North Dakota.

360     *"So long as the Indians abstain":* "The Indian War Scare," *The Brooklyn Daily Eagle,* November 29, 1890.

360     *"Sitting Bull should be captured":* "Ready to Fight," *The Brooklyn Daily Eagle,* December 2, 1890.

360     *he was to make no arrests:* R. V. Belt to McLaughlin, Washington, December 5, 1890, *Sixtieth Annual Report of the Commissioner of Indian Affairs,* 333. According to McLaughlin, he had plans in place for his Indian police to arrest Sitting Bull on December 6. Report of James McLaughlin, December 24, 1890, *Sixtieth Annual Report of the Commissioner of Indian Affairs,* 334.

361     *In a December 6 telegram:* McLaughlin to Gen. Ruger, Standing Rock Agency, December 6, 1890, *Sixtieth Annual Report of the Commissioner of Indian Affairs,* 333.

361     *well aware of McLaughlin's role:* Jerome A. Greene, *American Carnage: Wounded Knee, 1890* (Norman: University of Oklahoma Press, 2014), 175–76.

361     *"secure the person of Sitting Bull":* M. Barber to Commanding Officer, St. Paul, MN, December 12, 1890, *Sixtieth Annual Report of the Commissioner of Indian Affairs,* 333.

361     *McLaughlin suggested they wait:* Report of James McLaughlin, December 24, 1890, ibid., 334; and James McLaughlin to Mary Collins, Standing Rock Agency, December 26, 1890, in "The Words of Winona," *Akron Beacon and Republican,* Akron, OH, February 14, 1891.

362     *a letter from Sitting Bull:* The earliest extant version of this letter, a transcription by Walter Campbell, is in Typescript research correspondence regarding the death of Sitting Bull, CC, box 114, folder 6. See also Vestal, *Sitting Bull,* 283–84.

362     *McLaughlin responded with a long letter:* This letter, dated December 13, is reproduced in Usher L. Burdick, *The Last Days of Sitting Bull* (1941; reprint: Landisville, PA: Coachwhip Publications, 2011), 31–33.

362     *John M. Carignan:* "An Early Trader Is Ill," *The Kansas City Star,* January 22, 1929; "John M. Carignan, Indian Friend Dies," *Emmons County Record,* Linton, ND, July 16, 1931; and Frank Fiske to Elmo Scott Watson, Fort Yates, North Dakota, March 5, 1945, Watson Papers.

363     *Carignan dutifully wrote down:* John M. Carignan to James McLaughlin, Grand River, ND, December 14, 1890, in Vestal, *New Sources,* 13–14.

363     *proceed with the arrest at once:* W. F. Drum to Assistant Adjutant General, Fort Yates, ND, December 17, 1890, and James McLaughlin to Herbert Welsh, Standing Rock Agency, ND, January 12, 1891, both in John M. Carroll, ed., *The Arrest and Killing of Sitting Bull: A Documentary* (Glendale, CA: The Arthur H. Clark Company, 1986), 129 and 125, respectively.

363     *orders in English and Lakota:* The original orders may be viewed on the Welch Dakota Papers website: https://www.welchdakotapapers.com/2011/11/sitting -bull-his-last-days-2/.

364     *a short letter to Carignan:* James McLaughlin to J. M. Carignan, Standing Rock Agency, ND, December 14, 1890, in Vestal, *New Sources,* 14–15.

364     *Sitting Bull learned he would die:* One Bull told of Sitting Bull's premonition to an Elsia Craig, possibly an officer's wife at Fort Yates. See Elsia Craig, "Sitting Bull's Cabin," *Bismarck Daily Tribune,* February 28, 1891.

365     *Crow Foot, now sixteen, had an iron bed:* One Bull diagram of Sitting Bull's cabin, CC, box 105, folder 41.

365    **"Believing in the Ghost Dance":** As quoted in Pfaller, *James McLaughlin*, 398 n. 16. Years later, One Bull would claim that Bull Head falsely accused him of being "a believer." However, *Chicago Herald* reporter Sam Clover interviewed One Bull in early December 1890 and described him as "one of the leaders of the ghost dance." See One Bull interview, CC, box 104, folder 11; and "Among Ghost Dancers," *The Sunday Ledger*, Tacoma, WA, December 21, 1890, quoting the *Chicago Herald*.

365    **Early the next morning:** My reconstruction of the seriously bungled arrest of Sitting Bull, including quotations, is drawn primarily from these, mostly eyewitness, accounts: Red Tomahawk in A. B. Welch, "The Battle of Standing Rock," *The Clover Leaf* (February 1928): 33–39; Affidavit of Shoots Walking, January 6, 1925, E. D. Mossman Papers, #10173, State Historical Society of North Dakota; He Alone Is a Man statement in Vestal, *New Sources*, 45–55; Swift Hawk statement in "Swift Hawk's Story," *Akron Beacon and Republican*, OH, January 10, 1891; Scarlet Whirlwind Woman interview, CC, box 105, folder 41; One Bull interviews, CC, box 104, folder 11, and box 105, folder 41; Gray Eagle interview, CC, box 106, folder 54; Little Soldier interview, CC, box 104, folder 6; Weasel Bear interview, CC, box 105, folder 20; Otter Robe interview, CC, box 106, folder 54; White Bird interview, CC, box 105, folder 12; Grover Eagle Boy interview, CC, box 106, folder 54; One Elk interview, CC, box 106, folder 54; Old Bull interview, box 105, folder 36; Black Hills statement, E. D. Mossman Papers, #10173, State Historical Society of North Dakota; interviews of He Alone Is a Man, Four Robes, Gray Eagle, One Bull, and Scarlet Whirlwind Woman in Carroll, ed., *The Arrest and Killing of Sitting Bull*, 67–77; "Who Killed Sitting Bull?," *Bismarck Weekly Tribune*, December 26, 1890; John M. Carignan narrative in Fiske, *Life and Death of Sitting Bull*, 45–51; and James McLaughlin report, December 24, 1890, *Sixtieth Annual Report of the Commissioner of Indian Affairs*, 333–38.

368    **She was singing a brave song:** Historians and others have frequently written that Crow Foot goaded his father into resisting, and some Metal Breast accounts do claim this. However, the eyewitness accounts of Four Robes, Scarlet Whirlwind Woman, Good Voiced Eagle, Weasel Bear, and Gray Eagle state Crow Foot said nothing. The brave song quote is from Frank Zahn, in notes to an interview of One Bull he conducted on behalf of Walter Campbell. Zahn attributes the song to "one of Sitting Bull's wives." In a biographical sketch of Bull Head, Josephine Waggoner identifies her as "Sitting Bull's oldest wife," which was Whole Tribe Seeing Her. Zahn further states that the account of the wife singing the brave song was "verified by Little Soldier (living), also a number of others." Frank Zahn notes in One Bull interview, CC, box 104, folder 11; and Josephine Waggoner, "Lieut. Henry Bullhead Jr., Tatomkapa," Pioneer Biography Files.

369    **fired at Bull Head:** The vast majority of the eyewitness accounts state that Catch the Bear fired the opening shot. However, a very few accounts—Scarlet Whirlwind Woman being a prime example—claim that Bull Head shot Sitting Bull first, thus precipitating the fight.

369    **leaving a jagged, two-inch hole:** This comes from the Shoots Walking affidavit. As with all the accounts that have been left us from this episode, both Indian

and white, there are several contradictions in important details. McLaughlin wrote in his official report that Bull Head's slug entered on the left side between the tenth and eleventh ribs, and that there was no exit wound. Fred P. Caldwell, a member of the Eight Cavalry, recalled that Sitting Bull had a gunshot wound "in front and center of body about two inches below where neck joins body; I think it passed through lower part of collar bone." He was certain that the chief wasn't shot in the head. However, Caldwell also wrote that Sitting Bull's head was "pounded all out of shape," which causes one to wonder how he could determine there was no bullet wound in that bloody mess. F. P. Caldwell to W. M. Camp, Maltby, SD, May 12, 1914, Robert S. Ellison/Walter Camp Papers, DPL, box 1, folder 130.

370    *ride the Buffalo Bill horse:* An oft-repeated tale has the Buffalo Bill horse performing "tricks" when the shooting started, the gunfire supposedly fooling the horse into thinking it was back in Cody's Wild West. This myth first appears in Vestal's *Sitting Bull*, originally published in 1932, in which Vestal described the animal as a "circus horse." But Cody's gift to Sitting Bull wasn't a "circus horse" that performed tricks; it was a saddle mount. And not one of the many eyewitness accounts left by Metal Breasts and Sitting Bull's followers mention this strange performance. See William E. Lemons, "History by Unreliable Narrators: Sitting Bull's Circus Horse," *Montana The Magazine of Western History* 45 (Autumn–Winter 1995): 64–74.

371    *the command of Captain Edmond G. Fechet:* Capt. Fechet's official report on the operations of his battalion is found in Carroll, ed., *The Arrest and Killing of Sitting Bull*, 133–42. He later published an article titled "The True Story of the Death of Sitting Bull," *Cosmopolitan* 20 (March 1896): 493–501. I've also drawn on accounts left by those who served in Fechet's command. These are George B. DuBois to George Thomas, Fort Yates, December 18, 1890, George B. Dubois Collection, MSS 215, History Colorado; Lieut. Stephen Slocum interview in "Sitting Bull's Death," *The Cincinnati Enquirer*, OH, February 20, 1892; F. P. Caldwell to W. M. Camp, May 12 and June 6, 1914, Robert S. Ellison/Walter Camp Papers, DPL, Box 1, folder 130; and Steele, "The Death of Sitting Bull: A Reminiscence." The account of an unnamed newspaper correspondent who accompanied the battalion is "Who Killed Sitting Bull?," *Bismarck Weekly Tribune*, December 26, 1890. We also have a letter from a member of a detachment under command of Lieut. Col. Drum that met Fechet's returning column twenty-two miles from Fort Yates. See Allen Siegert to Friend Gaetke, Fort Yates, December 17, 1890, Allen Siegert Papers, #20603, State Historical Society of North Dakota.

373    *Both were taken prisoner:* James McLaughlin report on the capture and death of Sitting Bull, Standing Rock Agency, December 16, 1890, National Archives, Washington, D.C., available for viewing online at https://catalog.archives .gov/id/300326?q=sitting%20bull%20arrest; "Sitting Bull's Death," *The Evening Star*, December 22, 1890; and "Was Bull Murdered?," and "Who Killed Sitting Bull?," both in *Bismarck Weekly Tribune*, December 26, 1890. McLaughlin's original report doesn't name the son of Jumping Bull. He refers to him as "'Middle' son of Little Assiniboine [Jumping Bull]." Of Jumping Bull's three sons, the "middle" son was Protecting Others While Running, and he would have

been twenty-one or very close in December 1890. See Dickson, *The Sitting Bull Surrender Census*, 71. Matthew Steele wrote years later that it was Sitting Bull's deaf stepson, John Sitting Bull, who was hiding under the thick bedding. See his "The Death of Sitting Bull," and Matthew F. Steele to Elmo Scott Watson, Fargo, ND, February 15, 1944, Watson Papers.

374   *One Bull's freighting outfit:* Direct descendants of Sitting Bull have long believed that One Bull played a prominent role in Sitting Bull's death. Sitting Bull's great-grandson, Ernie LaPointe, writes that it was One Bull who delivered the news to Agent McLaughlin that Sitting Bull was preparing to leave for Pine Ridge. However, this claim is not supported by the evidence, which tells us that One Bull was engaged in freighting to Standing Rock at the time McLaughlin received word of Sitting Bull's plans. And McLaughlin clearly states that the report was delivered by Hawk Man, not One Bull. And while One Bull had indeed acted as an informer for McLaughlin in the past, as well as serving as a Metal Breast, it's clear that One Bull lost favor with McLaughlin by participating in the Ghost Dance. McLaughlin, as stated in my narrative, immediately removed One Bull from the force. Additional evidence of One Bull's association with the Ghost Dance comes from Red Tomahawk. In his account of the arrest attempt, Red Tomahawk refers to One Bull as "a hostile dancer." See LaPointe, *Sitting Bull*, 95–101; and Red Tomahawk in Welch, "The Battle of Standing Rock," 35.

375   *"Father, I thought you said we were all going to live":* As quoted in Frank Zahn to W. S. Campbell, August 6, 1933, Fort Yates, Zahn correspondence, CC, box 107, folder 5. Capt. Fechet mentioned this incident in his article for *Cosmopolitan*, cited above, and stated that the Ghost Dancer was later killed at Wounded Knee. Fechet's commander, Lieut. Col. Drum, also references the daring rider in a letter to McLaughlin of February 26, 1891, in Vestal, *New Sources*, 33. Zahn identifies him as Crow Woman. Interestingly, Sergeant George DuBois wrote that while he was on picket duty that day, a loan rider approached Sitting Bull's place. The "whole camp opened up" on him but missed. DuBois claimed to have fired three times at the rider at a distance of about five hundred yards. On the third shot, the rider threw up his hands, and DuBois saw a riderless pony going over the hills. According to DuBois, some Metal Breasts later took a wagon out and brought in a dead Indian. DuBois's claim of hitting a moving target at five hundred yards is extremely far-fetched, and Crow Woman is not among the list of Indians killed in McLaughlin's December 16 report. DuBois to George Thomas, Fort Yates, December 18, 1890, George B. Dubois Collection.

# Epilogue

377   *"But I think I understand him":* Henry Herbert Knibbs, "The Walking Man," in *Songs of the Outlands: Ballads of the Hoboes and Other Verse* (Boston: Houghton Miflin Company, 1914), 6.

377   *"Sometimes death can defeat disgrace":* Waggoner, "Lieut. Henry Bullhead Jr., Tatomkapa."

377　*At 4:30 p.m. on December 16:* Report of H. M. Deeble, post surgeon, Fort Yates, ND, January 23, 1891, in Burdick, *The Last Days of Sitting Bull,* 169.

377　*the post surgeon cut off a small braid:* "Sitting Bull's Death," *Buffalo Courier,* December 20, 1893. Sometime before June 30, 1896, Deeble donated the braid or scalp lock and leggings to the Smithsonian Institution. These items were returned to Sitting Bull's descendants in 2007. "List of Accessions," *Annual report of the Board of Regents of the Smithsonian Institution, showing the operations, expenditures, and condition of the institution for the year ending June 30, 1896; Report of the U.S. National Museum,* H. Doc. No. 352, 54th Cong., 2nd Sess., 121; LaPointe, *Sitting Bull,* 132–42; and "Property to Go to Warrior's Kin," *Detroit Free Press,* September 19, 2007.

377　*His breechclout, shirt, additional items:* T. J. Thompson interview, CC, box 106, folder 54.

377　*what remained of his hair:* August Von Clossman to *The St. Louis Times,* St. Louis, May 21, 1907, typescript, August Von Clossman Papers, H74-043, South Dakota State Historical Society, Pierre.

377　*retrieved two cabinet card photographs:* The hospital steward was forty-seven-year-old August Von Clossman (1843–1916). In his 1907 letter to *The St. Louis Times,* cited above, he wrote that he removed the two cabinet cards from Sitting Bull's "coat pocket." A contemporary ink inscription on the cabinet card picturing the child, presumably in Von Clossman's hand, also states that it came from the chief's pocket and that it was covered with his blood. The photographs are part of the August Von Clossman Papers. For biographical information on Von Clossman, see "Military Burial Given Veteran of Six Wars," *The St. Louis Star,* MO, October 25, 1916; and "Preferred Army Life and Her Home in Carondelet to European Honors," *St. Louis Post-Dispatch,* MO, January 14, 1901.

377　*autographed portrait of "Captain Jack":* Crawford inscribed the cabinet card to Sitting Bull, but he didn't date the inscription. The Poet Scout may have gifted the photo to the chief in September 1883. According to James McLaughlin, Crawford was in attendance at the laying of the cornerstone of the Dakota territorial capitol, at which time Crawford attempted to introduce Sitting Bull to former President Grant. Grant, claimed McLaughlin, "stared coldly at [Sitting Bull] and then at Crawford and without further notice of either of them, continued smiling and shaking hands with the crowd." "Maj. McLaughlin's Story," *The Sioux City Journal,* April 4, 1899.

378　*naked body was sewn up in canvas:* Report of H. M. Deeble, post surgeon, Fort Yates, ND, January 23, 1891.

378　*fabricated by the agency carpenter:* Edward Forte to Frank Fiske, Johnson City, TN, November 7, 1932, in Fiske, *Life and Death of Sitting Bull,* 53–56. In this letter, Forte writes, "I made the coffin in which Sitting Bull was buried, regardless of what anybody says about it." Forte received the appointment of agency carpenter in October 1890, notice of which is in R. V. Belt to McLaughlin, Washington, D.C., October 22, 1890, Standing Rock, Misc. Correspondence Received, 1864–, RG 75, NA-KC. Josephine Waggoner's husband, John Franklin "Frank" Waggoner, a soldier in the Twelfth U.S. Infantry at the time of

Sitting Bull's death, also claimed to have made the coffin. And he claimed that quicklime and acid were poured over the chief's body. However, I've not found Frank Waggoner to be at all reliable. In fact, Fort Yates photographer Frank Fiske considered Waggoner an outright liar. For Frank Waggoner's account, see Waggoner, *Witness*, 409. And for Frank Fiske's very low opinion of Waggoner's veracity, see Fiske to Elmo Scott Watson, Fort Yates, North Dakota, April 9, 1945, Watson Papers.

378     *northwest corner of the fort's graveyard:* Fiske, *Life and Death of Sitting Bull*, 53; Report of H. M. Deeble, post surgeon, Fort Yates, ND, January 23, 1891; and Plan of Post Cemetery, Fort Yates, in Waggoner, *Witness*, 412–13.

378     *Agent McLaughlin walked up:* Report of James McLaughlin, Fort Yates, January 27, 1891, in Burdick, *The Last Days of Sitting Bull*, 170.

378     *disappeared with his blanket-wrapped corpse:* Victoria Conroy statement in Hardorff, *The Oglala Lakota Crazy Horse*, 29–30; Horn Chips interview, Hardorff, ed., *Surrender and Death*, 86–88; and Red Feather interview, *Hinman Interviews*, 36.

378     *moving the chief's bones:* Horn Chips interview, Hardorff, ed., *Surrender and Death*, 86–88; and Horn Chips interview, Jensen, *Voices of the American West*, 1: 276–77.

378     *is an enduring mystery:* An interesting account of one person's quest to locate Crazy Horse's final resting place is Walstrom, *Search for the Lost Trail of Crazy Horse*.

379     *the man superintending the removal:* What follows is based on two letters by Frank J. Ecker: Ecker to W. M. Camp, Fort Yates, ND, December 29, 1909, in Kenneth Hammer, "Sitting Bull's Bones," *Research Review: The Journal of the Little Big Horn Associates* 15 (Winter 2001): 7–8; and Ecker to W. M. Camp, Humboldt, SK, Canada, May 25, 1914, Robert S. Ellison/Walter Camp Papers, DPL, Box 1, folder 128.

379     *Frank claimed the bones were stolen:* In his 1933 book, *Life and Death of Sitting Bull*, Frank Fiske spins a rather remarkable tale about how he and a friend dug down to Sitting Bull's coffin one night "several years" after Fort Yates was abandoned. Fiske wrote that they used a pick and a shovel, and they took turns digging so that one of them could always keep a lookout. Fiske claimed they dug a hole big enough for one person, and when the coffin was reached, the rotten side was pushed in and a large thigh bone and rib retrieved. They then replaced the dirt and the sod so that no one would ever know of their grave robbing. This story strains credulity. It hardly seems possible that the hole could be dug and refilled in the short time Fiske indicates (while a dance was taking place in the agency hall)—the grave was eight feet deep, per the report of the post surgeon. I have a strong suspicion that Fiske and his accomplice obtained their Sitting Bull "relics" when the grave was opened by Ecker in 1908—and very likely with Ecker's knowledge. According to the 1910 federal census for Standing Rock, Fiske and Ecker were next-door neighbors. And Fiske was the community's only professional photographer. One of Fiske's specialties was photographic postcards. Recall that Ecker claimed to have had photographic postcards made of Sitting Bull's bones. Ecker wrote in

the 1914 letter cited above that "I know the men that stole [the bones], and just who has them now." Fiske claimed in 1933 that he'd since reburied his thigh bone at Sitting Bull's grave. However, in a 1948 newspaper interview, Fiske said he still retained one of the chief's bones. A humerus donated to the State Historical Society of North Dakota by Fiske's widow in 1954 was determined to be from a female aged between seventeen and twenty-two years. "Thru the Hills," *Rapid City Journal*, May 6, 1948; and Robert C. Hollow Jr., "The History of Sitting Bull's Remains," typescript, box 28, folder 12, Historical Society Administration Superintendent's Correspondence, #3023, State Historical Society of North Dakota.

379    *the light of day in 1931:* Hollow, "The History of Sitting Bull's Remains"; Robert C. Hollow Jr. and Herbert T. Hoover, *The Last Years of Sitting Bull* (Bismarck: State Historical Society of North Dakota, 1984), 60; "Fort Yates Sitting Bull Monument Being Planned," *The Bismarck Tribune*, July 20, 1962; and Robb DeWall, *The Saga of Sitting Bull's Bones* (Crazy Horse, SD: Korczak's Heritage, Inc., 1984), 133.

380    *neglect shown their ancestor's grave:* The grave had indeed been neglected for decades. See "Sitting Bull's Grave Pathetic Spot on Prairie," *The Bismarck Tribune*, October 4, 1918.

380    *"the white man's red tape":* Clarence Gray Eagle quoted in the *Rapid City Journal*, April 9, 1953.

380    *off to a corner of the plot:* DeWall, *The Saga of Sitting Bull's Bones*, 133.

380    *but otherwise intact:* Ibid., 100. Information on the condition of the skull is contradictory. Some contemporary accounts state it was in pieces. However, DeWall's sources included individuals who participated in the removal of the bones.

380    *made national headlines:* See, for example, "Sitting Bull's Bones Make Bad Medicine for Dakotas," *Daily News*, New York, NY, April 19, 1953.

381    *"They did a pretty sloppy job":* "Indian Tries Selling Old Bones in Bismarck," *Rapid City Journal*, April 9, 1953.

381    *unearthed by the Corps of Engineers:* Hollow, "The History of Sitting Bull's Remains"; and "Does Anyone Know Where Sitting Bull Is?," *The Bismarck Tribune*, October 6, 1984. The flood mitigation work is referenced in "Bids Examined on Fort Yates Flood Project," *The Bismarck Tribune*, June 21, 1962.

381    *"17 hand and foot bones":* Hollow, "The History of Sitting Bull's Remains."

381    *In 2007, Sitting Bull's four surviving:* "Sacred Battle: Sitting Bull's Kin Seek Battlefield Home for Chief's Restless Bones," *The Billings Gazette*, February 22, 2007; and LaPointe, *Sitting Bull*, 118–21.

382    *"Basically remains should go back":* "Sitting Bull's Descendants Want Bones Moved," *The Billings Gazette*, July 9, 2008.

382    *he blamed the Indian Bureau:* Report of James McLaughlin, December 24, 1890, *Sixtieth Annual Report of the Commissioner of Indian Affairs*, 338.

382    *"the great good accomplished":* McLaughlin report on the capture and death of Sitting Bull, Standing Rock Agency, December 16, 1890.

382    *No less than two hundred Lakotas:* Report of Capt. Frank D. Baldwin, February 5, 1891, in Greene, *American Carnage*, 399–400.

383    *"sort of phosphorus hue at night"*: "His Cabin Deserted," *The Helena Independent*, February 16, 1891.

383    *move the cabin about a mile:* "Sitting Bull's Cabin," *The Bismarck Tribune*, February 28, 1891.

383    *In a long negotiation:* "The Relics of Bull," reprinted from an 1891 issue of *The Minneapolis Journal* in the *Mandan Pioneer*, April 27, 1969; and "Sitting Bull's Cabin," *The Atchison Champion*, KS, November 3, 1891.

383    *taken apart and each log marked:* Edward Forte to Frank Fiske, Johnson City, TN, November 7, 1932, in Fiske, *Life and Death of Sitting Bull*, 55.

384    *a contract with Buffalo Bill's Wild West: The Irish Standard*, Minneapolis and St. Paul, February 18, 1893.

384    *When the fair opened:* There are a number of contemporary news reports on the Sitting Bull cabin exhibit in Chicago during the summer of 1893. See the *Bismarck Weekly Tribune*, April 28, June 30, July 7, July 14, July 21, September 15, and November 10, 1893; the *Kansas Semi-Weekly Capital*, Topeka, May 25, 1893; the *Sun*, New York, July 9, 1893; "Indians and Ostriches," *Courier Democrat*, Langdon, ND, August 31, 1893; and the *Inter Ocean*, Chicago, October 6 and 19, and November 1, 1893.

385    *The Coney Island version:* See the *Bismarck Tribune*, May 26, May 31, and September 15, 1894; and the *Brooklyn Daily Eagle*, June 9, 10, and 11, August 6, and September 1 and 3, 1894.

385    *a "loaded cigar"*: "Gives an Indian a Loaded Cigar," *The Chicago Tribune*, July 2, 1894; and *The Standard Union*, July 2, 1894.

386    *a deal to purchase the log cabin:* "Mr. Forrester's New Fad," *The Brooklyn Daily Eagle*, September 7, 1894.

386    *promoted to U.S. Indian inspector:* Pfaller, *James McLaughlin*, 191; and "McLaughlin Popular with the Indians," *The Inter Ocean*, March 23, 1895.

387    *"preserve the heritage and bloodline"*: LaPointe, *Sitting Bull*, 113.

387    *touring with various Wild West shows:* "Cummins Show Here," *The Buffalo Commercial*, NY, May 21, 1906; "Cummins' Wild West Here," *Buffalo Courier*, May 21, 1906; and "Son of Sitting Bull to Appear," *New York Tribune*, November 25, 1906.

387    *"attitude throughout his life"*: Charles F. Larrabee to U.S. Indian Agent, Standing Rock Agency, Washington, D.C., May 2, 1908, typescript at http://www.primeau.org/sittingbull/wmsittingbull.html.

387    *"Naturally, Major McLaughlin would not"*: Frank Zahn to W. S. Campbell, Fort Yates, June 1, 1932.

388    *three of Weldon's letters:* These letters and her miscellaneous notes are in Vestal, *New Sources*, 103–17.

388    *"No one in the world was as happy"*: As quoted in "Among the Ghost Dancers," *The Sun*, December 28, 1890.

388    *her tragic death in 1921:* Caroline Weldon obituary, *The Standard Union*, March 16, 1921; "Pioneer Dies in Blaze in Eastern City," *The Bismarck Tribune*, March 21, 1921; and Eileen Pollack, *Woman Walking Ahead: In Search of Catherine Weldon and Sitting Bull* (Albuquerque: University of New Mexico Press, 2002), 316.

388    *two of her paintings of Sitting Bull:* A second Weldon painting is in the collec-

tions of the Historic Arkansas Museum, Little Rock. Like the painting at the North Dakota State Museum, it's also based on a photograph of the chief.

389 *"as fine a specimen of a warrior"*: As quoted in "Anent Chief Gall," *Bismarck Weekly Tribune*, December 21, 1894.

389 *"On all occasions [Gall] advises"*: B. M. Robinson, "The Indian," *The Chattanooga Daily Times*, TN, January 11, 1891.

389 *purchase a wagon for the chief*: McLaughlin to T. J. Morgan, Standing Rock, February 17, 1891, typescript at https://www.welchdakotapapers.com/2012/04 /james-mclaughlin-indian-agent-standing-rock-copybook-february-1891-82 -letters/#no-161; and R. V. Belt to McLaughlin, Washington, D.C., March 14, 1891, Standing Rock, Misc. Correspondence Received, 1864–, RG 75, NA-KC.

389 *a medal and a silver-headed cane*: Paul L. Hedren, "The Crazy Horse Medal: An Enigma from the Great Sioux War," *Nebraska History* 75 (Summer 1994): 195–99; Paul L. Hedren, "Postscript," *Nebraska History* 77 (Summer 1996): 114; and "How General Custer Died," *The Chicago Tribune*, December 7, 1890.

389 *report on Crazy Horse's bungled arrest*: Clark to General Crook, Camp Robinson, NE, September 5, 1877, in Hardorff, ed., *Surrender and Death*, 181.

389 *"with great satisfaction"*: "The Pipe of Peace," *The Leavenworth Times*, October 17, 1878.

389 *only when none of his fellow Lakotas*: "Bayonetted by a Soldier," *The Omaha Daily Bee*, September 2, 1888.

390 *Red Tomahawk took more and more credit*: "Tells How He Shot Down Sitting Bull," *The Bismarck Tribune*, April 29, 1911; "Barry Tells How Sitting Bull Met Death," *The Billings Gazette*, August 23, 1931; and "Relics of Days When Sioux Were Mighty, Knife and Two Rifles Owned by Sitting Bull, Are Now in Possession of Joseph Dixon," *The Bozeman Courier*, MT, January 12, 1934.

390 *audiences with three presidents*: "Met Red Tomahawk and the Rest of 'Em," *The Los Angeles Times*, April 8, 1903; "Choice May Be Peace or War," *Evening State Journal*, Lincoln, NE, September 10, 1919; and "Chief Tomahawk on Official Visit," *The Evening Star*, June 21, 1929.

390 *His many stops included:* "East Accorded Red Tomahawk Honors of Potentate on Historic Visit," *The Bismarck Tribune*, June 25, 1929.

390 *"There are mysterious flowers"*: Red Tomahawk interview, Fort Yates, 1915, https://www.welchdakotapapers.com/2012/04/red-tomahawk/.

391 *the money he made by cooperating*: DeBarthe, *Life and Adventures*, 175 and 178.

391 *married in the spring of 1895*: Her name was Belle Ostrander. Their marriage license, dated April 6, 1895, is found in the marriage records for Andrew County, Missouri. The couple had a son, Frank, in May 1896. Belle's brother, William Ostrander, was a printer employed at St. Joseph's Combe Printing Company, which published DeBarthe's *Life and Adventures*. For William Ostrander, see "Ostrander's Death to be Investigated," *St. Joseph News-Press*, July 30, 1909; and "Probe Death, But Find No Violence," *St. Joseph Gazette*, July 31, 1909.

391 *marriages in Sioux country*: Mari Sandoz to E. A. Brininstool, New York, May 3, 1947, and Sandoz to Eleanor Hinman, New York, December 10, 1947, Sandoz Collection; *Cheyenne Daily Leader*, January 10, 1882; Margaret Brock Hanson,

ed., *Frank Grouard, Army Scout* (Kaycee, WY: Margaret Brock Hanson, 1983), 187–88; and Hardorff, ed., *Surrender and Death*, 30–31 n. 9.

391  *"They are ready to go to war with Spain"*: "Will Lead the Sioux to War," *The World*, April 18, 1898.

391  *Frank's life ended*: *St. Joseph News-Press*, August 17 and 18, 1905.

392  *"white man's motives"*: As quoted in Ray Tassin, *Stanley Vestal: Champion of the Old West* (Glendale, CA: The Arthur H. Clark Company, 1973), 168.

392  *"a displacement of one immigrant people"*: Peter Cozzens, *The Earth Is Weeping: The Epic Story of the Indian Wars for the American West* (New York: Alfred A. Knopf, 2016), 9.

393  *"We owned the Black Hills"*: As quoted in "Sioux Would Fight Custer Battle Again For Freedom," *Rapid City Journal*, September 2, 1948.

394  *reportedly grown to nearly $2 billion*: Nick Estes, "The Battle for the Black Hills," *High Country News*, Paonia, CO, January 1, 2021, https://www.hcn.org/issues/53.1/indigenous-affairs-social-justice-the-battle-for-the-black-hills.

394  *"If we accept the money"*: Theresa Two Bulls as quoted in "Why the Sioux Are Refusing $1.3 Billion," August 24, 2011, https://www.pbs.org/newshour/arts/north_america-july-dec11-blackhills_08-23.

394  *"I want you to hold these grounds"*: One Bull and Mrs. One Bull interviews, CC, box 105, folder 19.

394  *"We won the battle against Custer"*: Lionel Bordeaux as quoted in "Why the Sioux Are Refusing $1.3 Billion."

## American Indian Informants

401  *"If the white historians"*: W. S. Campbell to "Dearest Girls," McLaughlin, SD, September 6, 1929, CC, box 104, folder 10.

# RESOURCES

## Manuscripts and Visual Resources

*Beinecke Rare Book and Manuscript Library, Yale University, New Haven, Connecticut*
Thomas M. Anderson manuscript, "Army Episodes and Anecdotes," WA MSS 6
George Bent Papers, 1904–1926, WA MSS 32

*Bent's Old Fort National Historic Site, La Junta, Colorado*
Thomas Fitzpatrick Letters, 1846–1853 (digital file)

*Buffalo Bill Center of the West, Cody, Wyoming*
Sitting Bull drawings, Pratt-Evans-Pettinger-Anderson Collection

*Buffalo Bill Center of the West, McCracken Research Library*
"David Humphreys Miller—Indians Who Fought Custer: Survivors of the Little
    Big Horn," MS007

*Colorado Springs Pioneers Museum, Colorado Springs, Colorado*
Francis W. Cragin Collection

*Denver Art Museum, Denver, Colorado*
Crazy Horse Ledger Book

*Denver Public Library, Colorado*
Robert S. Ellison, Walter M. Camp Papers

*History Colorado, Denver*
James R. Walker Collection, MSS 653
George B. Dubois Collection, MSS 215

*Kansas Historical Society, Topeka*
Joseph G. Masters Collection

*Merrill-Cazier Library Special Collections and Archives Division, Utah State University, Logan*
Addison Pratt family papers, 1830–1931

*Minnesota Historical Society, St. Paul*
James Boyd Hubbell Papers, 1865–1906, A/.H876

*Museum of the Fur Trade, Chadron, Nebraska*
Crazy Horse File
Josephine Waggoner Papers

*National Anthropological Archives, Smithsonian Institution, Washington, D.C.*
Four Horns copy of Sitting Bull and Jumping Bull drawings, Manuscript 1929A
Sitting Bull drawings, Manuscript 1929B

*National Archives at Kansas City, Missouri*
Record Group 75—Records of the Bureau of Indian Affairs

*Nebraska State Historical Society, Lincoln*
Eleanor Hamlin Hinman Papers, RG3200.AM
Charles Philander Jordan Papers, RG2095.AM

*The Newberry, Chicago, Illinois*
Elmo Scott Watson Papers, 1816–1951
Olin Dunbar Wheeler Papers, 1892–1924

*South Dakota State Historical Society, Pierre*
Crazy Horse Biography File
John R. Brennan Family Papers, H72-002
August Von Clossman Papers, H74-043
James McLaughlin Letter, 1920, H74-115
Tim Nowak Collection, H2010-094
Sitting Bull Biography File

*The State Historical Society of Missouri, Columbia*
John G. Neihardt Papers

*State Historical Society of North Dakota*
Frank Bennett Fiske Papers, 1850–1979, #10105
Historical Society Administration Superintendent's Correspondence, #3023
Eric C. Jacobsen Papers, 1883–1939, #10898
E. D. Mossman Papers, #10173
Allen Siegert Papers, #20603
Matthew Forney Steele Papers, #10115
Frank Zahn Papers, 1869–1948, #10162
Pioneer Biography Files, 1936–1940

*University of Nebraska-Lincoln Libraries, Archives & Special*
*Collections, Lincoln, Nebraska*
Mari Sandoz Collection

*University of Oklahoma, Western History Collections, Norman, Oklahoma*
Walter Stanley Campbell Collection

*Welch Dakota Papers*
https://www.welchdakotapapers.com/

*Yellowstone County Museum, Billings, Montana*
Ghost Dance shirts, dresses, and related artifacts on display in the exhibition
"Waiting for the Earth to Move: The 1890 Ghost Dance."

## Audio Recordings

Neihardt, John G. *Flaming Rainbow: Reflections and Recollections of an Epic Poet.*
Los Angeles, CA: United Artists Records, Inc., 1973.

## Private Collections

Larry Belitz, Hot Springs, South Dakota
James "Putt" Thompson, Crow Agency, Montana

## Theses and Dissertations

Pearson, Jeffrey V. "Crazy Horse and the Great Sioux War." M.A. thesis. University of New Mexico, History, 2001.
Posthumus, David C. "Transmitting Sacred Knowledge: Aspects of Historical and Contemporary Oglala Lakota Belief and Ritual." Ph.D. dissertation. Indiana University, Anthropology, 2015.

## Published Material

### Government Documents

Bourke, John Gregory. *The Medicine-Men of the Apache.* Washington: Government Printing Office, 1892.
*Condition of the Indian Tribes: Report of the Joint Special Committee Appointed Under Joint Resolution of March 3, 1865.* Washington: Government Printing Office, 1867.
Hewitt, J. N. B., ed. *Journal of Rudolph Friederich Kurz: An Account of His Experiences Among Fur Traders and American Indians on the Mississippi and the Upper Missouri Rivers During the Years 1846 to 1852.* Washington: Government Printing Office, 1937.
Schubert, Frank N., ed. *Explorer on the Northern Plains: Lieutenant Gouverneur K. Warren's Preliminary Report of Explorations in Nebraska and Dakota, in the Years 1855-'56-'57.* Washington: Government Printing Office, 1981.
*United States Congressional Serial Set.*
*The War of the Rebellion: A Compilation of the Official Records of the Union and Confederate Armies.* 70 vols. Washington: Government Printing Office, 1881–1901.

### Books and Articles

Adams, George Rollie. *General William S. Harney: Prince of Dragoons.* Lincoln: University of Nebraska Press, 2001.
Allison, E. H. "Sitting Bull's Birthplace." *South Dakota Historical Collections* 6 (1912): 270–72.
———. *The Surrender of Sitting Bull, Being a Full and Complete History of the Negotiations Conducted.* Dayton, OH: The Walker Litho and Printing Co., 1891.

Andersson, Rani-Henrik. *A Whirlwind Passed Through Our Country: Lakota Voices of the Ghost Dance.* Norman: University of Oklahoma Press, 2018.

Armstrong, William John. "Legacy of an Unlikely Friendship: Sitting Bull and a Michigan Family." *Michigan History Magazine* 79 (Jan.–Feb. 1995): 28–35.

Aspinwall, Jane L. *Alexander Gardner: The Western Photographs, 1867–1868.* Kansas City: The Hall Family Foundation and The Nelson-Atkins Museum of Art, 2014.

Bad Heart Bull, Amos, and Helen Blish. *A Pictographic History of the Oglala Sioux.* Lincoln: University of Nebraska Press, 1967.

Barbour, Barton H. *Fort Union and the Upper Missouri Fur Trade.* Norman: University of Oklahoma Press, 2001.

Barrett, Carole. "One Bull: A Man of Good Understanding." *North Dakota History: Journal of the Northern Plains* 66 (Summer/Fall 1999): 3–16.

Beard, Dewey (Iron Hail). "Dewey Bear: The Last Survivor," interview typescript (1955), in *Black Hills Nuggets, Commemorative Edition, 1776-1876-1976.* Rapid City, SD: The Rapid City Society for Genealogical Research, Inc., 1975.

Beck, Paul N. *Columns of Vengeance: Soldiers, Sioux, and the Punitive Expeditions, 1863–1864.* Norman: University of Oklahoma Press, 2013.

Belden, George P. *Belden, the White Chief, or Twelve Years Among the Wild Indians of the Plains.* Cincinnati: C. F. Vent, 1871.

Belitz, Larry. *The Buffalo Hide Tipi of the Sioux.* Sioux Falls, SD: Pine Hill Press, 2006.

———. *Chips Collection of Crazy Horse Medicines.* Hot Springs, SD: privately printed, n.d.

Bent, George. "Forty Years with the Cheyennes." Six installments. Edited by George Hyde. *The Frontier: A Magazine of the West* 4 (October 1905–March 1906).

Bettelyoun, Susan Bordeaux, and Josephine Waggoner. *With My Own Eyes: A Lakota Woman Tells Her People's History.* Edited by Emily Levine. Lincoln: University of Nebraska Press, 1998.

Bisbee, William Haymond. *Through Four American Wars: The Impressions and Experiences of Brigadier General William Henry Bisbee.* Boston: Meador Publishing Company, 1931.

Bishop, John S. "Ellen Howard's Tintype and the Crazy Horse Controversy." *The English Westerners' Society Tally Sheet* 50 (Summer 2004): 57–60.

Black Elk. *The Sacred Pipe: Black Elk's Account of the Seven Rites of the Oglala Sioux.* Recorded and edited by Joseph Epes Brown. Norman: University of Oklahoma Press, 1989.

Blackburn, William Maxwell. "Historical Sketch of North and South Dakota." *South Dakota Historical Collections* 1 (1902): 23–80.

Board of Commissioners. *Minnesota in the Civil and Indian Wars, 1861–1865.* 2 vols. St. Paul, MN: Pioneer Press Company, 1891.

Bordeaux, William J. *Conquering the Mighty Sioux.* Sioux Falls, SD: Author, 1929.

———. *Custer's Conqueror.* Sioux Falls, SD: Smith and Company, 1951.

Bourke, John G. *The Diaries of John Gregory Bourke.* Edited by Charles M. Robinson III. Vol. 2. Denton: University of North Texas Press, 2005.

———. *On the Border with Crook.* New York: Charles Scribner's Sons, 1891.

Bournichon, Joseph. *Sitting-Bull, Le Héros du Désert: Scènes de la Guerre Indienne aux Étas-Unis.* Tours, France: Cattier, 1879.

Bradley, James. H. *The March of the Montana Column: A Prelude to the Custer Disaster.* Edited by Edgar I. Stewart. Norman: University of Oklahoma Press, 1961.

Bray, Kingsley M. *Crazy Horse: A Lakota Life.* Norman: University of Oklahoma Press, 2006.

———. "Crazy Horse and the End of the Great Sioux War." *Nebraska History* 79 (Fall 1998): 94–115.

———. "Sitting Bull and Lakota Leadership." *English Westerners' Society Brand Book* 43 (Summer 2010): 13–24.

Brennan, John R. "Red Cloud—Marpiyaluta: A Brief History of the Most Celebrated Sioux Chief." *The Oglala Light* 3 (June 1907): 1–3.

Brill, Charles J. *Custer, Black Kettle, and the Fight on the Washita.* Norman: University of Oklahoma Press, 2001.

Brininstool, E. A. "Buffaloing Buffalo Bill." *Hunter, Trader, Trapper* 76 (April 1932): 17–18.

———, ed. *Crazy Horse: The Invincible Ogalalla Sioux Chief.* Los Angeles, CA: Wetzel Publishing Co., Inc., 1949.

Brown, Joseph Epes, ed. *Animals of the Soul: Sacred Animals of the Oglala Sioux.* Rockport, MA: Element Books, 1997.

Buechel, Eugene, compiler. *A Dictionary—Oie Wowapi Wan of Teton Sioux.* Pine Ridge, SD: Red Cloud Indian School, Inc., 1983.

Buecker, Thomas R. *Fort Robinson and the American West, 1874–1899.* Lincoln: Nebraska State Historical Society, 1999.

———. *Last Days of Red Cloud Agency: Peter T. Buckley's Photograph Collection, 1876–1877.* Lincoln: Nebraska State Historical Society, 2016.

———. "Lt. William Philo Clark's Sioux War Report." *Greasy Grass* 7 (May 1991): 11–20.

———. "The Search for the Elusive (and Improbable) Photo of Famous Oglala Chief." *Greasy Grass* 14 (May 1998): 27–36.

————, and R. Eli Paul, eds. *The Crazy Horse Surrender Ledger*. Lincoln: Nebraska State Historical Society, 1994.

Burdick, Usher L., ed. *David F. Barry's Indian Notes on "The Custer Battle."* Baltimore: Wirth Brothers, 1949.

————. *The Last Battle of the Sioux Nation*. Stevens Point, WI: Worzalla Publishing Co., 1929.

————. *The Last Days of Sitting Bull*. 1941. Reprint, Landisville, PA: Coachwhip Publications, 2011.

————. *Tales from Buffalo Land: The Story of Fort Buford*. Baltimore: Wirth Brothers, 1940.

Burnham, Philip. *Song of Dewey Beard: Last Survivor of the Little Bighorn*. Lincoln: University of Nebraska Press, 2014.

Carleton, Lieutenant J. Henry. *The Prairie Logbooks: Dragoon Campaigns to the Pawnee Villages in 1844, and to the Rocky Mountains in 1845*. Edited by Louis Pelzer. Lincoln: University of Nebraska Press, 1983.

Carrington, Frances C. *My Army Life on the Plains and the Fort Phil Kearney Massacre*. Philadelphia: J. B. Lippincott Company, 1910.

Carrington, Henry B. *The Indian Question*. 1884. Reprint, New York: Sol Lewis, 1973.

Carrington, Margaret. *Ab-Sa-Ra-Ka, Home of the Crows, Being the Experience of an Officer's Wife on the Plains*. Philadelphia: J. B. Lippincott & Co., 1868.

Carroll, John M., ed. *The Arrest and Killing of Sitting Bull: A Documentary*. Glendale, CA: The Arthur H. Clark Company, 1986.

Catlin, George. *Letters and Notes on the Manners, Customs, and Conditions of the North American Indians*. 2 vols. 1844. Reprint, New York: Dover Publications Inc., 1973.

Chaky, Doreen. *Terrible Justice: Sioux Chiefs and U.S. Soldiers on the Upper Missouri, 1854–1868*. Norman, OK: The Arthur H. Clark Company, 2012.

Chittenden, Hiram Martin, and Alfred Talbot Richardson, eds. *Life, Letters and Travels of Father Pierre-Jean De Smet, S. J., 1801–1873*. 4 vols. New York: Francis P. Harper, 1905.

Clark, Robert A., ed. *The Killing of Chief Crazy Horse, Three Eyewitness Views* . . . Glendale, CA: The Arthur H. Clark Company, 1976.

Clark, William Philo. *The Indian Sign Language*. Philadelphia: L. R. Hamersly & Co., 1885.

Clow, Richmond L. *Spotted Tail: Warrior and Statesman*. Pierre: South Dakota Historical Society Press, 2019.

Cody, William F. *An Autobiography of Buffalo Bill*. New York: Cosmopolitan Book Corporation, 1920.

Collins, Ethel A. "Pioneer Experiences of Horatio H. Larned." *Collections of the State Historical Society of North Dakota* 7 (1925): 1–58.

Collins, Mary C. "The Autobiography of Mary C. Collins, Missionary to the Western Sioux." Edited by Richmond L. Clow. *South Dakota Historical Collections* 41 (1982): 1–66.

Connell, Evan S. *Son of the Morning Star: Custer and the Little Bighorn.* San Francisco: North Point Press, 1984.

Coues, Elliott, ed. *Forty Years a Fur Trader on the Upper Missouri: The Personal Narrative of Charles Larpenteur, 1833–1872.* 2 vols. New York: Francis P. Harper, 1899.

Cowdrey, Mike. "A Winter Count of the Wajaje Lakota, 1758–59 to 1885–86." *Tribal Art* 19 (Autumn 2015): 128–33.

Cozzens, Peter. *The Earth Is Weeping: The Epic Story of the Indian Wars for the American West.* New York: Alfred A. Knopf, 2016.

———, ed. *Eyewitness to the Indian Wars, 1865–1890: The Long War for the Northern Plains.* Mechanicsburg, PA: Stackpole Books, 2004.

Crawford, Lewis F. *Rekindling Camp Fires: The Exploits of Ben Arnold (Connor).* Bismarck, ND: Capital Book Co., 1926.

Creelman, James. *On the Great Highway: The Wanderings and Adventures of a Special Correspondent.* Boston: Lothrop Publishing Company, 1901.

Cronau, Rudolf. "My Visit Among the Hostile Dakota Indians and How They Became My Friends." *South Dakota Historical Collections* 22 (1946): 410–25.

Curtis, Edward S. *The North American Indian.* Vol. 3. Cambridge, MA: The University Press, 1908.

Curtis, Natalie, ed. *The Indians' Book.* New York: Harper and Brothers, 1907.

DeBarthe, Joe. *The Life and Adventures of Frank Grouard, Chief of Scouts, U.S.A.* St. Joseph, MO: Combe Printing Company, 1894.

DeLand, Charles Edmund. "The Sioux Wars," *South Dakota Historical Collections* 15 (1930): 9–724.

Deloria, Philip J. *Becoming Mary Sully: Toward an American Indian Abstract.* Seattle: University of Washington Press, 2019.

DeMallie, Raymond J. "The Sioux in Dakota and Montana Territories: Cultural and Historical Background of the Ogden B. Read Collection," in Glenn E. Markoe, ed., *Vestiges of a Proud Nation: The Ogden B. Read Northern Plains Indian Collection.* Burlington, VT: Robert Hull Fleming Museum, 1986.

———, ed. *The Sixth Grandfather: Black Elk's Teachings Given to John G. Neihardt.* Lincoln: University of Nebraska Press, 1984.

———. "These Have No Ears: Narrative and the Ethnohistorical Method." *Ethnohistory* 40 (Autumn 1993): 515–38.

———. "Touching the Pen," in Roger L. Nichols, ed., *The American Indian, Past and Present*. Norman: University of Oklahoma Press, 2008.

———, Douglas R. Parks, and Robert Vézina, eds. *A Fur Trader on the Upper Missouri: The Journal and Description of Jean-Baptiste Truteau, 1794–1796*. Lincoln: University of Nebraska Press, 2017.

DeMontravel, Peter R. *A Hero to His Fighting Men: Nelson A. Miles, 1839–1925*. Kent, OH: Kent State University Press, 1998.

Denig, Edwin Thompson. *Five Indian Tribes of the Upper Missouri*. Edited by John C. Ewers. Norman: University of Oklahoma Press, 1961.

Denny, Cecil E. *The Law Marches West*. 1939. Reprint, Moreton-in-Marsh, UK: Denny Publishing Limited, 2000.

De Noyer, Charles. "The History of Fort Totten." *Collections of the State Historical Society of North Dakota* 3 (1910): 178–236.

De Smet, Pierre-Jean. *Western Missions and Missionaries: A Series of Letters*. New York: James B. Kirker, 1863.

DeWall, Robb. *The Saga of Sitting Bull's Bones*. Crazy Horse, SD, Korczak's Heritage, Inc., 1984.

Dickson, Ephriam D., III. "Crazy Horse: Who Really Wielded Bayonet That Killed the Oglala Leader." *Greasy Grass* 12 (May 1996): 2–10.

———. "George McAnulty's Account of the Death of Crazy Horse." *Little Big Horn Associates Newsletter* 39 (May 2005): 4–6.

———. "Prisoners in the Indian Camp: Kill Eagle's Band at Little Big Horn." *Greasy Grass* 27 (May 2011): 3–11.

———. "Reconstructing the Indian Village on the Little Bighorn: The Cankahuhan or Soreback Band, Oglala." *Greasy Grass* 22 (May 2006): 3–14.

———. *The Sitting Bull Surrender Census*. Pierre: South Dakota State Historical Society Press, 2010.

Diedrich, Mark, ed. *Sitting Bull: The Collected Speeches*. Rochester, MN: Coyote Books, 1998.

Dixon, Chris. "Crazy Horse and the Cheyenne," in Ronald H. Nichols, ed., *The Brian C. Pohanka 32nd Annual Symposium, Custer Battlefield Historical & Museum Assn., Inc., Held at Hardin, Montana, on June 22, 2018*. Fort Collins, CO: Citizen Printing Company, Inc., 2019.

Dixon, Joseph K. *The Vanishing Race: The Last Great Indian Council*. Garden City, NY: Doubleday, Page & Company, 1913.

Dodge, Grenville M. *The Battle of Atlanta and Other Campaigns, Addresses, Etc.* Council Bluffs, IA: The Monarch Printing Company, 1911.

Donahue, Michael N. *Drawing Battle Lines: The Map Testimony of Custer's Last Stand*. El Segundo, CA: Upton and Sons, 2009.

———. *Where the Rivers Ran Red: The Indian Fights of George Armstrong Custer*. Montrose, CO: San Juan Publishing, 2018.

Donovan, James. *A Terrible Glory: Custer and the Little Bighorn—The Last Great Battle of the American West* (New York: Little, Brown and Company, 2008).

Drips, J. H. *Three Years Among the Indians in Dakota*. Kimball, SD: Brule Index, 1894.

Eastman, Charles A. *Indian Heroes and Great Chieftains*. Boston: Little, Brown, and Company, 1918.

———. "Rain-In-The-Face: The Story of a Sioux Warrior." *The Outlook* 84 (Oct. 27, 1906): 507–12.

———. "The Story of the Little Big Horn (Told from the Indian standpoint by one of their race)." *The Chautauquan* 31 (July 1900): 353–58.

Eastman, Elaine Goodale. "The Ghost Dance War and Wounded Knee Massacre of 1890–91." *Nebraska History* 26 (January–March 1945): 26–42.

"Expeditions of Captain James L. Fisk to the Gold Mines of Idaho and Montana, 1864–1866." *Collections of the State Historical Society of North Dakota* 2 (1908): 421–61.

Fechet, Edmond G. "The True Story of the Death of Sitting Bull." *Cosmopolitan* 20 (March 1896): 493–501.

Finerty, John F. *War-Path and Bivouac, or the Conquest of the Sioux*. 1890. Reprint, Norman: University of Oklahoma Press, 1961.

Fiske, Frank Bennett. *Life and Death of Sitting Bull*. Fort Yates, ND: Pioneer-Arrow Print, 1933.

Fletcher, Alice C. "The Indian Woman and Her Problems." *The Southern Workman and Hampton School Record* 28 (May 1899): 172–76.

———. "The Shadow or Ghost Lodge: A Ceremony of the Ogallala Sioux." *Reports of the Peabody Museum of American Archaeology and Ethnology* 3 (1887): 296–307.

———. "The Sun Dance of the Ogalalla Sioux." *Proceedings of the American Association for the Advancement of Science, Thirty-First Meeting* (1883): 580–84.

Foley, Thomas W., ed. *At Standing Rock and Wounded Knee: The Journals and Papers of Father Francis M. Craft, 1888–1890*. Norman, OK: The Arthur H. Clark Company, 2009.

———. *Father Francis M. Craft: Missionary to the Sioux*. Lincoln: University of Nebraska Press, 2002.

Fremont, John C. *The Exploring Expedition to the Rocky Mountains*. Washington, D.C.: Smithsonian Institution Press, 1988.

Friesen, Steve, and François Chladiuk. *Lakota Performers in Europe: Their Culture and the Artifacts They Left Behind*. Norman: University of Oklahoma Press, 2017.

Frost, Lawrence A. *General Custer's Thoroughbreds: Racing, Riding, Hunting, and Fighting.* Mattituck, NY: J. M. Carroll & Co. 1986.

———, ed. *With Custer in '74: James Calhoun's Diary of the Black Hills Expedition.* Provo, UT: Brigham Young University Press, 1979.

Garavaglia, Louis A., and Charles G. Worman. *Firearms of the American West, 1803–1865.* Albuquerque: University of New Mexico Press, 1984.

Gardner, Mark Lee. *Fort Laramie National Historic Site.* Tucson, AZ: Western National Parks Association, 2007.

———. *George Armstrong Custer: A Biography.* Tucson, AZ: Western National Parks Association, 2005.

———. *Little Bighorn Battlefield National Monument.* Tucson: Western National Parks Association, 2005.

———. *Washita Battlefield National Historic Site.* Tucson: Western National Parks Association, 2002.

———. "'Where Buffalo Was Plenty': Bent, St. Vrain & Co. and the Robe Trade of the Southern Plains." *Museum of the Fur Trade Quarterly* 43 (Fall/Winter 2007): 22–35.

Garland, Hamlin. "General Custer's Last Fight as Seen by Two Moon[s]." *McClure's Magazine* 11 (Sept. 1898): 443–48.

Garraghan, Gilbert J., ed. "Father De Smet's Sioux Peace Mission of 1868 and the Journal of Charles Galpin." *Mid-America: An Historical Review* 13 (Oct. 1930): 141–63.

Gessner, Robert. *Massacre: A Survey of Today's American Indian.* New York: Jonathan Cape and Harrison Smith, 1931.

Gibbon, Guy. *The Sioux: The Dakota and Lakota Nations.* Oxford, UK: Blackwell Publishing, 2003.

Gilbert, James N. "The Death of Crazy Horse: A Contemporary Examination of the Homicidal Events of 5 September 1877." *Journal of the West* 32 (Jan. 1993): 5–21.

Goodale, Elaine. "An Indian's View of the Indian Question." *The Inter Ocean,* Chicago, Oct. 16, 1890.

Goodyear, Frank H., III. *Red Cloud: Photographs of a Lakota Chief.* Lincoln: University of Nebraska Press, 2003.

Graham, Col. W. A. *The Custer Myth: A Source Book of Custeriana.* Harrisburg, PA: The Stackpole Company, 1953.

Gray, John S. *Centennial Campaign: The Sioux War of 1876.* Ft. Collins, CO: The Old Army Press, 1976.

———. *Custer's Last Campaign: Mitch Boyer and the Little Bighorn Reconstructed.* Lincoln: University of Nebraska Press, 1991.

———. "The Story of Mrs. Picotte-Galpin, a Sioux Heroine: Eagle Woman Learns About White Ways and Racial Conflict, 1820–1868." *Montana The Magazine of Western History* 36 (Spring 1986): 3–21.

Greene, Candace S. "Verbal Meets Visual: Sitting Bull and the Representation of History." *Ethno History* 62 (April 2015): 217–40.

———, and Russell Thornton, eds. *The Year the Stars Fell: Lakota Winter Counts at the Smithsonian.* Lincoln: University of Nebraska Press, 2007.

Greene, Jerome A. *American Carnage: Wounded Knee, 1890.* Norman: University of Oklahoma Press, 2014.

———, ed. *Battles and Skirmishes of the Great Sioux War, 1876–1877: The Military View.* Norman: University of Oklahoma Press, 1993.

———. *Fort Randall on the Missouri, 1856–1892.* Pierre: South Dakota State Historical Society, 2005.

———. *Lakota and Cheyenne: Indian Views of the Great Sioux War, 1876–1877.* Norman: University of Oklahoma Press, 1994.

———. "'We Do Not Know What the Government Intends to Do . . .': Lt. Palmer Writes from the Bozeman Trail, 1867–68." *Montana The Magazine of Western History* (Summer 1978): 16–35.

———. *Yellowstone Command: Colonel Nelson A. Miles and the Great Sioux War, 1876–1877.* Lincoln: University of Nebraska Press, 1991.

Grimes, Richard S. "The Making of a Sioux Legend: The Historiography of Crazy Horse." *South Dakota History* 30 (Fall 2000): 277–302.

Grinnell, George Bird. *The Fighting Cheyennes.* New York: Charles Scribner's Sons, 1915.

Hafermehl, Louis N. "Chasing an Enigma: Frontier Photographer Orlando S. Goff." *North Dakota History* 81 (Summer 2016): 3–26.

Halaas, David Fridtjof, and Andrew E. Masich. *Halfbreed: The Remarkable True Story of George Bent, Caught Between the Worlds of the Indian and the White Man.* Cambridge, MA: Da Capo Press, 2004.

Hämäläinen, Pekka. *Lakota America: A New History of Indigenous Power.* New Haven, CT: Yale University Press, 2019.

Hamilton, Judge Charles C. "Address Before the Academy of Science and Letters of Sioux City, Iowa, November 27, 1928." *The Annals of Iowa* 41 (1972): 809–34.

Hammer, Kenneth, ed. *Custer in '76: Walter Camp's Notes on the Custer Fight.* Provo, UT: Brigham Young University Press, 1976.

———. *Men with Custer: Biographies of the 7th Cavalry.* Edited by Ronald H. Nichols. Hardin, MT: Custer Battlefield Historical and Museum Association, Inc., 1995.

————. "Sitting Bull's Bones." *Research Review: The Journal of the Little Big Horn Associates* 15 (Winter 2001): 2–8 and 31.

Hans, Fred M. *The Great Sioux Nation.* Chicago: M. A. Donohue and Company, 1907.

Hansen, Emma I. *Plains Indian Buffalo Cultures: Art from the Paul Dyck Collection.* Norman: University of Oklahoma Press, 2018.

Hanson, Charles E., Jr. *The David Adams Journals.* Chadron, NE: The Museum of the Fur Trade, 1994.

Hanson, James A. *Little Chief's Gatherings: The Smithsonian Institution's G. K. Warren 1855–1856 Plains Indian Collection and the New York State Library's 1855–1857 Warren Expeditions Journals.* Crawford, NE: The Fur Press, 1996.

————, ed. *Spotted Tail: Renaissance Man of the Lakotas.* Chadron, NE: Museum of the Fur Trade, 2020.

Hanson, Joseph Mills. *The Conquest of the Missouri, Being the Story of the Life and Exploits of Captain Grant Marsh.* Chicago: A. C. McClurg & Co., 1909.

Hanson, Margaret Brock, ed. *Frank Grouard, Army Scout.* Kaycee, WY: Margaret Brock Hanson, 1983.

Hardin, Barry E. *The Plains Warbonnet: Its Story and Construction.* Pottsboro, TX: Crazy Crow Trading Post, 2013.

Hardorff, Richard G. *Hokahey! A Good Day to Die! The Indian Casualties of the Custer Fight.* Spokane, WA: The Arthur H. Clark Company, 1993.

————, ed. *Indian Views of the Custer Fight: A Source Book.* Norman: University of Oklahoma Press, 2005.

————. *Lakota Recollections of the Custer Fight: New Sources of Indian-Military History.* Spokane, WA: The Arthur H. Clark Company, 1991.

————. *The Oglala Lakota Crazy Horse: A Preliminary Genealogical Study and An Annotated Listing of Primary Sources.* Matituck, NY: J. M. Carroll and Company, 1985.

————. *The Surrender and Death of Crazy Horse: A Source Book About a Tragic Episode in Lakota History.* Spokane, WA: The Arthur H. Clark Company, 1998.

Harrison, Peter. *Monahsetah: The Life of a Custer Captive.* Edited by Gary Leonard. London: The English Westerners' Society, 2014.

Hart, John, ed. *Bluecoat and Pioneer: The Recollections of John Benton Hart, 1864–1868.* Norman: University of Oklahoma Press, 2019.

Hassrick, Royal B. *The Sioux: Life and Customs of a Warrior Society.* Norman: University of Oklahoma Press, 1964.

Hebard, Grace Raymond, and E. A. Brininstool. *The Bozeman Trail: Historical Accounts of the Overland Routes into the Northwest and the Fights with Red Cloud's Warriors.* 2 vols. Cleveland, OH: The Arthur H. Clark Company, 1922.

Hedren, Paul L. "The Crazy Horse Medal: An Enigma from the Great Sioux War." *Nebraska History* 75 (Summer 1994): 195–99.

———, ed. *Ho! For the Black Hills: Captain Jack Crawford Reports the Black Hills Gold Rush and the Great Sioux War*. Pierre: South Dakota State Historical Society Press, 2012.

———. *John Finerty Reports the Sioux War*. Norman: University of Oklahoma Press, 2020.

———. "Postscript." *Nebraska History* 77 (Summer 1996): 114.

———. *Powder River: Disastrous Opening of the Great Sioux War*. Norman: University of Oklahoma Press, 2016.

———. *Rosebud, June 17, 1876: Prelude to the Little Big Horn*. Norman: University of Oklahoma Press, 2019.

———. *Sitting Bull's Surrender at Fort Buford: An Episode in American History*. Williston, ND: Fort Union Association, 1997.

———. *Traveler's Guide to the Great Sioux War: The Battlefields, Forts, and Related Sites of America's Greatest Indian War*. Helena: Montana Historical Society Press, 1996.

———. "Who Killed Crazy Horse: A Historiographical Review and Affirmation." *Nebraska History Magazine* 101 (Spring 2020): 2–17.

Heriard, Jack. "Debating Crazy Horse: Is This the Photo of the Famous Oglala?," *Whispering Wind* 34 (2004): 16–23.

Heski, Thomas M. *"Icastinyanka Cikala Hanzi" The Little Shadow Catcher, D. F. Barry, Celebrated Photographer of Famous Indians*. Seattle, WA: Superior Publishing Company, 1978.

Hilger, Sister H. Inez, ed. "The Narrative of Oscar One Bull." *Mid-America: An Historical Review* 28 (July 1946): 147–72.

Hilger, Nicholas. "General Alfred Sully's Expedition of 1864." *Contributions to the Historical Society of Montana* 2 (1896): 314–28.

Hill, Burton S. "The Great Indian Treaty Council of 1851." *Nebraska History* 47 (1966): 85–110.

Hinman, Eleanor. *The Eleanor H. Hinman Interviews on the Life and Death of Crazy Horse*. Edited by John M. Carroll. New Brunswick, NJ: The Gary Owen Press, 1976.

———. "Oglala Sources on the Life of Crazy Horse." *Nebraska History* 57 (Spring 1976): 1–51.

Holley, Frances Chamberlain. *Once Their Home, or Our Legacy from the Dahkotahs*. Chicago: Donohue & Henneberry, 1891.

Hollow, Robert C., Jr. "Sitting Bull: Artifact and Artifake." *North Dakota History: A Journal of the Northern Plains* 54 (Summer 1987): 3–14.

———, and Herbert T. Hoover. *The Last Years of Sitting Bull.* Bismarck: State Historical Society of North Dakota, 1984.

Hoover, Herbert T. "The Sioux Agreement of 1889 and Its Aftermath." *South Dakota History* 19 (1989): 56–94.

Hosmer, J. Allen. *A Trip to the States by Way of the Yellowstone and Missouri, with a Table of Distances.* Virginia City, MT: Beaver Head News Print, 1867.

Howard, James H., ed. *Lakota Warrior: Joseph White Bull.* Lincoln: University of Nebraska Press, 1998.

Hunt, David C., and Marsha V. Gallagher, eds. *Karl Bodmer's America.* N.p.: Joslyn Art Museum and University of Nebraska Press, 1984.

Hutton, Paul Andrew, ed. *The Custer Reader.* Lincoln: University of Nebraska Press, 1992.

Hyde, George E. *Life of George Bent: Written from His Letters.* Edited by Savoie Lottinville. Norman: University of Oklahoma Press, 1968.

———. *Red Cloud's Folk: A History of the Oglala Sioux Indians.* Norman: University of Oklahoma Press, 1957.

Jackson, Donald. *Custer's Gold: The United States Cavalry Expedition of 1874.* New Haven, CT: Yale University Press, 1966.

———. *Voyages of the Steamboat Yellow Stone.* New York: Ticknor & Fields, 1985.

Jackson, Joe. *Black Elk: The Life of an American Visionary.* New York: Farrar, Straus and Giroux, 2016.

Jensen, Richard E., ed. *Voices of the American West.* 2 vols. *The Indian Interviews of Eli S. Ricker, 1903–1919* (vol. 1) and *The Settler and Soldier Interviews of Eli S. Ricker, 1903–1919* (vol. 2). Lincoln: University of Nebraska Press, 2005.

Jensen, Richard E., and R. Eli Paul, and John E. Carter. *Eyewitness at Wounded Knee.* Lincoln: University of Nebraska Press, 2011.

Johnson, A. F. "Career of Captain George Sword." *The Oglala Light* 11 (Nov. 1910): 21–23.

Johnson, W. Fletcher. *The Red Record of the Sioux: Life of Sitting Bull and History of the Indian War of 1890-'91.* Philadelphia: Edgewood Publishing Company, 1891.

Jones, Robert Huhn. *Guarding the Overland Trails: The Eleventh Ohio Cavalry in the Civil War.* Spokane, WA: The Arthur H. Clark Company, 2005.

Judd, A. N. *Campaigning Against the Sioux.* 1906. Reprint, New York, Sol Lewis, 1973.

Kadlecek, Edward, and Mabell Kadlecek. *To Kill an Eagle: Indian Views on the Last Days of Crazy Horse.* Boulder, CO: Johnson Books, 1981.

Kane, Lucile, ed. *Military Life in Dakota: The Journal of Philippe Régis de Trobriand.* St. Paul, MN: Alvord Memorial Commission, 1951.

Kane, Randy. "What Did Crazy Horse Look Like?," *Nebraska History Magazine* 99 (Winter 2018): 224–33.

Karol, Joseph S., ed. *Red Horse Owner's Winter Count: The Oglala Sioux, 1786–1968.* Martin, SD: The Booster Publishing Co., 1969.

Keefe, Brian L. *The Battle at Rainy Butte: A Significant Sioux-Crow Encounter of 1858.* London: The English Westerners Society, 2006.

Keenan, Jerry. *The Wagon Box Fight: An Episode of Red Cloud's War.* Conshohocken, PA: Savas Publishing Company, 2000.

Kehoe, Alice Beck. *The Ghost Dance: Ethnohistory and Revitalization.* New York: Holt, Rinehart and Winston, 1989.

Kelly, Fanny. *Narrative of My Captivity Among the Sioux Indians.* Hartford, CT: Mutual Publishing Company, 1873.

Kimball, Maria Brace. *A Soldier-Doctor of our Army: James P. Kimball, Late Colonel and Assistant Surgeon-General, U.S. Army.* Boston: Hougton Mifflin Company, 1917.

Kime, Wayne R., ed. *The Black Hills Journals of Colonel Richard Irving Dodge.* Norman: University of Oklahoma Press, 1996.

King, Charles. *Campaigning with Crook and Stories of Army Life.* New York: Harper & Brothers, 1890.

———. "Custer's Last Battle." *Harper's New Monthly Magazine* 81 (Aug. 1890): 378–87.

Kingsbury, David L. "Sully's Expedition Against the Sioux in 1864." *Collections of the Minnesota Historical Society* 8 (1898): 449–62.

Lame Deer (Fire), John, and Richard Erdoes. *Lame Deer: Seeker of Visions.* New York: Simon & Schuster, 1972.

LaPointe, Ernie. *Sitting Bull: His Life and Legacy.* Salt Lake City: Gibbs Smith, 2009.

LaPointe, James. *Legends of the Lakota.* San Francisco: The Indian Historian Press, 1976.

Larson, Robert W. *Gall: Lakota War Chief.* Norman: University of Oklahoma Press, 2007.

———. *Red Cloud: Warrior-Statesman of the Lakota Sioux.* Norman: University of Oklahoma Press, 1997.

Lee, Jesse M. "The Capture and Death of an Indian Chieftain." *Journal of the Military Service Institution of the United States* 54 (May–June 1914): 323–40.

Lemly, H. R. "The Fight on the Rosebud." *Proceedings of the Annual Meeting and Dinner of the Order of Indian Wars of the United States,* 1917.

———. "The Passing of Crazy Horse." *Journal of the Military Service Institution of the United States* 54 (May–June 1914): 317–22.

Lemons, William E. "History by Unreliable Narrators: Sitting Bull's Circus Horse." *Montana The Magazine of Western History* 45 (Autumn–Winter 1995): 64–74.

Libby, O. G., ed. "The Arikara Narrative of the Campaign Against the Hostile Dakotas, June 1876." *North Dakota Historical Collections* 6 (1920): 9–209.

Liddic, Bruce R., and Paul Harbaugh, eds. *Custer and Company: Walter Camp's Notes on the Custer Fight*. Lincoln: University of Nebraska Press, 1998.

Limbaugh, Ronald H., ed. *Cheyenne and Sioux: The Reminiscences of Four Indians and a White Soldier*. Stockton, CA: Pacific Center for Western Historical Studies, 1973.

Linderman, Frank B. *American: The Life Story of a Great Indian*. Yonkers-on-Hudson, NY: World Book Company, 1930.

Lindner, Markus H. "Family, Politics, and Show Business: The Photographs of Sitting Bull." *North Dakota History* 72 (2005): 2–21.

Lubetkin, M. John, ed. *Before Custer: Surveying Custer: Surveying the Yellowstone, 1872*. Norman, OK: The Arthur H. Clark Company, 2015.

————. *Custer and the 1873 Yellowstone Survey: A Documentary History*. Norman, OK: The Arthur H. Clark Company, 2013.

————. *Jay Cooke's Gamble: The Northern Pacific Railroad, the Sioux, and the Panic of 1873*. Norman: University of Oklahoma Press, 2006.

————. *Road to War: The 1871 Yellowstone Survey*. Norman, OK: The Arthur H. Clark Company, 2016.

MacEwan, Grant. *Sitting Bull: The Years in Canada*. Edmonton, Canada: Hurtig Publishers, 1973.

MacLean, French L. *Sitting Bull, Crazy Horse, Gold, and Guns: The 1874 Yellowstone Wagon Road and Prospecting Expedition and the Battle of Lodge Grass Creek*. Atglen, PA: Schiffer Publishing, Ltd., 2016.

Maddra, Sam A. *Hostiles? The Lakota Ghost Dance and Buffalo Bill's Wild West*. Norman: University of Oklahoma Press, 2006.

Manhart, Paul I. *Lakota Tales and Texts in Translation*. Chamberlain, SD: Tipi Press, 1998.

Manzione, Joseph. *"I Am Looking to the North for My Life": Sitting Bull, 1876–1881*. Salt Lake City: University of Utah Press, 1991.

Mark, Joan. *A Stranger in Her Native Land: Alice Fletcher and the American Indians*. Lincoln: University of Nebraska Press, 1988.

Markoe, Glenn E., ed. *Vestiges of a Proud Nation: The Ogden B. Read Northern Plains Indian Collection*. Burlington, VT: Robert Hull Fleming Museum, 1986.

Marquis, Thomas B. *The Cheyennes of Montana*. Algonac, MI: Reference Publications, Inc., 1978.

———. *Custer, Cavalry and Crows: The Story of William White*. Fort Collins, CO: The Old Army Press, 1975.

———, as told by Thomas Leforge. *Memoirs of a White Crow Indian*. New York: The Century Company, 1928.

———, interpreter. *She Watched Custer's Last Battle*. 1933. Reprint, Scottsdale, AZ: Cactus Pony, c. 1969.

———. *A Warrior Who Fought Custer*. Minneapolis: The Midwest Company, 1931.

Marshall III, Joseph M. *The Journey of Crazy Horse: A Lakota History*. New York: Viking, 2004.

Masters, Joseph G. *Shadows Fall Across the Little Horn*. Laramie: University of Wyoming Library, 1951.

Mattes, Merrill J. *The Great Platte River Road*. Lincoln: Nebraska State Historical Society, 1969.

McCoy, Ron. "Four Horns: A Hunkpapa Lakota Warrior-Artist Commemorates His Relative's Valor." *American Indian Art Magazine* 39 (Spring 2014): 42–51.

———. "Sitting Bull: A Hunkpapa Lakota Chronicles His Life of Dauntless Courage." *American Indian Art Magazine* 40 (Winter 2014): 34–45.

McCrady, David G. *Living with Strangers: The Nineteenth-Century Sioux and the Canadian-American Borderlands*. Toronto, Canada: University of Toronto Press, 2010.

McCreight, M. I. *Chief Flying Hawk's Tales: The True Story of Custer's Last Fight as told by Chief Flying Hawk*. New York: The Alliance Press, 1936.

———. *Firewater and Forked Tongues: A Sioux Chief Interprets U.S. History*. Pasadena, CA: Trail's End Publishing Co., Inc., 1947.

McDermott, John D., ed. "Documents Relating to the Fetterman Fight." *Annals of Wyoming* 63 (Spring 1991): 68–72.

———. *Red Cloud's War: The Bozeman Trail, 1866–1868*. 2 vols. Norman: The Arthur H. Clark Company, 2010.

———, R. Eli Paul, and Sandra J. Lowry, eds. *All Because of a Mormon Cow: Historical Accounts of the Grattan Massacre, 1854–1855*. Norman: University of Oklahoma Press, 2018.

McLaughlin, James. *My Friend the Indian*. Boston: Houghton, Mifflin Company, 1926.

McMurtry, Larry. *Crazy Horse*. New York: Viking, 1999.

Merington, Marguerite, ed. *The Custer Story: The Life and Intimate Letters of General Custer and His Wife Elizabeth*. New York: The Devon-Adair Company, 1950.

Michno, Gregory F. *Lakota Noon: The Indian Narrative of Custer's Defeat*. Missoula, MT: Mountain Press Publishing Company, 1997.

Miles, Nelson A. "The Future of the Indian Question." *North American Review* 152 (Jan. 1891): 1–10.

———. *Personal Recollections and Observations of General Nelson A. Miles.* Chicago: The Werner Company, 1896.

———. *Serving the Republic: Memoirs of the Civil and Military Life of Nelson A. Miles.* New York: Harper & Brothers, 1911.

Millard, Bailey. "The Squaw Man as He Is." *Everybody's Magazine* 22 (March 1910): 369–79.

Miller, David Humphreys. *Custer's Fall: The Indian Side of the Story.* New York: Duell, Sloan and Pearce, 1957.

———. "Echoes of the Little Bighorn." *American Heritage* 22 (June 1971): 28–39.

———. *Ghost Dance.* New York: Duell, Sloan and Pearce, 1959.

———. "Sitting Bull's White Squaw." *Montana The Magazine of Western History* 14 (April 1964): 55–71.

Miller, David, Dennis Smith, Joseph McGeshick, James Shanley, and Caleb Shields. *The History of the Assiniboine and Sioux Tribes of the Fort Peck Indian Reservation, 1600–2012.* Poplar, MT: Fort Peck Community College, 2012.

Monnett, John H., ed. *Eyewitness to the Fetterman Fight: Indian Views.* Norman: University of Oklahoma Press, 2017.

———. *Where a Hundred Soldiers Were Killed: The Struggle for the Powder River Country in 1866 and the Making of the Fetterman Myth.* Albuquerque: University of New Mexico Press, 2008.

Mooney, James. "The Death of Sitting Bull." *De Lestry's Western Magazine* 1 (Jan. 1898): 129–35.

———. *The Ghost-Dance Religion and the Sioux Outbreak of 1890.* 1896. Reprint, Lincoln: University of Nebraska Press, 1991.

Moorehead, Warren K. *The American Indian in the United States, Period 1850–1914.* Andover, MA: The Andover Press, 1914.

Moses, L. C. *Wild West Shows and the Images of American Indians, 1883–1933.* Albuquerque: University of New Mexico Press, 1996.

Moulton, Candy. *Valentine T. McGillycuddy: Army Surgeon, Agent to the Sioux.* Norman, OK: The Arthur H. Clark Company, 2011.

Murray, Charles Augustus. *Travels in North America During the Years 1834, 1835, and 1836.* 2 vols. New York: Harper & Brothers, 1839.

Myers, Frank. *Soldiering in Dakota, Among the Indians, in 1863-4-5.* 1888. Reprint, Pierre, SD: State Historical Society, 1936

Nasatir, A. P., ed. *Before Lewis and Clark: Documents Illustrating the History of the Missouri, 1785–1804.* 2 vols. Lincoln: University of Nebraska Press, 1990.

Neihardt, John G. *Black Elk Speaks, Being the Life Story of a Holy Man of the Ogalala Sioux as told to John G. Neihardt.* New York: William Morrow & Company, 1932.

Nelson, Mark J. *White Hat: The Military Career of Captain William Philo Clark.* Norman: University of Oklahoma Press, 2018.

Nelson, Paul D. "'A Shady Pair' and 'An Attempt on His Life': Sitting Bull and His 1884 Visit to St. Paul." *Ramsey County History* 38 (Spring 2003): 4–12.

Newell, Cicero. *Indian Stories.* Boston: Silver, Burdett and Company, 1912.

Newson, T. M. *Thrilling Scenes Among the Indians.* Chicago: Belford, Clarke & Company, 1884.

Olson, James C. *Red Cloud and the Sioux Problem.* Lincoln: University of Nebraska Press, 1965.

Ostler, Jeffrey. *The Plains Sioux and U.S. Colonialism from Lewis and Clark to Wounded Knee.* New York: Cambridge University Press, 2004.

Paige, Darcy. "George W. Hill's Account of the Sioux Indian Sun Dance of 1866." *Plains Anthropologist* 25 (1979): 99–112.

Painter, C. C. *Cheyennes and Arapahoes Revisited.* Philadelphia: The Indian Rights Association, 1893.

Palmer, H. E. "History of the Powder River Expedition of 1865." *Transactions and Reports of the Nebraska State Historical Society* 2 (1887): 197–229.

Pattee, John. "Dakota Campaigns." *South Dakota Historical Collections* 5 (1910): 275–350.

Paul, R. Eli, ed. *Autobiography of Red Cloud: War Leader of the Oglalas.* Helena: Montana Historical Society Press, 1997.

———. "The Battle of Ash Hollow: The 1909–1910 Recollections of General N. A. M. Dudley." *Nebraska History* 62 (1981): 373–99.

———. *Blue Water Creek and the First Sioux War, 1854–1856.* Norman: University of Oklahoma Press, 2004.

———. "An Early Reference to Crazy Horse." *Nebraska History* 75 (1994): 189–90.

———. *The Frontier Army: Episodes from Dakota and the West.* Pierre: South Dakota Historical Society Press, 2019.

———. "Lester Beach Platt's Account of the Battle of Massacre Canyon." *Nebraska History* 67 (1986): 381–407.

Peterson, Jacqueline, with Laura Peers. *Sacred Encounters: Father De Smet and the Indians of the Rocky Mountain West.* Norman: University of Oklahoma Press, 1993.

Petter, Rodolphe. *English–Cheyenne Dictionary.* Kettle Falls, WA: Valdo Petter, 1915.

Pfaller, Louis L. *James McLaughlin: The Man with an Indian Heart.* New York: Vantage Press, 1978.

———. "Sully's Expedition of 1864, Featuring the Killdeer Mountain and Badlands Battles." *North Dakota History* 31 (Jan. 1964): 26–77.

Pickett, William D. "Memories of a Bear Hunter." In George Bird Grinnell, ed., *Hunting at High Altitudes: The Book of the Boone and Crockett Club*. New York: Harper & Brothers, 1913.

Pollack, Eileen. *Woman Walking Ahead: In Search of Catherine Weldon and Sitting Bull*. Albuquerque: University of New Mexico Press, 2002.

Poole, D. C. *Among the Sioux of Dakota: Eighteen Months' Experience as an Indian Agent, 1869–1870*. 1881. Reprint, St. Paul, MN: Minnesota Historical Society Press, 1988.

Pope, Dennis C. *Sitting Bull, Prisoner of War*. Pierre: South Dakota State Historical Society Press, 2010.

Potter, James E., ed. *"From Our Special Correspondent": Dispatches from the 1875 Black Hills Council at Red Cloud Agency, Nebraska*. Lincoln: Nebraska State Historical Society Books, 2016.

Powell, Peter J. *People of the Sacred Mountain: A History of the Northern Cheyenne Chiefs and Warrior Societies, 1830–1879, with an Epilogue, 1969–1974*. 2 vols. San Francisco: Harper & Row, 1981.

———. "Sacrifice Transformed into Victory: Standing Bear Portrays Sitting Bull's Sun Dance and the Final Summer of Lakota Freedom," in Evan M. Mauer, *Visions of the People: A Pictorial History of Plains Indian Life*. Minneapolis, MN: The Minneapolis Institute of Arts, 1992.

———. *Sweet Medicine: The Continuing Role of the Sacred Arrows, the Sun Dance, and the Sacred Buffalo Hat in Northern Cheyenne History*. 2 vols. Norman: University of Oklahoma Press, 1998.

Powers, Thomas. "The Crazy Horse Medicine Bundle." *Nebraska History* 95 (Spring 2014): 64–75.

———. *The Killing of Crazy Horse*. New York: Alfred A. Knopf, 2010.

Powers, William K. *Oglala Religion*. Lincoln: University of Nebraska Press, 1977.

———. "A Winter Count of the Oglala." *American Indian Tradition* 9 (1963): 27–37.

———. *Yuwipi: Vision and Experience in Oglala Ritual*. Lincoln: University of Nebraska Press, 1982.

Price, Catherine. *The Oglala People, 1841–1879: A Political History*. Lincoln: University of Nebraska Press, 1996.

*Proceedings of the Great Peace Commission of 1867–1868*. Washington, D.C.: The Institute for the Development of Indian Law, 1975.

Prucha, Francis Paul. *The Great Father: The United States Government and the American Indians*. Lincoln: University of Nebraska Press, 1995.

Quivey, Addison M. "The Yellowstone Expedition of 1874." *Contributions to the Historical Society of Montana* 1 (1876): 268–74.

Rappagliosi, Father Philip. *Letters from the Rocky Mountain Indian Missions*. Edited by Robert Bigart and Lisa Moore Nardini. Lincoln: University of Nebraska Press, 2003.

Red Shirt, Delphine. *George Sword's Warrior Narratives: Compositional Processes in Lakota Oral Tradition*. Lincoln: University of Nebraska Press, 2016.

Reese, Montana Lisle, ed. *Legends of the Mighty Sioux*. Chicago: Albert Whitman & Company, 1941.

Riley, Paul D. "The Battle of Massacre Canyon." *Nebraska History* 54 (1973): 220–24.

Robinson, De Lorme W. "Editorial Notes on Historical Sketch of North and South Dakota." *South Dakota Historical Collections* 1 (1902): 85–162.

Robinson, Doane. "The Education of Red Cloud." *South Dakota Historical Collections* 12 (1924): 156–78.

——. *A History of the Dakota or Sioux Indians*. 1904. Reprint, Minneapolis: Ross & Haines, Inc., 1974.

——. "The Rescue of Frances Kelly." *South Dakota Historical Collections* 6 (1908): 110–17.

——. "Some Sidelights on the Character of Sitting Bull." *Proceedings of the Mississippi Valley Historical Association for the Year 1909–1910* 3 (1911): 73–79.

Rodenbaugh, Theodore F., and William L. Haskin, eds. *The Army of the United State: Historical Sketches of Staff and Line with Portraits of Generals-in-Chief*. New York: Maynard, Merrill, & Co., 1896.

Sandoz, Mari. *Crazy Horse: The Strange Man of the Oglalas*. New York: Alfred A. Knopf, 1942.

Schmitt, Martin F., ed. *General George Crook, His Autobiography*. Norman: University of Oklahoma Press, 1946.

Schultz, James Willard. *William Jackson, Indian Scout: His True Story, Told by His Friend*. Boston: Houghton Mifflin Company, 1926.

Seitz, Don Carlos. *The Dreadful Decade: Detailing Some Phases in the History of the United States from Reconstruction to Resumption, 1869–1879*. Indianapolis: Bobbs-Merrill Company, 1926.

"Sioux on the War-Path." *The Illustrated American* 5 (Jan. 10, 1891): 263–72.

Slaughter, Linda W. "Fort Abercrombie," *Collections of the State Historical Society of North Dakota* 1 (1906): 412–23.

——. "Leaves from Northwestern History," *Collections of the State Historical Society of North Dakota* 1 (1906): 200–92.

Smith, De Cost. *Red Indian Experiences*. London: George Allen & Unwin Ltd., 1949.

Smith, Shannon D. *Give Me Eighty Men: Women and the Myth of the Fetterman Fight.* Lincoln: University of Nebraska Press, 2008.

Sprague, Donovin Arleigh. *Pine Ridge Reservation.* Charleston, SC: Arcadia Publishing, 2004.

———. *Standing Rock Sioux.* Charleston, SC: Arcadia Publishing, 2004.

Spring, Agnes Wright. *Caspar Collins: The Life and Exploits of an Indian Fighter of the Sixties.* New York: Columbia University Press, 1927.

———, ed. "Dr. McGillycuddy's Diary." *The Denver Brand Book* 9 (1953): 279–307.

———. "Old Letter Book Discloses Economic History of Fort Laramie, 1858–1871." *Annals of Wyoming* 13 (Oct. 1941): 237–330.

Standing Bear, Luther. *Land of the Spotted Eagle.* Boston: Houghton Mifflin Company, 1933.

———. *My People the Sioux.* Edited by E. A. Brininstool. Boston: Houghton Mifflin Company, 1928.

———. "One Indian the White Man Never Conquered." *Los Angeles Times Sunday Magazine,* January 22, 1933.

Stands in Timber, John, and Margot Liberty. *A Cheyenne Voice: The Complete John Stands in Timber Interviews.* Norman: University of Oklahoma Press, 2013.

Steele, Matthew F. "Buffalo Bill's Bluff." *South Dakota Historical Collections* 9 (1918): 475–85.

Sterling, M. W. *Three Pictographic Autobiographies of Sitting Bull.* Smithsonian Miscellaneous Publications. Vol. 97, No. 5. Washington, D.C.: Smithsonian Institution, 1938.

Szabo, Joyce M. "Mapped Battles and Visual Narrative: The Arrest and Killing of Sitting Bull." *American Indian Art Magazine* 21 (Autumn 1996): 64–75.

Tallent, Annie D. *The Black Hills; or, The Last Hunting Ground of the Dakotahs.* St. Louis: Nixon-Jones Printing Co., 1899.

Tankersley, Kenneth B., and Robert B. Pickering. *Sitting Bull's Pipe: Recovering the Man, Connecting the Myth.* Wyk auf Föehr, Germany: Tatanka Press, 2006.

Tassin, Ray. *Stanley Vestal: Champion of the Old West.* Glendale, CA: The Arthur H. Clark Company, 1973.

Taylor, Joseph Henry. *Sketches of Frontier and Indian Life on the Upper Missouri and Great Plains.* Washburn, ND: published by the author, 1895.

Thomas, Rodney G. *Rubbing Out Long Hair, Pehin Hanska Kasota: The American Indian Story of the Little Big Horn in Art and Word.* Spanaway, WA: Elk Plain Press, 2009.

Torrence, Gaylord. *The Plains Indians: Artists of Earth and Sky.* New York and Paris: Skira/Rizzoli/Musée du Quai Branly, 2014.

Traub, Peter E. "The First Act of the Last Sioux Campaign." *Journal of the United States Cavalry Association* 15 (April 1905): 872–79.

Unrau, William E., ed. *Tending the Talking Wire: A Buck Soldier's View of Indian Country, 1863–1866.* Salt Lake City: University of Utah Press, 1979.

Utley, Robert M. *Cavalier in Buckskin: George Armstrong Custer and the Western Military Frontier.* Norman: University of Oklahoma Press, 1988.

———. *The Lance and the Shield: The Life and Times of Sitting Bull.* New York: Henry Holt and Company, 1993.

———. *The Last Sovereigns: Sitting Bull and the Resistance of the Free Lakotas.* Lincoln: University of Nebraska Press, 2020.

———, ed. *The Reno Court of Inquiry.* Fort Collins, CO: Old Army Press, 1983.

Van den Broeck, Karl. "Everything We Know About Sitting Bull's Crucifix Is Wrong." *True West* 65 (Nov. 2018): 20–24.

Vaughn, J. W. *With Crook at the Rosebud.* Harrisburg, PA: The Stackpole Company, 1956.

Vestal, Stanley. "The Man Who Killed Custer." *American Heritage* 8 (Feb. 1957): 4–9 and 90–91.

———. *New Sources of Indian History, 1850–1891.* Norman: University of Oklahoma Press, 1934.

———. *Sitting Bull: Champion of the Sioux.* Norman: University of Oklahoma Press, 1957.

———. *Warpath: The True Story of the Fighting Sioux Told in a Biography of Chief White Bull.* New York: Houghton Mifflin Company, 1934.

Villard, Oswald Garrison. *Fighting Years: Memoirs of a Liberal Editor.* New York: Harcourt, Brace and Company, 1939.

Wade, F. C. "The Surrender of Sitting Bull: Jean Louise Legaré's Story." *Canadian Magazine* 24 (Feb. 1905): 335–44.

Waggoner, Josephine. *Witness: A Húŋkpapȟa Historian's Strong-Heart Song of the Lakotas.* Edited by Emily Levine. Lincoln: University of Nebraska, 2013.

Wagner, David E. *Powder River Odyssey: Nelson Cole's Western Campaign of 1865: The Journals of Lyman G. Bennett and Other Eyewitness Accounts.* Norman, OK: The Arthur H. Clark Company, 2009.

Wagner, Glendolin Damon. *Old Neutriment.* Boston: Ruth Hill, 1934.

Walker, James R. *Lakota Belief and Ritual.* Edited by Raymond J. DeMallie and Elaine A. Jahner. Lincoln: University of Nebraska Press, 1991.

———. *Lakota Society.* Edited by Raymond J. DeMallie. Lincoln: University of Nebraska Press, 1982.

———. "The Sun Dance and Other Ceremonies of the Oglala Division of the

Teton Dakota." *American Museum of Natural History Anthropological Papers* 16, pt. 2 (1917): 50–221.

Walker, Judson Elliott. *Campaigns of General Custer in the North-West, and the Final Surrender of Sitting Bull.* New York: Jenkins and Thomas, 1881.

Walstrom, Cleve. *Search for the Lost Trail of Crazy Horse.* Crete, NE: Dageford Publishing, Inc., 2003.

Warman, Cy. "The Flight of Sitting Bull." *The Indian School Journal* 7 (March 1907): 41–45.

Warren, Louis S. *Buffalo Bill's America: William Cody and the Wild West Show.* New York: Alfred A. Knopf, 2005.

Watson, Elmo Scott. "Crazy Horse—The Greatest Among Them," in Roderick Peattie, ed., *The Black Hills.* New York: The Vanguard Press, 1952.

———. "The Last Indian War, 1890–91: A Study of Newspaper Jingoism." *Journalism Quarterly* 20 (Sept. 1943): 205–19.

———. "Stirring War Tales Told in the Soft Syllables of Ogallalas by Big Chief." *The Colorado Springs Gazette.* August 13, 1922.

Welch, A. B. "The Battle of Standing Rock." *The Clover Leaf* (Feb. 1928): 33–39.

Werts, Keith T. *The Crazy Horse and Colonel Nelson Miles Fight of 1877: New Discoveries at the Battle of the Butte.* Spokane, WA: Werts Publishing, 2014.

———, and Stevan C. Booras. *The Crazy Horse and Crook Fight of 1876: New Discoveries at the Battle of the Rosebud.* Spokane Valley, WA: Werts Publishing, 2011.

White, David A., ed. *News of the Plains and Rockies, 1803–1865.* 8 vols. Spokane, WA: The Arthur H. Clark Company, 1996–2001.

Williams, J. Fletcher. *History of the Upper Mississippi Valley.* Minneapolis: Minnesota Historical Company, 1881.

Wilson, Garrett. *Frontier Farewell: The 1870s and the End of the Old West.* Regina, SK, Canada: Canadian Plains Research Center, University of Regina, 2007.

Wissler, Clark. "Societies and Ceremonial Associations in the Oglala Division of the Teton-Dakota." *American Museum of Natural History Anthropological Papers* 11, pt. 1 (1912): 2–99.

Witte, Stephen S., and Marsha V. Gallagher, eds. *The North American Journals of Prince Maximilian of Wied.* 3 vols. Norman: University of Oklahoma Press, 2008–2012.

Wunderlich, Gerold M. *Rudolf Cronau, 1855–1939, in "Wilden Westen": Views of the American West.* New York: Gerold Wunderlich & Co., 1996.

Yarborough, Leroy. "Tragic Life of Crazy Horse." *Real West* 6 (July 1963): 36–38 and 47–50.

Zincke, F. Barham. *Last Winter in the United States.* London: John Murray, 1868.

### Newspapers

The Abbeville Press and Banner (SC)

The Advertiser-Courier (Hermann, MO)

Akron Beacon and Republican (OH)

Army and Navy Journal (NY)

The Atchison Champion (KS)

The Baltimore Sun (MD)

Bangor Daily Whig and Courier (ME)

The Benton Record (Fort Benton, MT)

The Benton Weekly Record

The Billings Gazette (MT)

Bismarck Daily Tribune (ND)

The Bismarck Tribune (ND)

Bismarck Weekly Tribune (ND)

The Black Hills Pioneer (Deadwood, SD)

Black Hills Weekly Times (Deadwood, SD)

The Border Sentinel (Mound City, KS)

The Boston Daily Globe

The Boston Sunday Globe

Bozeman Avant Courier (MT)

The Bozeman Courier (MT)

Bradford Reporter (Towanda, PA)

The Brooklyn Daily Eagle (NY)

The Brooklyn Union (NY)

The Buffalo Commercial (NY)

Buffalo Courier (NY)

Buffalo Express (NY)

The Buffalo Sunday Morning News (NY)

Burlington Daily Times (VT)

The Canton Advocate (SD)

Capital Journal (SD)

Catholic Telegraph (Cincinnati, OH)

The Chadron Tribune (NE)

The Chattanooga Daily Times (TN)

Cheyenne Daily Leader (WY)

The Chicago Daily Tribune (IL) [masthead 1872 to 1886, when it again became The Chicago Tribune]

Chicago Herald (IL)

Chicago Times (IL)

Chicago Tribune/The Chicago Tribune [mastheads prior to 1872]

The Cincinnati Enquirer (OH)

Cleveland Morning Leader (OH)

The Colorado Springs Gazette (CO)

The Conrad Independent (Conrad, MT)

Courier Democrat (Langdon, ND)

The Courier-Journal (Louisville, KY)

The Daily Argus-Leader (Sioux Falls, SD)

The Daily Crescent (LA)

Daily Inter Mountain (Butte, MT)

The Daily Journal (Ogdensburg, NY)

The Daily Journal of Commerce (Kansas City, MO)

Daily National Intelligencer (D.C.)

Daily News (New York, NY)

Daily Ohio Statesman (Columbus, OH)

Dawes County Journal (Chadron, NE)

The Deadwood Daily Pioneer-Times (SD)

Denver Daily Tribune (CO)

Detroit Free Press (MI)

El Paso Morning Times (TX)

Emmons County Record (Linton, ND)

Evening Bulletin (San Francisco)

The Evening Star (D.C.)

Evening State Journal (Lincoln, NE)

The Evening Telegraph (Philadelphia, PA)

Frank Leslie's Illustrated Newspaper (NY)

Fremont Tri-Weekly Tribune (NE)

Friendship Weekly Register (Friendship, NY)

Frontier Scout (Fort Rice, ND)

The Glasgow Courier (MT)

Gold Hill Daily News (Gold Hill, NV)

The Great Falls Tribune (MT)

Harrisburg Daily Independent (PA)

Harrisburg Telegraph (PA)

Hartford Courant (CT)

The Helena Independent (MT)

Helena Weekly Herald (MT)

The High Country News (Paonia, CO)

The Highland News (Hillsborough, OH)

The Indianapolis Times (IN)

The Inter Ocean (Chicago)

The Irish Standard (Minneapolis and St. Paul)

Jamestown Alert (ND)

The Janesville Daily Gazette (WI)

Junction City Weekly Union (KS)

The Kansas Chief (White Cloud)

The Kansas City Star (MO)

The Kansas Herald of Freedom (Lawrence)

The Kansas Semi-Weekly Capital (Topeka)

The Lancaster Intelligencer (Lancaster, PA)

Leavenworth Daily Commercial (KS)

The Leavenworth Times (KS)

The Los Angeles Times (CA)

The Louisville Daily Courier (KY)

Mandan Pioneer (ND)

The Manhattan Nationalist (KS)

Memphis Daily Appeal (TN)

Milwaukee Daily Sentinel (WI)

The Mineral Independent (Superior, MT)

The Minneapolis Journal (MN)

The Minneapolis Tribune (MN)

The Montana Post (Virginia City, MT)

Morning Journal and Courier (New Haven, CT)

Muscatine Evening Journal (Iowa)

The National Tribune (D.C.)

Nebraska Herald (Plattsmouth, NE)

The Nebraska State Journal (Lincoln)

The New North-West (Deer Lodge, MT)

New Orleans Daily Crescent (LA)

The New York Herald

New York Times

New York Tribune

The Northern Pacific Farmer (Wadena, MN)

The Omaha Daily Bee (NE)

The Philadelphia Age (PA)

Philadelphia Daily Evening Bulletin (PA)

The Philadelphia Inquirer (PA)

The Pittsburgh Dispatch (PA)

The Pittsburgh Post (PA)

The Pittsfield Sun (MA)

Rapid City Journal (SD)

The Representative (Fox Lake, WI)

The Republican Journal (ME)

The River Press (Fort Benton, MT)

Rochester Democrat and Chronicle (NY)

Rock Island Daily Argus (IL)

Rocky Mountain Husbandman (Diamond City, MT)

Rocky Mountain News (Denver, CO)

Sacramento Daily Record-Union (CA)

St. Cloud Democrat (MN)

St. Joseph Gazette (MO)

The St. Joseph Herald (MO)

St. Joseph News-Press (MO)

St. Louis Dispatch (MO)

St. Louis Globe-Democrat (MO)

St. Louis Post-Dispatch (MO)

The St. Louis Star (MO)

The St. Paul Daily Globe (MN)

The Salt Lake Herald (UT)

Savannah Morning News (GA)

The Sioux City Journal (IA)

Sioux City Register (IA)

Sioux County Pioneer (Fort Yates, ND)

Springfield Daily Republic (OH)

The Standard Union (Brooklyn, NY)

The Sun (NY)

The Sunday Ledger (Tacoma, WA)

The Times (Philadelphia, PA)

The Topeka State Journal (KS)

Vermont Watchman and State Journal (Montpelier, VT)

The Washburn Leader (ND)

The Washington Post (D.C.)

Washington Sentinel (D.C.)

Wausau Daily Herald (WI)

The Weekly Free Press (Atchison, KS)

The Weekly New Era (Lancaster, PA)

The Weekly Pioneer and Democrat (MN)

Western Reserve Chronicle (Warren, OH)

Wheeling Sunday Register (WV)

Winnipeg Free Press (Manitoba, Canada)

Winona Daily Republican (MN)

The World (NY)

# INDEX